OREGON

A BEST PLACES® GUIDE
TO THE OUTDOORS

TERRY RICHARD

SASQUATCH
BOOKS
SEATTLE

Dedication

To my wife, Randi, who made this possible by joining me on my outings, putting up with my absence, and solving my computer problems.

First Edition

00 99 98   6 5 4 3 2 1

ISSN: 1097-6019
ISBN: 1-57061-124-6

Cover Photo: Tim Bieber/The Image Bank
Cover Design: Karen Schober
Interior Design: Lynne Faulk, Vashon Island, WA
Maps: GreenEye Design, Seattle, WA
Copy editor: Heath Lynn Silberfeld / Enough Said
Proofreader: Kris Fulsaas, Seattle, WA
Composition: Fay Bartels and Patrick David Barber

Important Note: Please use common sense. No guidebook can act as a substitute for experience, careful planning, and appropriate training. There is inherent danger in all the outdoor activities described in this book, and readers must assume responsibility for their own actions and safety. Changing or unfavorable conditions in weather, roads, trails, waterways, etc. cannot be anticipated by the author or publisher, but should be considered by any outdoor participants. The author and the publisher will not be responsible for the safety of users of this guide.

The information in this edition is based on facts available at press time and is subject to change. The author and publisher welcome information conveyed by users of this book, as long as they have no financial connection with the area, guide, outfitter, organization, or establishment concerned.

Sasquatch Books
615 Second Avenue, Suite 260
Seattle, Washington 98104
(206)467-4300
www.sasquatchbooks.com

Contents

How to Use this Book   v

Oregon Outdoor Primer   vi

About Best Places® Guidebooks   xvii

Willamette Valley   1
> Greater Portland   3
> Wine Country   39
> Cascade Foothills   56
> Salem and the Heart of the Valley   77
> Greater Eugene   97

Southern Valleys   123
> The Umpqua Valley   125
> The Rogue Valley   142

Oregon Coast   175
> Northern Beaches   177
> Tillamook   192
> Lincoln City   211
> Newport   222
> Oregon Dunes   239
> Bay Area   257
> Southern Coast   274

Columbia River   293
> Columbia Basin   295
> Hood River and the Gorge   307
> Lower Columbia   330

Northern Cascades and Central Oregon   347
> Mount Hood   349
> Lower Deschutes River   373
> Lower John Day River   391
> Mount Jefferson and the Metolius River   400
> Crooked River   412
> Santiam Pass and Mount Washington   429
> Bend and the Upper Deschutes River   441
> Three Sisters and Cascade Lakes   464

Southern Cascades and the Klamath Basin   479

   Willamette Pass   481
   Diamond Lake   494
   Crater Lake National Park   503
   Mountain Lakes   512
   Klamath Basin   525

Northeast Mountains   541

   Wallowas and Hells Canyon   543
   La Grande and the Grande Ronde River   560
   Baker County   574
   Pendleton Grain Belt   590
   Upper John Day River   602

Southeast High Desert   617

   Lake County   619
   Harney County   634
   Malheur County   647

Index   657

How to Use this Book

We have tried to make *Inside Out Oregon* an entertaining, informative, and easy-to-use guidebook. The state's geographical regions were divided into eight sections. Basic reference maps are featured at the beginning of each section. Each section is then subdivided into smaller, more manageable areas (or chapters) that are represented in the following manner.

Introduction

The introduction to each chapter offers a general description of the area and its primary towns and features. These sections should provide you with a sense of place and history, as well as give you an idea of what to expect when you visit. Directions to the area and transportation information are included in the **Getting There** sections, which are followed by **Adjoining Areas** to your destination that are found in this book.

Inside Out

The Inside Out sections make up the bulk of the book. We go to great pains to discover what the best year-round options are for outdoor activities in each area. We talk to locals, rangers, guides, and outdoor-store owners to get the scoop on the most popular trails, lakes, stretches of river, climbs, ski slopes, and more. And we reveal some lesser-known gems as well.

These sections are divided into individual sports and activities, listed in order of prominence and appeal. Most chapters include **Hiking, Biking, Fishing, Camping, Skiing,** and **Rafting/Kayaking**—things that can be enjoyed in many parts of the state. Other chapters feature specialized activities, such as **Windsurfing, Caving,** and **Hang Gliding.** Here, you can select your adventure and discover how to get out into the wilderness, outside, out-of-doors, just out! The Oregon Outdoor Primer, on the next page, also provides safety tips and essential information on outdoor recreation and travel.

Outside In

After a long day enjoying the outdoors, you need to know where to go for some inside fun. The **Attractions** sections tell you about museums, shops, and other sights in the area that will distract the kids, get you out of inclement weather, or are just great places. The **Restaurants** and **Lodgings** sections provide star-rated reviews of the best places to eat and sleep. (See the About Best Places Guidebooks segment on the following pages for a description of how we rate and choose our restaurants and lodgings.)

More Information

Finally, we wrap up each chapter with a list of useful phone numbers specific to that area. Ranger districts, chambers of commerce, visitors centers, and more are all included for your convenience.

Oregon Outdoor Primer

Despite how easy it is to get outdoors in Oregon, it's always best to plan ahead to make maximum use of your precious time for recreation. Following are some tips for getting the utmost out of the outdoors.

Camping

Oregon has a reputation for having some of the best **state park campgrounds** in the country. The Oregon Coast, in particular, is dotted with numerous places to pitch a tent or park a recreational vehicle. Most parks have their own facilities and activities—or are within a short drive of them—that will keep a camper busy for a week or more. The coast itself is ever changing and warrants exploring throughout the year. The addition of **yurts** to a dozen state park campgrounds (nine of them on the coast) makes off-season camping accessible to campers who might not otherwise get out during the rainy months. Yurt is an acronym short for year-round universal recreational tent, which in Oregon means a circular domed tent with a plywood floor, structural support, electricity, and a glass skylight.

An increasing number of Oregon campgrounds are being retrofitted with **barrier-free facilities,** a catchall term that means they meet standards for wheelchair access set by the Americans with Disabilities Act. Nearly 10 percent of the state's population has some type of disability. Families with baby strollers, the elderly with walkers, and even the healthy who are healing from injuries can benefit from the growing number of barrier-free facilities, which in addition to campsites include fishing piers, boat docks, and trails.

Although campgrounds decorate the landscape of Oregon, it seems there are never quite enough to go around on busy weekends. Signs saying "campground full" can be as common on a sunny summer weekend as umbrellas on a rainy winter day. (But believe me, being without a campground on a Saturday in July on the Oregon Coast will ruin you day more than being without an umbrella in December in Portland.)

Most public land in Oregon is available for **dispersed camping,** which means campers can pitch a tent or park an RV where they want, when they want. Regulations usually limit stays to 14 consecutive days and require certain common sense precautions—proper disposal of human waste, carrying out your garbage, having an axe, a shovel, and a bucket handy in the event of a fire. Land that is closed to camping will be posted as such. Fires outside developed campgrounds are usually banned during the June through September fire season. Dispersed camping is allowed on Oregon **coastal beaches**, except in certain cities (Seaside, Cannon Beach,

Manzanita, Rockaway Beach, Lincoln City, Newport, Bandon, and Gold Beach). Although dispersed camping is quite common, especially in the mountains and desert east of US 97, most campers want a little more comfort when they camp—picnic tables, fire rings, garbage collection, running water, electrical hookups, and especially hot showers. To guarantee a spot that offers some of the comforts of home, it's best to make a reservation.

Reservations

The ultimate camper's lament in Oregon is that, not only can they not make a campground reservation, but they can't even connect with the camping reservation service by telephone. Like so many other campers, they are probably calling **Reservations Northwest, (800) 452-5687**, during the busy season to book a last-minute spot. It's funny to hear someone complain that it took 250 attempts on their speed-redial telephone before they were able to connect. With everyone else using the same technique, it's no wonder the system is overwhelmed. Reservations Northwest is based in Portland and makes reservations for 25 campgrounds operated by the Oregon Department of Parks and Recreation (as well as 46 state parks in Washington). Additional parks are being added each year to the reservation system.

The service is open daily from 8am to 5pm weekdays, with **extended hours** until 8pm from May through August. Reservations may be made up to 11 months in advance, or as close as two days before your planned arrival. Oregon parks in the system take reservations for camping all year round, with the yurts, covered wagons, teepees, and house boats frequently in high demand. Reservations include a $6 nonrefundable reservation fee, as well as the first night's fee for each campsite. Payment can be made by credit card. The best time to get through is late in the day, especially during the extended hours of summer.

In addition to state parks, the US Forest Service is the major provider of campgrounds in Oregon. With 13 national forests in the state, **national forest campgrounds** are even more widespread than state parks. Most of the Forest Service campgrounds operate on a first-come basis. Reservations are most frequently available for campgrounds located near metropolitan areas of the Willamette Valley or on the Oregon Coast, for group sites, and for horse camps. Although horse camps are specially designed to accommodate horse owners, they are open to all campers. The noise, smell, and extra cost, however, tend to concentrate horse owners at horse campgrounds. To make a reservation up to 240 days in advance, call (800) 280-CAMP (280-2267). County parks and the Bureau of Land Management also operate campgrounds, usually available on a first-come basis.

Prices

Oregon's state park campgrounds are some of the most expensive in the nation. An on-going budget shortfall forces the Oregon Parks and Recreation Department to extract every possible dollar from those who choose to visit its parks. Campsites can cost up to $20 for a full hookup, or $17 just for a tent, per night. The **off season** from November to March, called the Discovery Season by park officials, offers nightly rates reduced from $3 to $5 per night from high-season rates. The state park system also has 24 parks that charge fees for day use—either $3 for the day or $25 for an annual permit valid for all parks. Day-use passes can be bought at parks where they are sold.

Oregon's state park system has been treading water, at best, in recent years since it was removed from dedicated funding through the Department of Transportation's budget. The state park system's average of 465 visitors per acre is by far the highest among western states, which average 70 visitors per acre. Back in 1980, Oregon had 2.6 million residents, 48 state park campgrounds, and 92,489 acres in the state park system. As the 20th century draws to a close, the state has grown to 3.2 million residents, the campground network has increased by one (to 49), and the size has shrunk to 92,006 acres. Oregon's state parks are still there to be enjoyed, but be prepared to enjoy them with a lot more users and to pay more for the privilege.

National forest campgrounds range widely in price, from $5 to $15, depending on amenities. Many campgrounds remain free, but don't expect to find running water or garbage collection. An increasing number of national forest day-use parks are also charging day-use fees. Expect to pay $3 for day-use parking at the Oregon Dunes National Recreation Area, or $5 to enter Newberry Crater National Volcanic Monument.

Hiking/Backpacking

Trails abound in Oregon. From short to long, from steep to flat, Oregon has hiking opportunities that appeal to all levels of outdoor users. The Pacific Crest National Scenic Trail (more commonly referred to as the Pacific Crest Trail, or PCT), follows the spine of the Cascades from Washington to California and is the granddaddy of the state's **long-distance trails.** Most use on the PCT, however, is on day hikes from highways that cross the trail, or short backpack trips. The same holds true for Oregon's other long-distance trails, including the Oregon Coast Trail, the North Umpqua Trail, and the Fremont National Recreation Trail. Individuals will need to decide for themselves the best way to use the long-distance routes. For **shorter trails,** most of which can be hiked in a single day, mileage and a difficulty rating are included. Trail mileage frequently includes a loop option (because hikers like to see different scenery), or the distance is given one-way to either a possible backpack camp or a turnaround point. Trails rated **easy** have minimal elevation changes. **Moderate** trails usually climb less than 1,000 feet, while **difficult** trails tend to gain more than 1,000 feet in elevation. Elevation, however, is only one way to compare trail difficulty. It all comes down to hikers knowing how hard they want to work for their enjoyment.

Most Oregon mountains can be climbed via a relatively simple "walk up" route. Even Mount Hood, tallest in the state at 11,235 feet, has a route where climbers of limited experience can achieve success. Many of the state's mountains also have technical routes that are beyond the scope of this book. All climbers should take normal precautions, no matter how simple the route. Leave word at home where you are going and when you will return. Bring a rope, an ice axe, and crampons, and use them in appropriate situations. Take the time to learn skills by climbing with experienced leaders, who are frequently available through mountaineering clubs or professional guide services. When climbing Mount Hood, bring a Mountain Locator Unit, a device designed to lead seachers to a beacon sent out by the unit. The locator units can be rented 24 hours a day from the Mount Hood Inn at Government Camp, as well as at Portland mountaineering stores. The unit is used only on Mount Hood because it requires sophisticated tracking equipment that is available only on Oregon's most frequently climbed mountain.

Many of the national forests in Oregon are part of the Region 6 **trailhead parking fee system.** Region 6 encompasses Oregon and Washington and an annual pass is good for all fee trailheads in the system. An annual pass costs $25 and a day pass costs $3. Passes are sold at ranger stations and at sporting goods and convenience stores near the fee trailheads. This is a trial program authorized by Congress to run through 1999, so expect changes in the future. The best way to be sure you have a pass when you need one is to purchase the annual permit, or to buy several day-use permits in advance and date them as instructed when you use them. Oregon national forests that participate in the program are the Deschutes, Mount Hood, Siskiyou, Siuslaw, Umatilla, Wallowa-Whitman, and Willamette, plus the Columbia River Gorge National Scenic Area. Forests that do not require the pass are Fremont, Malheur, Ochoco, Umpqua, and Winema.

Gear

Rain gear is pretty much part of the established routine for anyone who goes for a hike in Oregon. Oregon's **rainy season** lasts from November through June on the west side of the state. Eastern Oregon receives most of its moisture then, too, but it's a lot less than the west side (except the highest mountains). Summer frequently brings long periods of sunny days, although good weather should never be taken for granted during overnight trips. Summer afternoon thunderstorms are common in the mountains. A rain jacket and pants—even a folding umbrella—don't weigh much and the reassurance of having them along will allow you to spend more time on the trail.

Other items of clothing are a matter of personal choice. Wool or synthetics are far superior to cotton, especially in wet weather. A good pair of boots, well broken in, are vital for crossing snowfields. An increasing number of long-distance hikers are trading off the support afforded by hiking boots in favor of the comfort and lighter weight of a good pair of running shoes. Again, it's personal choice.

Every hiker should carry along the **"10 essentials,"** a tried-and-true list of equipment that can save a life in an emergency:

- **Map:** Make sure it's of the area you're visiting and that you know how to use it.
- **Compass:** An orienteering class (usually offered by local park-district recreation programs) is the best way to learn how to use a compass.
- **Sunglasses and sunscreen:** You need these even on cloudy days.
- **Extra food:** Bring enough food that doesn't require cooking to last an extra day.
- **Extra clothing:** This should include rain gear, underwear, hat, and mittens. Carry it in a plastic bag inside your pack.
- **Flashlight:** Even if you're sure you'll return before darkness, it's comforting to know you have a light along. Bring an extra bulb and a set of backup batteries.
- **First-aid kit:** Everyone should bring a basic kit, which can be purchased prepackaged in drug stores; a larger group should carry a more extensive kit. Know what's inside and how to use it.
- **Fire starter:** Candles, burning paste, or fire pellets work well, but if you're spending a lot of time on snow nothing beats a stove.
- **Matches:** Carry them in a waterproof container.
- **Pocket knife:** A Swiss Army knife, complete with the usual assortment of bells and whistles, can deal with most trail emergencies. Pocket tools are becoming increasingly popular.

Maps

Maps are a necessity and can be purchased as you travel at ranger stations and outdoor stores along the way. The best source for getting them in advance is the Nature of the Northwest store, a joint operation between the US Forest Service and the Oregon Department of Geology. The store carries all Forest Service and Bureau of Land Management maps for Oregon, plus all US Geological Survey maps of Oregon. Maps can be ordered over the telephone by calling (503) 731-4444, or by visiting the store at 800 NE Oregon, Suite 177, in the Lloyd District of Portland.

Another valuable map source is Powell's Travel Store, (503) 288-1108, in downtown Portland's Pioneer Courthouse Square at SW Sixth and Yamhill. The store has Oregon's most comprehensive inventory of travel literature and maps. Nautical charts of the Columbia River and Pacific Ocean are available from Captain's Nautical Supplies, (503) 227-1648, at 138 NW 10th also in downtown Portland.

Call first

The Oregon outdoors is a very dynamic place. Things change. Occasionally change comes quickly, such as difficult weather conditions or an altered landscape. Change can also happen slowly, such as the repair of road damage caused by a storm. It's always best to call ahead, or to stop by a ranger station or outdoor store and ask for the latest conditions. At the end of every chapter in this book is a list of sources for **More Information**, important phone numbers relevant to that area. Oregon Parks and Recreation (also referred to in this book as Oregon State Parks) can be reached at (800) 551-6949; an operator at that number can direct callers to the appropriate Forest Service or other number.

Biking

The seat of a bicycle is a glorious way to see Oregon. You may not know it when riding in Portland, but much of the state is lightly populated, has uncrowded roads and trails, and has residents that treat bicyclists courteously. State and city governments have actively been building facilities for bikers for more than two decades, giving the state an extensive network of **lanes and paths** dedicated for bicycle use. The US Forest Service and Bureau of Land Management also actively work to accommodate bicycles on its trail systems.

By law, bicycles are looked upon as motor vehicles and must obey the laws of the highway. **Helmets** are required on riders under 16 years of age and are always a good idea for everyone. Many government agencies and chambers of commerce publish the best guides, with local riding routes described in detail. Because some of these rides cover 50 miles or more on the road, or follow numerous twists and turns on the trail, complete detail is not possible in this book. Pick up copies of these local guides, usually at bike shops, ranger stations, or visitor centers, and supplement them with appropriate county or national forest maps.

Many of Oregon's hiking trails are open to **mountain bikes.** The major exceptions are the Pacific Crest Trail and all trails inside wilderness areas. Although it may be legal to ride a trail, the best places usually have some kind of development geared to make them friendly to bicycles. Those are the riding areas described in this book. Most towns of any size in Oregon have a bicycle shop. Many are listed here.

Rafting/Kayaking/Canoeing

Rowing and paddle sports are enjoyed nearly everywhere in Oregon. The state's numerous rivers, lakes, and bays provide a wealth of opportunities for self-outfitted boaters and commercial operations. Day trips abound, as well as multiday outings that can test the skills of expert boaters. Rafters can turn trips on the John Day and Owyhee Rivers into weeklong outings, or ocean surf paddlers can design the ultimate survival test by paddling offshore from the Columbia River to California.

Oregon has many commercial river guides (the lower Deschutes River alone has more than 130 licensed outfitters). Most companies run safe, enjoyable trips under the supervision of the Oregon Marine Board, the US Forest Service or the Bureau of Land Management. Fatalities to boaters on commercial trips are extremely rare. Outfitters listed in this guide tend to be local businesses, run by people who live near the river they specialize in.

Oregon's paddling season runs throughout the year. Each river has an optimum paddling season, however, with a fine line between being too low to run during the dry season and being too high to boat because of floods. To check the latest **river flow information** and the weather forecast, call the National Weather Service's recorded information line in Portland at (503) 261-9246.

Fishing/Boating

Oregon still has plenty of great fishing. Despite the highly publicized decline of salmon runs, the state has fishing opportunities that rank among the best in the country. Quite often, fishing and boating go hand in hand. Many of the state's marine facilities were built to accommodate fishermen and their boats. License revenue that goes into the Oregon Marine Board coffers for construction of boating facilities is far greater from the numerous small fishing boats than from the handful of large cabin cruisers that ply the waters of the Columbia and Willamette Rivers.

Oregon's renowned fisheries include the spring run of chinook salmon at the mouth of the Rogue River, the fall run of chinook at Tillamook Bay, the feisty redside trout taken each summer from the Deschutes River, the legendary summer steelhead of the North Umpqua River, the bass fishing in the lakes of the Oregon Dunes, and an emerging trophy walleye fishery of the mid-Columbia River.

Fishing regulations are outlined annually in a synopsis called *Oregon Sport Fishing Regulations,* published by the Oregon Department of Fish and Wildlife. The booklet is widely circulated at tackle and fly-fishing shops, outdoor stores, and visitors centers. Because of the numerous regulations and emergency closures, fishing is perhaps the most complicated of all outdoor pursuits. Read the synopsis carefully, or call the department information line in Portland at (503) 872-5268. All persons 14 years or older must have a **license** to fish in Oregon (special regulations apply on Native American reservations and in Crater Lake National Park), also widely available at tackle shops and outdoor stores.

Wildlife

Oregon no longer has grizzly bears, but it does have its share of wildlife, some of which can be trouble when it mixes with humans. Cougars, black bears, rattlesnakes, black widow spiders, ticks, and wasps can quickly turn an outing from enjoyable to life threatening. Thankfully, incidents are rare and usually can be avoided by exercising appropriate caution. Don't leave food around camp to attract bears, make a nightly check for ticks, and don't go poking in brush piles where snakes live—use common sense.

Oregon's birdlife is abundant. The Oregon Coast is part of the Pacific flyway and is a birders' delight. The Klamath Basin is the wintering ground for an estimated 3.5 million waterfowl. Even Portland, the state's largest city, has 40 bald eagles that spend winter nights in nearby hills and hunt by day in the Colombia River bottomlands within a dozen miles of the city's skyscrapers. Peregrine falcons nest on city bridges.

The safest way to enjoy wildlife, for both the viewer and the animals, is with a good pair of binoculars and a spotting scope. Always maintain a safe distance. Even the supposedly tame mule deer in Wallowa State Park have harmed people who got too friendly.

Skiing/Winter Sports

Oregon has the **longest lift-served ski season** in North America. End of discussion.

Timberline Ski Area at Mount Hood has the lift and snow capabilities to offer downhill skiing every day of the year. Due to maintenance and weather considerations, the ski lifts occasionally sit idle, but are usually open for business 330 days each year. A routine closure occurs in mid-September, when the ski area's upper lifts are closed for maintenance. The upper lifts reopen the last weekend of September and operate for the fall season, until snowfall allows the lower lifts to open. Skiing during **summer** is on the Palmer snowfield, an ancient field of snow on the south side of Mount Hood. (Though occasionally called a glacier, the snowfield lacks crevasses and other characteristics required to be a glacier.) Most activity during summer is by ski racers in training—nearly every US ski racer has trained at Mount Hood, as have many international stars—and by snowboard camps that attract participants from around the world.

Outside the summer season on Mount Hood, a typical Oregon ski season begins in early November. The snow pack usually lasts longer than skiers' enthusiasm. Most ski areas begin to close in mid-April. Mount Bachelor complements Mount Hood by staying open for skiing until July Fourth. Oregon ski areas frequently receive **500 inches** of snow annually, with 200 inches or more reported on the ground during late winter.

The **fluctuating weather** is the bane of skiing in Oregon. Located so close to the Pacific Ocean, the freezing level bounces up and down throughout the winter. Powder snow one day can turn to slush the next. Trial and error is the best way to learn when it's good to go skiing in Oregon.

Downhill

Skiing in Oregon is an odd-duck event compared to other Western states. The only mountainside resort in the state is Mount Hood's Timberline Lodge, which celebrated its 60th anniversary in 1997. The venerable hotel will be undergoing a facelift during the next several years as it is retrofitted to accommodate wheelchairs and its swimming pool is remodeled into a health spa for guests.

Despite the lack of lodging, Oregon's ski areas play the hand that is dealt them. With the exception of Govenment Camp on Mount Hood, most of the land near ski areas is owned by the federal government's national forest system. Despite occasional requests, permission has yet to be granted to construct new overnight lodges near chairlifts on national forest land. Although many of Oregon's 1.5 million annual ski visits are made by day trippers, most of the ski areas work with nearby resorts and motels to cater to overnight visitors. Mount Hood has Government Camp and Hood River, Mount Bachelor has Bend and Sunriver, Ski Ashland uses Ashland's large bed base that was built to accommodate the summer theater industry, and Willamette Pass and Hoodoo tap into nearby resorts that were built as summer fishing lodges. Skiers and snowboarders may not be able to stay at the base of the lifts, but the variety of nearby accommodations mitigate the inconvenience. For recorded information on **ski conditions,** call (503) 222-9951 in Portland, or check the yellow pages under Skiing for local numbers.

Cross-Country

The Mount Bachelor Nordic Center is frequently listed as one of the best on the West Coast. Its 56-kilometer trail system has staged national championships, and annual training sessions in May attract the nation's elite skiers. The center's location alongside Mount Bachelor's downhill ski runs make it ideal for families that want to mix the two types of skiing. Mount Hood Meadows has plans to construct a permanent, full-service Nordic center to replace facilities that have been housed in a trailer. The state's other Nordic centers operate mostly as adjuncts to downhill ski areas.

The state **sno-park system** blends roadside parking areas with cross-country ski and snowmobile trails. More than 100 sno-parks are spread around the state; see Driving, below.

Driving

Oregon's mountain passes are well cared for during winter by crews from the Oregon Department of Transportation (ODOT). Occasionally, snow-fall or traffic is so heavy that the plowing crews shut portions of highways temporarily (it usually happens only on Sunday afternoons when you're in a hurry to get home). Avalanches, the plague of winter travel in many other Western states, rarely impact Oregon's highways.

Most of the state's paved highways remain open all year. Major exceptions are Rim Drive in Crater Lake National Park, the Cascade Lakes Highway in Central Oregon, and the McKenzie Pass Highway (Highway 242), which are usually closed for the winter season from November until May or even June. Other local roads (the Clackamas-Breitenbush and Aufderheide byways of the western Cascades) have less formal closures dictated by local snow conditions.

The state's **traction device law** has a series of escalating requirements and applies to all state highways. At the minimum, drivers must carry chains or traction tires, when instructed to do so, while passing through the formally designated snow zones on most state highways that traverse mountains. During times of reduced traction, drivers may be instructed to install chains or traction tires. A **four-wheel drive vehicle** does not need to use chains if its unloaded weight is 6,500 pounds or less, and if it is operated with power to all wheels, is carrying chains, has all-weather tires on all wheels, is not towing another vehicle, and is not being operated in an unsafe manner. **Studded tires** are allowed on Oregon highways from November 1 to April 1. Although steel studs can no longer be sold in Oregon, their use remains legal in the state. (Tire stores now sell aluminum or polymer studs.)

Vehicles that park in the more than 100 designated ski and snow-play areas in Oregon must display a state **sno-park permit** from November 15 to April 1. Permits are available from ODOT Driver and Motor Vehicles (DMV) offices throughout the state, as well as from stores that sell winter sports gear or cater to skiers. Ski areas occasionally dispatch employees to sell the permits to arriving vehicles early in the season, but don't plan on purchasing a permit this way. Permits sell for about $2.50 for the day, $4 for three days, or $10.50 for the season, but the DMV charges 50 cents less. Washington, Idaho, and California sno-park permits are valid in Oregon. Violators are subject to a $10 fine. Money raised by the program pays for the plowing of the parking lots. Some winter resorts choose to plow their own parking lots and are not part of the sno-park program. Places where sno-park permits are not required include Mount Bachelor Ski and Summer Resort, Diamond Lake Resort, and Crater Lake National Park.

For a 24-hour **road report** in Oregon, call (541) 889-3999, or check out the Oregon Department of Transportation Web site at www.ODOT.state.or.us for real-time photos of road conditions on US 26 at Government Camp or US 20 at Santiam Pass.

Windsurfing/Surfing

Unlike most outdoor activities, windsurfing and surfing occur in the open where everyone can see them. During a windy summer day, travelers on Interstate 84 through the Columbia River Gorge must think half the people in the state are riding back and forth across the river on sailboards. A growing number of surfers and ocean windsurfers also attract the attention of travelers on US 101.

The numbers of participants in board sports are small compared to hikers and bikers, but windsurfers enjoy undisputed world-class sailing conditions in Oregon. The discovery of windsurfing in the early 1980s turned the sleepy orchard town of Hood River into one of the hottest multisport recreation destinations in the country.

Cold water offshore keeps Oregon from becoming overrun with surfers, but those who can bear the temperatures find some excellent waves to ride.

About Best Places® Guidebooks

The restaurant and lodging reviews in this book are condensed from Best Places guidebooks, a unique series written by and for locals. The best places in the region are the ones that denizens favor—establishments of good value, often independently owned, touched with local history, run by lively individuals, and graced with natural beauty. Best Places reviews are completely independent: no advertisers, no sponsors, no favors.

All evaluations are based on numerous reports from local and traveling inspectors. Best Places writers do not identify themselves when they review an establishment, and they accept no free meals, accommodations, or any other services. Every place featured in this book is recommended, even those with no stars.

Stars

Restaurants and lodgings are rated on a scale of zero to four stars, based on uniqueness, loyalty of local clientele, performance measured against goals, excellence of cooking, value, and professionalism of service. Reviews are listed alphabetically.

☆☆☆☆	The very best in the region
☆☆☆	Distinguished; many outstanding features
☆☆	Excellent; some wonderful qualities
☆	A good place
no stars	Worth knowing about, if nearby

Price Range

Prices are subject to change; contact the establishment directly to verify.

$$$	Expensive (more than $80 for dinner for two; more than $100 for lodgings for two)
$$	Moderate (between expensive and inexpensive)
$	Inexpensive (less than $30 for dinner for two; less than $70 for lodgings for two)

Directions

Basic directions are provided with each review; contact each business to confirm hours and location.

Cheaper Eats/Sleeps

The listings under Cheaper Eats and Cheaper Sleeps are for the budget-conscious traveler. While they are not star-rated, each establishment is recommended and is generally in the inexpensive price range (see above). These listings do not provide directions; call ahead to confirm location.

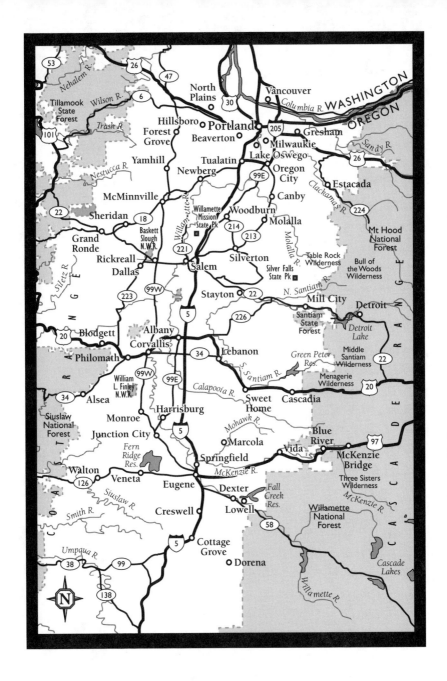

Willamette Valley

Greater Portland   3

Wine Country   39

Cascade Foothills   56

Salem and the Heart of the Valley   77

Greater Eugene   97

Willamette Valley

Greater Portland

From the Sandy River Gorge on the east, south to the Clackamas River, west into Washington County, and north through Forest Park to where the Columbia River forms Portland's northern boundary, including the cities of Portland, Troutdale, Gresham, Oregon City, Milwaukie, Lake Oswego, Tigard, Beaverton, and Aloha.

The City of Roses, the River City . . . Portland is just as sweet by any other name.

Officially home to 503,000 residents, the population of the Portland metro area swells to 1.7 million when the counts are combined for Multnomah, Washington, and Clackamas Counties in Oregon and Clark County, just across the Columbia River in Washington. Fully half of Oregon's 20 largest cities are inside Portland's Urban Growth Boundary. Although located in Washington state, Vancouver is an integral part of the Portland area, sending many workers south each day to earn a living in Oregon, and it has grown into the fourth-largest city in the Evergreen State.

Despite the Greater Portland area's population boom of the 1990s, the city has managed to maintain a livability envied by many other large cities. Portland's downtown, tied elegantly to the Willamette River waterfront, is vibrant and energetic both day and night. Several of the city's neighborhoods—NW 23rd Avenue, the Pearl District, Hawthorne, Hollywood, Multnomah, Sellwood, and St. Johns—have a fast-paced lifestyle all their own.

Portlanders are a hard people to pigeonhole. Residents don't rely too much on any one industry for their livelihoods, and weather downturns in the economy quite well. Portlanders love to drive their sports utility vehicles and show off the latest in Gore-Tex clothing, but they may just as easily be headed for the rivers to go fishing or to the mountains for some skiing. They love morning coffee and their after-work microbrews, easily the best selection of handcrafted beers in the country. They have two major league pro sports franchises, the Trail Blazers of the National Basketball Association, and the Portland Power of the new women's American Basketball League. All the major college sports teams are located elsewhere in the Willamette Valley. Instead of watching people play sports, Portlanders would just as soon do the performing themselves.

The commercial and industrial sides of Portland are kept livable by a system of neighborhood and regional parks and greenspaces, plus a network of foot, bicycle, and water trails that connect them. Called the 40-Mile Loop, Portland's interconnected trail system is gradually expanding into a 140-mile-long system that connects 30 parks.

Residents of the tri-county area spoke loud and clear to protect parks and greenspaces when they voted in 1995 to raise $135.6 million via property taxes to purchase undeveloped land and improve parks. Of the total, about $25 million was earmarked for local projects, either to develop or improve existing facilities or purchase land that adjoined existing parks. Metro, the regional government and managing body, used the remainder of the money to purchase 5,000 acres of undeveloped land that future generations will decide whether to convert into parks or keep as undeveloped greenspaces.

With growth comes inevitable congestion. Portland's highway system becomes noticeably more crowded every year. A recent survey by the Texas Transportation Institute of 39 U.S. cities ranked Portland as having the 15th most congested traffic system despite ranking 30th in population. Portland is trying to mitigate the congestion with an east-west light-rail line that runs from Gresham to Hillsboro. The city is also aggressively encouraging bicycle commuting and has been ranked number one among U.S. cities by a national cycling magazine for its variety of bicycle-friendly programs.

City traffic, so far, is usually only congested during the traditional rush hour, so anyone looking for some outdoor recreation should bear that in mind. Timing is critical for trips to Mount Hood, the Gorge, the Lower Columbia, the northern coast, and southwest Washington, the major day and weekend recreational play areas for Portland. When the freeways are too crowded to head out of town, Portland offers a wealth of outdoor recreation opportunities inside the metro area. How many other cities are there where fishermen can hook onto a bright spring chinook within sight of the downtown skyline?

Rafters and kayakers get whitewater thrills on the Sandy River between Dodge and Oxbow Parks, while canoeists enjoy the lower river from Oxbow to where it joins the Columbia River. The lower Clackamas is another popular spot with floaters, and hosts salmon fishing every bit as good as that of the Willamette River in downtown Portland.

Road cyclists have paths along the Columbia River, Interstate 205, and the Springwater Corridor. Mountain bikers need not leave the city to enjoy rides from the end of NW Thurman Street onto Leif Erikson Drive in Forest Park and on Powell Butte at SE 162nd Avenue and Powell Boulevard. Rock climbers have put up many routes on Rocky Butte and at Lewis and Clark State Park. Tent campers head for Oxbow Regional Park, sailors ply the waters of the Columbia River, and rowers streak across the Willamette River.

Added to the mix are an ever-growing number of decidedly urban sports—indoor climbing, indoor paintball, in-line skating, skateboarding, and a water park with wave pool.

Maybe Portland's name should be Fun City.

Getting There

Portland is the transportation hub of Oregon. Interstate 5 ties Portland to Oregon's western valley cities and California to the south. Interstate 84 connects Portland to a string of small towns as the freeway heads east to the Idaho border. Portland is linked to the northern Oregon coastal towns by US Highway 30 (US 30) to Astoria, US Highway 26 (US 26) to Seaside, and Highway 18/22 to Lincoln City. Portlanders traveling to Mount Hood and Central Oregon use US 26, which leaves the metro area at Gresham. Portland International Airport is a rapidly expanding airline hub, with Delta Airlines offering nonstop service to Asia. Alaska Airlines and its partner, Horizon, are the busiest regional and West Coast carriers. Most of the nation's other major airlines also serve the Portland airport. Union Station and the central bus terminal, both located at the north end of downtown, offer rail and bus service to regional and national destinations.

Burnside Street divides Portland into north and south. One-way distance east-to-west is 3.1 miles, a pleasant outing accessible by bus from anywhere in the city. Portland's other geographical dividing line is the Willamette River, which divides the city into east and west. The northeast part of town is divided further into North and northeast Portland by Williams Avenue, which acts as a northern extension of the east-west boundary where the river begins curving to the west.

Although it never hurts to have an automobile for access, the Greater Portland area has convenient and inexpensive bus service that can be used to reach many of the metropolitan area's recreation sites. For information about Tri-Met's bus routes, call (503) 231-3199 or stop at the transit agency's downtown information center at Pioneer Courthouse Square, 701 SW Sixth Avenue. Tri-Met also offers light-rail train service east from downtown Portland to Gresham and will soon be completing its westside line from Portland to Hillsboro.

Adjoining Areas

SOUTH: **Salem and the Heart of the Valley, Wine Country**

EAST: **Hood River and the Gorge, Mount Hood, Cascade Foothills**

WEST: **Lower Columbia**

Weather

Although weather can be nice enough for a picnic on any day of the year, Greater Portland has a fairly predictable weather pattern. The hot days of summer don't usually begin until around July 4. But once they set in, Portland can go well into October before the wet weather returns. November through March is usually very wet, although a week of clear, chilly weather is possible at any time. Spring showers linger from April through June, although it can clear up and stay nice for days at a time. The main complaint about Portland's weather is the preponderance of gray skies—Portland is famous for the all-day drizzle that results in an official measurement of a trace of rain for the day at the official measuring station.

Portland's average yearly precipitation is 36.3 inches, as measured at Portland International Airport. The wettest year ever was 1996, when 63.56 inches of rain were recorded. Portland usually hits 100 degrees a few times each summer and can dip into the teens during the winter. Snowfall is rare, but when it happens the city's traffic is paralyzed. It doesn't snow at all some years, but in others there may be three or four separate snow events.

The most hazardous weather is the ice storms that blow in from the Columbia River Gorge. The ice is easy to predict. When it's clear and below freezing for several days, warm moisture approaching from the Pacific Ocean is going to turn to ice. It's rare when Portland breaks out of a winter chill without going through an ice storm. The ice is usually worst near the mouth of the Columbia Gorge, where Troutdale can get covered by 1 to 2 inches in a few hours. Areas like Tigard, far enough away from the Gorge, rarely see more than a glazing of ice.

Hiking/Walking/Parks

Most big cities have good places to walk—at least they should have, what with the tons of concrete and blacktop that go into making cities. Greater Portland is a good place to walk but, more importantly, the city and its suburbs are a great place to hike. Portland's **parks** must have one of the largest systems of hiking trails of any urban area in America.

Forest Park, Lower Macleay Park, Hoyt Arboretum, and Washington Park, all in Portland's West Hills; Marquam Park, just south of downtown; Tryon Creek State Park and Marshall Park in southwest Portland; Mount Tabor Park and Powell Butte Nature Park in southeast Portland; and Oxbow Regional Park 6 miles east of Gresham have hiking trail systems where, just a few hundred yards from some trailheads, hikers may think they are in a national forest, not a city park.

Paved walkways offer long-distance walking along the Columbia River, the Willamette River Greenway, I-205, the Springwater Corridor, Terwilliger Blvd, and Beaverton's Greenway Park. These paved routes also are ideal locations for riding bicycles and are discussed under Cycling, below.

Many other parks have large grassy fields that encourage neighborhood residents to go for a walk after dinner on a summer evening. Some of the best are Pier Park and Kelley Point Park in North Portland; Laurelhurst Park in southeast Portland; George Rogers Park in Lake Oswego; Mary S. Young State Park in West Linn; Gabriel Park and Woods Park in southwest Portland; Hyland Forest Park and Tualatin Hills Nature Park in Beaverton; Commonwealth Lake Park in Cedar Hills; Cook Park in Tigard; Tualatin Community Park in Tualatin; and Wood Village City Park.

Walking opportunities in **manicured parks** include the Grotto, in northeast Portland, and the Leach Botanical Gardens and Crystal Springs Rhododendron Garden, both in southeast Portland. Even the Glendoveer and Rose City Golf Courses, both in northeast Portland, encourage walking for nongolfers. Glendoveer, (503) 253-7507, has a 2-mile walking fitness course around its 36 holes maintained by Metro. The 2.5-mile route around the Rose City Golf Course, (503) 253-4744, follows a footpath and city streets just outside the golf course fence.

It can be daunting figuring out where to hike in Portland. Most of the local parks and recreation districts ease the pain of decision making by scheduling regular tours of the town. A commercial outfit is Walking Tours of Portland, (503) 665-2558. For information on many of the parks listed here, call **Metro Regional Parks and Greenspaces,** (503) 797-1850, or **Portland Parks and Recreation,** (503) 823-2223.

Portland and its suburbs have dozens of outdoor stores, most of which are listed under "Sporting Goods" in the yellow pages. One store that has long been meeting the needs of a variety of recreationists, including rental equipment, is the Mountain Shop at 628 NE Broadway, (503) 288-6768.

Portland's West Hills

For hikers, **Forest Park,** (503) 823-4492, is the mother of all Portland parks. Forest Park's 4,700 acres stretch to the northwest from the west edge of central Portland, above the Tualatin Valley to the south and the Willamette River and Sauvie Island to the north. The **Wildwood Trail** begins at the Vietnam Veterans Memorial in Washington Park and runs for 27.5 miles. Most of the trail runs through Forest Park, one of the largest urban parks in the United States. The trail's northern terminus is beyond Germantown Rd at Firelane 12, but most use occurs far to the south because of more numerous access points. A guide to all of Portland's parks, as well as information on Forest Park, are available through the city's parks department, (503) 823-2223.

Forest Park is 8 miles long and 1.5 miles wide. Although several housing developments have defaced part of the forest in recent years, the Metro Greenspaces program provides additional protection that will guarantee the integrity of the park for future generations. Metro has recently purchased 361 acres, which could have otherwise been developed for housing, and transferred title to the city for additions to Forest Park.

Due to its length, the Wildwood Trail is usually visited in segments. Overnight use is not allowed, so backpacking is not a possibility. Joggers have undoubtedly run the entire distance in a day, but they probably missed some of the sights along the way. Most users locate a favorite trailhead, then return again and again to experience the changing seasons and to look for new loop hiking opportunities that a number of adjoining trails offer. Free maps of Forest Park and the Wildwood Trail are available throughout Portland. A good place to pick one up is the Hoyt Arboretum Visitor Center, located alongside the Wildwood Trail at 4000 SW Fairview Blvd.

The Wildwood Trail is easiest to access at its southern end in **Washington Park,** where it passes alongside the **Japanese Garden** and through **Hoyt Arboretum.** The trail crosses several neighborhood streets, including Fairview Blvd, before it reaches Burnside St and enters Forest Park. Tri-Met buses have convenient service from Portland to the trailhead at the Vietnam Veterans of Oregon Memorial and the trail's crossing of Burnside St. The memorial is located at the southern edge of the arboretum, next to the **World Forestry Center** and **Metro Washington Park Zoo.** The Wildwood Trail begins at the memorial, which provides a poignant reminder of the soldiers who may have been alive today to enjoy Oregon's outdoors if their country hadn't summoned them to war. The zoo is located at 4001 SW Canyon Rd, the World Forestry Center at 4033 SW Canyon Rd, and the Japanese Garden at 611 SW Kingston.

Hoyt Arboretum is 175 acres of woods and meadows and trails that connect Washington Park with Forest Park. When seen either on a map or in person, the three parks make up one big contiguous swath of green. The arboretum is home to more than 900 species of trees and shrubs from around the world that are planted among the native firs and cedars.

Portland's mild, moist climate is good for growing just about everything except desert and tropical plants. The arboretum's trail system includes 2 miles of the Wildwood Trail and the 1-mile paved **Bristlecone Pine Trail.** Access for people with disabilities is available off Fischer Lane. The arboretum's visitors center has information, exhibits, a horticultural library, and rest rooms. For information or to reserve the group picnic shelter, call (503) 796-5274.

Once the Wildwood Trail crosses to the north side of W Burnside St, it climbs steeply to reach the **Pittock Mansion,** a 16,000-square-foot chateau-type mansion that was completed in 1914, (503) 823-3624. The house and its antique furnishings are open to tour daily, except for some closures during winter. The mansion, located at 3229 NW Pittock Dr, has a commanding view of Portland from atop its perch in the city's West Hills. The surrounding grounds, with a sweeping view of the rivers and mountains that surround Portland, serve as a bird sanctuary and provide a marvelous setting for a picnic on a summer day.

From the Pittock Mansion, the Wildwood Trail continues winding its way to the northwest, taking a circuitous route to stay atop ridges and avoid dropping down to cross drainages. Access points along the way are at **Audubon House,** 5151 NW Cornell Rd, and where the trail passes along the spine of Forest Park and crosses Holman Lane, NW 53rd Dr, Saltzman Rd, Springville Rd, and Germantown Rd. Many of the trail's street crossings offer limited access, and parking can be congested on weekends.

Forest Park has another 35 miles of trail, including fire lanes, in addition to the Wildwood Trail. To become intimately familiar with the park requires lots of experience with the trail system and many miles of walking or riding a mountain bike. The trail system from **Macleay Park** is one of the major feeder routes onto the Wildwood Trail. Macleay Park is located at the west end of NW Upshur St, and is accessible via Tri-Met. The Lower Macleay Trail connects in less than a mile to the Wildwood Trail.

Marquam Nature Park

Tucked away in a ravine beneath "Pill Hill"—the collection of medical buildings just south of downtown Portland—Marquam Nature Park is one of those inner-city gems that every big city should have. The park is part of a greenway, mostly completed, that connects the Willamette River with the Wildwood Trail near the Washington Park Zoo.

The 2-mile **Marquam Park Trail** begins at the end of SW Marquam St, located just off SW Sam Jackson Rd .25 mile west of Terwilliger Blvd. Portland Parks and Recreation, (503) 823-2223, publishes a trail map of the park. The lower trail system follows a short nature path, complete with numbered stops that correspond to brochures available at an unstaffed nature shelter. The upper trail climbs through a ravine with signs of housing never far on either side. The fully leafed trees of summer provide a closed-in setting, but urban noise is never far away. After the trail crosses busy Sherwood Dr and Fairmont Blvd, it arrives atop **Council Crest Park,** the high point of Portland at 1,070 feet above sea level. Council Crest is a famous Portland picnic park with a view.

Tri-Met bus routes serve the Marquam Nature Park trail, both on Sam Jackson Rd (bus route 12) and near the summit of Council Crest (bus route 51). Using the bus to avoid a car shuttle is a popular way to hike on the long trail systems of west Portland.

The Marquam Park Trail is connected to the Willamette River by trails south along Terwilliger Blvd, east through **Himes Park,** crossing under Barbur Blvd and I-5 along Iowa St, south along Corbett Ave, and east along Nebraska St to the Willamette River at **Willamette Park.** The connection northwest from Council Crest to the zoo follows a patchwork of city streets and paths, but the recent reconstruction of US 26 during development of the westside light-rail passenger line improved bicycle and pedestrian access in the area.

Southwest Portland

Tryon Creek State Park, (503) 653-3166, is one of four day-use state parks in the Greater Portland area. Others are Mary S. Young State Park in West Linn and Dabney and Lewis and Clark State Parks near Troutdale along the Sandy River. The 635 acres of Tryon Creek are mostly covered with old-growth Douglas fir, interspersed with western hemlock, grand fir, and western red cedar. Many a Portland schoolchild has gotten a formal first brush with nature during a field trip to Tryon Creek. The park is located just south of the Lewis and Clark College campus at 11321 SW Terwilliger Blvd.

The park has 8 miles of hiking trails, 3.5 miles of horse trails, and a 3-mile paved bicycle path. The **Trillium Trail** is .33 mile long and is designed for people of all abilities. The trail system begins at the park's nature center, which has interpretive displays and regular programs that explain the natural history of the area. Tryon Creek is one of the last free-flowing creeks in the Portland area that is still suitable habitat for native cutthroat trout. The creek runs 5 miles from its beginning near I-5 through the park to the Willamette River at the north end of the town of Lake Oswego, which was developed around a lake of the same name (no public access).

Marshall Park, just upstream from Tryon Creek State Park, is another park that provides connecting greenspaces, a trademark of the Portland parks system. Marshall Park's 2-mile trail system is used heavily by neighborhood residents and also by cyclocross bicycle riders.

Southeast Portland

Hikers looking for some up-and-down walking on the east side of Portland usually head for the area's numerous volcanic buttes. Although they are in no danger of erupting, Mount Tabor and Powell Butte both show evidence of the geological past that witnessed the formation of dozens of volcanic vents and cones between the shores of the Willamette River and the slopes of Mount Hood. Like most Greater Portland parks, Mount Tabor (bus route 15) and Powell Butte (bus route 9) are well connected by the city's Tri-Met bus system.

Mount Tabor rises 600 feet above the residential areas of east Portland and covers half of a square mile. The park is home to several of the city's water reservoirs, as well as an informal trail system and plenty of big second-growth trees. The main entrance is just east of SE 60th Ave on Salmon St, where an inspiring view of downtown waits just behind the locked gate that keeps vehicles at bay.

The park is a haven for the city's dog owners, even though an experimental off-leash area proved to be a failure because of damage to the vegetation and contamination of the drinking water in the uncovered reservoirs. Dogs still roam the park in numbers that approach the count for human visitors, although most are back on leashes as the law requires them to be elsewhere. The city parks department has been working to open another part of the park for dogs to be allowed to run free.

The park's 2-mile trail system was developed informally over the years. Paths climb through the underbrush to the top of the butte for a view of Mount Hood. Only maintenance vehicles have used paved roads through the upper part of the park since the 1970s.

Powell Butte Nature Park is another city water storage area, but unlike Mount Tabor the water is stored underground in covered cisterns. The park's status as a Portland reservoir makes it part of the city limits, although its location at SE 162nd Ave and Powell Blvd puts it about 40 blocks farther east than the city limits boundary to the north.

Powell Butte is a 570-acre park with a dynamite view from its summit. The park's 9-mile trail system is popular with hikers and equestrians, as well as bikers who have opened up additional trails for single-track riding. The trails on the south side connect with the Springwater Corridor. The Mountain View Trail is paved for .6 mile and is barrier free, although wheelchairs may find its 5 percent grade to be steep. The 1.3-mile Meadowland Trail has a hardened surface for wheelchair use.

Sandy River

The Sandy River at the east edge of Portland gives the city a unique flair rarely found in large metropolitan areas. The Sandy, protected federally as a National Wild and Scenic River, has outstanding fishing for steelhead and chinook salmon, some exciting whitewater for rafting and kayaking, and the only tent camping in the Greater Portland area. Most hiking along the river occurs in Oxbow Regional Park, at Dabney and Lewis and Clark State Parks, and at the Sandy River Delta, an area under development for recreation and wildlife habitat by the management of Columbia River Gorge National Scenic Area.

Oxbow Regional Park has nearly 15 miles of trails that follow the meanders of the Sandy River and traverse the lush green walls of the river's gorge. Six miles of the park's trails are open to horses. Most of the trails are in the main part of the park along Oxbow Pkwy, accessible on the west side of the river from Gresham, but the park also has some lesser-used trails along Gordon Creek Rd, accessible through Troutdale on the east side of the park.

Sitting near the west end of the Columbia River Gorge, Oxbow Regional Park occasionally gets hammered by the ice storms that hit east Multnomah County. The park is not a pretty sight after an ice storm, although the park staff usually act quickly to reopen the roads. They usually wait to work on the trail system, keying the opening to the end of spring's wet weather in May.

Dabney State Park and **Lewis and Clark State Park,** both located down the Sandy River from Oxbow Regional Park near Troutdale, have short, informal trail systems. Dabney's trails follow the river's banks, while trails at Lewis and Clark head east to Broughton's Bluff and its popular rock climbing cliffs. Lewis and Clark State Park is located just south of the Sandy River interchange off I-84 at the east edge of Troutdale. Dabney State Park is 7 miles upriver from the freeway on SE Crown Point Hwy.

The **Sandy River Delta** is located on the northeast side of the Sandy River exit of I-84, just east of Troutdale. Formerly used for grazing, the 1,400 acres can be under a lot of water during years when the Columbia River is running high. Usually by midsummer, the land dries out and hikers can park in designated areas at the freeway interchange and hike a 2-mile trail to the sandy shores of the Columbia. Although used fairly heavily, probably because of its closeness to Portland and its undeveloped setting, the delta area isn't always a pleasant place to hike. When the wind is blowing from the east, jets from Portland International Airport take off to the east. While they cross the delta at a decent but noisy height, private planes from nearby Troutdale Airport are taking off in the same direction and flying much closer overhead.

The Sandy River Delta at the west end of the Columbia River Gorge is the gateway to an abundance of outdoor recreation just east of Portland (see Hood River and the Gorge and Mount Hood chapters). The best place in Portland to stock up with U.S. Forest Service maps and information is the **Nature of the Northwest Information Center,** (503) 731-4444, in northeast Portland's Lloyd District at 800 NE Oregon, Suite 177.

Other Greater Portland Parks

The **Camassia Natural Area,** a 27-acre preserve abutting West Linn High School, is just one of so many pleasant surprises in Portland where a hike of less than a mile can be as rejuvenating as miles clicked off on a forest trail. The Nature Conservancy purchased the natural area in 1962, the first in Oregon to be owned by the land preservation organization. (The conservancy's system has since grown to 32 preserves covering 35,000 acres in the state.) While the Camassia remains one of the group's smallest preserves in the state, its significance is magnified by the rapid urbanization of the Portland area. The natural area is an important home to rare native plants, as well as a tangled woodland of Douglas fir, madrona, and Oregon white oak. The natural area has a 2-mile trail system and visitors are asked to stay on it. A few parking spots are at the end of Walnut St, two blocks north of Sunset Ave in the southern part of West Linn. For information, call the conservancy, (503) 228-9561.

The **National Sanctuary of Our Sorrowful Mother,** also known simply as **The Grotto,** has a 1-mile trail system through its manicured gardens with views of the Columbia River and surrounding mountains. The major feature is a large cave carved in a cliff to house a Catholic shrine, a marble replica of Michelangelo's famous *Pieta*. The Grotto is especially popular during December when it's decked out for the holidays. The Grotto, (503) 254-7371, is open daily, except for Thanksgiving and Christmas. It's located at NE 85th Ave and Sandy Blvd.

Leach Botanical Garden, (503) 761-9503, is a 9-acre Portland park located at 6704 SE 122nd. The garden has a .75-mile trail that winds among the 1,500 labeled plant species. The Leach family began the garden in the 1930s and donated the land to the city in 1979. Other gardens with short walks among flowers and trees include the **Japanese Garden** and the **Rose Garden** in Washington Park; the **Berry Botanic Garden** in southwest Portland at 11505 SW Summerville Ave; and the **Crystal Springs Rhododendron Garden** in Portland's Eastmoreland district at SE 28th just north of Woodstock.

Elk Rock Island, just off the east bank of the Willamette River in the south end of Milwaukie, offers a scenic 1-mile hike opposite the exclusive Dunthorpe neighborhood of Portland. The island is accessible by foot when the river level is low, usually midsummer until late fall. The pathway begins at SE Sparrow St and 19th Ave.

Kelley Point Park at the northwest tip of Portland has a 1.1-mile loop trail that is designed for viewing the busy oceangoing ship traffic at the confluence of the Willamette and Columbia Rivers at the end of N Marine Dr.

Several of Portland's suburbs pride themselves on their walking path systems. **Lake Oswego,** (503) 636-0280, has been recognized nationally for its commitment to a city trail system. **Gresham,** (503) 669-2531, has a walking tour route designed to show off many of its significant trees.

Cycling

With 140 miles of bicycle lanes and paths, most added at a furious pace in the mid-1990s, Portland quickly transformed itself into a bicycle-friendly city. Several suburbs have done the same, especially in Hillsboro and Gresham, where the high-tech boom of Oregon's Silicon Forest has brought many new streets to serve the factories and housing that comes with them. No question, cycling is the activity undergoing the most rapid changes in Greater Portland.

The major barriers to cycling in Portland continue to be the West Hills, a steep climb on a bike, and the Willamette River. A 100 percent bicycle-rack-equipped fleet of **Tri-Met buses,** plus portage of bikes on MAX light-rail cars, is often the best ticket for cyclists to cross the West Hills between Portland and its western suburbs. The **Willamette River bridges** have been improved for cycling, but several bridges have such poor approaches or narrow sidewalks that there is little leeway for a cyclist. The best downtown bridges for cyclists are the Hawthorne, Burnside, and Broadway. Other places to cross are in West Linn, in Sellwood, and on the St. John's Bridge. The I-205 bike path over the Glen Jackson Bridge is a safe, albeit extremely noisy and unpleasant, way to cross the Columbia River between Portland and Vancouver. Cyclists are welcome, but not encouraged, to cross on the I-5 Interstate Bridge.

Many Portlanders ignore the beauty of the **Columbia River,** which makes up Portland's northern boundary and is the largest river in the American West. The Columbia tends to be out of sight, out of mind in a part of town without a lot of attractions. There are a few exceptions—most notably by boaters and bicyclists. Cyclists, as well as a few walkers, make use of a system of bike lanes, off-road bike paths, and the shoulders of busy **Marine Drive** to enjoy sights along the river. This 13-mile route stretches from NE 33rd Dr to 223rd Dr, where the road dips south of the river at the **Chinook Landing** boat launch and beyond to **Troutdale Community Park** on the Sandy River. Several segments of the bike paths are extremely pleasant, where the path is separated from the highway on the river side and dips down into the river dike where vehicle noise is muffled.

The **I-205 bike path**, constructed alongside Portland's eastern freeway in the early 1980s, runs for 11.5 miles from SE Evergreen Hwy and 120th Ave on the Vancouver side of the Columbia River to a mile south of Clackamas Town Center. Some creative riding can extend the route across a pedestrian/bicycle bridge over the Clackamas River in the High Rocks section of Gladstone. The cement-surfaced bike path is open to just about every form of nonmotorized travel. It's not particularly good for high-speed riding because of its varied use and its numerous direction changes as it works its way across east Portland's busy street network. All of the major intersections have traffic signals. The I-205 bike path connects via NE Fremont St to the I-84 bike path, a particularly gruesome stretch of concrete that may as well be part of the highway. The highway noise is deafening, and it's an uncommon sight when someone is spotted on the bike path.

The **Willamette River Greenway,** accessible from many streets that meet the river through the center of Portland, is another masterpiece in the making. When it is finished, cyclists will be able to ride on bike paths on both sides of the Willamette River between the Broadway and Sellwood Bridges and beyond. The west side already offers good access to Willamette Park, although a few pieces are still missing south of the downtown River-Place development. Tom McCall Waterfront Park, the grass and cement promenade along the Willamette River in downtown Portland, is closed to bicycles during Rose Festival. Heavy use by all kinds of visitors throughout the year requires a subdued pace on a bicycle.

The east side of the Willamette River has a paved shoreline path between the Burnside and Hawthorne Bridges, but it will take some cleaning up and some new connections to make it a pleasant place to ride. The Portland Office of Transportation is planning a bicycle crossing of the Steel Bridge that will involve a floating pier so that the eastside bike path won't get washed away by the next hundred-year flood.

Bike lanes along **Terwilliger Boulevard,** the city street that climbs south of downtown Portland past Oregon Health Sciences University, provide a way around the West Hills by connecting with bike lanes along the Beaverton-Hillsdale Hwy to Beaverton. Bike lanes continue south on Terwilliger, past Tryon Creek State Park, all the way to Lake Oswego. (Cyclists and joggers used to share an off-road path along Terwilliger, but the use got too heavy and the city moved the cyclists onto the street where they belong.)

Greenway Park, (503) 645-6433, follows a linear path between Beaverton and Tigard along Fanno Creek. The park covers 60 acres in a narrow strip from SW Denney Rd on the north and SW Scholls Ferry Rd on the south. A 2-mile paved path traverses the park, making it a popular spot for hikers and bikers from surrounding neighborhoods.

Portland's newest cycling showcase is the **Springwater Corridor,** a 16.8-mile rail-trail conversion that was dedicated in 1996. The old Bellrose rail line runs from near SE McLoughlin Blvd in Portland's Sellwood district all the way to Boring, a small community in Clackamas County southeast of Gresham. The Springwater Corridor has a hardened chip-sealed surface in Portland, a blacktop surface in Gresham, and a gravel surface for its last 4 miles to Boring. The trail draws an annual total of a million user days by cyclists, walkers, equestrians, in-line skaters, and wheelchair-users. The corridor's major trailheads are at SE 45th Ave and Johnson Creek Blvd in Portland and at Main City Park and at SE Hogan Rd in Gresham. The trail crosses many city streets, as well as the I-205 bike path, and is easy to access from most southern neighborhoods in Portland and Gresham. The trail's $2.5 million of improvements have brought marked crossings at all the major streets, permanent rest rooms at the Portland trailhead, and landscaping.

The Portland end of the trail passes through a long-neglected industrial area that is slowly showing signs of change. Some of the businesses are interested in adopting parts of the trail and landscaping it where it passes their facilities. The trail takes on a more rural feeling where it crosses Foster Rd and passes Beggars-tick Wildlife Refuge, Powell Butte Nature Park, and Gresham's Main City Park. The trail's west end butts up against an unbridged railroad track that will be connected to the Willamette River Greenway in the future. A pleasant spot near the west end is on Johnson Creek in inner southeast Portland at Tideman Johnson Park. The corridor has an excellent free map available from Portland Parks and Recreation, (503) 823-2223.

Despite Portland's rapid growth, the area still has a network of **country roads** that offer pleasant cycling. The best roads are found east of Gresham toward the Sandy River, south of Oregon City, and west of Beaverton. All are just beyond the Greater Portland area but close enough to reach on a bicycle. If all else fails, find a friend, get a permit to put your bikes on a Tri-Met bus, ride a bus to the end of the line, and cycle back into town. Permits require watching a short video and learning to use the bike rack on the bus. Check with Tri-Met, (503) 239-3044, for information on obtaining the $5 bike permit.

Portland's most active bicycling group is the **Portland Wheelmen Touring Club,** which leads rides almost every day of the year. Some of the rides are geared to train new cyclists in the rules of the road for group riding. On other rides, leaders pass out route maps and that's the last most cyclists will see of the fastest riders. To join any of the club's rides, all of which are open to nonmembers, call the hotline at (503) 257-7982.

A **bike shop** is never far away when riding through Portland's neighborhoods and its suburbs. The yellow pages have a complete listing under "Bicycles." Most bikers eventually find their way into one of the four Bike Gallery stores. The downtown Bike Gallery is at 821 SW 11th, (503) 222-3821. Portland's excellent **bicycle map**, published by Metro and called "Bike There," can be purchased for $3.95 at most bike stores.

Mountain Biking

With so many places to ride a road bike, you might think a mountain bike isn't necessary in Portland. Wrong! As elsewhere, mountains bikes or their hybrids make up the bulk of the bike market in Portland. Also as elsewhere, most mountain bikes in Portland are ridden in the city and never see a dirt trail or mud puddle, but it doesn't have to be that way.

Leif Erikson Drive, located in **Forest Park** at the west end of NW Thurman St, is a mecca for the city's hard-core mountain bikers. The road is closed to motor vehicles, except for the park maintenance staff, and gradually gets more difficult the farther up the 16-mile distance you ride. Popular loops are made on any of the fire lanes that crisscross the park. Forest Park (see Hiking/Walking/Parks, above) is also heavily used by hikers and runners, so bikers need to be alert to avoid accidents.

Powell Butte Nature Park in southeast Portland at 162nd and Powell Blvd is another spot high on the list of mountain-bike riders. The park's trail system is shorter than Forest Park's, but it mixes some difficult hill climbing with outstanding views. The park has 15 miles of single-track trails, with the most difficult riding in the woods.

Portland's main mountain-bike club is **Portland United Mountain Pedalers (PUMP),** (503) 223-3954. There are dozens of **bicycle shops** strategically located around the metro area. The Fat Tire Farm, (503) 222-3276, is a prominent mountain-bike shop located near the entrance to the Forest Park trail system at 2714 NW Thurman.

Camping

Besides skiing, one of the few forms of outdoor recreation in short supply in Greater Portland is tent camping. The only legal spot to pitch a tent in the metro area is **Oxbow Regional Park,** (503) 663-4708, 6 miles east of Gresham via Division St. The park is operated by Metro, and its 45 tent and small RV campsites (no hookups) are open all year on a first-come basis, as long as the winter weather isn't too severe. (On the few days each year when the weather is extreme, anyone voluntarily camping in a tent would be a little foolish anyway.)

Other campgrounds just outside the Greater Portland area are

Champoeg State Park on the Willamette River near Newberg (see Salem and the Heart of the Valley chapter); Barton County Park and McIver State Park near Estacada (see Cascade Foothills chapter); and Battle Ground Lake State Park, across the Columbia River 2 miles northeast of the town of Battle Ground in Washington's Clark County.

Recreational vehicles may be parked for the night in a selection of spots in Greater Portland. Among them are Jantzen Beach RV Park, (503) 289-7626, on Hayden Island in the Columbia River, 1503 N Hayden Island Dr; Fir Grove RV Park, (503) 252-9993, in northeast Portland, 5541 NE 72nd; and Trailer Park of Portland, (503) 692-0225, 66 SW Nyberg Rd, and Roamer's Rest RV Park, (503) 692-6350, 17585 SW Pacific Hwy, both in Tualatin.

Wildlife

The backyard is the first place Greater Portland area residents usually start watching for wildlife. The city's neighborhoods have a healthy population of opossums, raccoons, and squirrels. Some of the leafier parts of the city harbor coyotes and black-tailed deer. One year, two Roosevelt elk wandered into the city and took up residence. Outer reaches of the metro area see occasional visits by cougars and black bears.

Birds live throughout the Greater Portland area. The great blue heron, one of the tallest North American birds, is the city's official winged mascot. Bald eagles have been known to nest on Ross Island in the Willamette River. A spring outing to Oaks Bottom can easily result in spotting 30 or more bird species, including red-tailed hawks and osprey. Mount Tabor Park has a resident flock of ring-necked pheasants.

Portland's designated wildlife areas include the following:

Smith and Bybee Lakes is a marshy area in North Portland that covers 2,000 acres during winter and spring, then dries up to about half that size by late summer. The shallow lakes are one of the largest remaining river-bottom lands that remain along the Columbia River as it passes Greater Portland. Wildlife that the lakes harbor can be seen from canoes or a growing trail system with parking lots on N Portland Rd and N Marine Dr. The St. John's Landfill, formerly Portland's largest refuse depository, lies just south of Bybee Lake. The surface of the landfill is slowly being reclaimed for wildlife habitat even while methane gas is collected from the garbage buried deep in the ground. The parking lot for the lakes' canoe launch and 1-mile trail system is 2.5 miles west of I-5 on N Marine Dr. The lakes are home to beavers, river otters, ducks, herons, kingfishers, and great horned owls. The Western painted turtle is listed as a sensitive species and the lakes are one of its last strongholds in the Portland area. Fishing in the lakes is good for largemouth bass, crappie, and bluegills, although consumption is discouraged because of heavy-metal contamination and ongoing sewer overflows from Portland. The lakes are managed by Metro's Regional Parks and Greenspaces, (503) 797-1850.

Beggars-tick Wildlife Refuge, named after a species of native sunflower, is located on SE 111th St, just north of Foster Rd next to the Springwater Corridor. The 21-acre wetland, managed by the Metro Greenspaces program, can overflow with waters from the rising floodplain of Johnson Creek during winter, then turn bone dry at the end of a hot summer. The refuge is home to a variety of **wintering water birds,** including wood ducks and green-winged teal, and is claimed in summer by marsh wrens and red-winged blackbirds. It's even a good place to watch **dragonflies** feeding on the abundant insect population.

Oaks Bottom, a swampy area on the east bank of the Willamette River just south of downtown, is a Portland city park wildlife refuge known for its birdlife. Entry to the refuge is on trails from parking lots on SE Seventh and Sellwood Blvd in Sellwood Park, or from a new 10-car lot at the 5000 block of SE Milwaukie Blvd. Oaks Bottom is an outstanding birding location year-round, especially in early March when Portlanders are itching to get outside.

Bird species observed during one late winter outing included Canada goose, song sparrow, northern shoveler, green-winged teal, crow, starling, mourning dove, robin, mallard, cormorant, bufflehead, cinnamon teal, great blue heron, red-winged blackbird, swallow, downy woodpecker, black-capped chickadee, California gull, red-tailed hawk, wood duck, spotted towhee, scrub jay, yellow-rumped warbler, ruby-crowned kinglet, American widgeon, golden-crowned kinglet, lesser scaup, finch, flicker, and hairy woodpecker. Not bad for a wildlife refuge within sight of downtown Portland's tall buildings.

Now a few things to remember about Oaks Bottom: High water can make the trails around the bottom's east side impassable. The vast pools of standing water usually turn the place into Portland's biggest mosquito factory when the temperature warms up in June. The railroad track along the bottom's west side is closed to public access. (The city is negotiating for an easement, which would close the missing link of the trail system from Boring via the Springwater Corridor to downtown via the Hawthorne Bridge.)

The **Audubon Society**'s Portland headquarters at 5151 NW Cornell Rd sits at the edge of a 160-acre preserve set on Balch Creek at the edge of Forest Park. The nature store's telephone number is (503) 292-9453. The society maintains a collection of preserved animals and birds to show visitors and use in its educational programs. A good place to begin watching for wildlife is from inside the large meeting room where a bird feeder just beyond the windows attracts resident songbirds and squirrels. The society's bird sanctuary has 4 miles of forested trails that pass native flora and provide opportunities to view the fauna. Watch for **woodpeckers, nuthatches,** and **towhees.** The pond usually has **ducks** swimming above and **cutthroat** below. The society's preserve has three separate areas: the **Pittock Bird Sanctuary,** south across Cornell Rd, the **Collins Sanctuary,** northeast of Audubon House, and the Audubon Sanctuary, adjacent to the visitors center to the north.

The **Sandy River Gorge** is one of the true gems of the Greater Portland area. Set at the eastern edge of the Urban Growth Boundary, the gorge offers a feeling of remoteness despite the jet airplanes that fly over-head as they come and go from Portland International Airport. The Gorge and Oxbow Regional Park, the major park along the Sandy River, offer dependable sightings of **osprey, kingfishers, mergansers,** and **black-tailed deer.** The preserve is managed by the Salem District of the Bureau of Land Management (BLM), (503) 399-5646, and the Portland chapter of The Nature Conservancy, (503) 228-9561.

Greater Portland has many more places to watch for wildlife (see Hiking/Walking/Parks, above). Some of the best are Tryon Creek State Park at the boundary between Portland and Lake Oswego; Crystal Springs Rhodo-dendron Garden and Powell Butte Nature Park in southeast Portland; Elk Rock Island, which is surrounded by the Willamette River between Portland and Milwaukie but can be reached on foot during low water; virtually any-where along the Columbia, Willamette, Clackamas, and Tualatin Rivers; and, all in Portland's West Hills, the Metro Washington Park Zoo, Marquam Nature Park, and Forest Park.

Fishing

Every February, Portland's fishermen eagerly await the first sign of the return of the spring run of chinook salmon to the **Willamette River.** Moorages up and down the river come alive with activity as anglers scurry to tune up their boats after a winter of idleness and get them ready for the salmon. At least it used to be that way. The Willamette River's run of spring chinook has been on the wane, and fishery managers are trying to figure out why. When the salmon are in the river, boats are thick from downtown upstream to Willamette Falls at Oregon City. The season can be short, how-ever, because when a predetermined number of fish are caught the season ends. For the lucky few anglers who bag a spring chinook, they'll enjoy some of the best-tasting fish in the world. The most popular **boat launches** are Willamette Park on the river's west side at SW Macadam and Nebraska, and Clackamette and Meldrum Bar Parks on the river's east side on either side of the Clackamas River mouth between Gladstone and Oregon City.

Portland's fishermen also try their luck at landing a chinook in the **Columbia, Sandy,** and **Clackamas Rivers.** Chinook are in the Columbia from February through April, but, like the Willamette, the regulations and seasons change at the drop of a dime.

Fishing for chinook in the Sandy is best in April, then again for the fall run from August through October. Peak catches of chinook in the Clackamas usually occur in April and May. The area's best angling for steelhead in the Sandy is during winter, although fish are caught all year long. The Clackamas also has steelhead throughout the year, with peak success usually in December and January. **Columbia River boat launches** are operated by Metro, (503) 797-1850, at Chinook Landing and the James Gleason boat launch, both located along NE Marine Dr. The Gleason ramp is at 42nd Ave, and Chinook Landing is at 223rd. **Clackamas boat launches** are upriver at the town of Carver and near the river's mouth at Clackamette and Meldrum Bar Parks. Float fishermen access the Sandy River at Dodge Park, 5 miles northwest of Sandy on SE Lusted Rd and at Oxbow Regional Park (see Camping, above).

With the decline of the salmon runs, Portland fishermen have switched interest to other fisheries, most notably warm-water fishing in the sloughs and bays of the Columbia and Willamette. Sturgeon and shad are also sought in both rivers. The Oregon Department of Fish and Wildlife, (503) 229-5222, publishes a free booklet called "Guide to Warmwater Fishing in the Portland Metropolitan Area." Although some places are better than others, especially around pilings and piers of the Columbia and Willamette Rivers, fish have been pulled from just about every pool of water in the Greater Portland area. Portland has an abundance of fishing shops, most listed in the yellow pages under "Fishing." One of the largest-volume stores is Fisherman's Marine & Outdoor, with stores in Oregon City at 1900 McLoughlin Blvd and at 1120 N Hayden Meadows Dr in the Delta Park area of Portland. Kaufmann's Streamborn, (503) 639-6400, at 8861 SW Commercial in Tigard, is one of the state's largest suppliers of fly-fishing equipment.

Portland also has some good trout fishing, especially for hatchery fish stocked especially for the youngsters. Success rates can be quite high, especially a few days after a pond or lake has been stocked with legal-size trout. Some of the best places for trout are **Blue Lake** at 20500 NE Marine Dr, the **Mount Hood Community College pond** at 26000 SE Stark in Gresham, and **Roslyn Lake** at 41401 SE Thomas Rd near Sandy. Other good trout fishing is located nearby in Hood River and the Gorge, Cascade Foothills, and Lower Columbia (see Fishing in those chapters).

Boating

It's not anything to match Seattle, but Portland is a city of boaters. From big motor cruisers to the tiniest of sailboats, from oceangoing kayaks to river rafts, most Portlanders at least know someone who spends time in a boat on summer weekends. And yes, there are personal watercraft. The newest wave of water access is popular here, too, especially off the downtown Willamette River waterfront and the James Gleason boat launch on the Columbia River at NE 42nd Ave. Regardless of personal feelings toward the Jet-skis, they are here to stay and Oregon actively manages them. The main constraint on their use is a no-wake speed limit near the many houseboats that float on the Willamette and Columbia Rivers and on the Columbia Slough in northwest Portland.

Portland's rivers are filled with powerboats during the hot weekends of summer. The Coast Guard and county river patrol unit have their hands full keeping the peace, but things usually work out and don't get too rowdy. Boat campers head for **Government Island** in the Columbia River just north of Portland International Airport; picnickers head for **Powers Marine Park** on the Willamette's west shore south of the Sellwood Bridge; and water-skiers look for calm water wherever they can find it, usually on the Willamette from **Ross Island** south to the **Clackamas River.**

Major boat launches on the Columbia River are **Chinook Landing**, a 67-acre marine park operated by Metro near Troutdale, and the NE 42nd Ave launch by the airport (see Fishing, above). Also called the **James Gleason ramp,** the launch is adjacent to a sandy stretch of Columbia River known as Broughton Beach, and together they are the focus of a $4 million improvement project.

The Willamette River has many launch points. Most popular are **Swan Island,** (503) 249-4764, in the North Portland harbor at the Swan Island Lagoon; **Willamette Park** and **Sellwood Riverfront Park,** both Portland parks, (503) 823-2223, on either bank of the Willamette River just south of downtown; plus another half-dozen public launches scattered between Milwaukie upriver to Oregon City. **Meldrum Bar** and **Clackamette Park,** situated on either side of the mouth of the Clackamas River between Oregon City and Gladstone, are favored by fishermen. More than a dozen transient moorages are scattered around Portland, with **RiverPlace** just off downtown the most noticeable. Telephone for the RiverPlace marina's harbormaster is (503) 241-8283.

One place that isn't open to public boating in Greater Portland is **Lake Oswego,** one of the few natural lakes in the Portland area. Boating access is limited to the residents whose homes line the lake's shore in one of the most exclusive areas of Portland.

No trip in Portland is complete without a passage through the **Willamette Falls Locks** at West Linn off Willamette Falls Dr. The locks cater to the Willamette River's busy commercial traffic during the week, but plenty of pleasure craft pass through on weekends. The Willamette Falls Locks, (503) 656-3381, were opened in 1873 and are operated by the U.S. Army Corp of Engineers. Each of the four locks is 40 feet wide and 210 feet long. Average passage time is 45 minutes upstream and 30 minutes down. The locks are open daily from 7am to 11pm and are free of charge. Be sure to add some extra time to tour the museum. When approaching the locks, contact the lockmaster by radio or use the small boat alarm at the end of the lock. The lockmaster appreciates getting a phone call in advance when nonmotorized craft plan to pass.

Cruises

Portland will never be mistaken for Miami, but several cruise lines operate in and around the River City. The Willamette River past downtown Portland is a popular setting for harbor cruises, and the Columbia River on the north side of town carries cruise ships all the way from Astoria to Lewiston, Idaho.

The Portland Spirit, (503) 224-3900, offers dinner tours throughout the year on the **Willamette River.** Boarding is in Tom McCall Waterfront Park near Salmon Street Springs, the city's famous riverside fountain. The stern-wheeler *Columbia Gorge,* (503) 223-3928, plies the waters of the Willamette from October through June when it's not in the Columbia River Gorge. Boarding is at SW Naito Pkwy and Stark St.

Willamette Jetboat Excursions, (503) 231-1532, began operating tours of the Portland harbor in 1997. A subsidiary of the Hellgate jet-boat tours on the Rogue River out of Grants Pass in southern Oregon, the company uses the same type of jet-boat as the ones used on the Rogue River. The company provides the quickest way of any commercial operation to see the Willamette River, from the shipyards at Swan Island to Willamette Falls at Oregon City. The two-hour tour is offered four times daily from mid-May through mid-October. Tours begin at the docks adjacent to the Oregon Museum of Science and Industry, 1945 SE Water Ave, on the east side of the Willamette River across from the city's downtown skyline.

The Doubletree Hotel Jantzen Beach is the boarding place for day cruises on the **Columbia River** from Portland into the Gorge by Great Rivers Cruise Tours of Seattle, (800) 720-0012. The company also runs day tours on the Willamette River.

Sailing

Portland has an active population of sailors who usually spend summer evenings sailing on the **Columbia River** between Portland's two interstate-highway bridges. Yacht clubs on the Columbia River are Rose City, Tyee, and Portland. Waverly Yacht Club is on the **Willamette River.** Some sailing ships ply the waters of the Columbia all the way to Astoria, then continue offshore for trips as far away as Newport on the central Oregon Coast or Victoria, British Columbia. Sailors who have the most fun tend to be able to trailer their boats to surrounding locations where conditions are more exciting than the repeated tack and jibe between the Columbia's two bridges.

Rafting/Kayaking/Canoeing

Portland must be one of the few big cities with a fun **whitewater** river experience at the very edge of the metro area. The **Sandy River,** which runs from the glaciers of Mount Hood to join the Columbia at Troutdale, offers 8 miles of mellow rapids between Dodge Park near Sandy and Oxbow Regional Park near Gresham. The river's next 7.5 miles, to the takeout at Lewis and Clark State Park before it joins the Columbia, covers scenic Class I water. The most difficult rapids on the Dodge Park section is Pipeline, a Class III less than .5 mile from the launch. The rapid spills a few boaters, but a pool just below is a good spot to collect spilled gear. (The pool is also a favored spot for steelhead anglers.) The river alternates mellow rapids with placid water, but the scenery in the canyon is usually the major attraction. The only place to stop for lunch is a sandy beach on river right, about midway through the float and just below Blue Hole rapids.

The Sandy is usually too low to accommodate rafts after mid-June. The river is at its best when swollen by rain or snowmelt, but don't boat it when it gets too high—partially submerged trees can be a deadly surprise. The Sandy River at Troutdale is usually the setting of the most drownings each year in the Portland area. After a warm afternoon partying in the river's sand, someone (usually a young male) tries to swim across the river and doesn't make it. The water is always cold in the Sandy (it's fed by Mount Hood's glaciers during the summer) and the current is surprisingly strong.

Portland has an ardent group of **paddlers,** although they head beyond the metro area for quality trips. It's possible to paddle the Columbia and Willamette Rivers, but busy commercial barge and oceangoing traffic, plus powerboats, make the experience less than enjoyable.

Good places to paddle include the lower **Clackamas River,** from the town of Carver downstream to Clackamette Park at the confluence with the Willamette River; the lower **Sandy River,** between Oxbow Regional Park and Lewis and Clark State Park (see Hiking/Walking/Parks, above), and on **Blue** and **Roslyn Lakes** on Portland's east side (see Fishing, above). Wildlife viewing is good from a canoe or kayak on Smith and Bybee Lakes and the Columbia Slough, upstream from Kelley Point Park, all in North

Portland. The **Tualatin River** in Washington County makes for a long, lazy float in a canoe, except for the 5 miles above its confluence with the Willamette that shouldn't be run due to a dam and a rocky channel. The Tualatin River is slowly being rehabilitated from the decades of abuse it's received. A popular 11-mile trip runs from Shamberg Bridge, on Elsner Rd 2 miles west of Hwy 99W at Sherwood, to a takeout at Shipley Bridge on Stafford Rd 2 miles north of I-205 between Tualatin and West Linn.

Passage through the Willamette Falls Locks (see Boating, above) isn't limited to motorized craft. A Portland canoe club schedules a regular trip through the locks every spring, launching at West Linn's **Willamette Park,** passing through the locks, paddling upstream for a good view of Willamette Falls, then heading downstream for a takeout at Sportcraft Marina in Oregon City or the public marina just downstream on the Willamette's east bank.

Sportcraft Marina, (503) 656-6484, rents a variety of motor and paddle boats from its facilities at 1701 Clackamette Dr, Oregon City. Canoes and kayaks can also be rented from Alder Creek Kayak Supply, (503) 285-0464, 250 NE Tomahawk Island Dr in North Portland, and at Ebb and Flow Paddlesports, (503) 245-1756, 0604 SW Nebraska St in Portland. (The 0604 address is a quirk in Portland's street numbering system and designates an address east of Naito Pkwy—formerly Front Ave—but west of the Willamette River.)

A word about **Portland's water:** Stay away from the Willamette River during times of high runoff from rains. The city's storm runoff system is connected to its sewer system, and any big rainstorm produces too much flow for the sewage treatment system, so the water is flushed directly into the river. Portland is spending billions of dollars to clean up the mess and convert its sewer system, but it will be many years before the project is finished. The **Columbia Slough** is also notoriously polluted and Portland is trying to clean it up. Despite the slough's concentration of heavy metals, it's simply too outstanding a wildlife area for paddlers to ignore. Be sure to clean up big time after paddling on the slough and stay off it during periods of sewer overflow.

Rowing

Despite the Willamette River's heavy traffic, rowing is popular on it. And so are dragonboat paddling—an event staged for the city's annual Rose Festival celebration in June—and outrigger canoe paddling. The Station L Rowing Club, (503) 916-8100, 1466 NW Naito Pkwy, has a boathouse in northwest Portland near the Fremont Bridge and is always looking for new members. Club members also give lessons to newcomers to the sport, although people who want to learn how to row single sculls should check with RiverPlace Marina, (503) 241-8283, or the Lake Oswego Parks Department, (503) 636-0280.

Climbing

Indoor climbing wasn't invented in Portland, but it sure has been embraced warmly. The city has three commercial climbing gyms, plus climbing walls in grade schools, high schools, community colleges, and outdoor stores. Costco's SportsNation at 18120 SW Lower Boones Ferry Rd in Tigard, (503) 968-4500, one of the largest athletic clubs anywhere (140,000 square feet), mixes climbing walls with its 9 basketball courts and 13 volleyball courts.

The Portland Rock Gym was the first commercial climbing gym in Portland. It's grown to two locations—one at 2034 SE Sixth in Portland, (503) 232-8310, where top-roping allows climbs on a 35-foot-high wall, and another at 617 NW 13th in the Pearl District, (503) 796-9335, a bouldering gym designed to meet the needs of people with a busy downtown lifestyle. The Stoneworks Gym, (503) 644-3517, at 6775 SW 111th Ave in Beaverton, caters to climbers in Portland's western suburbs.

Climbers who want to practice their skills **outdoors** but don't want to drive a long way should head for Rocky Butte in northeast Portland, located on NE Rocky Butte Rd off 92nd and Fremont, and Broughton's Bluff in Lewis and Clark State Park near Troutdale (see Hiking/Walking/Parks, above). Both areas have many climbing routes to choose from and are often used as training grounds for more difficult climbing in central Oregon's Smith Rock State Park (see Crooked River chapter). Portland's climbing specialty store is Climb Max, (503) 797-1991, at 3341 SE Hawthorne Blvd.

In-line Skating/Skateboarding

Portland's wet weather puts the damper on outside skating during much of the year, but no problem: the action moves inside for weekly skates in **Memorial Coliseum** or to the area's major roller rinks at Portland's Oaks Amusement Park, located at the east end of the Sellwood Bridge, or Skate World in Gresham at 1220 NE Kelley Ave and Skate World in Hillsboro at 4395 SE Witch Hazel Rd. Portland's ice skaters use rinks at Lloyd Center, (503) 288-6073, and Clackamas Town Center, (503) 786-6000, two of the Portland area's three largest shopping malls, and Valley Ice Arena, 9250 SW Beaverton-Hillsdale Hwy in Beaverton.

In-line skaters are also welcome at the weekly Tuesday night bicycle races around the 1.9-mile track at Portland International Raceway. About the only place skaters aren't welcome is the downtown area, where a city ordinance was passed to ban all types of skating on sidewalks before in-line skating became a practical way to commute to work.

Portland's **skateboard parks**—one indoor and another outdoor—keep busy year-round. Many of the country's top skateboard pros pass through town on their way from California to give clinics at the big skate ramps that have been built around Government Camp as part of the off-slope activities for Mount Hood's summer ski and snowboard camps.

Portland's favorite skateboard park nestles under the east side of the **Burnside Bridge.** An informal arrangement between the parks department and the riders seems to work pretty well. The parks department allows the existence of the informal park, but the riders who use it must keep it clean and police the surrounding area. It's worth a visit by non-skateboarders just to see the latest trends in how the younger generation dresses, thinks, and acts.

Portland's long-established skateboard shop is Cal's Skateboards, (503) 248-0495, located downtown at 213 NW Couch.

Paintball

If you're looking for a place to go splat, Portland's got a spot. Called City Paintball, (503) 233-1105, the indoor paintball park is a popular way for workers to bond with their bosses after business hours. The park is located at 631 NE Grand Ave. Outdoor paintball action is available in Tigard at Hit-N-Run Paintball, (503) 968-9579, at 8900 SW Commercial and in Molalla at Splat Action Paintball Park, (503) 829-7311, at 32155 S Grimm Rd.

Swimming

Waters around Portland warm up by mid-July to allow plenty of outdoor swimming opportunities in the natural settings of Blue Lake Regional Park, Willamette Park, and the Sandy River at Oxbow Regional Park, but none of the rivers or lakes have a wave pool or water slide like the North Clackamas Aquatic Park, (503) 650-3483, in Milwaukie at 7300 SE Harmony Dr. The indoor water park has a 4-foot wave pool, plus three water slides. Local park districts offer a number of additional indoor and outdoor swimming pools. Biggest of all is the Tarpenning Recreation Complex, a 92-acre park and swimming facility operated by the Tualatin Hills Parks and Recreation District, (503) 645-6433, at 15707 SW Walker Rd in Beaverton.

Kite Flying

About the only urban sport that hasn't found a home indoors is kite flying. Other than during winter, when the east wind howls out of the Columbia

River Gorge, Portland isn't known as a particularly windy city. But it doesn't take a lot of wind to get a well-designed kite into the air, and Portland has several spots where kite fliers gather nightly during summer.

Some of the best places to fly a kite are **Blue Lake Regional Park** in northeast Portland; **West Delta Park** on the west side of I-5 just south of the Interstate Bridge; and **Broughton Beach** on the Columbia at NE 42nd Ave. When the wind is blowing strong, just about any place without overhead obstruction, such as a neighborhood football field or park, can be a good place to fly a kite. A kite specialty store is Paint the Sky Kites, (503) 222-5096, in northwest Portland at 828 NW 23rd.

Attractions

With its plethora of parks, charming downtown core, splendid westside riverfront, and proximity to so many of Oregon's finest diversions, **Portland** is a gem. Below is a glimpse of the Rose City (followed by reviews of its top restaurants and lodgings); for a more comprehensive city guide, see our series companion, *Portland Best Places.*

Music. Portlanders pack the city's beloved Arlene Schnitzer Concert Hall, at 1000 SW Broadway, 52 weeks a year. A variety of performers— classical, jazz, and rock—play the "Schnitz" each season; home to the Oregon Symphony Orchestra, under conductor James DePreist; (503) 228-1353. Chamber Music Northwest presents a five-week-long summer festival spanning four centuries of music; (503) 223-3202.

Theater and Dance. Neighboring the Schnitz is the Portland Center for Performing Arts, which contains two performance spaces. Its full-time resident company, Portland Center Stage, (503) 274-6588, began as an offshoot of the acclaimed Shakespeare Festival in Ashland, but is now wholly independent. PCS offers excellent production values, whatever the play (light comedies seem to play best). You can always be assured of work by Shakespeare with productions by Tygres Heart, (503) 222-9220, housed in the same facility. The Portland Repertory Theater, (503) 224-4491, puts on critically acclaimed productions in a theater just off Naito Pkwy. Musicals of any caliber land at Civic Auditorium (222 SW Clay St)—also home to the Portland Opera, (503) 241-1802. The Oregon Ballet Theater, (503) 227-6867, enlists youth and daring to serve the needs of Portland's ballet fans.

Museums and Visual Arts. The Oregon Museum of Science and Industry, (503) 797-OMSI, is a stunning facility—and not just for kids. Gallery walks once a month (on "First Thursdays") encourage Portlanders to visit their corner of the art world. The Portland Art Museum (1219 SW Park Ave, (503) 226-2811) takes center stage, but the city is popping with public art, too; just watch for it—or pick up the "Public Art: Walking Tour" booklet, free at the Regional Arts & Culture Council (309 SW Sixth Ave, Suite 100, (503) 823-5111) and hunt down these treasures. Pioneer Courthouse Square, off SW Broadway and Yamhill Sts, is a good place to begin your search, and the stunningly renovated Central Library, on SW 10th Ave, is a great place to end it; (503) 248-5123.

Literature. Powell's, the superpower of bookstores (1005 W Burnside, (800) 878-7323 out-of-state or (503) 228-4651 in-state), presides over literary Portland. It and many other excellent bookstores, as well as churches and colleges, present readings by local and visiting writers. Literary Arts, the Portland Arts and Lectures Series, produces a series of lectures by nationally known literary figures and although tickets are scarce you might get lucky; (503) 227-2583.

Nightlife. Check local newspapers' calendar listings for what's happening in the jazz world (*Willamette Week* is out each Wednesday; the *Oregonian's* entertainment section is in Friday's paper). One gig you can depend on is at the Portland Art Museum: its Museum After Hours programs on Wednesdays at 5:30pm are still going strong after a decade; (503) 226-2811. Rock fans get their licks at Berbati's Pan or La Luna, while folkies hang at the Aladdin. If you feel like dancing, head to the refurbished Crystal Ballroom on W Burnside, where the music—from reggae to ballroom—starts at 9pm.

Spectator Sports. The town's big-league action can be found at the shiny new Rose Garden Arena, home of the Portland Trail Blazers men's basketball team. The Trail Blazers usually manage to make the playoffs, although they haven't won the championship since 1977; call Ticketmaster, (503) 224-4400. Portland also has one of nine professional women's teams in the new American Basketball League: the Portland Power went 15–25 in their first season (the wins came after a coaching switch midseason); call Ticketmaster. The Portland Winter Hawks, a member of the Western Hockey League, hit the ice at home 36 times a season; call Ticketmaster.

Shopping. Crafts can be found weekends at Saturday Market under the Burnside Bridge. Pioneer Place is major downtown shopping complex starring Saks Fifth Avenue. Upscale specialty shops and eateries are also found at the Water Tower at John's Landing, at Lloyd Center, or at the suburban malls Clackamas Town Center and Washington Square. Northwest

Portland's 23rd Ave and SE Hawthorne Blvd between 20th and 50th feature great neighborhood merchants; NE Broadway and Multnomah (in southwest Portland) are also bright spots in the neighborhood shopping scene. Lots of antiques are found in Multnomah and Sellwood, in the city's southeast corner.

Restaurants

Al-Amir ☆☆   The elaborate Bishop's House hosts this elegant Lebanese outpost. Starring here are the smoky, intense baba ghanouj and the creamy hummus, but the kitchen's reach is extensive. Don't depart without trying the grape leaves. *223 SW Stark St (downtown between 2nd and 3rd), Portland; (503) 274-0010; $$.*

Alexis ☆☆   Most restaurants offer a meal; the family-run Alexis is a party. The welcome here is warm and the Greek food authentic and memorable. Regulars often order several appetizers for dinner. On weekends a Middle Eastern dancer performs. *215 W Burnside (between 2nd and 3rd), Portland; (503) 224-8577; $$.*

Assaggio ☆☆   This is the place for carbo-loading. For $10 a person, you'll receive three courses of pasta. You can skip their picks and explore the 20 pasta choices by yourself, and it's hard to go wrong. The rooms are carefully decorated. *7742 SE 13th Ave (in Sellwood, at 13th and Lambert), Portland; (503) 232-6151; $$.*

Atwater's ☆☆☆   This showcase restaurant looks Mount Hood in the eye and places its emphasis on local ingredients in a Continental-inspired menu. The menu changes seasonally, covering a lot of ground well. There's a more casual bar and a voluminous wine list. *111 SW 5th Ave (off W Burnside), Portland; (503) 275-3600; $$$.*

Avalon Grill ☆☆☆   Since its splashy opening, this dramatically designed and located restaurant has been rising. The chef seems more surefooted, matching signature dishes with lively innovations. In the postmodern bar, there's live jazz and cigars. *4630 SW Macadam Ave (near John's Landing), Portland; (503) 227-4630; $$.*

Bangkok Kitchen ☆☆   Crowds stream here for the unadorned basics of Southeast Asian cooking: hot-and-sour soups, curries, salads, and noodles. The funky, informal atmosphere has attracted a faithful following. Kids are more than welcome. *2534 SE Belmont St (at 25th Ave), Portland; (503) 236-7349; $.*

Bima ☆   The vaguely Caribbean menu has its fans, but the star here is the scene, architecturally and socially. In this dramatic space, warehouse walls tower, and splashes of color and asymmetrical furniture are everywhere. At night, the bar's lit up by an artsy crowd. *1338 NW Hoyt (between NW 13th and 14th), Portland; (503) 241-3465; $$.*

B. Moloch/The Heathman Bakery and Pub ☆☆ The Heathman's casual cousin is a hearty brewpub, with walls of windows and artful high ceilings. The food is meaty, though there are also salads, pastas, sandwiches, and one of the city's better breakfasts. *901 SW Salmon St (at the north end of the South Park Blocks), Portland; (503) 227-5700; $$.*

Brasserie Montmartre ☆☆ There's only one real restaurant after midnight in Portland. Brasserie offers everything from veal to eggs Benedict to caviar, all surprisingly consistent. The major ingredient, however, may be the scene—Doc Martens and suits, nightly jazz, dancing. *626 SW Park Ave (between Alder and Morrison), Portland; (503) 224-5552; $$.*

Bread and Ink Cafe ☆☆ Things are getting more ambitious in this Hawthorne neighborhood bistro. Longtime fans will still find impressive baked desserts, a Sunday-warming three-course Yiddish brunch, and a serious hamburger. Dinners aim higher. *3610 SE Hawthorne Blvd (corner of SE 36th), Portland; (503) 239-4756; $$.*

Bush Garden ☆☆ There's an extensive Japanese menu here. The most interesting options, however, come through the sushi bar, where you can rattle off words like uni, ama ebi, and toro; point and look hopeful; or just ask the chef to surprise you. *900 SW Morrison St (at 9th, near Nordstrom), Portland; (503) 226-7181; $$.*

Caffe Mingo ☆☆ This resolutely casual new trattoria on NW 21st rejects both reservations and high prices. Instead, it maintains a solid, inviting version of Italian cafe cuisine. The menu is limited but handled very well. *807 NW 21st (between Johnson and Kearney), Portland; (503) 226-4646; $$.*

Campbell's Barbecue ☆☆ What packs the place is an exuberant vision of barbecue. People come into this little house and just inhale. The dining area is quaint, the servers cheerful, and the side dishes inviting. *8701 SE Powell Blvd (exit off I-205, corner SE 85th), Portland; (503) 777-9795; $.*

Caprial's Bistro and Wine ☆☆ Hot regional chef Caprial Pence has been raising her profile and the result is no loss of imagination and more consistency at her bistro. Vivid flavors shoot around the storefront, sandwiches and salads are creative, and desserts are intense. *7015 SE Milwaukie Ave (just south of Bybee), Portland; (503) 236-6457; $$.*

Casablanca ☆ This Moroccan hot spot spellbinds diners with elaborate atmosphere and decoration, and food that provides its own richness. Dinner begins with enticing appetizers and entrees run to couscous, kababs, and intense Moroccan stews. Baklava is rich and flaky. *2221 SE Hawthorne (at 22nd Ave), Portland; (503) 233-4400; $$.*

Delfina's ☆☆   Once a popular pizza-and-pasta place, the menu here is now smaller and oft-changing, and the results are pleasing. Ambience consists of low lighting and Italian language lessons broadcast in the restaurant. *2112 NW Kearney St (corner of NW 21st), Portland; (503) 221-1195; $$.*

Doris' Cafe ☆   Doris' is a full-scale soul-food restaurant. The cool, attractive space is a meeting place—one of the few places around where all races mingle. The smoky barbecue sauce is more sweet than angry, and fried chicken wings are killer. *325 NE Russell (near Rose Quarter exit off I-5 northbound), Portland; (503) 287-9249; $.*

Esparza's Tex-Mex Cafe ☆☆☆   This rollicking hangout, the best Tex-Mex restaurant in Portland, has loads of atmosphere. The menu and specials have the reach of Texas. It's all hand-smoked and hand-designed. *2725 SE Ankeny St (1 block south of E Burnside, on the corner of SE 28th), Portland; (503) 234-7909; $$.*

Fiddleheads ☆☆☆   This Western regional cuisine is based on dishes that existed before anybody called it the West (Shoshone corn dumplings, fry bread). A skilled hand with all kinds of local fare is present in this compact, elegant space adorned with Northwest Indian art. *6716 SE Milwaukie (in Westmoreland, near corner of Bybee), Portland; (503) 233-1547; $$.*

Fong Chong ☆☆   This has been Portland's brightest dim sum place for a long time, but along with sticky rice in a lotus leaf, you might find something surprising, such as shallot dumplings. It's fun, inexpensive, and tasty. *301 NW 4th Ave (at Everett), Portland; (503) 220-0235; $.*

Genoa ☆☆☆☆   For 25 years, elaborate seven-course meals (with a fewer-course option on weekdays) have provided the Portland dining scene with elegance and artistry. The pasta course can stop you in your tracks, and the three-hour affair leaves you seduced, not overwhelmed. *2832 SE Belmont St (at NE 29th), Portland; (503) 238-1464; $$$.*

The Heathman Restaurant and Bar ☆☆☆☆   The chef doesn't exactly merge classic French cuisine with Pacific Northwest trends; rather, he expands the classics to absorb local ingredients. Incredible in-house pastries add to the effect. Evenings bring jazz. *1009 SW Broadway (at Salmon), Portland; (503) 241-4100; $$$.*

Higgins ☆☆☆   Here is a seasonal Northwest menu, strong on local meats, poultry, and especially seafood. Spectacular presentation endures. Thinner wallets appreciate Higgins's bar next door. A rare fine restaurant that welcomes kids. *1239 SW Broadway (at SW Jefferson), Portland; (503) 222-9070; $$$.*

Hunan ☆ After 20 years, Hunan still produces some of the most consistently good Chinese cooking and at reasonable cost. The chicken in tangy sauce is unbelievable, and versions of the spicy standards are pungent and massively popular. *515 SW Broadway (between Washington and Alder), Portland; (503) 224-8063; $$.*

Il Fornaio ☆☆ It's a California chain. But once you forgive it that, you'll notice that the skill of its chefs is undeniable. The pasta and entree menu is substantial, and the menu goes on an annual tour of Italy; every month features offerings from different areas. *115 NW 22nd Ave (just north of Burnside), Portland; (503) 248-9400; $$.*

Indigine ☆☆ Weekdays, Northwest ingredients are blended with Eastern spices and other inspirations at hearteningly reasonable prices. On Saturdays is a blowout East Indian feast. Not everything bursts with flavor, but the dessert tray will have you purring. *3725 SE Division St (at 37th St), Portland; (503) 238-1470; $$.*

Jake's Famous Crawfish ☆☆ Some of the best seafood in the city is served in this century-old restaurant. A combination of old tradition and new ideas applied to very fresh seafood could keep the landmark going for another century. *401 SW 12th Ave (at SW Stark), Portland; (503) 226-1419; $$.*

Jarra's Ethiopian Restaurant ☆☆ Jarra's will teach you what's wat: the wat (stews) are deep red, and packed with peppery after-kicks. Dinners come with stewed meats and vegetables, all permeated with vibrant spices. *1435 SE Hawthorne Blvd (at SE 14th), Portland; (503) 230-8990; $.*

L'Auberge ☆☆☆ This establishment has a menu nearly as French as its name. There are actually several menus—a four-course fixed-price special; à la carte offerings; a French provincial special; and the more laid-back bar menu. *2601 NW Vaughn St (at 26th), Portland; (503) 223-3302; $$$.*

Lemongrass ☆☆☆ The menu is limited (dazzling curries and seafood), but the focus is powerful. There's a choice of heat intensity, but getting much past mild takes you into a place of pain. You'll wait for a table (there are no reservations), but you'll come back to wait again. *1705 NE Couch (turn on NE 17th off Burnside), Portland; (503) 231-5780; $$.*

McCormick & Schmick's Seafood Restaurant ☆☆☆ The original M&S still retains its excitement, and a kitchen that skillfully handles its extensive fresh list. The place is frequently jammed, offering a lively bar scene and a wide selection of single-malt Scotches. *235 SW 1st Ave (at Oak St), Portland; (503) 224-7522; $$.* ■ *9945 SW Beaverton-Hillsdale Hwy (1 mile east on Hwy 10 from Hwy 217), Beaverton; (503) 643-1322.*

Montage ☆☆   Portland's definitively hip late-night hangout is now open for lunch for the same unexpectedly good Southern/Cajun cuisine. Dinners are both ambitious and unique. The loud hum of conversation and music fuels the late-night energy. *301 SE Morrison St (underneath the Morrison St Bridge), Portland; (503) 234-1324; $.*

Murata ☆☆☆   Murata is the best Japanese restaurant in Portland. Once someone has translated the specials, they're often worth the culinary gamble. Murata has recently branched out with its own bento parlor. *200 SW Market (downtown, between 2nd and 3rd), Portland; (503) 227-0080; $$.*

Opus Too ☆☆   The cooks at the mesquite-fed grill are equally deft with fish and red meat. Fish is simply prepared, but a few sauces prevail, along with Cajun possibilities, daily specials, and lunchtime sandwiches. There's a long bar and live jazz floats in from Jazz de Opus next door. *33 NW 2nd Ave (NW Couch and 2nd, Old Town district), Portland; (503) 222-6077; $$.*

The Original Pancake House ☆☆   People wait patiently outside this landmark restaurant, which hums from 7am until it closes in midafternoon. Omelets big enough for two arrive with a short stack. Service is cheerful and efficient. *8600 SW Barbur Blvd (Barbur Blvd exit from I-5 south; at SW 24th), Portland; (503) 246-9007; $.*

Paley's Place ☆☆☆   In just a few years, this intimate dining room has established itself as a premier Portland restaurant. The food is best described as exquisite, with Northwestern freshness married to a real artistic sensibility. Menus change with the harvests. *1204 NW 21st Ave (corner of Northrup), Portland; (503) 243-2403; $$$.*

The Ringside ☆☆   People come here for beef, and they get it in large, juicy slabs—the only question is which cut. Still, the onion rings are what singlehandedly made this place famous. Waiters are dignified and professional. *2165 W Burnside (2 blocks west of Civic Stadium), Portland; (503) 223-1513; $$.*

Sweetwater's Jam House ☆☆   This lively Caribbean spot, now in large, cool digs in the Belmont area, has lost none of its fire or its fun. Sides are stunning (ethereal coconut rice!). There is an extensive list of Caribbean rums. *3350 SE Morrison (1 block north of SE Belmont, in the renovated Belmont Dairy), Portland; (503) 233-0333; $.*

Tapeo ☆☆   As close to Spain as you'll get in Portland. Thirty different tapas—small plates designed for casual munching—and 20 different sherries are served in an unhurried atmosphere. First, combine a few cold tapas with some hot items. Then retrieve the menu and explore further. *2764 NW Thurman (corner of NW 27th), Portland; (503) 226-0409; $$.*

3 Doors Down ☆☆☆   This austere storefront has made an impact on the neighborhood both because of its mingling of Northwest seafood and Italian instincts, and because there's often a line waiting out on the street. The small, spare room has a warm atmosphere, if a considerable noise level. *1429 SE 37th Ave (north of Hawthorne), Portland; (503) 236-6886; $$.*

Toulouse ☆☆   The cassoulet, a southern French bean stew, is a specialty. But Toulouse also offers impressive items out of its wood oven and makes forays into other parts of the European continent. The big warm room, with a bar next door, is becoming a hangout. *71 SW 2nd Ave (just south of Burnside), Portland; (503) 241-4343; $$.*

Typhoon ☆☆   This Thai cuisine has more colors than curry, and the menu is a kaleidoscope of inspired seafood dishes and pungent noodle dishes. A particularly deft hand with shrimp and fish allows the delicate flavors to surmount serious spices. *2310 NW Everett (in Everett Market, just off NW 23rd Ave), Portland; (503) 243-7557; $.*

Wildwood ☆☆☆   The chef/owner goes deeper into Northwest cuisine by filling his oven with regional ingredients and his own imagination. Specialties include designer pizzas and seductive desserts. Wildwood feels like San Francisco but tastes like the best of Oregon. *1221 NW 21st Ave (corner of Overton), Portland; (503) 248-9663; $$$.*

Yen Ha ☆   Portland's most extensive Vietnamese menu offers a range of possibilities that invite exploration. Some local Vietnamese mutter that the menu has become Americanized, but crowds are consistently multicultural. The ambience is Formica and Budweiser. *6820 NE Sandy Blvd (at 68th Ave), Portland; (503) 287-3698; $.*

Zefiro ☆☆☆☆   After dazzling with a Mediterranean menu, this exciting restaurant is migrating toward Asia. Eastern inspirations with a creative twist appear, but the menu never forgets its Riviera roots. This is one of the city's liveliest people-watching (and celeb-spotting) stops. *500 NW 21st (corner of Glisan), Portland; (503) 226-3394; $$$.*

Zell's: An American Cafe ☆☆   Pile into one of the best breakfasts in this time zone: fruit waffles, a range of pancakes, and inspired eggs. And expect a warm welcome. There's a lunch menu, of course, but breakfasts are tough to beat. *1300 SE Morrison St (13 blocks east of the Willamette Bridge), Portland; (503) 239-0196; $.*

Lodgings

5th Avenue Suites ☆☆☆   This is a pleasant stay for business travelers and well-to-do families both. Most of the rooms are spacious suites, but all have a sense of grandeur. The staff is gracious (they welcome dogs) and the lobby is stunning but welcoming. The Red Star Tavern & Roast House is an excellent open-spaced bistro. *506 SW Washington (5th and Washington), Portland, OR 97204; (503) 222-0001 or (800) 771-2971; $$$.*

The Governor Hotel ☆☆☆   This hotel's lobby features a mural depicting the Lewis and Clark journey, plus mahogany and a large fireplace. The list of amenities is long (access to an athletic club and to the business center, whirlpool tubs, and more). The restaurant downstairs, Jake's Grill, provides the ultimate room-service fare. *611 SW 10th Ave (downtown, at Alder), Portland, OR 97205; (503) 224-3400 or (800) 554-3456; $$$.*

The Heathman Hotel ☆☆☆☆   Many consider this intimate hotel Portland's best. It offers excellent business services, a central location, artistic details, and exceptional service. The lobby lounge is elegant, and a library and fitness suite are available. Just steps away is a four-star restaurant, the Heathman Restaurant and Bar. *1001 SW Broadway (downtown, at Salmon), Portland, OR 97205; (503) 241-4100 or (800) 551-0011; $$$.*

Hotel Vintage Plaza ☆☆☆☆   This refined hotel is elegant but not opulent. We like the intimate scale, the gracious staff, and the complimentary wines and piano music. Attention shows in the details. Rooms come with continental breakfast and newspaper. Pazzo Ristorante on the main floor serves excellent Northern Italian cuisine. *422 SW Broadway (downtown, at Washington), Portland, OR 97205; (503) 228-1212 or (800) 243-0555; $$$.*

The Lion and the Rose ☆☆☆   Portland's most elegant B&B is a 1906 mansion with gracious hosts who let few details go unchecked (from candles in the baths to fresh cookies). It's indisputably decorated. Breakfast is lavish and a lovely afternoon tea is offered. *1810 NE 15th Ave (1 block north of NE Broadway), Portland, OR 97212; (503) 287-9245 or (800) 955-1647; $$$.*

MacMaster House ☆☆   The florid furnishings and eclectic art here reflect the personality of an amiable host. An imposing exterior gives way to seven rooms, all of which house antiques. Lavish breakfasts are served, too. All this in a great location (two blocks from Washington Park). *1041 SW Vista Ave (4 blocks south of W Burnside), Portland, OR 97205; (503) 223-7362; $$.*

Mallory Motor Hotel ☆   Just west of the downtown core is this beloved hotel. It's an older establishment in *every* sense; it's also one of the best bargains in town—reserve in advance. Have breakfast in the restaurant; park in the free garage. The cocktail lounge draws both the older and retro crowds. *729 SW 15th Ave (at SW Yamhill), Portland, OR 97205; (503) 223-6311 or (800) 228-8657; $$.*

Marriott Residence Inn/Lloyd Center ☆   This hotel is geared toward longer stays and rates drop accordingly. Each suite has a full kitchen, a sitting area with a couch, and a desk. Jacuzzis and a heated outdoor pool are on the premises. *1710 NE Multnomah (2 blocks east of Lloyd Center), Portland, OR 97232; (503) 288-1400; $$$.*

Portland Guest House ☆☆   This urban retreat has white carpets, antique linens, and the classiness of an intimate hotel. The owner drops in mornings to serve breakfast. Each room has its own phone and clock, making this a good place for business travelers, too. *1720 NE 15th Ave (off NE Broadway), Portland, OR 97212; (503) 282-1402; $$.*

Portland's White House ☆☆   This place looks a bit like its Washington, D.C., namesake, complete with circular driveway. Japanese maples flank the columns at the mansion's entrance. Inside are six exquisite rooms. New owners converted the carriage house into new guest rooms. *1914 NE 22nd Ave (2 blocks north of NE Broadway), Portland, OR 97212; (503) 287-7131; $$$.*

RiverPlace Hotel ☆☆☆   This lovely luxury hotel fronts the Willamette River and has some glorious views. Inside are plush furnishings; massage and spa treatments are available. Wide paths lead from the hotel through Tom McCall Waterfront Park. Downstairs, the Esplanade restaurant makes a stunning location for a meal. *1510 SW Harbor Way (off SW Naito Pkwy), Portland, OR 97201; (503) 228-3233 or (800) 227-1333; $$$.*

More Information

Beaverton Area Chamber of Commerce, Beaverton: *(503) 644-0123.*
Bicycle Transportation Alliance, Portland: *(503) 226-0676.*
Bureau of Land Management, Oregon State Office, Portland: *(503) 952-6002.*
Bureau of Land Management, Salem (Sandy River Gorge): *(503) 399-5646.*
Clackamas County Tourism Development Council, West Linn: *(800) 647-3843.*
Gresham Area Chamber of Commerce, Gresham: *(503) 665-1131.*
Gresham Parks and Recreation, Gresham: *(503) 669-2531.*
Lake Oswego Parks and Recreation, Lake Oswego: *(503) 636-0280.*
Metro Regional Parks and Greenspaces, Portland: *(503) 797-1850.*
The Nature Conservancy, Portland: *(503) 228-9561.*
Nature of the Northwest Information Center, Portland: *(503) 872-2750.*
North Clackamas County Chamber of Commerce, Milwaukie: *(503) 654-7777.*

North Clackamas Parks and Recreation District, Milwaukie: *(503) 794-8002.*

Oregon City Chamber of Commerce, Oregon City: *(800) 424-3002.*

Oregon Department of Fish and Wildlife, Portland: *(503) 229-5222.*

Oregon Parks and Recreation, Portland: *(503) 731-3411 and (800) 551-6949.*

Portland Audubon Society, Portland: *(503) 292-6855.*

Portland Oregon Visitors Association, Portland: *(800) 962-3700.*

Portland Parks and Recreation, Portland: *(503) 823-2223.*

Portland Parks Outdoor Recreation, Portland: *(503) 823-5132.*

Portland Wheelmen Touring Club, Portland: *(503) 257-7982.*

Tualatin Hills Parks and Recreation District, Beaverton: *(503) 645-6433.*

U.S. Forest Service Region 6 headquarters, Portland: *(503) 808-2644*

Washington County Visitors Association, Beaverton: *(800) 537-3149.*

Wine Country

From the Washington-Columbia county line on the north, east to the west edge of the Portland metropolitan area, south to the Polk-Benton county line and west to the crest of the Coast Range, including the cities of Hillsboro, Forest Grove, Sherwood, Newberg, McMinnville, and Dallas.

It's easy to get distracted in Oregon's Wine Country, a region of bountiful agriculture but comparatively little opportunity to enjoy outdoor recreation, mostly because the counties have a shortage of public lands, so abundant elsewhere in Oregon. Despite a lack of hiking trails and whitewater rivers, the Wine Country has some recreation opportunities that shouldn't be overlooked by visitors as they travel around the most productive grape-growing region north of California's Napa Valley. Tours of the vineyards attract many visitors to the region, but the savvy ones return to enjoy some of the rare recreational jewels offered by the region.

An even bigger draw (and distraction) than the region's vineyards is Spirit Mountain Casino near the Polk County town of Grand Ronde. The casino attracts an estimated 2.5 million visitors every year, making it one of the busiest tourist attractions in the state.

Wine Country is a great place to go for a hot-air-balloon or glider flight around Newberg and McMinnville. Henry Hagg Lake at Scoggins Valley Park near Forest Grove, just a short drive from Portland, is one of the most diverse, and popular, places for outdoor recreation. So what if the park doesn't offer overnight camping? The Flying M Ranch in the Coast Range foothills west of Yamhill is a mecca for all sorts of activities, including horseback riding, black powder and mountain man festivals and camping by airplane (black powder refers to target shooting with a ball and musket). Paddle trips are popular on the Tualatin and Yamhill Rivers, and bird-watching is a year-round activity at the region's many wetlands. Warm-water fishing can be good where there is public access, and trout fishing is usually hot after the lakes and ponds are stocked with hatchery fish.

Despite this apparent largesse, the region will always be known for its grapes and the wine they produce. Many of Oregon's best-known vineyards—Knudsen Erath, Sokol Blosser, Oak Knoll, and Elk Cove among them—are justifiably famous for their production of some of the country's best pinot noir, pinot gris, and chardonnay wines.

With road signs pointing to vineyards open for touring around just about every bend, it's difficult to stay committed to making that long bicycle tour or that canoe trip through Oregon's Wine Country. The surest way to stay focused is to get up early, get the recreation out of the way by midafternoon, and stop in for a couple of wine tastings on the way home. With as many vineyards as there are in Washington, Yamhill, and Polk Counties, this approach is a virtual guarantee that you'll test out just about every form of the region's outdoor recreation opportunities before you run out of new vineyards to visit. This approach may be a little distracting, but it can be a powerful incentive for making repeat visits to Oregon's Wine Country.

Getting There

Hillsboro, the seat of Washington County, lies at the west edge of the Portland metro area, easily accessible via US Highway 26 (US 26), Tri-Met's new MAX light-rail passenger line, or Highway 8 (the Tualatin Valley Highway) from Beaverton. McMinnville, the county seat of Yamhill County, lies near the center of Oregon's largest grape growing region. Portland is a 38-mile drive from McMinnville via Highway 99W. Dallas, the seat of Polk County, is 15 miles west of Salem off Highway 22. A network of county roads leads into the rural areas where Oregon's most productive vineyards are located, as well as into the second-growth forests of the Coast Range. The forests west of the mid-Willamette Valley are mostly privately owned but have a mix of Bureau of Land Management (BLM) and Oregon Department of Forestry lands.

Adjoining Areas

NORTH: **Lower Columbia, Greater Portland**

EAST: **Salem and the Heart of the Valley**

WEST: **Lincoln City, Tillamook**

inside out

Hiking

Bring a raincoat! In addition to a comparative shortage of public land in Oregon's Wine Country, there's one other good reason why the region isn't the mother lode of outdoor recreation in Oregon. It rains in the mountains just west of Wine Country—it rains a lot.

During Oregon's notoriously wet 1996 calendar year, a Federal Aviation Administration radar station atop **Laurel Mountain** in the Polk County area of the Oregon Coast Range recorded 204.12 inches of precipitation. The rainfall shattered the previous state record set in 1937 of 168.88 inches, also in the northern Coast Range. Actually, the state climatologist believes it rains 10 percent more on a nearby ridge, but Laurel Mountain has the only monitoring station in the area.

At 3,589 feet, Laurel Mountain is the highest elevation point in Polk County. Other high points in Wine Country counties are 3,283-foot Saddle Mountain in Washington County, 6 miles south of the Coast Range summit on Hwy 6, and 3,424-foot Trask Mountain in Yamhill County, 5 miles west of the Flying M Ranch. The hike up Saddle Mountain is described in the Northern Beaches chapter, and the other mountains can be reached by driving the maze of logging roads shown on the BLM Salem District's Westside map.

If you still want to pass up the wineries and go for a hike in Wine Country, there are a few interesting places to go.

The high-tech boom in Hillsboro has brought some interesting developments to Washington County, including **Dawson Creek Park.** The private park along NE Brookwood Pkwy was built by the Tektronix Master Retirement Trust as part of a high-class development. Parking access is limited to employees, but the public is welcome to access the park on foot (park in front of the barricades that are interspersed along Brookwood Pkwy) and enjoy the 4.5 miles of pathways that wind through a series of ponds designed to control flooding.

The Tualatin Hills Park and Recreation District maintains a series of public pathways on the **Jenkins Estate,** a 68-acre country farm that dates to 1913. The estate's nature trails begin at the main house, accessible off Grabhorn Rd. Head southwest from Beaverton for 4 miles on Farmington Rd to reach the estate, (503) 642-3855. Where Farmington Rd intersects SW 209th Ave on the right, turn left onto Grabhorn Rd and drive 300 yards to the estate entrance.

The **Magness Memorial Tree Farm,** (503) 625-7471, operated by the World Forestry Center of Portland, is 4 miles south of Sherwood off Ladd Hill Rd. The 70-acre forest has 2 miles of trail, including the .5-mile **John Nagle Trail** that is paved for use by the physically challenged. An attraction of the farm is a climb to the top of a 60-foot fire tower for a panoramic view of the Cascade Mountains.

The Tualatin River has its headwaters in the eastern Coast Range, the next drainage south of Scoggins Creek and the reservoir that creates Hagg Lake. A road follows the Tualatin River upstream from the community of Cherry Grove to two waterfalls. **Little Lee Falls** is a pleasant 10-foot drop into a large pool and **Lee Falls** is about twice as high. To reach Cherry Grove, drive Hwy 8 for 6 miles south of Forest Grove or 11 miles north of Yamhill. Drive 6 miles west of the highway and continue through Cherry Grove to the end of pavement on Summit Ave. At the end of the pavement, turn west on a dirt road and drive .8 mile to an unmarked turnout for the short walk to Little Lee Falls. Continue hiking up the drainage on a dirt road for 1.5 miles for a view of Lee Falls.

The **Delbert Hunter Arboretum and Botanic Garden,** (503) 623-3651, is a 35-acre city park in Dallas at the intersection of Park and Douglas Sts, a pleasant spot for a picnic or a short walk. Trails wander through the displays of plants, mostly native to the Northwest, in the park set alongside Rickreall Creek.

Falls City, a logging community in the Coast Range foothills 5 miles southwest of Dallas on Hwy 223, is named for a 30-foot-high cascade on the **Little Luckiamute River.** The falls is on the west side of town at **Michael Harding Park.** A walking tour of Falls City leads to the falls, to the upper park along the river, to a pair of footbridges that connect north and south Main St and to a loop around the town's stately old homes. Park downtown and look for signs. Farther up the Little Luckiamute, 5 miles west of Falls City on Black Rock Rd, a trail leads 12 miles into the Coast Range from **Gerlinger Park.**

Other long hiking opportunities in Oregon's Wine Country can be found at the **Banks-Vernonia Linear State Park** and **Hagg Lake,** both in Washington County and described under Biking and Parks. The local hiking expert is Hillsboro's Bike 'N' Hike, (503) 681-0594. A four-store chain in the Portland area, the Hillsboro shop is at 156 SE Fourth Ave.

Biking

Oregon's first rails-to-trails conversion, the **Banks-Vernonia Linear State Park,** attracts plenty of cyclists, hikers, and equestrians to sample the pleasures that can be found along the 20-mile trail. The northern 6 miles of the trail are paved and are located in Columbia County (see Lower Columbia chapter). The rest of the trail has a hardened gravel surface and is best for mountain bikes, but the state parks department continues to extend the pavement as funding allows.

The Washington County section of the trail begins near the Tophill trailhead at milepost 8, which is 8 miles south of Vernonia on Hwy 47, and extends into Banks where it meets an inglorious ending a few hundred yards short of its intended destination.

Additional public access into Banks is required for completion of the trail, which also needs some major rehabilitation along the way due to some recent severe winter storms. Other trailheads in Washington County are at the community of Buxton (2 miles north of US 26), at Manning alongside US 26, and on Pongrantz Rd between Manning and Buxton. Equestrians use Tophill and Buxton. Camping is not allowed along the 8-foot-wide trail.

Rural western Washington County is perhaps the most popular location for road cycling from the Portland metro area. The county's network of paved roads leads past scenic farms and small communities. Popular tour routes pass through the communities of West Union, North Plains, Kansas City, Gaston, Farmington, and Scholls. A Washington County map will keep cyclists from getting lost while they learn their favorite roads to ride. Tri-Met buses haul bikes all the way to Hillsboro or Forest Grove, a good way to start a ride without having to contend with a lot of traffic (see Cycling in Greater Portland chapter for information on obtaining a bus/bike permit). The Washington County Wine Country Scenic Loop brochure and a free guide with detailed information of six bike tours are both available by calling (800) 537-3149. Ask for the "Biking in Washington County" brochure. (See the listing for Hillsboro's Bike 'N' Hike shop under Hiking.)

Yamhill County offers outstanding road-bike tours around its wine country, including **Chehalem Mountain, Lafayette,** and the **Upper Yamhill Valley.** Expect to climb significantly more than in Washington County. The Yamhill Wineries Association, (503) 434-5814, publishes a brochure. Polk County's favorite riding areas are around **Rickreall** and the **Luckiamute forks** near Falls City.

It might be tempting to head out into the forest for a **mountain-bike ride,** but very little of the land is publicly owned in sufficiently large blocks to allow off-road riding. It's best to stay on forest roads, many of which are closed to public use Monday through Friday while logging is in progress.

Camping

The **Flying M Ranch,** (503) 662-3222, is a historic landmark that continues to serve travelers to western Yamhill County. The ranch's history dates back more than a hundred years to when a hotel was built along the Trask River as a rest haven for travelers on a stagecoach route between the Yamhill Valley and the Oregon Coast. The ranch has been operated by the same family since 1922.

An airstrip right in front of the big central building is a good indication that the ranch goes out of its way to cater to travelers. Facilities include a tent campground, RV park, horseback rides, motels, cabins, group picnics, restaurant, and live entertainment on weekends. The ranch's trail system leads all the way through the mountains to the coast, so it's best to ride along with a ranch wrangler to learn the way home. To locate the Flying M, drive west out of either Yamhill or Carlton and watch for the red and white signs (see Lodgings in this chapter).

The Forest Grove unit of the Tillamook State Forest, (503) 357-2191, operates **Gales Creek Campground,** 2 miles west of the Coast Range summit on Hwy 6 at milepost 35. The 23-unit campground is open during summer season and offers the only public campground tent camping in Washington County. A 2-mile trail, open to hikers and bikers, climbs 600 feet from the campground to the Coast Range summit, where it crosses the highway and continues as the historical wagon trail into Tillamook County. The .5-mile **Rippling Waters Nature Trail** is 10 miles downstream from the campground along Gales Creek via Hwy 6 and Hwy 8. An interpretation booklet is available from the Forest Grove unit of the Tillamook State Forest. The trail is on the south side of Hwy 8, about 5 miles northwest of Forest Grove.

RV camping is available at the Washington County Fairgrounds, (503) 648-1416, at 872 NE 28th Ave in Hillsboro; Fernwood RV Park, (503) 357-9494, at 57625 NW Wilson River Hwy west of Forest Grove; and Rose Grove, (503) 357-7817, at 3839 Pacific Ave in Forest Grove.

BLM holdings are scattered in checkerboard fashion around the west fringe of Wine Country, a legacy of a land giveaway to a railroad that was never built. The scattered square-mile blocks have few developed facilities, so don't go searching for big, sprawling campgrounds. The BLM's Salem District, (503) 375-5646, maintains a small campground at **Mill Creek Recreation Site,** 5 miles northwest of Dallas, plus the 48-mile Nestucca River National Back Country Byway. The east end of the byway is accessible from the towns of Yamhill and Carlton, but all of the developed facilities are in the Tillamook County section of the byway (see Tillamook chapter).

Sheridan Viewpoint, 10 miles northwest of the towns of Yamhill and

Sheridan via a maze of BLM logging roads, has an outstanding view of the Cascades to the east. The roads in the area pass through a large block of BLM land (be sure to bring a Salem District Westside map) and is one of the few good places for dispersed camping in Wine Country. Take your pick, but be warned that the road system is complicated and difficult to follow even with a map. Bring along a compass so you can tell north from south when the famous fogs of Oregon's northern Coast Range mess up your directional sense.

Western Yamhill County contains some land administered by the Siuslaw National Forest, but its recreation facilities in the **Mount Hebo** area are most easily approached from the Tillamook side (see Tillamook chapter).

Polk County's fair board operates a 40-unit campground at the fairgrounds in Rickreall, at the south edge of town on Hwy 99W. For reservations, call (503) 623-3048.

Parks

Henry Hagg Lake at **Scoggins Valley Park,** (503) 648-8715, near Forest Grove is the mother of all picnic areas a short drive from Portland. The Bureau of Reclamation constructed the lake's dam in the mid-1970s as a flood control, irrigation, and water quality–control project. The park is managed by Washington County. Except for camping, the park offers just about every type of summer recreation. To reach the park, head south for 4 miles from Forest Grove on Hwy 47 and turn west on Scoggins Valley Park Rd for 3 miles to the entrance.

The dam is at the southeast side of the lake. A paved road circles the lake, connecting several recreation areas, all well spaced around the lake, that have boat launches and picnic grounds. A buoy line across the center of the lake divides it into two speed zones. Water-skiers head for the east part of the lake near the dam and windsurfers and sailors use the upper part of the lake to the west. Fishermen go wherever the fish are biting.

The 1,113-acre lake is circled by 15 miles of hiking trails. Cyclists have 11 miles of bicycle lanes on the road that circles the lake. The park is open from late April through October, but the road is open all year. For winter bird-watching, park outside the locked gates at the recreation areas and walk to the trail that circles the lake. The park also has a 520-foot hiking and wildlife-viewing trail that's handicapped accessible at the south side of the dam, as well as barrier-free comfort stations and picnic areas throughout the park.

Other popular picnic parks in Washington County are **Lincoln Park,** (503) 359-3239, between Main St and Sunset Dr in Forest Grove; **Harleman Park,** (503) 357-3011, on S 10th Ave and Heather St in Cornelius;

Shute Park, (503) 681-6120, at 10th and Maple in Hillsboro; and **Stella Olsen Park,** (503) 625-5722, on Meinecke Rd in Sherwood. Stella Olsen is the largest at 30 acres and has some hiking trails through wildlife habitat.

Bald Peak State Park, a 26-acre preserve atop the 1,633-foot summit of the Chehalem Mountains, is just south of the Washington County line in Yamhill County. Drive north 4 miles from Newberg on Hwy 219, turn and drive east for 9 miles on signed Bald Peak Rd. The day-use park has an outstanding view of the Cascade Mountains and the Tualatin Valley. The pace of residential construction so obvious from atop Bald Peak is nothing short of frightening.

Yamhill County's park system has 10 day-use parks, including **Ed Grenfell, Deer Creek,** and **Huber,** all within a 10-mile drive of McMinnville. For information and driving directions over the network of county roads, call (503) 434-7515. **Erratic Rock Wayside** is a state natural site where a boulder from eastern Washington was deposited by an Ice Age flood. The park is .5 mile north of Hwy 18, about 6 miles east of Sheridan. The county's **Stuart Grenfell Park,** 3 miles southwest of Sheridan, is a popular rest room stop midway between Portland and the coast on Hwy 18.

Polk County is home to the **Ritner Creek covered bridge,** 3 miles south of Pedee alongside Hwy 223. The bridge was built in 1926 for $6,963 and was restored for $26,031 in 1975. The bridge has a small park next to it, a shady spot for a picnic among the towering fir, maple, and alder.

Nesmith Park adjoins the county fairgrounds on Hwy 99W at Rickreall, offering picnic facilities and swimming for the kids. **Gerlinger County Park,** 5 miles west of Falls City on Black Rock Rd, is a pleasant spot on the Little Luckiamute River.

Wildlife

Bird-watchers take heart. Feathered creatures enjoy Oregon's Wine Country nearly as much as do summer tourists. Birders who live on the west side of the Portland area need not travel far to pursue their favorite activity. The City of Hillsboro's 650-acre **Jackson Bottom Wetlands Preserve,** (503) 681-6206, is a long-established birding destination that will soon be rivaled by the new 3,000-acre multi-unit Tualatin River National Wildlife Refuge near Sherwood (see below).

Jackson Bottom, located at the southwest edge of Hillsboro on the east side of Hwy 219, is bordered on the south by the Tualatin River. The site contains freshwater marshes and forested wetlands. Winter flooding is supplemented by treated wastewater from the Hillsboro sewage treatment plant, so the bottomland stays wet all year. More than 130 bird species have been counted here, with spring's migration the peak time to spot birds. A recent March day of watching accounted for 47 species, led by 300 **Canada geese,** 100 **American coots,** and 100 **mallards.** The list also included **ring-necked duck, ring-necked pheasant, pied-billed grebe,** and **varied thrush.** Mammals such as **otter, mink, beaver,** and **raccoon** can be seen from the 1-mile-long nature trail that begins at the south viewing area on the Tualatin River. Best viewing is from Hwy 219 near the north and south ends of the marsh.

The **Tualatin River National Wildlife Refuge,** (503) 625-4377, was created by Congress in 1993 with refuge headquarters at 20555 SW Gerda Lane, Sherwood, and its nature trails will open to the public in 1999. The refuge includes several blocks of land along the Tualatin River north of Sherwood on either side of Hwy 99. Viewing of the same bird species that frequent Jackson Bottom is best from Sherwood-Scholls Rd.

Winter is a good time to watch for ducks on **Hagg Lake,** when Scoggins Valley Park is empty and forlorn of people (see Parks, above, for more information). Watch for loons, grebes, and all types of diving ducks. Rarities are **red-throated loons** and **red-necked grebes.** The best birding areas are at the north end of the reservoir near Tanner and Scoggins Creeks. Owls live around the lake all year and common sightings include **great horned owl** and **screech owl.** Forest Grove's sewage treatment plant is nearby on Fern Hill Rd and is a popular gathering spot for **tundra swans** in winter.

Large congregations of **Canada geese** spend the winter at **Baskett Slough National Wildlife Refuge,** (503) 757-7236, a 2,492-acre preserve 2 miles west of Rickreall on Hwy 22 where a roadside kiosk describes the features of the refuge. The refuge is one of three that comprise the Western Oregon complex, which was created to protect wintering habitat for dusky Canada geese. In addition to a variety of birds, the refuge is home to 30 species of mammals, 10 species of reptiles, and 8 species of amphibians. The main access points into the refuge are on Smithfield and Colville Rds, both off Hwy 99 2 miles north of Rickreall. Access is limited to licensed hunters from October 1 through April 30, except for a short loop around Baskett Butte in the southern part of the refuge off Colville Rd. The high point of the refuge is Mount Baldy, all of 414 feet above sea level.

Fishing

Hagg Lake, the largest fishing opportunity in Oregon's second most populous county, gets plenty of attention from the Oregon Department of Fish and Wildlife. (See the Oregon Outdoor Primer for information on regulations and seasons.) This water playground is stocked early in the fishing season with legal-size rainbow trout before warming waters of the lake turn angler interest from trout to smallmouth bass. Best trout fishing, including native cutthroat that spawn in the tributaries, is in the Scoggins Creek and Sain Creek arms. A state-record 7-pound, 4.5-ounce smallmouth bass was caught in Hagg Lake in 1994. Fishing picks up in July when the water hits the 60-degree mark. Yellow perch, bluegill, and crappie are also plentiful, especially in the Tanner Creek arm on the northeast side. (See Parks, above, for more information on the lake.)

Scoggins Creek, before it's impounded to create Hagg Lake, has fair angling for wild cutthroat early in the season before the creek flow dwindles in June. The runout below the dam is also productive. **Gales Creek,** the next drainage north of Scoggins Creek, is managed for wild steelhead, but its production has dwindled. The creek is also home to native cutthroat. The BLM's Salem District Westside map shows access routes. A highway pond on the south side of Hwy 6 just west of the US 26 junction is stocked with trout and sees plenty of fishing activity early in the season. The local fly-fishing expert is T. K. Fly Supply, (503) 359-1325, located at 2635 Pacific Ave in Forest Grove.

The **Tualatin River** is a 75-mile meandering stream that has good angling for cutthroat above Gaston on Patton Valley Rd, but access is limited due to private ownership. Most angling in the lower river is for bass and panfish near any of several bridges and from small boats. A popular drift-boat launch is from the Hwy 210 bridge at North Scholls.

The **Yamhill River** is 60 miles long and follows the same angling pattern as the Tualatin—good for trout in the spring in its tributaries and for warm-water fish lower down during summer. The added bonus during winter is a run of cutthroat spawners from the Willamette. **Willamina Creek** near Sheridan has good spring trout fishing and a run of winter steelhead. **Willamina Pond** in Willamina's Huddeston Park is a popular kids' fishing spot for stocked rainbow, plus bullhead and perch.

The **forks of the Luckiamute** offer good early-season trout fishing above Falls City, where a waterfall is a natural barrier on the Little Fork for spawning fish from the Willamette. Much of the fishery is catch-and-release wild trout and steelhead. Rainbows are stocked early in the season. The BLM's Salem District Westside map is necessary to scout out creek fishing throughout Wine Country.

For a managed fly-fishing outing, try Red Hills Lake, (503) 864-3453, a commercial operation located in the hills northwest of Hwy 99W near Dundee at 19606 NE Archery Summit Rd. The 4-acre lake is stocked with Kamloops trout from Canada and steelhead, with the big ones growing to 25 inches and 10 pounds.

Boating/Canoeing

Hagg Lake sees it all: small-boat sailing, canoeing, waterskiing, wind-surfing, personal watercraft, and fishing. Recreation Area A West sees most of the motor activity, while Recreation Area C is best for nonmotor-ized craft and those who want to cruise at less than 10mph with a motor. (See Parks, above, for more information.)

The **Willamette River** helps take the pressure off Hagg Lake and keeps it from being overrun on summer weekends. **Rogers Landing Park,** (503) 538-2014, in Newberg is the busiest Willamette access between Portland and Salem. The Yamhill County park is a busy boat launch and water-ski area and has pleasant riverside picnicking and hiking opportunities. The park is 1 mile south of downtown Newberg on River St and Rogers Landing Rd.

Wine Country has a pair of paddling opportunities that beckon canoeists and flatwater kayakers from around the Willamette Valley. Both are usually boated during the November through May rainy season. The National Weather Service in Portland, (503) 261-9246, option 1, reports levels on selected rivers, but you'll need to learn to judge the Yamhill and Tualatin from how other rivers are flowing. The lower **Yamhill River** com-bines with the Willamette for a 12-mile float from near McMinnville to Newberg. The **Tualatin River** has 22 miles of paddling from Scholls to Lake Oswego, with the Schamberg Bridge dividing the float in two.

The Yamhill float begins at Yamhill Locks Park at Lafayette and ends on the Willamette River in Newberg. The locks were built in 1900 and accommodated river traffic until the 1950s. The launch is just below a remains of the locks and a minor rapids in Lafayette on Hwy 99 between Newberg and McMinnville. The Yamhill has little pep to it during summer, so paddlers need to work pretty hard until the Willamette is joined 5 miles above Newberg. The take-out is at Rogers Landing Park (see above).

The Tualatin offers a soupy-green 22-mile float during summer between the launch where Hwy 210 crosses the river at North Scholls to a takeout at Shipley Bridge on Stafford Rd just north of I-205 between Lake Oswego and Tualatin. The Schamberg Bridge on Elsner Rd 3 miles north-west of Sherwood divides the float in the middle. The river's lower 5 miles to its confluence with the Willamette has a dangerous dam followed by a rocky channel and should not be boated.

Hot Air Ballooning

The sun is just beginning to peek over the shoulder of Mount Hood far to the east and already the balloon captains of Yamhill County are unfurling their high-tech bags that will carry a gondola of awestruck tourists aloft over Wine Country.

With the hot air balloon safely laid out on a grassy field, the propane burners are fired up and the balloon begins to rise in the still morning air. The balloon's envelope collects the hot air and begins rising into the sky. Inflated to near capacity, only the balloon's tethers and sacks of sand keep it from taking off. When the pilots sees that everything is ready, passengers climb over the wicker sides of the gondola, ropes are untied, weight is tossed aside, and the balloon lifts off. The bag of hot air climbs swiftly to a couple thousand feet over the launch point at Newberg's **Sportsman Airpark** on St. Paul Rd at the west edge of town. The pilot keeps track of the winds and compensates with a blast of hot air from the burner. The flight is over too soon, naturally, but the view will last a lifetime. The landing is always a bit of a guessing game, but somehow the pilot manages to touch down in the predetermined open space.

For a hot-air-balloon ride over Wine Country, check out Vista Balloon Adventures of Newberg, (800) 622-2309; Rex Hill Winery of Newberg, (503) 538-0666; or American Hot Air Lines of Wilsonville, (503) 224-1179. Expect to pay about $175 for a three-hour tour, which includes instruction and preparation on the ground. Hot-air-balloon rides are not entirely without risk. A well-publicized accident in 1997 left one passenger dead on an American Hot Air Lines flight, but such incidents are extremely rare.

Gliding

A hot air balloon isn't the only way to fly over Wine Country. Non-motorized gliding, also called soaring, is another way to get into the skies. The Willamette Soaring Club, (503) 647-0913, operates out of an airstrip just north of the Dersham Rd exit of US 26 at North Plains. Club members use their sailplanes to give nonmembers rides for about $50 on Wednesdays, Saturdays, and Sundays from April through October.

Commercial glider rides are available at the McMinnville Airport from Cascade Soaring, (503) 472-8805.

Attractions

So many of the **Willamette Valley wineries'** pinot noirs have achieved international renown that many of the better-known bottlings are quite pricey; however, the ardent wine explorer can still find the up-and-coming producers cheerfully selling fabulous wine at reasonable prices out the winery's front door. The greatest concentration of wineries is in Yamhill County, mostly between Newberg and McMinnville. Here, among rolling oak-covered hills, are increasing numbers of vineyards and enough wineries to keep the touring wine lover tipsy for a week.

The Oregon Wine Advisory Board publishes a free wineries guide; call (503) 228-8336 or (800) 242-2363. Each county wine association also offers Thanksgiving and Memorial Day weekend touring maps and information: Yamhill County, (503) 434-5814; Polk County, (503) 581-0355; and Washington County, (503) 648-8198 or (503) 357-5005. Pick up a free copy of the monthly *Oregon Wine* newspaper, available at most Wine Country lodgings, restaurants, and wine shops, as well as at numerous Portland wine shops and hotels.

In fine weather take along a picnic lunch: many wineries have tables outside, and some sell chilled wine and picnic supplies.

Pacific University is why most people come to **Forest Grove,** and the towering firs on the small campus do justice to the town's name. But there's also quite a collection of local wineries, making the area worth exploring, perhaps on your way to the ocean. **Bellevue,** a tiny crossroads, is the site of three fine establishments, all under one roof. The **Oregon Wine Tasting Room,** (503) 843-3787, offers tastes of the best bottlings from two dozen Oregon wineries. The Lawrence Gallery, (503) 843-3633, is an excellent showcase of fine regional talent in all mediums. Upstairs is Augustine's, one of the region's better restaurants (see Restaurants, below).

McMinnville is growing up: the feed stores and steel mill are still here, but so are the high-tech companies and espresso hangouts. The growing wine industry has had a positive effect, especially on the food scene: there's a better concentration of interesting places to eat here than elsewhere in Wine Country. Along with its central location, that makes this town a good headquarters for wine touring. Serious wine lovers can overdose on great wine and food while hobnobbing with wine celebrities (including some of France's hot young winemakers) at the three-day **International Pinot Noir Celebration** in late July or early August on the grounds of gracious old Linfield College; call (503) 472-8964 for information.

Restaurants

Augustine's ☆☆ This informal space has scenic views out both sides: farmland on one side and down into the Lawrence Gallery on the other. The seasonal seafood (salmon fillet, sturgeon) is the chef's real focus. *19706 Hwy 18 (7 miles west of McMinnville), Bellevue; (503) 843-3225; $$.*

Cafe Azul ☆☆ Exotic flavors from southern Mexico (along with rich moles and handmade tortillas) make for a constantly changing menu of great creativity. Desserts are divine. The storefront location isn't quite up to the food. Reserve ahead. *313 3rd St (right downtown), McMinnville; (503) 435-1234; $$.*

Golden Valley Brewpub and Restaurant ☆ This former warehouse is the happening place in McMinnville. Half is pub, half is restaurant, but you can eat in either. The menu is extensive—stick with the basics. There's a good selection of their own brews. *980 E 4th St (at E 3rd and N Johnson), McMinnville; (503) 472-2739; $.*

Ixtapa ☆ Enter this colorful, lively little restaurant for fresh, light, not-too-spicy Mexican food. The service really hustles. *307 E 1st St (on Hwy 99W northbound, in town), Newberg; (503) 538-5956; $.*

Kame ☆ McMinnvilleites aren't used to getting their change counted out in Japanese, but for food this good and this inexpensive, they don't seem to mind one bit. Kame has white walls, plain tables, and simple Japanese food—graciously served and reasonably priced. *228 N Evans (at 3rd), McMinnville; (503) 434-4326; $.*

Nick's Italian Cafe ☆☆☆ Nick's is both a local institution and winemakers' culinary headquarters. The five-course Northern Italian meal amazes, and a seasonal antipasto, the housemade pasta, and the entree are always delicious. It's not fancy but the food and the wine list pack 'em in. *521 E 3rd St (downtown, across from the movie theater), McMinnville; (503) 434-4471; $$.*

Red Hills Provincial Dining ☆☆☆ You'll be received warmly in this country restaurant. The dinner menu of a half-dozen items changes weekly, and the choices are all intriguing. It's the best of European country cooking—simple but flavorful. Outstanding wine list. *276 Hwy 99W (at north edge of town), Dundee; (503) 538-8224; $$.*

Third Street Grill ☆☆ This elegant Victorian-style house has intimate nooks and crannies. The menu is oriented toward meats, but with interesting combinations of flavors. Portions are generous, and the wine list contains an excellent selection of local wines. *729 E 3rd St (just east of downtown), McMinnville; (503) 435-1745; $$.*

Tina's ☆☆ The owners work magic in a small building by the side of the road: tiny garden outside, plain walls inside. Food is creative—try a rabbit risotto or cream of cucumber soup. Unwind here after a day on the road. *760 Hwy 99W (center of town, across from fire station), Dundee; (503) 538-8880; $$.*

Cheaper Eats

Alf's Nostalgia or a craving for good grease and thick shakes will lead you to this old-fashioned soda shop. Settle in to enjoy ice cream or a thick burger. For entertainment, go watch the live monkeys cavorting. *1250 S Baker St, McMinnville; (503) 472-7314; $.*

El Ranchero A south-of-the-border stop that offers a more expansive menu and presentation than most. Dive into the seafood options, and fill up on the spilling-over platters of rice and beans. *2628 NE Hwy 99W, McMinnville; (503) 434-9525; $.*

Etcetera All the area winemakers pile in for lunch, and everybody calls this tiny place Alice's—her meatloaf sandwiches are always in demand and her early-morning scones disappear quickly. Stop here for picnic fixings (salads, sandwiches, terrific desserts). *976 Hwy 99W, Dundee; (503) 537-9340; $.*

Panadaria y Videos González Head through the grocery store to the back walk-up window for very authentic, tasty Mexican sandwiches, tacos, and traditional dishes. Even if you overorder, you probably won't spend more than five bucks. *508 E 1st Ave, Newberg; (503) 538-0306; $.*

Lodgings

Flying M Ranch ☆☆ The setting is terrific—nothing but mountains and forest. There are ponds for swimming and fishing, tennis courts, and hiking and horse trails (cowboys can take you trail riding). Rooms are motel-style—savvy visitors rent a rustic cabin with a kitchen (and budget travelers camp and get access to facilities). Large groups might check out the lodge on Trask Mountain. There's a Western-style lounge and a mostly standard-fare restaurant. *23029 NW Flying M Rd (10 miles west of Yamhill; follow the little red flying Ms), Yamhill, OR 97148; (503) 662-3222; $–$$.*

Mattey House ☆☆ This Victorian farmhouse has been restored to its original elegance but with a lighter, more country feel. Rooms are (authentically) small, with nice touches. Wander through the small vineyard—you'll feel you're in the middle of the country. *10221 NE Mattey Lane (just south of Lafayette on Hwy 99W), McMinnville, OR 97128; (503) 434-5058; $$.*

The Partridge Farm Bed & Breakfast Inn ☆ They raise partridges here, and other birds, so you get fresh eggs for breakfast. A broad lawn helps one feel out in the country. Three rooms have antiques and in-room sinks. Romantics can take a hot-air-balloon ride. *4300 E Portland Rd (just off Hwy 99W, north of Newberg), Newberg, OR 97132; (503) 538-2050; $$.*

Safari Motor Inn ☆ For location and price, it's hard to beat this long-established, unassuming motor lodge. Nothing fancy here, but it's a nice alternative for visitors who shy away from B&Bs. Rooms are quiet and beds are comfortable. *345 N Hwy 99W (at 19th St), McMinnville, OR 97128; (503) 472-5187; $.*

Sheridan Country Inn This old house on the outskirts of town is now a friendly inn with large rooms (eight in the funky but spacious mansion, four in duplexes). Some rooms have microwaves, private baths, and TVs. Kids are welcome. *1330 W Main (1 mile west of Bridge St on Hwy 18 business loop), Sheridan, OR 97378; (503) 843-3151; $$.*

Springbrook Hazelnut Farm ☆☆ This colorfully elegant farmhouse has a dining room that feels like an Italian palazzo, and a spacious guest wing. There's a library, a TV room, a great carriage-house apartment, and an orchard, pool, and tennis courts. *30295 N Hwy 99W (just off Hwy 99W, north of Newberg), Newberg, OR 97132; (503) 538-4606 or (800) 793-8528; $$$.*

Steiger Haus Inn ☆☆ This house was designed as a B&B, and downstairs rooms all have decks. This peaceful creekside oasis has a Northwest feel, with lots of light. A full breakfast includes coffee roasted especially for the inn. *360 Wilson St (from Hwy 99W, turn east on Cowls at the hospital), McMinnville, OR 97128; (503) 472-0821; $$.*

Wine Country Farm ☆ Surrounded by vineyards in Dundee, this 1910 stucco home has three bedrooms with spectacular views. The owner can take you on an Arabian horse-and-buggy ride. Breakfast is home-baked goodies, and the attached winery is open for tasting. *6855 Breyman Orchards Rd (call for directions), Dayton, OR 97114; (503) 864-3446 or (800) 261-3446; $$.*

Youngberg Hill Vineyard Bed & Breakfast ☆☆ This place is back in business: new owners fell for the gorgeous property and are determined to make it a first-class establishment. A vineyard skirts the rambling house, and all rooms have stunning views. The quiet is deeply refreshing. *10660 Youngberg Hill Rd (call for directions), McMinnville, OR 97128; (503) 472-2727; $$$.*

Cheaper Sleeps

Baker Street Inn With only four rooms (and one cottage out of budget range), the feel at this inn is warm and cozy. The price includes breakfast (a major meal), which helps keep this high-end "bargain" within budget. *129 SE Baker St, McMinnville, OR 97128; (503) 472-5575 or (800) 870-5575; $.*

Best Western Vineyard Inn This motel's location sure isn't glamorous and the rooms are rather utilitarian, but the central location and dinky swimming pool make this place worth knowing about. *2035 S Hwy 99W, McMinnville, OR 97128; (503) 472-4900 or (800) 285-6242; $.*

More Information

Bureau of Land Management, Salem: *(503) 375-5646.*
Dallas Area Chamber of Commerce, Dallas: *(503) 623-2564.*
Greater Hillsboro Chamber of Commerce, Hillsboro: *(503) 648-1102.*
McMinnville Chamber of Commerce, McMinnville: *(503) 472-6196.*
Northwest Oregon Tourism Alliance, Portland: *(800) 962-3700.*
Tillamook State Forest, Forest Grove: *(503) 357-2191.*
Tualatin Hills Park and Recreation District, Beaverton: *(503) 645-6433.*
The Visit Group, Salem: *(503) 399-7199.*
Washington County Visitors Association, Beaverton: *(800) 537-3149.*
West Valley Chamber of Commerce, Sheridan: *(503) 843-4964.*
Yamhill County Wineries Association, McMinnville: *(503) 434-5814.*

Cascade
Foothills

From the Clackamas River on the north, east to the western slopes of the Mount Hood and Willamette National Forests, south to the Calapooia River, and west to the Willamette Valley lowlands, including the towns of Estacada, Lyons, Detroit, and Sweet Home.

Oregonians, perhaps more than any other Northwesterners, have a love affair with their rivers. Idaho is more famous for its whitewater boating. Washington's rivers, especially on the Olympic Peninsula, overwhelm with their sheer number. And Alaska is in a different league entirely. But when it comes to the formal protection of rivers, Oregon is the nation's leader. Residents have fought hard against development over the years to place 56 rivers, creeks, and forks on the National Wild and Scenic Rivers and the State Scenic Waterways Programs. In fact, the Rogue River in southern Oregon was one of the original waterways protected when the federal system was created in 1968. Many Oregon rivers also have multiple segments of their main stem and tributaries protected.

The Cascade Foothills are a showcase for the state's rivers. Within the west slope of the Oregon Cascades and the Willamette Valley, the federal program protects parts of the Clackamas River and its tributary, the Roaring River; the Little North Fork Santiam River and its tributary, Elkhorn Creek; and Quartzville Creek, while the State Scenic Waterways Program includes much of the Clackamas River, and the Little North Fork and Battle Ax Creek, both tributaries of the North Santiam River.

Conversely, the Cascade Foothills are also a showcase for what can happen to rivers that are not protected. Major dams, all built by the US Army Corps of Engineers to control flooding, have created reservoirs on the North, Middle, and South Forks of the Santiam

River, which have more than paid for themselves in the amount of flood damage they've prevented. But that cost has also meant the death of the river and its fish runs upstream and the artificial manipulation of the river downstream.

Oregon's shortage of natural lakes, especially in the western valleys between the Coast and Cascade Ranges, is mitigated, however, by the lakeside recreation offered by these reservoirs. Detroit Lake on the North Santiam, Green Peter Reservoir on the Middle Santiam, and Foster Reservoir on the South Santiam all come alive with fishermen, water-skiers, and swimmers when summer's heat causes an exodus from the cities in the valley. Just don't bother visiting them in the fall when the reservoirs are drawn down in preparation for winter. The view of wide, muddy shorelines, littered with stumps of trees harvested before the reservoirs were filled, leaves one wondering whether the river would have looked better if it had been protected rather than dammed.

Getting There

Portlanders zip into the Cascade Foothills a few minutes from Interstate 205 by taking exit 12 on Interstate 205 onto Highway 224 (Clackamas Highway) and driving southeast 20 miles to Estacada. Salem's getaway to the Cascade Foothills is Highway 22, a 52-mile drive east to Detroit and the North Fork of the Santiam River. Visitors from central Willamette Valley towns, including Albany and Lebanon, head east on US Highway 20 (US 20) to Sweet Home, the gateway to the Middle and South Forks of the Santiam River. Campgrounds and access points to national forest lands become frequent within 30 to 50 miles from any of these cities.

Adjoining Areas

NORTH: **Greater Portland**

SOUTH: **Greater Eugene**

EAST: **Mount Hood, Mount Jefferson and the Metolius River, Santiam Pass and Mount Washington**

WEST: **Salem and the Heart of the Valley**

inside out

Camping

With the majority of Oregon's population only an hour's drive away, the valleys of the Cascade Foothills fill up with campers on weekends from May into September. From Portland on the north to Eugene on the south,

they come to camp, fish, hike, pan for gold, ride bikes, and just relax and
escape the noise and congestion of the cities where they live.

Dispersed camping is popular along the **Collawash River** in the
Clackamas River drainage within Mount Hood National Forest; along
the **Molalla River,** on Bureau of Land Management (BLM) land upstream
from Molalla; along the **Little North Santiam River,** on a mix of BLM
and Willamette National Forest land upstream from Mehama on Hwy 22;
and, in particular, along **Quartzville Creek,** another mix of BLM and
Willamette National Forest land upstream from Sweet Home on US 20.

Clackamas River

Campers from Portland heading for the hills don't need to drive very far out
of town before finding spots to pitch a tent or park an RV. With so many
campgrounds to choose from, it takes some time to learn which meet individual needs the best. Boaters like Lazy Bend, Fish Creek, and Indian Henry
because all are near launch or take-out sites. Hikers and bikers head for Fish
Creek and Indian Henry for the convenient access to the Clackamas River
Trail. Both have barrier-free facilities. Riverside is popular because it is near
Big Bottom and Alder Flat, both scenic natural areas with short paths
through old-growth forests. Most campgrounds in the Clackamas River
drainage are on the national reservations system and can be reserved by calling (800) 280-2267. Most camps are gated and closed during the off-season
(October through April), although several are usually kept open throughout
the winter without services. Best bets to be open for winter camping are the
smallest campgrounds, such as Armstrong, Sunstrip, and Riverford. Two of
the better campgrounds in the entire Cascade Foothills country are located
alongside the Clackamas River near Estacada: Clackamas County's **Barton
Park** and **Milo McIver State Park.** Both parks have busy boat launches.

The Barton campground has 90 sites, including 39 brand-new state-
of-the-art sites for large recreational vehicles. The park also has picnic
areas large enough to accommodate 1,000, ball fields, a playground, horseshoe pits, and showers. The park is located on the Clackamas River, 9.4
miles west of Estacada, and is popular with fishermen and floaters. The
Clackamas River is relatively mellow as it flows from Estacada to join the
Willamette River at Gladstone, but all boaters should take standard precautions and treat the river with respect.

To reach Barton Park, as well as all the other recreation opportunities
up the Clackamas River drainage, drive I-205 to exit 12 at Clackamas.
Travel east on Hwy 212/224 for 3.2 miles to where it splits at Rock Creek
Junction. The left fork leads to Sandy and Mount Hood, while the right
fork heads to Estacada and the Clackamas River. Follow Hwy 224 for 6.4
miles toward Estacada and watch for the signed entry to Barton Park on

Bakers Ferry Rd. Clackamas County keeps its campgrounds open from May 1 through the end of September. Call (503) 650-3484 for reservations and information for all Clackamas County parks. Another Clackamas County campground in the Cascade Foothills is **Metzler Park,** a 69-unit facility on Clear Creek south of Estacada on Metzler Park Rd.

McIver State Park is located on the south side of the Clackamas River off Springwater Rd, 4 miles northwest of Estacada. The park's facilities include 44 electrical sites, 4 primitive tent sites, and 1 site accessible for those with disabilities. As with most large state park campgrounds, McIver offers hot showers for its campers. McIver Park's 951 acres offer large grassy play areas, a 7-mile trail system for hikers and equestrians, a boat launch, plenty of Clackamas River frontage, and a panoramic viewpoint that takes in the rapidly urbanizing area southeast of Portland as well as Mounts Hood, Adams, and St. Helens. The park is open for day use all year and the camping season runs March through November. For camping reservations, call (800) 452-5687.

Traveling upriver from Estacada on Hwy 224, **Promontory Park** comes first at 5 miles, followed by a string of Mount Hood National Forest campgrounds that begin with Lazy Bend and continue up the drainage for 40 miles. Promontory Park has 52 campsites and is operated by a concessionaire for Portland General Electric. The park has full services, including boat rentals and groceries, and a sign warns about the last gasoline available for 70 miles up the Clackamas River Highway to Detroit. For camping reservations at Promontory Park, call (503) 464-8515.

Campgrounds become numerous as travelers work their way up the Clackamas along the 75-mile Clackamas-Breitenbush National Forest Scenic Byway, which links state and national forest highways for a scenic route through the foothills between Estacada and Detroit. Campgrounds (and the number of sites) are **Lazy Bend** (21), **Lockaby** (30), **Armstrong** (12), **Fish Creek** (24), **Roaring River** (19), **Sunstrip** (9), and **Indian Henry** (86). Upriver from Indian Henry Campground at Ripplebrook Ranger Station, the Clackamas divides into three branches: the Oak Grove Fork comes down from Timothy Lake in the Mount Hood country, the main stem comes from the Olallie Lake Scenic Area in the Mount Jefferson/Metolius country, and the Collawash River fork drains the Bull of the Woods Wilderness Area in the Cascade foothills. Campgrounds in the foothills country upstream from Ripplebrook are **Rainbow** (17 sites), **Riverside** (16), **Riverford** (9), **Raab** (27), and **Kingfisher** (23). The forest highway switches numbers from 46 to 63 to 70, but keep following signs to Bagby Hot Springs and stay on pavement.

North Santiam

Campers heading east out of Salem on Hwy 22 up the North Santiam River Canyon have a couple of main campgrounds to pick from and a whole lot of others that help ease the pressure on the major parks. Smaller county, BLM, and national forest camps are located up the Little North Fork canyon of the Santiam, up the Breitenbush River, around Detroit Lake, and farther up the North Santiam.

Fishermen's Bend Recreation Site, 30 miles east of Salem, is the showcase park in the BLM's Salem District. It has 38 fee campsites, plus river access for fishing, a boat ramp, picnic sites, an amphitheater, and a nature trail. The recreation area also has group camping and picnicking facilities. Call (503) 897-2406 for group reservations. When traveling from the west, Fishermen's Bend is one of the first in a long line of recreation facilities in the North Santiam corridor that stretch all the way to Santiam Pass and beyond in the Santiam Pass/Mount Washington country.

Detroit Lake State Recreation Area, 50 miles east of Salem, is one of the biggest lake-based recreation facilities in the Oregon state park system, with 134 tent sites, 70 electrical sites, and 107 trailer spaces with full utility hookups. Two campsites are reserved for campers with disabilities. Reservations are accepted throughout the camping season, which runs from March 1 through late November, by calling (800) 452-5687. Park information is available at (503) 854-3346. The campground must have something special to offer in order to be so large—and it does. Its water facilities include floating boat docks, fishing docks, and a designated swimming area. Water-skiers from the Willamette Valley flock here as an alternative to skiing on the Willamette River. The park has evening interpretive programs in an outdoor amphitheater. Be prepared for rain because Detroit Dam collected 138.85 inches in 1996, an extraordinarily wet year in Oregon.

Willamette National Forest campgrounds within 5 miles of Detroit are **Hoover, South Shore, Cove Creek, Upper Arm,** and **Piety.** Hoover, located on the south shore of Detroit on Forest Rd 10, is the largest, with 37 sites and barrier-free facilities. Piety is a 12-unit campground located on an island in the lake and is accessible by boat only. Launch at the state park and paddle or motor south 1 mile to the island. Farther up the North Santiam, campers head for **Whispering Falls, Riverside,** and **Marion Forks.** Riverside is the largest, with 37 sites. All of the forest service campgrounds in the area are operated on a first-come basis. Call the Detroit Ranger Station, (503) 854-3366, for information.

The Little North Fork Canyon enters the North Santiam near the town of Mehama, 23 miles up Hwy 22 east of Salem. The county, BLM, and national forest roads that follow the Little North Fork pass numerous day-use recreation sites before the road ends at a locked gate at the Opal Creek area. Campgrounds are located at the BLM's **Elkhorn Valley,** (503) 375-5646, 8.3 miles from Hwy 22 up the Elkhorn Valley Highway from Mehama, and at the Forest Service's **Shady Cove,** (503) 854-3366, 18.3 miles up the canyon. Linn County, (541) 967-3917, has 40 campsites in **John Neal Campground** at Mehama on Hwy 22. Elkhorn Valley Campground often operates to capacity in its 24 sites during good weather periods of summer and has the best facilities near Opal Creek Wilderness, which was created by Congress in 1996. Campers use holes in the Little North Fork for swimming and fishing.

The Breitenbush River flows out of the Mount Jefferson area to join the North Santiam at Detroit. The Detroit Ranger Station, (503) 854-3366, maintains 60 campsites in its **Breitenbush, Humbug,** and **Cleator Bend Campgrounds** east of Detroit on Forest Rd 46 in the Breitenbush Valley. **Elk Lake Campground** is 5 miles north of Detroit at the southern edge of the Bull of the Woods Wilderness. The camp has only 14 sites but campers persistent enough to drive the backroads to reach it are rewarded with a beautiful lakeside setting at 4,000 feet in elevation. The campground is at the end of Forest Rd 4697. Turn north at Humbug Campground in the Breitenbush Valley.

The Breitenbush drainage is perhaps best known for its hot springs, the largest flow of hot water in Oregon's western Cascades. **Breitenbush Hot Springs,** (503) 854-3314, is a rustic old resort 10 miles up the Breitenbush Valley on Forest Road 46 north of Detroit. The historic hot springs are now operated as a holistic retreat and conference center (see Cheaper Sleeps in this chapter). Breitenbush Hot Springs accepts day visitors for a fee, but it's best to call ahead for a reservation because special functions occasionally cause the facilities to be closed to all but conference attendees.

Middle Santiam

Camping along the Middle Fork of the Santiam River means driving county, BLM, and national forest roads between Foster Reservoir on the west, Green Peter Reservoir in the middle, and the Quartzville Creek National Wild and Scenic River and recreation corridor to the east. Foster Dam backs up the Middle and South Forks of the Santiam River near Sweet Home, where Linn County operates Sunnyside Park. Green Peter Dam upstream creates an even larger lake on the Middle Santiam where Whitcomb Creek Campground is also operated by Linn County. Quartzville Creek is the main tributary of the Middle Santiam, and its main campground is the BLM's Yellowbottom. Quartzville Creek is also famous for its many beautiful dispersed camping sites.

Sunnyside Park is the showcase park in an impressive system of camping parks operated by Linn County. More than just a campground, a camping park also has some type of sports facilities for team play, such as volleyball. For information and group camping reservations, call the Linn County Parks Department at (541) 967-3917. Sunnyside Park has 165 sites, most with water and electricity hookups, as well as barrier-free rest rooms and showers. With fees ranging from $12 to $14, expect to pay about $5 less per site than at a state park campground. Camping season is April 1 until November 1. Besides a volleyball court, the park has water facilities that include a boat ramp, moorage, waterskiing, fishing, and swimming. Sunnyside Park is 3 miles east of Sweet Home on Quartzville Rd at the head of Foster Reservoir.

Whitcomb Creek Park, (541) 967-3917, accessible via the county road that follows the north shore of Green Peter Reservoir, is 9 miles northeast of Sunnyside Park. The park has 39 sites, none with hookups. Its camping fee is about $10, and its season is late April until early October. Boaters enjoy exploring the arms and bays of Green Peter Lake.

The BLM's **Yellowbottom Campground,** (503) 375-5646, is located in an old-growth forest, a dozen miles up Quartzville Creek from Green Peter Lake via BLM Rds 29.1 and 35.3. The BLM's road number system is usually bewildering to decipher, so just stay on the main road and keep heading in the direction that looks right. In this case, it will be. With Yellowbottom's 22 sites, only the lucky few get to stay overnight there, so everyone else camps out in a wide choice of dispersed sites. The Rhododendron Trail within the campground winds uphill through a colorful understory of rhododendrons, which usually bloom in May at their elevation of 1,500 feet.

South Santiam

Cascadia State Park, (541) 854-3406, is the first campground to greet travelers heading east from Sweet Home on US 20, the South Santiam Highway. Cascadia, 12 miles east of Sweet Home, has 25 primitive campsites, picnic tables, fireplaces, and water. The park does not take reservations and is open March through November. Park trails lead to the South Santiam River, where clear water and smooth rocks attract visitors to fish and swim. A 1.5-mile round-trip hike leads through the lush forest of Soda Creek to a view of 150-foot-high Lower Soda Creek Falls. The 105-foot-long Short Covered Bridge is located nearby the park on the north side of US 20.

Continuing upriver along US 20, in the 25 miles east of Cascadia State Park, the Sweet Home Ranger District, (541) 367-5168, offers small campgrounds at **Trout Creek, Yukwah, Fernview, House Rock,** and **Lost Prairie.** All are situated near hiking trails and fishing holes. Yukwah has the best RV facilities, House Rock is located in a grove of old-growth forest, and Trout Creek is located near the historic Old Santiam Wagon Road, a pioneer route through the north-central Cascades. Rooster Rock trailhead across US 20 from Fernview is the portal for the Menagerie Wilderness (see Hiking, below).

Picnics

While a lot of visitors to the Cascade Foothills make their visit a weekend affair, plenty also head up for the day to enjoy a picnic or to find a shady lunch stop as they drive between the Willamette Valley and central Oregon. Most of the campgrounds in the foothills have picnic facilities, and there are also plenty of day-use-only parks.

In addition to its campground at **Promontory Park,** Portland General Electric operates two day-use parks near Estacada as part of its hydroelectric projects on the Clackamas River. **River Mill Park,** 1 mile west of Estacada off Hwy 224, is closest to Portland. The park is located on a 2-mile-long reservoir on Estacada Lake behind River Mill Dam and is popular for picnicking, fishing, and boating. **Faraday Park,** 1 mile southeast of Estacada on Hwy 224, was developed to provide fishing access, not as a picnic area. But, hey, even fishermen have to stop for lunch, as long as the fish aren't biting.

Eagle Fern Park, operated by Clackamas County on Eagle Creek, is a popular summer picnic spot 4.3 miles east of Hwy 224 and the community of Eagle Creek, on Eagle Fern Rd. The park dates to the 1930s and is set amid a grove of towering western red cedar and Douglas fir. Covered picnic areas can accommodate large groups. The park is open daily, although it was closed recently for a short time when a statewide election limited property taxes. (Increasingly run by statewide voter initiatives, Oregon has become accustomed to voters from 300 miles away cutting off funding to local governments and school districts. Parks are frequently first to feel budget constraints.)

Most of the campgrounds along the Clackamas River are also good for picnicking. A couple of special places to try are **Carter Bridge,** a campground converted into a picnic area, at the confluence of the Clackamas and Collawash Rivers on Forest Rd 46, 3 miles upstream from the Ripplebrook Ranger Station (Hwy 224 changes from a state road to a national forest road at Ripplebrook). Carter Bridge also is the site of a Class IV rapids on the Clackamas River and can provide some interesting viewing when rafters are running the river during spring. The Collawash and Clackamas Rivers merge 3 miles upstream from Ripplebrook. The Collawash has some of the best summer swimming hole opportunities of any river close to Portland. The Clackamas River Highway (Hwy 224 and

Forest Rd 46) has a history of washing out during major winter flooding events. The Oregon Department of Transportation has spent millions of dollars repairing the road in recent years, but it's only inevitable that some other section will wash out in the future.

The Little North Santiam Recreation Area out of Mehama, which follows a series of county, BLM, and national forest roads up the Elkhorn Valley, is lined with many day-use areas used by picnickers, swimmers, and fishermen. Turning off Hwy 22 and heading upstream northeast from Mehama, watch for Marion County's **North Fork Park** at 2 miles, the BLM's **Canyon Creek Park** at 7.2 miles, the county's park at **Salmon Creek Falls** at 13.7 miles, and the Detroit Ranger Station's **Three Pools** swimming hole at 17.3 miles. The Little North Santiam is famous far and wide for its beautiful swimming holes and fishing spots. The Opal Creek Wilderness awaits near the end of the road (see Hiking, below), a popular spot for hikers and anyone interested in seeing a 500-year-old forest. Perhaps the best spot for a picnic is on one of the tables that overlook the Little North Santiam at Canyon Creek Park.

The canyon of the North Santiam upriver from Mehama on Hwy 22 invites travelers to stop for a picnic at **North Santiam State Park; Minto, Packsaddle,** and **Niagara County Parks;** and **Mongold State Park,** all well signed along the road between Mehama and Detroit. The day-use areas are strung out along Hwy 22 over a 25-mile stretch of highway between Mehama and Detroit Lake. Niagara is known for its scenic waterfalls and steep-walled canyon along the North Santiam, while Mongold offers day-use access to Detroit Lake away from the busy state park campground a mile farther up the highway. Packsaddle Park is used by boaters for access to the North Santiam, and Minto Park has an extensive trail system along the river.

The Middle and South Forks of the Santiam have most of their developed picnic opportunities within the campgrounds. Additional day-use areas include Linn County's **Lewis Creek Park** and the US Army Corps of Engineers' **Gedney Creek Park,** both on Foster Reservoir, and the BLM's **Dogwood Park** on Quartzville Creek. **House Rock and Lost Prairie Campgrounds** along US 20 have day-use facilities that are wheelchair accessible.

Hiking

Beautiful Opal Creek, a "line in the sand" between preservationists and logging interests when it comes to the battle over old-growth timber harvesting, was protected by Congress in 1996 as the 20,300-acre **Opal Creek Wilderness** and 13,640-acre scenic recreation area along the Little North

Santiam River. The area's protected status guarantees that its 500-year-old Douglas fir, western red cedar, and western hemlock forest will continue to follow nature's course. Opal Creek, managed by the Detroit Ranger Station, (503) 854-3366, had been the last unprotected low-elevation valley in Oregon's Cascades with most of its ancient forest intact.

To reach the Opal Creek trailhead drive Hwy 22 for 23.2 miles east of Salem to Mehama and turn northeast into the Little North Santiam Recreation Area. Drive 15.2 miles to where the road surface switches to gravel and continue 1.3 miles to a junction. The left junction (Forest Rd 2209) leads in 4.1 miles to a locked gate and the hiking entrance to the Opal Creek area. The right junction (Forest Rd 2207) reaches the turnoff to Three Pools after .8 mile and Shady Grove Campground and the Little North Santiam trailhead in 1.8 miles. The road continues all the way to Detroit (follow signs), passing the Opal Lake trailhead at 10 miles and reaching Hwy 22 at 19.7 miles. The **Little North Santiam Trail** (easy; 4.2 miles) follows the river downstream to its lower trailhead off Forest Rd 2209-201.

The access trail to the Opal Creek Trail follows an old mining road that continues to be used by the Forest Service and the Friends of Opal Creek, the nonprofit group that owns the old mine at **Jawbone Flats.** The public is not allowed to drive on the road, although visitors with accessibility problems can arrange for a ride with the Friends group by calling (503) 897-2921. From the locked gate, a Douglas fir estimated to be a thousand years old lives 100 feet south of the road, .2 mile from the gate. The road passes the trail to **Whetstone Mountain** (difficult; 4.5 miles one way, 3,000-foot elevation gain) at .9 mile, then passes through a grove of 500-year-old Douglas firs at 1.7 miles. At 2 miles from the gate, an opening in the forest to the south leads to Merten Mill and a path to a waterfall called **Cascadia de Los Niños** on the Little North Santiam River. The **Opal Creek Trail** (easy; 2.5 miles one way) begins 2.2 miles on the right from the locked gate. Jawbone Flats, an actively used collection of old mining buildings, comes at 3.3 miles on the road where Battle Ax and Opal Creeks join to form the Little North Santiam.

To reach **Opal Pool,** the most famous attraction in the area, walk past Jawbone Flats to a bridge over Battle Ax Creek. Turn right and hike .2 mile to Opal Pool, a 100-yard-long chasm cut by Opal Creek through bedrock. The emerald-colored pool is at the bottom of a 30-foot waterfall at the end of the chasm.

The **Bull of the Woods Wilderness** is adjacent to and north of Opal Creek. Bull of the Woods was designated as a wilderness in 1984 by Congress, and 7,500 of its 34,885 acres were shifted to the Opal Creek

Wilderness in 1996. The transfer was made so that all of Bull of the Woods, located in the Clackamas River drainage, is managed by the Mount Hood National Forest, (503) 630-6861, and Opal Creek, with all of it in the Santiam River drainage, is managed by the Willamette National Forest, (503) 854-3366.

Bull of the Woods also protects a significant area of old-growth forest, but much of its terrain is significantly higher than Opal Creek. Elevations in Bull of the Woods range from 2,500 feet to 5,523, while the Jawbone Flats area of Opal Creek lies at 1,400 feet. Bull of the Woods is popular for a weekend backpack trip or day hiking. The **Dickey Creek Trail** (difficult; 5.9 miles one way) leads from near the Collawash River to the old fire lookout at the summit of Bull of the Woods. Access is from the north on the Clackamas River Highway and Forest Rds 46, 63, 6330, and 6340; pick up a Mount Hood National Forest map for navigation.

The Clackamas River area is festooned with trails, although floods and resulting trail and road washouts have left the system a mess. Call the Clackamas River Ranger District, (503) 630-6861, for current conditions. The **Clackamas River Trail** (moderate; 7.8 miles one way), located on Hwy 224 between Fish Creek and Indian Henry Campgrounds, continues to be an all-time favorite in the drainage because the trail stays relatively level as it follows within earshot of the river. Be sure to visit Pup Creek Falls just south of the trail's midpoint. The **Riverside Trail** (easy; 4 miles) follows the river upstream between its trailheads in Rainbow and Riverside Campgrounds. The Clackamas River Ranger District has a long-range goal of completing the **Urban Link Trail,** which could connect downtown Portland with the Pacific Crest Trail near Olallie Lake by following Portland's Springwater Corridor, the Clackamas River Trail, and the **Rhododendron Ridge Trail.** Also called the Rho Ridge Trail (difficult; 8.4 miles one way), the route follows a ridge top that divides the Clackamas from the Collawash. The northern trailhead is on Forest Rd 6350 (get a Mount Hood National Forest map for directions to this lightly used part of the forest). The most popular hike on the Collawash is up the Hot Springs Fork to **Bagby Hot Springs,** a rustic bathing area with bathhouses and a soaking pool. The hot springs is 1.5 miles from Forest Rd 70, but the trail continues 12.5 miles into and through the Bull of the Woods Wilderness. Other short hikes with plenty to see in the Clackamas drainage are the **Big Bottom** area, along the river 12 miles upstream from Ripplebrook Ranger Station, and **Alder Flat,** an area of old-growth forest .25 mile north of Ripplebrook.

Table Rock Wilderness Area, one of the few managed by the BLM in Oregon, lies 19 miles southeast of Molalla. Head for the Hardy Creek mountain bike trailhead (see Cycling, below) and keep going upstream.

Where the road branches at 19 miles, the main trailhead is another 3 miles up the Middle Fork road to the left, then 5 miles to the right up the Table Rock roads. The **Table Rock Trail** (moderate; 2.3 miles one way) climbs 1,000 feet to reach the summit of 4,881-foot Table Rock and its outstanding views of the Cascade Range.

Other wilderness areas in the Cascade Foothills are the 5,000-acre **Menagerie** and the 8,542-acre **Middle Santiam Wildernesses.** The Menagerie, an area of unusual rock outcrops favored by rock climbers until they discovered Smith Rock State Park in central Oregon, is easily reached off US 20 about 20 miles east of Sweet Home. The **Rooster Rock Trail** (difficult; 2.2 miles one way) begins near Fernview Campground and climbs 2,255 feet for views of the rock cliffs that rise above the forest of the Menagerie. The **McQuade Creek Trail** (difficult; 6.1 miles one way to 100 feet below the 4,965-foot summit of Chimney Peak) leads into the Middle Santiam Wilderness from the upper Quartzville Creek drainage. Two miles after driving east off BLM land in the upper Quartzville drainage onto forest service land, turn south on Forest Rd 1142 and drive 2 miles to the trailhead. The McQuade Creek Trail reaches the wilderness boundary in 4 miles, has a spur to just beneath the summit of Chimney Peak at 6.1 miles, and continues as a long-distance through route (10 miles or more) to three other trailheads on the east side of the Middle Santiam Wilderness. The Swamp Peak, Gordon Peak, and Chimney Peak trailheads are accessible over a network of logging roads, and anyone trying to locate them needs maps of the Willamette National Forest and the Middle Santiam Wilderness.

The Quartzville Creek corridor provides access to one shouldn't-miss hike into the BLM's **Crabtree Valley,** an isolated grove of giant 500-year-old trees. The 2-square-mile grove is 42 miles east of Albany and varies in elevation from 2,850 feet to 4,443 feet. Crabtree Lake is the central attraction, but it's the surrounding trees that make the valley special. Reaching the valley requires precisely following a maze of BLM roads, plus a 0.7-mile hike should you be so fortunate as to find the proper place to park. Contact the BLM's Salem office, (503) 375-5646, for driving directions.

A couple of nature trails not to miss while traveling from the Willamette Valley through the Cascade Foothills are the **Cal Leitch Nature Trail** at the Maples Wayside on Hwy 22 and the **Hackleman Creek Old-Growth Trail** on Hwy 22. The Maples Wayside is 35 miles east of Salem, conveniently located for a quick stop off the highway and a short tour of the 12 interpretive stations along the North Santiam River. The Hackleman Trail is located 40 miles east of Sweet Home and features a self-guided interpretive hike through an ancient grove of trees. The 1.2-mile loop portion of the trail is barrier free but moderately difficult for wheelchair users.

Biking

With all the hills in the Cascade Foothills, it's hard to make a case for anything that resembles convenient, easy road-bike rides. **Cyclists** can use the paved roads that head out of the Willamette Valley into the foothills, but the riding is so much better in the valley itself that few choose to do so. One ride that is worth a try, but only with a shuttle vehicle, is a 55-mile paved descent on **Willamette National Forest Road 11** from near Marion Fork (2 miles south on Hwy 22), down the Quartzville Creek corridor and out to Sweet Home. The road is heavily traveled by vehicles only on its lower portion along Foster Reservoir.

The Cascade Foothills are increasingly being opened to **mountain-bike riding.** The **Molalla River** trail system has gone from nothing but some overgrown logging roads to 20 miles of singletrack in a few years. Trails are managed by the BLM, (503) 375-5646, and are maintained by volunteers from local mountain-bike clubs. To reach the **Hardy Creek** trailhead, drive east from Salem on Hwy 211 and turn north at a Y intersection at the east edge of Molalla onto Feyrer Park Rd. At the next junction turn right onto Dickey Prairie Rd, then turn right to cross the Molalla River on the Glen Avon Bridge. Watch for the trailhead on the south side of the road, 9 miles southeast of Molalla. The Clackamas Ranger District of the Mount Hood National Forest sees some mountain-bike use, but much of the riding is on trails built for hiking and have steep climbs. An exception is the 7.8-mile **Clackamas River Trail** (see Hiking, above). Although the trail has little climbing, it's rated moderate because of its many technical sections and the unforgiving basalt rock it passes through.

The **Opal Creek Trail** may be one of the best bike rides for beginning mountain-bike riders in the Cascade Foothills. Rather than on a singletrack, the ride is on a 3-mile dirt road that was improved in 1997 to allow passage of large trucks for hauling out mining debris. The ride begins at a locked gate on Willamette National Forest Rd 2209 in the upper Little North Santiam River Valley. More so than the ride itself, it's really the sights along the way and the short side hikes that make the Opal Creek area an outstanding bike ride. (See Hiking, above, for directions and more information.)

Fishing

The **Clackamas River** flows 85 miles before entering the Willamette River at the town of Gladstone. Fortunately for Portland-area anglers, much of the best fishing is located nearby in the lower part of the river below Estacada. When fish are in the river, small motorboats and drift boats ply the river's lower waters. With near-continuous runs of salmon and steelhead, fish are almost always in the river.

The Clackamas has runs of spring and fall chinook, plus summer and winter steelhead. (More than a few corporate anglers make use of liberal sick-leave policies when the salmon and steelhead are biting!) Best access below Estacada is from **Carver** and **Barton Parks** (see Camping and Picnics, above). Continuing upstream, undeveloped **Bonnie Lure State Park,** located at the confluence with **Eagle Creek,** offers some good bank angling. Other access points near Estacada are **McIver State Park** and Portland General Electric's **River Mill** and **Faraday Lake Parks.**

Four-mile-long **North Fork Reservoir,** 7 miles south of Estacada, is stocked with rainbow throughout the season. Best fishing is at the upper end. Fishing pressure in the Clackamas River above the reservoir is much less intense than below, but steelhead fishing and wild trout can be good upriver and in the tributaries. Fishing in the Clackamas is managed by the Oregon Department of Fish and Wildlife's Columbia Region office in Clackamas, (503) 657-2000.

The **Santiam River** and its many forks provide a varied and quality fishery. The **North Fork** has winter and summer runs of steelhead, spring chinook, and plenty of trout; the **Middle Fork** is a fine trout stream above its reservoirs, and the **South Fork** is another good producer of summer steelhead and spring chinook. The parks described above in Camping and in Picnics provide the best access. Check with Creekside Fly, (503) 395-2565, in Salem for information and call the Oregon Department of Fish and Wildlife's fishing line, (503) 872-5263, for regulations.

Reservoirs on the Santiam offer some good fishing in their variety. **Detroit Lake** is stocked regularly throughout the season with catchable rainbow trout and also produces kokanee and brown bullhead. **Foster Reservoir** is stocked with catchable rainbow, and illegally introduced largemouth bass and bluegill also proliferate. **Green Peter Reservoir** is the least heavily fished of the three reservoirs but is popular for its naturally occurring kokanee. (See Camping, above, for directions and phone numbers for campgrounds on these lakes.)

Barrier-free access to good fishing for the handicapped is available in the Cascade Foothills at the Detroit Ranger Station's **Hoover Campground** on Detroit Lake, where a 200-foot-long fishing pier is built over the edge of the lake. A short nature trail winds through a dense forest between the campground and the fishing pier. Best barrier-free fishing opportunities in the Clackamas River Ranger District are at **Two Rivers,** where the Clackamas and Collawash meet near Ripplebrook Ranger Station; at **Fish Creek Campground** on the Clackamas River Highway above Estacada; and at **Lake Harriet,** 4 miles up the Oak Grove Fork from Ripplebrook, just beyond the Cascade Foothills in the Mount Hood country.

The Willamette National Forest has more than 350 lakes, most of which were void of fish populations before the Oregon Department of Fish and Wildlife began its stock program in the 1920s. Heavily fished lakes are stocked annually, while the more isolated lakes are planted every few years. Fingerlings are usually stocked in the lakes, so it will take a year or more of growth to bring the trout to a catchable size. Check with the Detroit Ranger Station, (503) 854-3366, or the Sweet Home Ranger Station, (541) 367-5168, for the best fishing opportunities.

Wildlife

Although abundant with wildlife, the Cascade Foothills is one of the few regions of Oregon without an area formally protected as a national or state wildlife refuge. Without a designated place to look, it pays to keep an eye out all the time because wildlife is all around. The forests have **black-tailed deer** and **Roosevelt elk,** plus lots of little critters like **raccoons, rabbits,** and **squirrels.**

The **Walton Ranch Interpretive Trail** 20 miles east of Sweet Home offers a good chance to view a resident herd of **elk** during winter when they gather to graze the pastureland and escape the mountain snows. Elk can be seen from December through May, usually mornings and evenings. Viewing is best from platforms strategically placed along the trail, a 400-yard barrier-free walk with interpretive signs. To locate the trail, drive east of Sweet Home for 20 miles on US 20 and watch for signs to the Trout Creek trailhead on the north side of the highway and the beginning of the trail.

The best spots for bird-watching are around open water where breaks in the forest make it possible to spot activity. Foster Reservoir (see Camping, above) near Sweet Home is a good place to watch for species like **Swainson's thrush, black-headed grosbeak,** and **rufous hummingbird** during summers; migrating **harlequin ducks** during May; and **goldeneyes** and **bufflehead ducks** during winter. **Osprey, common merganser,** and **American dippers** are frequently seen in and around the water. Farther upstream in the mountains, watch for **blue grouse, pileated woodpeckers,** and **Steller's and gray jays**.

The Cascade Foothills' lack of wildlife refuges is more than made up for by the number of its **fish hatcheries.** Many of the streams have their own fish hatcheries that raise chinook and coho salmon, plus steelhead, for local release, as well as trout for stocking nearby lakes and ponds. A fish hatchery is, to say the least, an unnatural place to learn about the life habits of the area's fish, but despite the artificial setting, a hatchery can be the best place because of the difficulty of seeing them in a natural setting. Many of the hatcheries offer tours to groups and school classes by appointment. Each has a somewhat unique production schedule, so certain times of the year are best for watching returning fish and egg gathering.

The US Fish and Wildlife Service operates the Eagle Creek National Fish Hatchery, (503) 231-6828, on a tributary of the Clackamas River 40 miles southeast of Portland. Signs pinpoint the remote location of the hatchery, 5 miles east of Eagle Fern Park from Hwy 224 (see Camping, above). The best time to view spawning **steelhead** operations is March through June.

The Oregon Department of Fish and Wildlife operates four hatcheries in the area as well. The Clackamas Hatchery, (503) 630-7210, is located inside McIver State Park near Estacada. It has an inside display area with viewing into the incubation room. The Roaring River Hatchery, (541) 394-2496, is 8 miles east of Hwy 226 near Crabtree on Fish Hatchery Dr. The hatchery is known for its display pond that contains 15-pound **rainbow trout.** The Marion Forks Hatchery, (541) 854-3522, is alongside Hwy 22, about 18 miles east of Detroit Lake. The South Santiam Hatchery, (541) 367-3437, is 5 miles east of Sweet Home along the South Santiam River on US 20 just below Foster Dam. Spawning occurs in September when adult **spring chinook** return and during the winter when **steelhead** arrive.

One of the best places in Oregon to view naturally **spawning chinook salmon** is in a large pool of the Clackamas River, about 2,000 feet downstream by trail from Riverside Campground (see Camping, above). Spawning usually occurs from mid-September through early October. Forest Service staff are usually available to answer questions at the lookout when the fish are in the river. Another spot to watch for spawning chinook at the same time of the year is along Forest Rd 46 at a pullout 2.5 miles southeast of Ripplebrook Ranger Station.

Cross-Country Skiing

Due to their relatively low elevation, the Cascade Foothills' winter sports opportunities are fairly limited. An exception is the big winter cold snap, when snow drops all the way down to the floor of the Willamette Valley to the west. Cross-country skiers who are brave enough to venture out in those conditions need only to drive to the nearest unplowed road and go to work.

The only three designated state sno-parks (see Oregon Outdoor Primer) in the Cascade Foothills are strung out on US 20 as the highway makes its climb to Santiam Pass. When traveling from the west, **Tombstone Summit** comes first, 11 miles before Santiam Junction, and is followed by **Lost Prairie** (7.5 miles from the junction) and **Lava Lake** (4 miles from the junction). Tombstone Summit, 63 miles east of Albany, has a relatively lofty elevation at 4,236 feet, but it lies well west of the Cascade crest and it can be mighty wet. The area has several short but scenic ski tours when conditions are good. Lost Prairie, although farther east toward the crest of the Cascades, is nearly a thousand feet lower than Tombstone Summit. The two sno-parks are connected by a 5-mile ski trail on the south side of the highway. Lava Lake has only 5.5 miles of marked trail, but it offers interesting skiing through old-growth forests with views of six Cascade volcanoes.

Other ski opportunities await at the end of unplowed roads along the Clackamas and Breitenbush river drainages. The Clackamas attracts curious skiers and sledders from Portland, who soon learn why most everyone heads to Mount Hood. The Clackamas River Valley is too low in elevation to have good snow conditions very often, but when the freezing level drops below 2,000 feet it can have some fun play spots. The **Breitenbush Gorge** offers backcountry skiers a route into the Mount Jefferson high country. The trailhead is southeast of Breitenbush Hot Springs (see Camping, above), where snow closes Forest Rd 4685. The 6-mile ski trip up to Jefferson Park follows the South Breitenbush Trail.

Rafting/Kayaking/Canoeing

The rivers of the Cascade Foothills don't offer long, multiday trips like those possible on other Oregon rivers. But what the **Clackamas and Molalla Rivers** and the **forks of the Santiam** lack in distance, they more than make up for in intensity. The upper parts of the rivers can offer extreme challenges, usually tackled only by the very best rafters and kayakers during the spring rain and snowmelt season. Intermediate boaters can enjoy middle segments of the rivers, while canoeists and inner-tubers are safe on the lower sections.

Finding an outfitter can be difficult here. Because of the shortness of the river-running season, guides come and go with about the same frequency as Oregon's spring rainstorms. Check with the local ranger district to see if anyone is operating commercially on the Santiam, (503) 854-3366, or the Clackamas, (503) 630-6861.

Clackamas River

The Clackamas has two major sections of interest to boaters—the 21.5 miles from McIver State Park to the river's mouth at Gladstone and the 13 miles from Three Lynx Power Station to North Fork Reservoir. Three dams near Estacada separate the runs into the lower and upper sections. The Clackamas Ranger District asks all boaters to fill out a registration form at their launch site.

The **lower Clackamas** has one lively Class II rapids right out of the box at McIver, then flows with a much easier gait all the way to the

Willamette. Boat access points along the way are at Barton and Carver (see Camping and Picnics, above) and Clackamette Park (see Greater Portland chapter) at the river's mouth. The river usually carries enough water all year for safe boating. The high water of spring can be dangerous because of the river's cold temperature, its surprisingly strong current, and unexpected snags that wash down with each flood. Shuttle logistics are easy because roads closely follow the river, except where it runs through a deep, scenic canyon just downstream from McIver State Park. More than a few Portland rafters have cut their teeth on this section of the Clackamas.

The **upper Clackamas** takes on a decidedly different character than the lower. Without reservoirs to feed it throughout the summer, the river-running season usually lasts from November into June. The river charges through several big rapids, mostly Class III but at least one Class IV at Carter Bridge. Bob's Hole, 3 miles above North Fork Reservoir, is a popular play spot for kayakers. Popular launches are at Three Lynx Power Station and Fish Creek Campground, with Big Eddy and Lazy Bend boat ramps serving as the main takeouts. The river above Three Lynx is also run, but Killer Fang rapids just below Alder Flat Campground is usually a mandatory portage. Kayakers also play in the Collawash River, the Oak Grove Fork of the Clackamas, Eagle Creek, and Clear Creek.

Molalla River

The **Molalla River** is an often overlooked recreational gem within easy reach of Willamette Valley towns. There are limited facilities as the river passes through BLM and private timber company land between Table Rock Wilderness and its meeting with the Willamette River near Canby. A 13-mile section of the river from Table Rock Fork to Glen Avon Bridge runs through a scenic canyon that is seldom far from Molalla River Rd. The moss-covered basalt cliffs near the Three Bears rapids are beautiful enough to distract you from the business at hand. Three Bears can grow into a Class IV rapids during heavy spring snowmelt. The danger of fallen trees lying across the river demands respect when running the Molalla. The launch is down the bank from the road wherever the boater feels comfortable, and the takeout is just upstream of Glen Avon Bridge.

The **lower Molalla**, from the Glen Avon Bridge downstream for 12 miles to the Hwy 213 crossing, is ideal canoe water. Feyrer County Park divides the trip in half. All of the Class II rapids in this section are confined to the upper part of the run.

Santiam River Forks

Expert paddlers challenge various segments of the Santiam forks, but intermediates pretty much are restricted to the 15 miles between Packsaddle County Park and Mehama on the **North Santiam.** The biggest challenges are Class II Spencer's Hole at Gates and the 6-foot drop at Mill City Falls. With a dependable summer flow due to release of water from Big Cliff Dam upstream, the North Santiam is one Oregon river that is nowhere near its boating potential. As use is being squeezed on the Deschutes River near Maupin, rental raft companies have been setting up shop on the North Santiam on late summer weekends. Check with All-Star Rafting and Kayaking, (800) 909-7238, for rentals and guided trips.

Kayakers have run just about everything that carries sufficient water in the area—Class V sections of the **South Santiam** above and below Foster Dam, the wilderness run on the **Middle Santiam, Quartzville Creek,** the **North Santiam** above Detroit Lake, and the **Calapooia River** in the foothills southeast of Sweet Home. All require some local knowledge before they can be run safely. The rivers can be scouted from the road, but it's best to talk to someone who has just finished a trip before embarking on a first descent.

Canoeists lacking the skill to paddle whitewater need only to wait for the rivers to reach flatter ground, where they can paddle to their hearts' content as the rivers flow into the Heart of the Valley country to join the Willamette River.

Waterskiing

The Cascade Foothills is water-ski country for much of the northern Willamette Valley, other than the Willamette River itself. Skiers looking to carve some wakes behind a powerful speedboat pretty much need to head for the reservoirs of the foothills. As with all Willamette tributary reservoirs, submerged stumps, logs, and rocks are always present. Be especially watchful for obstructions near the shoreline, which can rise and fall by a dozen or more feet throughout the year. Reservoirs are usually lowered beginning in September to create storage room for the winter rains and spring snowmelt.

North Fork Reservoir is a 350-acre impoundment of the Clackamas River 7 miles south of Estacada on Hwy 224. The reservoir is very popular with a variety of user groups, and water-skiers are considered a nuisance by fishermen. The upper 2.5 miles of the reservoir have a 10mph speed limit to protect the resort area at Promontory Park from speeding boats and their noise. If the truth be known, water-skiers are better served by heading north into Washington, 30 miles from Portland on I-5 to Woodland, to splash in the three reservoirs of the Lewis River that begin 25 miles east of the freeway.

Detroit Dam creates a 3,500-acre lake, when full, on the North Santiam River. The reservoir is 9 miles long with 32 miles of shoreline. The reservoir behind the 463-foot-high dam is frequently used for water-ski shows. Boat launches are available at Detroit Lake State Park (see Camping, above) and from Willamette National Forest campgrounds along the lake. Big Cliff Dam, a 191-foot-high structure, is 3 miles downstream from Detroit Dam and acts as a re-regulating reservoir to control the flow of water in the North Santiam. Boating is not allowed on Big Cliff Reservoir.

Sweet Home turns into a big waterskiing center on summer weekends when hot residents of the Willamette Valley head for the waters of **Foster Reservoir** and **Green Peter Reservoir** to cool off. The 126-foot-high Foster Dam creates a 1,220-acre, 3.5-mile-long lake. Green Peter is one of the US Army Corps of Engineer's largest lakes in Oregon. A 327-foot-high dam backs up water for 10 miles and floods 3,720 acres.

Gold Panning

There's gold in those hills. **Quartzville Creek** is one of four designated recreational gold panning areas on Oregon's public lands and is the only one within easy reach of the Willamette Valley. Mining on Quartzville Creek is along the lower section of the drainage on BLM land. The upper creek on Willamette National Forest land is privately claimed. Check with the BLM, (503) 375-5168, for a brochure that shows designated mining areas.

Gold was discovered in Quartzville Creek in 1863. During its 30 years of productivity, more than $200,000 of gold and silver were extracted. Recreational mining began after World War II and continues to be productive. The designated mining quarter is open to public use, except for two small private claims. Miners usually concentrate on areas known as gold traps, spots of the river where the current slows down enough to allow the gold to settle to the bottom. The best panning spots are usually the insides of curves, areas of stream overflow, and the downstream side of boulders and other obstructions.

Skydiving

The Cascade Foothills are especially beautiful from the air, even though skydivers have more important things to occupy their time than enjoying the pretty scenery. The **Beaver Oaks Airport,** off Heiple Rd 3 miles north of Estacada on Hwy 224, has been helping people fall to earth for nearly 40 years. Neighbors keep trying to get the county to shut the airport down because of the noise of the planes, but canopies continue to brighten up the sky overhead. The skydiving service at the airport teaches beginners on static line and gives tandem jumps. To schedule the fastest minute of your life, call (503) 630-5867.

Cheaper Sleeps

Breitenbush Hot Springs This old mountain spa offers a quiet, cleansing time in the woods. Soak in the outdoor pools or sweat in a sauna. Yoga, meditation, and forest walks are offered. Sleep in tiny, heated cabins ($10 more with toilets) or camp out. Meals are family-style and vegetarian. Bring bedding and towels. You may pop in for a daytime soak, but call ahead to check on availability. *PO Box 578, Detroit, OR 97342; (503) 854-3314; $.*

More Information

Bureau of Land Management, Salem: *(503) 375-5646.*
Clackamas County Parks Department, Oregon City: *(503) 650-3507.*
Clackamas County Tourism Development Council, Oregon City: *(800) 547-3843.*
Clackamas River Ranger District, Estacada: *(503) 630-6861.*
Detroit Ranger District, Detroit: *(503) 854-3366.*
Estacada/Clackamas River Area Chamber of Commerce, Estacada: *(503) 630-3483.*
Linn County Parks Department, Albany: *(541) 967-3917.*
Marion County Regional Parks, Salem: *(503) 588-6261.*
Mount Hood National Forest, Gresham: *(503) 668-1700.*
North Santiam Visitor Information Center, Mill City: *(503) 897-2865.*
Sweet Home Chamber of Commerce, Sweet Home: *(541) 367-6186.*
Sweet Home Ranger District, Sweet Home: *(541) 367-5168.*
Willamette National Forest, Eugene: *(541) 465-6521.*
Willamette Valley Visitors Association, Albany: *(800) 526-2256.*

Salem
and the Heart
of the Valley

From Wilsonville at the south edge of the Portland metropolitan area, east to the Cascade foothills, south to the Linn-Lane county line at Harrisburg, and west into the Coast Range of Benton County and the Willamette Valley lowlands, including Silver Falls State Park and the cities of Woodburn, Silverton, Salem, Albany, Corvallis, and Lebanon.

Thousands of pioneers couldn't have been wrong: there must be something special about the Willamette Valley. When the wave of emigrants began trekking toward Oregon in the 1840s, they weren't thinking about fun things to do on their weekends. They were mostly interested in the rich soil, the sunny summer growing season, and the mild winters. It wasn't until the valley was divided up, settled, and planted that the settlers from the East began thinking of leisure activities. In the early years, a good old-fashioned barn raising was probably how the pioneers spent their free time on summer weekends while they waited for their crops to mature.

Nowadays, residents of the Willamette Valley are a little more sophisticated in their tastes for outdoor recreation. They have to be, because they are lured in so many different directions. Those who live in the Heart of the Valley, from Harrisburg north to Wilsonville, are tugged toward the east by the allure of the Cascades and to the west by the magic of the Pacific Coast. Both are convenient destinations, close enough to enjoy on a day's outing without worrying about finding a place to stay overnight.

But residents here shouldn't overlook—and most don't—what they have even closer at hand. Despite a comparative shortage of publicly owned land, the Heart of the Valley is filled with opportunities for road and mountain-bike riding; canoeing, kayaking, and other types of boating; wildlife watching; camping; and hiking.

Two of inland Oregon's most beloved state parks—Champoeg near Wilsonville and Silver Falls near Silverton—are located in the Heart of the Valley. Champoeg State Park is rife with history, dating to 1813 when a post was established nearby to serve French-Canadian trappers attracted by the beaver trade. The park's visitors center describes Champoeg's role in the birth of American government in the Oregon Territory. Silver Falls State Park is situated on a tributary of the Willamette in the tree-covered hills east of Salem. The park's famous Trail of Ten Falls through Silver Creek Canyon offers one of the most spectacular hiking opportunities in the state, often overlooked in lieu of the impressive waterfalls of the Columbia River Gorge.

Other attractions in the Heart of the Valley include Mary's Peak, a 4,097-foot summit that looms over the west edge of Corvallis; the annual migration of waterfowl to the Ankeny and William L. Finley National Wildlife Refuges; and paddling opportunities in the Willamette, Pudding, Santiam, and Calapooia Rivers.

With a population of 120,835, Oregon's capital city of Salem is the state's third-largest city behind Portland and Eugene. The city and surrounding area are home to 13,000 full-time state government employees. Food processing is the other major industry. Salem isn't always looked upon fondly by the rest of the state, especially early in the odd-numbered years when the state legislature is in session, but its location makes it an attractive place to live. Close enough to Portland to be within reach of big-city attractions, Salem is less congested and retains a degree of livability that Portland began losing a decade ago as growth began overwhelming its transportation corridors.

The pioneers were right when they headed to the Willamette Valley a century and a half ago and made Salem the capital in 1851. There really is something special about the place.

Getting There

Interstate 5 runs north and south through the Heart of the Valley. Wilsonville is 20 miles south of Portland, Salem is 45 miles south of Portland, and Harrisburg is 90 miles away. Highway 99E, the old federal highway that connected Willamette Valley towns before the coming of Interstate 5, offers a less hectic way to explore the Heart of the Valley's east side. Highway 99W offers access to the west side. US Highway 20 (US 20) threads its way through the southern part of the valley as it makes its run from the Pacific Ocean to Idaho, connecting Corvallis, Albany, and Lebanon.

Adjoining Areas

NORTH: **Greater Portland**

SOUTH: **Greater Eugene**

EAST: **Cascade Foothills**

WEST: **Wine Country, Newport**

Parks/Hiking/Walking

For a place that shouldn't have much to brag about when the subject is hiking, Salem and the Heart of the Valley have some surprisingly pleasant spots to go for a hike. From the incredible Silver Falls State Park to urban walks through some of Oregon's oldest towns, life in the Heart of the Valley doesn't necessarily mean driving to the mountains or the coast to enjoy a hike.

Compared to other parts of Oregon, the Heart of the Valley has relatively little publicly owned land—which limits hiking to paved urban corridors or small pockets of rural land. But that's enough to allow some memorable walking opportunities, especially at Silver Falls, Champoeg, and Willamette Mission State Parks; on Mary's Peak; and on the trails shared with mountain bikers in the McDonald State Forest near Corvallis.

Silver Falls State Park

Silver Falls State Park has topography that you might expect to find in the Cascade Foothills, but the park's lack of connecting roads into the forest to the east make the park a part of the Heart of the Valley. Few if any visitors to the park view it as an entryway to the Cascades. Highway 214 makes a 40-mile loop as it swings through the park from Silverton and automatically funnels visitors back to Salem. Drive Hwy 214 either southeast from Silverton or east from Salem to reach the 8,700-acre park, the largest state park in Oregon. The major visitors center is the **South Falls** day-use area, well signed as you enter the park from the south. For park information, call (503) 873-8681.

Silver Creek Canyon's **Trail of Ten Falls** (moderate; 7.5-mile loop), one of the most scenic trails in Oregon, begins at South Falls but can also be reached from the Canyon and North Falls trailheads (see below). The trail is also known as the **Silver Creek Canyon Trail** or, more simply, the Canyon Trail. The South Falls trailhead begins at the visitors center on the southwest side of the park, the Canyon trailhead is near the center of the trail east of South Falls, and the North Falls trailhead is located farther east where Hwy 214 makes its prominent bend. All trailheads have easily visible signs along the highway.

Spring, obviously, is the best time of year to experience the trails because the waterfalls are at their biggest due to snowmelt. Summer is also popular because the shade offers a respite from the heat. Fall can be spectacular with the changing color of the leaves, which when they drop leave open, unobstructed views of the falls. Winter can be the most exotic time of all when the falls are covered with ice, although the roads and trails can be especially treacherous.

The trail's 10 named **waterfalls** and their heights in feet are South Falls (177), Lower South Falls (93), Lower North Falls (30), Double Falls (178), Drake Falls (27), Middle North Falls (106), Winter Falls (134), Twin Falls (31), North Falls (136), and Upper North Falls (65). Most spectacular are South Falls and North Falls, especially when the trail takes you behind the cascades of water.

The Civilian Conservation Corps built the Silver Creek Canyon Trail in the 1930s. Flooding in the mid-1990s impacted the trail severely and only recently have bridges been rebuilt and the trail reopened over its entire length.

Beginning at the park visitors center and day-use area, the trail leads .25 mile to a footbridge over Silver Creek and continues behind South Falls. Lower South Falls is another mile downstream, about half the height of South Falls but significantly wider. Lower North, Drake, and Middle North Falls are all clustered at the bottom of the canyon in the center of the trail system. Double Falls is .1 mile off the main trail on Hult Creek. Winter Falls is tucked beneath the canyon rim near the Canyon trailhead, an alternate access point that allows hikers to shorten the Silver Creek Canyon Trail by half. Upper North Falls and North Falls are each about .25 mile from the North Falls trailhead, the northeast entrance to the Silver Creek Canyon Trail. Twin Falls is .9 mile downstream from North Falls.

While the Silver Creek Canyon Trail receives the bulk of its use from hikers in the state park, by no means is it the only place to go for a hike in the area. The park also has a 3-mile jogging trail, a 4-mile bike trail, and 14 miles of equestrian trails that are also open to hikers. The park campground (see Camping, below) is located south of Hwy 214, away from the South Falls day-use area, and is conveniently located near the park's other trails.

With so many waterfalls on Silver Creek, a thinking person might surmise that there are other waterfalls in the area. Yes, there are, but they are little known to other than the locals and can be difficult to locate. Two of the most scenic are 70-foot **Abiqua Falls,** a spectacular falls set in a basalt amphitheater canyon that is painted green, yellow, and orange by moss and lichen and is the next drainage north of Silver Creek. **Butte Creek Falls,** an 80-foot cascade north of Abiqua, has several other smaller falls above and below. Locating state-owned Butte Creek Falls is a major help in being able to find Abiqua Falls, which is owned by the monks of the Mount Angel Abbey.

To locate Butte Creek Falls, use an Oregon highway map to find the small community of Scotts Mills, 15 miles southeast of Woodburn off Hwy 213. Drive southeast from the center of Scotts Mills on Crooked Finger Rd for 9.3 miles to the end of pavement. Continue 2.2 miles and turn left on road CF400. Drive 1.9 miles and look for an unsigned parking area on the left in the Santiam State Forest. Follow an unsigned trail down to the creek and continue walking downstream for .25 mile to a view of Butte Creek Falls.

To find Abiqua Falls, drive Crooked Finger Rd as above to the end of pavement and continue 1.5 miles. Turn south on an unsigned road, pass through a gate, and begin descending. Drive 2.5 miles to a second gate. Stay right, then left, at junctions along the way between the gates. If the first gate is locked, you'll need to hike 2.5 miles to the second gate. From the second gate, notice a spur road to the left. Hike south for 100 yards on the spur road, then look for a path into the forest on the left. Follow the path down, reaching the creek in .25 mile, then follow the creek upstream 300 yards to one of Oregon's most spectacular waterfalls. Not all explorers are lucky enough to find Abiqua Falls on their first visit to the area.

More State Parks

Champoeg State Park can be a great place to hike when other places are cut off by bad weather. When Mount Hood is blanketed by snow and the Columbia River Gorge is cloaked in ice, Champoeg can be an attractive destination for hikers who simply have to get out of the house during winter. Of course, Champoeg can have its own problems, like during the famous February 1996 floods when the Willamette River covered parts of the park under 10 feet of water. At such times there's little to do besides wait for the water to subside, give the park staff time to clean up the mess, and go for a hike during the summer. Come to think about it, summer is another great time to hike in Champoeg.

Prior to the arrival of the white settlers, the Champoeg prairie was the home of the Calapooya Indians, who used the area to hunt, fish, and gather bulbs of the camas lily. Beginning in 1841, early white settlers began holding meetings to discuss predator control problems. From the meetings, the first vote was held to establish the first organized provisional government in the Pacific Northwest. Within a year, the seat of government had moved to Oregon City, but the seed had been sown at Champoeg. The area's key location astride the Willamette River made it a stopping point for steamboats and stagecoaches until the flood of 1861 washed away most traces of civilization.

The 615-acre park has a 1.5-mile hiking trail that winds through a historic townsite, a prairie, and a wooded area. Hikers roam at will on the park's large grassy lawns, which are a popular place for orienteering clubs to stage meets. The park also has 4 miles of bicycle trails, which can also be used by hikers, including a 2.5-mile connector downstream on the Willamette to Butteville. The Riverside day-use area is the most popular beginning point for strolls around the park and can be reached by taking I-5 exit 278 between Salem and Portland and following the signs on the county roads 5 miles northwest to the park; call (503) 633-8170 for park information.

Willamette Mission State Park is 27 miles upstream of Champoeg when counting every curve and bend of the Willamette River. To reach its 1,686 acres, drive I-5 to exit 263 at Brooks. Drive west of the freeway for 1.75 miles on Brooklake Rd and turn north on Wheatland Rd for 2.5 miles to the park entrance. The Wheatland Ferry crosses the Willamette River at the north edge of the park. Call (503) 393-1172 for park information.

Willamette Mission has 4 miles of bike paths, 5 miles of horse trails, and a 1-mile jogging path, all of which are open to hikers and walkers. The paved bike path around the Filbert Grove day-use area is accessible for people with disabilities. The park has the largest black cottonwood tree in the nation, measuring 26 feet, 8 inches in circumference. The 250-year-old tree is 156 feet high. Other park attractions are its outstanding wildlife viewing opportunities and its respite from the hustle and bustle of the I-5 corridor. The park is named for a mission established in 1834 by the Methodists. The great flood of 1861 damaged much of the mission site and changed the course of the river to its present channel.

Molalla River State Park covers 567 acres where the Molalla River joins the Willamette River at Canby. The park has a .75-mile hiking trail from the parking area down to the Willamette River and upstream for a short way before the brush gets too thick for hiking. Only those who want to bushwhack through brush and wetlands actually see the Molalla River as it passes the park's western boundary. Grassy play fields and wetlands with good wildlife viewing opportunities are major attractions of the park. To reach the park, drive north from Hwy 99E in Canby for 2 miles on Holly St toward the Canby Ferry. The park area is .25 mile west of Holly St. For another adventure, hop aboard the Canby Ferry for a ride across the Willamette River. The Canby, Wheatland (near Willamette Mission State Park), and Buena Vista (near Independence) Ferries are the last of the free, half-dozen car-size ferries that ply the Willamette.

Marys Peak Scenic Botanical Area

Heart of the Valley hikers who want to escape the heat of a Willamette Valley summer don't need to head for the Cascades to get high enough to feel cool mountain breezes. Marys Peak, a big, rounded hump bordering the southern part of the valley to the west, is 4,097 feet high—tall enough to provide a change in temperature. A Siuslaw National Forest road leads to the summit, which can also be reached by trails. For those who want to enjoy the outstanding view of the Willamette Valley with minimal effort, the **Marys Peak Road** leaves Hwy 34 about 10 miles west of Philomath. Turn north and drive Forest Rd 30 and its Marys Peak spur for 9.3 miles to the observation point parking lot. The summit is another .7-mile walk to the south.

Marys Peak Trail (difficult; 3.6 miles one way) climbs the north side from Woods Creek Rd. Drive US 20 for 1.8 miles west of Philomath, turn south onto County Rd 26440, and drive 6 miles to a locked gate and parking area. The trail climbs 2,300 feet out of the typical coastal Douglas fir forest into the noble fir stands of the Marys Peak Scenic Botanical Area before ending at the observation point parking lot near the summit.

The **East Ridge Marys Peak Trail** (moderate; 2.4 miles one way) gains 1,100 feet from a parking lot along Marys Peak Rd. A 1.2-mile **Tie Trail** connects the two summit hikes (via the East Ridge and the main Marys Peak Trails), while the 1.6-mile **Meadow Edge Trail** traverses the top of the peak. Call Siuslaw National Forest's Alsea Ranger District, (541) 487-5811, for information.

The **Corvallis-to-the-Sea Trail** represents a long-standing dream to connect the southern Willamette Valley with the central Oregon Coast. While the Bureau of Land Management (BLM) continues to work on segments of the proposed 105-mile trail, current use is limited to the Marys Peak segment, the Corvallis-to-Philomath bike path, and trails on the west side of the Coast Range near Newport. Call the BLM, (503) 375-5646, for information.

Gardens, Towns, and Parks

Hiking in the Heart of the Valley more often means walking through urban developments than hiking through wilderness areas. The result can be the same—tired feet, aching muscles, and a sense of accomplishment. Depending on a hiker's taste, civilized developments may be even more beautiful than the run-of-the-mill sights in nature. Oregon, after all, has so many outstanding locations that the average ones can seem pretty bland.

A Willamette Valley flower garden during the spring bloom will never appear bland. The Willamette Valley is laced with orchards, vineyards, and gardens that welcome visitors in season, even though actual hiking opportunities are limited. While feet may not get a workout, the eyes, nose, and taste buds will. The area around **Woodburn** and **Silverton** is known for its acres of spring flower blooms; Aurora is famous for its hazelnuts; Woodburn has the World's Berry Center Museum; Wilsonville has an herb festival; and iris gardens paint the fields purple around Salem. For a sample of the short hikes available in Oregon's gardens, try out the .25-mile nature trail at Fir Point Farms, (503) 678-2455, 2 miles north of Aurora at 14601 Arndt Rd.

The Oregon Garden, perhaps the next great West Coast botanic garden, is under construction south of Silverton on the Cascade Highway. Ground was broken and the first plantings were made in late 1997. Organizers had already raised $10 million at the time and were seeking an additional $6 million to complete the first phase and open the garden in the summer of 2000.

The forestry industry is also on display in the Heart of the Valley. **Starker Forests,** a Philomath company, has a nine-stop nature trail on its tree farm off US 20 south of Blodgett on Tum Tum Rd. The .25-mile trail helps explain how forestry practices that are taught at Oregon State University are applied in an Oregon forest. For information about the site, call the company at (541) 929-2477.

Living history is on display throughout the Heart of the Valley, particularly in the cities where great pride is taken to preserve and restore historic landmarks. Salem has a historic tour that is long enough to be designated as a driving route, but the best way to get a feel for the history is to make occasional stops and to get out and see the sights on foot. The walking route includes tours of the **Court-Chemeketa** and **Gaiety Hill/Bush's Pasture Park** historic districts. For a detailed guide of Salem's historic sites, check with the visitors association at 1313 Mill St SE, Salem, (800) 874-7012.

Silverton, located along Hwys 213 and 214 on the way to Silver Falls State Park, has plenty of sights to see before heading out of town. The town's .8-mile historic walking tour passes several buildings that were constructed in the late 1800s. Other Heart of the Valley towns with historic buildings that can best be seen on foot include **Aurora, Albany, Philomath, Corvallis,** and **Independence.**

Camping

Close enough to visit on day trips, state park campgrounds in the Heart of the Valley aren't incredibly large like those along the coast. **Champoeg State Park** has 46 tent sites, 48 electrical sites, and 12 walk-in sites. **Silver Falls State Park** has 51 tent sites and 54 electrical sites. **Willamette**

Mission State Park has camping for groups only. Champoeg and Silver Falls have camping year-round and accept reservations at (800) 452-5687. For information on fees charged at specific parks, call the State Parks information line, (800) 551-6949. (See Parks/Hiking/Walking above, for directions and additional information on these state parks.) Yurt camping is available at Champoeg, which also has two electrical campsites that are barrier free for use by disabled campers.

On the north end of the Heart of the Valley, Clackamas County maintains a campground 1 mile east of Molalla at **Feyrer Park,** where 27 acres along the Molalla River provide 20 RV and 8 tent sites, ball fields, and play areas. To reach the park, from Hwy 211 in Molalla, follow Dickey Prairie Rd to Feyrer Park Rd. For reservations, call (503) 655-8521.

On the east side near the center of the valley, Linn County offers **Waterloo Campground** 20 miles east of Lebanon just off US 20. The park has 60 sites, 50 with hookups, as well as fishing, swimming, and hiking trails along 1.25 miles of the South Santiam River. Some of the sites are barrier free.

Benton County offers camping at several areas in the south end of the Heart of the Valley, each operated by a different agency. The county manages **Salmonberry Campground,** (541) 757-6871, a 19-unit camp located 6 miles west of Alsea .5 mile south of Hwy 34 on Salmonberry Rd. RV parking spaces are 60 feet long and rest rooms are accessible. **Benton County Fairgrounds,** (541) 757-1521, on the northwest side of Corvallis, has unlimited sites without hookups. **Willamette Park Campground,** (541) 753-3119, has 15 sites 1 mile south of Corvallis on Goodnight Rd and is operated by the city parks department. **Marys Peak Campground,** (541) 487-5811, is a 6-site tent camp managed by Siuslaw National Forest near the summit. (See Parks/Hiking/Walking, above.) The BLM, (503) 375-5646, operates 16 sites at **Alsea Falls Campground,** 29 miles south of Corvallis on the South Fork access road, a national back country byway that follows the Alsea River between the communities of Alpine on the east and Alsea on the west.

Cycling

Although mountain bikes have become the bike of choice in the Heart of the Valley as they are elsewhere, it's the high-speed road bike that really comes in handy. The outstanding scenery, from farms to wildlife refuges and covered bridges, beckons cyclists to rack up the miles. Quiet country roads make it easy to enjoy the sights without having to worry about what's coming up from behind.

Corvallis has a well-deserved reputation as one of Oregon's most bicycle-friendly cities. The town is flat, only 224 feet above sea level, and its street pattern is so well laid out so that many workers and students from Oregon State University use a bicycle whenever they can. The city has 60 miles of bike paths and lanes. Check with the Corvallis Parks Department, (541) 757-6918, for information. The Heart of the Valley has many other outstanding bike-ride opportunities, including **bike trail systems in the three major state parks** and the paved 7-mile **Corvallis-to-Philomath bike path.** The path follows US 20, and several parking lots serve as trailheads on the south side of the highway. Peak Sports, (541) 754-6444, in downtown Corvallis rents bicycles.

The **Willamette Valley Bicycle Loop** is a designated 195-mile ride that covers much of the territory on the west side of I-5 between Willamette Mission State Park and Eugene. A brochure that describes the route in detail is available from visitors centers in the valley, or call the Willamette Valley Visitors Association at (800) 526-2256. The Albany Parks Department has published the "Albany and Mid-Willamette Valley Bicycle Map," which sells for $4 in local bike stores. Call (541) 926-1517 to order the map.

The Heart of the Valley is covered-bridge country with 13 of the scenic treasures located in Benton, Marion, and Linn Counties. Linn has the most with 9. Many of Linn County's **covered bridges** are clustered northeast of Albany, the county seat. A free brochure published by the Albany Visitors Commission, located at 435 W First Ave, (541) 926-1517, describes a route that leads to covered bridges in Stayton, Jordan, Scio, Crabtree, Albany, and Larwood. The **Larwood Bridge** is next to a scenic picnic park and fine swimming hole on Crabtree Creek. To locate the bridge, drive Hwy 226 east of Albany for 9 miles to where it turns north. Soon after the highway changes direction, turn east on Hatchery Rd and drive 6 miles to Larwood Park.

Salem is hopping aboard the bicycle wagon and has plans to develop a 205-mile bike-path and -lane system by early next century. Nearly a third of the facilities are already in place. Call the Salem Department of Community Services at (503) 588-6261 for information. Bicycle shops are numerous in Corvallis, Salem, and Albany. Check with each city's visitors center (see More Information, below).

McDonald State Forest, managed by Oregon State University, has an extensive system of roads and singletracks of varying difficulty for mountain bikers. The farther in you go, the more difficult the riding is. To reach the forest from Corvallis, ride west on Harrison Blvd to where it changes to Oak Creek Dr. Continue to ride to the end of the road, 6 miles northwest of Corvallis, and park near Oak Creek Laboratory of Biology. The 7,000-acre forest has more than 60 miles of roads and trails. Its high point is 2,178-foot **McCulloch Peak.** The forest is dedicated to research, not recreation, and university officials have become concerned about the amount of use. Bikers need to obey all rules to avoid more use restrictions in the future.

For an even more challenging ride, bikers climb **Marys Peak** via the East Ridge Trail. A loop is possible by using the Tie Trail, which connects to the upper part of the North Ridge Trail (see Parks/Hiking/Walking above).

Canoeing/Boating

The placid **Willamette River** is ideal for **canoeing, kayaking, waterskiing,** and **motorboat cruising.** The state has joined with most cities and counties along the way to develop a system of moorages, day-use parks, campgrounds, and marinas to serve the needs of the river's many boaters. Signs identify public facilities along the river's shore. The Willamette River Greenway program in Salem, (503) 378-6378, is the state park agency in charge of coordinating resources along the river. With three counties and a half-dozen major cities along the way, who's in charge of what gets complicated, especially when approaching from the water. The Oregon Marine Board published a Willamette River recreation guide in 1995, but the free booklet was so popular that it went out of print within two years. Another printing of the comprehensive guide depends on whether funds are available.

Despite the river's calm appearance, it can hide a variety of **hazards** to navigation, including shallow and rocky shoals, narrow side channels, dead-heads, and strainers. The river also flows with a powerful current, and the waterfall at Oregon City must be bypassed via the locks system. The river runs 185 miles from where its forks join at Springfield to its confluence with the Columbia River at Portland. The Heart of the Valley section begins at river mile 161 near Harrisburg in the south and ends at river mile 34 at the Canby Ferry in the north.

Harrisburg Park has full **river facilities** along a section of river known for its wildlife viewing opportunities. McCartney Park downstream 5 miles off Cartney Dr has camping accessible by boat and vehicles. Peoria Park is another Linn County camping park with river access near mile 141 on Peoria Rd. The Corvallis area has a string of parks, including Willamette, Crystal Lake, Pioneer Boat Basin, Waterfront, and Michael's Landing. (Corvallis is an active boating town, including a collegiate rowing program.)

Oregon State Parks operates several riverside parks downstream to Albany. Truax Island has auto access along Riverside Dr, but the others are for use by river travelers. River parks at Albany with river access and other facilities include Bryant, Monteith, Bowman, and Takena Landing. Luckiamute Landing is a large state park at the Willamette's confluence with the Santiam, where a boat is required for access.

Polk County operates Buena Vista and Wells Island Parks on either side of the Buena Vista Ferry, which crosses the river 10 miles southeast of Independence. The City of Independence operates Independence River-view Park where River Road Bridge crosses the river. Most boating traffic at Salem is concentrated at **Wallace Marine Park,** one of the busiest access points along the river. Park facilities downstream to Newberg include Sponges Landing, on the east bank 7 miles from Salem; Spring Valley, across the river from Willamette Mission State Park; and Rogers Landing in Newberg.

Champoeg State Park has a public dock for transient moorage. Boat Works Marina serves boaters on the river beneath the I-5 bridge at Wilsonville. Clackamas County operates Hebb Park, a day-use facility with a boat launch, at the north side of the Canby Ferry. If you don't have any luck finding a copy of the Marine Board's out-of-print Willamette River recreation guide, the next-best map for locating moorage facilities on the Willamette River is the BLM's Salem Westside Recreation Map. Boating is permitted on Oregon's navigable streams that run through private property, but there is no active management by state or federal agencies. Call the valley's visitors centers for names of local stores that sell boating equipment.

The **Calapooia River** is the Cascade drainage between the McKenzie River on the south and the Santiam River on the north. The Calapooia River's lower portion provides a popular canoe trip from the Hwy 34 bridge between Corvallis and Lebanon and Bryant Park in Albany. As with all shallow, meandering rivers on Oregon's west side, log jams and strainers are always a possibility on the Calapooia.

Other canoe trips on Willamette tributaries include the lower 9.5 miles of the **Santiam River,** from Jefferson to the Buena Vista Ferry; 14 miles of the **Luckiamute River** to the Willamette, plus a 1-mile upstream paddle to the Buena Vista Ferry; 8 miles on the **Yamhill River,** from Yamhill Lock Park at Dayton, plus 5 miles downstream on the Willamette to Rogers Park in Newberg; and 7 miles down the **Pudding River,** from near Hwy 99E to Molalla River State Park. Canoeists and kayakers look-ing for a little more zip head to the **Marys River,** a 19-mile Class II run during spring from Blodgett to Philomath.

Fishing

The **Willamette River** is famous for its salmon and steelhead angling, but the section that flows through the Heart of the Valley has become better known for its warm-water fishing. The anadromous fish continue to swim upriver, but conditions in the Willamette make it difficult to catch them so most anglers wait for them to arrive in spawning tributaries.

The Willamette, above the falls at Oregon City to Harrisburg, has numerous boat launches (see Boating, above) and other angling opportunities. Success often requires a boat, although bank angling can be productive under logs and brush piles in sloughs and at the edges of the main current. Fishing is usually best when the river drops during summer and fall. Besides bass and bluegill, the river produces a few sturgeon from its deep holes, cutthroat trout near the mouth of the tributaries during spring, and rainbow trout upriver from Peoria.

Streams in the Willamette Valley are managed by the Oregon Department of Fish and Wildlife's Northwest Region office in Corvallis, (541) 757-4186. For information on what's biting, check in Salem with Valley Fly Fishers, (541) 375-3721, or in Corvallis at the Scarlet Ibis, (541) 754-1544.

Bryant Park at Albany has good bank and small-boat fishing, with bass, crappie, bluegill, and bullhead catfish among the catch. The **Buena Vista Ferry** is another hot fishing spot, but a boat is necessary to reach the best fishing 2 miles upstream. **Horseshoe Lake** is a productive oxbow cutoff of the river near St. Paul. The **Peoria** area is a popular all-day drift. **Willamette Mission State Park** is a good family fishing site, with fish replenished seasonally by winter floods that fill the park's oxbow, which was once part of the river. **Molalla River State Park** can be productive for those who can battle through the brush to reach either the **Molalla** or **Willamette Rivers.** The Heart of the Valley also has good fishing in some ponds scattered around the valley, including **St. Louis** and **Woodburn Ponds** near Woodburn and **Wilsonville Pond** near Wilsonville.

Wildlife

The **dusky Canada goose,** one of five subspecies of North America's most common goose, winters almost exclusively in the Willamette Valley. Three national wildlife refuges, all reached by calling (541) 757-7236, were created in the 1960s to provide wintering habitat for the species of goose that spends its summer in Alaska's Copper River Delta country. The 5,325-acre **William L. Finley National Wildlife Refuge** is 10 miles south of Corvallis on Hwy 99W. The 2,796-acre **Ankeny National Wildlife Refuge** is 10 miles north of Albany. The 2,492-acre **Baskett Slough National Wildlife Refuge** (see Wine Country chapter) is 2 miles north of Rickreall.

The Finley refuge produces fields of crops designated for wildlife while protecting four types of historic habitats in the Willamette Valley: Oregon white oak savannah, meandering creeks with Oregon ash bottomland forest, old-growth big-leaf maple, and native prairie. The Ankeny refuge is an area of farm fields, hedgerows, forests, and wetlands near the confluence of the Willamette and Santiam Rivers. Both refuges have trail systems that traverse their varied habitats, as well as viewing from roads and designated wildlife watching areas. Public access is allowed May 1 through September 30 at Ankeny and a month longer at Finley. Hunting is allowed in season according to state regulations.

To the untrained eye, the dusky Canada goose is almost indistinguishable from the **Great Basin Canada goose,** the most common subspecies in Oregon. While hunters are required to take a goose identification class, casual observers rely on the dusky's larger size and darker color to distinguish it from other Canada geese.

Best wildlife-viewing times are early and late in the day. Northward migration begins in March when the **geese, ducks,** and **swans** leave the refuges. They are followed by shorebirds in April and songbirds in May. Summer residents include **mergansers, wood ducks, turtles,** and **black-tailed deer.** Songbirds begin to return south in August, and the geese begin to arrive in late September. **Roosevelt elk** still live in the Willamette Valley and can be heard bugling at Finley during the autumn rut. The majority of the waterfowl arrive by November and many spend the winter, accompanied by **bald eagles, peregrine falcons,** and **other raptors.**

Finley can be reached by driving south for 10 miles from Corvallis on Hwy 99W. Turn west at the refuge entrance sign and drive 2 miles. Ankeny is 10 miles north of Albany or 12 miles south of Salem off I-5. Take exit 243, drive .25 mile west, and turn north on Ankeny Hill Rd for 1.5 miles to an information kiosk.

The Oregon Department of Fish and Wildlife maintains the 1,600-acre E. E. Wilson Wildlife Area 10 miles north of Corvallis on Hwy 99W. Turn east at Camp Adair to reach the headquarters, which has show pens that are open for viewing upland game birds all year. The facility raises **Sichuan pheasants** for release in suitable habitat. Paved roads that are good for biking and an interpretive trail help visitors become familiar with the area. The wildlife area has a fishing pond stocked with trout that is open from February through September. Disabled hunters are allowed to hunt rabbits in February.

The state maintains a fish hatchery in the Heart of the Valley near Alsea in the Coast Range beneath Marys Peak. The hatchery, (541) 487-7240, raises coastal **cutthroat trout** and **winter steelhead.** Adult **white sturgeon,** cutthroat, and **rainbow trout** are present for viewing all year. Best season to visit is winter, when adult steelhead return. To reach the hatchery, drive 21 miles west on Hwy 34 from Corvallis to milepost 43. Turn north for .25 mile to the hatchery entrance.

Oregon's capital city of Salem has a population of 120,000, but the city has many greenspaces that have good wildlife-viewing opportunities. Cascade Gateway Park at the intersection of I-5 and Hwy 22 has two lakes, an oak grove, and some open grassy areas where **wood ducks,**

nuthatches, and **woodpeckers** reside. Minto-Brown Island Park is located in the Willamette River floodplain a mile southwest of Salem on River Rd. The park is host to wintering flocks of **Canada geese** and is used for nesting by **mourning doves** and **green-backed herons.** McGilchrist Pond, located near the intersection of McGilchrist Rd and 25th St, is a good spot to watch for **water birds. Raptors** use the undeveloped grassland around Salem airport, especially during winter.

Cross-Country Skiing

Marys Peak offers the closest dependable snow for any town in the Heart of the Valley (see Parks/Hiking/Walking, above). The 4,097-foot peak, the notable western landmark from throughout the southern Willamette Valley, is the highest coastal mountain between the Olympic Peninsula of Washington and the Siskiyou Mountains of southern Oregon. The summit road to the snow line can be reached by driving 16 miles southwest of Corvallis on Hwy 34 and turning north on Forest Rd 30 in Siuslaw National Forest. A large sno-park is 5 miles up the road at 2,570 feet in elevation.

Because the snow line fluctuates widely during winter, most skiers drive as high up the road as they can and begin skiing where snow conditions are adequate. The summit is another 5 miles above the lower sno-park. Check with the Alsea Ranger District, (541) 487-5811, for an update on snow conditions.

Horseback Riding

There's nothing better than hopping aboard a trusty steed and going for a ride along a river or through a wooded glade on a warm summer day. Hiking along with a llama that carries your load isn't bad either.

Most Oregon cities and resort areas aren't far away from trail-riding opportunities. For those who live in the Heart of the Valley, a jaunt atop a horse usually means visiting one or two close-by state parks and joining a wrangler for a trail ride. The outfitter at **Silver Falls State Park** and **Willamette Mission State Park** is a nonprofit organization called Horses for the Physically Challenged.

With its stables located at Scotts Mills near Silverton, the outfitter has expanded its operation to become one of the first to offer trail rides for all abilities. The group began as an adaptive riding program for disabled adults and children but has expanded its operation into the two state parks. Riders who need a wheelchair to maneuver across land usually learn very quickly how to cover the same territory with a horse. The smiles on their faces usually say they would exchange a horse for a wheelchair any day, if only the horse could duck inside doorways and didn't eat so many oats.

Trail rides are available in these state parks during summer. For information and reservations, contact Horses for the Physically Challenged, (503) 873-3890. The company also does business as the Adaptive Riding Institute. Riders without disabilities are welcome to take part in the rides. The organization continues to operate under its primary mission outside the state park trail-ride program, leading trips and giving lessons to riders with physical disabilities, training horses to give rides to the disabled, and developing specialized equipment to help disabled riders enjoy themselves while in the saddle.

Salem Area Llama Encounters and Mascots leads **llama treks** through Silver Falls State Park. The treks are operated by Wiley Woods Ranch, (503) 362-0873, and range from three to nine hours.

Attractions

The 1938 state capitol in **Salem** has an art-deco-cum-grandiose-classical look and is worth a visit, especially since the fix-up from earthquake damage earlier this decade. Handsome parks flank the building, and just behind is **Willamette University**, the oldest university in the West. The campus is a happy blend of old and new brick buildings, with a small stream, Mill Creek, nicely incorporated into the landscape. It's a pleasant place to stroll, and plant lovers should visit the small but well-tended botanical gardens on the east side of the campus.

Across the road from Willamette University is **Historic Mission Mill Village,** 1313 Mill St SE, (503) 585-7012. The impressive 42-acre cluster of restored buildings from the 1800s includes a woolen mill, a parsonage, a Presbyterian church, and several homes. The mill, which drew its power from Mill Creek, now houses a museum that literally makes the sounds of the factory come alive. The Jason Lee House, dating from 1841, is the oldest remaining frame house in the Northwest; regular tours of the premises run from 10am to 4:30pm, Tuesday through Saturday. The Salem Visitors Information Center is part of the complex, as are several shops selling handcrafted clothing, gifts, and antiques.

Bush House, 600 Mission St SE, (503) 363-4714, is a Victorian home built in 1877 by pioneer newspaper publisher Asahel Bush. It sits in a large park complete with conservatory, rose gardens, hiking paths, and barn turned art gallery. Tours are available.

Gilbert House Children's Museum, (503) 371-3631, on the downtown Salem riverfront between the bridges, has a variety of hands-on learning activities for young children. Children also appreciate **Enchanted Forest,** (503) 371-4242, a nicely wooded storybook park with space for picnicking, just off I-5 south of town.

Old-fashioned **ferries,** operated by cable, still cross the Willamette River in a few places and offer a fun alternative to bridges, if you have some extra time. Two run in the Salem area: the Wheatland ferry, just north of town in Keizer (follow Hwy 219 north from downtown and turn off on Wheatland Rd), and the Buena Vista (from I-5 take exit 243 and follow Talbot Rd west). They run every day (except during storms or high water) and cost very little.

Mount Angel Abbey, a 100-year-old Benedictine seminary northeast of Salem, is picturesque on a foggy morning, when its beautiful setting atop a butte sacred to local Native Americans makes it seem as if it's floating in the clouds. Don't miss the library, a gem by the internationally celebrated Finnish architect Alvar Aalto. For hours, call (503) 845-3030.

Time and I-5 have both bypassed **Albany,** which is probably a blessing. Once you get off the freeway (ignore the smell of the nearby pulp mill), you'll discover a fine representative of the small-town Oregon of an earlier era, with broad, quiet streets, neat houses, and a slow pace. Once an important transportation hub in the Willamette Valley, the town has an unequaled selection of historic homes and buildings in a wide variety of styles, many of them lovingly restored.

A self-guided tour of **historic buildings** displays 13 distinct architectural styles in the 50-block, 368-building Monteith Historic District alone. Then there are the Hackleman District (28 blocks, 210 buildings) and downtown (9.5 blocks, 80 buildings). Many of the buildings are open for inspection on annual tours offered the last Saturday in July and the Sunday evening before Christmas Eve. A handy guide is available free of charge from the Albany Chamber of Commerce, 435 W First Ave, (541) 926-1517, or the Albany Convention and Visitors Center at 300 SW Second, PO Box 965, Albany, OR 97321, (800) 526-2256.

The **covered bridges** that were so characteristic of this area are disappearing. From 450 their number has dwindled to fewer than 50, but that's still more than in any state west of the Mississippi. Most of the remaining bridges are in the Willamette Valley counties of Lane, Linn, and Lincoln, and local preservationists are fighting to save them. Best starting points for easy-to-follow circuits of the bridges are Albany, Eugene, and Cottage Grove. In addition, many handsome bridges dot the woods of the Oregon Coast Range. Six of these bridges lie within an 8-mile radius of Scio, northeast of Albany. For a map, contact the Albany Convention and Visitors Center, (800) 526-2256. For other tours, send a self-addressed, stamped envelope with two first-class stamps to the Covered Bridge Society of Oregon, PO Box 1804, Newport, OR 97365, or call (541) 265-2934.

Corvallis is a pleasant mix of old river town and funky university burg. The Willamette River lines the small downtown area, which is noticeably livelier than most small towns of the area. You can poke around in interesting shops and stop in for an outrageously big pastry and a cup of coffee at **New Morning Bakery**, 219 SW Second, (503) 754-0181, where you can also get a light lunch or dinner. The **Oregon State University** (OSU) campus is typical of Northwest megaversities, with a gracious core of old buildings, magnificent giant trees, and lots of open space, surrounded by a maze of modern, boxlike classroom and residential buildings of little character. Sports are big here, especially basketball and gymnastics, but the basement of Gill Coliseum also houses the **Horner Museum,** which has a wonderfully eclectic, rather dilapidated collection that relates the history of Oregon's development from Native Americans to the Oregon Trail to economic growth—a grand place for kids, with lots of nooks and crannies and large artifacts from yesteryear. Unfortunately, it's only open weekends; (541) 737-2951. Tree lovers may also enjoy OSU's 40-acre **Peavy Arboretum**, 8 miles north of town on Hwy 99W—it has hiking trails and picnic facilities. A local **winery** of interest is Tyee Wine Cellars, (541) 753-8754, a small producer of impeccable quality, just south of the airport off Hwy 99W.

Restaurants

Alessandro's Park Plaza ☆☆ This oasis is the most elegant place to eat in Salem. Call it upscale Italian, with professional service and a menu emphasizing pasta and seafood dishes. Classics are done with flair. *325 High St SE (at Trade St), Salem; (503) 370-9951; $$.*

Bombs Away Cafe ☆ This taqueria with an attitude has all your Tex-Mex favorites, but with a wholesome twist: heaps of herb-flavored brown rice, hardly any fat in sight, and lots of vegetarian choices. *2527 NW Monroe (at 25th), Corvallis; (541) 757-7221; $.*

DaVinci's ☆ At this very popular pizza place in a brick-and-dark-wood building, individual pizzas come with an assortment of toppings, and there are different homemade whole-wheat pastas each day. *180 High St (near Ferry St), Salem; (503) 399-1413; $$.*

The Gables ☆☆ The best place for more formal occasions resides in a strip mall, but the exterior belies a crisp-linen interior. The menu is tried and true; dinners are huge, with all the trimmings. Expect perfectly cooked meat and quietly efficient service. *1121 NW 9th St (follow Harrison to 9th), Corvallis; (541) 752-3364; $$.*

La Margarita ☆ With mirrors to make it look bigger than it is and music to keep it hopping, this is definitely one of the livelier spots downtown. The specialty is mesquite grilling. Margaritas are mammoth. *545 Ferry St SE (near corner of High and Church Sts), Salem; (503) 362-8861; $.*

McGrath's Publick Fish House ☆ Crowds pack this sharp-looking restaurant with the diverse menu and good prices. Order the seafood off the daily fresh sheet. The young wait staff lacks expertise but is eager. *350 Chemeketa (at Liberty St), Salem; (503) 362-0736; $$.*

Morton's Bistro Northwest ☆ You sit below road level in an intimate interior and look out on an attractive courtyard. The ambitious menu is mostly Northwest cuisine with international influence—fresh seafood, veal, and a few pasta dishes. Expert service. *1128 Edgewater (across Marion St bridge from downtown), West Salem; (503) 585-1113; $$.*

Nearly Normal's ☆ There's nothing normal about this joint, which advertises its food as "gonzo cuisine": vegetarian food, organically grown, prepared with originality and panache. This place can get crowded, and you bus your own dishes. *109 NW 15th St (near corner of Monroe), Corvallis; (541) 753-0791; $.*

Novak's Hungarian Paprikas ☆☆ Don't be put off by the strip-mall setting of this friendly family-run Hungarian spot. Housemade sausages and sides of spiced cabbage are wonderful. Huge servings come with lots of vegetables and potatoes, and small prices. *2835 Santiam Hwy SE (take exit 233 toward town), Albany; (541) 967-9488; $.*

Lodgings

Hanson Country Inn ☆☆ This wood-and-brick farmhouse is a registered historic home often used for weddings. The living room gleams, and the four guest rooms have luxurious linens. Explore the formal lawn and garden. A two-bedroom cottage with a kitchen is perfect for families. *795 SW Hanson St (5 minutes west of town off West Hills at 35th), Corvallis, OR 97333; (541) 752-2919; $$.*

Marquee House Bed and Breakfast ☆ This B&B has a movies theme: Stay in the "Topper" room, with a collection of old hats, or among Western memorabilia in the "Blazing Saddles" room. Evenings, settle back for movies and popcorn. Breakfast is fresh and plentiful. *333 Wyatt Ct NE (off Center St, just west of intersection with 17th), Salem, OR 97301; (503) 391-0837; $$.*

Cheaper Sleeps

Howell House Bed and Breakfast This former 1891 rooming house is full of period antiques; there's an old coal stove, too. The immaculate high-ceilinged rooms may be small, but the breakfasts aren't. Enjoy the heirloom roses, covered spa, and gazebo outside. *212 N Knox St, Monmouth, OR 97361; (503) 838-2085; $.*

More Information

Albany Chamber of Commerce, Albany: *(541) 926-1517.*
Alsea Ranger District, Alsea: *(541) 487-5811.*
Benton County Parks Department, Corvallis: *(541) 757-6871.*
Bureau of Land Management, Salem: *(503) 375-5646.*
Canby Area Chamber of Commerce, Canby: *(503) 266-4600.*
Corvallis Visitors Bureau, Corvallis: *(800) 334-8118.*
Linn County Parks Department, Albany: *(541) 967-3917.*
Marion County Regional Parks, Salem: *(503) 588-6261.*
Molalla Area Chamber of Commerce, Molalla: *(503) 829-6941.*
Monmouth-Independence Chamber of Commerce, Independence: *(800) 772-2806.*
Oregon Department of Fish and Wildlife, Portland: *(503) 872-5268.*
Oregon Department of Forestry, Salem: *(503) 945-7200.*
Oregon Parks and Recreation Department, Salem: *(800) 551-6949.*
Oregon State Marine Board, Salem: *(503) 378-8587.*
Oregon Tourism Commission, Salem: *(503) 986-0000.*
Salem Convention and Visitors Association, Salem: *(800) 874-7012.*
Silverton Area Visitor Information Center, Silverton: *(503) 873-5615.*
Siuslaw National Forest, Corvallis: *(541) 750-7000.*
Stayton/Sublimity Chamber of Commerce, Stayton: *(503) 769-3464.*
Willamette Valley Visitors Association, Albany: *(800) 526-2256.*
Woodburn Area Chamber of Commerce, Woodburn: *(503) 982-8221.*

Greater
Eugene

From the Lane-Benton county line on the north, east to McKenzie Bridge and the western foothills of the Cascades, south to the divide between the Willamette and Umpqua Rivers, and west to the tide-water of the Siuslaw River near Mapleton, including the McKenzie River Valley and the cities of Junction City, Eugene, Springfield, and Cottage Grove.

Residents of Greater Eugene can be excused if they exude a certain air of smugness. In a state known for its diverse beauty, Eugene and surrounding Lane County lay claim to just about every type of topography in the state (except for desert).

Lane is the only county outside of Alaska that reaches from ocean beach (at Florence) to mountain glacier (the Three Sisters). The western and eastern sections of Lane County are described in other chapters of this book, but the center of the county around Eugene has plenty of outdoor attractions of its own. Eugene is the state's second-largest city, with a population of 126,325, and its sister city of Springfield is eighth largest, with 50,140.

So why should Eugene residents feel smug? For one, they rarely need to worry about the traffic problems that afflict Portland. Traveling from Eugene to the beach, to a river, or to the mountains rarely means enduring a traffic jam. As home to the University of Oregon, Eugene residents have access to many outstanding services, including the college's active outdoor recreation program and its library's vast inventory of maps.

About the only drawback to living in Eugene is its abundant rainfall. During the abnormally wet year of 1996, a rain gauge at Eugene Airport recorded an amazing 101.93 inches of rain; a newer automated gauge, however, recorded only 77.17 inches during the same year. The discrepancy, as it turned out, occurred because the automated gauge collected only 0.01 inch of rain before tipping over and feeding information to a computer. It seems that the new gauge was overwhelmed so frequently during November and December that the older-style gauge recorded 17 inches more rain during those months than the new gauge. No matter how much rain fell in 1996, the total most surely broke the city's record of 65.56 inches, which had been set in another abnormally wet year, 1995. Back-to-back records should make Eugene ready for some drier years, and bring the averages back down to a more normal 50 inches.

The best way to experience Eugene is on the seat of a bicycle. The city is widely known for its system of bike paths and lanes, as well as its bike bridges over the Willamette River. Although Eugene has been forced in recent years to sharing its bicycle-friendly reputation with Corvallis and Portland, Eugene residents know they were first and set the standard for bike facilities in Oregon.

Eugene's fat-tire crowd also has plenty of places to ride nearby, even though the Willamette Valley is not famous for its hills farther north. Closer to the Willamette's headwaters, Eugene is surrounded on three sides by buttes and hills. Only to the north does the valley stretch out long and flat.

The forks of the Willamette River join on the southeast outskirts of Eugene, where the river changes character from a clear mountain stream to the broad river that continues all the way to its meeting with the Columbia River at Portland. Rafts and river kayaks are popular upstream of Eugene, especially on the McKenzie River, while canoes and sea kayaks rule the waters downstream

The McKenzie is another of those magical rivers that make Oregon famous. It flows west out of the Cascades, providing a multitude of recreation opportunities easily accessible along Highway 126, until it joins the Willamette at the north edge of Eugene. Camping, hiking, fishing, and biking aren't complete around Eugene unless the McKenzie is part of the plans. After a weekend on the McKenzie, visitors are hard to distinguish from residents because they all wear the same smug look.

Getting There

Eugene is 110 miles south of Portland via Interstate 5, the main north-south highway in Lane County. Highway 126 runs east-west through the county, from the Pacific Coast at Florence and along the McKenzie River into the Cascades. Highway 58 heads southeast of Eugene, passing through Oakridge and then climbing to the crest of the Cascades and Willamette Pass, before dropping into the Klamath Basin. Eugene Airport serves regional and commuter airlines.

Adjoining Areas
> NORTH: **Salem and the Heart of the Valley**
> SOUTH: **The Umpqua Valley**
> EAST: **Three Sisters and Cascade Lakes, Willamette Pass**
> WEST: **Oregon Dunes**

inside out

Biking

Greater Eugene is one of the most bicycle-friendly areas in the country. The city itself has more than 100 miles of bike lanes and paths, four bicycle/pedestrian bridges over the Willamette River, 20 shops that sell bikes, a couple of small bicycle manufacturers (Green Gear and Co-Motion Cycles), bike racks on all the transit system's buses, and a citizenry that accepts the bicycle as a legitimate form of transportation.

Eugene is surrounded by outstanding riding opportunities, both on road and off. The Willamette Valley to the north has ample flat, cruising opportunities, while the rolling hills on the other three sides of town keep cyclists from getting too lazy. Mountain-bike rides are plentiful, both in town and in the countryside. The Willamette National Forest's Lowell Ranger District, (541) 937-2129, actively manages for mountain-bike recreation, as does the Bureau of Land Management (BLM) at its Shotgun Park near Marcola, (541) 683-6600.

Some Eugene **bike shops** that can help with information and equipment are Cycle Bi, (541) 687-0288, 1330 Willamette; Second Nature Bicycles, (541) 343-5362, 446 E 13th St; Collins Cycle, (541) 342-4878, 60 E 11th St; and Pedal Power, (541) 342-4878, 535 High St. The stores sell one of the state's better bike maps, which covers Eugene-Springfield and the southern Willamette Valley.

Cycling

Eugene has one of the state's oldest (and most beautiful) bike path systems, which can be traced to the 1971 passage of Oregon's bikeway bill, a law that mandates 1 percent of Oregon's gasoline tax receipts be devoted to planning, constructing, and maintaining bike and pedestrian facilities.

Eugene's paved bike/pedestrian trail winds along the **Willamette River Greenway,** a system of parks and greenspaces on both sides of the river from I-5 on the east in Springfield to Belt Line Rd to the northwest in Santa Clara. The greenway's eastern trailhead is in Springfield's Island Park, where Main St crosses the Willamette River. The trail continues west through Eugene on both sides of the river, well marked all the way, then bends north to the suburb of Santa Clara where it fans out onto city-street bike lanes from the Owosso Bike Bridge over the Willamette.

The central part of the 11.3-mile trail system passes through **Alton Baker Park,** a wide strip of green on the Willamette's north bank just north of the University of Oregon. The trail system crosses back and forth along the river by using four bridges that don't allow automobiles. Access points are numerous along the trail; just follow a street toward the river.

Knickerbocker Bike Bridge is farthest east, just beneath the I-5 bridge that crosses the Willamette between Eugene and Springfield. Heading downstream, cyclists can cross the river at Autzen, Greenway, and Owosso Bike Bridges. **Autzen Bike Bridge** connects Alton Baker Park on the north bank of the Willamette with the University of Oregon along Franklin Boulevard on the south. The **Greenway Bike Bridge** crosses the river behind Valley River Center, the largest shopping mall in Eugene, on Valley River Dr. The **Owosso Bike Bridge** crosses just south of Belt Line Rd, the freeway that serves the northwest part of Eugene. The city has been negotiating with Marist High School to allow an easement to complete the bikeway on the right bank of the river near Owosso Bike Bridge. For information, contact the Eugene bike program, (541) 687-5298, the Springfield bike program, (541) 726-3759, or the Willamalane Park and Recreation District, (541) 726-4335.

The BLM's 14-mile **Row River Trail,** which became a showcase for rail-trail conversion in Oregon when it was paved in 1997, begins at Mosby Creek and extends to Culp Creek. The route follows the Row River, passing Dorena Reservoir, with three covered bridges and three parks along the way. The city of Cottage Grove plans to extend the trail west 3 miles to downtown. To reach the Row River trailhead at Mosby Creek, use exit 174 from I-5, north Cottage Grove, and drive southeast for 1 mile on Row River Rd. Turn south on Mosby Creek Rd and drive another mile to the trailhead.

Constructed in 1902, the Row River Trail's corridor was used as a railroad to haul ore from the Bohemia mines and lumber from the Culp Creek mill to Cottage Grove. The railroad was no longer needed when the mill closed in 1991 and was abandoned in 1993. The tracks were removed in 1994 when the BLM assumed management and began converting the trail into a nonmotorized corridor for use by cyclists, walkers, runners, skaters, and equestrians. The trail provides an outstanding recreation opportunity for travelers along the I-5 corridor. For information, contact the Eugene District of the BLM, (541) 683-6600.

Rural riding opportunities abound in Lane County, with many rides passing through or by the county's numerous covered bridges. Of the 51 **covered bridges** that still stand in Oregon, 20 are in Lane County, the most of any county west of the Mississippi River. Other than Eugene itself, just about every part of Lane County has a covered bridge or two. Cottage Grove has the most, with four in the hills east of town and another three west of town, including the **Mosby Creek Bridge** (see Row River Trail, above).

Four bridges are located along Hwy 58 between Springfield and Westfir, including the 65-foot-long **Lowell Bridge.** The bridge provides a scenic site in its can't-miss location just north of the busy cross-Cascades highway along Dexter Reservoir, 10 miles southeast of I-5. The **Office Bridge,** located 1 mile north of Hwy 58 in the tiny town of Westfir, is the longest covered bridge in the state, at 180 feet. The bridge crosses the North Fork of the Middle Fork of the Willamette River, 40 miles southeast of Eugene.

The area around Mapleton in western Lane County has three covered bridges. For information on all of Oregon's covered bridges, including location, length, the year they were built, and their world guide number, pick up the brochure called "Oregon's Covered Bridges" at any Willamette Valley visitors bureau. The Eugene Visitors Bureau, (541) 484-5307, is located at 305 W Seventh. Lane County Public Works Department, (541) 682-6911, publishes a brochure called "20 Covered Bridges."

Eugene is a popular goal for Willamette Valley cyclists who want to endure the torture of a double century by riding back and forth between Portland (220 miles round trip) in a weekend.

Mountain Biking

Newcomers to single-track bike riding often take their first spill on one of the close-in trails to Eugene. If the experience isn't too disheartening, they often wind up farther afield at any of the off-road riding opportunities that abound on nearby public land.

The **Ridgeline Trail** at the south end of Eugene was built to alleviate user conflicts on urban trails. This trail dedicated to mountain bikes is only a mile long, but the views and the opportunity to ride singletrack in the city keep it busy. The Ridgeline Trail system is also used heavily by hikers as they wander among the three lobes of **Spencer Butte Park.** To reach the mountain-bike trailhead, drive Fox Hollow Rd to the south edge of town and look for the trailhead where the road passes through East Spencer Butte Park.

Hendricks Park, Eugene's oldest park, lies at the southeast edge of Eugene. Bikers from the nearby University of Oregon campus head for the park for a quick tour. Fairmount Blvd passes through the park and connects to a pair of trailheads for the 1.5-mile trail system.

The **Fox Swale Area,** south of Eugene between Fox Hollow Rd and Camas Swale Rd, has 15 miles of trail and dirt-road riding. To reach the area, ride or drive south of Eugene on Fox Hollow Rd for 9.5 miles, over a summit, and down into a valley to BLM Rd 14-4-4, on the left and easy to miss. Park and begin riding through a complicated network of private and BLM logging roads and trails. Most of the land is owned by International Paper Company, which allows public riding. Bring along a copy of the Eugene District BLM map to help stay oriented. The map is available from the BLM office at 2890 Chad Dr.

Just west of Eugene, the **Skinner's Classic** ride is a 3-mile loop built as a racecourse. The ride begins in west Eugene off Needham Rd. To reach the trailhead, drive south on Chambers St over the top to Lorane Hwy. Turn right and travel 1.1 miles down Lorane Hwy to Needham Rd (located at the same intersection as Blanton Rd). Follow this gravel road for .8 mile to where it ends in a clearing and begin riding.

A step up in challenge is the **Winberry Divide Trail,** a 5-mile one-way ride in the Lowell Ranger District. The trail rolls along a ridgeline above Lookout Point Reservoir. Drive the North Shore Rd from Lookout Dam, located just north of Hwy 58 near Lowell, for 11 miles. Turn north on School Creek Rd and drive 4 miles to the top of the ridge and the signed trailhead. If you're not ready to turn back after 5 miles, climb another 1,250 feet to the 4,000-foot top of **Tire Mountain.** The descent is one of the most fun rides around and makes the climb worth every drop of sweat.

The Cottage Grove Ranger District of the Umpqua National Forest has some good riding, including the 5.5-mile **Brice Creek Trail,** the 12-mile **Crawfish Trail,** and the 27-mile **Fairview Peak** loop. Brice Creek is good for beginners, but the other two have big climbs and only experts should apply. The Brice Creek trailhead is 2 miles inside the forest boundary on Forest Rd 22, which can be reached by leaving I-5 at the north Cottage Grove exit and by driving southeast along Dorena Reservoir on County Rd 2400 for 23 miles to the beginning of the Umpqua National Forest. The trailhead is at the west side of a bridge that crosses Brice Creek. The trail follows the north bank of the creek and climbs 380 feet. Crawfish Trail involves a 3,400-foot climb and begins at Cedar Creek Campground, 1 mile farther into the forest from Brice Creek Trail. The Fairview Trail requires a 4,010-foot climb and begins 3 miles farther into the forest from Cedar Creek Campground. The Cottage Grove Ranger District, (541) 942-5591, provides information sheets describing its recreation opportunities.

A mixture of BLM, state, and private logging company lands awaits bikers west of Eugene. A complex system of roads and trails begins atop a ridge on **Nelson Mountain Rd,** 21 miles west of Eugene via Hwy 126. Just west of the town of Walton, turn north on Nelson Mountain Road and drive 6.7 miles to the ridge top. The BLM's Eugene District map will be a big help in staying found.

The BLM's **Shotgun Recreation Site** has 20 acres that are developed and 240 more that are undeveloped, and is adjacent to BLM land that is used for timber production. The area is laced with 50 miles of single-track trail and fire roads. The park is located 12 miles northeast of Springfield up Mohawk Valley Rd.

The 27-mile **McKenzie River Trail** is open to mountain bikes. The upper part of the trail, which is located in the Santiam Pass and Mount Washington country, is steeper and more technical than the lower trail. To reach the western trailhead, drive Hwy 126 east from Eugene for 50 miles to the town of McKenzie Bridge. Continue driving east another 2 miles on Hwy 126 to parking areas along the river on the north side of the highway. A good turnaround is at Trail Bridge Campground near the trail's midway point.

Another popular ride in the McKenzie River Valley is the **Olallie Trail,** which has loop rides of 11.5 to 29 miles. The trail is famous for its panoramic view of the Cascades from South Sister to Mount Hood and for its wildflowers. To locate the lower trailhead, turn south on Horse Creek Rd just east of the McKenzie Bridge store on Hwy 126. Turn south after 2 miles on Forest Rd 1993. The lower trailhead is at 3 miles and another is located at 6.5 miles up the road.

Camping

Greater Eugene has plenty of campgrounds to choose from, starting about a dozen miles east and west of town and continuing up into the Cascades and all the way to the coast. The major concentration of campgrounds is along the McKenzie River Highway, the Robert Aufderheide Memorial Drive (see Scenic Drives, below), Fall Creek and Lookout Point Reservoirs near Lowell, and along Dorena Reservoir up into the Umpqua National Forest. The west side of Lane County has a scattering of campgrounds, until the Oregon Dunes country on the coast. One thing the interior of Lane County lacks is a state park campground. All the county's state park facilities are for day use only, except on the coast.

Camping begins on the McKenzie River Highway (Hwy 126) at **Delta Campground,** midway between Blue River and McKenzie Bridge on Hwy 126. With 39 sites, it's the second-largest Willamette National Forest campground in the Greater Eugene area. The campground is famous for its grove of old-growth Douglas fir and western red cedar trees, some up to 500 years old. **McKenzie Bridge Campground** is next upriver, with 20 sites, then comes **Paradise Campground.** With 64 sites, Paradise is the largest campground in the area and is located 1 mile west of the Hwy 126–242 junction. The campgrounds are managed by the McKenzie River Ranger District, (541) 822-3381.

Blue River Lake, a reservoir 1 mile north of Hwy 126 near McKenzie Bridge, has 23 campsites at **Mona Campground.** The campground is in the Blue River Ranger District, (541) 822-3317.

Other than group campgrounds, only McKenzie Bridge and Paradise Campgrounds can be reserved through the national reservations system, by calling (800) 280-2267. Concessionaires staff most of the campgrounds in the area under contract with the Forest Service and are working to make more sites available by reservation.

Aufderheide Drive (Forest Rd 19) is a 70-mile paved route that connects Hwy 126 near McKenzie Bridge on the north to Hwy 58 near Oakridge on the south. Camps within the first 25 miles of the northern part of the drive are **Slide Creek Campground** on Cougar reservoir and **French Pete, Homestead, and Frissell Crossing Campgrounds,** all on the South Fork of the McKenzie River. Each is signed along the way and all are small (Frissell Crossing is the largest, with 17 sites). The horse camp at **Box Canyon,** midway along the drive at the pass between the McKenzie and Willamette drainages, was built by the Civilian Conservation Corps in the 1930s. Campers who don't have horses are welcome to use the horse camp's 11 sites, but as a matter of courtesy it's better to stay at another campground because horse owners need the corrals. **Kiahanie** has 19 sites on the byway's southern section along the North Fork of the Middle Fork of the Willamette, 20 miles north of Oakridge. The Blue River Ranger District, (541) 822-3317, manages the northern half of Aufderheide Dr and the Oakridge Ranger District, (541) 782-2291, is in charge of the southern part.

Fall Creek Reservoir and Lookout Point Reservoir, both large artificial lakes near Lowell on Hwy 58, are part of the US Army Corps of Engineers' 10 multipurpose water projects in the Willamette Valley. Fall Creek Reservoir has camping at **Upper End Park** (drive 2 miles north of Lowell on County Rd 6220, then 7 miles east along the reservoir's north shore on County Rd 6204) and at other mini-campsites scattered along the lakeshore. **Cascara Campground** in Upper End Park has 55 sites, plus a boat launch. Call the Corps' office at Lowell, (541) 937-2131, for information. Farther east above the reservoir on Forest Rd 18, the Lowell Ranger District, (541) 947-2129, maintains five tiny campgrounds, plus a group camping site at **Clark Creek.**

Lookout Point Reservoir, at 14.2 miles long, is one of the largest lakes in the Army Corps' Willamette Valley system. Camping is available only at the head of the lake at **Hampton Campground** (5 sites) and **Black Canyon Campground,** both on the north side of Hwy 58. Black Canyon has 75 campsites, a nature trail accessible in a wheelchair, and 4 paved campsites. **Shady Dell Campground** (9 sites) is another 2 miles up Hwy 58 where the Middle Fork of the Willamette River flows freely before joining the reservoir. All are managed by the Lowell Ranger District, (541) 937-2129.

Cottage Grove is the gateway to camping opportunities at Cottage Grove Reservoir, 5 miles south of town on London Rd, and at Dorena Reservoir, 5 miles east of town on Government Rd. The Cottage Grove Ranger District has more camping southeast of town up the Row River drainage from Dorena Reservoir. The US Army Corps of Engineers maintains **Pine Meadows Campgrounds** (93 sites with hookups) on the east side of Cottage Grove Reservoir and **Schwarz Park** (190 sites, 35 with hookups) on the Row River just below Dorena Reservoir Dam. Lane County has camping at **Baker Bay Park** (51 sites, no hookups) on the south shore of Dorena Reservoir. Both parks on Dorena Reservoir have campsites for disabled campers. Reservations are taken only for group camping. For information, contact the Corps' Cottage Grove Lake office, (541) 942-5631, or Lane County Parks, (541) 682-6940.

The Umpqua National Forest has five campgrounds upstream from Dorena Reservoir. Follow the Row River Rd southeast upstream toward the forest boundary (see Cycling, above). The road branches 2 miles before entering the forest (the north branch becomes Forest Rd 17 and the south branch becomes Forest Rd 22). The largest campground in the district is **Rujada,** with 10 sites, just inside the forest boundary on Forest Rd 17. For information, contact the Cottage Grove Ranger District, (541) 942-5591. The BLM, (541) 683-6600, has 10 campsites, including one that is barrier free, at **Sharps Creek,** 10 miles above the end of Dorena Reservoir on Sharps Creek Rd (County Rd 2460). The area is a designated site for recreational gold panning.

On the west side of Eugene, Fern Ridge Reservoir has camping on the northwest shore at the county's **Richardson Park.** One of the most highly developed campgrounds in the county, the park's 50 sites have water and electric hookups, and can be reserved by calling (541) 935-2005. Camping facilities are available for the disabled. To reach the reservoir, drive west of Eugene on Hwy 126 for 15 miles to Veneta. Turn north on Territorial Rd, which follows the reservoir's west shore and reaches Richardson Park after 6 miles.

Farther west of Eugene, the BLM has campgrounds on Siuslaw River

Rd, which heads south off Hwy 126 3 miles west of Walton. **Whittaker Creek Park Campground,** only a mile south of the highway, has 31 camp units. The Whittaker Creek Old-Growth Ridge Trail is a 1.3-mile trail built to display several forest systems typical of Western Oregon's Coast Range. The park also has a 1.5-mile hiking trail, a swimming area, and a boat landing for drift boats. The BLM's **Clay Creek Park Campground** is another 10 miles up the Siuslaw River. It has 21 sites, covered picnic areas, a ball field, and a swimming area. For information, call the BLM at (541) 683-6600.

Parks/Picnics

With an abundance of reservoirs and the lakeside recreation they provide, the Greater Eugene area is well endowed with day-use parks just perfect for summer picnics. Eight US Army Corps of Engineers reservoirs, built mainly to control flooding but available for a multitude of uses, are sprinkled around the area. Even away from the man-made lakes, travelers in the Greater Eugene area are never far from day-use parks. The Willamette, McKenzie, and Siuslaw Rivers have many parks and boat launches lining their banks. A drive up the McKenzie River can be a very slow drive indeed when one stops at all the day-use facilities along the way.

Fern Ridge Reservoir west of Eugene has a half-dozen parks, including Lane County's Richardson Park, Orchard Point Park, and Zumwalt Park, (541) 682-6940). All have picnic facilities, and Richardson and Orchard Point have swimming beaches. The Corps of Engineers, (541) 937-2131, operates Perkins Peninsula Park and Kirk Park, two prime wildlife viewing areas on the north and south sides of Fern Ridge Reservoir. A private concessionaire operates Fern Ridge Shores, (541) 484-5307, which combines day-use facilities with camping. The main access to Fern Ridge Reservoir is through Veneta (see Camping, above). Clear Creek Rd, which heads west from 99W 1 mile north of Belt Line Rd in Eugene, accesses the north shore of the reservoir. In a clockwise direction beginning from the south on Hwy 126, parks are Perkins Peninsula, Zumwalt, Fern Ridge Shores, Richardson, Kirk, and Orchard Point. (See Boating/Water Activities and Fishing, below).

Blue River Reservoir (see Camping, above), located a mile north off Hwy 126 near McKenzie Bridge, has limited road access. Mona Campground provides the best picnic opportunity. **Cougar Reservoir** (see Camping, above), 3 miles south of Hwy 126 also near McKenzie Bridge, has many dispersed recreation opportunities on roads that follow both shores of the lake. Picnicking with developed facilities is best in the campgrounds.

The Fall Creek, Lookout Point, and Dexter Reservoirs complex off Hwy 58, a dozen miles southeast of Eugene, has picnic opportunities along much of the shoreline. State, county, and national forest roads follow the shores of all three reservoirs, which are accessed from the town of Lowell. The most developed day-use parks are **Lowell and Dexter Parks** on Dexter Reservoir, **Ivan Oakes Park** on Lookout Point Reservoir, and **Winberry Park** on Fall Creek Reservoir. Lowell County Park covers 45 acres and has large summer play facilities with horseshoes, swimming, and a multi-use sports court.

Jasper County Park, located 20 miles east of Eugene on the Middle Fork of the Willamette below Dexter Reservoir, is a 60-acre park with enough facilities to supply the needs of group picnics up to 150 people. All of these parks are operated by Lane County, (541) 682-6940, and are shown on the Willamette National Forest map (stop at the Lowell Ranger Station at 60 Pioneer in Lowell to pick up a copy).

Cottage Grove Reservoir has picnic facilities at Lakeside, Shortridge, and Wilson Creek Parks, all operated by the Corps of Engineers, (541) 942-5631. In addition to picnic facilities, Wilson Creek and Lakeside have boat ramps. **Dorena Reservoir** has picnic grounds and boat ramps at Harms and Baker Bay Parks, both operated by Lake County, (541) 682-6940.

In addition to the BLM's campgrounds, the major recreation facility it operates in Greater Eugene is the **Shotgun Recreation Site** in the hills near Marcola, 24 miles northeast of Eugene on Mohawk Valley Rd. Popular for its mountain-bike trails, the park also has 5 miles of hiking trails, a ball field, horseshoe pits, and a swimming area on Shotgun Creek. Two group picnic shelters have enough room to seat 112 people.

A string of parks lines the **Willamette River Greenway** (see Cycling, above) as it passes through Springfield and Eugene. The river's major forks, the Coast and Middle, join at the south side of the metro area near I-5. The string of greenway parks begins with Island Park in Springfield and continues in Eugene with Alton Baker, Skinner Butte, Owen Rose Garden, and East Basin. Hendricks and Spencer Butte Parks (see Cycling, above) are popular picnic sites on Eugene's south end.

What it lacks in camping facilities in the Greater Eugene area, the Oregon State Parks system more than makes up for with its day-use parks. Several state parks line the McKenzie River, beginning with **Armitage State Recreation Site** near the McKenzie's confluence with the Willamette, 5 miles north of Eugene on Coburg Rd. Continuing east up the river to McKenzie Bridge, state parks encountered by visitors are **Hendricks Bridge** (7 miles east of Springfield), **Ben and Kay Dorris** (21 miles east of Springfield), **Howard J. Morton** (40 miles east of Springfield), and **Jennie B. Harris** (1 mile east of McKenzie Bridge). Many parks were named after the people who donated the land to the state parks system. All have picnic facilities and fishing access. Armitage has a nature center with exhibits, plus a 1-mile trail. Armitage and Hendricks Bridge charge day-use fees. The parks are managed by the Willamette Valley office in Gervais, (503) 393-1172.

Elijah Bristow State Park, located 15 miles southeast of Eugene on Hwy 58, makes picnickers work up an appetite by enticing them onto its 10-mile trail system. The park is developed along the Middle Fork of the Willamette River near the Dexter Reservoir Dam. Its trails for walkers, bikers, and equestrians wind along the Willamette River through dense wooded areas.

The state maintains the **Washburne Wayside,** 4 miles northwest of Junction City on Hwy 99W, and the **Alderwood Wayside,** 15 miles southwest of Junction City on Hwy 36. Both waysides have short walking opportunities, and Alderwood has fishing in the Long Tom River. Junction City got its name because it is located where the two branches of the highway that predate I-5 meet. Hwy 99W travels down the west side of the Willamette Valley from Portland, while Hwy 99E travels down the east side of the valley from Portland, merging with I-5 between Salem and Albany and crossing the Willamette River at Harrisburg.

Scenic Drives

Aufderheide Drive, which connects the McKenzie and Willamette Rivers through the heavily forested western Cascades, is designated by the Willamette National Forest as a national scenic byway. The 70-mile route is paved all the way from where it heads south of Hwy 126 near McKenzie Bridge to its junction with Hwy 58 near Oakridge. Traveling from the north, the byway passes Cougar Reservoir and the South Fork of the McKenzie River (see Camping, above); climbs to the divide between the two river systems at the historic Box Canyon horse camp; passes through the Constitution Grove of old-growth Douglas fir and the gorge of the Wild and Scenic North Fork of the Middle Fork of the Willamette River; and ends at the covered bridge in Westfir (see Cycling, above).

The Forest Service has a cassette tape that describes highlights of the drive either north to south or south to north. Pick up the tape at the ranger station at either end, listen to it along the way, and drop it back at one of the ranger stations. For information, call the Blue River Ranger District, (541) 822-3317, or the Oakridge Ranger District, (541) 782-2291.

The tour is named for Robert Aufderheide, who devoted his life to forestry. Aufderheide was supervisor of the Willamette National Forest from 1954 until his death in 1959. In addition to its numerous fishing, hiking, and camping opportunities along the way, the drive passes the Constitution old-growth grove 30 miles out of Oakridge. The grove was dedicated by the Forest Service in 1987 to commemorate the 200th anniversary of the signing of the *U.S. Constitution*. Plaques bearing the names of the *Constitution* signers can be found along a .125-mile loop trail through the grove.

Also, see Cycling, above, for information on the area's **covered bridges,** which can make lovely driving destinations.

Hiking/Backpacking

Mount Pisgah in Burford Park, the 1,516-foot peak that anchors the southeast corner of the Eugene metro area, has a summit trail used by hikers, joggers, picnickers, and bird-watchers. At the base of the peak, the Mount Pisgah Aboretum, (541) 747-3817, has a self-guided nature trail. To reach the trailhead, drive I-5 to the Hwy 58 exit at the south end of Eugene. A quarter mile east of the freeway, turn north off Hwy 58 onto Seavy Loop Rd and follow signs for 2 miles to Burford Park and the aboretum. The **Mount Pisgah Trail** (moderate; 1.6 miles one way) has outstanding views of the confluence of the Willamette Middle and Coast Forks. Don't be surprised to find several other hikers on the summit because other trails also climb to the top from neighborhoods on different sides of the peak. The spring wildflower display can be impressive, but keep a wary eye out for poison oak.

The **Eugene to the Pacific Crest Trail** is a 95-mile route that was partially completed in the mid-1990s along the ridges on the north side of the Middle Fork of the Willamette River. The trail's western terminus is near the Ferry Street Bridge in downtown Eugene on the south-bank bike path along the Willamette River. The trail gains a mile in elevation by its eastern terminus at the Pacific Crest Trail near Waldo Lake. Final construction of the trail depends on obtaining easements to cross private land between Springfield and Dexter Reservoir. The 68 miles east of Dexter follow ridgelines that offer outstanding views and shorter day-hiking opportunities. Check with the Lowell Ranger District, (541) 937-2129, for a comprehensive guide that was published when the national forest segments were linked in 1994.

The **McKenzie River National Recreation Trail** follows the upper McKenzie River for 26.5 miles, beginning 1.5 miles west of the McKenzie River Ranger Station on Hwy 126 and continuing northeast to the river's headwaters in Clear Lake. Day hikes are easily accessible from the campgrounds (see Camping, above) and from numerous marked trailheads along Hwy 126. The most scenic parts of the trail are near the Clear Lake end (see Santiam Pass and Mount Washington chapter). Delta Campground near McKenzie Bridge has a .5-mile nature trail with informational stops that explain the dynamics of its old-growth forest.

Aufderheide Scenic Byway between McKenzie Bridge and Westfir passes several trailheads that lead into the **Three Sisters Wilderness.** Self-issuing permits are available (and required) at the trailheads. This is the largest unlogged forest on the west side of the Oregon Cascades; backpackers will need to hike as much as 20 miles to reach the high-country lakes that are more easily accessible from the east (see Three Sisters and Cascade Lakes chapter). Trails up **French Pete** and **Rebel Creek** begin a few miles south of Cougar Reservoir and head 20 miles or more into the wilderness. The **Erma Bell** area, located 3 miles up Forest Rd 1957 from Box Canyon horse camp, was the first wilderness trail in the Pacific Northwest modified to accommodate wheelchair use. The 1.5-mile trail provides access to the Lower Erma Bell Lake in the Three Sisters Wilderness. (The trail still provides some challenging terrain and is not recommended for electric wheelchairs.) The small Skookum Creek Campground at the trailhead has some barrier-free campsites. Hikers heading into the wilderness should carry the Three Sisters Wilderness map, available from Forest Service offices and sporting goods stores.

The **Fall Creek National Recreation Trail,** located 30 miles east of Eugene and Fall Creek Reservoir on Forest Rd 18, follows the creek for 14 miles. Trailheads are reached by driving east from the reservoir (see Camping, above) to Dolly Varden Campground, Broken Bowl Picnic Area, Big Pool Campground, Clark Creek Nature Trail, Johnny Creek Nature Trail, Bedrock Campground, Puma Campground, and trail's end on Puma Creek. Trail elevations range from 960 feet to 1,385 feet, making the trail accessible throughout most of the year. Major attractions include Fall Creek, which is within view much of the way, the numerous small campgrounds, and the Marine Creek grove of old-growth trees. The **Johnny Creek Nature Trail** is a .5-mile-long trail and is designed to be accessible by wheelchair users. A popular spur from the main trail is the 5.8-mile **Jones Trail,** which heads north .75 mile east of Bedrock Campground.

The Cottage Grove Ranger District of the Umpqua National Forest receives relatively light use compared to the Willamette National Forest east of Eugene. Three paved roads (see Camping, above) reach the forest boundary 25 miles southeast of Cottage Grove. Popular hikes lead to the summits of 5,987-foot **Bohemia Mountain** (moderate; .8 mile one way), 4,616-foot **Mount June** (difficult; 1.1 miles one way), and **Swastika Mountain** (easy; .75 mile one way). The **Swordfern Trail** (easy; 1.4-mile loop) is a popular hike from Rujada Campground, while the **Fairview Creek Trail** (difficult; 1 mile one way) begins at Mineral Camp and leads through a ravine of old-growth Douglas fir. The **Moonfalls Trail** (easy; .5 mile one way) leads to a 125-foot-high waterfall on Alex Creek. Stop at the Cottage Grove Ranger Station, (541) 942-5581, 78404 Cedar Park Rd in Cottage Grove, for recreation opportunity guides that describe the trails in detail.

Rafting/Kayaking/Canoeing

The **McKenzie River** is one of Oregon's most heavily used recreational rivers, with everything from rafts, canoes, and inner tubes plying its waters throughout the summer. Release of water from Blue River Reservoir and two others higher up helps keep much of the river available for recreation through the summer. The major whitewater run on the river is on the upper river in the Santiam Pass and Mount Washington country, but the river can be floated in the Greater Eugene area from Paradise Campground near McKenzie Bridge to its confluence with the Willamette near Eugene. Leaburg Dam near Leaburg is a mandatory portage. The river is managed jointly by the McKenzie Ranger District, (541) 822-3381, the Blue River Ranger District, (541) 822-3317, and the Eugene District of the BLM, (541) 683-6600.

The 9-mile section of river above Paradise Campground is the most challenging on the river (see Santiam Pass and Mount Washington chapter). The 33 miles from Paradise (see Camping, above) down to Leaburg Dam are Class II, with the lower 15 miles being the bread-and-butter run of the McKenzie. The 15-mile run begins at Finn Rock, 2.5 miles west of Blue River on Hwy 126, and continues downstream to Prince Helfrich landing on the south side of the river 1 mile below Ben and Kay Doris State Park (see Parks/Picnics, above). The river has 38 miles of easy Class II water below Leaburg Dam to Armitage Park, near the confluence with the Willamette at Eugene (see Parks/Picnics, above).

Despite the amount of use, the McKenzie is not a river to take lightly. The section that begins at Finn Rock has several rapids that can flip a raft or swamp a canoe. Brown's Hole and Marten's Rapids have plenty of river booty lying beneath the whitewater at the bottom of their pools.

On the McKenzie more than a dozen companies offer whitewater-rafting trips throughout the summer. Jim's Oregon Whitewater, (541) 822-6003, has an office alongside Hwy 126 at McKenzie Bridge. Pontoon float trips are offered by McKenzie Pontoon Trips, (541) 741-1905, of Springfield.

The **Willamette River** also packs enough punch as it flows through Springfield and Eugene to attract whitewater boaters. Local guide services that offer trips on the Willamette include Al's Wild Water Adventures, (541) 895-4465, of Creswell and the Oregon Paddler, (800) 267-6848, of Springfield. A 2-hour trip goes for less than $30. The best river access points are Dexter Dam, Jasper County Park, and Alton Baker Park (see Parks/Picnics, above).

Leisurely canoe trips down the Willamette, from Eugene all the way to Oregon City (see Salem and the Heart of the Valley chapter), can begin on the northwest side of Eugene at the city's Whiteley Landing, (541) 687-

5252. Other spring whitewater opportunities include runs on the **Mohawk, South Fork McKenzie, and Blue Rivers.** For help getting on the rivers, check with the McKenzie River Paddlers in Fall Creek at 38305 Jasper-Lowell Rd.

Boating/Water Activities

Most Willamette Valley reservoirs offer outstanding boating opportunities, and the ones in the Greater Eugene area are no exception. Water levels in all the Willamette Valley reservoirs fluctuate widely throughout the year. Pools are typically full by late spring, then begin to drop as water is released during summer to meet the needs of irrigators below and to keep the rivers clean, cool, and fresh. Reservoirs are drawn down to their lowest levels during late fall in order to have storage capacity available during winter and spring floods. Shorelines are covered with mud and debris during their low-water season, but shorebirds and other wildlife benefit from the change in the water level.

Fern Ridge Reservoir (see Camping, above) has marinas at Richardson, Orchard Point, and Fern Ridge Shores Parks. Richardson Park has 286 slips with daily, weekly, monthly, and seasonal moorage. Fern Ridge is well known as a beginner **windsurfing** site, a place Eugene sailors learn the ropes before heading to the Pacific Coast at Florence or to the Columbia River Gorge. The reservoir is also good for **water-skiers,** although with a maximum depth of only 44 feet they need to be cautious around the shoreline.

Blue River Reservoir (see Camping, above) doesn't have a marina, but it has boat launches at Lookout Creek and Saddle Dam. The reservoir is popular for **fishing** and **waterskiing.** Drive Forest Rd 1506 along the southern part of the reservoir beginning at Delta Campground on Hwy 126. The 270-foot-high Saddle Dam creates a 6.4-mile-long reservoir that covers 1,420 acres.

Boats can launch onto **Cougar Reservoir** (see Camping, above) at Echo Park, Slide Creek campground, and Sunnyside, all along East Side Rd. Cougar Dam is 452 feet high and its 6-mile lake covers 1,280 acres. Slide Creek has a **swimming** beach and the reservoir is used by **float plane** pilots, **fishermen,** and **water-skiers.**

Fall Creek Reservoir (see Camping, above) has boat ramps at North Shore Park on the north side of Fall Creek Dam, Winberry Park on the south side of the dam, and Upper End Park at the head of the reservoir. Fall Creek is primarily a **fishing** lake. The dam is 180 feet high and the 6.8-mile lake covers 1,820 acres.

Off the two reservoirs located along Hwy 58 near Lowell, **water-**

skiers prefer **Dexter Reservoir** to **Lookout Point Reservoir** (see Camping, above) because it gets less wind. Dexter Dam is 93 feet high and impounds 1,024 acres in a 2.8-mile lake. Lookout Point Dam, just upstream from Dexter, is 276 feet high and backs up water for 14.2 miles over 14,360 acres. Boat ramps are available at Lowell and Dexter Parks (see Parks/Picnics, above) on Dexter Reservoir. Lowell Park has a **swimming** beach. Water access for Lookout Point Reservoir is from North Shore Boat Ramp, located on the north side of the dam, and from Hampton and Black Canyon Campgrounds on the south side of the reservoir along Hwy 58. Dexter is popular with **speedboat racers, waterskiers,** and **sailors.** The wind can make boating dangerous on Lookout Point Reservoir, so check in advance with the project manager at (541) 937-2131.

    Dorena Reservoir covers 1,749 acres and is 5 miles long. Its dam is 145 feet high. Baker Bay Park (see Camping, above) has a **boat ramp** and **swimming** beach. Harms Park, located on Row River Rd along the north shore of the lake, has a **boat ramp.** The dam at **Cottage Grove Reservoir** (see Camping, above) is 95 feet high and its 3-mile-long lake covers 1,158 acres. Wilson Creek Park on the east shore and Lakeside Park on the west side of the dam have **boat launches** and **swimming beaches.**

Fishing

The **McKenzie River** runs 90 miles from its birth on the west slope of the Cascades at Clear Lake to its confluence with the Willamette River near Armitage State Park at the north edge of Eugene. Running clear and fast most of the way, the McKenzie is one of Oregon's most storied fishing streams. One of the finer trout streams in Oregon, the river gives its name to the McKenzie River drift boat, the type of river fishing boat that is used extensively on rivers throughout the West because it draws so little water.

    The McKenzie is known for its large native redside rainbow trout, as well as its spring run of chinook salmon and its summer run of steelhead. Most fishermen find they need a boat for access to the river's most productive holes, although plenty of bank angling goes on near the three dozen boat ramps that line the river. Public access points and boat ramps are marked along the length of Hwy 126 from Springfield to the Cascades (see Parks/Picnics above).

    Best fishing for wild rainbow and cutthroat trout is during March and April. The river is stocked with catchable rainbow throughout the summer. Native chinook begin to arrive in May and the run usually peaks in June. Success is best in the lower river. Fishing for hatchery steelhead is best during the heat of summer. For information and regulations, check with the Corvallis office of the Oregon Department of Fish and Wildlife, (541) 757-4186. Regulations are detailed in the annual book of *Oregon Sport Fishing Regulations* available through fishing license outlets. Fly-fishing shops in Eugene are Caddis Fly, (541) 342-7005, 168 W Sixth Ave, and Homewaters Fly, (541) 342-6691, 444 W Third Ave.

The **South Fork of the McKenzie River** above Cougar Reservoir is stocked with legal-size rainbow. Wild rainbow, cutthroat, and bull trout are available in the upper river, but they must be released. Boat fishing is most productive in **Cougar Reservoir,** and bank anglers take some rainbow from the coves. Blue River and its reservoir, another McKenzie tributary, are also good for stocked rainbow. The **Mohawk River,** which joins the McKenzie at Springfield, is the most productive stream in the McKenzie basin for wild cutthroat.

The **Willamette River** and its **Middle Fork** below Dexter Dam have some good fishing for spring chinook and summer steelhead. Dexter and Lookout Point Reservoirs are both infested with squawfish, so fishing pressure is light. **Fall Creek Reservoir** is used for rearing chinook, so fingerling rainbow are not stocked. Fishing above the reservoir in Fall Creek is good for hatchery trout and wild cutthroat. The **North Fork of the Middle Fork of the Willamette River,** along Aufderheide Scenic Byway north of Westfir, is managed for wild trout and is open for fly-fishing only. The **Coast Fork of the Willamette** is one of the least productive streams in the river's upper drainage.

Cottage Grove Reservoir is managed as a trophy bass fishing lake, with catch-and-release required on the big ones over 15 inches. Bluegill, black crappie, and brown bullhead are also present, along with stocked rainbow. **Dorena Reservoir** supports a similar mix of fish.

Fern Ridge Reservoir supports a variety of warm-water fish and some cutthroat, but the best fishing is in the **Long Tom River** below Fern Ridge Dam. Largemouth bass, white crappie, and brown bullhead are common catches, but the most prized possession is one of the wild cutthroat trout that grow large in the reservoir and are most easily caught in the river.

The **Siuslaw River** above tidewater at Mapleton is productive for fall chinook and winter steelhead. **Lake Creek,** the Siuslaw's major tributary, is also productive. **Triangle Lake,** located 25 miles west of Junction City on Hwy 36, flows into Lake Creek and is productive for largemouth bass, bluebell, and yellow perch. The lake covers 280 acres and is surrounded by private land. The lake is heavily used for water sports, both from the public boat ramp and the many private ramps belonging to the homes that line the lake.

Wildlife

Fern Ridge Reservoir, a 9,000-acre lake and wetland just west of Eugene, offers some of the most varied birding opportunities in the Willamette Valley. Thousands of wintering waterfowl and raptors, songbirds, and migrating shorebirds and gulls make the reservoir worth visiting at any time of the year. Because of the lake's size and its extensive summer mudflats, a spotting scope is a big help when trying to add birds to a life list. More than 250 species have been documented.

The lake is surrounded by the Oregon Department of Fish and Wildlife's **Fern Ridge Wildlife Area,** (541) 935-2591. The protected area covers 17,726 acres. Access to the south side of the wildlife area is along either side of Hwy 126, 6 miles west of Eugene. The 44-foot-high, 6,330-foot-long dam is reached by driving Clear Lake Rd along the north side of the lake, 3 miles west of Eugene Airport.

Habitats are characteristic of the type of wetlands that covered the Willamette Valley before farmers began draining the fields to plant crops. Cattail marshes, canary grass, and alder and willow thickets mix with groves of Douglas fir and oak-covered uplands. Viewing is best from a boat, especially a canoe that can be used to paddle along the edges of the reservoir, or from any of the roads that approach the water. Favored viewing spots include the dam area, Richardson Park on the northwest side, Zumwalt Park on the southwest, and Perkins Peninsula Park on the south.

Geese, swans, and **ducks** flock to the area to spend the coldest months of winter. The concentration of waterfowl also draws birds of prey, including a few **bald eagles, red-tailed hawks,** and **northern harriers. Sharp-shinned hawks** and **Cooper's hawks** spend time in the woodlands below the dam around Kirk Park. Summer brings **osprey, yellow warblers,** and **cedar waxwings** below the dam.

Much of the land between Fern Ridge Reservoir and Eugene is managed as the **West Eugene Wetland,** (541) 683-6413, a cooperative project managed by the BLM. A management plan was adopted in 1992 with the goal of protecting 4,000 acres of one of the most endangered plant communities in the nation: the Willamette Valley wet prairie. The wetland will protect wildlife and plant habitats that connect the city of Eugene with Fern Ridge Wildlife Area. Public use is allowed, but the priority is on protecting the area's natural resources. Land is acquired as it becomes available from willing sellers.

The many buttes around Eugene in the south end of the Willamette Valley can provide outstanding wildlife viewing opportunities. Mount Pisgah and its arboretum, located on the southeast edge of the Eugene metro area (see Hiking/Backpacking, above), is famous for its variety of birds as well as for its trees. Spencer Butte, an undeveloped forested hill at the south edge of town on Willamette St (see Cycling, above), has a resident flock of **mountain quail.** A 1-mile hiking trail leads to the summit. Skinner Butte is a developed park in the center of Eugene on the south bank of the Willamette River where **pygmy owls** and **screech owls** live.

Other good close-in wildlife areas are Alton Baker Park along the Willamette River, the open fields and hedgerows around Eugene Airport, and Danebo Pond just west of the city limits.

State fish hatcheries in the Greater Eugene area include Dexter Ponds, (541) 937-2714, just below Dexter Dam near Lowell. Leaburg, (541) 896-3294, and McKenzie, (541) 896-3513, are both located on the McKenzie River on either side of Leaburg along Hwy 126. The Dexter hatchery raises **spring chinook,** and viewing of adult fish is excellent during summer. Leaburg's grounds are landscaped to resemble a Japanese garden. Adult **sturgeon** and **trout** are on display in hatchery ponds. The McKenzie hatchery has a picnic area and visitors center that overlooks the spawning area, which is usually busiest in September.

Hot Springs

The McKenzie Bridge area of eastern Lane County has long been a place to relax sore, tired muscles in a hot springs after a hard day of recreation.

Belknap Springs Resort, (541) 822-3512, is one of Oregon's best-known commercial hot springs. Located along the McKenzie River on Hwy 126, 6 miles northeast of McKenzie Bridge, the resort has lodge rooms and cabins, as well as tent and RV camping. Bathing is available in two pools of water that comes out of the ground at 196°F. Warmed by an underground lava flow, the water is cooled and chlorinated before piped into the pools.

Bigelow Hot Springs, also known as Deer Creek or McKenzie Hot Springs, is a small rock and sand pool located beneath a fern grotto at the edge of the McKenzie River that offers more rustic bathing opportunities. A small flow of 130° water keeps the pool temperatures at about 100°. The pool is 9 miles northeast of McKenzie Bridge off Hwy 126. Turn west on Forest Rd 2654 and park just beyond a bridge over the river. Follow the McKenzie River Trail south 200 yards and take the second steep path on the left that drops down the bank to the riverside pool.

Also known as Cougar Hot Springs, **Terwilliger Pool** is located up Rider Creek a short way from Cougar Reservoir. From near the town of Blue River, turn south from Hwy 126 onto Forest Rd 19, which follows the west side of Cougar Reservoir. Drive 7 miles from the highway and watch for the trailhead sign. The hot springs is a .25-mile hike west of the road. The springs' six rock-sided pools are very popular. The stonework around the pool, a carving in one of the rocks, and a covered structure to hang clothes show that the springs has had a lot of tender loving care over the years. In order to control vandalism and rowdy parties, the parking area and hot springs are closed at night.

outside in

Attractions

Although it's the state's second-largest urban area, **Eugene** is still very much Portland's sleepy sister to the south. There's no skyline here—unless you count the grain elevator (well, okay, there's a 12-story Hilton, too)—and a Eugenean's idea of a traffic jam is when it takes more than five minutes to traverse downtown. There's always parking; people smile at you on the street; and, even in its urban heart, Eugene is more treed than paved. Still, this overgrown town has a sophisticated indigenous culture, from its own symphony to homegrown ballet, opera, and theater companies. There are more speakers and events (courtesy of the University of Oregon, the state's flagship institution) than one could possibly ever attend. There are good **bookstores**—don't miss Smith Family Bookstore, (541) 345-1651 or (541) 343-4714)—the requisite number of **coffeehouses,** trendy **brewpubs**—try Steelhead in Station Square, (541) 686-2739, or the new local favorite, The Wild Duck, on W Sixth, (541) 485-3825)—and enough local color from persevering hippies to backcountry loggers to make life interesting.

Spend a morning at **Saturday Market,** the state's oldest outdoor crafts fair and the ultimate Eugene experience: unique crafts sold by the artisans themselves, Continental noshing, eclectic music, and inspired people-watching; open April through December on High St at Broadway. While away an afternoon shopping and eating your way through the **Fifth Street Public Market,** three levels of shops and upscale crafts booths surrounding a pretty brick courtyard; Metropol, the city's best bakery, is on the ground floor. Finish with an evening at the **Hult Center for the Performing Arts,** a world-class concert facility with two architecturally striking halls. The 24-hour concert line is (541) 342-5746. If you're in town in early July, don't miss the area's oldest and wildest countercultural celebration, the **Oregon Country Fair**; (541) 484-1314.

The **University of Oregon** features a lovely art museum with a permanent collection of Orientalia, a natural history museum, several historic landmark buildings, and a wide variety of speakers and events; (541) 346-3111. The university has a good bookstore, too; (541) 346-4331. **Wistec,** a small but nicely conceived hands-on science and technology museum (with accompanying laser light-show planetarium), is the place to take kids on rainy afternoons; 2300 Leo Harris Pkwy, (541) 687-3619.

Tokatee Golf Club, 3 miles west of McKenzie Bridge, is commonly rated one of the five finest in the Northwest: lots of trees, rolling terrain, and distracting views of the scenery; (541) 822-3220 or (800) 452-6376. It's open February through November.

Restaurants

Adam's Place ☆☆☆ Eugene's most elegant restaurant, this is a quietly sophisticated place, with attentive service, lovely presentation, and inventive cuisine. There's a nice selection of Oregon and California wines. *30 E Broadway (on downtown mall), Eugene; (541) 344-6948; $$.*

Ambrosia ☆ The pizzas (with trendy toppings) are wonderful here. But the pasta dishes and fresh fish specials prove that Ambrosia is much more than a designer pizzeria. Gelato cools the evening. *174 E Broadway (corner of Pearl), Eugene; (541) 342-4141; $.*

Cafe Navarro ☆ This restaurant is a rich cross-cultural experience, with dishes ranging from Africa and Spain to Cuba and the Caribbean. Navarro freely combines cuisines, often arriving at extraordinary results. There are no bad choices. *454 Willamette St (at the foot of Willamette St), Eugene; (541) 344-0943; $.*

Cafe Soriah ☆☆ Locals love this classy but unpretentious Mediterranean and Middle Eastern restaurant where they feel equally at home in Saturday-night finery or jeans. The popular owner makes the best baba ghanouj and stuffed grape leaves this side of Beirut. *384 W 13th (corner of Lawrence), Eugene; (541) 342-4410; $$.*

Chanterelle ☆☆☆ Understated, sophisticated, and wonderful, this intimate spot offers ultra-fresh ingredients cooked with respect and imagination. A small menu is supplemented by specials—plus extraordinary desserts—and the chef comes out at the end of the night to greet loyal patrons. *207 E 5th (across from Fifth Street Public Market), Eugene; (541) 484-4065; $$.*

Keystone Cafe Where you get back to where you once belonged. If that makes no sense to you, then Keystone isn't your kind of eatery. Mingle with the counterculturalists and dig into the best breakfast in town. In back is an organic bakery. *395 W 5th (corner of Lawrence), Eugene; (541) 342-2075; $.*

The LocoMotive Restaurant ☆☆ The owners come to Eugene via Israel, the Caribbean, and Manhattan, and bring sophistication and subtlety to their menu, which is 100 percent vegetarian, with ingredients that are 100 percent organic. The results are 100 percent delicious. *291 E 5th (across from Fifth Street Public Market), Eugene; (541) 465-4754; $$.*

Log Cabin Inn Home cooking and clean, comfortable lodgings are found here in eight remodeled cabins on the water. Dinners are popular and offer a broad range—from wild boar to prime rib. Don't skip the marionberry cobbler. *56483 McKenzie Hwy (50 miles east of I-5 on Hwy 126), McKenzie Bridge; (541) 822-3432; $$.*

Mekala's ☆ A pretty Thai restaurant overlooking a courtyard, Mekala's features more than 12 fiery curries and 24 vegetarian dishes. The inventive chef/owner shows sensitivity to a wide range of palates. *296 E 5th St (in Fifth Street Public Market), Eugene; (541) 342-4872; $.*

Mona Lizza ☆ Come for a designer pizza, a glass of the local microbrew, and a game of pool. Or come and choose from a diverse nouveau-Italian menu. Renditions of the Mona Lisa line the walls, all painted by local artists. *830 Olive St (on downtown mall), Eugene; (541) 345-1072; $.*

Shiki ☆ With its extensive sushi bar, authentic menu, and subtle service, Shiki is Eugene's first noteworthy Japanese restaurant. The location is the only unpromising feature—inside, the menu has something for everyone. *81 Coburg Rd (Ferry St Bridge to Coburg), Eugene; (541) 343-1936; $.*

Spring Garden ☆ This resolutely uncharming spot on Springfield's Main Street serves some of the best Chinese food south of Portland. Feast on a variety of fresh, flavorful entrees, and ignore those around you who order the combination plates. *215 Main St (downtown), Springfield; (541) 747-0338; $.*

Zenon Cafe ☆☆☆ Imagination and consistency have made this one of the best restaurants in Eugene. Noisy, crowded, and invariably interesting, ever-changing menu features Italian, Greek, Middle Eastern, Cajun, Thai, and Northwest cuisines. Nothing disappoints. Desserts are fantastic. *898 Pearl St (corner of E Broadway), Eugene; (541) 343-3005; $$.*

Cheaper Eats

Glenwood Restaurant Campus Cafe This breakfast hot-spot has fantastic food for next to nothing. The whole-wheat waffles are a must at a whopping $2, and the skillets (scrambled eggs with vegetables and ham or bacon) are quite good. Lunch and dinner are served here, too; on weekend nights, stop in for a microbrew and live music. *1340 Alder, Eugene; (541) 687-0355; $.*

La Tiendita & Taco Loco Part art gallery, part retail shop, and part restaurant, this is not your typical burrito take-out spot, but it is Mexican kitsch all the way. The menu, a combination of Mexican and El Salvadoran dishes, rumbas with unusual variations on old favorites. *764 Blair Blvd, Eugene; (541) 683-5531; $.*

Lodgings

Campbell House ☆☆☆ This restored 1892 inn has everything: a quiet, lovely location, elegant rooms (four-poster beds, VCRs, phones), and attentive service. Each room has a private bath, some have fireplaces. Coffee and tea brought to your room are followed by a full breakfast. *252 Pearl St (2 blocks north of Fifth Street Public Market), Eugene, OR 97401; (541) 343-1119 or (800) 264-2519; $$$.*

Eagle Rock Lodge ☆ This laid-back, classy lodge is great for a weekend retreat during the river-rafting season. Bring a bottle of wine and stretch out in front of the fire. A masseur is available. Breakfast is included with the room all year; winters, dinner is too. *49198 McKenzie Hwy (36 miles east of I-5 on Hwy 126), Vida, OR 97488; (541) 822-3962 or (800) 230-4966; $$.*

Eugene Hilton For convenience to downtown, the Hilton fills the bill. The rooms are predictable, but some have views. Amenities include a (very small) indoor pool along with a sauna, Jacuzzi, and fitness room. *66 E 6th Ave (exit 194B off I-5, then exit 1 to city center), Eugene, OR 97401; (541) 342-2000; $$$.*

Excelsior Inn ☆☆ Sitting atop a restaurant is this European-style inn. The 14 suites, all charmingly decorated, feature vaulted ceilings and private baths. All rooms have TVs and VCRs. Complimentary breakfast is served at the restaurant. *754 E 13th (2 blocks west of the university), Eugene, OR 97403; (541) 342-6963; $$$.*

Holiday Farm ☆ The resort encloses 90 acres and several hidden lakes, though you wouldn't know it at first glance. There's a main house and riverside cottages with decks and views, and the restaurant makes an enjoyable dining stop. *54455 McKenzie River Dr (3 miles west of McKenzie Bridge), Blue River, OR 97413; (541) 822-3715; $$$.*

McGillivray's Log Home Bed and Breakfast ☆ This spacious log home on 5 wooded acres makes for a pastoral retreat. Two guest rooms (one with a king-size bed and two twins—perfect for families) both have private baths. A hearty breakfast is prepared on the wood cookstove. *88680 Evers Rd (14 miles west of Eugene off Hwy 126), Elmira, OR 97437; (541) 935-3564; $$.*

The Oval Door ☆ This spacious home with wraparound porch sits on a quiet street close to downtown. Four rooms have private baths. Indulge in the Jacuzzi room with oversize tub, heated towels, and soft music. A full breakfast is served. *988 Lawrence St (corner of 10th), Eugene, OR 97401; (541) 683-3160 or (800) 882-3160; $$.*

Phoenix Inn   This is one of a small chain of hotels, and it sits close to the university campus. Rooms are large and each has a microwave. There's an indoor pool with spa and a small fitness center. *850 Franklin Blvd (exit 194B off I-5, then university exit to Franklin Blvd), Eugene, OR 97403; (541) 344-0001 or (800) 344-0131; $$.*

Valley River Inn   ☆☆   Next door is a shopping mall, but the inn looks toward the Willamette River. With courtyards, plantings, and an inviting pool area, this sprawling complex creates a world of its own. The rooms are oversize and well decorated. *1000 Valley River Way (exit 194B off I-5 to 105 west to exit 1), Eugene, OR 97401; (541) 687-0123; $$$.*

Cheaper Sleeps

Campus Inn   Toward the top end of the cheaper-sleep price range, this inn is worth the couple of extra bucks. Convenient to both the university and downtown, this newer, unassuming motel has 58 units and no seasonal rate changes. *390 E Broadway, Eugene; (541) 343-3376; $.*

Courtesy Inn   For a little extra cash, this inn lets your pets take you with them when they travel. In most other respects, however, it's an average, modestly priced motel. Easy to find and convenient to downtown; the rooms are clean and nicely furnished. *345 W 6th Ave, Eugene; (541) 345-3391; $.*

Eugene International Hostel   This converted home can accommodate 20 people in dormitory and private rooms. (Plan ahead if you want a room to yourself.) Truly the best deal in town (around $20 for a dormitory bed, $40 for a private room); rates include access to the kitchen and a continental breakfast. *2352 Willamette St, Eugene; (541) 349-0589; $.*

McKenzie River Inn   This simple, riverside B&B should satisfy your longing for quiet. Bedrooms all have private baths and a cottage sports a kitchen. A public boat launch is downstream and a big, hot breakfast is included. *49164 McKenzie River Hwy, Vida, OR 97488; (541) 822-6260; $.*

More Information

Blue River Ranger District, Blue River: *(541) 822-3317.*
Bureau of Land Management, Eugene: *(541) 683-6600.*
Bureau of Land Management, Roseburg: *(541) 440-4930.*

Cottage Grove Chamber of Commerce, Cottage Grove: *(541) 942-2411.*
Cottage Grove Ranger District, Cottage Grove: *(541) 942-5591.*
Creswell Visitors Center, Creswell: *(541) 895-5161.*
Eugene/Lane County Visitors Association, Eugene: *(800) 547-5445.*
Junction City/Harrisburg Area Chamber of Commerce: *(541) 998-6154.*
Lane County Parks Department, Eugene: *(541) 682-6940.*
Lowell Ranger District, Lowell: *(541) 937-2129.*
McKenzie Ranger District, McKenzie Bridge: *(541) 822-3381.*
McKenzie River Chamber of Commerce, Leaburg: *(541) 896-3330.*
Oakridge Ranger District, Oakridge: *(541) 782-2291.*
Springfield Area Chamber of Commerce, Springfield: *(541) 746-1651.*
Umpqua National Forest, Roseburg: *(541) 672-6601.*
US Army Corps of Engineers, Lowell: *(541) 937-2131.*
Willamette National Forest, Eugene: *(541) 465-6521.*

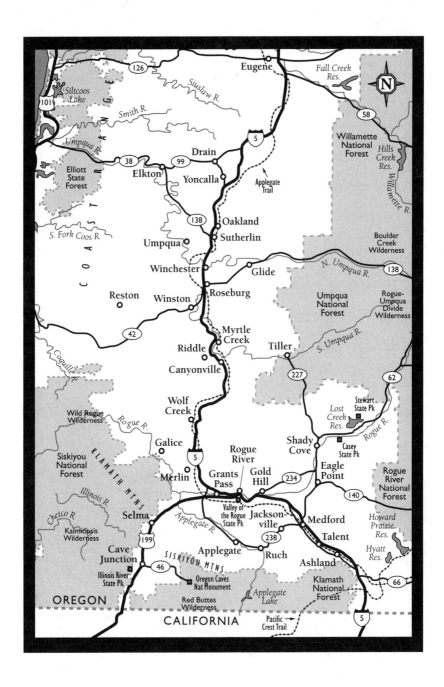

Southern Valleys

The Umpqua Valley   125

The Rogue Valley   142

Southern
Valleys

The Umpqua Valley

From the divide between the Umpqua and Willamette Rivers on the north, east to the forested slopes of the western Cascades, south to the Umpqua-Rogue divide, and west to the Coast Range and tidewater on the Umpqua River at Scottsburg, including the valleys of the Umpqua, the Boulder Creek and Rogue-Umpqua Divide Wilderness Areas, and the towns of Sutherlin, Roseburg, Winston, Myrtle Creek, and Canyonville.

A thunderstorm can happen just about anywhere during an Oregon summer. This one happened on the North Umpqua River at Island Campground, the popular takeout point for day trips on the river just above Steamboat Inn.

The heat of a July day began to build by noon. The air was humid and muggy, a rare occurrence in Oregon where high humidity is usually limited to the fall-through-spring rainy season. By 3pm, clouds had begun to build in the narrow slot of sky that is visible from the bottom of the deep canyon. But these clouds were different from most. While the clouds covered the north side of the canyon like a big down comforter, blue sky continued to dominate the ridges on the southern side. As the afternoon wore on, the clouds began to change color from white to gray, to dark gray, to black. Something big was about to cut loose, but only on the north side of the canyon, because the southern sky remained clear.

With a bolt of lightning and a crack of thunder, the sky opened wide and doused the north side of the canyon with rain. The few campers and fishermen on the river's north bank scrambled for cover, while rain descended in sheets for a few minutes, then slowed to a trickle. The moisture was welcome because it scoured the heat out of the canyon and the humidity again became bearable. Reports on the radio the next morning said more than a hundred lightning strikes had touched down on the north side of the North Umpqua, although none of the fires they sparked burned out of control.

The storm's unusual clear edge, although an isolated occurrence, served as a powerful reminder of a geographical division in Western Oregon. The Umpqua Valley is a lot different from the Willamette Valley a few miles to the north. While the two may be indistinguishable during a long, rainy winter, even the eye of an untrained observer can tell the difference during summer.

When you drive Interstate 5, the scenery slowly begins to change a few miles south of Cottage Grove where the Coast Fork of the Willamette River gives way to the Umpqua drainage. At first the change is barely noticeable, but after a few miles it becomes obvious.

The Umpqua marks the beginning of the transition from the wet Pacific Northwest climate to the drier Mediterranean-like climate found farther south in California. While Douglas fir and western red cedar can still be found in the Umpqua Valley, the understory of the Umpqua's lower mountain slopes has more open grassy spots than the thick underbrush farther north. Scrub oak dominates the slopes of the lower hills.

The difference is fairly subtle, but enough to make even a summer thunderstorm drench one side of a canyon while leaving the other side dry.

Getting There

Roseburg, county seat of Douglas County, is 177 miles south of Portland on Interstate 5. Douglas County and the Umpqua Valley are crossed east to west by Highway 138, a primary route through the Cascades. Both Highways 38 and 42 lead west from Interstate 5 to coastal beaches. Douglas County and the Umpqua National Forest have extensive road systems that lead to most parts of the Umpqua Valley, including the Umpqua National Forest's Rogue-Umpqua Scenic Byway. Commercial air traffic goes through airports at Eugene and Medford.

Adjoining Areas

NORTH: **Greater Eugene**

SOUTH: **The Rogue Valley**

EAST: **Willamette Pass, Diamond Lake, Crater Lake National Park**

WEST: **Bay Area, Oregon Dunes**

inside out

Fishing

The **North Umpqua River** occupies a warm spot in the heart of many an angler from around the world. Whether they've been to the river or not, serious fly-fishermen learn about the Umpqua like big-game hunters learn about the Serengeti Plain of eastern Africa and mountain climbers learn about Mount Everest in Nepal. The North Umpqua is the subject of many a tall fishing tale, as well as a regular presence among coffee-table fishing books on the fine art of making a wary, wild fish rise to a tantalizingly placed artificial fly.

The North Umpqua rises along the crest of the Cascades at Maidu Lake near the resort area of Diamond Lake. The river flows through a beautiful, picturesque canyon for 100 miles to where it joins the South Umpqua River, 10 miles northwest of the Douglas County seat of Roseburg. The forks join in the farmland outside Roseburg and together flow another 100 miles to mix with the waters of the Pacific Ocean at Winchester Bay near Reedsport. The North Umpqua River is the site of a Pacific Power and Light hydroelectric project, but most fishermen who access the river from Hwy 138 would never know it. The water impoundment projects are located on the upper river, north of the highway, and are drawn down during summer to keep the water of the river fresh, cool, and blue-green. The river below the hydro projects is protected as Wild and Scenic, the only river in the Umpqua Valley within the national river protection program.

The North Umpqua is followed throughout much of its length by the 79 miles of the **North Umpqua Trail,** a route used by hikers, bikers, and equestrians, as well as fishermen. A lot of the fishermen head all the way up the river's drainage to Diamond Lake, where the trout fishing for planted rainbow is easier than in the fly-fishing-only zone on the North Umpqua (see Diamond Lake chapter). The North Umpqua's 31-mile fly-fishing-only zone begins at **Rock Creek,** 5.6 miles east on Hwy 138 from the Colliding Rivers Information Center, (541) 496-0157, at Glide.

The run of **summer steelhead** gives the North Umpqua its reputation. A mixture of wild and hatchery fish, 8 to 12 pounds, are common from July through November. A wild run follows during winter. A 25-inch steelhead weighs about 5 pounds, with another pound added for each additional inch in length. The North Umpqua's fly-fishing section, from Rock Creek for 31 miles upriver to Soda Springs Dam, is closed for trout but is open for steelhead all year. One wild steelhead, with the adipose fin still intact, can be kept daily, with a maximum of 5 per year. Up to 2 fin-clipped hatchery steelhead can be kept each day, up to 10 per year. For regulations, check the state fishing synopsis or call the Roseburg office of the Oregon Department of Fish and Wildlife, (541) 440-3353.

Steamboat Inn, which operates on a special-use permit from the Umpqua National Forest similar to the ones granted to ski resorts higher in the Cascades, attracts fishermen from all around to enjoy its superior lodgings and great fishing. The inn also has some impressive bronze sculptures of the elusive steelhead in its lobby and library. Steamboat Inn, (541) 498-2411, is 39 miles upriver from Roseburg on Hwy 138 (see Lodgings, below).

Steamboat Creek enters the North Umpqua nearby. The creek is the main spawning ground for the river's wild summer steelhead and has been closed to all fishing since 1932. Summer steelhead enter the Umpqua River system in May when the water temperature begins to rise. The fish spend the summer in the cooler pools of the river and wait to spawn until late the next winter. Winter steelhead, the more numerous of the two wild runs, head upstream during fall when rain makes the rivers rise.

The North Umpqua's spring chinook run begins in February and extends into June. Spawning occurs in late summer. The fall run of chinook enters the river in September. The state record chinook of 83 pounds was taken from the Umpqua River in 1910.

The summer run of coho salmon at the mouth of the Umpqua at Winchester Bay (see Oregon Dunes chapter) is one of the strongest in the state (but that's not saying much in an era of dwindling numbers of wild coho). The coho enter the Umpqua with the fall rains and are most common in the main stem of the Umpqua and the South Umpqua.

The **South Umpqua** flows 95 miles from its headwaters in the Rogue-Umpqua Divide Wilderness to its meeting with the North Umpqua near Roseburg. While logging has adversely impacted much of the upper South Umpqua's fishery, the lower South Umpqua River remains one of the most productive in Oregon for smallmouth bass. Smallmouth bass are relative newcomers to the Umpqua Basin, but they are a popular target on the Umpqua and South Umpqua when it's too hot for anything else to bite.

Shad are common in the Umpqua system in May and June, especially in the main river and the South Umpqua. Shad have a reputation as fighters. Although bony, their meat is usually smoked and canned and the roe is considered a delicacy.

Striped bass reside in the lower Umpqua and Smith Rivers in western Douglas County, as well as Winchester Bay. The Umpqua is about the farthest north that striped bass live in the cold waters of the Pacific. The state record is 64 pounds, set in 1973 and taken from the Umpqua. A more typical catch is 15 pounds.

The Umpqua Basin's main population of kokanee, a landlocked coho salmon, is in **Hemlock Lake,** 10 air miles south of Steamboat Inn. Drive south on Hwy 138 from Apple Creek Bridge across the North Umpqua on Forest Rd 4714 to reach the lake, one of the few in the lower part of Umpqua National Forest. Another approach is from Glide via County Rd 17C, which becomes Forest Rd 27.

Compared to the Willamette and Rogue Valleys, **lake fishing** is limited in Douglas County, except near the crest of the Cascades (see Diamond Lake chapter). Fishermen use small boats on 640-acre **Galesville Reservoir,** an impoundment on Cow Creek near Canyonville east of I-5 on County Rd 36, and on **Ben Irving Reservoir,** a 250-acre irrigation reservoir 7 miles south of Tenmile on County Rd 365.

For the stocking schedule in the Umpqua Basin, call the Roseburg office of the Oregon Department of Fish and Wildlife, (541) 440-3353.

Douglas County and Roseburg are home to more than a dozen professional **fishing guides** that help visitors hook onto the big ones. Most interest is in drift-boat fishing for the steelhead of the North Umpqua, but guides also go after salmon, bass, and sturgeon. For a list of outfitters, contact the Roseburg Visitors and Convention Bureau, (800) 444-9584, or the Oregon Guides and Packers Association, (800) 747-9552.

Scenic Drives

The **North Umpqua Highway** (Hwy 138) is part of the 172-mile Rogue River-Umpqua National Forest scenic byways system. In a state filled with beautiful rivers, the North Umpqua ranks high on the list. The river's corridor is liberally sprinkled with campgrounds and picnic areas, natural sites that include colliding rivers, dizzying waterfalls, and Indian artifacts.

Traveling east from Roseburg, Hwy 138 joins the North Umpqua in 17 miles at Colliding Rivers, where the North Umpqua and Little River meet head on before continuing as one. The North Umpqua Ranger District, (541) 496-3532, and the Colliding Rivers Information Center, (541) 496-0157, are both within walking distance of the Colliding Rivers Viewpoint within the town of Glide.

The North Umpqua Highway continues east from Colliding Rivers, following the Wild and Scenic North Umpqua River. Idleyld Park, a small resort community, is 4 miles east of Colliding Rivers. Steamboat Inn, 22 miles east of Colliding Rivers, is another landmark and is followed by the turnoff for Toketee Ranger Station at 42 miles, Diamond Lake Resort at 66 miles (see Diamond Lake chapter), and a viewpoint of Crater Lake at 79 miles (see Crater Lake National Park chapter). After looping around Diamond Lake, the byway follows Hwys 230 and 62 along the Rogue River toward Medford (see The Rogue Valley chapter). For information on the byway, contact the Umpqua National Forest, (541) 672-6601, at 2900 NW Stewart Pkwy in Roseburg.

Wildlife

Douglas County and the Umpqua Valley are a wildlife watcher's paradise, although it takes some effort because of a lack of designated viewing sites. Other than the Bureau of Land Management's (BLM) Dean Creek Elk Viewing Area in western Douglas County (see Oregon Dunes chapter), viewers are pretty much on their own to figure out what lives where. The diverse vegetation in the Umpqua Valley supports big mammals like **Roosevelt elk** and **black-tailed deer,** plus **wild turkeys, cougars,** and plenty of **black bear.**

Other than birds overhead, steelhead are about the easiest creatures to see in the Umpqua Valley. The **Deadline Falls Fish Overlook** is a gathering spot for steelhead and chinook salmon as the fish make their way up the North Umpqua River to their spawning grounds. Fish gather in the pool beneath the falls, then jump in an effort to get themselves into calmer water above. More often than not, the fish come up short, get swept back into the pool, and have to try again. Best viewing times are early and late in the day from June through August. To find the overlook, drive 6 miles east of Colliding Rivers on Hwy 138 (see Scenic Drives, above) to the turnoff to Swiftwater Park. Turn south, cross Swiftwater Bridge, and park in the lot on the left on the south bank of the North Umpqua River. Hike the North Umpqua Trail from the north side of the parking lot east for 400 yards to the viewing platform, which sits in a forest of old-growth Douglas fir, western red cedar, and sugar pine.

To see chinook salmon spawning during September and October, drive past Colliding Rivers on Hwy 138 to milepost 49 and watch for fish in the gravel beds of the North Umpqua.

The state's **Rock Creek Fish Hatchery,** (541) 496-4484, is located .75 mile north of Idleyld Park on Rock Creek Rd. The hatchery raises coho and spring chinook, as well as summer steelhead and rainbow trout. The hatchery has a wheelchair-accessible trail with interpretive signs leading to a viewing deck.

The **Winchester fish ladder** provides an opportunity to view adult fish swimming upstream on the North Umpqua River. Located 6 miles north of Roseburg on I-5, exit 129, the fish ladder is on the north side of the river along Hwy 99 near the town of Winchester. Depending on the time of year, viewing includes steelhead, chinook and coho salmon, trout, lamprey, squawfish, and suckers.

The BLM maintains the **Miner Wolf** watchable wildlife site for fish viewing on **Wolf Creek,** a tributary of the Umpqua River. The area is being rebuilt to enhance habitat for coho, steelhead, and cutthroat trout. The site, 33 miles northwest of Roseburg, has a nature trail and picnic table. Head for the town of Umpqua on County Rd 9 west of Sutherlin. Turn northwest on County Rd 33 for 11 miles to the Tyee Bridge. Cross the Umpqua River on BLM Rd 25-7-5.1 and continue 3 miles to the site. The BLM's Roseburg District, (541) 440-4930, has information sheets on most of its recreation opportunities, even though it will be one of the last Oregon BLM districts to publish a comprehensive map of the land it manages. The office is located in Roseburg at 777 NW Garden Valley Blvd.

Birding is good throughout the Umpqua Valley, with many of the most productive places found in the river lowlands where riparian areas mix with farmlands and forests. Productive areas during spring and fall migrations include farm and log ponds between Sutherlin and Winchester; Stewart Park, on Stewart Pkwy—Roseburg's main park on the right bank of the South Umpqua River; and the Umpqua Community College grounds several miles north of Roseburg between Wilber and Winchester, east of I-5, exit 129, on College Rd.

For wildlife watching of a different sort, head for Wildlife Safari's 600-acre, drive-through exotic-animal park. Visitors tour one of the oldest parks of its kind in the comfort of their own vehicles. One of the park's rules is to keep the windows rolled up when you're visiting the **lions.** For information, call Wildlife Safari, (541) 679-6761. The park is located outside Winston. From I-5, exit 119, just south of Roseburg, drive west 4 miles on Hwy 42 and watch for signs to the park.

Rafting/Kayaking/Canoeing

The forks of the Umpqua River host just about every type of river boating. Expert **kayakers** can run white-knuckle whitewater in the upper reaches of the South Umpqua or take the 20-foot plunge over Steamboat Falls on Steamboat Creek. Commercial paddle-raft operations keep a 16-mile stretch of the North Umpqua busy with boaters even during the low water of summer because of reservoir releases. Self-outfitted **rafters** run the same stretch, then tack on a second day to the outing by continuing another 16 miles below Steamboat Inn before a boating closure that begins July 15. **Canoeists** out for some of the longest flatwater river-paddling opportunities in Oregon head for the Umpqua River below where the north and south forks join.

A local outfitter on the North Umpqua is Oregon Ridge and River Excursions of Glide, (541) 496-3333. The North Umpqua Ranger District can supply a list of an additional dozen whitewater **guide services** that split time on the North Umpqua with other Oregon rivers. Recreation on the North Umpqua is managed in its upper section by the North Umpqua Ranger District, (541) 496-3532, and in its lower section by the Roseburg District of the BLM, (541) 440-4930.

Commercial whitewater trips on the **North Umpqua** usually begin at Boulder Flat Campground, 36 miles east of Colliding Rivers, and run downstream 14.5 miles to a takeout at Gravel Bin, 1.5 miles above Steamboat Inn. (River mileage and highway mileage rarely correspond.) Regular releases from the PacifiCorp reservoirs at Toketee and Lemolo Reservoirs keep the river lively with rapids even during summer, when the only rain that hits the Umpqua for weeks at a time comes from a stray thunderstorm.

An information board at the Boulder Flat launch site lists 12 Class III rapids, as well as a Class IV called Pinball. Much of the river can be scouted from the road, although it takes a .3-mile hike downstream on the North Umpqua River from the south side of the Apple Creek Bridge to get an advance look at Pinball. The river flows swiftly in its upper reaches, with few breaks between rapids. Most of the action comes from dodging rocks and other obstructions, rather than from big waves. Pinball is a boulder-choked drop, but it offers a safe way through for rowers and paddlers who can make quick maneuvers.

During fishing season, boating is restricted to the hours from 10am to 6pm to let anglers enjoy the river during the prime morning and evening hours. Below Gravel Bin for 17.5 miles to Bogus Creek, the river is closed to boating from July 15 to October 31 to protect the fishing. Before the annual closure, the North Umpqua offers a 32-mile run that some boaters make as a two-day trip. Camping is at riverside campgrounds along Hwy 138 that are also accessible by automobile (see Camping, below).

The North Umpqua below Gravel Bin is less lively than the river's upper 14.5-mile section, but long flat stretches are punctuated by some powerful rapids. Rapids called Steamboat, Bathtub, and Little Niagara are Class III and can be difficult to run because of low water. The takeout at Cable Crossing is easy to miss and should be scouted from the road beforehand. Located near the BLM's Swiftwater picnic area, Cable Crossing is just above Rock Creek Falls and the Narrows, both usually run by experts only.

Expert kayakers have some winter rain and spring runoff boating on the lower portions of **Canton** and **Steamboat Creeks,** which join the North Umpqua near Steamboat Inn. Both have waterfall drops of 20 feet that would have been outside the realm of navigability not too long ago but are within the ability of a growing number of extreme creek paddlers. Be sure to obtain the advice of local paddlers (if any happen to be on the water when you decide to run it) before running either creek.

While the North Umpqua begins to change character near Glide, it by no means becomes a lazy Sunday afternoon paddle. Below the Narrows in the town of Idleyld Park, the river offers 30 miles of Class II and III water, depending on the river's flow. This section is popular with fishermen in drift boats and canoeists with confidence and skill. Launches are available down the bank at Idleyld Park below the Narrows or, for drift boats, at Colliding Rivers. The river begins its transition from a forested canyon to grassy farmlands below Colliding Rivers, but still packs Class III punch at Whistler Falls and Dixson Falls before the portage around Winchester Dam. Below Winchester, the river has another 6 miles of Class II water before joining the South Umpqua at River Forks Park.

The upper **South Umpqua River** offers 33 miles of Class III and IV paddling above Canyonville. The navigable portion begins along Forest Rd 28 just above Campbell Falls, a 15-foot drop that's a good indicator of what type of paddler (Class IV) should attempt the upper river.

The South Umpqua has long stretches of placid water punctuated by Class II rapids as it descends from Canyonville to its confluence with the North Umpqua. The South Umpqua flows through Roseburg, while the North Umpqua passes 4 miles north of town.

At River Forks Park, the name of the river drops the North and South names and becomes simply the Umpqua. The united **Umpqua River** flows 84 miles, from where the north and south forks join 5 miles northwest of Roseburg, to tidewater near Scottsburg. The river flows slowly through its many meanders, but higher flows and unexpected hazards can cause trouble along the way. Sawyers Rapids packs Class III punch surprisingly far down the river between Elkton and Scottsburg. To run Sawyers Rapids, launch from a turnout at milepost 27 on Hwy 138 and take out at milepost 24.5. The lower river has numerous access points that are marked along the highway.

Camping

It's rarely more than a few miles that campers have to travel to find a scenic spot to pitch a tent or park an RV in the Umpqua Valley. While campgrounds are numerous, most are on the small side—but most campers don't consider that a problem.

Campers who want to sleep close to Roseburg usually drive east on Hwy 138 up the valley of the North Umpqua. Beginning near Colliding Rivers at Glide, campgrounds come fast and furious. Sizes range from 5 to

30 sites. Because reservations are not taken, it can be a little frustrating to locate an open spot on a warm Friday night during summer. Perseverance usually pays off. If the North Umpqua looks too busy, Little River Rd (County Rd 17C), which heads southeast from Glide, has a half-dozen other places to look. Dispersed camping outside of campgrounds is also popular. The North Umpqua Ranger District, (541) 496-3532, at Glide has recreation opportunity guides that point the way to the best locations.

National forest campgrounds located along the North Umpqua River begin 18.5 miles east of Glide with **Bogus Creek.** They continue with **Canton Creek, Island, Apple Creek, Horseshoe Bend, Eagle Rock, Boulder Flat,** and **Toketee,** at 42 miles east of Glide. More campgrounds line the highway as it continues east (see Diamond Lake chapter). The best bets for RV campers are Bogus Creek and Horseshoe Bend, 30 miles east of Glide. Both can take trailers up to 35 feet long. Most North Umpqua River campgrounds were free until Congress passed the National Fee Demonstration Program in 1996. Most of the new $5 overnight charge is put to good use maintaining and developing facilities where the money is collected. The **Hemlock Lake** area (see Fishing, above) is the most popular camping location up the Little River tributary of the North Umpqua.

The Tiller Ranger District, (541) 825-3201, located in the southern part of the Umpqua National Forest, receives far less use than its more famous northern neighbor, the North Umpqua Ranger District. Locals like that just fine when they head up the forks of the South Umpqua River for quiet camping opportunities. The Tiller District has a half-dozen developed campgrounds, all with fewer than 10 sites.

The ranger district has two fire lookouts for rent: **Acker Rock Lookout** from June through October and **Pickett Butte Lookout** from November through May. Both rent for $40 per night. Contact the ranger district for directions and rental information. Expect to provide your own food, bedding, and drinking water. Available during summer, Acker Rock Lookout can be reached via a .4-mile hike from the parking area. Pickett Butte Lookout, located at 3,200 feet in elevation, may require skis or a snowmobile to approach it in winter.

The BLM is co-manager with the Forest Service of the North Umpqua's Wild and Scenic River corridor and has some campgrounds of its own. **Susan Creek Campground,** (541) 440-4930, located 12.5 miles east of Glide on Hwy 138, is one of the prettiest in the area. The 31-unit campground has several short trails that lead to the North Umpqua, 50-foot Susan Creek Falls, and Susan Creek Indian Mounds where moss-covered rocks are believed to be a spiritual site visited by Indian boys approaching manhood. The campground has showers and the best camping facilities for the handicapped among the valley's BLM and Forest Service sites. RV size is 35 feet.

Other smaller BLM campgrounds in the area include **Scaredman Campground,** a free site open year-round on Canton Creek 40 miles east of Roseburg on Steamboat Creek Rd; **Rock Creek** and **Millpond Campgrounds,** both north up Rock Creek Rd, which leaves the North Umpqua Hwy 6 miles east of Glide; **Cavitt Creek Campground,** the site of a popular swimming hole and a 10-foot waterfall up the Little River Rd (6.7 miles from Hwy 138 at Glide and 3.2 miles on Cavitt Creek Rd); and **Tyee Campground,** located on the main stem of the Umpqua 12 miles west of Sutherlin off Hwy 138. All are managed by the Roseburg BLM District, (541) 440-4930.

Douglas County fills in where national forest and BLM land ends in the Umpqua Valley. **Whistler's Bend** is the closest campground along the North Umpqua River east of Roseburg. Only 15 miles from town on Hwy 138, the county park has 23 campsites and 30 picnic tables. RV travelers looking for guaranteed space can stay right in Roseburg at the 50-unit **Douglas County Fairgrounds RV Park,** (541) 440-4505, at the southeast side of exit 123 from I-5. Other county parks with camping along I-5 are **Pass Creek,** at exit 163 near Drain; **Amacher,** 5 miles north of Roseburg at the Winchester exit; and **Charles Stanton,** located at the north Canyonville exit. All have RV hookups. For information, call the Douglas County Parks Department at (541) 957-7001.

Parks

A good place to stop is right in the center of Roseburg at **Riverside Park,** a shady spot along the South Umpqua River as it winds its way through downtown. The park is on Spruce St, on the east bank of the river beneath the Hwy 138 bridge. While enjoying a respite from the heat of a summer day, you may as well stop at the Roseburg Visitors Information Center, (800) 444-9584, in Riverside Park at 410 SE Spruce. **Stewart Park,** (541) 672-9731, is located in the west part of Roseburg on Stewart Park Dr. Roseburg's main city park, it has 230 acres devoted to all types of recreation, including an 8.5-mile paved bicycle/jogging trail. Roseburg is also known for its outstanding youth sports programs, including American Legion Ball Park in Stewart Park, where the nation's best youth baseball teams regularly compete for state, regional, and national championships.

At 1,100 acres, **Mildred Kanipe Memorial Park,** (541) 459-9567, is one of Oregon's larger county parks. Picnic sites and other facilities are located among a historic ranch house and outbuildings 7 miles northeast of Oakland. The park has an extensive trail system beyond the day-use area, and dispersed camping is allowed by permit from the park office. To reach the park, take I-5, exit 138, into Oakland and drive east on Oak St, which becomes County Rd 22. Drive 4 miles, then turn left on County Rd 50 and drive 3 miles to the park's entrance.

Other popular county parks are **River Forks,** where the North and South Umpqua join northwest of Roseburg on River Forks Rd; **Ben Irving Reservoir,** an 11,250-acre lake 5 miles south of Tenmile via County Rds 141, 140, and 365; **Chief Miwaleta Park,** located on Galesville Reservoir southeast of Canyonville (take I-5, exit 88, turn east on Starveout Creek Rd to County Rd 36, turn left, and follow it for 5 miles to the reservoir); and **Cooper Creek Reservoir,** at the east edge of Sutherlin on County Rd 120.

Hiking

The 79 miles of the **North Umpqua Trail,** from near Idleyld Park on the west to Miller Lake east across the Cascades, is a difficult trail to avoid. Most campgrounds, picnic areas, and scenic locations in the North Umpqua Valley are threaded together by the North Umpqua Trail. Whether kayakers are scouting rapids, fishermen are eyeing a new steelhead hole, or bathers are headed for Umpqua Hot Springs, they are all using parts of the North Umpqua Trail. The trail is jointly administered by the BLM, (541) 440-4930, the Umpqua National Forest, (541) 672-6601, and Douglas County Parks, (541) 440-4500.

The trail's western end is at the BLM's **Swiftwater** picnic area, 6 miles east of Glide on Hwy 138. Known as the Tioga segment, the first 11 miles of the trail wind through a mature forest of Douglas fir, western red cedar, hemlock, and pine, some up to 6 feet in diameter. The first .25 mile of the trail is barrier free and leads to the Deadline Falls watchable wildlife site, where steelhead and salmon gather from May through October to jump the falls (see Wildlife, above).

As the trail continues east, segment names change to Fox, Mott, Panther, Calf Creek, Marsters, Jessie Wright, Boulder Creek, Deer Leap, Hot Springs, Dread and Terror, Lemolo, and Maidu. Bikers are allowed on the trail as well as hikers. Vigorous stands of poison oak are common along the trail. The managing agencies publish a free map that describes each of the trail segments in detail. Pick up a copy at the Colliding Rivers Information Center at Glide or any other ranger station or visitors center.

With so many miles to cover, hikers usually narrow down their choices of what they want to see. It's sort of like going into the store that sells 31 flavors of ice cream—everyone has his or her own idea of what is best and it's hard to make a mistake.

The river canyon's numerous waterfalls are frequent side-trip destinations along the North Umpqua Trail. **Watson Falls,** at 272 feet the third highest in Oregon, is .5 mile south of the North Umpqua in the Toketee area, a collection of buildings that house Forest Service employees and staff from the Pacific Power and Light power station. The turnoff to Watson Falls is 48 miles east of Colliding Rivers on Hwy 138, or 2.2 miles east of Toketee Lake. Turn south on Forest Rd 37, drive .2 mile to the trailhead, park, and walk .3 mile to a view of the falls.

Toketee Falls is only a few miles away, so make a point of walking the .5 mile of the North Umpqua Trail to view the 90-foot lower drop and the 30-foot upper drop on the North Umpqua River. To find the trailhead, turn north off Hwy 138 onto Forest Rd 34, which goes to the Diamond Lake Ranger Station at Toketee. Where the road crosses the North Umpqua River, less than a mile from Hwy 134, park and hike west downstream on the North Umpqua Trail for a view of the falls.

Umpqua Hot Springs is located 4 miles northwest of Hwy 138 from Toketee via Forest Rds 34 and 3401. From the trailhead the bathhouse is .25 mile along the North Umpqua Trail. Small but popular, the hot springs is perched on a wooded bluff overlooking the North Umpqua River. At 2,600 feet, it's usually accessible throughout the year. A three-sided bathhouse covers the 6-foot-by-6-foot pool that is filled by a 108° spring.

The Little River, which joins the North Umpqua at Colliding Rivers near Glide, offers a number of scenic waterfalls as it tumbles down the west slope of the Cascades from Hemlock Lake. Access the drainage by driving southeast on County Rd 17C, which becomes Forest Rd 27 at the Umpqua National Forest boundary. Driving up river from Glide, **Wolf Creek Falls** comes first. The two-tiered, 125-foot falls is on BLM land 10.6 miles up Little River Rd from Glide. An easy trail leads 2 miles to the falls. **Cedar Creek Falls** is signed 12.1 miles farther up Little River Rd and can be viewed from the road. A .7-mile trail leads to the base of 70-foot-high **Yakso Falls.** It begins at the entrance to Lake in the Woods Campground.

The 19,500-acre **Boulder Creek Wilderness** surrounds Boulder Creek, a major tributary of the North Umpqua 50 miles east of Roseburg. The 10.6-mile **Boulder Creek Trail** traverses the wilderness north to south one way, while the North Umpqua Trail skirts a small part of the southern edge of the wilderness. The towering rock pillars that can be seen along Hwy 138 at the south edge of the wilderness attract a few rock climbers. The Boulder Creek Trail begins across from Boulder Flat Campground along Hwy 138, but there's the small matter of getting across the North Umpqua. The river is never safe to ford, so hikers need to drive to bridges east or west of the campground and get on the North Umpqua Trail. To reach the Soda Springs Trailhead, 2 miles east of the Boulder Creek Trail, turn north off Hwy 138 onto Forest Rd 4775. Immediately turn left on the Soda Springs Dam access road (Forest Rd 4775-011) and drive 1.3 miles to the trailhead's parking area. Begin walking west on a gated road, 1.2 miles to the powerhouse and 2 miles to the beginning of the Boulder Creek Trail. The trail that heads north through the wilderness is a difficult hike with numerous stream crossings.

Many visitors to the South Umpqua Valley pay homage to **South Umpqua Falls,** 20 miles northeast of the Tiller Ranger Station on Forest Rd 28. The ranger station is in the community of Tiller, 21 miles east of I-5 at Canyonville on County Rd 1. The 15-foot-high falls can be seen from the South Umpqua Falls picnic area, where short trails lead to the best viewpoints. The most popular location in the ranger district, the observation deck overlooks the falls while providing protection for a fish ladder. Trespassing on the fish ladder or angling within 200 feet of it is prohibited.

The Umpqua Valley shares the 33,000-acre **Rogue-Umpqua Divide Wilderness** with the Diamond Lake area. The 31.4-mile **Rogue-Umpqua Divide Trail** can be reached from a half-dozen trailheads from the west near the headwaters of the South Umpqua River. Most popular is the **Fish Lake Trail** (difficult; 8 miles one way), which leads to 90-acre Fish Lake. Located at 3,350 feet in elevation, the 140-foot-deep lake has good backcountry fishing for rainbow and brook trout. To reach the Fish Lake Trail, continue driving past South Umpqua Falls on Forest Rd 28 for 4 miles to Forest Rd 2823. Turn right, drive to Forest Rd 2830, turn right, drive to Forest Rd 2840 and turn left, and drive .5 mile to the trailhead, 28 miles in all from the Tiller Ranger Station. The area is administered by the Tiller Ranger District, (541) 825-3201. All three Umpqua National Forest wilderness areas (including Mount Thielsen in the Diamond Lake chapter) are described on the same map, which is available from ranger stations.

Biking

For many years, Douglas County has been active in promoting cycling, and publishes a free map called the **Douglas County Bicycling Guide.** For a copy, call the Roseburg Visitors Information Center, (800) 444-9584. Despite the county's advocacy of bicycling, it would be a mistake to compare the Umpqua Valley with the Willamette Valley when it comes to cycling. Pedaling around the Willamette Valley is relatively easy and the larger population means cyclists can be seen everywhere, while the Umpqua Valley has many more rolling hills and cycling is more difficult. With only 98,600 residents spread among its 5,071 square miles, Douglas County has comparatively few cyclists. Log-hauling trucks still dominate traffic on the county's narrow, two-lane roads, so cyclists always need to ride with caution.

Stewart Park, Roseburg's main city park, is a starting spot for a variety of rides in town (see Parks, above). Located along the South Umpqua River in the west-center of town, the park is connected by bike paths to downtown and nearby neighborhoods. Bike lanes link the park to a 14-mile rural loop on country roads northwest of town where the forks of the Umpqua join at River Forks Park.

With a half-dozen covered bridges, two designated scenic byways, dozens of historic barns and houses, and plenty of small, friendly towns, Douglas County and the Umpqua Valley can be a rewarding place to cycle for those who enjoy getting off the beaten path to explore.

Myrtle Creek, located along I-5 16 miles south of Roseburg, has two of the county's covered bridges. **Horse Creek Covered Bridge,** 105 feet long, was renovated in 1991. The bridge spans Myrtle Creek and connects the town's Millsite Park on Second Ave and Park St with parking areas for cyclists and pedestrians. **Neal Lane Covered Bridge** spans South Myrtle Creek and is still in use by automobiles at the intersection of County Rds 42 and 124. Backroads between Myrtle Creek, Canyonville, and Riddle provide scenic rural cycling opportunities. Pick up a free map of Douglas County at any visitors center.

The BLM's 45-mile **Cow Creek National Back Country Byway** begins near Glendale along I-5, makes a loop through the Coast Range west of the freeway, and returns to the freeway downstream at Riddle to the north. The byway is lightly traveled and offers paved road riding. Downstream south to north is best, if you can arrange a shuttle. The **Cow Creek Recreational Gold Panning Area** is 21 miles southwest of Riddle. A 1,300-foot segment of the creek was withdrawn from private mining claims to offer public recreational gold panning. The site has the only developed recreation facilities along the byway, a day-use area with picnic tables, rest rooms, and an information board.

A tour of Douglas County wouldn't be complete without noticing some of the county's **historical barns.** The Roseburg Visitors Information Center, (800) 444-9584, can provide a detailed brochure that describes the best-preserved barns and the architecture that makes them interesting. Bikers can reach several clusters of the old buildings by riding rural roads between Sutherlin and Umpqua west of I-5, between Melrose and Winston west of Roseburg, and between Canyonville and Days Creek east of I-5. Each location has several barns of interest, including one each that is on the National Register of Historic Places.

The 79 miles of the **North Umpqua Trail** (see Hiking, above), which parallels Hwy 138 much of the way, is open to **mountain bikes,** but it's anything but an easy ride. Cyclists usually figure out their tolerance level by going for short rides on the trail from any of the numerous campgrounds or day-use areas. The most forgiving part of the trail is the 16-mile Tioga section, located at the west end of the trail on BLM land. Begin on the west at Swiftwater Park (see Wildlife, above) and ride east to the Wright Creek Trailhead on Forest Rd 4711 on the south side of the river along Hwy 138. Less difficult mountain-bike riding is available farther east on Hwy 138 at Diamond Lake (see Diamond Lake chapter).

outside in

Attractions

The **Roseburg** area now has several **wineries** open for tours and tastings much of the year. Henry, 687 Hubbard Creek Rd, Umpqua, (541) 459-5120, and HillCrest, 240 Vineyard Lane, (541) 673-3709, are open all year. The others have more limited hours in winter. La Garza, 491 Winery Lane, (541) 679-9654, also has a tasting-room restaurant, the first in the region, serving lunch Wednesday through Sunday, May through September.

The **Douglas County Museum of History and Natural History** imaginatively displays logging, fur-trapping, and pioneer items in one of the handsomest contemporary structures you'll find. There's a modest admission charge. It's open daily; off I-5 at the fairgrounds, exit 123, (541) 440-4507.

What started out as the Cow Creek Indians' bingo parlor has grown into the **Seven Feathers Hotel and Gaming Resort** in Canyonville (pop. 1,500), about 25 miles south of Roseburg. It features hundreds of slots, other gaming tables, and a four-story, 156-room hotel that opened in 1996.

Restaurants

Teske's Germania ☆ German restaurants are an endangered species in southern Oregon. If you hunger for sauerbraten, red cabbage, and homemade spaetzle, this is the place to go. The fare is hearty and surprisingly inexpensive. *647 SE Jackson (near Cass, downtown), Roseburg; (541) 672-5401; $.*

Tolly's ☆ Tolly's is an oddity. Downstairs is an ice cream parlor, candy counter, and antique gift shop. Upstairs is a special-occasion place for locals. The execution of dishes like bacon-wrapped filet mignon is respectably consistent. Extensive wine list. *115 NE Locust St (exit 138 off I-5 to middle of town), Oakland; (541) 459-3796; $$.*

Lodgings

House of Hunter ☆ Roseburg's best B&B is a 1900 Italianate home, with five bedrooms. Some rooms may seem a bit small and ordinary, but the public grand room downstairs is bright and pleasant. Homemade baked goods make for a hearty breakfast. No pets. *813 SE Kane St (near downtown), Roseburg, OR 97470; (541) 672-2335 or (800) 540-7704; $.*

Steamboat Inn ☆ On the banks of a fly-fishing-only stream is this seemingly plain lodge and local landmark. Stay in a small knotty-pine cabin, a cottage with a kitchen, or a riverside suite. Meals are served in the main building every day (remarkably good family-style dinners by reservation only). Call for seasonal closures. *42705 N Umpqua Hwy (Hwy 138, 38 miles east of Roseburg), Steamboat, OR 97447-9703; (800) 840-8825; $$$.*

Cheaper Sleeps

Acker Lookout This fire lookout has only one cot, but you can fit three other people on the floor in sleeping bags. A .5 mile hike offers pleasant rewards: views of the Rogue Basin from sheer cliffs (be careful). The Forest Service provides the wood stove, propane refrigerator, stove, and oven, and you provide the rest. For $40 a night (three-night maximum), it's not a bad deal. For directions or reservations, call the Tiller Ranger District, (541) 825-3201.

More Information

Bureau of Land Management, Roseburg: *(541) 440-4930.*
Canyonville Information Center, Canyonville: *(541) 839-4258.*
Colliding Rivers Information Center, Glide: *(541) 496-0157.*
Diamond Lake Ranger Station, Toketee: *(541) 498-2531.*
Douglas County Parks Department, Roseburg: *(541) 957-7001.*
Myrtle Creek Information Center, Myrtle Creek: *(541) 863-3171.*
North Umpqua Ranger District, Glide: *(541) 496-3532.*
Roseburg Visitors Information Center, Roseburg: *(800) 444-9584.*
Southern Oregon Visitors Association, Medford: *(800) 448-4856.*
Sutherlin Visitors Center, Sutherlin: *(800) 371-5829.*
Tiller Ranger District, Tiller: *(541) 825-3201.*
Umpqua National Forest, Roseburg: *(541) 672-6601.*
Winston Information Center, Winston: *(541) 679-6739.*

The Rogue Valley

From the Rogue-Umpqua divide on the north, east to the edge of the Cascades, south to the California border, and west to the crest of the Siskiyou Mountains, including the Wild Rogue and Red Buttes Wildernesses, the east slope of the Kalmiopsis Wilderness, and the cities of Grants Pass, Cave Junction, Medford, Jacksonville, and Ashland.

Wandering, wild, and mischievous, Oregon's Rogue River is synonymous around the country with outstanding white-water rafting and kayaking, but could just as well be famous for its outstanding hiking, fishing, and camping. The Rogue Valley just about has it all when it comes to outdoor recreation.

Rogue River rises in three forks in the Cascade Mountains near Crater Lake National Park. The forks join by the time they disappear into Lost Creek Lake, the Rogue River reservoir that allows dependable rafting downstream when water flow would otherwise trickle to a near halt during the dry months of summer. Soon after leaving Lost Creek Lake, the Rogue passes near the most populous parts of Jackson County (Medford, Ashland, and Eagle Point) before entering Josephine County and flowing through the county seat of Grants Pass.

Up to this point, the Rogue isn't much different from Oregon's other major Cascade rivers: it runs through a spectacular canyon with waterfalls, is dammed into a lake, and is splashed in by the multitudes during the heat of summer. Pretty regular stuff.

All that begins to change west of Grants Pass, where the Rogue enters the Siskiyou Mountains. The canyon the river carves as it rushes to join the Pacific Ocean at Gold Beach is unique in many ways. The only coastal mountain canyon that can compare to the

Rogue is the canyon of the Illinois River, a tributary of the Rogue and another of Oregon's most spectacular rivers.

The Rogue's Hellgate section begins just downstream from Grants Pass. Followed closely by a paved highway and traveled heavily by jet-boats, Hellgate Canyon will never be confused for a wilderness area. Development along the river means more users wind up in this section than in the Rogue's wild section that begins farther downstream beneath the Grave Creek Bridge.

Access to the wild Rogue is tightly controlled, with about 150 rafters and kayakers allowed to enter the canyon each day during summer's regulated season. Jet-boat traffic is not allowed at all during summer, but a few brave pilots run all the rapids when the river is flush with water during winter. Boundaries of the Wild Rogue Wilderness were set just above the river corridor to allow continued use of motorized craft in the canyon.

Hikers face no limits on use of the riverside Rogue River National Recreation Trail, but summer's heat keeps it from being very busy with foot traffic. For the river's next 35 miles below the Grave Creek Bridge, only one windy, narrow, steep dirt road open to the public reaches the river's shore at Rogue River Ranch and Marial Lodge on the river's north bank.

The Rogue's wild section is famous among river runners around the world. Rapids like Rainie Falls, Mule Creek Canyon, Blossom Bar, and Devil's Staircase are subjects of many a tall tale around a riverside fire. Despite the Rogue's well-deserved reputation as a challenging whitewater river, its difficulty pales in comparison to the feisty Illinois River, which can only be run during a short rainy season in spring.

The Illinois, the Rogue's major tributary, joins the Rogue near Agness after its run through the Kalmiopsis Wilderness. The vast network of wilderness is proposed every few years for a national park, but emotions are mixed among local residents and no one has been willing to lead the charge through Congress. Whether it becomes a national park or not, the Rogue will continue working its magic on everyone who visits it.

Getting There

The Rogue River at Grants Pass is a 245-mile drive south from Portland on Interstate 5. Medford is 29 miles farther south from Grants Pass. Ashland is 12 miles beyond Medford, and the California border is 15 miles south of Ashland. East-west travel through the Rogue Valley is via US Highway 199 (US 199), also known as the Redwoods Highway, and on three state highways that head east of Interstate 5 into the Cascades: Highways 62, 140, and 66. County, National Forest, and Bureau of Land Management (BLM) roads fan out from the major highways. Medford-Jackson County Airport serves regional and commuter airlines.

Adjoining Areas

NORTH: **The Umpqua Valley**
EAST: **Crater Lake National Park, Mountain Lakes**
WEST: **Southern Coast**

inside out

Rafting/Kayaking

Rogue River: Wild Section

Despite a reputation that far exceeds the quality of its whitewater, the Rogue River still manages to send countless visitors away with smiles on their faces. The river's wild section, which passes through the coastal Siskiyou Mountains, has only two rapids that rank with the best in the West: Rainie Falls, which is usually passed through a channel built to help passage of fish, and Blossom Bar, a bona fide Class IV with more than its share of river booty at the bottom of the river. Use of the river is managed by the BLM staff at the **Rand Visitors Center,** (541) 479-3735. The place to check for **outfitters,** canceled private **permits,** current **conditions,** and **shuttle services,** the visitors center is 18 miles west of Merlin on County Rd 2400, which follows the Rogue River downstream and is called Merlin-Galice Rd (see Scenic Drives, below, for information on shuttle routes).

Getting on the river is the first order of business. Commercial clients who want to go with a guide service usually can find a spot on short notice, but it doesn't hurt to reserve well in advance for the most popular float periods. Self-outfitted boaters must go through a lottery system, or hope to pick up a canceled permit on short notice.

Access to the wild section of the Rogue during its controlled season, which begins May 15 and ends October 15, is evenly divided between private and commercial boaters. Total use averages 14,500 people per year during the regulated season when the bulk of the boating occurs. Use is not limited during the off-season, although rafting parties still need to obtain a permit and obey regulations regarding fire and human waste disposal.

The annual application season for Rogue River **permits for self-outfitted boaters** runs from December 1 through January 31. Tioga Resources of Roseburg, (541) 672-4168, which accepts applications in December and January, manages the lottery system on the Rogue as a concessionaire for the BLM. Recreation on the Rogue River is managed by the Medford District of the BLM, (541) 770-2200, which does not issue the original lottery permits but reissues canceled permits through the Rand Visitors Center.

About 7,200 applications are received from private boaters each year and about 900 permits are awarded. That's about a 12.5 percent success rate, but the percentage of satisfied customers is usually much higher because of multiple applications by party members and the availability of canceled permits. More than a few boaters take a gamble, show up at the Rand Visitors Center at 8am, pick up a canceled permit, and are on the river the same day.

Trips on the Rogue's wild section frequently begin at **Almeda Bar,** although some parties launch at the end of the road beneath the **Grave Creek Bridge.** Both sites can be reached by continuing on County Rd 2400 from the Rand Visitors Center. The takeout is at **Foster Bar,** a 30-mile drive upriver from Gold Beach on the Oregon coast via the Lower Rogue River Hwy. The 40-mile float through the wild section of the Rogue usually takes three or four days, although kayakers in a hurry have been known to push through in one long day. Boat launches can be reached by driving the Merlin-Galice Rd downstream from Merlin, the small town on I-5 3 miles north of Grants Pass.

Although many a beginner has rowed a raft or paddled a kayak down the Rogue River, an experienced party leader is usually a necessity because of the trouble the big rapids can cause. Rainie Falls, a 12-foot drop about 3 miles downstream from the Grave Creek Bridge, is usually run via a narrow fish ladder along the river's north bank during typical summer flows. Many boaters run straight through it during the big water of spring, but more than a few are fished out by buddies after their boats flip.

The Rogue has many Class II rapids and a few Class III over the next 16 miles to Rogue River Ranch, a national historic site managed by the Forest Service, and Marial Lodge, a private resort (see Rogue River Lodges, below, and Southern Coast chapter). Most parties stop along the way to tour a cabin used by Zane Grey when he wrote many of his colorful novels of Western adventure and settlement. The 4 miles below Marial to Paradise Bar Lodge are the most intense on the Rogue. The river passes through **Mule Creek Canyon,** a narrow slot in the bedrock that forces the entire flow of the river into its narrow channel. The whitewater is hardly noticeable, but the river's hydraulics and boils have enough power to take control of a raft and do whatever it wants with it.

Blossom Bar Rapids, usually the highlight of the trip, awaits 2 miles downstream of Mule Creek Canyon. Nearly everyone stops to scout the rapids, if only to watch how much trouble other river parties can get into as they pass through. A successful run requires entry on the left, then a hard pull back over to the right, and then a move toward the center. The section of river immediately below Blossom Bar magnifies the problems. The rare drownings on the Rogue usually occur here when swimmers can't be retrieved in time to avoid swimming the next mile of serious white-water through **Devils Staircase Rapids.** Paradise Bar Lodge is a popular stopping point just below Devils Staircase. The final 10 miles below the lodge to Foster Bar has many Class II rapids that seem anticlimactic. If the wind is blowing upriver from the Pacific, it can feel like a long stretch indeed.

As the hub of southern Oregon's river-running industry, the Rogue offers a trip for just about everyone. Numerous commercial outfitters lead **guided trips,** taking care of everything from rowing to cooking and set-ting up camp. Some even offer overnight trips in the Rogue River lodges, a unique river experience in the West. Commercial trips on the Rogue River are available from many outfitters in southern Oregon. Among those based in Josephine County are River Adventure Float Trips of Grants Pass, (800) 790-7238; Rogue River Guide Service of Grants Pass, (541) 476-2941; and Rogue Wilderness Adventures of Merlin, (800) 336-1647. Many of the Rogue's whitewater outfitters also design trips that cater to fisher-men when steelhead and chinook are in the river. For those who want to get themselves down the river but need some coaching and equipment, kayak classes are offered by Running Wild of Ashland, (541) 482-9283, and Siskiyou Kayak School of Jacksonville, (541) 772-9743.

A unique way to get downriver is in a vinyl kayak called an "orange torpedo." The little craft, more widely known as a Tahiti, is amazingly stable and may offer the most lively, bouncy ride of any whitewater boat. Oregon Torpedo Trips of Grants Pass, (541) 479-5061, began on the Rogue in the 1970s and has expanded to offer trips in similar equipment on rivers such as the Colorado in Arizona, the Salmon in Idaho, and the North Umpqua in Oregon. Paddlers usually spend a fair amount of time swimming while they learn the ropes, but the Rogue is a pool-and-drop river that makes it easy to collect gear at the bottom of rapids. Rainie Falls and Blossom Bar are easy to walk around and let the guides paddle through if you choose.

Rogue River: Hellgate Section and Upper Rogue

The Rogue River's **Hellgate Section** runs 34 miles downstream from the west edge of Grants Pass to Grave Creek and the beginning of the river's federally designated Wild and Scenic section. Part of the Hellgate section was protected as a recreational river in 1968 when 84 miles of the Rogue became one of eight rivers originally protected by Congress under the Wild and Scenic Rivers Act.

The Rogue's designated recreational section, which runs 27 miles from the **Applegate River** to **Grave Creek,** fits the definition of a recreation river to a T. The river receives intense recreational use by fishermen, rafters, and jet-boaters. The recreational section is closely followed by roads and has many parks and a few lodges on its shore. Hollywood has even taken note of the beauty by filming an occasional movie along the Rogue's Hellgate section, including part of *River Wild* with Meryl Streep and Kevin Bacon.

The Hellgate section has three main floating trips, although each can be combined or shortened by using any of the numerous parks and boat launches along the way. **Lathrop Landing,** located 5 miles west of Grants Pass on the Rogue River Loop Hwy on the north side of the river, offers a 14-mile float, mostly over flat water to **Hog Creek.** The 14 miles from Hog Creek to Grave Creek is the bread-and-butter run of the Hellgate section, flowing through many Class II rapids along the way. Many boaters reduce the section by floating the 4 miles between Almeda Park to Grave Creek, enjoying a near-continuous stretch of Class II water without having to deal with the permit system in place on the wild river below Grave Creek. At present, private recreational use is unlimited in the Hellgate section. Rafters should beware of the steady stream of jet-boat traffic that plies the waters of this stretch.

The Rogue River above Grants Pass also receives intense use, although much of the use is by fishermen and jet-boats pilots. Savage Rapids Dam, an irrigation diversion project, restricts navigability 4 miles east of Grants Pass. A lot of people are ready to tear the dam out, but the economic benefits provided by its irrigation pool are difficult to overcome. The river above the dam provides an enjoyable beginner float, plus an adrenaline-pumping Class IV drop over **Nugget Falls** just upstream of Gold Hill. This section is popular because of its easy access to I-5 at the town of Rogue River and the shorter time commitment than runs on the Hellgate and wild section. Local outfitters for this section include Arrowhead River Adventures of Eagle Point, (541) 830-3388, and Raft the Rogue in Shady Cove, (541) 878-3623.

Rental equipment for all parts of the river is available from Whitewater Cowboys of Merlin, (541) 479-0132, and Rogue Raft Rentals in Shady Cove, (541) 878-3623.

Illinois River

Now that you've run the Rogue, it's time to get serious and start thinking about running the Illinois. Along with the upper Owyhee and its forks in southeast Oregon, the Illinois is Oregon's most challenging stretch of whitewater that is run by commercial outfitters. Oregon, of course, has many difficult rivers and creeks that expert paddlers and kayakers enjoy, but the Illinois is one of the few rivers where novices can hop aboard a multiday commercial expedition and know that when it comes to white-water, they've had their money's worth.

The 79-mile-long Illinois River rises in Northern California's Klamath Mountains (basically the same range that is called the Siskiyou Mountains in Oregon), flows through the Kalmiopsis Wilderness, and joins the Rogue River about 25 miles above Gold Beach and the Pacific Ocean. The Illinois is an extremely unpredictable river and can usually be run only during the early spring rain and snowmelt season. That often means cold and uncomfortable camping during the three- or four-day trip, but rafters and kayakers occasionally need to do a little suffering to enjoy life in the big leagues of whitewater river running. A couple of **commercial outfitters** offer trips on the Illinois River, but the rain-driven nature of the river makes the river-running situation volatile; check with the **river manager** at the Siskiyou National Forest's Gold Beach Ranger District, (541) 247-3600, for a list of outfitters.

The district has been developing a limited-entry **permit** system for self-outfitted boaters on the Illinois. The plan, which should be in place for the 1999 boating season, would restrict access to two parties a day on Friday through Sunday during the spring season. Contact the ranger station listed above for answers to questions regarding individual access to the river; the Illinois is not a river that boaters can just hop on and run without up-to-date information on conditions, so anyone contemplating a float should take the time to obtain all pertinent information in advance.

The Illinois is totally at the mercy of the weather gods. Even though it may not rain on the river's rafting section, a pounding rainstorm on the headwaters in California can turn the river into an unrunnable torrent overnight. The only alternative may be to wait several days to get back on the river, or to hike out over some of Oregon's most rugged terrain without the benefit of a trail. And part of such a hike is likely to be through snow because usually winter hasn't let go of its grip on the mountains above the river while the boating season is in progress. Many rafters who have left their equipment deep in the canyon, thinking it would be safe to come back and retrieve it, have returned to find the best parts of their gear co-opted by the hermits and hillbillies who live in the Kalmiopsis. (If Oregon can ever match the rigors of *Deliverance,* possibly the best-known movie made about rafting, it's in the canyon of the Illinois.)

Trips on the Illinois begin with mandatory **registration** at the Selma Market, a store that, as its name suggests, is located in Selma on US 199 about 22 miles southwest of Grants Pass. The launch site is 15 miles north of the market on Forest Service roads. As for the Rogue River, contact the managing agency for authorized shuttle services. The Illinois River may be the only river in the world where rafters begin and end at places with the same name. The launch at (south) **Oak Flat** is at river mile 35. The take-out, also called (north) **Oak Flat**, is 31 miles downstream and 4 miles above the confluence with the Rogue.

With the river's quick rise and fall due to rain, every decision along the way can have an impact on a successful run or a miserable trip. But when things work out right, the Illinois can provide one of the ultimate whitewater experiences in Oregon.

The river has too many Class II rapids to count, three dozen Class III rapids, a dozen Class IV rapids, and one Class V, **Green Wall.** It's the level of the river at Green Wall that worries boaters. If the water is too low, the rapid can be too rocky to run or portage. If the water is too high, the waves and holes can be too big to survive in the event of a mishap. The favored flow is 800 to 2,500 cubic feet per second, although kayakers run it at much lower water in summer and rafters boast about squeezing past at double the maximum recommended flow. It's up to the party on the river to decide, but you can see why the Rogue might feel comfortable after a trip on the Illinois.

Weekend Tip: A weekend trip is possible from Portland, as well as from other cities of similar distance. Drive to Grants Pass on Friday after work and stay in a motel. Rise early on Saturday, register at the Selma Market, set up the shuttle, and drive to the launch. Run the upper part of the river on Saturday, finish the trip on Sunday, and drive home from Gold Beach. It's not the most relaxing way to spend a weekend, but few people at work on Monday morning will have better stories to tell.

Rogue River Lodges

Rustic lodges that line the banks of the Rogue River can turn just another river camping trip into an elegant experience, complete with hot showers, comfortable accommodations, and restaurant meals. The trouble with a lodge rafting trip on the Rogue is that you may never be satisfied with a river camping trip again. The wild section of the Rogue has three strategically placed lodges that can alleviate the need to bring along a tent, rain tarps, and cooking stoves. Unfortunately, the lodges are no secret and are often booked to capacity by long-time clients, mainly commercial outfitters and fishing guides. Small private parties, especially one or two boats, can occasionally sneak into an empty cabin or two that the larger parties don't need. The only way to find out for sure is to call for a reservation.

The Galice Resort, (541) 476-3818, located 15 miles west of Merlin on County Rd 2400, is upriver from the wild section of the Rogue but nevertheless caters to an assortment of river travelers. Unlike the next three lodges downstream, Galice Resort has convenient automobile access. Many a rafting party gathers at the resort for breakfast and to prepare shuttles before beginning the trip downriver.

Black Bar Lodge, located 10 miles below the Grave Creek launch, is the key to a successful lodge trip on the Rogue because it's strategically located as a first-night stop. If Black Bar has space available, either Marial or Paradise Bar Lodge downstream should be able to accommodate you for the second night on the river. Black Bar Lodge, (541) 479-6507, is located on the south bank of the river and relies on a gated road to provide supplies for the many rafting parties that stay in its cabins and chow down in its dining room. Even hikers on the Rogue River National Recreation Trail across the river make use of the lodge by scheduling the lodge staff to row across the river and pick them up.

Marial Lodge, (541) 474-2057, located 20 miles downstream from Grave Creek, sits just above the entrance to Mule Creek Canyon, one of the Rogue's more notorious stretches. The lodge can be reached by public road from the north, but it's a long, bumpy ride via the BLM's gravel road system. Management of the Rogue changes near Marial Lodge from the BLM on the east to the Siskiyou National Forest on the west. River users probably won't notice the difference.

Paradise Bar Lodge, (800) 525-2161, is 4 miles downstream from Marial and 24 miles down from Grave Creek. It sounds like a short distance, but rafters must negotiate Mule Creek Canyon, Blossom Bar, and Devils Staircase Rapids to get there. Access to Paradise Bar Lodge is easier than the lodges upstream because of a small airplane landing strip and a dock that caters to the jet-boat traffic on the lower river. Paradise Bar Lodge is a mandatory stopping place, whether a rafting party is staying overnight or not, because of its full-service saloon.

Other lodges downstream to the takeout are **Half Moon Bar Lodge,** (541) 247-6968, .5 mile below Paradise Bar Lodge; **Clay Hill Lodge,** (800) 228-3198, 5 miles farther down; and **Wild River Lodge,** (800) 228-3198, 31 miles below Grave Creek. **Santa Anita Lodge,** (541) 247-6884, is .25 mile downstream from the takeout at Foster Bar. All can shuttle non-boaters upriver from Gold Beach for overnight accommodations.

Rogue River floaters who can't find space in the lodges can choose from among the 52 designated **campgrounds** on a first-come basis, accessible either by boat or from the Rogue River Trail. The Rand Visitors Center, (541) 479-3735, issues a list of the campgrounds when boaters register.

Boating

To many visitors, the **Rogue River** is synonymous with **jet-boats** rather than rafts. While much of the jet-boat traffic plies the river upstream from Gold Beach in the Southern Coast country, Grants Pass is just too close to the busy vacation travel on I-5 not to cash in on the tourist jet-boat trade.

Tour boats leave docks just off downtown Grants Pass and run the river for 37.5 miles downstream to where the wild river begins at Grave Creek. Even for a rafter, a jet-boat ride is a great way to see the river. Pilots become intimately familiar with the river during their frequent trips and know exactly where to watch for wildlife and how to spot it. An all-day ride in a jet-boat can easily provide more wildlife sightings than a three-day raft trip because of the experience of the pilot. The largest jet-boat tour company on the upper river is Hellgate Jet Boat Excursions of Grants Pass, (800) 648-4874. Despite the tourist draw, jet-boats are not universally loved, to say the least, by residents of the river. The boats' noise can be unpleasant and their wakes can cause erosion. The BLM deals with the problem by tightly controlling the number and times of the launches by the commercial companies. Most pilots go out of their way to avoid conflict by cutting their engines and steering to direct their wake away from other river traffic.

Lake boaters spend most of their time in the Rogue Valley at **Lake Selmac,** a Josephine County Park and reservoir on McMullin Creek 2 miles east of Selma, and at **Applegate** and **Lost Creek Reservoirs,** both US Army Corps of Engineers irrigation projects. More boating, especially attractive to water-skiers, is available 20 miles east of Ashland at Hyatt and Howard Prairie Reservoirs (see Mountain Lakes chapter).

Lake fishermen use the same three lakes, but are especially attracted to **Applegate Lake.** The 988-acre impoundment on the Applegate River, 15 miles south of Jacksonville, has a 10mph speed limit that makes water-skiers go elsewhere. **Lost Creek Reservoir,** a 3,430-acre impoundment on the Rogue River 30 miles northeast of Medford, has a Corps of Engineers boat launch at Takelma and another at Stewart State Recreation Area. (For more on the lakes, see Camping and Parks, below.)

Camping

State and County Parks

With 1,389,544 visitor days during a recent two-year biennium, **Valley of the Rogue State Park** ranked second behind Yaquina Bay as the most popular park in the Oregon system. Of course, the park's location a short drive from I-5 near the town of Rogue River doesn't hurt business. The park is divided into four camping loops, one strictly for tents and another loop with six yurts tucked among the RV units. The park has 146 RV sites and 21 tent sites, as well as picnic facilities shaded by large madrona and oak trees along 3 miles of Rogue River frontage. It also has a boat launch, a 1-mile interpretive trail, and evening programs during the summer. Valley of the Rogue is open year-round and accepts reservations at (800) 452-5687; for general information, call (541) 582-1118. The park is located just off I-5 at exit 45.

Stewart State Park, the recreation gateway to the Rogue River's Lost Creek Reservoir, is 35 miles north of I-5 on Hwy 62, midway between Medford and the south entrance to Crater Lake National Park. The campground is open from February 1 through October 31 but does not accept reservations (except for group sites). The park has a large, lakeside day-use area, plus a boat launch used by fishermen and water-skiers. A marina includes a large mooring facility, plus a store and cafe. Stewart State Park is located on the 10-mile hiking trail system maintained by the US Army Corps of Engineers on Lost Creek Reservoir.

Jackson County operates two campgrounds in the Rogue Valley— Emigrant Lake and Cantrall-Buckley—while Josephine County maintains five.

Emigrant Lake Park, 5 miles south of Ashland at exit 14 off I-5, has 42 camping units, a twin-tube 280-foot water slide, and 12.5 miles of lake shoreline. **Cantrall-Buckley Park,** 7 miles southwest of Jacksonville on Hwy 238, has 1.75 miles of frontage on the Applegate River. The county's park system is also funded by renting out the pavilion in Jacksonville where the Britt Festival stages music concerts throughout the summer. For information on these county parks and group camping reservations, call (541) 776-7001.

Josephine County has campgrounds along the Rogue River, beginning 3 miles west of Grants Pass with **Schroeder Park** and continuing downstream with **Whitehorse, Griffin, Indian Mary,** and **Almeda.** All are on the river's south bank, accessible via the Rogue River Loop Hwy, which is on Lower River Rd. Indian Mary is the pride of the county and is the largest, with 90 camping units. Call Josephine County Parks, (541) 776-7001, for information.

Away from the Rogue River, the county has campgrounds at **Lake Selmac** (see Boating, above) and **Wolf Creek** on Lower Wolf Creek Rd. Lake Selmac has 90 campsites and Wolf Creek 40. For equestrians who don't have a horse, **guided horseback rides** are available from Lake Selmac Trail Rides, (541) 597-4610, at Lake Selmac Park.

US Forest Service and BLM Campgrounds

The Applegate Ranger District, (541) 899-1812, is based in Jacksonville and is part of the Rogue River National Forest. The Applegate District has numerous small campgrounds, mostly with a dozen sites or fewer, in the national forest southwest of Ashland just north of the California border. Most of the campgrounds surrounding Applegate Lake are situated on a nearby stream. Rarely do they fill up, but just in case **reservations** are available at five campgrounds by calling the Hart-Tish store at (541) 899-1544 on **Applegate Lake.** Campers looking for wheelchair access should try **Hart-Tish Park** for day use and camping and **Swayne Viewpoint** for its accessible pathway and view.

The Galice Ranger District, (541) 471-6500, is part of the Siskiyou National Forest and manages recreation on national forest land west of Grants Pass. All of its campgrounds are small, with fewer than 10 sites, except for the 27 sites at **Sam Brown Campground.** Sam Brown and other campgrounds are located along Forest Rd 25, which leaves the Merlin-Galice Rd 1 mile west of Indian Mary County Park. Forest Rd 25 is the main recreational access to this part of the Siskiyou National Forest, other than the Rogue River itself. **Big Pine Campground,** named for a 250-foot-high ponderosa pine, has four short nature loops. The longest, a .75-mile sloping trail, is called Challenge Loop. The campground is 12 miles south of the Rogue River on Forest Rd 25.

The Illinois Valley Ranger District, (541) 592-2166, also part of the Siskiyou National Forest, has some campgrounds in the US 199 corridor that are busy because of their location en route to Oregon Caves National Monument (see Hiking/Backpacking, below). The only overnight accommodations in the national monument are at **Oregon Caves Chateau,** (541) 596-3400. Campgrounds along the Oregon Caves Highway (Hwy 46), which leaves US 199 at Cave Junction and travels 20 miles east to the national monument, are **Grayback** and **Cave Creek.** The road beyond Grayback is narrow and winding, so leave the RV in the campground. Grayback is the only campground in the Siskiyou National Forest on the national reservations system. To guarantee a spot, call (800) 280-2267. Grayback, 12 miles east of US 199, has 39 sites and Cave Creek, 3 miles farther, has 18.

The BLM plays only a minor role in the Rogue Valley camping scene and its two campgrounds are rather remote. **Elderberry Flat Campground** is 20 miles north of Gold Hill, 20 miles east of Wolf Creek, 20 miles south of Milo, and 20 miles west of Shady Cove—in other words, 20 miles deep into the middle of nowhere. Elderberry Flat is 19 miles northeast of the town of Rogue River and I-5, then 9 miles north on W Evans Creek Rd. The 9 camp units are kept busy by off-road-vehicle riders and by hunters during the fall. The creek has some nice swimming holes, and the campground has barrier-free facilities.

Tucker Flat Campground is even smaller than Elderberry Flat. It has 8 sites, is even more remote, and is one of the most beautiful locations accessible by car in the Rogue Valley. The campground is located on the north shore of the Rogue River near Marial Lodge (see Rogue River Lodges, above) at the end of the 33-mile Grave Creek–to–Marial BLM byway.

Scenic Drives

The BLM's **Grave Creek to Marial National Back Country Byway** begins at the Grave Creek Bridge (see Rafting/Kayaking, above) at the entrance to the wild section of the Rogue River. The one-lane gravel road with turnouts is well marked along the way, but having a BLM Medford District map in hand provides a good measure of reassurance. The BLM maps are sold in sporting goods stores, at the BLM office in Medford, and at the Rand Visitors Center (see Rafting/Kayaking, above). A full tank of gas and a spare tire with plenty of air also help ease the strain on the brain. All designated BLM byways are designed to accommodate passenger autos. The byway climbs through the high country along the north side of the river before dropping to the river to reach Tucker Flat Campground and Marial Lodge (see Rogue River Lodges, above). Rogue River Ranch, a national historic site managed by the BLM, is just upriver from the lodge. From the campground it's a short walk downstream to the beginning of Mule Creek Canyon, one of the most spectacular sections along the Rogue. Also within a 4-mile one-way hike west on the Rogue River Trail are Blossom Bar Rapids and Paradise Bar Lodge. Walk toward the river from the campground to find the trail. This is one BLM byway that makes it deep into the backcountry.

The road along the north rim of the Wild Rogue Wilderness used to be an alternate shuttle for raft trips, but the connecting leg between Powers and Agness was washed away by a 1997 flood and may take years to rebuild (see Southern Coast chapter). Other shuttle routes are via the Redwoods Highway through California, a 200-mile trip used only when winter snow blocks the other route, and the BLM's **Galice-Hellgate National Back Country Byway.** The byway begins at I-5 near Merlin and travels west toward Galice Resort as County Rd 2400, also called Merlin-Galice Hwy (see Rafting/Kayaking, above). The byway branches when it reaches Forest Rd 25 (see Camping, above). The branch that follows the Rogue continues to Grave Creek, where it joins Grave Creek to Marial Byway. The southern branch heads up into the mountains out of Galice and comes out 50 miles later near the Foster Bar takeout, where float trips on the Rogue River end. The road along this southern rim of the Wild Rogue Wilderness is paved all the way but is only one lane wide with frequent pullouts.

Parks

Jackson County has a string of picnic parks along the Rogue River downstream from Shady Cove. First comes **Upper Rogue Park,** followed by **Takelma** and **Dodge Bridge.** All are on the north bank of the river, on Rogue River Dr. The county also operates **Sports Park,** 13 miles northeast of Medford via Hwy 62, Hwy 140, and Kershaw Rd, where activities include a shooting range, drag strip, go-cart track, softball fields, and fishing ponds.

As part of its recreation facilities on Lost Creek Reservoir, the US Army Corps of Engineers also has a park called **Takelma Park.** The Corps also has picnic grounds at **River's Edge** and **McGregor** on Lost Creek, which is 35 miles northeast of Medford on Hwy 62.

Designed by the creator of San Francisco's Golden Gate Park, **Lithia Park** on Pioneer Ave in downtown Ashland was one of the most graceful city parks in the state until the 1997 floods left it a muddy mess. The park has been rebuilt and is once again the city's showplace, visited by many who attend the annual Oregon Shakespeare Festival. The park runs for 100 acres behind the outdoor theater, providing a lovely mix of duck ponds, Japanese gardens, grassy lawns, playgrounds, groomed or dirt trails for hiking and jogging, and the pungent mineral water that gave the park its name. There's even an ice-skating rink in winter.

Josephine County has a dozen day-use parks along the Rogue, in addition to day-use facilities in most of its campgrounds (see Camping, above). The busiest is **Tom Pearce Park,** located on the east side of Grants Pass. From Grants Pass Pkwy, turn south on Agness and follow directions to Foothill. Go under the I-5 overpass and follow signs to the park, which offers a large picnic area, jogging trails, and facilities for disc golf, horseshoes, and volleyball.

Oregon state parks with day-use facilities in the Rogue Valley are **Casey,** just below the dam at Lost Creek Reservoir on Hwy 62; **Tou Velle,** on the Rogue River 9 miles north of Medford off Hwy 62; **Ben Hur Lampman,** 16 miles east of Grants Pass along I-5; and **Illinois River Forks,** 1 mile south of Cave Junction on US 199. All offer picnicking and fishing.

The BLM manages the **Gold Nugget Picnic Area** on the Rogue River 1 mile east of Gold Hill on Hwy 234, plus the **Little Applegate** and

Kenney Meadows Picnic Areas up the Little Applegate River south of Medford (see Camping, above). All three can accommodate wheelchair users and Little Applegate has an accessible nature trail.

The **Applegate Trail,** a southern branch of the Oregon Trail, is signed along highway parks throughout its course through Oregon. The trail split off from the California Trail along the Humboldt River in Nevada and worked its way past what would become Klamath Falls, Medford, and Grants Pass to its terminus in the Willamette Valley town of Dallas. The trail celebrated its 150th anniversary in 1996. It blazed the route for what was to become I-5, the most traveled corridor in the Pacific West.

No visit to the Rogue Valley is complete without a stop at **Hellgate Overlook,** which sits high on the cliffs above Hellgate Canyon and offers outstanding views of the Rogue River. The BLM overlook is 9.2 miles west of Merlin on Merlin-Galice Rd, just east of the Hellgate Bridge over the river. Parking is available in a small lot adjacent to the road. Although the site is not designed for picnicking, a quick bite while enjoying the beauty of the canyon wouldn't be out of order.

The Forest Service's Applegate Ranger District has a 45-site picnic ground at **McKee Bridge,** the first of many recreation facilities that line County Rd 859 between Jacksonville and Applegate Lake.

Hiking/Backpacking

Table Rocks is a 3,042-acre area cooperatively managed by the BLM, (541) 770-2200, and The Nature Conservancy. The upper and lower rock mesas (the upper is to the east and the lower to the west) rise 800 feet above the Rogue Valley, 5 miles north of Medford's exit 30 from I-5 on Table Rock Rd. The **Upper Table Rock Trail** (moderate; 1.25 miles one way) is off Modoc Rd, which veers east of Table Rock Rd at the base of the 800-foot-high mesa. At the intersection of Modoc Rd, continue on Table Rock Rd as it veers west to reach the **Lower Table Rock Trail** (moderate; 1.75 miles one way). The rocks and their vegetation are managed as an outdoor classroom for the many children who make field trips to the area. Unfortunately, the vegetation includes vigorous stands of poison oak. Watch out also for ticks and rattlesnakes and the cliffs at the edges of the tabletops. The Nature Conservancy owns a 500-acre preserve near Table Rocks where 150 acres of an Oregon white oak savanna still survive, one of the last oak groves on the floor of the Rogue Valley. The conservancy is working to open the area to the public.

Jacksonville, the mining town that dates to 1851, is the site of the **Sarah Zigler Interpretive Trail.** The trail begins at the Britt Gardens in town and leads past scenic creekside settings on Jackson Creek, where an 1854 gold strike was made, and into the Zigler Woods.

The **Sterling Mine Ditch Trail System** has 20 miles of trail 11 miles southeast of Ruch in the Little Applegate Valley on County Rd 859. Gold was discovered on Sterling Creek, 8 miles southeast of Jacksonville, in 1854. The trail system spreads throughout the Little Applegate Valley and includes the Sterling Mine Ditch, Wolf Gap, Bear Gulch, and Tunnel Ridge Trails. The Ditch Trail itself is fairly flat and begins at the BLM's Little Applegate Recreation Area. The trail system is open to hikers, bikers, and equestrians. Check with the Medford BLM, (541) 770-2200, for information sheets on its major recreation opportunities in the Rogue Valley.

For a bird's-eye view of the Rogue Valley and the city of Ashland, hike the **Grizzly Peak Trail** (moderate; 3 miles one way) to the 5,922-foot summit. The view also includes the Cascade volcanoes from Diamond Peak to Mount Shasta. To reach the trailhead, leave I-5 at exit 14 in Ashland and drive east on Dead Indian Memorial Hwy for 7.2 miles. Turn north on Shale Creek Rd and watch for signs to the trailhead. At BLM Rd 38-2E-9.2, drive 4.8 miles to begin the hike.

The BLM's **King Mountain Rock Garden,** located midway between Elderberry Flat (see Camping, above) and Wolf Creek on I-5, is an area of critical environmental concern regarding protection of its serpentine habitat. Occurring in only a few places around the world, serpentine outcroppings occur as islands of rocky soil and sparse vegetation set amid an area of lush vegetation. The area has a relatively high elevation for Western Oregon (5,265 feet at the top of King Mountain) and supports two protected species of plants (Siskiyou fritillaria and Umpqua phacelia) that flower in the spring shortly after the snow melts. To reach the rock garden, take exit 76 from I-5 at Wolf Creek and drive east on BLM Rd 33-5-21. Called Coyote Creek Rd, follow it east for 8 miles, turn north on BLM Rd 33-5-26, and drive 2 miles to the undeveloped parking area just below the summit. The area is open only to foot traffic.

Rogue River Trail

The 40-mile-long **Rogue River National Recreation Trail** offers a somewhat unique one-way hiking experience. Most long-distance trails require an oftentimes difficult shuttle arrangement before or after a trip, or a start at both ends with exchange of car keys along the way. That's not the case with the Rogue. Due to the demand for shuttles by rafters, it's easy for hikers to arrange in advance for a ride back to where they started. The river trail also offers a lodge-to-lodge hiking opportunity, thus alleviating the need to carry tents, sleeping bags, and cooking gear. Contact the BLM's Rand Visitors Center, (541) 479-3735, for **information** on the trail, a free guide booklet, a list of shuttle services, and a directory of campsites along the way. Permits are not required.

The Rogue River Trail can be hiked in either direction: beginning on the west at Foster Bar or the east at Grave Creek (see Scenic Drives, above). It may seem easiest to walk it downhill east to west, but it doesn't really matter due to the 700 feet of ups and downs along the way. The trail is on the north side of the river, so boat access to lodges on the other side must be arranged in advance (see Rogue River Lodges, above). While the trail is surrounded on either side of the river by the 36,000-acre Wild Rogue Wilderness, the bottom of the canyon itself was left outside the wilderness area to allow for special management of motorized boats, lodges, and the high volume of recreation.

Beginning at **Grave Creek** and hiking downstream, 12-foot-high Rainie Falls is the first major sight at 1.8 miles. Whiskey Creek Cabin comes at 3.1 miles, .25 mile up the creek from the river. The cabin was built by a miner in 1880 and is on the National Register of Historic Places. All cabins located along the Rogue, except the commercial lodges, are for viewing only, as they are historic sites or private.

Black Bar Lodge (see Rogue River Lodges, above) lies across the river at 9.6 miles. Battle Bar, site of a battle between the cavalry and the Takelma Indians in 1855, is at 16.6 miles. Winkle Bar, the cabin where Zane Grey lived, comes at 17.5 miles. The historic Kelsey Pack Trail, which begins near Winkle Bar, makes a 4.5-mile loop before returning to the main trail at Quail Creek. Rogue River Ranch, built by a settler in 1803, comes at 23 miles, where attractions become more numerous. The ranch, also listed on the National Register, is followed by Marial Lodge at 24.3 miles, Mule Creek Canyon at 24.4 miles, the end of Marial Rd at 25 miles, Blossom Bar Rapids at 27.1 miles, Paradise Bar Lodge at 28.3 miles, and the parking lot at **Foster Bar** at 40 miles (see Rafting/Kayaking, above).

The Rogue River can be blistering hot during summer, so most long-distance hikes occur during spring or fall. Black bears are frequently seen along the river and will take any opportunity to pilfer food along the way. The canyon is also home to rattlesnakes.

The best way to see **Rainie Falls,** a congregating point for spawning salmon and steelhead, is by hiking a 2-mile trail on the south bank of the Rogue from the Grave Creek Bridge, rather than the main Rogue River Trail on the river's north side. Since the main part of the falls is on the south part of the river, the view of rafters plotting a way through or around the falls is best from the north bank. Park at the Grave Creek Bridge (see Rafting/Kayaking, above) and follow the south bank of the river to the west.

Pacific Crest Trail

The 2,638-mile **Pacific Crest National Scenic Trail** (PCT) enters Oregon in the Rogue River National Forest about 24 miles south of Medford.

Somewhat surprisingly, the trail is on the west side of I-5 through much of Northern California, before it crosses back east of the freeway at Siskiyou Summit. The trail covers 30 miles above the Rogue Valley before it enters the Mountain Lakes country 10 miles east of the freeway near Soda Mountain. The trail is jointly managed by the Ashland Ranger District, (541) 482-3333, and California's Klamath National Forest, (916) 842-6131, which covers a small slice of Oregon.

The PCT crosses Siskiyou National Forest Rd 2025 almost at the point where it enters Oregon. Rds are never far from the trail until after it crosses I-5 and begins the transition from the Siskiyous to the Cascades. The system of roads makes the trail easy to reach, but the trail's wilderness feel found elsewhere is lacking.

Popular day hikes along the Siskiyou part of the trail are **Wrangle Gap** east to **Siskiyou Gap** (moderate; 3.8 miles one way), both easily accessible by Forest Rds 20 and 22, and **Grouse Gap** on Forest Rd 20 east to the national forest boundary on County Rd 1151 (easy; 3.5 miles one way). The trail closely follows the north side of County Rd 1151, which connects the **Mount Ashland** ski area with I-5, as it winds its way to the east. **Pilot Rock,** a 5,908-foot-high outcrop, is a well-known landmark near the trail 2 miles east of I-5.

Kalmiopsis and Red Buttes Wildernesses

The 180,000-acre **Kalmiopsis Wilderness** is one of Oregon's largest tracts of unspoiled land. A harsh, rugged country, the area's rocks prevented large tracts of forests from growing. The lack of soil, coupled with the quick runoff after a rainstorm, spared the land from timber harvest. The wilderness is named for the kalmiopsis shrub, a pre–Ice Age relic that resembles a small rhododendron. The kalmiopsis blooms pink during June.

The eastern portion of the wilderness has three main entry points: south Oak Flat, Briggs Creek, and McCaleb Ranch. (The Illinois River float trips begin and end at places that are both called Oak Flat. They are 31 river miles apart.) The north Oak Flat trailhead for the **Illinois River Trail** (difficult; 27 miles one way) is at the float-trip takeout and is managed by the Gold Beach Ranger District, (541) 247-3600. To reach the trailhead, drive 27 miles east of Gold Beach along Lower Rogue River Rd. Where the road crosses the Illinois River, turn south and follow the Illinois 4 miles upriver to the trail-head. The wilderness boundary is 8 miles upriver at Silver Creek, so back-packing is mandatory to spend much time in the wilderness. The trail continues to the Briggs Creek trailhead on the east side of the wilderness.

The **Briggs Creek** trailhead is 2 miles north of the south Oak Flat boat launch. The final 2 miles of road beyond south Oak Flat are suitable only in a four-wheel drive. To reach the trailhead, turn northeast off US

199 at Selma, drive Illinois River Rd 17 miles to south Oak Flat, and walk the final 2 miles to the trailhead. The 27-mile Illinois River Trail is the only well-maintained, long-distance hiking route in the Kalmiopsis Wilderness. It crosses over the summit of 3,975-foot Bald Mountain as it makes its way between Briggs Creek and south Oak Flat.

The turnoff for McCaleb Ranch trailhead comes 5 miles before south Oak Flat. A Boy Scout Camp is located at the ranch, where a .5-mile trail leads to a thrilling suspension footbridge across the Illinois River. The McCaleb Ranch and Briggs Creek trailheads are located within the Illinois Valley Ranger District, (541) 592-2166.

Due to the remoteness of the country, overnight trips are safest when arrangements are made in advance to be dropped off at a trailhead and picked up at another. Hikes on seldom maintained trails across the wilderness using this technique are possible, but stream crossings are problematic during late summer. Many of the hiking routes follow trails to mining claims that are still being operated within the wilderness boundary.

Red Buttes Wilderness covers 20,323 acres, mostly along the Siskiyou Mountains crest, with 80 percent of it inside California. The western lobe of the wilderness is in Oregon and has four trailheads on a network of national forest roads that wind their way toward the California border. Red Buttes is 4 miles south of Oregon Caves National Monument, but the state highway that leads to the caves ends there and doesn't approach the wilderness. The most popular destinations in the Oregon part of the wilderness are **Tannen Lake,** a steep hike of 1 mile from the farthest west trailhead in the wilderness, and the old-growth western red cedar forest along **Sucker Creek.** The 18-mile **Boundary Trail** connects Tannen Lake with **Grayback Mountain** 6 miles north of the wilderness boundary. At 7,048 feet, Grayback is the highest peak in Josephine County, and the trail climbs right over the top. Maps for the Siskiyou National Forest and the Red Buttes Wilderness are essential for exploring the area. Pick them up at the Illinois Valley Ranger District, (541) 592-2166, in Cave Junction.

Oregon Caves National Monument

Though Oregon is famous for its lava tubes in the Cascades (see Bend and the Upper Deschutes River chapter), Oregon's most spectacular cave is enshrined as Oregon Caves National Monument in the Siskiyou Mountains. The Siskiyou National Forest surrounds the 480-acre preserve. Oregon Caves is 50 miles south of Grants Pass via Hwy 199, the Redwoods Highway, which continues on to Crescent City. Turn south at Cave Junction and drive Hwy 46 to Oregon's oldest national monument, dating to 1909.

Cave tours are offered daily, except on Thanksgiving and Christmas. Tours last for 1.5 hours and are not recommended for those with heart, breathing, or walking difficulties. The cave tour covers 500 stair steps, most of which are steep and wet, and the trail that leads back to the visitors center at the end of the tour drops with a grade of 16 percent. Children must be able to climb a set of test stairs unassisted and must be at least 42 inches tall to join a tour. Cost is about $6 for adults and $3.75 for children under 12.

Tours begin whenever groups of 16 are formed, except during winter when five tours depart on a set schedule. Park information is available from monument headquarters, (541) 592-2100, or the Illinois Valley Visitors Center, (541) 592-2631. The visitors center is located in Cave Junction, near where the cave access road leaves US 199.

The cave tour leads through a series of grottos and passageways, many of them filled by fantastic limestone formations. The National Park Service has worked diligently in recent years to restore damage done to the cave by early visitors who thought nothing of breaking off a sample and taking it home. Among the most interesting features are the Petrified Garden, Niagara Falls, the Grand Column, and the Ghost Room. The cave continues to add to its stalactites and stalagmites, although the process is too slow for humans to notice.

While a visit to the cave requires the accompaniment of a tour guide, the national monument has a 6-mile trail system that visitors are welcome to explore on their own. The **No Name Trail** (easy; 1.5-mile loop) passes tumbling mountain streams and mossy cliffs set amid a dense forest. The **Cliff Nature Trail** (easy; 1-mile loop) has trailside signs that describe natural features, including conifer forests, marble rock outcrops, and mountain vistas. The **Big Tree Trail** (moderate; 3.5-mile loop) climbs 1,100 feet to one of the largest Douglas fir trees in Oregon. The trail wanders through an old-growth forest with vistas down into the surrounding valleys.

Biking

The Rogue Valley has an ardent corps of **mountain bikers,** who have helped establish one of Oregon's better trail systems. Beware, however, that much of the riding is on the hills that surround the river and is on the steep side. Most rides are rated difficult. With the numerous roads that head into the mountains above the Rogue Valley, road-bike riding opportunities are nearly unlimited. Many national forest trails allow access to mountain bikes, but not the Rogue River Trail. Check with the Applegate Ranger District, (541) 899-1812, in Jacksonville or the Ashland Ranger District, (541) 482-3333, in Ashland for detailed descriptions of the best national forest rides.

One exception to the difficult-is-king rule is the loop trail system that circles Applegate Lake, the reservoir on the **Applegate River** south of Jacksonville (see Camping, above). An 18-mile system of singletrack and paved and gravel roads circles the lake. Elevation varies only 200 feet, but the trail has plenty of ups and downs along the way. A frequent starting point is **French Gulch** trailhead, 25 miles south of Medford just east of the Applegate Dam on County Rd 859. The east shore of the lake is most scenic because roads approach the shoreline in only a few places. For some additional distance, the 2.8-mile **Grouse Loop Trail** makes a loop into the forest from the lakeside Hart-Tish Picnic Area. The 7.5-mile **Stein Butte Trail** climbs from the upper end of the lake east to the 4,400-foot level of Stein Butte.

Ashland's mountain bikers don't even need to drive out of town to begin their rides. **Lithia Park** downtown (see Parks, above) is the beginning of the **Lithia Loop** mountain-bike route through the Ashland watershed. The 25-mile loop has an unfortunate circumstance in that most of its 3,000 feet of climbing begin in the first 5 miles.

Conversely, the 15-mile one-way **Siskiyou Crest Trail** begins high, at the 6,600-foot level in the Mount Ashland ski-area parking lot (take exit 6 from I-5 and drive 8 miles west on Mount Ashland Rd), and is only moderately difficult to Dutchman Peak. If you continue riding beyond Dutchman Peak rather than retracing the trail back to the ski area, you'll learn why the local mountain-bike race is called Revenge of the Siskiyous.

Southern Oregon is a hotbed for road-bike riders, who rack up the miles by riding the **paved roads** in the lower elevations of the Rogue Valley. Because of the colorful blossoms, Medford's annual Pear Blossom Festival, (541) 734-7327, in early April is one of the more popular times to see the valley from the seat of a bicycle. Medford has a busy 3-mile bicycle/pedestrian path through the heart of town along **Bear Creek Greenway,** accessible a few blocks east of downtown.

Fishing

The **Rogue River** continues to offer some of the West's best fishing. Although fishing is not as good as it used to be (it never is, is it?), the Rogue still draws anglers from distant reaches of the planet for the chance to hook a wild chinook or coho salmon, or the mighty steelhead of late summer. Fishing on the river is managed by the Oregon Department of Fish and Wildlife's Roseburg office, (541) 440-3353. Check the statewide synopsis, available at tackle stores, for regulations.

As the fish migrate upriver, anglers in the Southern Coast country have easy access to the river from roads and motorized boats. The situation changes in the wild section, where drift boats, rafts, and the Rogue

River Trail are the main forms of access from Foster Bar upriver to Grave Creek. Above Grave Creek, the river is never far from a road all the way to its headwaters in the Mountain Lakes country. (Jet-boats, however, are allowed in the Rogue from Foster Bar upriver to Blossom Bar all year and can run the entire river, should their pilots be so daring, outside the May 15 to October 15 regulated-use season (see Rafting/Kayaking and Boating, above).

The Rogue has runs of spring and fall chinook, summer and winter steelhead, and hatchery steelhead. Wild trout and coho are available but must be released unharmed. The fish runs in the river intermingle between seasons and upriver destinations, so there is usually something available for the taking all year long. Fishing for steelhead is best from September through February. Chinook fishing is best in August and September, while coho are most abundant in October. Migrating fish are usually easiest to catch in pools below and above rapids.

Guided fishing trips through the river's wild section should be arranged well in advance, especially trips that use the riverside lodges rather than tent camping. Check with the lodges for outfitters who offer trips, or obtain a list of Rogue River guide services from the Oregon Outdoors Association, formerly the Oregon Guides and Packers Association. The association's booklet of members and services is called the "Oregon Outdoor Recreation Guide," and a copy is available by calling the Oregon Tourism Commission at (800) 547-7842. Local visitors centers will have brochures of the numerous guide services.

Fishing on the Rogue below Grants Pass is concentrated from the mouth of the Applegate River downstream to Almeda Bar. Bank access is convenient at the numerous parks that line the river. Above Grants Pass, **Pierce Riffle County Park,** 3 miles east of town on Foothill Blvd, is a popular spot for spring chinook, as is the **Gold Ray Pool** just downstream from Tou Velle State Park (see Parks, above). The river has a significant catch-and-release fishery for trophy-size trout just below Lost Creek Dam at Casey State Park, 35 miles northeast of Medford on Hwy 62.

Reservoir fishing in the Rogue Valley often means bass. The relatively low elevations of **Lost Creek Reservoir** (1,872 feet above sea level) and **Applegate Lake** (1,987 feet) let the fish grow fast and big (see Boating, above). Lost Creek Lake is a well-known producer of largemouth bass, with lots of fish around 5 pounds and big ones up to a former state record of 11 pounds. Both reservoirs have wild and hatchery trout, smallmouth bass, and a variety of panfish. Trolling is usually most productive, although bank anglers find a way to fill their creels. With a 10mph speed limit, fishing on Applegate doesn't mean contending with the water-ski and cruising traffic that Lost Creek Reservoir gets.

While the Rogue and the reservoirs in its system attract the bulk of the fishing interest, a number of smaller streams are productive for trout fishing with flies. A good source on fly-fishing is the Ashland Fly Fishing Guide Service, (541) 482-1430.

Wildlife

The lower Rogue River is a wildlife watcher's dream, with **black-tailed deer** and **wild turkeys** so accustomed to the comings and goings of people that they are easy to photograph close up. Paradise Bar Lodge (see Rogue River Lodges, above), just below the end of the Rogue's wild section, is a good place to rise early and walk amid a flock of gobbling turkeys. Jet-boat rides on the river often give passengers a rare opportunity to see a **black bear** in the wild, as well as **river otters** playing on the bank or **osprey** diving for a meal. **Steelhead** and **chinook salmon,** anxious to get upriver to spawn, leap from the water as they try to swim past Rainie Falls.

Closer to the cities of the Rogue Valley, the state's **Denman Wildlife Area,** (541) 826-8774, provides water habitat for nesting and migrating waterfowl, as well as habitat for upland game birds. The area has a short self-guided interpretive trail with excellent wildlife viewing throughout the year. To reach the area, take exit 31 from I-5 in Medford and drive north on Table Rock Rd for 4 miles. Turn east on East Gregory Rd and drive 1 mile to the wildlife area.

The state also maintains a **fish hatchery** just below Lost Creek Dam on the Rogue River, 9 miles east of Shady Cove on Hwy 62. The Cole M. Rivers Fish Hatchery, (541) 878-2235, raises rainbow trout, coho, spring and fall chinook, and summer and winter steelhead. The observation deck overlooks a collection pond and other ponds that hold adult salmon. A viewing room also overlooks the spawning area and display ponds feature trout and steelhead. A nearby platform on Butte Creek provides viewing of naturally spawning spring chinook. March through October is the best time to see the variety of activities.

The varied park system that surrounds the cities of the Rogue Valley provides outstanding **birding.** Whitehorse County Park, 6 miles west of Grants Pass on Lower River Rd, mixes **forest birds** with **water birds** that live along the Rogue River. Lake Selmac County Park, 22 miles southwest of Grants Pass on US 199, is home to a variety of forest birds, including **ruffed and blue grouse, mountain quail,** and **screech owls.** Medford's Prescott Park includes 3,571-foot Roxy Ann Butte, 6 miles east of town off Hillcrest Rd. Most forest birds that nest in southern Oregon can be found along the rough 2-mile road that leads to the summit. Tou Velle State Park, located 4.5 miles north of the Medford Airport on Table Rock Rd, mixes riparian and forested habitats. Lower and Upper Table Rocks, a short drive farther north, attract birds that prefer a dry, deciduous habitat with oaks and brush.

Downhill Skiing

With all the other forms of outdoor recreation available in the valley of the Rogue, it stands to reason that the relatively dry valley would be nowhere close to a good ski area. Wrong! **Ski Ashland,** the medium-size ski area that simply refused to die, offers some of Oregon's most challenging downhill skiing and snowboard terrain atop 7,533-foot-high Mount Ashland.

After a series of dry winters during the early 1990s, owners of the ski area were ready to dismantle the chairlifts and ship them to a ski area they owned at Stevens Pass, Washington. That would have been the end of lift-served skiing at Mount Ashland. Before the lifts were packed up and shipped north, the owner gave the citizens of the Rogue Valley the opportunity to purchase the ski area. After a furious fund-raising effort, $1.7 million was collected just in time to stop the lift from heading north on I-5. The Ashland Parks Department took title to the ski area, turned management over to a private concessionaire (the same group that had been running the ski area all along), and snow returned in abundance as Oregon's climate changed to a wet cycle in the mid-1990s.

When conditions are good, weekend crowds from the Rogue Valley and as far south as Redding, California, can swamp the lifts and lodge. The money paid for acquisition of the ski area didn't cover the expense of converting the lifts to high-speed quads, like the ones at Mount Bachelor and Mount Hood. Another chairlift, to serve intermediate terrain west of the existing lifts, is planned for 1999 because the ski area has been banking money since the change in ownership.

When conditions are bad at Ski Ashland, they can be really bad because the summit bears the initial brunt of Pacific storms. Trees can snap, power lines can go dead, and the road can require hours to plow. The ski area will always have its ups and downs, due to insufficient snow or high freezing levels that bring rain, but the new ownership means that it will be ready for skiers of the Rogue Valley when conditions are good.

Ski Ashland is only 18 miles from Ashland, with the first 10 miles on I-5 south of town to exit 6 at the Siskiyou Summit. From the exit, drive 8 miles west on the Mount Ashland Rd. It has four chairlifts and an interesting old lodge that looks like it would have been at home in 16th-century England. Shakespeare's influence extends from the festival in Ashland all the way to the highest peak in Oregon's Siskiyou Mountains.

The Ariel double chair climbs to just below the summit of the mountain, serving an open bowl and some steep runs. The Windsor chair doesn't climb quite so high and is more protected when winds howl across the summit from the nearby Pacific Ocean. The Sonnet and Comer chairs serve beginners and some short intermediate trails near the lodge. The ski area operates daily and for night skiing Thursday through Saturday. For ski area information, call (541) 482-2897; for snow conditions call (541) 482-2754.

Hot Air Balloons

Not all the hot air is trapped at the bottom of the Rogue Valley during the heat of a summer day. Some air is intentionally made hot, usually just after dawn, to fill the envelope of a hot air balloon and send adventurers aloft for a unique perspective from a couple thousand feet in the air. Oregon Adventures Aloft, (800) 238-0700, runs its hot-air-balloon adventures from the Rogue River. Every day is a new adventure in a balloon, which gets its mobility at the whim of the wind, but a flight may offer views of Rogue River rapids, fields of wildflowers, or, if the balloon gets high enough, a comprehensive view of one of Oregon's most beautiful valleys.

Gold Panning

Along with the Blue Mountains of Eastern Oregon, the Siskiyou Mountains that rise above the Rogue Valley were and still are among the most productive places for gold mining in the state. Most of the big stakes have long since been discovered and worked for all they're worth, but there's still enough gold in the tributaries of the Rogue to keep a steady stream of recreational miners coming to the valley.

The **Butte Falls Recreational Panning Area** has two sites that are managed by the Medford District of the BLM, (541) 770-2200. The Gold Nugget site is 2 miles north of Gold Hill on Hwy 234, and the Tunnel Ridge site is a dozen miles up the Little Applegate River from Ruch. Gold panning is permitted on nearly all streams and rivers that run through campgrounds managed by the BLM or Forest Service. It is also allowed on state lands below the vegetation line on navigable rivers and ocean beaches. It is not allowed, however, indiscriminately on federal land, unless permission is granted from the holder of a mining claim. Rather than panning blindly, most new prospectors begin by visiting areas that are known to be productive, which include Gold Nugget and Tunnel Ridge. Other gold panning and dredging sites reserved for the public include **Little Applegate,** just upstream from Tunnel Ridge, and Rogue River in the Hellgate recreation section.

The Applegate Ranger District, (541) 899-1812, maintains 4 fee sites where it costs a dollar a day to pan in areas adjacent to campgrounds. All the sites are located along Rogue River Forest Rd 10, which travels from Ruch up the Applegate Valley to Applegate Lake.

outside in

Attractions

The remarkable success of the Oregon Shakespeare Festival, now well over 50 years old, has transformed sleepy **Ashland** into a town with, per capita, the best tourist amenities in the region. The festival draws a total audience of some 350,000 through the nine-month season to this town of 18,000. Amazingly, the town still has its soul: for the most part, it seems a happy little college town, set amid lovely ranch country, that just happens to house one of the largest theater companies in the land.

The **Oregon Shakespeare Festival** mounts plays in three theaters. In the outdoor Elizabethan Theater, which seats 1,200, appear the famous and authentic nighttime productions of Shakespeare (three different plays each summer). Stretching from February to October, the season for the two indoor theaters includes comedies, contemporary fare, and some experimental works. Visit the exhibit center, where you can clown around in costumes from plays past. There are also lectures and concerts at noon, excellent backstage tours each morning, and Renaissance music and dance nightly in the courtyard. The best way to get information and tickets (last-minute tickets in the summer are rare) is through a comprehensive agency: Southern Oregon Reservation Center, (541) 488-1011 or (800) 547-8052, PO Box 477, Ashland, OR 97520. The festival's box office phone is (541) 482-4331, or try www.mind.net/osf/.

Schneider Museum of Art, at the south end of the Southern Oregon State College campus, is the town's best art gallery, usually with several rotating exhibits. It's open Tuesday through Saturday, (541) 552-6245. The **Pacific Northwest Museum of Natural History** offers 16,000 square feet of dioramas, hands-on science labs, and interactive exhibits popular with school groups. There's a modest admission charge at 1500 E Main St, daily (closed Monday and Tuesday in winter), (541) 488-1084.

Medford, southern Oregon's largest city, may not win any contests with nearby towns for prettiness, but it is the center of things in this part of the world. The city is well known across the nation, due to the marketing efforts of Harry and David's, the mail-order giant known for its pears, other fruits, and condiments. **Harry and David's Original Country**

Store, South Gateway shopping center near Medford's southern I-5 exit (1314 Center Dr), offers "seconds" from gift packs and numerous other items, as well as tours of the complex, which is also the home of Jackson & Perkins, the world's largest rose growers; (541) 776-2277.

The town of **Jacksonville** started with a boom when gold was discovered in Ruch Gulch in 1851. Then the railroad bypassed it, and the tidy little city struggled to avoid becoming a ghost town. Much of the 19th-century architecture has been restored; Jacksonville now boasts 85 historic homes and buildings, some of which are open to the public. The strip of authentic Gold Rush–era shops, hotels, and saloons along California St has become a popular stage set for films. Jacksonville is also renowned for antique shops.

The **Britt Festival,** an outdoor music and arts series, runs from late June through September on the hillside field where Peter Britt, a famous local photographer and horticulturist, used to have his home. Listeners gather on benches or flop onto blankets on the grass to enjoy open-stage performances of jazz, bluegrass, folk, country, and classical music, as well as musical theater and dance. Quality of performances varies, but the series includes big-name artists from the various categories, and listening to the music under a twinkling night sky makes for a memorable evening. Begun in 1963, the festival now draws some 50,000 viewers throughout the summer. For tickets and information, contact the Britt Festival office, (541) 773-6077 or (800) 882-7488; brittfest@aol.com; www.mind.net/britt.

Jacksonville Museum, housed in the stately 1883 courthouse, follows the history of the Rogue Valley with plenty of photos and artifacts. Another section displays some works by Peter Britt. The adjacent children's museum lets kids walk through various miniaturized pioneer settings (jail, tepee, schoolhouse). There's a small admission charge for nonresidents; (541) 773-6536.

Valley View Winery, the area's oldest, is at Ruch, 5 miles west of Jacksonville; (541) 899-8468. The **winery** maintains another tasting room in town, in Anna Maria's, 130 W California St, (541) 899-1001. The Cave Junction area is home to two of Oregon's better wineries: Foris, 654 Kendall Rd, (541) 592-3752, and Bridgeview, 4210 Holland Loop Rd, (541) 592-4688. Both have tasting rooms open daily.

Restaurants

Bel Di's ☆☆ This lovely country dinner house has a grand view of the Rogue River. The ambience, attentive service, and soups are more special than many of the entrees. *21900 Hwy 62 (north side of Shady Cove's bridge), Shady Cove; (541) 878-2010; $$.*

Bella Union ☆ This restaurant, in a century-old saloon, has everything from pizza and pasta to elegant dinners to picnic baskets for the summertime Britt Festival. Lots of wines by the glass, too. *170 W California St (center of town), Jacksonville; (541) 899-1770; $$.*

Chateaulin ☆☆☆ A block from the theaters is this romantic cafe that bustles with before-and-after crowds gathered for the fine French cuisine. House specialties are pâtés and veal dishes, but seafood and poultry are also impressive. Service is always polished. *50 E Main St (down walkway from Angus Bowmer Theater), Ashland; (541) 482-2264; $$.*

Firefly ☆☆ Prepare for a visual feast as well as interesting fare at this storefront dinner house—presentation is extremely artistic. Fish, lamb, salmon, chicken, and duck entrees show up on the menu, and portions tend to be more than ample. *15 N First St (.5 block from Main), Ashland; (541) 488-3212; $$.*

Genessee Place ☆ Genessee is an oasis. Try quiche or potpies for lunch. Dinner entrees might be homemade cannelloni, fresh seafood, or veal specialties. There's a second Genessee in Grants Pass. *203 Genessee St (2 blocks east of I-5, between Main and Jackson Sts), Medford; (541) 772-5581; $$.*

Hamilton House ☆ Count on the salmon being exquisite at this handsome dinner house. A daily fresh sheet is likely to feature fish, and there are the usual steaks. Two can often get by for $30. *344 NE Terry Lane (south Grants Pass exit off I-5, 3 blocks to Terry Lane, left 1 block), Grants Pass; (541) 479-3938; $.*

Hungry Woodsman ☆ The Woodsman is a testimonial to the forest products industry (old saws and logging memorabilia adorn the walls). The menu is pretty basic: steak, prime rib, shrimp, lobster. Locals like it. *2001 N Pacific Hwy (3 blocks west of Rogue Valley Mall), Medford; (541) 772-2050; $$.*

Il Giardino ☆ Order the divine risotto when you place your reservation. It's not on the menu and it's time-consuming, but they love to cook here and are anxious to please. The place is intimate and can seem crowded. *5 Granite St (1 block from Shakespeare Festival), Ashland; (541) 488-0816; $$.*

Jacksonville Inn ☆☆☆ Often considered the area's best, this inn's intimate dining room serves continental and vegetarian cuisine. Order dinner in seven courses or à la carte; there's a well-stocked wine cellar, too. Upstairs, rooms boast four-poster beds; there are also three cottages. Reserve rooms in advance. *175 E California St (town's main thoroughfare), Jacksonville; (541) 899-1900; $$.*

Monet ☆☆ This gentrified French restaurant in a gracious house has become the talk of Ashland. The owners, established restaurateurs, go out of their way to make interesting vegetarian choices. The wine list goes on and on. Try for outdoor dining in summer. *36 S 2nd St (.5 block from Main St), Ashland; (541) 482-1339; $$.*

The Winchester Country Inn ☆☆ This century-old home, now a restaurant and inn, has gardens, gazebo, and country furnishings. The menu is ambitious, from Vietnamese to lamb to salmon du jour. In addition, there are 18 pretty guest rooms. Pampered guests get a full breakfast. *35 S 2nd St (.5 block from Main St), Ashland; (541) 488-1115; $$.*

Cheaper Eats

Ali's Thai Kitchen Atmosphere is zilch at this hole-in-the-wall, but the food's good, it's cheap, and there's a lot to choose from. The spring rolls are grand. Ditto the phad Thai. Beef entrees are better ignored. *2392 N Pacific Hwy, Medford; (541) 770-3104; $.*

Brothers Breakfast is the most popular meal at this deli and restaurant. No wonder: there are 20 omelets, and potato pancakes, breakfast burritos, and bagels and lox. Lunch and dinner too. *95 N Main St, Ashland; (541) 482-9671; $.*

Geppeto's Here's a lower-cost alternative with something for everyone. Locals describe the menu as "Italian-Ashland." Loosely translated, that would mean a multitude of pastas and fussier fare sharing billing with veg-head favorites. *345 E Main St, Ashland; (541) 482-1138; $.*

Mac's Diner Mac's is a paean to the '50s with neon and pictures of James Dean and Marilyn. You might try one of the "convertibles"—hot sandwiches with their tops down. Don't miss the mashed potatoes. *22251 Hwy 62, Shady Cove; (541) 878-6227; $.*

Wild River Brewing Company What started as a microbrewery has grown into an appropriately noisy and decidedly decent pizza and pasta joint. The house bread is nice stuff. *595 NE E St, Grants Pass; (541) 471-7487; $.*

Lodgings

(For Rogue River Lodges, check listings here and under Rafting/ Kayaking, above; see also Lodgings in Southern Coast chapter.)

Ashland Clearinghouse This reservation service for lodging in the area mainly handles the more pricey B&Bs. It's worth a call regardless, for two reasons: (1) these folks know their stuff and can make suggestions, and (2) they also represent a number of house rentals, available by the night or week. You might be able to get a good deal on a place for a party of six or eight. Off-season, they can find you some bargains at the better lodgings at rates as low as $55. *(541) 488-0338 or (800) 588-0338.*

Country Willows ☆☆☆ This country home close to downtown offers a peaceful view, several lodging options (including a cottage), and a pool and hot tub. There are running and hiking trails and ducks and goats on the property. *1313 Clay St (4 blocks south on Clay St from Siskiyou Blvd), Ashland, OR 97520; (541) 488-1590 or (800) 945-5697; $$$.*

Morical House Garden Inn ☆ With lovely rooms in the main house and two garden suites with spas, this inn is a good bet. Views of fields and mountains and a hearty breakfast, along with a garden with waterfalls and roses, don't hurt. *668 N Main St (1 mile north of downtown and theaters), Ashland, OR 97520; (541) 482-2254 or (800) 208-0960; $$.*

Morrison's Rogue River Lodge ☆ This Rogue River lodge, favored by fishermen, can actually be reached via a paved road. There are guest rooms and cottages—most people prefer the latter. A four-course dinner and breakfast are included. Closed December through April. *8500 Galice Rd (15 miles west of I-5, Merlin exit), Merlin, OR 97532; (541) 476-3825 or (800) 826-1963; $$.*

Mount Ashland Inn ☆☆☆ There's now an outdoor spa at this huge, posh cedar-log cabin with beamed ceilings, stone fireplace, and stained-glass windows. Beds are covered with quilts, and each unit has a private bath. *550 Mt Ashland Rd (follow signs to Mt Ashland Ski Area), Ashland, OR 97520; (541) 482-8707 or (800) 830-8707; $$$.*

Oregon Caves Chateau ☆ Set in a deep canyon, this restful old lodge has splendid views, fireplaces, and down-home cooking. The rooms are nothing fancy, but they're clean. Both the dining room and the lodge are open seasonally—call ahead. *Oregon Caves National Monument (Rte 46, 20 miles east of Cave Junction, follow signs), Cave Junction, OR 97523; (541) 592-3400; $$.*

Paradise Resort ☆ The one-time dude ranch is now a full-service resort, and activities abound: swimming, boating, tennis, golfing, biking or hiking, relaxing in a hot tub. The 15 large rooms have no TVs or phones—the emphasis is on peace and quiet. *7000-D Monument Dr (Hugo or Merlin exit off I-5, west to Monument Dr), Grants Pass, OR 97526; (541) 479-4333; $$.*

Peerless Hotel ☆☆ Old rooms in this 1900 hotel have been merged into new B&B units, two of them suites, and filled with eclectic antiques. All have high ceilings and oversize bathrooms; several have Jacuzzis. *243 4th St (between A and B Sts), Ashland, OR 97520; (541) 488-1082 or (800) 460-8758; $$$.*

Romeo Inn ☆☆☆   This imposing home has plush rooms and suites decorated with contemporary and antique furnishings. The rooms all have
phones and private baths. The heated pool and hot tub are open year-
round. Breakfast reportedly satisfies through dinnertime. *295 Idaho St (at
Holly), Ashland, OR 97520; (541) 488-0884 or (800) 915-8899; $$$.*

TouVelle House ☆☆   This three-story mansion is a Jacksonville landmark
with tons of floor space and a pool and spa out back. Catering to the cor-
porate trade, the innkeeper will even handle your laundry. Come morning,
she'll feast you and catch you up on town gossip. *455 N Oregon St (4 blocks
north of California St), Jacksonville, OR 97530; (541) 899-8938 or (800)
846-8422; $$.*

Under the Greenwood Tree ☆☆☆   This farm with its orchard, riding
ring, rose gardens, old trees, and antique buildings is a popular wedding
site. Each room has a private bath and Persian rug. Breakfasts (the
innkeeper is a Cordon Bleu chef) are elaborate affairs. Celebrities like it
here. *3045 Bellinger Lane (exit 27 off I-5, Barnett to Stewart, left on Hull,
right on Bellinger), Medford, OR 97501; (541) 776-0000; $$$.*

Windmill's Ashland Hills Inn   If you prefer motels to B&Bs, this is
Ashland's best, with 159 rooms, several suites, a pool, and tennis courts.
There is a nonsmoking unit with 60 suites; rates include breakfast. *2525
Ashland St (Hwy 66 exit from I-5, 1 block east), Ashland, OR 97520; (541)
482-8310 or (800) 547-4747; $$.*

Woods House ☆   This 1908 home boasts a setting with terraced English
gardens. Out front is a busy street, so try for a carriage-house unit. Rooms
have private baths, the theaters are within walking distance, and the hosts
are gracious. *333 N Main St (4 blocks north of theaters), Ashland, OR 97520;
(541) 488-1598 or (800) 435-8260; $$.*

Cheaper Sleeps

Ashland Hostel   This hostel's dormitory-style rooms are open to all ages.
(If you're lucky, you might get a private room.) Hours are strict, and guests
share a common kitchen. The building is pleasant, and the theaters are
only blocks away. *150 N Main St, Ashland, OR 97520; (541) 482-9217; $.*

Green Springs Inn   If you don't mind driving 17 miles up a mountain
highway, this rustic lodge is one of the Ashland area's best values. The
motel sits behind a restaurant that offers great fresh pasta. The forest set-
ting is beautiful. *11470 Hwy 66, Ashland OR 97520; (541) 482-0614; $.*

Palm Motel and Houses   The Palm's 13 cabinlike units are on the cutesy
side, with white walls and green trim. Out back are several two- and three-

bedroom houses for rent in summer only. There's a small swimming pool. *1065 Siskiyou Blvd, Ashland, OR 97520; (541) 482-2636; $.*

Phoenix Motel If Ashland motels are booked, try this small, older motel about 6 miles north on old Hwy 99. It's been remodeled and has a tidy look. Some of the 22 rooms have kitchens. There's a swimming pool. *510 N Main St, Phoenix, OR 97535; (541) 535-1555; $.*

Royal Coachman Motel One of the best motels on the upper Rogue, offering basic, clean accommodations; some rooms have a river view (but no-view rooms are cheaper). Next door is a great restaurant, Bel Di's. *21906 Hwy 62, Shady Cove, OR 97539; (541) 878-2481; $.*

Timbers Motel It may be Ashland's best older motel, across the street from Southern Oregon University. The two-story structure has clean, comfortable rooms, and there's a small swimming pool on the premises. *1450 Ashland St, Ashland, OR 97520; (541) 482-4242; $.*

Wolf Creek Tavern This 1880s inn (a historic stagecoach stop and a state heritage site) is a charmer. The 8 rooms and 1 suite all have bathrooms. Downstairs is a homey parlor and a decent, inexpensive restaurant. *100 Front St, Wolf Creek, OR 97497; (541) 866-2474; $.*

More Information

Applegate Ranger District, Jacksonville: *(541) 899-1812.*
Ashland Chamber of Commerce, Ashland: *(541) 482-3486.*
Ashland Ranger District, Ashland: *(541) 482-3333.*
Bureau of Land Management, Medford: *(541) 770-2200.*
Galice Ranger District, Galice: *(541) 471-6500.*
Grants Pass–Josephine County Chamber of Commerce,
    Grants Pass: *(800) 547-5927.*
Illinois Valley Chamber of Commerce, Cave Junction: *(541) 592-2631.*
Illinois Valley Ranger District, Cave Junction: *(541) 592-2166.*
Jackson County Parks Department, Medford: *(541) 776-7001.*
Jacksonville Chamber of Commerce, Jacksonville: *(541) 899-8118.*
Josephine County Parks, Grants Pass: *(541) 474-5285.*
Medford Visitors Bureau, Medford: *(800) 469-6307.*
Rand Visitors Center (Rogue River Information Office),
    Galice: *(541) 479-3735.*
Rogue River Chamber of Commerce, Rogue River: *(541) 582-0242.*
Rogue River National Forest, Medford: *(541) 858-2200.*
Siskiyou National Forest, Grants Pass: *(541) 471-6500.*
Southern Oregon Visitors Association, Medford: *(800) 448-4856.*

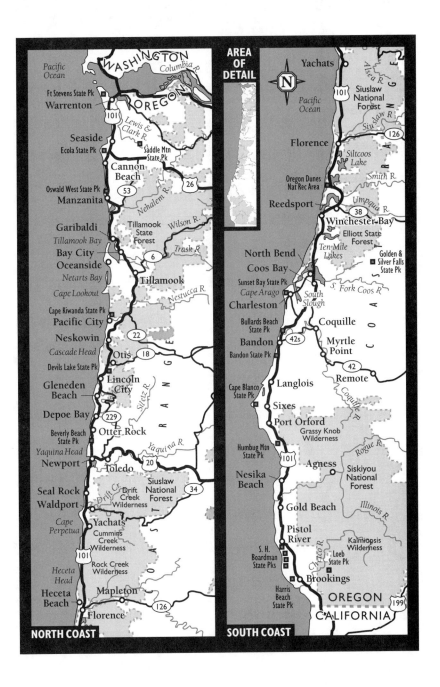

NORTH COAST

SOUTH COAST

Oregon
Coast

Northern Beaches   177

Tillamook   192

Lincoln City   211

Newport   222

Oregon Dunes   239

Bay Area   257

Southern Coast   274

Oregon
Coast

Northern Beaches

From the Clatsop Spit at the mouth of the Columbia River on the north, east to the crest of the Coast Range in Clatsop County, south to Cape Falcon near the Clatsop-Tillamook county line, and west to the Pacific Ocean, including the towns of Warrenton, Gearhart, Seaside, and Cannon Beach.

When Lewis and Clark established a winter camp at Fort Clatsop nearly 200 years ago, the only sign of Europeans off the Oregon Coast was the occasional passage of a sailing ship. How quickly times change in a couple of centuries.

As the nation looks toward the bicentennial celebration, beginning in 2004, of the explorers' journey, the Oregon Coast has become lined with strip malls, fast-food joints, and trophy homes that command stunning ocean views. The explorers' winter encampment in 1805–1806 is a rare protected enclave set amid the busy tourist strip between Seaside and Astoria. The explorers were also among the first Europeans to set foot on Oregon's Northern Beaches when they built a salt works at what would become the beach town of Seaside.

Despite the inevitable degradation of natural resources that follows human settlement, Oregon somehow managed to avoid some of the mistakes made elsewhere in the rush to develop the state's coastline. Visitors to the long, sandy beach strips have two governors to thank for their free and unfettered access to the beaches.

First was Oswald West, who in 1912 took the bold step of declaring all of Oregon's coastlines a public highway. Back before US Highway 101 plied the Oregon Coast from California to Washington, the beaches were the best way to travel long distances past the rocky head-lands and brushy coastal forests. With an eye at protecting more than a transportation corridor, West claimed everything below the high tide line to be public property.

While West's proclamation held developers at bay for more than a half century, the coast came under increasing pressure from developers to meet the growing second-home and recreation industries. When a motel fenced off part of the beach at Cannon Beach, citizens became outraged. Governor Tom McCall took the fight to the state legislature and helped pass the Oregon Beach Bill in 1967. The bill guarantees free and uninter-rupted use by the public of the entire shore to a surveyed line that follows the 16-foot elevation contour. The result is that residents, as well as visi-tors from around the world, have unrestricted use of one of the most beautiful coastlines in North America.

To better understand the significance of Oregon's coastal protection, just try walking along the coast in California, where private owners charge steep fees or close off access altogether to the coastal sand.

If Lewis and Clark could see what their journey of discovery led to, they would probably be a little disgusted by the congestion along the coastal highway and the fencing off of headlands by private owners. But at the same time, they would have to be pleased at how the public still retains its right to enjoy the coastal surf.

Getting There

Seaside, the center of the Northern Beaches, is a 79-mile drive northwest of Portland. US Highway 101 (US 101) is the main access to coastal beaches and towns.

Adjoining Areas

SOUTH: **Tillamook**

EAST: **Lower Columbia**

inside out

Camping

In the Northern Beaches, camping is usually synonymous with **Fort Stevens State Park.** The largest state park campground west of the Rockies, Fort Stevens has 253 tent campsites, 128 electrical sites, 213 RV sites with full utility hookups, and 9 yurts. Several campsites and 1 yurt are accessible by the disabled and are located near barrier-free rest rooms.

When fully occupied, as is frequently the case on summer weekends, Fort Stevens can be jammed by a couple thousand overnight guests and an equal number of day visitors. The result can be a crowded, noisy campground, complete with barking dogs, screaming children, and wailing sirens as the park staff attempts to keep order. It's not the pristine, lakeside camping that campers enjoy in central Oregon, but at least it puts lots of people close to miles of sandy Pacific Ocean beach.

Located 10 miles west of Astoria near the south jetty of the Columbia River, Fort Stevens's 3,763 acres are a 95-mile drive from Portland via Seaside and US 26. As the northern gateway to Oregon's coast, Fort Stevens also sees plenty of visitors from Washington's Puget Sound area, who find it relatively easy to get to and less developed than their own coastal vacation strip at Ocean Shores. Camping reservations can be made by calling Reservations Northwest, (800) 452-5687. Reservations are strongly advised on summer weekends, although it's always possible to pick up a cancellation. A KOA campground is located across the entry road to Fort Stevens and more than a few campers have found it to be more convenient and more accessible; call (800) 762-3443 for reservations.

In addition to all the camping space, Fort Stevens has two swimming areas at freshwater Coffenbury Lake, 5 miles of hiking trails, 9 miles of bike trails, viewing platforms at the south jetty of the Columbia River, and the military legacy of the Fort Stevens Military Reservation, which guarded the mouth of the Columbia from the Civil War through World War II and became part of the state park in 1976. The remnants of the *Peter Iredale,* an English sailing ship that ran aground during a storm in 1906, is a signature landmark in the park at the main day-use beach access area. Motor vehicles are allowed on the beach year-round south of the *Peter Iredale* to the town of Gearhart. They are also allowed to drive north of the shipwreck to the south jetty from May 1 to September 15, except from noon to midnight.

Fort Stevens is popular for good reason: except for a scattering of private RV parks, it's just about the only place to camp along Oregon's Northern Beaches. Other state park camping is limited to **Saddle Mountain State Park,** which has 10 tent sites 8 miles north of US 26 and Necanicum Junction on the Saddle Mountain turnoff, and **Oswald West State Park,** where 36 primitive campsites are .33 mile by trail from the parking area. Saddle Mountain, (503) 861-1671, like most of the smaller Oregon state parks, doesn't take reservations. The park's main attraction is a hiking trail to the mountain's summit (see Hiking/ Backpacking, below).

At Oswald West, the park staff offers wheelbarrows to campers to help them transport supplies from the parking area. The wheelbarrows keep the campground one of the most secluded of the Oregon coastal state parks system because this type of camping isn't for everyone. Named after the governor who claimed Oregon's beaches as public transportation corridors, Oswald West State Park, (503) 368-5154, is located on Cape Falcon 10 miles south of Cannon Beach on US 101. The campsites are tucked in the woods alongside Short Sand Creek, a short walk from Short Sand Beach. The park does not take reservations.

Camping drops off drastically during winter when the Northern Beaches receive the bulk of their annual rainfall. Just how much does it rain? Well, in 1996, an unusually wet year even by Oregon standards, Astoria collected 92.86 inches of moisture, nearly 30 inches above normal. All of it was rain because it's rarely cold enough to snow along the Oregon Coast.

Parks/Beaches

Oregon's beaches were made for picnickers. Because the water is too cold for most swimmers to enjoy, many beachgoers enjoy the coast by locating a scenic spot, having lunch, and watching the scenery change throughout the day. Although the work of man has done little to improve the beauty of Oregon's coast, construction of highways and beach parks have made it easy to enjoy. Because all of Oregon's beaches are publicly owned, all it takes is a parking area and a trail to reach what amounts to one of the largest public parks in the country.

Fort Stevens State Park begins the north–south parade of Oregon's coastal parks. The largest state park campground in Oregon, Fort Stevens also has four beach access points for day use. The parking lots are designated with letters A through D, beginning from the south at the main entry road and continuing north to the mouth of the Columbia. An observation platform at road's end at parking lot C gives viewers a close-up look at the busy Columbia River shipping lanes and the grass-covered dunes of Clatsop Spit. When it comes times for lunch, it may be best to head inland into designated tree-sheltered picnic areas where the wind doesn't blow as strongly as on the beach and where sand isn't another layer of a sandwich. (See Camping, above, for details on Fort Stevens.)

Heading south from Fort Stevens on US 101, major beach access state parks are **Del Rey Beach,** 3 miles south of the Fort Stevens turnoff and 2 miles north of Gearhart; **Ecola State Park,** 2 miles north of Cannon Beach where US 101 enters town; **Tolovana Beach,** 1 mile south of downtown Cannon Beach; **Arcadia Beach,** 3 miles south of Cannon Beach; **Hug Point,** 5 miles south of Cannon Beach; and **Oswald West State Park,** 10 miles south of Cannon Beach. The towns of **Gearhart** and **Seaside,** Oregon's largest coastal vacation destination, also provide access to miles of sandy beaches. All of the beaches are worth visiting; it's usually a matter of which one is closest to where you are when you want to hear the sound of crashing waves.

Besides Fort Stevens and Oswald West, Ecola State Park is the other gem of the Oregon parks system along the Northern Beaches because of its outstanding views, its pocket beaches, and its trail system. The 1,310-acre park caps a headland just north of Cannon Beach and is famous around the world for the stunning photographs that are taken there. Views include **Tillamook Rock,** a mile offshore with an inactive lighthouse perched atop its steep cliffs (the former light station was built offshore more than 100 years ago and abandoned in 1957; today it's a columbarium named "Eternity at Sea"), and **Haystack Rock,** the signature landmark of Cannon Beach that is accessible during low tide. One of the largest off-shore monoliths along the Oregon Coast, Haystack Rock has some inter-esting tide pools at low tide. Climbing is strictly prohibited because, in the past, too many people have been stranded by high tide.

Ecola State Park has a hikers' camp 1.5 miles north of the road end at Indian Beach picnic area. The trail to the camp continues north over Tilla-mook Head and comes out at Seaside (see Hiking/Backpacking, below).

Hiking/Backpacking

The **Oregon Coast Trail** is a 350-mile route that closely follows the coast-line between the Columbia River on the north and the California border on the south. For a free trail guide, call the State Parks information center at (800) 551-6949. The trail provides a variety of experiences, everything from hiking a footpath through coastal forests and walking on miles of sandy beach to hoofing it on city sidewalks and streets in order to cross coastal rivers and estuaries.

Although a few hikers occasionally boast of walking the entire dis-tance in a single, nonstop trip, that's not the way most walkers experience the trail. Virtually all of the coastline can be divided into short day-hike opportunities, leaving hikers plenty of time to explore tide pools, soak in the view from headlands, and avoid hiking when high tides make condi-tions dangerous. Although parts of the Oregon Coast Trail are suitable for backpacking, a lack of campgrounds, unreliable fresh water, frequent detours to highways, and lack of solitude make a backpacking experience less than ideal. All of Oregon's state park areas along the coast are well signed along the highway, either on US 101 or its spurs that more closely approach the coast. Most parking lots have rest rooms and trails that lead to beaches. The thick coastal vegetation has been tromped down over the years so that informal paths exist where developed trails are absent.

The northern 16 miles of the Oregon Coast Trail are along wide, sandy beaches between **Clatsop Spit** and **Gearhart**. To reach the beginning of the trail at the Columbia River, drive to the last day-use parking area in Fort Stevens State Park (see Parks/Beaches, above). The beaches were built by sand deposited by the Columbia River, the same way the famous Long Beach Peninsula on the Washington side of the river was created. The Coast Trail veers inland to cross several streams on city streets in Gearhart and Seaside, before rejoining the beach and heading south to Tillamook Head at the south end of **Seaside.** The trail passes a monument in Seaside where members of the Lewis and Clark expedition spent the early part of 1806 boiling seawater to make salt for preserving meat during their homeward journey.

The **Tillamook Head Trail** (moderate; 6 miles one way), part of the Oregon Coast Trail, begins at the south end of Seaside and climbs 900 feet over Tillamook Head before joining the trail system in Ecola State Park north of Cannon Beach. The trail's northern terminus is at the end of Sunset Blvd in Seaside and its southern end is at the end of the road in Ecola State Park. The trail offers occasional ocean views, but the forest is often too thick to see much more than what lies immediately ahead. Clark's Viewpoint at 3.7 miles south of Seaside is thought to be the southernmost point of exploration by the Lewis and Clark expedition.

South of Ecola State Park, beach hiking extends at low tide for 9 miles past Cannon Beach to Arch Cape. **Hug Point,** 5 miles south of Cannon Beach, offers a fascinating look at how early settlers used the coast as a travel corridor. Hug Point could be used as a wagon road at low tide, but only after some judicious blasting cleared enough space to cross the headland. High tide will make hikers scramble up the beach to the highway to pass Hug Point.

Arch Cape marks the northern end of Cape Falcon, which is a well-known navigational landmark that juts 1.5 miles into the Pacific Ocean. The Oregon Coast Trail veers to the inland side of US 101 before crossing the highway as it makes the climb to Cape Falcon. The 8-mile segment of trail south from Arch Cape is the longest unbroken forested stretch of the Oregon Coast Trail. The **Cape Falcon Trail** (easy; 2 miles one way to the tip of the cape) begins at the day-use area in Oswald West State Park (see Camping, above), climbs 300 feet through an old-growth grove of Sitka spruce, and ends at the tip of Cape Falcon. The end of the cape offers views south to 1,631-foot Neahkahnie Mountain, also part of Oswald West State Park (see Tillamook chapter).

Despite all the hiking temptations on the coast, one of the best hiking opportunities is inland from the beaches at **Saddle Mountain.** At 3,283 feet, the mountain is the tallest in the northern Oregon Coast Range and is easily accessible off US 26. Turn north from US 26 about 1.5 miles east of the Necanicum junction and drive 7 miles on a steep, paved road to the small state park campground and trailhead. The **Saddle Mountain Trail** (difficult; 2.5 miles one way) climbs to 1,633 feet to views of the Pacific Ocean, the Columbia River, and the Cascade volcanoes. The trail has numerous switchbacks and passes many sensitive grassy meadows, so hikers should remain on the trail at all times.

Another unusual location nearby is the **Four-County Point Trail** (easy; 1.5 miles round trip), the only place in Oregon where the corners of four counties touch. The trailhead is on the north side of US 26, 3 miles west of the turnoff to Timber. A green and white roadside hiker sign marks the trailhead. The trail ends at a marker that notes the spot where Columbia, Clatsop, Tillamook, and Washington Counties meet. The **Sunset Rest Area** is located alongside US 26 another 6 miles northwest of the Four-County Point Trail. The rest area has a 1-mile nature loop trail.

Fort Stevens State Park (see Camping, above) has an outstanding pedestrian/bicycle trail system that allows hikers to keep their vehicles parked for the weekend if they choose. The park has 9 miles of hiking trails and 8.5 miles of paved bicycle paths that connect the campground with the beaches and the historic military museum. Trails lead to the wildlife-viewing areas of Trestle Bay just inside the Columbia River at Youngs Bay and through the 36 interpretive stops that explain the Civil War construction of Fort Stevens. Coffenbury Lake, the park's popular swimming and fishing spot, is circled by a 2-mile trail.

A string of parks between Warrenton and Hammond are connected by the **Warrenton Waterfront Trail.** Accessible from several locations along the waterfront, the flat trail skirts the Columbia River estuary along old railroad beds, dikes, and roads.

Cycling

The coast has a designated long-distance route for cyclists, the **Oregon Coast Bike Route.** Beginning on the north with the crossing of the Astoria-Megler Bridge from Washington, the route follows US 101 south to the California border. The total length is 368 miles, although that varies depending on the number of side roads ridden. Through-cyclists are encouraged to ride north to south because they will get a boost from prevailing winds to help them climb the 16,000 feet of total elevation they will encounter along the way. Trips that cover 50 to 60 miles per day average six to eight days.

Although logistically easier to complete than a coastal hiking trip, the Oregon Coast Bike Route is not without its unpleasantries. Bikers don't have the problems finding drinking water and campsites that hikers do, but they will need a high tolerance for heavy commercial and recreation traffic as they make their way along US 101 on its unmarked shoulder bikeway. Most drivers are accustomed to seeing cyclists along the highway and go out of their way to be courteous. The Oregon Department of Transportation's Bicycle/Pedestrian Program—Room 210, Transportation Bldg, Salem, OR 97310; (503) 378-3432—publishes a free map of the Oregon Coast Bike Route.

September is often the best month to cycle the Oregon Coast. Often dry and sunny, September also has less highway traffic than July and August. Cyclists beginning the trip from the north should check for the latest information with Bike and Beyond, 1089 Marine Dr, Astoria, (503) 325-2961.

Aside from long-distance cycling, biking the relatively flat roads around the Northern Beaches is a popular vacation activity. Roads and trails around Fort Stevens, Seaside, and Cannon Beach are busy with cyclists who are looking to escape the coastal fog. When the sun comes out on **Seaside's beach,** rental bikes designed to be ridden in sand are popular and are available either on the beach or from tourist shops at Seaside and Cannon Beach.

Canoeing/Kayaking

America's ultimate exploratory expedition, much of it made in dugout canoes, reached its chronological midway point when Lewis and Clark set up camp for the winter of 1805–1806 at Fort Clatsop. Located 3 miles up the Lewis and Clark River in the Youngs Bay section of the Columbia River estuary, Fort Clatsop was built by the explorers as their winter home as they prepared to retrace their journey the following summer to Missouri. Their fort has been reconstructed by the National Park Service and serves as the focal point of **Fort Clatsop National Memorial,** (503) 861-2471. The fort is 3 miles east of US 101 at a signed turnoff 3 miles south of Astoria.

In addition to the reconstructed fort, the park maintains the historical canoe landing near the spot where expedition members stored their five canoes during their winter encampment when it rained on 94 of 106 days. The park also offers modern canoeing facilities and may one day become the termination of the **Lewis and Clark Columbia River Water Trail** (see Lower Columbia chapter). The water trail is being built to connect Portland with the mouth of the Columbia via a series of campgrounds and shallow-draft boat facilities through the Lower Columbia country in time for the bicentennial celebration of the Lewis and Clark journey.

The Columbia estuary is popular with paddlers—both canoeists and sea kayakers—although a certain amount of experience is advised because of the river's current, the heavy shipping traffic, and the mudflats that appear at low tides. The Fort Clatsop canoe launch is a good spot for beginners because it's relatively sheltered from the estuary's challenges and still provides some interesting paddling both upstream and downstream.

Paddlers also use **Coffenbury Lake** in Fort Stevens State Park (see Camping, above) and a Clatsop County boat launch at **Cullaby Lake,** a small freshwater lake just east of US 101 midway between Gearhart and Warrenton. Dories occasionally launch at **Tolovana Beach** at the south end of Cannon Beach, as do surf kayakers (see Surfing/Windsurfing, below). Major boat harbors are located at marinas in **Warrenton** and **Hammond,** where experienced Columbia River charter fishing boat pilots wait to take fishermen across one of the most dangerous river bars in the world (see Fishing, below).

Fishing

Formerly one of the world's largest producers of Pacific salmon, the **Columbia River** has fallen on hard times recently. Loss of habitat and overfishing have combined to sharply reduce the river's production of chinook and especially coho salmon. Federal and state fishery managers have taken steps in recent years to reduce the harvest of fish, but they are having less success restoring spawning beds and making the river's dams less deadly to migrating fish.

Until the situation changes, salmon fishing **offshore** from the Northern Beaches will continue to be highly volatile. Most years will see short seasons, with strict quotas and limited fishing opportunities. When the designated number of fish are caught, usually coho, the season ends and fishermen need to switch to more plentiful **bottom fish,** which include ugly creatures such as cabezon and greenling, tasty swimmers such as lingcod and Pacific halibut, and the catchall category of rockfish: sea bass, snapper, and rock cod. The rockfish all taste about the same, but it takes a fisheries biologist to tell them apart.

Oregon still produces some individually large chinook salmon and sizable runs of coho, but upriver runs are so depleted that most fish are allowed to pass through coastal waters without facing the temptation of a hook. An exception is the famous **Buoy 10** season, when a designated area just inside the mouth of the Columbia usually sees a short, furious salmon season in August. For information, call the Oregon Department of Fish and Wildlife's information line, (503) 872-5263, or its Marine Region office at Newport, (541) 867-4741. Again, the situation is highly volatile and changes year to year. Coho salmon reared in net pens, where they are contained until they grow large enough to have enhanced opportunities to survive in the wild, have become a supplementary fishery in **Youngs Bay** and elsewhere in Oregon.

Other fish that spend their lives between fresh water and salt water include steelhead, sea-run cutthroat trout, sturgeon, and striped bass. Sturgeon are commonly taken in the Columbia estuary. Charter companies that operate offshore and inside the Columbia estuary, depending on the season and what type of fish are biting, include Deep Sea Charters out of Warrenton, (503) 861-2429, and Corkey's out of Hammond, (503) 861-2088).

Coastal **surf casting** is usually for a variety of bottom fish, as well as various types of surf perch. Albacore tuna usually run off Oregon's shore during summer, but it takes an unusually warm current to pull them to 50 miles from shore, where it's feasible for sport fishing charters to seek them.

Clam digging for razor clams is usually good on the beaches of Clatsop County, especially the beaches of Fort Stevens State Park. Best digging is during the lowest tides. The season runs daily from September 1 through July 15, but can be closed on short notice due to health dangers from eating the clams. Bag limit is 24 clams dug daily, regardless of size. A license is not necessary. Clams are taken from the Columbia estuary, but not nearly as many as from inland waters farther south along the coast. Many gas stations along US 101 rent shovels.

Trout fishing in the Northern Beaches country is mostly limited to the few freshwater lakes along the coast. **Coffenbury Lake** in Fort Stevens State Park (see Camping, above) is stocked annually with legal-size trout. **Cullaby Lake** on the east side of US 101 at Gearhart is a better bet for warm-water pan fish. The 22-mile **Necanicum River,** which joins the Pacific at Seaside, provides fair fishing for steelhead during the winter and spring drift-boat season. In order to rebuild the native cutthroat population, northern coastal streams are closed to fishing until late May and all trout fishing is catch-and-release.

Wildlife

With its location astride the Pacific flyway, Fort Stevens State Park is a good place for bird-watching. Because the park lacks a headland, however, birders usually combine a trip to the shores and estuary of Fort Stevens with a visit to the headlands of Ecola State Park or Cape Falcon to see all the birds that use the flyway.

Surprise sightings at Fort Stevens State Park (see Camping, above) have included **yellow-billed loons, Mongolian plovers,** and **Wilson's storm-petrel. Sandpipers, pelicans,** and **cormorants** are common along the shores and in the estuary. Parking lot D, located at the north end of Fort Stevens at Trestle Bay, has a short trail that leads to a blind with a choice location at the edge of the Columbia estuary. Parking lot C, located nearby at the South Jetty of the Columbia, overlooks the ocean and is a designated whale-watching site. The platform, however, is not high enough above the surf to provide consistent sightings of the **California gray whales** that swim by, going south in December and north in March. **Snowy owls** from the Canadian arctic show up in northwest Oregon every seven to eight years when their population booms and they are forced to expand their range. The owls' most recent appearance in significant numbers was 1997.

Ecola State Park is another of Oregon's 29 designated **whale-watching** sites. The park's headlands provide a good perch for watching for the mammals. The system of islands that make up Oregon's federal **coastal wildlife refuge** (see Tillamook chapter) begins offshore at Ecola. Bird sightings include **common murre, American black oystercatcher, rhinoceros auklet,** and **tufted puffin.**

Tide pools, rare along the Northern Beaches, can be found at Ecola Point in Ecola State Park and at Haystack Rock at the south end of Cannon Beach.

Surfing/Windsurfing

The best surfing sites in Oregon tend to be closely guarded secrets, although the surfers already know about them. The regulars rarely take the time to give pointers to newcomers. The water off Oregon's Pacific beaches is cold, usually between 50° to 60° throughout the year, but that doesn't stop surfers, windsurfers, and surf kayakers from playing in the waves. They tough it out by wearing thick neoprene wet suits and booties and go out for as long as they can stand it. If the waves or winds are just right, that could mean several hours.

The beaches of **Clatsop Spit,** just south of the Columbia River's South Jetty (see Parks/Beaches, above), attract some surfers and windsurfers throughout the year. It seems that conditions are at their worst during the good weather of summer, so Oregon's ocean sports enthusiasts have to be ready for the waves when the waves are ready for them. Spring is usually a good time for wind and waves.

Windsurfers not yet ready for the ocean surf can often find windy conditions inside **Youngs Bay.** They launch from the Warrenton Moorage Basin and can be seen sailing alongside US 101 as it crosses the Youngs Bay Bridge. When the wind doesn't cooperate, windsurfers can enjoy the trail and string of parks that connect Warrenton with Hammond by the Warrenton Waterfront Trail (see Hiking/Backpacking, above). A local windsurf shop is Pacific Wave, 2021 US 101, Warrenton, (503) 861-0866.

Some of Oregon's best surfing conditions are found at the **Seaside Cove** and point break, at the south end of Seaside at the intersection of Sunset Blvd and Ocean Vista Ave. The surf is protected from direct exposure to large winter swells by Tillamook Head. As the swells travel around the point, waves become more regular and surfers ride some of the biggest waves in the state. Waves 10 feet high are common under prime conditions.

Other surfing spots along the Northern Beaches include **Indian Beach** at Ecola State Park; **Haystack Beach** in Cannon Beach; several breaks between Cannon Beach and Arch Cape; and the famous **Short Sands Beach** on the south side of Cape Falcon in Oswald West State Park (see Camping, above). A good place for beginning surfers, Short Sands has enough variety throughout the year to also attract experts.

outside in

Attractions

Surely **Gearhart,** with its assortment of weathered-wood beachfront homes in shades of gray and white, is the town with the most (and the best) examples of Oregon Coast architecture. Fashionable Portlanders put their summer cottages here—some of which are substantial dwellings—when the coast was first "discovered." Unlike other coastal towns, Gearhart is mostly residential. The wide beach is backed by lovely dunes. **Gearhart Golf Course,** which opened in 1892, is the second-oldest course in the West—a 6,089-yard layout with sandy soil that dries quickly—and is open to the public, (503) 738-3538.

Seaside, the Oregon Coast's first resort town, has become quite crowded (its snarly summer traffic is second only to Lincoln City's). The hordes mill along Broadway, eyeing the entertainment parlors, taffy concessions, and bumper cars, and then emerge at **the Prom,** the 2-mile-long cement "boardwalk" that's ideal for strolling. Lately, they also head for the newly constructed outlet mall along US 101 on the town's north end. To escape the bustle, browse the shelves at Charlie's Turnaround Books, 111 Broadway, (503) 738-3211, or sip something soothing at Cafe Espresso, 600 Broadway, (503) 738-6169, a cozy coffeehouse overlooking the Necanicum River.

Cannon Beach is the Carmel of the Northwest, an artsy community with a hip ambience and strict building codes that ensure only aesthetically pleasing structures are built, usually of cedar and weathered wood.

Still, the town is tourist-oriented, and during the summer (and most winter weekends as well) it explodes with visitors who come to browse the galleries and crafts shops clustered on Hemlock St.

The main draw, however, continues to be the wide-open, white-sand beach, dominated by **Haystack Rock**, one of the world's largest coastal monoliths (see Parks/Beaches, above).

Discover a surprisingly extensive selection of books at Cannon Beach Book Company, 132 N Hemlock, (503) 436-1301. For picnic supplies, try Osburn's Ice Creamery & Deli, 240 N Hemlock, (503) 436-2234, or the Cannon Beach Bakery, 144 N Hemlock, (503) 436-2592, which has one of the few remaining brick oil-fired hearth ovens on the West Coast. For take-out or eat-on-premises fish, try Ecola Seafood Market, 208 N Spruce, (503) 436-9130.

Restaurants

The Bistro ☆ It's hard to find, but once inside you'll enjoy both its intimate interior and its fresh, simply prepared seafood (though service can be slow, and some specials can seem uninspired). The adjacent bar is a relaxing spot for a brew and crab cakes. *263 N Hemlock (opposite Spruce, downtown), Cannon Beach; (503) 436-2661; $$.*

Café de la Mer ☆☆ This post-'60s coffeehouse became Cannon Beach's first fine-dining establishment 20 years ago and has won a considerable following. The atmosphere is warm, and the food is lovingly purveyed. Seafood is its raison d'être. Desserts can be sensational. *1287 S Hemlock (at Dawes), Cannon Beach; (503) 436-1179; $$$.*

Dooger's This place is popular. Outside, there's often a line. Inside, it's a clean, smokeless, family place with friendly service. Stick with the simpler offerings. Most fish can be prepared a number of ways. The largest of the Dooger's branches is in Cannon Beach. *1371 S Hemlock (corner of Sunset), Cannon Beach; (503) 436-2225; $$.* ■ *505 Broadway (at Franklin), Seaside; (503) 738-3773; $$.*

Homegrown Cafe ☆ Hip, nutritious, and delicious, this joint's reminiscent of a '60s-style healthnik eatery, but with a spiffed-up atmosphere and chow with pizzazz (like English muffins topped with hot spiced apples). *3301 S Hemlock (across from Tolovana Wayside Park), Tolovana Park; (503) 436-1803; $.*

Lazy Susan Cafe ☆ Everyone in town seems to gather at this airy, sunny, double-deck restaurant. The interior is bright, the tunes are New Age, and the service is mellow. Breakfast is the best time here. Lunch (and occasionally dinner) options include quiche and salads. *126 N Hemlock (downtown at Coaster Square), Cannon Beach; (503) 436-2816; $.*

Pacific Way Bakery and Cafe ☆☆ This airy cafe, with hip service and plenty of espresso, is the only restaurant downtown. Breakfast is Continental-style, lunch is savory, and pizzas and nightly specials round out the appealing menu. *601 Pacific Way (downtown, corner of Cottage), Gearhart; (503) 738-0245; $$.*

The Stand Small, tidy, and austere, the Stand serves seriously satisfying Tex-Mex chow and is patronized by a young skate-surf crowd (who appreciate the low prices and no-hassle service). You'll like the fresh corn tortillas and salsas and the many burrito options. *220 Ave U (1 block from beach), Seaside; (503) 738-6592; $.*

Cheaper Eats

Pizza 'a fetta This pint-size pizzeria, scrunched amid shops and galleries, serves Cannon Beach's best pizza, from a basic three-cheese pie to a white-clam concoction. Or create your own masterpiece. Slices, too. *231 N Hemlock, Cannon Beach; (503) 436-0333; $.*

Premier Pasta Buy pasta by the bag or the plate at this Necanicum riverfront noodle joint. A dozen herb varieties are yours for the asking. The owners are *Seinfeld* fans, and there's a painting of Kramer on the wall. *1530 S Holladay Dr, Seaside; (503) 738-5062; $.*

Lodgings

Anderson's Boarding House ☆ This solid Victorian fronts a busy street, but the backyard slopes gently to the Necanicum River—convenient and close to the beach. All six guest rooms have private baths, and there's also a cottage. Full breakfasts included. *208 N Holladay Dr (at 3rd), Seaside, OR 97138; (503) 738-9055 or (800) 995-4013; $$.*

The Argonauta Inn ☆ This cluster of residences has pleasant furnishings and fireplaces, and most have kitchens. All units are nonsmoking. If the Argonauta is full, inquire about the Waves or the White Heron Lodge, nearby and under the same management. *188 W 2nd (corner of Larch), Cannon Beach; PO Box 3, Cannon Beach, OR 97110; (503) 436-2601 or (800) 822-2468; $$.*

Cannon Beach Hotel ☆ This tidy nonsmoking hotel has a European flavor. There's a cheery lobby, and a newspaper and light breakfast are brought to your door. The more spendy Courtyard, a jointly managed lodging, offers more seclusion. *1116 S Hemlock (corner of Gower), Cannon Beach; PO Box 943, Cannon Beach, OR 97110; (503) 436-1392; $$.*

Gilbert Inn ☆ Built in 1892, this visually refreshing Victorian offers 10 guest rooms, all with period furnishings, private baths, and a full breakfast. Tongue-and-groove fir, cushy couches, and a large fireplace highlight the parlor. *341 Beach Dr (1 block off the Prom), Seaside, OR 97138; (503) 738-9770 or (800) 410-9770; $$.*

Sea Sprite Guest Lodgings ☆ This cute, always-popular oceanfront motel is a good choice for couples or families (but not pets). Each of the five small but homey attached units includes a kitchen, color TV, and VCR. Most have wood stoves. *280 Nebesna St (at Oceanfront), Tolovana Park; PO Box 933, Cannon Beach, OR 97110; (503) 436-2266; $$.*

Stephanie Inn ☆☆ This gorgeous oceanfront lodging radiates elegance; the emphasis is on pampered and purposeful service. Most rooms include fireplaces, Jacuzzis, VCRs, and stunning furnishings. A buffet-style breakfast is complimentary, and prix-fixe dinners are available to guests. Some minimum-stay requirements. *2740 S Pacific (on beach, at Matanuska), Tolovana Park; PO Box 219, Cannon Beach, OR 97110; (503) 436-2221 or (800) 633-3466; $$$.*

Cheaper Sleeps

McBee Motel Cottages These charming attached cottages are clean, comfy, and available for less than $50. All enjoy willow furniture and homey comforters; some have kitchens and fireplaces. Downtown and the beach are nearby. In winter, inquire about midweek, three-night specials. *888 S Hemlock (PO Box 943), Cannon Beach, OR 97110; (503) 436-2569; $.*

Riverside Inn Bed and Breakfast Seaside's best bargain for traditional lodging has cottages that are spacious and clean. The front faces a busy street, but the rear recedes to the Necanicum River, and the long riverfront deck is perfect for fishing and sunbathing. The beach is only blocks away. *430 S Holladay Dr, Seaside, OR 97138; (503) 738-8254 or (800) 826-6151; $.*

More Information

Astoria/Warrenton Visitors Center, Astoria: *(503) 861-1031.*
Cannon Beach Chamber of Commerce, Cannon Beach: *(503) 436-2623.*
Fort Stevens State Park, Warrenton: *(503) 861-1671.*
Northwest Oregon Tourism Alliance, Portland: *(800) 962-3700.*
Seaside Visitors Bureau, Seaside: *(800) 444-6740.*

Tillamook

From Neahkahnie Mountain near Manzanita and the Tillamook-Clatsop county line on the north, east along the Tillamook County line in the Coast Range, south to Cascade Head, and west to the Pacific Ocean, including the towns of Manzanita, Nehalem, Rockaway Beach, Garibaldi, Tillamook, Oceanside, Pacific City, and Neskowin.

The gentle coastal breeze carried a strange sound to the trail that traverses the crest of Cape Lookout, a 2-mile headland that juts into the Pacific Ocean in Tillamook County. Something was gasping for air, something that was 500 feet below the trail and swimming in the ocean. It could only be a California gray whale.

Rushing to an opening in the trees, hikers who heard the sound needed to wait only a minute or two for the whale to appear. Without warning, a 20-foot plume of spray broke the surface of the ocean and the mammoth mammal's head came into view. The whale began taking air in as its body broke the surface of the water. When its massive tail appeared, the whale was ready to dive and soon disappeared from sight. It was only a matter of a few minutes before the whale would have to reappear. The mammal's need for air nearly led to its extinction during the whaling heydays of the 19th century.

After swimming underwater for about four minutes, the whale again rose to the surface and repeated its breathing procedure. Obviously in no hurry to move on, the whale dived and resurfaced again and again, usually at four-minute intervals.

The spectacle took place just beyond the rocks on the south side of the cape, within easy view and earshot of the trail. Sooner or later other hikers were bound to come along and it would be time to have some fun. A couple of young brothers appeared on the trail, in a hurry to reach the end of the cape. It was going to be difficult to get them to stand still long enough to see the whale.

A whale is going to pop to the surface of the ocean in 2 minutes and 20 seconds, I told them. They must have thought something fishy was going on, but they slowed down long enough to search the surface of the ocean with their own eyes.

"A minute and a half," I updated them. They were obviously in a hurry and didn't believe it, but what if the story I told were true?

Just as they were about to continue hiking, I started a 10-second countdown. Almost to the second, the whale appeared at the ocean's surface, went through its exhale-inhale procedure and slapped the water with its tail as it went for another deep dive. The boys' eyes bugged out and their mouths opened in astonishment.

Seeing a California gray whale off the Oregon Coast doesn't need to be so surprising. Cape Lookout is only one of 29 designated state whale-watching sites where trained volunteers help visitors spot the mammals during their northward migration during March and southern migration during December.

Being close enough to hear their breathing is awe-inspiring. Being able to guarantee a whale's presence is a special treat.

Getting There

Tillamook, the county seat, is 74 miles west of Portland via Highway 6, the Wilson River Highway. Coastal beaches are several miles west of Tillamook and can be reached from US Highway 101 (US 101) and its scenic spur road called the Three Capes Scenic Highway.

Adjoining Areas

NORTH: **Northern Beaches**

SOUTH: **Lincoln City**

EAST: **Wine Country**

Camping

Coastal beaches

Situated due west of the Portland metro area, Tillamook County somehow manages to maintain a less crowded, more laid-back ambience than the coastal counties that border it to the north and south. Most coastal visitors from Portland make a beeline to the Pacific Ocean either northwest from Portland on US 26 to Seaside or southwest on Hwy 18 to Lincoln City. That leaves the winding, scenic western route on Hwy 6 to Tillamook for coastal explorers who aren't in such a hurry.

It makes you wonder what the coastal travelers are thinking about. Instead of the scenic headlands, quiet beaches, and fish-filled estuaries of Tillamook County, most prefer the miles of coastal development that clutter Clatsop and Lincoln Counties. Go figure.

Although much of the development in Tillamook County is well inland from the coast, two large state park campgrounds are within walking distance of the beach. **Nehalem Bay State Park,** located in the northern part of the county near Manzanita, lies on a spit of land that separates the ocean from the bay. It's a wonderfully diverse park with 284 campsites (all with electricity), 9 yurts, a horse camp with 17 sites and corrals, a hiker/biker camp, and even a fly-in camp adjacent to an airstrip. The 890-acre park has a 6-mile equestrian trail, a 1.5-mile hiking trail, and a 2-mile loop bicycle path. Coastal hikers can walk the 4-mile length of the sandy Nehalem Spit, then cross inland and return to the campground by walking at the edge of the tide flats of the bay. The park is also near some of the north coast's best clamming and crabbing areas in Nehalem Bay, and windsurfers love the ocean waves just north of the Nehalem Spit at Manzanita. Call (503) 368-5154 for information.

Cape Lookout State Park, located 12 miles southwest of Tillamook, has its campsites separated from the beach only by a thin strip of coastal forest. The park is located on Three Capes Scenic Highway, a scenic spur route that follows the coastline closely while US 101 runs well inland. The route is designated with frequent signs from Tillamook as it passes Cape Meares, Cape Lookout, and Cape Kiwanda. Each cape has a state park, but only Lookout has a campground.

The park has 55 sites for RVs and 191 for tents, 4 yurts to rent, and a hiker/biker camp. With 2,014 acres, Cape Lookout has ample room to spread out and enjoy the solitude of the Oregon Coast. Park trails include a .25-mile self-guided nature trail, which has 16 stations that describe coastal vegetation, plus the Cape Lookout Trail (moderate; 2.5 miles one way). When whales are migrating and it's not too stormy, the end of the cape is one of the best places to watch for them in Oregon. The park also has trails that lead up from the campground to the cape and down to the beach on the south, plus 5 miles of beach walking north along Netarts Spit. Call (503) 842-4981 for information.

Sites at both campgrounds can be reserved by calling Reservations Northwest at (800) 452-5687. Both have facilities to accommodate the disabled.

Barview Jetty County Park, a 160-acre full-service campground, serves campers wanting to be close to the fishing in Tillamook Bay. Located 2 miles north of Garibaldi just off US 101 near the bay's north jetty, the campground has 249 sites, 40 with full hookups. Reservations are available by calling (503) 322-3522. The county maintains two other smaller campgrounds near the beach. **Whalin Island Park** is 4.5 miles north of Cape Kiwanda on Three Capes Scenic Hwy and **Webb Park** is .25 mile east of the cape. Each has 30 sites that can be reserved by calling (503) 965-5001.

National forest land along the Oregon Coast begins on the north near Cape Lookout and intermittently extends south to the California border. The Forest Service campground farthest north along the Oregon Coast is **Sand Lake,** 8 miles north of Pacific City on Three Capes Scenic Hwy. The 101-unit campground is frequently filled by dune-buggy owners, who flock to the Sand Lake area. Although referred to as a postage stamp in size compared to the dune riding opportunities on the central coast, Sand Lake can get very crowded because it's so close to Portland. The Sand Lake area has many attractions for those who don't ride dune buggies, so the Forest Service designates part of the campground as a quiet zone. Siuslaw National Forest land in Tillamook County is managed by the Hebo Ranger District, (503) 392-3161.

Coastal mountains

When the coastline is foggy and cool, as it frequently is during summer, the Tillamook area has a wealth of camping opportunities a few miles inland where the sun has been known to shine once in a while. Siuslaw National Forest caters to inland campers in its Mount Hebo area, a 3,176-foot peak 10 miles east of Hebo. Turn east from US 101, where Forest Rd 1400 leads to all the recreation facilities in the Mount Hebo area. **Hebo Lake** campground comes first, halfway up the mountain on Forest Rd 1400, and has 16 sites. **Mount Hebo and South Lake Campgrounds,** both located near the mountain's top, have several primitive campsites that are popular with hikers and wildlife watchers. The Forest Service also maintains small, primitive campgrounds at **Castle Rock,** 4.2 miles south of Hebo on Hwy 22, and at **Rocky Bend,** the campground farthest west along the Nestucca River National Back Country Byway. Call the Hebo Ranger District, (503) 392-3161, for campground information.

The 48-mile Nestucca River National Back Country Byway can be reached from the east via Yamhill or Carlton (see Wine Country chapter), or from the west by turning east off US 101 at Beaver into the Coast Range toward Blaine. All but 3 miles of the byway are paved and the gravel portion is suitable for the family car. When approaching from the west, parks run by the Bureau of Land Management (BLM) are **Alder Glen, Elk Bend,**

Fan Creek, and **Dovre,** clustered near the middle of the byway. The campgrounds are small—fewer than a dozen sites—and Elk Bend is for picnicking only. All are located in delightful forested settings near the banks of the Nestucca. Fishing, wildlife watching, and swimming are the major attractions, in addition to the feeling of being away from it all. For information on BLM camps, call (503) 815-1100.

Tillamook County offers riverside camping along the Kilchis and Trask Rivers, two of the five rivers that drain into Tillamook Bay and make the bay so productive as a fishery. The 20-acre **Kilchis River Park** is 5 miles northeast of Tillamook on Kilchis River Rd off US 101 and has 34 campsites. **Trask River Park,** 12 miles east of Tillamook on Trask River Rd off Hwy 6, sits on 30 acres of forested land and has 60 campsites within an easy walk of the river. Reservations can by made by calling (503) 842-6694 for Kilchis and (503) 842-4559 for Trask.

The other major player in the camping business here is the Oregon Department of Forestry, which manages the 364,000 acres of the **Tillamook State Forest.** Once the location of a series of fires known collectively as the Tillamook Burn, the forest has been rehabilitated and is widely used for recreation and timber production. The largest fire occurred in 1933 when 240,000 acres went up in smoke. By the time a series of three more fires ended in 1951, 335,000 acres had been blackened. Although the area is now covered with young trees, the charred trunks of mammoth old-growth trees are a constant reminder of the fires of the mid-1900s.

Tillamook State Forest is best known for its off-road-vehicle riding opportunities for four-wheel drives, four-wheelers, and motorcycles (see Off-Road Vehicles, below). Vehicles driving west from the Portland area on Hwy 6 on Saturday mornings are usually part of a parade of RVs and trailers laden with colorful ORVs. Despite the noise the vehicles make, Tillamook State Forest is a very large place capable of comfortably handling hikers, equestrians, mountain bikers, and fishermen along with the ORV crowd. Managers of the state forest have worked diligently in recent years to improve the tawdry image of the campgrounds and have developed parts of the forest as safe havens for family camping.

The first thing to keep in mind about Tillamook State Forest is that just because something is called a camp doesn't mean that it is a campground. Many of the forest's recreation facilities were named after logging camps of the 1920s and may or may not be a campground today. The discrepancy becomes obvious when arriving at the east end of Tillamook County at the Coast Range's 1,581-foot Wilson River Summit on Hwy 6. While **Rogers Camp**, .5 mile south of the summit, is a day-use staging area for off-road vehicles, **Browns Camp,** located 2 miles to the south (follow signs to Scoggins Creek Rd), is a 29-unit campground with a day-use staging area. Browns Camp was rebuilt in 1997 and provides quiet, designated campsites away from the main riding area. In season, a camp host keeps an eye out for troublemakers and sheriff's deputies make regular patrols.

Other camps near the highway summit are **Elk Creek,** 4 miles west of the summit on the north side of Hwy 6, and **Stagecoach,** 5 miles west of Hwy 6 on University Falls Rd, which parallels the highway 1 mile to the south and begins at the Coast Range Summit turnoff. Elk Creek campground has 15 walk-in sites a few yards from the parking lot and is designed for hikers climbing Elk and Kings Mountains. Stagecoach is primarily used as a horse camp and was built in part by volunteers from Oregon Equestrian Trails. The camp has 10 sites, a hitching post, and two loop riding trails.

The turnoff to **Jones Creek Campground** is on Hwy 6, 54 miles west of Portland and .5 mile west of Lees Camp Store. (No, Lees Camp doesn't have a campground, and the store is out of business.) Located .5 mile north of Hwy 6 along the Wilson River, the 37-unit campground has good fishing access and some popular summer swimming holes. **Diamond Mill** and **Keening Creek** are smaller, no-fee campgrounds near Jones Creek, north of Hwy 6 on Diamond Mill Rd. Call the forestry department's Forest Grove office, (503) 357-2191, for more information on all the Coast Summit and Wilson River recreation sites, plus a free recreation map of the forest.

Nehalem Falls Campground was rebuilt in 1997. The 15-unit campground is 7 miles up Foss Rd along the Nehalem River from Mohler at the junction of US 101 and Hwy 53. The camp is managed by the forestry department's Tillamook office, (503) 842-2545.

Parks/Beaches

Oregon's magnificent string of coastal state parks continues unabated in Tillamook County. It seems that for every full-blown camping park along the beach, the state maintains a half-dozen or more scenic waysides that offer picnic spots and beach access. When the state parks system went through a budget crisis in the 1996–97 biennium, many of the beach wayside parks were targeted for closure. Although the Oregon legislature hasn't been known for its progressive thinking since the Governor Tom McCall era ended in the early 1970s, government leaders somehow found the funds to keep the parks open because they feared the wrath of beach-going voters.

What they didn't find, however, was a permanent, reliable way to fund the state parks system. Budget shortfalls can be expected in the future, and parks may be temporarily closed, especially during the winter season. Until a funding mechanism is found, Oregon state parks will continue to have some of the highest camping and day-use fees among any of the state park systems in the 50 states.

The north end of Tillamook County is anchored by **Nehalem Bay State Park,** which mixes picnic and beachcombing opportunities with its extensive overnight facilities (see Camping, above). Heading south down the coast, **Manhattan Beach State Recreation Site** is midway between the entrance to Nehalem Bay and the town of Rockaway Beach, Tillamook County's main beach resort. Although small compared to Seaside and Lincoln City, **Rockaway Beach** has a solid corps of admirers who return again and again to the white sandy shores at the edge of town.

Cape Meares, the headland above the southern end of Tillamook Bay and the farthest north of numerous parks along Three Capes Scenic Hwy, is known for its views of offshore islands and the Cape Meares lighthouse that crowns the point. Trained volunteers keep the lighthouse open for tours daily from May through September and on weekends in October, March, and April. A small museum describes the role lighthouses played to keep shipping safe along the Oregon Coast beginning in the 1860s. The 38-foot tower is the shortest on the Oregon Coast, but it has a commanding presence on the headland 217 feet above the ocean. The light was replaced by an automated beacon in 1963. Beach walkers head north from Cape Meares to a parking area at the south end of **Bay Ocean Peninsula,** the 4-mile-long peninsula that separates Tillamook Bay from the Pacific Ocean, and hike the beach from there.

Oceanside, a small community tucked into the southern cliffs of Cape Meares, has state park access to a strand of sandy beach that stretches south to a view of the magnificent Three Arch Rocks offshore. South beyond the camping parks at Cape Lookout and Sand Lake, the beaches of **Pacific City** and **Cape Kiwanda** attract visitors to the southern end of Tillamook County. Cape Kiwanda, at the north end of Pacific City, is known for its dory fleet, its hang-gliding launch for beginners, its gentle surfing waves, and its 4 miles of beach that reach south along the Nestucca Spit. A lot of film has been burned up by photographers trying for the perfect photo of the sun setting over the rugged cape and offshore islands. **Robert Straub State Park,** named after a 1970s governor, sits at the south edge of Pacific City. State parks along Three Capes Scenic Hwy are managed by the staff at Cape Lookout State Park, (503) 842-4981.

The community of **Neskowin** and its state beachside recreation area provide the last beach access before Tillamook County climbs up **Cascade Head** and the intense development of Lincoln County begins across the **Salmon River.** The 4 miles of beach north of Cascade Head have little adjacent development in the coastal forest and are a good place to wander away from crowds. A public access point is near the end of the road to Camp Winema, on the west side of US 101 midway between Pacific City and Neskowin.

Wildlife

Although whales are the star attraction, just about anywhere on the coast is a spot to watch for wildlife. From tide pools to offshore islands and inland fish hatcheries, Tillamook County has abundant opportunities for encounters with wildlife.

Oregon's **tide pools** tend to be challenging to reach. The abundant marine life forms that are displayed so well in Washington's inland waterways are more hidden in Oregon. Tide pools around Tillamook can be found on the south sides of each of the three capes—Meares, Lookout, and Kiwanda. The Kiwanda tide pools are relatively easy to reach from the beach, but the Meares tide pools require a hike north of Short Beach, which is 1 mile north of Oceanside, and the Lookout tide pools are 2.5 miles south from the trailhead where the Three Capes Scenic Hwy crosses the headland. Maxwell Point at Oceanside offers easy access to tide pools.

Many offshore coastal islands are part of the four-unit Oregon Islands National Wildlife Refuge, including the Cape Meares and Three Arch Rocks refuges in Tillamook County. While public entry to Oregon's offshore rocks, islands, and reefs is strictly prohibited, a good pair of binoculars and a spotting scope help bring the impressive **seabird colonies** into easy view. **Tufted puffins** are among the most popular birds on display. The refuge is managed from the Corvallis office of the Western Oregon National Wildlife Refuge Complex, (541) 757-7236.

State **fish hatcheries** supplement Tillamook County's abundant supply of wild salmon and steelhead. The Trask Hatchery, (503) 842-4090, 8 miles southeast of Tillamook at 15020 Chance Rd, has excellent viewing of returning **salmon** during fall. The Nehalem Hatchery, (503) 368-6828, located 8 miles northeast of Mohler on Hwy 53, raises **coho** and **steelhead** and has a fishing platform for those who hold wheelchair or blind angling licenses.

Whale Watching

Trained volunteers, working in cooperation with the Oregon Department of Fish and Wildlife and the Oregon Parks and Recreation Department, are on hand twice each year at 29 sites along the Oregon Coast to help visitors spot migrating **California gray whales.** Although the whale migration lasts several weeks and a few whales are year-round residents, Oregon's whale-watching weeks are timed to coincide with school holidays: the week between Christmas and New Year's for the southward migration and March spring break for the northward trip. Migrating whales can be seen for two or three weeks on either side of the official whale-watching weeks. The whale-watch program is run by the Department of Fish and Wildlife's Newport office, (541) 867-4741.

Whales are typically a mile or more offshore, so it takes a powerful pair of binoculars to locate them. Observers watch for plumes of spray the whales exhale from their blowholes when they surface to breathe. Whales can occasionally be seen much closer to shore, especially where they round headlands that jut far out into the ocean. One of the best places is the tip of Cape Lookout (see Camping, above), accessible by a 2.5-mile trail from the mainland. The trail has several good views down into the ocean on the south side of the cape, as well as expansive views to the south and west. Official whale-watching weeks happen during the middle of the coastal winter and spring storm seasons, so not every day is a good day to look for whales.

Other designated whale-watching sites in Tillamook County are at the historic marker turnout on US 101 on Neahkahnie Mountain north of Manzanita and the lighthouse at Cape Meares State Park on Three Capes Scenic Hwy (see Parks/Beaches above). Because resident whales frequently frolic in the kelp beds near shore, it's always wise to watch for them anytime you visit the coast. Several coastal charter boat services have expanded their business to include **whale-watching trips.** Check with D&D Charters in Garibaldi, (503) 322-0381.

Hiking

Tillamook County has a pleasant mix of beach hiking, mountain hikes, and short walks along its many beautiful rivers.

The beaches are easiest to access: just get on one and go. **Nehalem Spit** near Manzanita has a 5-mile stretch of sand; the beach that fronts the town of **Rockaway Beach** is 7 miles long; **Bay Ocean Peninsula** on the south side of Tillamook Bay covers 4 miles of sand; **Netarts Spit** on the north side of Cape Lookout is 4 miles long; the beach from **Cape Lookout** to **Sand Lake** is 8 miles; **Cape Kiwanda** sits near the middle of 8 miles of sandy beach; and the beaches north of Neskowin cover another 4 miles.

Hikers wanting an experience other than sand in their shoes can try Neahkahnie Mountain. The **Neahkahnie Mountain Trail** (moderate; 1.5 miles one way) climbs 1,100 feet to the mountain's 1,631-foot summit where the view takes in an impressive swath of coastline to the south. The trailhead is just off the east side of US 101, 1.2 miles north of the exit to Neahkahnie Beach.

Mount Hebo, site of some small Siuslaw National Forest camp-grounds (see Camping, above), has a road that crosses its 3,176-foot summit. Despite the road, hikers still find several trails to enjoy. The **Pioneer-Indian Trail** (difficult; 8 miles one way) connects Hebo Lake and Mount Hebo Campgrounds. The trail through **Hebo Plantation** just west of Hebo Lake Campground provides a lesson in forestry over its 2-mile length.

While the trail to the tip of Cape Lookout—in the state park by the same name—is popular with campers, the even-more-beautiful trail system on **Cascade Head** appeals to day visitors from Lincoln City and Pacific City. Cascade Head, the dominant coastal headland at the south end of Tillamook County, juts a mile into the ocean in a rounded arch, 10 miles south of Pacific City. The Siuslaw National Forest has trailheads for hiking to the Cascade Head Scenic Research Area and to Harts Cove. Both are accessible from Forest Rd 1861, which heads west from a signed turn-off as US 101 crosses the high point of Cascade Head. The **Harts Cove Trail** (moderate; 3 miles one way) drops 800 feet from the end of Forest Rd 1861 and ends on a bluff overlooking the inaccessible shores of the cove. The gravel forest road that leads to the trailheads comes to an end 1 mile east of the ocean. National forest land atop Cascade Head is managed by the Hebo Ranger District, (503) 392-3161.

The Nature Conservancy, which owns much of the grassy portions on the southern side of Cascade Head, has a trailhead at the west end of Three Rocks Rd, the road that follows the southern side of Cascade Head on the north side of the Salmon River estuary. Three Rocks Rd begins on the west side of US 101, 1.3 miles north of its junction with Hwy 18 and US 101. The **Cascade Head Nature Conservancy Trail** (moderate; 3.5 miles one way) crosses the head as it connects the southern Nature Conservancy trailhead with the northern Forest Service trailhead.

Six miles of the **Oregon Coast Trail** run inland from Cascade Head, just west of US 101. Trailheads for the coastal trail are signed 2 miles south of Neskowin on US 101 and at the east end of Three Rocks Rd.

The Wilson River Highway, which runs between Tillamook and Forest Grove on Hwys 6 and 8, is one of the most beautiful ways to cross the Coast Range in Oregon. The highway passes many tempting riverside settings, as well as hiking trails up two of the finest mountains in the Coast Range. The **Elk Mountain Trail** (difficult; 2 miles one way) climbs 1,900 feet to the mountain's 2,788-foot summit. It begins at Elk Mountain Campground, on the north side of Hwy 6, 5 miles west of the Coast Range Summit. The **King's Mountain Trail** (difficult; 2.5 miles one way) climbs 2,600 feet to the mountain's 3,226-foot summit. The trailhead is on the north side of the highway, 2 miles west of Elk Mountain. Note that the Tillamook State Forest is generally open to off-road vehicles south of Hwy 6 and closed on the north side of the highway (although they are allowed to travel on roads north of the highway). Hwy 6 is a convenient dividing line for the two different types of recreation.

More than anything, Tillamook County is a land of rivers. Some of the most beautiful settings in the county are along its rivers: the Wilson, Trask, Kilchis, Nehalem, and Nestucca. Although developed trail systems are rare, fishermen have pounded many a trail into the riverside banks over the years. Hikers can follow their footsteps to locate hidden swimming holes or other scenic spots where the water runs clear and deep. The **Peninsula Trail** (easy; 1-mile loop) is one of the few developed riverside trails. Located 6 miles up Trask River Rd east of Tillamook, the trail loops around a narrow peninsula that juts into one of the river's bends. A half-dozen picnic tables overlook the river in secluded spots.

At 266 feet high, **Munson Creek Waterfall** is the highest in Oregon's Coast Range. The .5-mile trail to the waterfall begins at Munson Falls County Park, 1.6 miles east of US 101 at the community of Pleasant Valley (7 miles south of Tillamook). The trail is rough in spots and suffers from lack of maintenance. **Niagara Falls,** a pair of 100-foot falls on Pheasant Creek, is a popular hiking destination in the Siuslaw National Forest. The trailhead is off Forest Rd 8533 near the western end of the Nestucca River National Back Country Byway near US 101 and Beaver. From road's end, the base of the falls is .7 mile away on an easy trail.

Biking

With all the motorcycles used in Tillamook State Forest, it might come as a surprise to see more than a few **mountain bikes**. The 9-mile **Wilson River Wagon Route Trail,** which follows the south side of Hwy 6, is open to bicycles, horses, and hikers but is one of the few along the highway's south side that is off-limits to motorized vehicles.

The trail begins across Hwy 6 from the entrance to Elk Creek Campground. At 48 miles west of Portland, it's one of the closest places to the west side of the metro area for a true mountain-bike experience. **University Falls** plunges 65 feet down a basalt cliff a short walk north of the Wagon Route Trail and University Falls Rd, 4.4 miles west of the Coast Range Summit on Hwy 6.

Long-distance **cyclists** on the Oregon Coast Bike Route (see Northern Beaches chapter) have 80 miles of pedaling in Tillamook County, including a detour off US 101 onto the **Three Capes Scenic Route.** The detour adds 10 miles to the trip, but it's worth it because of the scenery it passes and a narrow, dangerous section of US 101 it avoids. Designated biker camps are available in the two major state parks, Nehalem Bay and Cape Lookout (see Camping, above).

Off-Road Vehicles

Nearly two-thirds of Tillamook State Forest's 365,000 acres are open to off-road-vehicle travel. The sheer enormity sounds like the situation could be chaos—and it frequently was a decade ago—but in recent years the recreation plan for the forest has been implemented incrementally and things have settled down. Most of the riding and driving routes are designated. If they aren't exactly plotted on a map that can be passed out to the riders, they are at least implanted in the brains of the regulars and the forest rangers who keep an eye on things. For information on riding regulations, contact the Forest Grove office of Tillamook State Forest at (503) 357-2191.

While off-road vehicles are frequently looked at with disdain by hikers, they are a legitimate form of outdoor recreation that has an ardent corps of followers. A day spent on an off-road motorcycle or even inside a four-wheel-drive truck can be every bit as exhausting as a day on a hiking trail. And it's important to point out that much of the trail construction and campground improvements in Tillamook State Forest have been made through the volunteer efforts of the region's ORV clubs.

Most trail riding begins out of **Rogers** and **Browns Camps,** both on the south side of Hwy 6 near the Coast Range Summit. The virtual maze of trails—hundreds of miles of backroads, winding dirt tracks through the forest and hill climbs—is impossible to describe. Newcomers can show up at one of the staging areas and explain their plight to anyone who will listen, and usually will be able to locate someone to ride with. Unlike hiking, solitude is not usually a major attraction for off-road riding. Other meeting spots are the handful of restaurants and country stores that line the east end of Hwy 6 before it begins to climb from the Willamette Valley to the Coast Range Summit.

Sand Lake, the Siuslaw National Forest park near Pacific City, provides a different type of off-road experience. Instead of muddy trails and a maze of roads, 500 acres of coastal sand dunes attract the same types of vehicles as Tillamook State Forest. Sand Lake sounds pretty small in comparison, but it's large enough to keep the ORV crowd happy as they drive back and forth climbing 200-foot-high dunes. With so much of the coast off-limits to vehicles, Sand Lake provides a valuable recreation opportunity for those who want it. Nearly all of Tillamook County's coastal beaches are closed to vehicles, except for small sections near Sand Lake and Pacific City. The Oregon Department of Transportation's state highway map shows current coastal beach driving restrictions.

Fishing

Tillamook Bay and the rivers that feed it comprise one of the most active fisheries in the state. Depending on the latest set of regulations, which are tailored each year to ensure healthy reproduction of the anadromous fish runs, the waters of Oregon's second-largest bay come to life each fall as anglers arrive from throughout the Northwest to fish for big chinook. Regulations are published annually in the *Oregon Sport Fishing Regulations* synopsis and are updated on the Oregon Department of Fish and Wildlife's information line at (503) 872-5263. The synopsis is widely available around the state at sporting goods stores, visitors centers, and country grocery stores that sell fishing tackle.

Although Tillamook Bay's state chinook record of 83 pounds is no longer challenged, chinook half that size (even as large as 60 pounds) are occasionally taken during the fall run. The fishery lasts from late August through late October. Spring chinook are available in April and May.

With the onset of Oregon's fall rains, chinook and coho salmon, steelhead, and sea-run cutthroat trout begin to move up the bay's five rivers: the **Miami, Kilchis, Wilson, Trask,** and **Tillamook.** Angling is good throughout the fall and winter, although regulations vary and fishing for some stocks of wild fish may be catch-and-release. Check the latest synopsis of *Oregon Sport Fishing Regulations.*

Among Oregon rivers, the **Wilson River** is consistently a top producer of salmon and steelhead. Never far from Hwy 6, the river has good access. Angling from drift boats when the river is up during the winter can be productive. Most of the Tillamook Bay rivers have spring runs, but the fall runs tend to be bigger and last longer. Steelhead are in the rivers year-round, although winter is the most productive time. The Guide Shop, located at 12140 Wilson River Hwy near Tillamook, (503) 842-3474, keeps close watch on fish runs in the local rivers.

Tillamook Bay is also productive for sturgeon, as well as surf perch and bottom fish. **Surf casting** from rocks along the mouth of the bay can produce lingcod, especially during winter.

Pier's End fishing pier in Garibaldi offers wheelchair access out over deep water for bottom fishing. Scuba divers also make use of the pier, one of the few dive sites in Oregon that doesn't require a boat. Tidal currents can be strong near the mouth of the bay, and divers should be experienced. Garibaldi is also the headquarters of the bay's large fleet of charter boats. Although salmon continue to be sought offshore, many of the trips seek bottom fish and halibut. One of Oregon's most productive halibut areas lies 20 miles off the entry to Tillamook Bay. For the latest information on what's biting and which charter services are running trips, check with Garibaldi Marina, (503) 322-3312.

Clams and crabs are numerous in Tillamook Bay, as well as in the other bays of Tillamook County: **Nehalem, Netarts,** and **Nestucca.** Species of bay clams include cockle, littleneck, butter, and softshell. Razor clams are usually found on sandy stretches of coastal beaches. Oregon's food crabs are Dungeness and red rock. Licenses are not required to take clams and crabs, but each has its long list of regulations (see *Oregon Sport Fishing Regulations*) that must be observed. Harvest of native oysters is not allowed in Oregon and cultured oysters are private property that require the owner's permission to collect.

There is plenty of fishing action away from Tillamook Bay, especially on the **Nestucca and Nehalem Rivers.** Seasons on the Nestucca mirror the Tillamook Bay rivers: a spring run of chinook followed by a larger fall run, with steelhead in the river throughout the year. At 100 miles long, the Nehalem is one of the longer rivers that originate in the Coast Range. The Nehalem is most productive for the fall chinook run in the bay and for a winter run of steelhead. The BLM's Salem District Westside recreation map shows the road systems that follow the rivers; contact them at (503) 375-5646.

The **Salmonberry River,** a tributary of the Nehalem in northern Tillamook County, has been virtually inaccessible over the years due to a lack of roads that approach it. Railroad tracks follow the river, and an easement along 15 miles of the track was recently acquired to allow anglers, hunters, and hikers foot access via Camp 10 Rd from US 26. Fishing is catch-and-release for the river's winter run of steelhead.

Perhaps the ultimate fishing trip in Tillamook County, even in all of Oregon, is to launch from the beach in a **Pacific City dory.** The Haystack Fishing Club, (503) 965-7555, offers trips through the surf in a Pacific City dory. Fishing is for salmon, halibut, lingcod, and bottom fish. Non-fishing rides are also available. The highly mobile dory fleet also schedules whale-watching tours that begin on the beach at Pacific City, plus dory rides on local rivers and river fishing trips. Although dories can be launched elsewhere along the coast, Pacific City is the only U.S. town on the Pacific Ocean that is home to a commercial fleet of dories.

Kayaking

As if Tillamook County didn't already have enough to offer, the local bays and rivers have some of the state's best sea and river kayaking. Many of Oregon's sea kayakers get their first taste of salt water on **Nehalem Bay.** For a boost of excitement to help keep them sane until spring, river kayakers, from beginners to experts, wait for winter rains to fill the bay's rivers.

The launch facilities at **Wheeler Marina,** on the west side of US 101 in the center of town, are ideal for sea kayaking, and the marshlands of the bay are wonderful for exploring. This is no San Juan Islands experience, like kayakers get in Washington, but it's still plenty of fun. Annie's Kayaks, (503) 368-6055, has set up shop on Nehalem Bay at the marina in Wheeler and rents kayaks throughout the year. Saturday-morning clinics are offered during summer, both for conventional closed sea kayaks and the open cockpit models. After graduating from Nehalem Bay, kayakers head for bigger adventures in **Tillamook, Netarts,** and **Nestucca Bays.**

Sit-atop kayaks have opened up the north-coast rivers to local residents who have found that the same model of boat can be used for paddling in the surf and down whitewater rivers. The key is to learn where to do it safely. Beginning surf paddlers usually head for the south side of **Cape Kiwanda,** where the wave size is moderate and the rip tide isn't dangerous. Paddlers can have a lot of fun learning skills inside the break before they venture far enough out to reach the ocean's swells.

The **Nehalem, Kilchis, Wilson, Trask,** and **Nestucca Rivers** are popular during Oregon's rainy season (November through May). Kayakers, rafters, drift-boat fishermen, and whitewater canoeists flock to Tillamook when the rivers are right. Each river has a fine line between flood stage and too little water to enjoy. More than a few boaters have driven all the way from Portland only to find the rivers in flood stage and unrunnable. The only thing to do is to return another day.

Beginning paddlers should take lessons and travel with experienced boaters, but most of the rivers offer ways to learn skills without too much danger. Scout the lower section of a river from the road, looking for a flat stretch of river, followed by a drop and a quiet pool. Fishermen will already have made trails up and down the banks. After dressing properly with a wet suit and life jacket, carry the kayak above the drop and jump in. As long as the river doesn't have any obstructions, this can be a safe way to learn skills in all types of boats, especially if the water is lively enough to send you swimming. The first thing a sit-atop kayaker needs to learn is to stay with the boat after a flip, turn it upright, and reenter while on the water. The **Trask River** has a perfect spot to practice kayak reentry called Dam Drop Hole, 2 miles downstream on Trask River Rd from the Peninsula day-use park.

Hang Gliding/Paragliding

Hang gliding and paragliding are recreation pursuits that demand professional instruction, so no one should be tempted to launch without proper training and the accompaniment of a local pilot who knows the intricacies of the area. Tillamook is a favorite among Oregon's self-launched pilots. From the back-and-forth flying over the coastal headland at Oceanside to the teaching hill at Cape Kiwanda, just about everyone who flies in Oregon winds up here.

The north side of **Cape Kiwanda**—away from the dory fleet, the beach walkers, and the surfers—has long been a preferred teaching hill for hang gliding and paragliding. The prevailing winds out of the west give just enough lift to get a novice airborne without their having to worry about being blown out over the ocean. The Hang Gliding and Paragliding School of Oregon, (503) 223-7448, gives most of its beginner lessons at Cape Kiwanda.

Pilots with at least intermediate skills usually head for coastal-ridge soaring sites at **Anderson's Viewpoint** and **Oceanside.** Both launches receive a large number of tourists who pause to watch the pilots in action. The Anderson's Viewpoint launch is accessed from a roadside pullout on Three Capes Scenic Hwy on the north side of Cape Lookout, 12 miles southwest of Tillamook. The Oceanside launch is reached from the bluff that overlooks the north end of town; the landing is on the beach.

outside in

Attractions

Resting mostly on a sandy peninsula with undulating dunes covered in beach grass, shore pine, and Scotch broom, **Manzanita** is a lazy but growing community gaining popularity as a coastal getaway for in-the-know urbanites. For sweet treats and espresso, visit Manzanita News and Espresso at 500 Laneda Ave, (503) 368-7450.

Tillamook Bay is one of the homes for the summer salmon-fishing fleet, and good places to find **fresh seafood** abound. Drive out on the pier at Bay City's Pacific Oyster Co. on the west side of US 101, (503) 377-2323, for 'sters and a view. In Garibaldi, stop by Miller Seafood on US 101, (503) 322-0355, or Smith's Pacific Shrimp Co. at 608 Commercial Dr, (503) 322-3316, and ask what's fresh.

A tiny seaside resort that defines "quaint," **Oceanside** lies 8 miles west of Tillamook along the 22-mile Three Capes Scenic Hwy, which traces one of Oregon's most beautiful stretches of coastline (see Camping, above).

Tillamook is best known as dairy country. On the north end of town along US 101 sits the home of **Tillamook cheese,** the Tillamook County Creamery Association plant and visitors center, 4175 US 101 N, (503) 842-4481. The tour is self-guided but interesting. Afterward, nibble the free cheese samples, buy a scoop of Tillamook ice cream, or visit the restaurant and gift shop. Be prepared for hordes of tourists year-round. Bear Creek Artichokes in Hemlock, 11.5 miles south of Tillamook and closed in winter, (503) 398-5411, features a first-class selection of fruits, veggies, and herbs.

A diminutive, mostly residential community lying in the lee of Cascade Head, **Neskowin** is the final port of refuge before the touristy "20 Miracle Miles" (as the stretch from Lincoln City to Newport used to be called). The beach here is narrower but less crowded than other locales. Proposal Rock, an offshore island, can be reached at very low tides. The **Sitka Center for Art and Ecology** operates on the south side of Cascade Head and offers seasonal classes on many subjects, plus numerous talks and exhibits; (503) 994-5485. The Hawk Creek Cafe, 4505 Salem, (503) 392-3838, is a good bet for enjoying a beer or snack on an outdoor view deck.

Restaurants

ArtSpace Gallery Cafe ☆ Combining an avant-garde art gallery with an eatery, this bistrolike spot has a young, attentive waitstaff serving meals like succulent Tillamook Bay oysters (the limited menu's star attraction), or fettuccine, fresh fish, enlightening soups, and simple salads. *9120 5th (US 101 and 5th), Bay City; (503) 377-2782; $.*

Blue Sky Cafe ☆☆☆ This cafe purveys a blend of cutting-edge Northwest, Southwest, Mediterranean, and Asian cuisines. Even the decor is eclectic (lighted skeletons line the wine rack). It's as far away from pretentious as you can get but has incredibly inventive food. *154 Laneda Ave (at 2nd), Manzanita; (503) 368-5712; $$$.*

Cassandra's ☆☆ An overall exceptional eatery (and the finest pizzeria on the coast), colorful Cassandra's uses organic produce and meats and flour with no preservatives in its pizzas and salads, which range from traditional to way-different. *60 Laneda Ave (1 block off beach), Manzanita; (503) 368-5593; $.*

Grateful Bread Bakery ☆ Tempting you with robust breads, muffins, and an array of sweets, this bakery also offers extensive breakfast and lunch menus, such as lasagne, pancakes, hearty soups, and sandwiches. Enjoy your coffee on the deck. Closed in January. *34805 Brooten Rd (on Pacific City loop road), Pacific City; (503) 965-7337; $.*

Jarboe's ☆☆☆ Outside and inside, decor is unassuming—nothing whatsoever is allowed to upstage the French-inspired cuisine. The limited à la carte menu changes depending on what's available. Look for intricate colors and flavors, and expect lots of mesquite-grilled meats and seafood. *137 Laneda Ave (at Carmel), Manzanita; (503) 368-5113; $$$.*

Pelican Pub & Brewery The best spot for soaking up Cape Kiwanda's geographical splendor is this airy beachfront pub with in-house craft brews, finger foods, beefy chili, a tempting sandwich lineup, and thin-crusted pizzas. *33180 Cape Kiwanda Dr (on beach at Cape Kiwanda), Pacific City; (503) 965-7007; $.*

Roseanna's Oceanside Cafe ☆ Polished service and an upscale menu lend an urbane air to this converted country grocery (with a funky facade). Tillamook Bay oysters, steaks, pasta, and chowder are menu stalwarts. Dining-room ocean views are wonderful. *1490 Pacific St (on Oceanside's main drag), Oceanside; (503) 842-7351; $$.*

Cheaper Eats

Downie's Cafe Step back into the '50s in this neighborhood cafe offering down-home service and food, and filled mostly with locals clamoring for the clam chowder. Fish 'n chips are greasy-good, the burgers are huge, and the pies are delish. *9320 5th St, Bay City; (503) 377-2220; $.*

Lodgings

The Chelan ☆ This attractive adobe structure's nine condo units (all with ocean views and fireplaces) feel like getaway retreats. There are lush gardens and a secluded atmosphere. Most have two bedrooms; some enjoy private balconies. *48750 Breakers Blvd (just off Salem Blvd), Neskowin, OR 97149; (503) 392-3270; $$$.*

Eagle's View Bed & Breakfast Eagles may perch at this secluded B&B (it's high enough), but it's more likely you'll encounter a Siamese cat. All five guest rooms have private baths and handcrafted quilts; three enjoy spas, and one is wheelchair-accessible. Full breakfasts are served. *37975 Brooten Rd (.5 mile east of US 101), Pacific City; PO Box 901, Pacific City, OR 97135; (503) 965-7600 or (888)846-3292; $$.*

House on the Hill Bring your binoculars. The setting, on a bluff overlooking Three Arch Rocks and the Pacific, is unbeatable. This collection of buildings is nothing fancy, but all units have ocean vistas. Kids are fine (call ahead). *1816 Maxwell Mountain Rd (at Maxwell Point), Oceanside; PO Box 187, Oceanside, OR 97134; (503) 842-6030; $$.*

Hudson House Bed & Breakfast ☆☆ Perched on a bluff in the middle of nowhere, this Victorian farmhouse is picturesque. Guest rooms look out on forested hillsides surrounding a pastoral valley. Breakfasts are exceptional. Pacific City, Cape Kiwanda, and the ocean are 3 miles away. *37700 US 101 S (2.5 miles south of Cloverdale and east of Pacific City), Cloverdale, OR 97112; (503) 392-3533; $$.*

The Inn at Manzanita ☆☆ One block off the beach, occupying a multi-level, woodsy setting, is this tranquil retreat. Each of the nonsmoking units has a spa, a TV with VCR, and fresh flowers; most have treetop ocean views. Two-night reservations required in summer. *67 Laneda Ave (1 block from beach), Manzanita, OR 97130; (503) 368-6754; $$$.*

Ocean Inn ☆☆ You'd have to sleep on the beach to get any closer than this to the ocean. The 1-bedroom units are remodeled and ultra-attractive; the cottagelike older units are nearer the ocean. Some minimum-stay requirements. *20 Laneda Ave (on beach), Manzanita; PO Box 162, Manzanita, OR 97130; (503) 368-6797 or (800) 579-9801; $$$.*

Pacific Sands A stone's throw from breaking waves, this well-maintained condo-motel has a bland exterior but a super setting. The 10 roomy condos for rent have fireplaces and kitchens. Opt for a beachfront unit. *48250 Breakers Blvd (at Amity), Neskowin; PO Box 356, Neskowin, OR 97149; (503) 392-3101; $$.*

More Information

Bureau of Land Management, Tillamook: *(503) 815-1100.*
Garibaldi Chamber of Commerce, Garibaldi: *(503) 322-0301.*
Hebo Ranger District, Hebo: *(503) 392-3161.*
Nehalem Bay Area Chamber of Commerce, Nehalem: *(503) 368-5100.*
Nestucca Valley Chamber of Commerce, Cloverdale: *(503) 392-4499.*
Northwest Oregon Tourism Alliance, Portland: *(800) 962-3700.*
Rockaway Beach Chamber of Commerce, Rockaway Beach:
      (800) 331-5928.
Siuslaw National Forest, Corvallis: *(541) 750-7000.*
Tillamook Chamber of Commerce, Tillamook: *(503) 842-7525.*
Tillamook County Parks Department, Tillamook: *(503) 322-3477.*
Tillamook State Forest, Forest Grove: *(503) 357-2191.*
Tillamook State Forest, Tillamook: *(503) 842-2545.*

Lincoln City

From the Salmon River estuary near the north end of Lincoln City on the north, east to the crest of the Coast Range near the Lincoln-Polk county line, south to Otter Rock, and west to the Pacific Ocean, including the towns of Lincoln City, Gleneden Beach, and Depoe Bay.

The breeze usually begins to pick up around noon on the beaches of the Oregon Coast. Usually a light breeze to begin with, it frequently blows briskly enough by midafternoon to lift a dizzying array of colorful flying things into the sky.

Located almost directly on the 45th parallel, halfway between the Equator and the North Pole, Lincoln City was the first Oregon coastal town to take note of the dependable winds it receives. Until the late 1970s, kites were usually sold in Oregon in variety and sporting goods stores, along with bats and balls and lawn chairs. In 1979, Lincoln City staged its first kite festival, about the same time kite specialty stores began sprouting up along the coast. Kite stores now are about as common on the coast as Sunday afternoon traffic jams in Lincoln City, and kite festivals draw as many people to the coast as fishing.

Lincoln City usually stages kite festivals in the spring and fall at the D River Wayside, one of the smallest but busiest Oregon state parks. Really little more than a highway rest area, the park offers access to Lincoln City's miles of coastal sand and is the fourth-busiest park in the state system, with 1.2 million visitors during a recent two-year cycle used for state park budgeting. The kite fanatics come to fly their own creations and see designs that others have created. While stunt kites are the kites of choice among recreational fliers, the more experienced kiters play with

12-string puppet kites, art-deco kites, Indian fighter kites, and even old-style box kites.

Each festival usually tries to see how many kites can be airborne at the same time (a nice round number is 3,000) and how large a windsock the breeze can lift each day (how does 200 feet sound?). Night flying is also popular, with glow sticks attached to kites that light up the sky.

While some people take kite flying very seriously, most enjoy it as a simple recreational pastime. With Oregon's beaches usually too cold for swimming or sunbathing, beachgoers need something to do and it may as well be flying a kite.

The roads in and through Lincoln City are often thick with traffic, not the most relaxing place to spend time on a vacation or weekend. Its nickname, as bestowed by the Chamber of Commerce, is the "20 Miracle Miles," in reference to the long strip of development from Devil's Lake on the north to Gleneden Beach on the south. Not so fondly, visitors call it the "20 Miserable Miles," in reference to what used to be heavy weekend traffic that has turned into congestion just about whenever the sun shines.

The best way to enjoy Lincoln City is to drive into town, park your car at one of the many beachside lodges, don't even think of driving anywhere until it's time to head home . . . and go fly a kite.

Getting There

Lincoln City is an 88-mile drive southwest of Portland via Highway 99W to McMinnville, then Highway 18 to its junction with US Highway 101 (US 101) at the north edge of Lincoln City. Salem is 57 miles from Lincoln City via Highways 22 and 18. US 101 travels the Lincoln City area north to south.

Adjoining Areas

NORTH: **Tillamook**

SOUTH: **Newport**

EAST: **Wine Country**

inside out

Beaches/Kite Flying

Miles of sandy beaches are Lincoln City's trademark. Whether flying a kite or simply strolling in the breeze, most visitors here spend their outdoor recreation hours on the beach. With 6 miles of beach to the north and another 6 miles to the south, the strands of sand are more than enough to handle the crowds from the Willamette Valley that pour in most weekends.

The narrow opening of Siletz Bay at the south end of Lincoln City divides the beach sections in the middle. Vehicles are not allowed on the beach from north of Lincoln City near Neskowin all the way south to Florence.

With the smell of salt water in the air, drivers can make a beeline for **D River Wayside State Park** and its beach near the center of the strip of development that is called Lincoln City. While D River Wayside is the busiest parking access to the beach, it's by no means the only one. D River Wayside is the location of Lincoln City's three annual **kite festivals,** in the spring, summer, and fall. Call the Lincoln City Visitors Bureau, (800) 452-2151, for annual dates. Catch the Wind kite store is located nearby at 266 SE US 101, (541) 994-9500.

A far better choice for solitude is to turn north off US 101 onto Logan Rd at the north entrance to town and drive 1 mile to **Roads End State Wayside.** Once you're past the crowds coming and going from Chinook Winds Casino, cares of the journey fall away and the beautiful beach beckons. Walk the beach north 1 mile from Roads End to the base of a headland where the beach comes to an abrupt halt. No two houses that line the coastal bluff here look quite the same architecturally. The beach extends south through Lincoln City to Siletz Bay. You'll pass numerous lodges where most visitors stay, because the only state park campground in the immediate area is away from the ocean on Devil's Lake on Lincoln City's east side (see Camping, below). A less crowded and even more scenic location is at the south end of town, where the city's **Taft Waterfront Park** sits at the north end of Siletz Bay only a short walk from the coastal beach. A pod of harbor seals frequently pulls up and basks in the sun at the southern entrance to Siletz Bay. The seals can be seen with binoculars from Taft Park.

A 3-mile beach called the **Salishan Spit** protects the southern side of Siletz Bay. The beach is lined with some of Oregon's most expensive coastal houses, and vehicle access is restricted to property owners and guests. Because of Oregon's public beach law, however, everyone is allowed to hike the sand in front of the houses. The best access to Salishan Spit begins at **Gleneden Beach State Wayside,** a day-use park 1 mile south of Salishan Lodge on US 101. Turn west on Laurel Rd and drive less than a mile to the large parking lot at the beach. Walk north 3 miles to the end of the spit. Another 3 miles of beach stretches south to Fogarty Creek State Park, where a series of rocky headlands interrupt the sand until the south side of Otter Rock (see Newport chapter).

Hiking

With limited public land, the inland areas of northern Lincoln County have few hiking opportunities. The private timber companies that own much of the forest allow public access, but they ask that visitors stay off the roads weekdays when log trucks are in use. The private land is usually open for public recreation from Saturday morning to Sunday evening, plus Monday holidays. Camping and campfires are not permitted.

One hike that shouldn't be missed is the **Valley of the Giants,** a 47-acre old-growth forest preserve managed by the Bureau of Land Management (BLM). Actually located just east of the Lincoln County line in Polk County, the Valley of the Giants can be reached by driving logging roads up the Siletz River from the west or from Falls City on the east. It's rare when a first-time visitor actually locates the valley because of the maze of unmarked logging roads that needs to be negotiated. Access was especially bad following the 1996 floods that washed away large chunks of road and severely damaged two vehicle bridges. An incredible sight awaits the adventuresome travelers lucky enough to locate the valley. Home to some of Oregon's oldest trees, the valley has a dozen Douglas fir and western hemlock with 25-foot girths. Warnick Creek runs clear and cold at the bottom of the grove.

To find the Valley of the Giants from the town of Siletz, drive east on County Rd 410 for 5 miles to Logsden. Turn north on County Rd 307 and pass **Moonshine County Park** in 3.5 miles. Follow the Siletz River upstream from the park, winding north and then east for 15.1 miles to where the river's north and south forks merge. Turn north and follow the north fork for 4 miles to where the road begins to wind west. Cross two bridges and either walk or drive (if the road is open to vehicles) 1.5 miles to the trailhead. (Where the road forks, take the branch that goes north.) Although most of the road junctions are not marked, the trailhead is. The hiking loop through the Valley of the Giants is 1.7 miles long and drops 200 feet from the trailhead. The BLM has plans to mark the road access and publishes a map with driving directions. Contact the BLM's Mary's Peak Resource Area, Salem, (503) 375-5646, for directions. The BLM Salem District's Westside recreation map is a valuable tool for negotiating the roads of northwest Oregon, but even it is no guarantee that you'll find the Valley of the Giants. The Coast Range roads have a notorious reputation for puncturing tires, so be prepared with an extra spare. A recent trip resulted in four flat tires among four vehicles.

Siletz Falls, a series of cascades where the Siletz River carves its way through a basalt canyon, is a short walk downhill on a service road that is locked to keep out vehicles. Park along Siletz River Rd 13.4 miles upstream from Moonshine Park (see driving directions to Valley of the Giants, above), just before a painted mark on a tree that says 13.5. (Log-truck drivers make their way through the forest by following mileage markers painted on trees.) The Georgia-Pacific Corporation owns most of the land on the west side of the range, while Boise-Cascade holds much of the property on the east slope.

The Siuslaw National Forest completed construction in 1997 of a 1.5-mile trail to **Drift Creek** in the Coast Range east of Lincoln City. The trail gives Lincoln City hikers an alternative destination to Cascade Head, the beautiful but busy coastal headland nearby (see Tillamook chapter). To reach the Drift Creek trailhead, turn east from US 101 on Drift Creek Rd at the south end of Lincoln City. Turn right on S Drift Creek Rd after 1.5 miles and drive .25 mile to Forest Rd 17. Turn left and drive 10 miles east on the paved, single-lane road to the trailhead. The trail leads to a 75-foot waterfall and crosses a 240-foot suspension bridge. The trail begins at 911 feet in elevation, descends to 630 feet at the bridge, and scramblers can continue down to the creek's edge at 532 feet. The pool depth at the base of the falls varies from 6 inches to 2 feet during the summer and swells to 6 feet during the rainy season.

Camping

Devil's Lake State Park, (541) 994-2002, covers 104 acres, with camping on the west shore of the lake and day-use areas .75 mile away on the east shore. Both park areas are just east of US 101 on E Devil's Lake Rd. The campground has 32 sites with full hookups, 68 tent sites, and a hiker-biker camp. The campsites are separated from the lake by trees and a wet-land area, so don't expect a waterfront view. Devil's Lake is connected to the D River State Wayside (see Beaches/Kite Flying) on the beach by the 400-foot-long D River, which is said to be the shortest river in the world. State park facilities for the disabled include two campsites, rest rooms, and a fishing dock. The shallow lake is rife with underwater vegetation during the summer growth season, but that doesn't stop a wide variety of boating activities. Campground reservations are available by calling (800) 452-5687. Lincoln City also has one commercial RV park, the Tree 'N' Sea Trailer Park, (541) 996-3801.

Local residents who know how hard it is to get a campsite at Devil's Lake on the weekend head 35 miles up the Siletz River to **Moonshine County Park** (see Hiking, above, for directions). The 18-acre park has 8 sites with hookups, plus large grassy areas where it's hard to pitch too many tents. The park fronts a beautiful stretch of the Siletz River, famous for its summer swimming and inner-tube floating. Steelhead are in the river throughout the year, although most action occurs above the park. Picnickers have 36 tables to choose from, as well as a variety of ball fields where they can work off their lunch.

Jack Morgan County Park has 5 primitive campsites on the Siletz River, 5 miles downstream from Siletz when driving north on Hwy 229.

Parks

With the state playing lead fiddle in developing ocean-access parks, Lincoln County has concentrated much of its efforts inland or in places beyond the reach of the state. The county's **Knight Park,** a 2-acre boat launch and dock on the Lower Salmon River, provides the only public access to the 270-acre Salmon River estuary at the southern base of Cascade Head. The park can be reached by driving northwest 2 miles on Lower Salmon River Rd at a turnoff from US 101.

The Siletz River is lined with county parks, most with boat launches, on the way upriver from Siletz Bay. First comes **Strome Landing,** followed by **Morgan Park, Twin Bridges,** and **Moonshine.** State and county roads closely follow the river, one of the most circuitous in the Coast Range. Roads are well maintained up to Moonshine, where the narrow logging roads begin. Twin Bridges, 3 miles east of Siletz, has a deep hole beneath the bridge where youngsters of the county prove their moxie by jumping.

Another string of day-use state parks begins where the long stretch of sand ends 3 miles south of Gleneden Beach on US 101. The first is **Fogarty Creek State Park,** located 2 miles north of Depoe Bay, with a sheltered beach picnic area. The 142-acre park is a good spot for watching powerful waves that break against the fingers of rock that jut into the ocean. A short trail leads under the highway from the parking area to the beach. **Boiler Bay Wayside** is another mile down the coast. Located atop a grassy headland open to the ocean, blustery winds can make an outdoor picnic unpleasant. Because the view is so outstanding, plan to snack in your car anyway. A steep scramble trail leads down to the bay, where low tide allows examination of the tide pools.

The southern end of the Lincoln City area is crowned by another one of those spectacular sections of coastline that are so common in Oregon. A 2-mile spur road leaves US 101 just south of Depoe Bay, climbs 400 feet to the top of **Cape Foulweather,** and rejoins the highway at Otter Rock.

Although Cape Foulweather is too rugged for hiking, the view from the gift shop parking lot (accessible from the Otter Rock town loop, a 1-mile spur road west of US 101) is too good to miss. Binoculars can usually help spot sea lions basking on the offshore islands to the southwest. Otter Rock is the site of **Devils Punch Bowl State Park,** where a trail from the parking lot leads north to the tide pools. The "Punch Bowl" is dangerous at high tide because of how the waves are forced into the narrow constriction in the rock. The 1-mile trail that leads south from Otter Rock to Beverly Beach is popular with surfers and beach hikers. It's a long way to carry a surfboard, but the waves are among the best in Oregon and make the hike worthwhile.

Fishing

Depoe Bay is a small saltwater bay that offers little in shore fishing but has good access to the Pacific. **Offshore fishing** is productive for salmon, halibut, and many species of rockfish. Albacore occasionally swim close enough to shore for the fishing fleet to make a 20-mile or more journey out to sea to seek them. Prominent **charter boat companies** are Dockside Charters, (800) 733-8915, and Tradewind Charters, (800) 445-8730. Depoe Bay pumps out an average 50,000 angler trips per year, and the average catch is one of the highest on the Oregon Coast.

Surf casting around Lincoln City is best from state parks at **Boiler Bay** (see Parks, above) and **Rocky Creek,** 2 miles south of Depoe Bay on US 101. Northern Lincoln County's river estuaries—the **Salmon River** and **Siletz Bay** (see Parks, above)—see moderate fishing inside the bay. Both have convenient boat launch facilities, but bar crossings are rare. The Salmon River has a run of fall chinook, while Siletz Bay is most productive for crabs and clams.

The **Siletz River** upstream from tidewater is an all-around productive river, with angling for trout, fall chinook, and summer and winter steelhead. The lower river from Moonshine Park down to tidewater is usually fished from drift boats launched at any of the numerous parks and moorages. The upper segments of the 70-mile river run through private timber lands, but fishermen are numerous on weekends when steelhead peak in June, October, and the middle of winter.

Devil's Lake, which covers 700 acres on the east side of Lincoln City, is the area's best bet for bass and panfish. The lake is stocked with catchable rainbow trout (see Camping, above). The Lincoln City area has some other productive streams, including **Drift Creek** on the east side of Siletz Bay, but trout fishing in all local streams is restricted to catch-and-release in an effort to rebuild the native cutthroat trout population.

Boating/Kayaking/Surfing

The waters around Lincoln City see all types of boating, from children's paddle boats on **Devil's Lake** (see Camping, above) to charter fishing boats that operate out of Depoe Bay.

Depoe Bay offers a quick—and reasonably safe—way for charter and private boats to reach the open waters of the Pacific. Although normal navigation precautions need to be taken, the narrow channel that leads from the bay is one of the safest ways to enter the ocean from Oregon and is used heavily from June through October. The boat basin within the bay itself, operated by the Port of Depoe Bay, (541) 765-2361, is 390 feet by 750 feet, just large enough to accommodate most boats that seek its sheltered waters.

Rafters and **kayakers** run 11 miles of the **upper Siletz River,** from Elk Creek to Moonshine Park, but the river is extremely fickle, rising and falling after each rainstorm. Rapids change quickly from Class III to V and are no place for beginners. The 10 miles of the river below Moonshine Park to the town of Siletz is a good run for beginners and locals who want to get out for a quick river outing. Unlike most other Oregon rivers, rather than rushing straight to the sea the Siletz makes a big oxbow turn around the town of Siletz. Canoeists and kayakers find they can enjoy a scenic, 2-hour paddle on Class I water, then walk 15 minutes from the north side of town to pick up their vehicles at the launch site on the south side of town.

Surfing conditions tend to be marginal on Lincoln City's beaches, although a few locals can be seen riding the waves offshore when conditions are good. **Gleneden Beach** (see Beaches/Kite Flying, above) is the best place to try, both for surf kayaks and surfboards. Beverly Beach south of Otter Rock (see Parks, above) is a popular hike-to-surfing spot. Check with Oregon Surf Shop, (541) 996-3957, at 4933 S Hwy 101 in Lincoln City for information and equipment. **Siletz Bay** sees a few **windsurfers,** but the bay's tides are tricky and occasionally take the unwary out to sea where the county's water rescue unit is called on to make a retrieval.

Wildlife

The Lincoln City area offers a better-than-average chance to spot the **California gray whale** migrations during winter and spring. With a half-dozen designated whale-watching sites within 20 miles of each other, more than a few watchers spend the day driving back and forth trying to find out which location is luckiest. Call (541) 563-2002 for information.

Watchers don't even need to brave the elements at the site farthest north. The Inn at Spanish Head, which perches on a cliff at the southern end of Lincoln City, commands an impressive view of the ocean. Heading south, the next designated site is Boiler Bay, followed by the Depoe Bay seawall, Rocky Creek State Park just south of Depoe Bay, Cape Foulweather, and the Devil's Punch Bowl at Otter Rock. Whales are spotted at each location, but close-in sightings at Boiler Bay and the Depoe Bay seawall will be remembered longest. Several fishing charters in Depoe Bay offer whale-watching tours, both during the height of the migrations and during summer to view resident whales. Tradewind Charters, (541) 765-2345, and Deep Sea Trollers, (541) 765-2248, are two of several whale-watching cruise operations to try.

With so many miles of sandy beach, **tide pools** are a rarity in northern Lincoln County. Two of the easiest to reach are at Boiler Bay and Devil's Punch Bowl State Parks, but both are extremely hazardous areas when the tide begins to change. All of Oregon's tide pools are protected by Oregon Department of Fish and Wildlife; a good rule of thumb is to look, touch, but don't collect.

With its typical mix of headlands, marshes, and forests, the Lincoln County country is another one of the fine **birding** spots on the Oregon Coast. Siletz Bay National Wildlife Refuge, a priceless wetland buffer between development at Lincoln City and Gleneden Beach, is used regularly by three species of **loons, cormorants, pelicans,** and **bay and sea ducks.** Best viewing is from just outside the refuge at Taft Waterfront Park at the south end of Lincoln City and from parking spots along US 101 as it passes the east side of the bay.

The Salmon River, which lies between Lincoln City and Cascade Head, provides a variety of habitats for fish and mammals. **Roosevelt elk** are frequently spotted along the estuary and in the pastures along US 101. Hunters used to cause quite a stir when they legally shot big bulls while tourists admired what they thought was a protected herd. Elk are so common that they are considered a nuisance on Lincoln City golf courses.

outside in

Attractions

There is no off-season in **Lincoln City.** Every weekend is crowded, and traffic can be the pits. A slew of factory outlets located halfway through town and gaming casinos (to the north and east) have added to the gridlock. The good news is that the restaurant, lodging, and activity choices have never been so favorable. You can seek some solitude on the 7 miles of continuous sandy beach that begin at Roads End (at the north end of town) and continue south all the way to Siletz Bay.

Barnacle Bill's seafood store, 2174 NE US 101, (541) 994-3022, is well known (and open daily) for fresh and smoked seafood: salmon, sturgeon, albacore tuna, black cod, crab, and shrimp. On the north end of town, **Lighthouse Brewpub,** 4157 N US 101, (541) 994-7238, handcrafts some alluring ales and offers 25 beers on tap. **Ryan Gallery,** north of town at 4270 US 101, (541) 994-5391, exhibits mixed media, including fine Northwest watercolors and oils. **Mossy Creek Pottery** in Kernville, just south of Lincoln City, .5 mile up Immonen Rd, (541) 996-2415, sells some of the area's best locally made, high-fired stoneware and porcelain.

In **Gleneden Beach,** across the highway from Salishan Lodge, a cluster of shops includes the Gallery at Salishan, (800) 764-2318, which exhibits superlative paintings, sculpture, and pottery. Farther south along US 101, the Lincoln Beach Bagel Company, 3930 US 101, (541) 764-3882, is a good stop for a snack.

Once a charming coastal community, **Depoe Bay** is today mostly an extension of Lincoln City's strip development. Fortunately, some of the original town, including its picturesque and tiny harbor (surely one of the smallest anywhere), remains intact. The **Channel Bookstore** on US 101, one block south of the bridge, (541) 765-2352, is a used-book paradise. The **O'Connell Gallery,** 42 N US 101, (541) 765-3331, features environmental art and a great water-level view.

Restaurants

Bay House ☆☆☆ Here's a shoreside restaurant with a spectacular view that actually serves wonderful food. The ambience is traditional and the seasonal menu features mostly seafood, sometimes in imaginative preparations. Desserts are ethereal. *5911 SW Hwy 101 (at south edge of town), Lincoln City; (541) 996-3222; $$$.*

Chameleon Cafe ☆ This small cafe packs a culinary punch with plenty of variety. Reggae or Caribbean tunes emanate from the interior, decorated with outrageous art and patrolled by hip waitresses. The menu is an intriguing mix. *2145 NW US 101 (on west side of US 101), Lincoln City; (541) 994-8422; $.*

Chez Jeannette ☆☆☆ The food at this country inn restaurant is traditionally French: butter and cream are used in abundance and most entrees are carefully sauced. Veal, filet mignon, and a nightly game selection are wonderful, but seafood can also be superb. *7150 Old US 101 (.25 mile south of Salishan Lodge on the old highway), Gleneden Beach; (541) 764-3434; $$$.*

Dory Cove Crowds flock to this place, rain or shine. Hearty American fare, Oregon Coast–style, is the theme: seafood, steak, chowder, and 20-plus kinds of burgers. Go for the homemade pie à la mode. *5819 Logan Rd (next to state park), Lincoln City; (541) 994-5180; $.*

Salmon River Cafe ☆ Part deli, part bistro, this is the place for picnic fixings. A glass case displays salads, pastas, and desserts. Service is cheerful, and breakfast, lunch (try Lincoln City's finest cheeseburgers), and dinner will entice you to return. *40798 NW Logan Rd (at north end of town, next to Safeway), Lincoln City; (541) 996-3663; $.*

Tidal Raves ☆ Diners rave about the imaginatively prepared seafood served in this enticing cliffside restaurant. The menu is extensive, and every table in the attractive interior overlooks sculpted cliffs and crashing waves. *279 NW US 101 (on west side of highway), Depoe Bay; (541) 765-2995; $$.*

Lodgings

Channel House ☆ Situated on a cliff overlooking the ocean and the Depoe Bay channel, this inn has 12 rooms, all with private baths and ocean views. Some units have decks with private spas. Be sure to bring your binoculars during whale-watching season. *35 Ellingson St (at end of Ellingson St, above ocean), Depoe Bay; PO Box 56, Depoe Bay, OR 97341; (541) 765-2140 or (800) 447-2140; $$$.*

Inlet Garden Oceanview Bed & Breakfast ☆ Inlet Garden is an ideal alternative to Lincoln City's glitzy oceanfront lodgings. The house has lots of windows, exposed wood, and an ocean-view deck. Guest suites are bright and airy, and three-course breakfasts are memorable. *646 NW Inlet (.25 mile north of D River Wayside), Lincoln City, OR 97367; (541) 994-7932; $$.*

Inn at Otter Crest ☆ This rambling resort at Cape Foulweather is lushly landscaped. Breathtaking views abound, but fog often enshrouds these units that have fireplaces, kitchens, and ocean vistas (all have decks). Other amenities include a pool (with sauna and spa), tennis courts, and an isolated beach. *301 Otter Crest Loop (2 miles south of Depoe Bay), Otter Rock; PO Box 50, Otter Rock, OR 97369; (541) 765-2111 or (800) 452-2101; $$$.*

Salishan Lodge ☆☆☆ The Coast's preeminent resort sprawls over 350 acres and offers 205 guest rooms, an 18-hole golf course, a covered pool, tennis courts, a fitness center, a sauna, and forested trails. The huge lodge houses restaurants, a nightclub, and meeting rooms; kids have their own game room. Guest units are tastefully furnished, Northwest cuisine dominates the main dining room's menu. *On US 101 in Gleneden Beach; PO Box 118, Gleneden Beach, OR 97388; (541) 764-3600 or (800) 452-2300; $$$.*

More Information

Bureau of Land Management, Salem: *(503) 375-5646.*
Central Oregon Coast Association, Newport: *(800) 767-2064.*
Depoe Bay Chamber of Commerce, Depoe Bay: *(541) 765-2889.*
Hebo Ranger District, Hebo: *(541) 392-3161.*
Lincoln City Visitors Bureau, Lincoln City: *(800) 452-2151.*
Lincoln County Parks Department, Newport: *(541) 265-5747.*
Siuslaw National Forest, Corvallis: *(541) 750-7000.*

Newport

From Otter Rock on the north, east to the Lincoln-Benton county line in the Coast Range, south to Heceta Head and the Sea Lion Caves, and west to the Pacific Ocean, including the towns of Newport, Toledo, Seal Rock, Waldport, and Yachats.

A whale from Mexico City helped put Newport on the map. Long a fishing port and the center of a marvelous stretch of coastline, Newport wasn't exactly the hidden gem of the Oregon Coast. The city usually bustled with activity when the weather was good, but its location a little farther away from Portland than Seaside and Lincoln City tended to save it from the weekend influx of visitors.

That all changed on January 7, 1996, when Keiko the killer whale arrived from Mexico City. The star of two *Free Willy* motion pictures, Keiko was transferred from Mexico to his own tank on the Oregon Coast, and Newport hasn't been the same since. The whale's arrival received worldwide publicity, to say nothing of thousands of fan letters from adoring school children from around the country. The Oregon Coast Aquarium has received a constant stream of visitors ever since the whale began calling the place home. The long-term goal is to release Keiko into the wild, but it's hard to find someone who seriously thinks it will happen. Until that day, Keiko will continue to put on weight and thrill the multitudes who get to look through an underwater window while he swims around his tank. Regarding one of Oregon's biggest tourist attractions, emotions are divided on whether he would survive if he were released or whether it's best to keep him safe where he is. It doesn't say much about Oregon that its best-known resident is a penned-up whale, but that's another story.

Certainly Keiko's presence draws attention to the plight of whales around the world. He may even help spawn a new generation of humans who will be more interested in preserving endangered species than recent generations. Keiko also brings visitors to a spectacular part of the state, where an hour of watching a whale is just the first item on the long list of things to do. Newport is blessed with so many sights and activities that it would take the stamina of a whale to see them all.

The Newport area is a great place if you like to camp, surf, comb beaches for booty, hike on long strips of coastal sand or in wilderness areas, dig for clams, go fishing in the ocean, coastal bays, or rivers, or take a flight in a hang glider.

South Beach and Beverly Beach are two of Oregon's most popular coastal campgrounds. Surfing at Moolack Beach north of town is usually as good as it gets in Oregon. Beachcombers have long stretches of sand on the north and south sides of Yaquina Bay, as well as tide pools to check out at Cape Perpetua. Fishing is still productive in Yaquina Bay, as well as out to sea and up the Yaquina and Alsea Rivers. Human flight is possible off Yaquina Head—a hundred thousand seagulls can't be wrong.

In fact, about the only toy you have to leave home when you go to Newport is your dune buggy, because the town is at the heart of the longest vehicle-free strip of coast in Oregon. No wonder the world's most famous orca lives here.

Getting There

Portlanders usually drive the 114 miles to Newport by heading for Lincoln City, then following US Highway 101 (US 101) down the coast. US 20 connects Newport to the mid-Willamette Valley, a 53-mile drive to Corvallis. US 101 follows the coast north to south.

Adjoining Areas

NORTH: **Lincoln City, Wine Country**

SOUTH: **Oregon Dunes**

EAST: **Salem and the Heart of the Valley**

Hiking/Backpacking

The hub for marine-based educational facilities along the Oregon Coast, Newport attracts first-time visitors with its aquarium and other displays of sea life, then keeps them coming back to enjoy the area's numerous recreational opportunities. Perhaps nowhere else on the Oregon Coast is there such a fine mix of hiking opportunities as those found at Newport. Long strolls on sandy beaches, short walks to scenic lighthouses, awe-inspiring views from rocky headlands, and trails into three designated wildernesses entice hikers to return again and again to the Newport area in southern Lincoln County and northern Lane County.

A few backpackers attempt to walk the entire coastline each year. If they want fresh water in camp, they usually need to stay in developed campgrounds accessible to automobiles. Most of the major state park campgrounds have camping loops dedicated to backpackers and long-distance cyclists. Camping on the beach is legal in Oregon, except within the city limits of a half-dozen coastal cities (see Oregon Outdoor Primer and Bay Area chapter). Campfires are allowed on beaches but must be built away from driftwood piles and more than 25 feet from wooden structures.

Coast hikes/beachcombing

Hikers approaching Newport from the north can get a view of what lies ahead from the top of Otter Rock in **Devils Punch Bowl State Park,** west of US 101 off Otter Rock Loop Rd (see Lincoln City chapter). Newport and Yaquina Bay lie 9 miles to the south. A staircase leads south down to the beach, where 4 miles of sand await hikers on **Moolack Beach. Beverly Beach State Park,** 1 mile south of Otter Rock, offers convenient access to the same beach from alongside US 101.

Yaquina Head Outstanding Natural Area is a 100-acre preserve at the tip of Yaquina Head, 3 miles north of US 101 (turn west on Lighthouse Dr). The Bureau of Land Management (BLM) maintains several short interpretive trails on the peninsula, including the wheelchair-accessible **Quarry Cove Tide Pools Trail.** Dedicated in 1994, the .25-mile-long trail was the world's first barrier-free path through a tide pool. The paved trail is under water during high tide, but when the tide goes out the sea life comes into view. Starfish, sea urchins, and sea cucumbers have slowly been moving back into the tide pool since its construction. Each tidal sequence deposits some sand and aquatic vegetation, so all visitors need to be cautious of the slippery surface.

Yaquina Head Lighthouse at the tip of the cape is 93 feet high, and the tallest on the Oregon Coast. The lighthouse, which began operation in 1873, has daily tours during summer. Call (541) 265-2863 for a current schedule. The **Yaquina Head Interpretive Center,** which opened in 1997, sits on the site of an old gravel quarry. The **Yaquina Head Summit Trail** (easy; .3 mile one way) gains 160 feet as it climbs to the top of the head from the east end of the parking loop. The BLM park on the cape is compact and well signed.

Agate and Nye Beaches front the ocean along residential areas of Newport. **Agate Beach State Wayside,** just west of US 101 on the north side of town on Ocean Dr, provides access to Newport's 3 miles of beaches. **Nye Beach** marks the end of Newport's beaches at the north jetty of Yaquina Bay, where the busiest state park in Oregon crowns a 100-foot-high coastal bluff that overlooks Newport harbor. The 32-acre **Yaquina Bay State Park,** located just off US 101 at the north end of the Yaquina Bay Bridge, attracted nearly 1.4 million visitors during a recent 2-year period. **Yaquina Bay Lighthouse,** within the park, commands an impressive view of the entry to the bay, one of Oregon's busiest boating harbors. The state's only lighthouse that still combines living quarters with the light tower is open for tours daily during summer and on weekends the rest of the year.

South Beach State Park, located near the south jetty of Yaquina Bay, marks the beginning of 15 miles of beach that end at Waldport and Alsea Bay. The only detours from the beach are at the crossing of the mouth of Beaver Creek and Seal Rock, both midway between Newport and Waldport.

Located on Alsea Bay, Waldport is an overlooked coastal destination that has all the outdoor activities of the more famous towns. The 4 miles of beach on the north side of town are a good place to look for booty from the sea.

Waldport is connected to Yachats by 8 miles of beach, plus a few minor headlands, before Cape Perpetua interrupts the sandy shores. Yachats has a paved path at the edge of the ocean from downtown and north past its residential areas.

The **Cape Perpetua Scenic Area,** (503) 547-3289, is managed by the Siuslaw National Forest and contains the highest concentration of hiking trails along the Oregon Coast. The visitors center is 2.6 miles south of Yachats on the east side of US 101. Due to the ruggedness of the terrain, most of the trails are inland from the coast where they climb to viewpoints or traverse long ridges well away from the beach. Coast access is available on the **Trail of Restless Waters** (easy; .4-mile loop) and the **Captain Cook Trail** (easy; .6-mile loop). Both are accessible just off US 101. The Captain Cook Trail begins at the visitors center and leads to tide pools filled with marine life. The Spouting Horn, a hole in the rocks that spouts water like a whale when waves hit it just right, can be seen at high tide across Cooks Chasm. The paved Trail of Restless Waters begins .25 mile south of the visitors center and leads to the Devil's Churn overlook. Stairs descend to a rocky tidal shelf, but surprise waves make the area dangerous. The paved **Cape Cove Trail** (easy; .3 mile one way) connects the two trails.

Carl G. Washburne Memorial State Park, 8 miles south of Cape Perpetua on US 101, offers the next convenient access to long stretches of sand. The park's 2 miles of beach, accessible from trailheads in the campground and the day-use area, extend south and end at the tide pools on the north side of Heceta Head. The **Valley Trail** (easy; 1.5 miles one way) begins in the campground near the camp host's site and parallels US 101 on the east side of the highway. Hike the Valley Trail south and come to the **Hobbit Trail** (easy; .5 mile one way), which leads west to the beach. Hike north on the beach for a 4-mile loop.

Heceta Head Lighthouse, located 12 miles north of Florence, sits 205 feet above the ocean at the west edge of 1,000-foot-high Heceta Head. The lighthouse is believed to be the most photographed of the nine lighthouses on the Oregon Coast. The .5-mile trail to Oregon's most powerful coastal light begins at **Devil's Elbow State Park** on the south side of Heceta Head just west of US 101. The lighthouse is open for tours daily during summer and the lightkeeper's house operates as a bed and breakfast; call (541) 547-3696 for reservations.

Sea Lion Caves, a popular tourist attraction, is 1 mile south of Heceta Head (see Wildlife, below). Just south of the caves, the impressive headlands of the central coast give way to the long stretch of sand that runs uninterrupted all the way to the mouth of Coos Bay.

Inland hikes

Three small wilderness areas, along with the Cape Perpetua Scenic Area's trail systems, provide most of the hiking opportunities in the Coast Range around Newport. The trails and wilderness areas are managed by the Waldport Ranger District, (541) 563-3211. Siuslaw National Forest publishes topographic maps of the Drift Creek Wilderness, plus the Cummins Creek Wilderness and Cape Perpetua Scenic Area.

The 18-square-mile **Drift Creek Wilderness** is located 7 miles inland in the hills northeast of Waldport. The Drift Creek watershed has some of the largest remaining stands of old-growth forest in the Coast Range. Douglas fir and western hemlock have been growing for hundreds of years and have reached heights in excess of 200 feet, especially in the north part of the wilderness. Although small compared to wilderness areas in the Cascades, the Drift Creek area is attractive enough to appeal to backpackers.

Three trailheads provide access to the wilderness: Horse Creek north, accessible from national forest roads off US 101, and Horse Creek south and Harris Ranch, accessible from national forest roads off Hwy 34. When Drift Creek runs low during late summer and fall, the creek can be forded and hikes across the pocket wilderness are possible. The **southern part of**

Horse Creek Trail (moderate; 2 miles to Drift Creek) drops 1,200 feet to the creek from the trailhead at the end of Forest Rd 3464. The **north side of Horse Creek Trail** (moderate; 3 miles to Drift Creek) begins at the end of Forest Rd 5087. The **Harris Ranch Trail** (moderate; 3.5 miles to Drift Creek) begins at the end of Forest Rd 346, runs 2 miles to a meadow where the Harris family homesteaded in the 1930s, and continues to Drift Creek. The Harris homestead has the best backpack camping opportunities. Drift Creek is known for its fall runs of chinook salmon and steelhead.

The **Cummins Creek Wilderness** extends east into the Coast Range from Cape Perpetua and is accessible by the 6.2-mile **Cummins Ridge Trail.** The trail traverses the wilderness from the end of Forest Rd 1051 on the west to Forest Rd 5694 near the summit of 2,479-foot Cummins Peak on the east. The first 3.5 miles from the west follow an abandoned road through the ridge-top forest of ancient Sitka spruce trees. Together with the **Rock Creek Wilderness,** it covers 26 miles on the east side of US 101. Easy access to Rock Creek is limited to a .5-mile fisherman's trail from the west. Animal trails and bushwhacking routes are the only other ways to penetrate the thick forest. The fisherman's trail begins at Siuslaw National Forest's Rock Creek Campground.

The Cape Perpetua Scenic Area (see Coast hikes/beachcombing, above) is laced with trails, some busy with hikers near the Cape Perpetua Visitors Center and others far enough away from US 101 to see little use. On the east side of US 101, the cape's trail system leads to the lookout at Cape Perpetua Overlook and deep into the forest along tops of ridges. The **Giant Spruce Trail** (easy; 2 miles round trip) leads from the visitors center to a 500-year-old Sitka spruce. The **St. Perpetua Trail** (moderate; 2.6 miles round trip) climbs 600 feet, also from the visitors center, in switchbacks to a viewpoint that is also accessible by road. The **Whispering Spruce Trail** (easy; .25-mile loop) leads from the parking lot atop Cape Perpetua to a viewpoint at a stone shelter, at 800 feet one of the highest points so close to the pounding surf. The **Discovery Loop Trail** (easy; 1 mile) makes a circuit through the forest behind the visitors center. Loop hikes of 7 to 10 miles are possible by hiking east and then west on the **Cooks Ridge Trail,** the **Gwynn Creek Trail,** and the **Cummins Creek Trail.** The 1.3 miles of the **Oregon Coast Trail,** which parallels the east side of US 101 south of the visitors center, connect with each of the trails' western ends.

Lincoln County maintains the 1.5-mile **Mike Miller Park Educational Trail,** an interpretive trail through a Northwest coast Sitka spruce forest. The trail has 15 numbered posts that describe sand dunes, nurse logs, blowdowns, and snags. To find the park, drive south on US 101 1.2 miles past the Yaquina Bay Bridge and turn east on the park's gravel access road.

Biking

The 50 miles of the **Oregon Coast Bike Route** from Otter Rock on the north to Sea Lion Caves on the south is a challenging mix of climbs over headlands, busy city traffic, and narrow highway shoulders. Long cruising straightaways pass miles of sandy beaches and make the ride rewarding. With so many fantastic views of the ocean, cyclists can all too easily have their attention attracted away from the road where it needs to be focused. The busy section of US 101 through the north end of Newport can be bypassed by riding city streets to the north entrance to Yaquina Bay Bridge, beginning with Ocean View Dr.

Southern Lincoln County has three covered bridges, each a scenic ride inland from a coastal city. The 96-foot **Chitwood Covered Bridge** is just off US 20, about 18 miles east of Newport. The 72-foot **Fisher School Covered Bridge** is 20 miles east of Waldport on Hwy 34, then 10 miles south on Fisher–Five Rivers Rd. The **North Fork of the Yachats Covered Bridge** is 7 miles east of Yachats on Yachats River Rd. County Rd 804 follows the Yachats River and is part of a designated paved tour route that combines with Forest Rd 55 for auto/bike loops through the Coast Range foothills east of Cape Perpetua.

Mountain bikers can ride Forest Rd 55 east 4 miles from the Cape Perpetua Visitors Center to the upper Cook Ridge trailhead. Follow the single-track trail uphill .25 mile, then turn and ride west for 4.5 miles along the **Cooks Ridge Trail** to US 101. The upper part of the singletrack is steep and technical, but the lower 3 miles follow an abandoned roadbed.

Lanham Campground, alongside US 101 about 10 miles south of Yachats, has 10 campsites that were designed by Siuslaw National Forest for use by cyclists and hikers.

Camping

Four Oregon state parks offer camping near the beach in the Newport region. Each has campsites accessible to the handicapped, and all but Washburne take reservations at (800) 452-5687.

Beverly Beach State Park, (541) 265-9278, has camping 7 miles north of Newport on US 101. The park's camping mixture includes 56 RV spaces with full hookups, 76 electrical sites, 136 tent sites, 14 yurts, and a hiker/biker camp. The 130-acre park has its campsites strung out along Spencer Creek. A nature trail leads along the creekside campsites and connects with an underpass beneath US 101 to access Moolack Beach.

South Beach State Park, (541) 867-4715, covers 434 acres just west of US 101 at the south entrance to Yaquina Bay. The park has 244 camp-sites, all with electricity, 10 yurts, and a hiker/biker camp. A trio of short pathways lead from campsites to miles of sandy beach and views of the busy entrance of Yaquina Bay. The park has convenient access to all the major attractions in Newport, including the Mark O. Hatfield Marine Science Center and the Oregon Coast Aquarium on the south side of Yaquina Bay.

Beachside State Park, (541) 563-3220, is 4 miles south of Waldport on US 101. Small in comparison to other coastal state park campgrounds (32 electrical sites and 50 tent sites), the 17-acre park is one of two in the Oregon state parks system with ocean-view campsites. The 9 beachfront campsites at Beachside are available all year (the ones at Cape Lookout near Tillamook are only available during summer), and winter storms can make beachfront camping a memorable experience, indeed.

Washburne State Park, (503) 997-3641, is 14 miles north of Florence on US 101. With 1,089 acres, it's one of the larger coastal parks to explore. RV campers can choose from 58 full hookup sites. Tent campers have 2 sites reserved, plus 6 walk-in sites and a hiker/biker camp. Washburne is ideally situated between two of the Oregon Coast's most photogenic headlands: Cape Perpetua to the north and Heceta Head to the south.

Siuslaw National Forest is one of only two national forests in the contiguous 48 states with land that borders the Pacific Ocean. (The other is California's Los Padres National Forest.) It has 3 coastal campgrounds in the Newport area, but most of its overnight facilities are concentrated farther south (see Oregon Dunes chapter). **Tillicum Beach Campground,** 4.7 miles south of Waldport on US 101, is the largest, with 59 sites, and is open all year. **Cape Perpetua Campground,** 2.7 miles south of Yachats, and **Rock Creek Campground,** 10 miles south of Yachats, close for the winter around November 1. Cape Perpetua has 37 sites and Rock Creek 17. All are managed by the Waldport Ranger District, (551) 563-3211.

Ten Mile Creek and **Canal Creek** are inland Forest Service campgrounds that cater to hikers. Both have fewer than 10 sites and are managed by the Waldport Ranger District. Ten Mile Creek is situated between the Cummins Creek and Rock Creek Wildernesses on Forest Rd 56, while Canal Creek is 4 miles south of the Alsea River on Forest Rd 3462.

Parks/Picnics

Oregon's central coast is lined with pretty spots to pull off US 101, break out the picnic basket, and enjoy lunch with a view. Many of the state park waysides along the way also have beach access, so you can stretch your legs and burn calories if you eat too much.

Beverly Beach State Park begins the parade of roadside picnic tables. Located 7 miles north of Newport on US 101, the park is the state's second-busiest campground next to Fort Stevens near Warrenton. If so many campers scare off would-be picnickers, **Agate Beach State Recreation Site** is 6 miles to the south. Located at the southern end of Yaquina Head, Agate Beach has a good view of the Yaquina Head Lighthouse and a path to the beach. Named for the silica-filled rocks that can be picked from the sand, Agate Beach is just one of many places along the Oregon Coast that are productive for **rockhounds.** Other beachside rock collecting areas in the Newport country can be found at Moolack Shores and the north jetty of Yaquina Bay near Newport, Seal Rock near Waldport, and Bayshore and the mouth of the Yachats River in Yachats.

Yaquina Bay is a large estuary with many scenic settings accessible by automobile. The main roads give the bay a wide berth, but several lesser roads follow the bay shore closely before veering away. Any wide parking spot can be a good place to watch the comings and goings of the tide while having a bite to eat. Toledo, located on the Yaquina River 7 miles east of Newport, has picnicking at **Toledo City Park.**

The coast south from Newport to Heceta Head is lined with day-use state parks along US 101. Nearly all have picnic facilities and access to the beach. Day-use parks between Newport and Waldport are **Lost Creek, Ona Beach, Seal Rock,** and **Driftwood Beach. W. B. Nelson** is 1 mile east of Waldport on Hwy 34. **Governor Patterson Memorial** is the first park south of Waldport and is followed by **Smelt Sands,** several sites at **Yachats, Neptune, Stonefield Beach,** and **Devil's Elbow.** The most popular spots are the 237-acre park at Ona Beach, where Beaver Creek empties into the Pacific; 94-acre Yachats State Park, where a paved trail on the bluff above the beach gives wheelchair access to ocean views; 302-acre Neptune Park, with its access to tide pools and Cape Perpetua; and 546-acre Devil's Elbow, where Cape Cove provides a spectacular setting for Heceta Head Lighthouse at the top of the bluff to the north.

Siuslaw National Forest has beachside picnic facilities at **Devil's Churn** and **Cape Perpetua,** both 2.6 miles south of Yachats on US 101, and at **Ocean Beach,** 7 miles south of Cape Perpetua near Rock Creek Campground.

Fishing

Yaquina Bay, one of the busiest fishing spots on the Oregon Coast, meets the Pacific Ocean at Newport. Formed by the Yaquina River, the bay covers 1,700 acres and has tidewater inland for 13 miles. The south side of the bay is served by the Newport Marina at South Beach, (541) 867-3321, a Port of Newport facility with a public boat launch at 2301 SE Marine Science Dr. One of the largest marine harbors on the Oregon Coast, the marina has 600 moorage slips, as well as parking for recreational vehicles and a complete line of support facilities.

A charter boat fleet operates out of Newport for fishing and whale-watching tours. Check with Newport Tradewinds, (541) 265-2101, Newport Sportfishing, (800) 828-8777, or Sea Gull Charters, (541) 265-7441. All are located on Bay Blvd on the north side of the bay near the Embarcadero Marina, (541) 265-5435. Depending on current regulations, the primary catch is salmon, halibut, and bottom fish. Some years bring warm water close enough to shore to support charter albacore trips. Fishing in the bay itself is best for sea perch, lingcod, and flounder. The bay is also noted for its crabbing and clam digging.

The **Yaquina River** supports a strong run of fall chinook, with most action happening in the lower river and bay. Sturgeon are occasionally taken in the bay during winter and spring.

Alsea Bay at Waldport sees most fishing action inside the bay due to rough bar conditions and limited charter boat facilities. The bay is productive for chinook during the fall and for sea perch and flounder throughout the year. The **Alsea River,** 55 miles long, is noted for its winter runs of steelhead and coho. The bay and lower river are served by a half-dozen marinas, many of which cater to those who want to cash in on the bay's productive **crabbing** grounds. The Port of Alsea, (541) 563-3872, has a 500-foot transient dock plus a handful of open wet slips in town at the end of Mill St.

Southern Lincoln County has few other coastal streams capable of supporting runs of salmon and steelhead. Most stream fishing is for wild cutthroat trout, but regulations require catch-and-release to help rebuild the population. Planted rainbow trout can be caught in the two **Big Creek Reservoirs** on the east side of Newport, **Olalla Reservoir** near Toledo, and **Eckman Lake** at the W. B. Nelson State Wayside in Waldport.

Kayaking/Canoeing

Sea kayakers mix with fishing boats when they paddle the waters of Yaquina and Alsea Bays. Both bays have scenic and interesting paddling opportunities that are made convenient by the many public and private boat launches in the area.

The **Yaquina River** offers paddling trips of 10 miles or more with sea kayaks and canoes, from Elk City downstream to tidewater at Toledo or all the way into Newport. The **Alsea River** is one of the most heavily boated medium-size rivers along the Oregon Coast. The lower river is busy with fishermen in drift boats, especially during winter when the river's main run of steelhead is present and during fall when chinook are in the river.

Boat landings are numerous along the river and can be used for launching canoes and sea kayaks for trips to the bay. The Alsea River offers a 32-mile float, usually Class I but occasionally Class II, from the Mill Creek Park launch 2 miles west of Alsea on Hwy 34 in Benton County downstream to the town of Tidewater, 10 miles east of Waldport.

Wildlife

When it comes to looking at wildlife, sometimes it's best to bite the bullet, pay the entry fee, and enjoy. The Newport area has some of the best wildlife-watching opportunities in Oregon, especially at commercial operations where everything from killer whales to octopus are on display.

Keiko the **killer whale** lives in Newport at the **Oregon Coast Aquarium** on the south side of Yaquina Bay. Captured in waters off Iceland in the late 1970s, Keiko lived at Marineland in Niagara Falls, Ontario, until he was purchased and moved to Mexico City in 1986. He starred in the *Free Willy* movies without ever leaving his tank in Mexico. Keiko was moved to Newport in 1996 because he was having health problems in his Mexico tank, which was too small and had trouble keeping the water cold enough. Although Keiko came to Oregon for rehabilitation, not exhibition, he has become one of the biggest tourist draws in the state and perhaps Oregon's best-known resident. The 32-acre aquarium has plenty of other interesting exhibits, including **sea otters, sea lions, sea birds, jellyfish,** and the critters that call tide pools home. The aquarium is open daily. For information, call (541) 867-4931. The aquarium is located at 2820 SE Ferry Slip Rd, 1 mile east of US 101 on the south side of Yaquina Bay.

The **Hatfield Marine Science Center,** (541) 867-3011, is located near the aquarium on Marine Science Dr. The science center was built in 1965, while the aquarium opened in 1992. Visitor interest has shifted in recent years, but the science center continues to welcome visitors daily and helps teach them about the coastal environment. The Undersea Garden, (541) 265-2206, is a commercial display of sea creatures on the north side of Yaquina Bay at Newport's downtown waterfront.

Sea Lion Caves, located at the last rocky headland before the coast slips south into a long stretch of sand, is North America's largest sea cave. The cave is the site of a commercial operation that uses an elevator to carry visitors 208 feet down through solid rock to a refuge used by **Steller sea lions.** The marine mammals visit the cave in their greatest numbers during winter storms. During summer when most tourists are in the area, the caves may be visited by only a few sea lions. Either way, the voyage into the cavern is worth the price of admission. The caves' owner has helped keep a refuge open for the sea lions over the years and played an important role in protecting the animals until Congress passed the Marine

Mammals Protection Act. For information on the cave, call (541) 547-3111. Located near the midpoint of the Oregon Coast, the cave is 38 miles south of Newport and 11 miles north of Florence on US 101. The cave entrance and visitors center is on the west side of the highway and parking is on the east side.

The Newport country has a wealth of other wildlife-viewing opportunities. Designated spots for the **California gray whale** migration, staffed by volunteers during Christmas and spring-break weeks, are located at Pacific Shore RV Park and Yaquina Head Lighthouse, both 3 miles north of Newport on US 101; the Donald A. Davis City Kiosk in Newport; Yaquina Bay State Park; Devil's Churn, Cook's Chasm, and the overlook and visitors center at Cape Perpetua; and the Sea Lion Caves turnout along US 101.

Newport companies that specialize in **whale-watching tours** are Marine Discovery Tours, (800) 903-2628, at 345 SW Bay Blvd, and Sea Gull Charters, (541) 265-7441, at 343 SW Bay Blvd.

The central Oregon Coast has perhaps the greatest number of easily accessible **tide pools** in Oregon. From the north, the pools are found at the quarry on the south side of Yaquina Head, at Seal Rock, at Yachats State Park, at Cape Perpetua, and at two locations in Neptune State Park. The tide comes and goes twice every 24 hours and 50 minutes along the Oregon Coast. A tide table should be consulted to determine the best time to anticipate low tide, which is when residents of the tide pools are not covered by water. Annual tide tables are often printed in local telephone books and are available at sporting goods stores, visitors centers, and motels.

Several of the islands of the Oregon Islands National Wildlife Refuge are located offshore from the central coast. Gull, Otter, Whaleback, and Yaquina Head Rocks are all offshore north of Newport, while Seal Rocks are 4 miles north of Waldport. The 575 acres of the 1,400 offshore rocks, islands, and reefs in the coastal refuge system are home to large numbers of **seabirds** and **marine mammals**. It's illegal to set foot on the islands, but their animal life can be seen through binoculars from highway pullouts the length of the Oregon Coast.

The comings and goings of a variety of sea- and shorebirds can be seen from Yaquina Head, Yaquina and Alsea Bays, Yachats, and Cape Perpetua. While **gulls, murres,** and **puffins** prefer the coastal islands, the bays are filled with **mergansers, buffleheads,** and **red-necked grebes.** All three species of **West Coast loons** pass through regularly, including the rare **yellow-billed loon.**

Trails inland from Cape Perpetua (see Hiking/Backpacking, above) are productive for viewing mammals, including **Roosevelt elk, black bear,** and even an occasional **cougar.** It pays to keep both eyes open for possible wildlife activity anywhere in the Newport region.

Surfing

Moolack Beach, which melds into one with Beverly Beach and extends north of Newport from Yaquina Head to Otter Rock, usually attracts a steady following of surfers when conditions are good. Access is usually down a staircase from the parking lot at Otter Rock State Wayside or from pullouts alongside US 101 2 miles north of Yaquina Head. **Yaquina Head Cove,** on the south side of Yaquina Head, is known for its consistent surf, though rip currents can make the area dangerous during winter. The cove can be reached by hiking downhill to the beach from a paved parking lot just south of Yaquina Head off US 101, 4 miles north of Newport. Surfers also ride the waves at the **south jetty of Yaquina Bay** in South Beach State Park (see Camping, above). The rip current is known to be hazardous in winter surf conditions here, too.

Attractions

The most popular tourist destination on the Oregon Coast, **Newport** blends tasteful development (the Performing Arts Center, for example) with unending shopping-center sprawl. Lately, the furor over **Keiko** (the famous *Free Willy* killer whale residing at the Oregon Coast Aquarium; see Wildlife, above) has engulfed Newport like the wind and sideways rain of a winter sou'wester, and the tourist season is unending. To discover all that Newport has to offer, steer away from US 101's commercial chaos. Head for the **bay front,** a working harbor going full tilt, where fishing boats of all types—trollers, trawlers, shrimpers, and crabbers—berth year-round.

After a day on the water, quaff a native beer at the **Rogue Ales Public House,** 748 SW Bay Blvd, (541) 265-3188, home of the local microbrewery. Or sample the fresh catch at the **Taste of Newport,** 837 SW Bay Blvd, (541) 574-9450, which offers indoor and outdoor dining (and is a great stop for kids). **Oceanic Arts Center,** 444 SW Bay Blvd, (541) 265-5963, and the **Wood Gallery,** 818 SW Bay Blvd, (541) 265-6843, both on the bay front, are galleries worth visiting. The former offers mostly jewelry, paintings, pottery, and sculpture; the latter offers functional sculpture, woodwork, pottery, and weaving.

The **Nye Beach** area, on the ocean side of the highway, has fewer tourists and more of an arts-community feel, housing a potpourri of writers, artists, tourists, and fishermen. The **Newport Performing Arts Center,** 777 S Olive, (541) 265-ARTS, is an attractive wooden structure that hosts music, theater, and other events, some of national caliber. The **Visual Arts Center** at 839 NW Beach, (541) 265-5133, offers an ocean-front setting for exhibits and classes.

Artists and others seeking elbow room have moved to **Seal Rock** from crowded Newport. It's still not much more than a patch of strip development along US 101, but within that patch are a few keepers. Some interesting chain-saw art is being created at **Seal Rock Woodworks** along US 101, (541) 563-2452. Also along the highway, a tiny storefront with a sign proclaiming "Fudge" sells a variety of light and dark fudge and some tasty ice cream; (541) 563-2766. Farther south, **Art on the Rocks,** 5667 NW Pacific Coast Hwy, 2 miles north of the Alsea Bay Bridge, (541) 563-3920, has paintings, carvings, crafts, and jewelry.

Waldport is a town in coastal limbo, overshadowed by its larger, better-known neighbors—Newport to the north and Yachats to the south. Not to worry; Waldport has much to recommend it, including the lovely Alsea River estuary, untrampled beaches at either end of town, and a city center unspoiled by tourism. At the south end of the Alsea Bay Bridge (beautifully rebuilt in 1991) is an **interpretive center** with historic transportation displays.

Yachats (pronounced "ya-hots") means "at the foot of the mountain." The town has a hip, arts-community flavor, with an interesting mix of aging counterculturalists, yups, and tourists. Good local galleries include **Earthworks Gallery,** 2222 N US 101, (541) 547-4300, and **Backporch Gallery,** Fourth and US 101, (541) 547-4500.

Yachats is situated at the threshold of the spectacular 2,700-acre **Cape Perpetua Scenic Area.** Driving along US 101 provides an exhilarating journey, packed with panoramas of rugged cliffs abutting the ever-changing Pacific. The Cape Perpetua Visitors Center at 2400 S US 101, (541) 547-3289, offers films, displays, maps, and a logical starting point (see also Hiking/Backpacking, above).

Restaurants

Canyon Way Restaurant and Bookstore ☆☆ This eatery is actually an emporium, with a bookstore, gift shop, deli, and restaurant on the premises. The diverse menu is loaded with seafood and fresh pasta plates. *1216 SW Canyon Way (between Hurbert St and Bay Blvd), Newport; (541) 265-8319; $$.*

Cosmos Cafe & Gallery A step inside this hip eatery is like a step into outer space: the deep-blue ceilings feature heavenly bodies. Order from the counter, then enjoy the choices of salads, sandwiches, pastas, omelets, and Tex-Mex concoctions. The adjacent gallery is fun. *740 W Olive St (across from the Performing Arts Center), Newport; (541) 265-7511; $.*

La Serre ☆ This is one of the central coast's better restaurants. A plethora of plants highlights a dining area with skylights and a beamed ceiling. Seafood's a good bet, vegetarian dishes are top drawer, and, on Sunday, this is breakfast headquarters. Closed January. *160 W 2nd (2nd and Beach, downtown), Yachats; (541) 547-3420; $$.*

New Morning Coffeehouse ☆ A cross section of Yachats society frequents this homey retreat. Muffins, pies, and coffee cakes are superb; soups and chili are typical luncheon fare. During summer, New Morning whips up good pasta dinners and weekend live music. *373 N US 101 (at 4th St), Yachats; (541) 547-3848; $.*

Whale's Tale ☆ Serving up good food in Newport for more than 20 years, this spot's whale-motif interior is a bit ragged around the edges. Customers remain a mix of fishermen, hippies, and tourists. *452 SW Bay Blvd (at Hurbert), Newport; (541) 265-8660; $$.*

Yuzen ☆ A Japanese restaurant in a Bavarian-style building, located in a town with a Wild West motif, this place may sound unreal, but it sure isn't. The splendid sukiyaki, sushi, and tempura dishes are proof that this is the finest Japanese cuisine on the coast. *US 101 (8 miles south of Newport), Seal Rock; (541) 563-4766; $$.*

Lodgings

The Adobe Resort ☆ Ensconced in a parklike setting, the resort fans out around the edge of a basalt shore. Most of the sizable rooms have ocean views. All guests have access to a Jacuzzi and sauna. Children are welcome, and the on-site restaurant is *very* oceanfront. *1555 US 101 (downtown), Yachats; PO Box 219, Yachats, OR 97498; (541) 547-3141 or (800) 522-3623; $$.*

Cape Cod Cottages ☆ These cottages occupy 300 feet of quiet ocean frontage with easy beach access. Ten cozy, spic-and-span units come with kitchens, fireplaces, decks, and views. Some units sleep eight. Children are welcome. *4150 SW Pacific Coast Hwy (2.5 miles south of Waldport, on US 101), Waldport, OR 97394; (541) 563-2106; $$.*

Edgewater Cottages ☆ These varied cottages (popular with honeymooners) all have a beachy feel, ocean views, kitchens, and sun decks. They book up early and there are minimum-stay requirements. Kids and pets are fine (the latter by prior approval only). *3978 SW Pacific Coast Hwy (2.5 miles south of Waldport, on US 101), Waldport, OR 97394; (541) 563-2240; $$.*

Nye Beach Hotel & Cafe ☆ This place has a funky, '50s feel (narrow halls sport wildly shaped mirrors and succulents). All 18 rooms feature private baths, balconies, and views. The hotel's lobby has a tiny bar. A suave waitstaff serves all meals in a bistrolike setting. *219 NW Cliff St (just south of Sylvia Beach Hotel), Newport, OR 97365; (541) 265-3334; $$.*

Ocean House ☆ The setting overlooks a beach and a lighthouse, and the host is the epitome of congeniality. Guest rooms (all with private baths and views) are comfortable, not luxurious. If it's booked, try the ocean-front Tyee Lodge across the street. *4920 NW Woody Way (just off US 101 N in Agate Beach, 1 block south of Yaquina Head Lighthouse Rd), Newport, OR 97365; (541) 265-6158 or (800) 56BANDB; $$$.*

Sea Quest Bed & Breakfast ☆☆ This estatelike structure is located on a sandy bluff above the ocean. Most rooms have spas in their baths, queen-size beds, private entrances, and ocean views. There are miles of Pacific vistas. *95354 US 101 (6.5 miles south of Yachats on west side of US 101, between mile markers 171 and 172), Yachats; PO Box 448, Yachats, OR 97498; (541) 547-3782 or (800) 341-4878; $$$.*

Shamrock Lodgettes These rustic "lodgettes" (some are cabins, but most are rooms) are located on a grassy, oceanfront terrace. All are cozy and comfortable and enjoy fireplaces; some have kitchens. A sauna and spa are open to all guests. Pets are welcome. *On US 101 S (just south of Yachats River Bridge), Yachats; PO Box 346, Yachats, OR 97498; (541) 546-3312 or (800) 845-5028; $$.*

Sylvia Beach Hotel ☆☆ This bluff-top hotel is dedicated to bookworms and their literary heroes and heroines. Book one of the three "classics"— the "bestsellers" (views) and the "novels" (nonviews) are small but equally imaginative. Breakfast is included; dinner is by reservation only. *267 NW Cliff St (west on NW 3rd off US 101, 6 blocks to NW Cliff), Newport, OR 97365; (541) 265-5428; $$.*

Cheaper Sleeps

The See Vue With miles of Pacific panoramas, this place lives up to its name. Each unit in this cedar-shake lodging is differently appointed. The Salish offers the sweetest deal, but most rooms are less than $60. Wander down to the uncrowded beach. *95590 US 101 S, Yachats, OR 97498; (541) 547-3227; $.*

The Vikings These rustic cottages occupy an oceanfront bluff (steep stairs lead down to the beach). All have TVs; some have fireplaces and kitchens. Off-season rates begin at $50. The "crow's nest" is great for couples, but prices creep beyond bargain range in summer. *729 NW Coast St, Newport, OR 97365; (541) 265-2477 or (800) 480-2477; $.*

More Information

Alsea Ranger District, Alsea: *(541) 487-5811.*

Bureau of Land Management, Salem: *(503) 375-5646.*

Cape Perpetua Visitors Center, Yachats: *(541) 547-3289.*

Central Oregon Coast Association, Newport: *(800) 767-2064.*

Greater Newport Chamber of Commerce, Newport: *(800) 262-7844.*

Lincoln County Parks Department, Newport: *(541) 265-5747.*

Mapleton Ranger District, Mapleton: *(541) 268-4473.*

Siuslaw National Forest, Corvallis: *(541) 750-7000.*

Toledo Area Chamber of Commerce, Toledo: *(541) 336-3183.*

Waldport Ranger District, Waldport: *(541) 563-3211.*

Waldport Visitors Center, Waldport: *(541) 563-2133.*

Yachats Area Visitors Center, Yachats: *(541) 547-3530.*

Yaquina Head Outstanding Natural Area, BLM, Newport:
   (541) 265-2863.

Oregon Dunes

From Heceta Head on the north, east to the Coast Range divide in Lane and Douglas Counties, south to the south end of Oregon Dunes National Recreation Area in Coos County, and west to the Pacific Ocean, including the towns of Florence, Gardiner, Reedsport, and Winchester Bay.

T he dune buggy is still king of the beach at the Oregon Dunes. In a world that increasingly restricts personal freedom, here recreationists are allowed to zoom over one of the nation's largest coastal sand dunes (45 miles long) with something bordering on impunity.

Allowing driving on the dunes drives some environmentalists crazy, but the people who maneuver the noisy machines sure love it. Much of the 53 miles of coastal plain, from Florence on the north to the mouth of the Coos River on the south, is open to off-road-vehicle driving. A dune buggy is a catchall term that includes vehicles of varying shapes and sizes—from the classic rail (a buggy with an engine, a couple of seats, four tires, and a body that looks like it was made from old hand railings) to street-legal four-wheel-drive trucks, off-road motorcycles, and all-terrain four-wheelers.

It's hard to know who is having the most fun. Speed and climbing ability may be the objective for the young male crowd, but dune-buggy drivers are just as apt to be people over 50 and their grandchildren. Don't be surprised when a driver of an ATV takes off a helmet and reveals the head of an eight-year-old. It's all legal on the Oregon Dunes and its staging areas—even on some paved roads where someone that age would never be allowed to drive a car.

Visitors to the Oregon Dunes don't need to bring their own buggies to enjoy the mountain of sand. Rental outfits are as common as ·mushrooms after a fall rain. As with mushrooms, the more knowledge someone has about dune buggy–riding the safer the activity is. Rangers for the Oregon Dunes National Recreation Area (NRA) regularly patrol the dunes, looking for rule breakers and troublemakers. But mainly they're making the rounds in order to quickly respond to accidents. It's a rare summer day when there isn't some type of accident. Fortunately, most are no more serious than broken bones. Remember that dune buggy–riding is supposed to be a fun sport.

While dune buggies dominate the Oregon Dunes, they are by no means the only way to have a good time in the sand. Winchester Bay, located at the mouth of the Umpqua River, is situated near the middle of the dunes and provides some of Oregon's most outstanding coastal and estuary fishing. A nearby string of lakes, cut off from the ocean long ago by the growing piles of sand, offer some of the best bass fishing in the state. And enough coastal sand is off-limits to dune buggies to provide outstanding coastal hiking, horseback riding, and a little peace.

At the end of a long day, you'll find dune buggies can also be kings of the campground. Visitors to the Oregon Dunes who don't appreciate the noise of motors need to carefully pick their spot to place their pillow. The dunes are a big place—and they've been accommodating a diverse variety of visitors for many years.

Getting There

Florence is the gateway to the northern part of the Oregon Dunes, while Reedsport is centrally located in the dunes. Florence is 164 miles southwest of Portland, with an option of leaving Interstate 5 and driving west from Junction City on meandering and scenic Highway 36 or by exiting Interstate 5 at Eugene and using the more direct Highway 126. Visitors heading directly to Reedsport, 197 miles from Portland, drive south on Interstate 5 to the Drain exit 30 miles south of Eugene, then head 57 miles west to Reedsport via Highway 38. Although Reedsport is more than twice as far from Portland and Lincoln City as Florence, the freeway access makes it a viable alternative route to the area during times of crowded traffic on peak summer weekends. US Highway 101 (US 101) follows the coast north to south.

Adjoining Areas

NORTH: **Newport**

SOUTH: **Bay Area**

EAST: **Greater Eugene, The Umpqua Valley**

inside out

Dune Buggies

The first thing to do is get legal. Renters at any of the numerous dune-buggy centers from Florence to Reedsport don't usually need to worry. The company they rent from is obligated to abide by the regulations and to have a special-use permit for operating in Siuslaw National Forest. Those who bring their own vehicles to the dunes should stop at the national recreation area headquarters in Reedsport, (541) 271-3611, at 855 Highway Ave, to pick up the informative brochure called "Off-Road Vehicle Guide to the Sand Areas of the Siuslaw National Forest." The brochure explains in detail the legal requirements for off-road riding and the best places to enjoy it.

Vehicles must be registered, and their operators should either have a driver's license or have completed an all-terrain-vehicle training course. All vehicles must display a raised flag and be equipped with mufflers, brakes, lights, and seat belts. Some variance is given to off-road motorcycles.

The Oregon Dunes National Recreation Area stretches for 45 miles along the coast, from the south jetty of the Siuslaw River near Florence to the Horsfall area at the north end of Coos Bay near North Bend. The dunes vary in width from 1 to 2 miles. Because of the shifting sand, much of the dunes lacks paved roads. Because walking can be very difficult in dry sand, an off-road vehicle can be the best way to cover the territory and become intimately familiar with the dunes. While most of the dunes are open throughout the year to vehicles, some portions have summer closures and other parts are closed permanently. Although most closed areas are signed, it's the driver's responsibility to know where riding is allowed around the three major staging areas: North Siltcoos, High Dunes, and South Dunes.

The **North Siltcoos** off-road-vehicle area is at the north end of the dunes near Florence. The South Jetty access road has staging areas at Good Pasture and South Jetty on the north side of the open area. The Siltcoos River west of Westlake is an even busier staging area on the south end of the North Siltcoos riding area. Riding is pretty much open 6 miles to the south, except for a small closure around Cleawox Lake to avoid conflict with pedestrians.

The **High Dunes** riding area begins on the south side of the Umpqua River. Staging areas are located along Umpqua Beach Rd, although beach riding is allowed only in a small section from October 1 through April 30. Although this is the least popular of the dunes' three staging areas, it's still much larger than the Sand Lake area in Tillamook County, the other designated off-road riding area on the coast, and offers plenty of riding opportunities.

The **South Dunes** is the largest and busiest off-road-vehicle area on the Oregon Coast. Stretching for 12 miles between the ocean and US 101, the South Dunes staging areas are Spinreel in the north, Hauser in the middle, and Horsfall Rd in the south. The area includes a number of scattered parcels of private property that are closed to public use.

Off-road-vehicle drivers tend to congregate in certain campgrounds so they can share war stories and look at each other's rigs. Favorite campgrounds where riding from camp is legal are Driftwood II and Waxmyrtle near Siltcoos River, Spinreel near Lakeside, and Horsfall near North Bend. Horsfall has large open camping areas that really pack in the campers and riders during peak times (see Camping, below).

Dune buggy–riding is a lot of fun, or it wouldn't be such a big business on the central Oregon Coast. Whether powering up a 200-foot sand dune or cruising the posted speed limit on the beach, it's an activity that provides a high dose of adrenaline. It's easy for nonmotorized recreationists to look at it with disgust, but that attitude often changes once they give it a try.

For those who just want to see the dunes, **guided tours** in large passenger vehicles may be the way to go. Escorted tours, as well as vehicle rentals, are offered by Sand Dunes Frontier and Theme Park of Florence, (541) 997-3544; Dune Buggy Adventures of Winchester Bay, (541) 271-6972; Pacific Coast Recreation of North Bend (Hauser), (541) 756-7183; and Spinreel Dune Buggy Rentals of North Bend, (541) 759-3313. Tours start as low as $15.

Other companies that **rent vehicles** include Sandland Adventures of Florence, (541) 997-8087; Dune Odyssey of Winchester Bay, (541) 271-3863, and Winchester Bay Rentals of Winchester Bay, (541) 271-9357. Four-wheel all-terrain vehicles rent for $20 for a half hour up to $175 for the day. The rental companies have lots of hidden charges for damages, rescues, cleanup, and deposits, so compare prices carefully, be safe, and have fun.

Hiking

Dunes and beaches

It's not all dune buggies at the dunes. Hikers have plenty of places to explore far from the sound of motor vehicles. Dunes hiking, however, is different from the beach walking that is so common elsewhere on the Oregon Coast. Walking along the beach usually requires nothing more than locating a trail or path, following it to the wave-washed sand, turning, and heading up or down the coastline. When dunes hiking, you may need to hike 2 miles through the dunes to reach the shore.

Always make note of **landmarks,** especially trees, when hiking on the dunes. A compass can come in handy when the fog comes in and confuses your directional sense. Wind and rain can quickly erase your footprints. Wear lightweight **tennis shoes** rather than hiking boots, which can break through the surface of the sand and make hiking exhausting. Save long hikes for when the surface of the sand is wet, because dry sand is extremely tiresome to walk on. Expect to encounter shallow streams and boggy areas, which make it difficult to keep your feet dry and your clothes clean. **Quicksand** is also present during the rainy season. The Oregon Dunes receive an average of 75 inches of rainfall each year.

Dunes and beach hiking begin on the north at **Baker Beach,** a Siuslaw National Forest trailhead 9 miles north of Florence. Baker Beach is in the Mapleton Ranger District, (541) 268-4473, outside the boundaries of the Oregon Dunes National Recreation Area, but it offers essentially the same type of hiking experience as the dunes to the south. Baker Beach, **Sutton Beach,** and **Heceta Beach** all run together for 6 miles, forming an unbroken line of coastal sand from Sea Lion Caves on the north to the north jetty of the Siuslaw River on the south near Florence. Sutton Creek midway along can be difficult to cross during high water. The road to Baker Beach leaves US 101 about 2.5 miles north of Sutton Lake. Drive west for .75 mile to the end of the road, then hike .5 mile through the foredunes to the beach. The southern part of the beach can be reached by driving from Florence to the community of Heceta Beach or to the north jetty.

Recreation facilities in the nearby **Sutton Lake complex** include a 7-mile trail that connects Sutton and Alder Dunes Campgrounds with the boat ramp on Sutton Lake and a viewing deck along Sutton Creek.

The **Oregon Dunes National Recreation Area** covers 32,000 acres and offers outstanding opportunities for solitary hiking in areas closed to motor vehicles. Don't expect to find a wide, manicured trail everywhere because it's impossible to build such a thing through ever-changing sand dunes. On the other hand, expect to end the day every bit as tired after walking through miles of sand with little elevation change as after a much longer hike on a mountain. Stop by the Oregon Dunes headquarters, which also serves as the visitors center, in Reedsport for a free guide to the hiking trails of the dunes. The visitors center, (541) 271-3611, is on the west side of US 101 at the intersection with Hwy 38.

The **Oregon Coast Trail** follows the beach from beneath Sea Lion Caves to the Horsfall area near North Bend. The trail veers inland at Florence, Reedsport, and North Bend to cross the major rivers on highway bridges.

While the beach works well as a through hiking route, many parts are a long way away from US 101 parking areas. Several trails and hiking routes lead from the campgrounds along the highway through the dunes to the beach.

The Siltcoos River campgrounds (see Camping, below), 7 miles south of Florence west of US 101, are popular as a staging area for off-road vehicles, but they also access hiking opportunities in areas closed to riding. The **Waxmyrtle Trail** (easy; 1.5 miles one way) begins along the Siltcoos River at Waxmyrtle Campground. The trail follows the river's estuary before ending at the beach. The **Chief Siltcoos Trail** (easy; 1.25-mile loop) begins at Stagecoach trailhead, located on the south side of Siltcoos River Rd .5 mile before it ends at the beach. The trail circles through a thick coastal evergreen forest that includes shore pines, huckleberries, and rhododendrons. The **Lagoon Trail** (easy; 1-mile loop) circles Lagoon Campground and offers views of wildlife in a bend of the Siltcoos River that was isolated by construction of a road.

Carter and Taylor Lakes, 7.5 miles south of Florence on the west side of US 101, have a 2-mile trail system that leads to a viewing deck for an overlook of the dunes and continues on to the beach. Wooden posts mark the hiking route through open sand. This part of the dunes is closed to motor vehicles, although the beach is open for driving from September 16 through March 14.

The **Oregon Dunes Overlook Trail** (difficult; 3.5-mile loop) begins 10 miles south of Florence on the west side of US 101. The overlook parking area has a wooden boardwalk and viewing platform, plus a trailhead for a loop through the dunes. The beach is 1 mile away on the **Overlook Beach Trail.** To make the loop, hike south 1 mile on the beach, watch for a trail marker on the foredune, and return on the **Tahkenitch Loop Trail.**

The **Tahkenitch Creek Trail** 11 miles south of Florence begins at a day-use trailhead on the west side of US 101. The trail has three separate loops of 1.5, 2.5 and 4 miles, increasing from easy to difficult because walking through sand is tiring. The trail wanders through the dunes and is usually within view of the wildlife that inhabit the creek. The beach is not accessible because of the creek.

Tahkenitch Campground, 12.5 miles south of Florence (see Camping, below), is the trailhead for the **Tahkenitch Dunes Trail** (moderate; 2 miles one way) and the **Threemile Lake Trail** (difficult; 3 miles one way). Both trails reach the beach and can be hiked as a 6.5-mile loop by making the connection along the beach. Wooden posts with blue bands on the top mark the points where the trails reach the beach. The fresh water of Threemile Lake makes this a possible backpack outing. Off-trail parts of the dunes are closed to protect nesting habitat of the snowy plover from March 15 through September 15.

The **Umpqua Dunes Trail** (moderate; 1.5 miles one way), which leads through the **Umpqua Scenic Dunes,** is the most popular hike in the southern dunes between Reedsport and North Bend. The area has a special protected status within the Oregon Dunes NRA and its large dunes are off-limits to motor vehicles. The trail begins at Eel Creek Campground (see Camping, below), or from a nearby day-use parking area along US 101, both about 10.5 miles south of Reedsport. The trail leads through some of the highest dunes on the Oregon Coast before ending at the beach. The **Eel Trail** (easy; .75 mile one way) begins at campsite 50 in the Eel Creek Campground and connects with the Umpqua Dunes Trail.

The **Horsfall area,** 4 miles north of North Bend, is the dunes' busiest staging area for off-road vehicles. Hikers waiting for riders in their family to return can enjoy the **Bluebill Trail** (easy; 1-mile loop), which begins at Bluebill Campground. The trail circles a 40-acre lakebed, which dries out during summer but turns into a marsh during rainy periods.

Some **off-trail** spots to try in the Oregon Dunes NRA are the **Goodpasture Dunes** from Cleawox Lake; **north spit of the Umpqua River** from the end of the road west of Gardiner; the **High Dunes** from the last parking lot on the coast road south of Winchester Bay; the **Umpqua Scenic Dunes** from North Eel Campground; and **Tenmile Creek** from Spinreel Campground.

Inland hiking

As in the north, the Coast Range is frequently overlooked as a recreation destination east of the Oregon Dunes. Most travelers hurry right past as they head west from I-5 for their date with the coastal sand. Local residents know better. While the dunes are crowded with people, or enshrouded by a cold summer fog, the valleys of the Coast Range can offer an unhurried respite from whatever problems beset the beach.

Lacking its own coastal estuary, the **Smith River** might just be the least-known major Coast Range river. The river and its tributaries flow through a mixture of land managed by Siuslaw National Forest and the Bureau of Land Management (BLM), as well as private timber lands owned by International Paper, before joining the Umpqua River at Reedsport.

Kentucky Falls, managed as a special-interest area by Siuslaw National Forest, is 17 miles inland from the coast midway between Florence and Reedsport. Kentucky Creek, a tributary of the Smith River's north fork, has three 80- to 100-foot waterfalls A network of national forest and county roads give access to the Kentucky Falls trailhead, 7 miles southeast of Mapleton as the crow flies but much farther by road. Cross the bridge over the Siuslaw River in Mapleton and follow the river's south bank for 4 miles on County Rd 5036. Turn south and head into the national forest as the number switches to Forest Rd 48. Drive 10 miles and turn east on Forest Rd 23, following it 7 miles to the trailhead. The **Kentucky Falls Trail** (moderate; 2 miles one way with a 1,000-foot drop in elevation) ends at the base of the two lower falls, which drop together for 60 feet before splitting into a pair of 20-foot plunges. The upper falls is seen .75 mile along the trail, and the 60-foot north fork falls can be seen from the end of the trail. The Forest Service has plans to extend the trail 5 miles downstream along the North Fork of the Smith River.

The **Sweet Creek Trail** (easy; 1 mile one way), just across the Siuslaw River divide from Kentucky Falls, has four access points for viewing 11 waterfalls that drop from 5 to 90 feet along the trail. To reach the trailhead, drive the south bank road of the Siuslaw River west of Mapleton, and then 5 miles south on County Rd 5036 to the trailhead just inside the national forest boundary.

Farther north in the forest, the **Pawn Trail** (easy; .7 mile one way) leads through a grove of 500-year-old Douglas fir, western red cedar, and western hemlock. The trailhead is located up North Fork Siuslaw River Rd, 15 miles northeast of Florence. The **Enchanted Valley Trail** (easy; 2 miles one way) heads up Bailey Creek from an arm of Mercer Lake, 8 miles northeast of Florence.

Biking

With all that sand around, off-road biking is one type of recreation that isn't widespread in the Oregon Dunes country. Every rule has an exception, so don't necessarily leave the **mountain bike** home on the next trip to the dunes. The **Siltcoos Lake Trail,** a 4.5-mile singletrack, is a worthy challenge on the east side of US 101 7 miles south of Florence. The trail is also popular with hikers, so be sure to share. About halfway to the lake from the highway, the trail divides and provides some variety. The north loop leads to 5 backcountry campsites and the south loop to 1, so expect to encounter some backpackers along the way. The trail shouldn't be ridden during the rainy season because of the damage a bike can do to the tread. Expect to gain a surprising 900 feet on an out-and-back trip because of the divide that separates the lake from the highway.

Cyclists can make any number of road loops in the Smith and Siuslaw drainages. The **North Fork Siuslaw River Road** has a popular 15-mile one-way trip that can be ridden year-round. It heads northeast from Florence on County Rd 5070 through second- and old-growth forest.

The **Oregon Coast Bike Route** covers 54 miles here from Sea Lion Caves to North Bend. While the route on US 101 is relatively wide, what it gains in safety it loses in scenery. As the highway makes its run past the

Oregon Dunes, it offers fewer ocean views than just about anywhere along the Oregon Coast.

Horseback Riding

The back of a horse can be a great place from which to watch the surf roll in and the wind blow across the dunes. Oregon's beaches are free and open to horseback riding. One Tillamook County town used to have its beaches closed to horses, but it petitioned the Oregon State Parks Department to rescind the ban. That leaves the entire coast open to horseback riding.

The busiest beach of all for horseback riding is **Baker Beach,** 9 miles north of Florence, because it has a commercial stable alongside US 101, a parking lot developed for unloading horses near the beach, and a nearby inland trail system. The beach is managed as an equestrian trailhead by the Siuslaw National Forest's Mapleton Ranger District, (541) 268-4473. Weekend cowboys tow horse trailers from the Willamette Valley, pull into the parking lot, and set up camp for the weekend. The .5-mile ride through the coastal foredune leads to a 6-mile stretch of beach, bounded on the north by Sea Lion Point and on the south by the Siuslaw River.

Riders without their own horses can **rent** a mount from C&M Stables, (541) 997-7540, located 8 miles north of Florence on the east side of US 101. The stables are open year-round, but it's always best to call in advance for a reservation. Rides to the beach cross the highway and follow backroads to the Baker Beach trailhead. Although this is trail riding, where the guide keeps light control of the group at all times, the stable allows competent guests to canter their horses on the hard-packed sand of the beach. The stable also has rides into the surrounding coastal mountains, the location of Siuslaw National Forest's Coast Horse Trail system.

The **Coast Horse Trail** system loops through the forest 3 miles east of US 101. Access is from Forest Rds 58 and 789, both marked along US 101 between C&M Stables and Sea Lion Caves. Trailheads are at Horse Creek Campground and Dry Lake day-use area in the mountains east of US 101. The campground has barrier-free facilities and a mounting platform.

Horses for the Physically Challenged, a nonprofit organization that trains horses and designs adaptive riding equipment, leads an annual outing to Baker Beach and the Coast Horse Trail system each September for disabled riders. The program is based in the Willamette Valley town of Scotts Mills and can be reached at (503) 873-3890.

Equestrians who want to ride in the southern part of the Oregon Dunes head for **Wild Mare Campground,** a 12-site camp with corrals on Horsfall Rd off US 101 near North Bend. Reservations are available by calling (800) 280-2267. The campground got its name years ago when it was common for ranchers to graze horses in the Horsfall area for the summer before they were needed for the hunting season. A young mare was accidentally left behind one year and roamed the dunes for a quarter century. Although many tried to catch her, she remained free until she died of old age. Her passage was noted when her body was discovered in the dunes. Unlike Baker Beach to the north, where off-road vehicles aren't allowed, around Wild Mare Campground dune buggies mix with horseback riders, though the campground itself is off-limits to off-road vehicles.

Camping

The Oregon Dunes really do have a lot of campgrounds. It just seems like there are not enough on peak summer weekends or when trying to make a reservation on short notice.

When traveling from the north, Siuslaw National Forest's **Sutton Lake Recreation Complex,** (541) 268-4473, comes first. Located at the beginning of the sand 4 miles south of Sea Lion Caves (see Newport chapter), the complex mixes lakeside recreation with dune hiking and horseback riding. More than 150 campsites are spread among campgrounds at **Alder Lake Dune, Sutton Lake,** and **Sutton Creek,** all clustered together 5 miles north of Florence. A road leads to Holman Vista for views of the dunes and a trail to the beach. Alder and Dune Lakes are stocked with trout, and Sutton and Mercer Lakes have boat launches.

Lane County enters the campground picture with **Harbor Vista Park** near the north jetty of the Siuslaw River in Florence. One of the few coastal campgrounds with an ocean view, the 15-acre park has 7 tent sites and 31 RV sites, plus a view structure that overlooks the north jetty and the Pacific Ocean. For reservations, call (541) 997-5987.

Jessie M. Honeyman Memorial State Park, 3 miles south of Florence on US 101, is one of the most beloved in the Oregon parks system. The campground offers swimming and fishing in Cleawox Lake, at the edge of the campground, plus waterskiing across the highway in Woahink Lake. Jet-ski rentals are available on Woahink Lake from M&M Seaplanes, (541) 997-6567. The 522-acre park has 237 tent sites, 141 sites for RVs, 4 yurts, and barrier-free campsites. Reservations are available at Honeyman by calling (800) 452-5687. The park's telephone number is (541) 997-3641.

The **Siltcoos River,** 6 miles south of Florence, has a cluster of campgrounds on the west side of US 101 that serve as staging areas for dune buggies. **Driftwood II, Lagoon,** and **Waxmyrtle** have nearly 200 sites among them, some of which can be reserved by calling the National Forest

Service reservations system at (800) 280-4496. The reservations system usually holds back some campsites on a daily basis for first-come use. **Tyee Campground,** with 13 campsites on the east side of US 101 near Siltcoos Lake, is a better bet for quiet afternoons because there won't be any dune buggies around.

All Siuslaw National Forest campgrounds on the Oregon Dunes are managed by the Oregon Dunes National Recreation Area, (541) 271-3611, in Reedsport (see Hiking, above).

Carter Lake Campground, a Forest Service facility 8 miles south of Florence on US 101, has 24 sites that serve boaters on the typical coastal dune lake. One mile long, Carter Lake is 200 yards at its widest.

Tahkenitch Lake, a many-tentacled body of water 7 miles north of Reedsport on the east side of US 101, has more than 60 Forest Service campsites at **Tahkenitch and Tahkenitch Landing Campgrounds.** Campers are attracted by the lake's outstanding fishing, floating dock, and boat launch.

Windy Cove A and B, both Douglas County campgrounds, have 97 sites for tent and trailer camping and are a short walk to the marina at Salmon Harbor in Winchester Bay. For information and reservations, call (541) 271-4138. Reedsport and Winchester Bay are also home to numerous private RV parks because of the activity in the dunes and the bay's busy fishing port.

Umpqua Lighthouse State Park, (541) 271-4118, has 42 tent campsites and 22 RV spaces with full hookups. The park is 6 miles south of Reedsport just west of US 101, a short drive from Winchester Bay. The nearby Umpqua River Lighthouse commands an impressive view of the south jetty of the Umpqua River. Lighthouse tours can be arranged through Douglas County Parks, (541) 271-4631.

W. M. Tugman State Park, (541) 888-4902, 8 miles south of Reedsport on US 101, has 115 campsites with electricity, a hiker/biker camp, and 2 barrier-free sites. The 560-acre park is on the east side of US 101 on Eel Lake. The Umpqua Dunes Trail, one of the best in the Oregon Dunes, is 1 mile away across the highway (see Hiking, above).

The Forest Service offers camping at **Eel Creek Campground,** on the west side of US 101 9 miles south of Reedsport. The campground's 78 campsites are popular with hikers who want to escape the noise of dune buggies. Some of the sites, however, are only a few feet off US 101. The Umpqua Scenic Dunes area is connected to the campgrounds by a trail (see Hiking, above).

Spinreel Campground is a popular off-road-vehicle staging area, 13 miles south of Reedsport. The camp's 27 sites are .5 mile west of US 101 on a sandy road. The Horsfall staging area, located at the south end of

Oregon Dunes National Recreation Area 5 miles north of North Bend off US 101, has 90 campsites at **Horsfall and Bluebill Campgrounds,** plus large overflow areas that handle crowds on summer weekends.

With one exception, inland camping in the Coast Range tends to be in small campgrounds set on the numerous creeks and rivers that carve valleys deep in the mountains. The Siuslaw River has camping at the **North Fork,** 15 miles northeast of Florence on North Fork Siuslaw Rd (see Biking, above), and at **Archie Knowles,** 3 miles east of Mapleton on Hwy 126. Camps scattered around the Smith River drainage are the BLM's **Smith River Falls, Twin Sisters Creek, Vincent Creek, Fawn Creek,** and **Clay Creek,** all out-of-the way spots that cater to local fishermen. The Mapleton Ranger District, (503) 268-4473, manages the Forest Service camps and the Eugene District, (541) 683-6600, manages the BLM camps.

The exception to the small campground rule is **Loon Lake Recreation Site,** a multifaceted park operated by the Coos Bay District of the BLM, (541) 683-6600. Loon Lake is 20 miles east of Reedsport on Hwy 38. Turn south on Mill Creek Rd, 3 miles west of Scottsburg, and drive 7 miles to the recreation area. Created 1,400 years ago by a landslide, the 260-acre lake is 190 feet deep and 2 miles long. Facilities include a lodge, interpretive program, swimming beach, boat launch, and water-ski dock. Two dozen picnic tables line the lake's beach area, and the campground has 53 sites, plus a large meadow for tent campers. For a less hectic pace, campers head for the 8 tent sites nearby at the BLM's **East Shore Campground.** Loon Lake Lodge, (541) 599-2244, located on the lake 2 miles from the main campground, is open year-round. The lodge has a small motel, restaurant, store, more than 50 RV campsites, and several large group camping sites.

Picnics

Perhaps more so than anywhere else on the Oregon Coast, US 101 is relatively isolated from the beach as it passes the Oregon Dunes. The numerous state wayside parking areas common elsewhere on the coast are mostly absent on the dunes because of the mile or more of sand that separates the highway from the beach. Because of the separation, most picnic facilities tend to be located alongside the campgrounds of the dunes.

There are always exceptions, of course, and for the dunes it's the **south jetties.** The best opportunities for day-use recreation accessible by automobile, whether it's picnicking, kite flying, or beachcombing, are located along 4 miles of road that run along the beach to its end at the south jetty of the Siuslaw River in Florence, or along the 2.5 miles of road that dead-end in the dunes south of the Umpqua River in Reedsport. The two beaches are where visitors go when they want to see the ocean while visiting the two towns on the river estuary.

Darlingtonia State Wayside, 6 miles north of Florence on the east side of US 101, offers a forested setting for a picnic where insects are on the menu. Many a picnic has been spoiled by swarming insects, but the darlingtonia plants help even the score. The insect-eating plants are 8 to 24 inches high and grow in boggy areas of southwest Oregon and northwest California. Also known as the cobra lily, the plant lures insects into its leaf opening with nectar and colorful petal-like appendages. Once inside, an insect becomes confused and gradually slides into a pool of liquid at the base of the leaf where it is digested and absorbed as food. The wayside is Oregon's only designated **rare plant sanctuary.**

Fishing

Winchester Bay and the **Umpqua River estuary** comprise one of Oregon's most diverse fisheries, combining offshore angling for salmon, halibut, and bottom fish with outstanding bay fishing year-round for nearly all of Oregon's fish species. The bay is also good for clams and crabs. Some of the world's tastiest oysters come from commercial beds located in a triangle formed by jetties off the mouth of the Umpqua.

Salmon Harbor Marina, located in Winchester Bay, is home to a large fleet of charter boats that offer fishing and whale-watching trips. As Oregon's coastal bars go, the entry to Umpqua River is relatively benign and can be used throughout much of the year. One of the largest marinas on the West Coast, Salmon Harbor is a department of Douglas County. Information on charter fishing opportunities is available by calling the marina at (541) 271-3407. The marina has more than 900 boat slips with access to fresh water, electricity, showers, and sewage disposal.

Anglers with their own boats can launch from public facilities at Winchester Bay, **Reedsport, Gardiner, and Scottsburg.** (Nearly all Oregon boat launches are marked by signs along the highway.) The lower **Umpqua River** has fishing in season for sturgeon, spring and fall chinook salmon, striped bass, and perch. The state-record striped bass of 64 pounds, 8 ounces, was taken from the Umpqua. The bay is a good producer of Dungeness crab, as well as gaper, razor, and softshell clams. Clam diggers without a boat usually visit the beach in front of Gardiner or the mudflats at the mouth of the **Smith River.**

The mouth of the **Siuslaw River** near Florence has plenty of fishing opportunities, but a relatively difficult bar crossing has limited the development of a charter-fishing industry. Most fishing occurs inside the bay, rather than offshore, for fall chinook, shad, perch, and the occasional striped bass. Public launches are located at Florence and upriver at

Tiernan and Mapleton. The largest is C & D Dock, (541) 268-9950, located 3 miles west of Mapleton on Hwy 126. The best **crabbing** is just inside the river's mouth on incoming tides. Tidal mudflats just east of Florence are big producers of softshell clams.

With 32 lakes, **Oregon Dunes National Recreation Area** attracts more fishermen than off-road-vehicle riders. The dunes are lined by all types of lakes, from the 3,000 acres covered by Siltcoos Lake to the famous clear waters of 82-acre Cleawox Lake in Honeyman State Park.

Siltcoos Lake, 6 miles south of Florence on US 101, is one of Oregon's best warm-water fisheries, with ample fishing opportunities for bass, bluegill, trout, yellow perch, crappie, and bullhead. Salmon and steelhead have access to the lake through the Siltcoos River. The town of Westlake, located on US 101 at the west end of Siltcoos Lake, has a public boat ramp with a wheelchair-accessible fishing pier. Ada County Park, accessible from the east off County Rd 5334, serves the east shore of the vast lake. The lake appeals to all types of fishermen, from the small fry seeking their first nibble by a hatchery trout to serious bass fishermen. The lake holds the state record for coho salmon (25 pounds, 5 ounces) and sea-run cutthroat trout (6 pounds, 4 ounces).

Other large lakes of the Oregon Dunes are **Tahkenitch Lake,** 11 miles south of Florence on US 101, and **TenmileLake,** one of the most heavily fished lakes in Coos County (see Bay Area chapter). Tahkenitch Lake sprawls over 1,500 acres. Primary access is a public boat ramp alongside US 101 at Tahkenitch Landing Campground (see Camping, above). Fishing requires a boat, because of the brushy banks. Crappie, bluegill, and yellow perch are the lake's primary yield.

Other productive fishing lakes in the Oregon Dunes country are **Sutton, Mercer,** and **Munsel** north of Florence (see Sutton Lake Recreation Complex in Camping, above); **Woahink, Cleawox, Carter,** and **Threemile** in the Oregon Dunes NRA between Florence and Reedsport; and **Clear, Eel,** and **Saunders,** also in the dunes between Reedsport and North Bend. **Horsfall Lake** at the south end of the dunes is occasionally very large but is always very shallow. As with other shallow dunes lakes, it varies in size depending on the water table. The lake contains yellow perch, brown bullhead, and largemouth bass, but fishing opportunities vary widely throughout the year.

Loon Lake, 20 miles southeast of Reedsport (see Camping, above), provides the best mountain lake fishing in the Oregon Dunes country. Other inland fishing opportunities abound in the **Siuslaw, Umpqua,** and **Smith Rivers** and their tributaries.

Boating/Kayaking

When it comes to boating opportunities, **Florence** and **Reedsport** are on a short list of special places in Oregon that combine river, bay, and ocean boating. Both cities have their downtown business districts set on riverfronts that are strongly influenced by ocean tides, and their bays' mudflats aren't far away. Both cities have commercial **harbor tours** that introduce visitors to the various water-recreation opportunities.

The *Westward Ho* stern-wheeler operates out of the dock in Old Town Florence. Tours include historical expeditions, jaunts into the bay, and weekend sunset dinner cruises. The *Westward Ho* can by reached by calling (541) 997-9691. Reedsport's harbor and bay tours are offered by Umpqua Jet Adventures, (541) 271-5694, at 423 Riverfront Way. The 13-mile upriver tour focuses on the wildlife of the Umpqua, while a 2-hour bay cruise downriver to Salmon Harbor shows off the recreational and industrial areas of the lower Umpqua.

Sea kayaks ply the waters of the **lower Umpqua and Siuslaw Rivers,** although tides and mudflats are constant considerations. The rivers offer long stretches of placid paddling from tidewater: Mapleton on Hwy 26 for the Siuslaw and Scottsburg on Hwy 38 for the Umpqua.

Wildlife

Because the Oregon Dunes lack a coastal headland, wildlife watching here requires a different approach from elsewhere along the coast. Instead of marine animals, the dunes are a place to look for **black bear, bobcat, deer, skunk,** and **raccoons.** The animals may be difficult to spot, but their tracks in the sand are a telltale sign of their presence.

More than 240 species of birds have been sighted in the Oregon Dunes, with 130 species present during practically any time of the year. For a copy of a bird checklist, stop at the Oregon Dunes National Recreation Area headquarters, (541) 271-3611, at 855 Highway Ave in Reedsport. Rather than the seabirds the coast is famous for, the dunes harbor **herons, grouse, woodpeckers, warblers,** and **finches.** It pays to keep a bird book and binoculars handy when visiting the Oregon Dunes. **Shorebirds** are easy to spot south of the Siuslaw River's south jetty.

The only designated spot for watching **California gray whales** is the Umpqua River Lighthouse, located atop a bluff on the south side of the Umpqua River (see Camping, above). The lighthouse is more than .5 mile away from the beach, so it's not the most productive of the designated spots to see California gray whales in Oregon. Because of all the sand, tide pools are virtually nonexistent along the Oregon Dunes. Boaters, however, frequently spot **harbor seals** in Umpqua and Siuslaw Bays.

While the ocean off the Oregon Dunes hides its marine wildlife well, a short trip inland provides travelers with one of the best opportunities to view **Roosevelt elk** in Oregon. The BLM's Dean Creek Elk Viewing Area, a 1,040-acre preserve on the south side of Hwy 38, has a herd of 60 to 100 elk that can be viewed throughout the year. Located 3 miles east of Reedsport, the viewing area has an interpretive building that describes the wildlife that lives at the edge of the coastal mountains and the marshy areas along the Umpqua River. Best viewing is early and late in the day. Favorite times are mid-June, when cows bring their newborn calves into the meadows, and mid-September and early October when the bulls are bugling and fighting for dominance.

Windsurfing/Surfing

The Florence area has become a graduation area for windsurfers who learn inland, especially on Fern Ridge Reservoir near Eugene, and want to step up to sailing on salt water. The mouth of the **Siuslaw River** frequently has adequate winds for sailing on a short board, but the real challenge is to head offshore into the waves along the south-jetty beach. As is the case at other Oregon jetties, a strong rip current flows seaward along the jetty during heavy winter surf.

Surfers and surf kayakers also play in the waves at the **Siuslaw's south jetty,** as well as the **south jetty of the Umpqua.** The Umpqua has one of Oregon's best jetty breaks, but the river's productive fishery also tends to attract **sharks.** Shark attacks are rare in Oregon, but they occur with enough frequency to give those who play in the surf reason to be cautious. Attacks by great white sharks usually get widespread publicity every five years or so.

Woahink Lake along US 101 south of Florence has winds throughout the year, but windsurfing is usually on a long board. Nearby **Siltcoos Lake** may be a better choice during summer because the prevailing wind pattern makes it difficult to return to the launch on Woahink Lake.

Central Coast Watersports, (541) 997-1812, in Florence has the latest gear and information for surfers, sea kayakers, and scuba divers.

Attractions

Florence, intersected by the deep, green Siuslaw River, is surrounded by the beauty of the Oregon Dunes National Recreation Area. The town has transformed itself from a sleepy fishing village to a tourist mecca, but the local catch can still be had at **Weber's Fish Market** on the main strip, 802 US 101, (541) 997-8886. The revitalized **Old Town,** a continually upgraded few blocks of shops, restaurants, and some of the town's oldest structures, has become visitor oriented without selling out to schlock.

Reedsport is a port town on the Umpqua River a few miles inland, while Winchester Bay is at the river's mouth. Because you can catch only glimpses of the 53-mile-long Oregon Dunes NRA from the highway, plan to stop and explore on foot. Headquarters are in Reedsport at the intersection of US 101 and Hwy 38; 855 Highway Ave, (541) 271-3611. (See Dune Buggies, Hiking, and Wildlife, above, for additional information.)

The former Antarctic research vessel *Hero* is moored on the Reedsport riverfront and is open to the public (summer only). Adjacent is the **Umpqua Discovery Center Museum,** which features a weather station and exhibits on marine life, ocean beaches, and logging; 409 Riverfront Way, (541) 271-4816.

Restaurants

Blue Hen Cafe ☆ Okay, so there are blue chickens everywhere. What's important is that the place is friendly, the prices are reasonable, the food is tasty, and there's lots of it. Chicken dominates the menu, but there's other stuff, too. *1675 Hwy 101 (in north part of town), Florence; (541) 997-3907; $.*

International C-Food Market ☆ Catch it, cook it fresh, and keep it simple is the plan at this sprawling seafood operation on the Siuslaw River pier. The fishing fleet is just outside: fresh fish, crabs, oysters, and clams are served any way you like 'em. *1498 Bay St (at Siuslaw River), Florence; (541) 997-9646; $$.*

Lodgings

Coast House ☆☆ This exclusive house is rented to only one or two couples at a time. Set on a forested oceanfront cliff, this spectacular structure features two skylit sleeping lofts, and all necessities except food are provided; there's no phone or TV. *10 miles north of Florence (call for details), Florence; PO Box 930, Florence, OR 97439; (541) 997-7888; $$$.*

Johnson House Bed & Breakfast ☆☆ Standards are high at this popular B&B. The library is strong on natural history, politics, essays, and poetry, and breakfasts are among the best on the coast. The hosts also own Moonset, a spendy, couples-only retreat. *216 Maple St (1 block north of river in Old Town), Florence; PO Box 1892, Florence, OR 97439; (541) 997-8000 or (800) 768-9488; $$.*

Cheaper Sleeps

Ocean Haven   This spot's cliffside location overlooking the ocean is near-perfect. The Shag's Nest ($50) is a one-room cabin with kitchenette, deck, and 360-degree view (book in advance; the bath's in the lodge). Lodge units aren't as cheap. *94770 US 101, Florence, OR 97439; (541) 547-3583; $.*

More Information

Bureau of Land Management, Coos Bay: *(541) 756-0100.*
Bureau of Land Management, Eugene: *(541) 683-6600.*
Central Oregon Coast Association, Newport: *(800) 767-2064.*
Douglas County Parks Department, Winchester: *(541) 957-7001.*
Florence Area Chamber of Commerce, Florence: *(541) 997-3128.*
Lane County Parks Department, Eugene: *(541) 682-6940.*
Mapleton Ranger District, Mapleton: *(541) 268-4473.*
Oregon Dunes National Recreation Area, Reedsport: *(541) 271-3611.*
Reedsport/Winchester Bay Chamber of Commerce: *(541) 271-3495.*
Siuslaw National Forest, Corvallis: *(541) 750-7000.*

Bay Area

From Coos Bay on the north, east into the Coast Range along the Coos-Douglas county line, south to the Coos-Curry county line, and west to the Pacific Ocean, including the towns of Lakeside, North Bend, Coos Bay, Charleston, Coquille, Bandon, and Myrtle Point.

When driving US Highway 101 (US 101) north to south, something special begins to happen around Coos Bay. As you approach North Bend and the entrance to Oregon's Bay Area, the highway veers inland away from the Pacific Ocean. Coos Bay–North Bend, with 26,405 residents, is the largest population center on the Oregon Coast. Unlike Seaside, Lincoln City, and Newport, however, in the Bay Area most of the residential development is several miles away from the coastal shore.

As US 101 continues south toward Bandon, it heads well inland, with finger roads branching west and ending at remote beaches—two words rarely used together in Oregon. The atmosphere seriously begins to change, when the coastal highway then hits Bandon. A few miles south of town, the myrtlewood shops and other tourist attractions begin to disappear. Impressive seastacks rise out of the pounding surf, providing a constantly changing panorama that continues all the way to Brookings and the California border. The highway becomes lonely, feeling more like a road in Eastern Oregon than one of the most scenic drives in the country.

Even away from its rugged coastline, Oregon's Bay Area is full of surprises. Little out-of-the-way campgrounds are set amid towering trees and clear-running streams. One of the area's towns is called Remote, because it is. Some of the nation's largest trees still stand in the surrounding forests.

Coos Bay itself is a long, narrow estuary. Its southern branch, which is called the South Slough, is one of the best places to go for a canoe trip in Oregon. Birds love the South Slough as much as butter clams love Coos Bay. In 1974 South Slough became the country's first estuary to be protected by Congress.

Not to be mistaken for California's Bay Area, the Bay Area of Oregon does possess a few places capable of attracting a crowd during summer vacation. The string of state parks—Sunset Bay, Shore Acres, and Cape Arago—accessible along the Cape Arago Highway south of Charleston offer about as fine a package of parks as can be found. Sunset Bay is simply breathtaking and wouldn't look out of place in Hawaii (minus the palm trees). Shore Acres is a cultivated garden that blooms around an old estate, while Cape Arago lies at the northern edge of one of the least accessible parts of the Oregon Coast.

The Bay Area is one part of the coast that has it both ways—civilized and tame in its cities and parks but rugged and wild in its beaches and forests. That's usually the precise mixture for something special.

Getting There

Interstate 5 is connected to Oregon's Bay Area by Highway 38 to Reedsport and Highway 42 to Bandon. Coos Bay is 212 miles from Portland via Reedsport. US 101 and its scenic spur roads traverse the Bay Area north to south. The Cape Arago Highway leaves US 101 at the southern end of the town of Coos Bay, heading first toward Charleston and continuing through a string of state parks before ending atop Cape Arago. North Bend Municipal Airport is served by commuter airlines.

Adjoining Areas

NORTH: **Oregon Dunes**

SOUTH: **Southern Coast**

EAST: **The Umpqua Valley, The Rogue Valley**

Kayaking/Canoeing

The **South Slough National Estuarine Research Reserve** is a paddler's paradise. Located at the southern end of Coos Bay, the slough is an interesting mixture of saltwater marshes, freshwater streams, forested islands, and the abundant variety of plants and animals that inhabit them. In 1974, the 4,400-acre reserve became the nation's first estuary to be preserved and is funded through a partnership between the state of Oregon and the National Oceanic and Atmospheric Administration.

The South Slough drains 26 square miles of land directly south of the Port of Charleston. The slough has 600 acres of tidelands and channels. The reserve is reached by turning south on Seven Devils Rd from Charleston, 5 miles west of US 101. An interpretive center is located on the slough's west side, and is open weekdays throughout the year, plus weekends from June through August. The center maintains educational displays and nature trails and can provide information on tides and weather. The reserve's telephone number is (541) 888-5558.

The **tide** is the major factor when planning a canoe or kayak trip in the slough. Incoming tides lead paddlers toward the slough's southern reaches where the freshwater creeks join the estuary. An outgoing tide carries boats north toward the main part of Coos Bay and the ocean. Paddlers should stay in channels where water is the deepest to avoid running aground on mudflats and sandbars. Stay in the canoe or you might get stuck above your knees while walking through the soft mud. With the proper tide, the 4-mile-long slough is a 2-hour paddle in either direction.

The closest **launch** to Charleston is the Port of Coos Bay's industrial annex landing, located where the Cape Arago Hwy crosses the mouth of the slough at its north end. The southern launch is on Hinch Rd, located just east of Seven Devils Rd 5 miles south of Charleston. The county launch facility on Hinch Rd has a small flow of water during low tide, so plan accordingly. The Hinch Rd launch is on the **Winchester arm** of the slough, the western of its two major arms. The eastern **Sengtacken arm** has no launch facility, so paddle north on the western arm for 2 miles to enter the top of the eastern arm. Both arms have expansive beds of eelgrass that provide food and hiding places for small fish and the kingfishers and great blue herons that hunt them. A popular destination in the slough is 23-acre **Valino Island,** site of a former casino and saloon.

Another popular paddling spot in the Bay Area is the **lower Coquille River** as it passes through the **Bandon Marsh Wildlife Refuge,** (541) 757-7236 (see Wildlife, below). The refuge is just north of Bandon on US 101, between the Coquille River and the highway. Whitewater kayaking is available during the rainy season on the west fork of the **Millicoma River,** the south fork of the **Coos River,** and the south fork of the **Coquille River.** The river water levels rise and fall quickly, and it's best to find someone with local experience to boat with. The best way to locate local boaters is to drive the roads along the rivers on a weekend during the rainy season (November through May).

Boating

Oregon's Bay Area is a haven for all types of boaters—from large ocean-going sailboats that visit the Charleston harbor to the small fishing boats that can be rented in area lakes. The cities of Coos Bay and North Bend maintain a half-dozen boat launches that give access to the bay, but the area's major marina is the **Charleston Boat Basin** just inside the bar. This Port of Coos Bay facility has 566 open slips that can be reserved by calling (541) 888-2549.

The Coquille River at Bandon has a major marina operated by the Port of Bandon, but the bar crossing on the Coquille is more difficult than the one at Coos Bay. The **Port of Bandon Marina,** (541) 347-3206, has 90 slips.

Tenmile Lakes, one of the best freshwater fishing areas along the coast, are 11 miles north of North Bend on the east side of US 101 at Lakeside. The lakes are in Coos County, just east of the Oregon Dunes National Recreation Area boundary. The twin lakes have 5 private marinas, accessible by car from Lakeside or North Lake Dr or from a boat. The marinas have wet slips, dry storage, boathouses, boat rentals, and all the related amenities. The largest is La Playa Marina, (541) 759-4775, at 2200 North Lake Rd. Small-boat launch facilities are liberally sprinkled around the Bay Area, including at **Powers Park** in Powers, at **Empire Lakes** in Coos Bay, and along the **Coos, Millicoma, and Coquille Rivers.**

The north side of Coos Bay has a major boating facility at the **North Spit Boat Launch,** (541) 756-0100. Managed by the Bureau of Land Management (BLM), the park has a variety of outdoor activities, including surf fishing, wildlife viewing, beach hiking, windsurfing, and off-road-vehicle driving. Located on the Coos Bay Spit immediately south of the Oregon Dunes National Recreation Area, the launch is reached by crossing Coos Bay on US 101 north, turning west, and driving 6 miles on the Trans-Pacific Highway.

Hiking/Beaches

Beach walking in Oregon's Bay Area is regularly broken up by coastal headlands and bays, much more so than the coast to the north. Even the Oregon Coast Trail spends most of its time on pavement when traversing the rugged coastline of Coos County.

The **north spit of Coos Bay** has 6 miles of sandy beach south of the Oregon Dunes, but the beach doesn't do through-hikers much good because it ends at an impassable bay. The beach is also open to off-road vehicles. The next sand to the south of Coos Bay is found in pocket beaches at **Bastendorff** and **Sunset Bay,** on the Cape Arago Hwy south of Charleston (see Camping, below), and **Seven Devils Wayside** off US 101 on Seven Devils Rd north of Bandon. The long strand of sand returns at **Whisky Run Beach,** a county park 8 miles north of Bandon, and continues all the way through **Bullards Beach State Park** at the north end of Bandon and the mouth of the Coquille River. The sand gives way to rocky headlands in southern Coos County around Bandon, but returns 3 miles south of town where the beaches of **Bandon State Park** begin. Sand continues all the way to the Curry County line (see Southern Coast chapter). Beaches along the **New River,** which runs parallel to the ocean for 9 miles near Langlois, are some of the loneliest in the state. To reach them turn west from US 101 on Lower Fourmile Creek Rd, 8 miles south of Bandon.

Finding a good viewpoint of **Cape Arago Lighthouse** is one of the most difficult propositions along the Oregon Coast. Each of the coast's eight other publicly owned lighthouses are easy to view from a road or a short trail, but that's not the case with the lighthouse that guards the southern entrance to Coos Bay. The easiest spot to view the light is from a Coast Guard housing project just north of **Sunset Bay State Park** (see Camping, below), but the federal government maintains it as a residential area and visitors are not welcome unless invited by a resident. For the best view of the lighthouse from publicly accessible land, park at the day-use area on the northeast side of the sculpted half circle made by Sunset Bay. An unmaintained trail leads west along the north shore of the bay, then turns north along the edge of an oceanside bluff. The lighthouse can be seen offshore after a 1-mile hike through a tangle of coastal vegetation. Be careful along the way where the path passes close to the edge of the coastal bluff. The lighthouse can also be seen from a scenic wayside along Cape Arago Hwy, although it's best to use binoculars to bring it up close. (Cape Arago State Park is 2 miles south of the lighthouse, so don't look for it there.)

The **Oregon Coast Trail** runs for 4 miles between the highway and the ocean, connecting Sunset Bay State Park with Cape Arago State Park. The trail begins at the south end of the Sunset Bay day-use area on the bay, passes near the gardens of Shore Acres State Park, and ends atop Cape Arago where an impassible headland bars travel farther to the south. Shore Acres was built by a California shipping and timber baron. Its gardens are a beautiful place for a stroll, and trails to the cliffs above the ocean end at spectacular viewpoints (see Parks/Picnics, below). Cape Arago has a paved path down to North Cove and a trail down to tide pools at South Cove.

The city of Coos Bay has several short hiking trails near the town's business and residential districts. The paved **Bay Front Walk** is .66 mile long on the city's waterfront. The **Mingus Park Pond Walk** is a .5-mile circle of the pond, Chinese gardens, picnic areas, and playground on 10th St, two blocks north of Central Ave. Fishermen, walkers, and joggers use the 2-mile trail around **Empire Lakes.** The trail is adjacent to the campus of Southwestern Oregon Community College.

The South Slough National Estuarine Reserve (see Kayaking/ Canoeing, above) south of Charleston isn't only for canoeists. The **Estuary Study Trail,** the **Wasson Creek Trail,** and the **Winchester Creek Trail,** each a designated nature walk with interpretive stops along the way, thread the reserve's extensive stand of coastal forest. Trails begin at the interpretive center, located on the west side of the slough 4 miles south of Charleston, and vary in length from 1.3 to 3 miles.

Oregon State Parks has a 1.4-mile loop trail system that shows off the twin falls of **Golden and Silver Falls State Park,** 24 miles northeast of Coos Bay in the Millicoma River drainage. From the south end of Coos Bay on US 101, follow a signed county road to Allegany and continue another 10 miles to the park. The **Millicoma Marsh Interpretive Trail,** located where the river joins the Coos Bay estuary, is a 1-mile trail that begins at Millicoma Middle School in Coos Bay.

The **Doerner Fir Trail,** a 1.5-mile round trip, leads to the largest coastal Douglas fir tree in Oregon. The trail has several steep sections and is slippery when wet. It's located near Sitkum on the self-guided **Growing Forest Driving Tour,** an adventure developed by the BLM. The six-stop tour through the central Coast Range between Bandon and Roseburg takes most of a day to finish. A free illustrated booklet is available from the BLM, (541) 756-0100, or at the Fairview store in Fairview (5 miles east of Coquille). The Doerner Fir is the largest known Douglas fir in the world— 329 feet tall and 11.5 feet in diameter.

The Powers Ranger District, (541) 439-3011, of Siskiyou National Forest has several short trails that lead to scenic locations. **Elk Creek Falls** drops 100 feet, a short walk by trail 9 miles south of Powers on Forest Rd 33. Powers is 18 miles south of Hwy 42 at Myrtle Point on County Rd 219. From the same trailhead, visit the world's largest **Port Orford cedar,** 1.25 miles by trail from the road. The cedar is 219 feet high and has a circumference of 38 feet. **Coquille River Falls** drops 50 feet, 12 miles farther up the Coquille drainage from Elk Creek Falls. The Coquille Falls is a steep .5 mile by trail from Forest Rd 3348, the main road that branches from Forest Rd 33 and continues up the South Fork Coquille drainage.

Mount Bolivar, at 4,319 feet the highest peak in Coos County, lies at the northern tip of the Wild Rogue Wilderness. A 1.4-mile trail leads to the summit, where a spectacular view awaits of the Rogue River as it cuts its way through the Siskiyou Mountains to the Pacific Ocean. The summit is crowned with a plaque that was placed on September 22, 1984, in honor of Simón Bolívar, the liberator of Venezuela. To reach the trailhead, continue driving Forest Rd 3348 past Coquille Falls to the summit of the Coast Range.

Other trails in the Powers Ranger District are the **Iron Mountain Trail** (difficult; 2.7 miles one way), **Panther Ridge Trail** (difficult; 10.8 miles one way), and **Azalea Lake Trail** (easy; 1.2 miles one way). Check with the ranger district for information sheets on all of its trails.

Biking

Two cycling detours away from US 101 make pedaling the 31 miles of the **Oregon Coast Bike Route** from North Bend to Bandon one of the most interesting sections along its 368-mile length.

The detour when pedaling south along US 101 comes just after crossing the Coos Bay Bridge. Rather than fighting the heavy traffic through the business districts of North Bend and Coos Bay, the designated route veers to the west at Florida Ave. Follow the signed route south on Monroe Ave, west on Virginia Ave, and south on Broadway to its junction with the **Cape Arago Highway.** Turn west and continue along the east side of Coos Bay to Charleston. Because the Cape Arago Highway dead-ends at Cape Arago State Park, turn south at Charleston on **Seven Devils Road** for the through route that rejoins US 101 north of Bandon. Ride south to the first junction, then take the eastern of two choices to avoid crossing seven deep ravines on the south side of Cape Arago that gave the area its name. The road across the ravines turns to gravel and is unsuitable for a road bike. The detour route continues south until it veers west onto E Humphreys Rd and eventually rejoins the southern end of Seven Devils Rd. Continue riding to US 101 to complete the 26.7-mile detour. A side trip through Charleston on the Cape Arago Hwy leads to many of the Bay Area's most scenic destinations (see Hiking/Beaches, above).

The second detour through Bandon is even more scenic. Near milepost 260 on US 101, 2 miles north of town, veer southwest on Riverside Dr into central Bandon. Follow First St and Ocean Dr along the mouth of the Coquille River to the Bandon oceanfront. Continue south on **Beach Loop Road,** which eventually turns east to rejoin US 101 after a 17.5-mile detour. Beach Loop Rd offers many stunning views of the offshore rocks and islands that make Bandon one of the most scenic spots on the Oregon Coast. The most famous of all is Face Rock, which was named after an Indian legend that tells about a maiden lost at sea.

In 1997 Siskiyou National Forest completed paving a 72-mile bicycle tour route called the **Powers to Glendale Bike Route,** (541) 439-3011. The route uses one-lane, paved Forest Service and BLM roads as it travels between Coos County on the west and Douglas County on the east in the mountains north of the Wild Rogue Wilderness. Although open to motor-vehicle traffic, the route is seldom traveled. Improvements included widening parts of the road to make it safer for bicycles and developing some campgrounds for use by cyclists. Siskiyou National Forest expects the route to be used by bicycle tour companies that send equipment vans ahead to establish camp and carry gear for paying cyclists.

Mountain bikers have discovered some interesting riding on trails through the coastal forest on bluffs above **Sunset Bay** and **Whisky Run Beach.** The **Euphoria Ridge Trail** near Bridge, 10 miles east of Myrtle Point on Hwy 42, and the **Winchester Road Trail Area,** at milepost 251 off US 101, are favorite riding places for the local crowd of riders. Moe's Bicycle Shop, (541) 756-7536, of North Bend is a good place to learn more.

Camping

With two major bays and two major state park campgrounds (Sunset Bay near Coos Bay and Bullards Beach near Coquille Bay), Oregon's Bay Area keeps visitors' choices simple.

Coos Bay itself is an industrial estuary that flows like the curve of a bell between the towns of North Bend and Coos Bay. The bay's best recreation opportunities lie just to the south of its entry, on the stretch of highway that runs from Charleston to its end atop Cape Arago. **Sunset Bay State Park,** 12 miles from Coos Bay on Cape Arago Hwy, has 63 RV campsites, 72 tent sites, 4 yurts, a hike/biker camp, and 11 group tent areas that cater to local families. The 395-acre park's day-use area is centered on an exquisite bay; the steep cliffs to the north and south allow the bay's water to warm slightly during summer, providing the warmest coastal swimming experience in Oregon. Of course, warm in Oregon means the low 60s, too cold for staying in very long. The campsites are located east across Cape Arago Hwy alongside Big Creek. The park's telephone number is (541) 888-4902, but reservations are taken only at (800) 452-5687. The campground has 2 full hookup sites for persons with disabilities.

The Coquille River bay at Bandon is the site of **Bullards Beach State Park,** one of the gems in the long string of magnificent state parks that dot the Oregon Coast. The 1,289-acre park has 92 full hookup campsites and another 99 electrical sites. It also has 6 yurts, a horse camp, a hiker/biker camp, and 2 barrier-free campsites and rest rooms. The park has a boat launch on the Coquille River, plus 4 miles of sandy beach and coastal dunes. The park's signature feature is the **Coquille River Lighthouse,** which was built at the mouth of the Coquille River in 1896. The light has not been in service since 1939 but acts as an ornamental beacon across the river from downtown Bandon. The lighthouse is accessible by vehicles, and tours are offered Wednesday through Sunday from mid-May through mid-October. The campground has one of the best horse camps of the coastal state parks, with corrals and three horse trails that lead from camp to the beach.

Camping on coastal beaches in Oregon is allowed, except where cities request that the Oregon Parks and Recreation Department prohibit it. Bandon is the only Bay Area city where ocean beach camping is not allowed (see Oregon Outdoor Primer).

Bastendorff Beach Park, located 2 miles west of Charleston just off the Cape Arago Hwy, provides an alternative to camping at Sunset Bay State Park. Famous for its surfing waves, the county's Bastendorff Park has 56 RV sites and 25 tent sites. The 91-acre park has extensive picnic facilities, lawns for games, a basketball court, and fish-cleaning facilities. A day-use parking area overlooks the beach and the south jetty of Coos Bay. For information, call (541) 888-5353.

The county's 350-acre **La Verne Park** is located on the North Fork of the Coquille River, 15 miles northeast of Coquille on the north fork road. The park's 84 campsites, 20 with full hookups, are popular with fishermen who take crawfish, fall chinook, and winter steelhead in the river. The park also has large picnic and sports field facilities. West La Verne Park is nearby and can take group picnics up to 300 people in size. For information on the parks call (541) 396-2344.

Powers County Park is located within the city limits of Powers, a logging community 18 miles south of Myrtle Point on the South Fork of the Coquille River. The 70-acre park has 30 campsites with electrical and water hookups. The park borders a 40-acre lake that has fishing for trout, bass, and crappie. The park converts its picnic lawns to camp spaces, so it always has room for another camper on big summer weekends. Day-use facilities include tennis, basketball, and volleyball courts. Contact the park at (541) 439-2791.

The Coos County parks department, (503) 396-3121, ext. 354, also has primitive camping facilities at **Nesika Park** near Golden and Silver Falls State Park (see Parks/Picnics, below); **Frona Park** near Dora, in the foothills east of Coquille; and at **Rooke-Higgins Park** up the Millicoma River from Coos Bay, where a boat ramp provides access for fishing. These parks are off the beaten path and used primarily by county residents. Check with the parks department for directions if the coast is foggy and you want to head inland for some sunshine.

The BLM, (541) 756-0100, maintains a couple of small campgrounds near the old **Coos Bay Wagon Road.** Pioneered in 1872, the road still connects Bandon on the west to Roseburg on the east. The old wagon road is located north of Hwy 42, the main east-west route through the area today, and south of the Growing Forest Driving Tour (see Hiking, above). Paved most of the way, the route follows the track used by wagons. To drive the road, leave US 101 just south of Coos Bay at the Sumner turnoff. The wagon road heads southeast to Sumner, then east through Dora, Sitkum, and Lookingglass on its way to Roseburg. BLM camps midway along the route are **Skeeter Creek** and **Park Creek.**

Bear Creek is another small BLM campground on Hwy 42 near the east end of Coos County, 48 miles east of Coos Bay. The **Sandy Creek Bridge,** the only covered bridge left in Coos County, is located along the way near the village of Remote on Hwy 42. The county maintains a picnic area at the bridge.

Siskiyou National Forest has a half-dozen small campgrounds, most with fewer than a dozen sites, on its maze of logging roads that lead up the South Fork of the Coquille River from Powers. A portion of the 82-mile **Rogue-Coquille Scenic Byway** was blown out during a massive landslide in November 1996, turning what had been a through-route from Myrtle Point to Gold Beach into a dead end 19 miles south of Powers. The damage was so severe that the earliest the road may reopen is 1999. The project was turned over by the Forest Service to the Federal Highway Administration, which is better able to handle such a large reconstruction project. Campgrounds still accessible upriver from Powers are **Myrtle Grove, Daphne Grove, Rock Creek, Eden Valley, Squaw Lake,** and several other small, secluded spots. Until the road is repaired, the Coquille's upper south fork will remain one of the most remote getaways in all of Oregon's counties. Check with the Powers Ranger District, (541) 439-3011, for the latest conditions.

Parks/Picnics

Shore Acres State Park is one of the most beautiful day-use facilities in Oregon's park system. Located on Cape Arago Dr, the park is 13 miles south of Coos Bay, and was originally a country home for lumber and shipping magnate Louis Simpson. The park has a 7-acre garden (reconstructed from Simpson's original formal garden) where groundskeepers work hard to keep something blooming throughout the year. Covering 743 acres, the state park has hiking trails, beach access, picnic grounds, and, above all, outstanding wave watching—winter waves breaking against the headlands of Shore Acres have graced many pages in books and magazines. The gardens at Shore Acres feature more than 5,000 tulips blooming in late March and April; hundreds of rhododendrons and azaleas blooming in April and May; 5,000 flowering plants and 900 rosebushes blooming during summer; and 150,000 lights decorating the gardens during the Christmas season.

Cape Arago State Park, located at the end of the road 1 mile south of Shore Acres, covers 134 acres on top of the 200-foot-high coastal bluff. Picnic tables are spread among openings in the thick coastal forest. Hiking trails lead down to the beach of North Cove.

Other coastal day-use parks in the Bay Area are **Seven Devils Wayside,** a beachside picnic area 10 miles north of Bandon on Seven Devils Rd, and the numerous scenic viewpoints at **Face Rock** and **Bandon State Park,** a 900-acre string of waysides and beaches that stretch along the coast for 5 miles south of Bandon. Off US 101 a popular way to experience Bandon's beach is to take a **horseback ride** with Bandon Beach Riding Stables, (541) 347-3423.

Although Oregon's coastal state parks command most of the attention, several inland parks are worth the time it takes to visit. **Golden and Silver Falls State Park,** a state natural area 24 miles northeast of Coos Bay up the Millicoma River (see Hiking/Beaches, above), is the setting for a pair of 100-foot waterfalls. A 1.4-mile loop trail wanders through the park's 157 acres of old-growth forest to viewpoints of Golden Falls, located on Glenn Creek, and Silver Falls on Silver Creek.

The **Coquille Myrtle Grove,** 14 miles south of Myrtle Point off Hwy 42, is a 7-acre grove managed by state parks to preserve a lovely stand of **old myrtlewood trees.** Travelers soon learn that the Oregon Bay Area is myrtlewood country. From the numerous crafts shops that specialize in myrtlewood to the trees themselves, this famous hardwood is never far from sight. An evergreen and the only tree of the genus *Umbellaria*, the myrtlewood belongs to the laurel family and produces tiny yellow flowers in late winter. The wood is highly prized for carvings and used for everything from grandfather clocks to tacky souvenirs. It's hard to leave the Bay Area without buying something made from myrtlewood. The Coquille Myrtle Grove is a picnic area set amid the stand along the Coquille River. A brochure entitled "Discovering Oregon's Evergreen Hardwood" is available from local chambers of commerce to guide visitors to 28 areas, from the Umpqua River to the California border, where myrtlewood grows in public areas.

Other day-use state parks in the Bay Area are **Hoffman Memorial State Wayside,** located 3 miles south of Myrtle Point on Hwy 42, and **Conde B. McCullough State Recreation Site,** which offers boating access off Old US 101 a mile north of North Bend.

Whisky Run Beach, located off Seven Devils Rd 8 miles north of Bandon, is another fine Coos County park. The beach begins where the creek joins the Pacific and continues south all the way to the north jetty of the Coquille River in Bullards Beach State Park. Other county day-use parks can be found at **Tenmile Lake** near Lakeside on US 101; 3 miles up the Coquille River on Hwy 42S from Bandon at **Judith Parker Park;** on the **south jetty at Bandon;** on Bandon's waterfront on **Kronenberg Beach;** and at the **Charleston Fishing Dock.**

Fishing/Clamming

At first glance, Charleston Harbor at the mouth of Coos Bay appears to be the busiest fishing spot in Oregon's Bay Area. Although Charleston is the county's base for saltwater fishing, at the end of the season Tenmile Lakes in the northern part of the county probably clocks in the greatest number of fishing days.

North and South Tenmile Lakes cover 2,200 acres east of US 101 at Lakeside. The lakes are among the state's biggest producers of bass, with catch-and-release tournaments producing as many as 50 fish on a single rod in a day. The many-tentacled lakes are no more than 15 feet deep, which allows their water to warm to an unheard of temperature of 70° along the coast, and fishing is best from May through September. (How convenient.) Trout are stocked annually to give the small fry something to keep them interested. The lakes have five marinas with nearly 250 mooring slips, plus a wide array of recreation facilities from pedal boats to waterskiing. Resort camping is available at Northlake Resort and Marina, (541) 759-3515, and at Sunlake Marina, (541) 759-3869. Coos County operates Tenmile Lake Park in Lakeside at the south end of 11th St and Park Ave. Connected by the shallow North Lake Canal, the lakes' expanse of water makes them the state's fourth-largest body of fresh water. The county park has five boat ramps, a fish-cleaning stand, and a swimming and wading area for the small fry who have given up on landing a trout.

Boats leaving **Charleston Harbor** are well protected by jetties on both sides of the mouth of Coos Bay. Charters work the ocean for chinook and coho salmon, as regulations allow, and switch to bottom fish when the salmon are out of season. The Charleston Fish Dock produces surf perch and cod during summer for anglers without boats. Betty Kay Charters, (800) 752-6303, operates out of Charleston for salmon, halibut, tuna, and bottom fish. **Coos Bay** itself is one of Oregon's most productive areas for Dungeness crab and a variety of clams. Coos Bay and the nearby ocean beaches have gaper, cockle, softshell, butter, littleneck, and razor clams. Minus tides of .4 or more are the best digging times.

The **Coquille River estuary** at Bandon is also productive for crabs and clams. Salmon fishing is good inside the river's mouth from mid-September until fall rains allow the fish to move upstream in mid-November. Angling is good for sea perch off the jetties and striped bass are taken in the sloughs. For offshore charters at Bandon, call Port o' Call Charters, (800) 634-9080.

The forks of the **Coquille,** the **Millicoma,** and the **South Fork of the Coos** have runs of fall chinook from September through November and winter steelhead from November through March. Shad is another popular fish taken from the bays and rivers of Oregon's Bay Area. Cutthroat trout are native to many of the area's clearest streams.

Wildlife

The estuaries are where it's at when it comes to watching for wildlife in the Bay Area. Coos Bay is Oregon's largest estuary south of the Columbia River and has good **birding** throughout the year. The habitat changes from salt marshes to tidal mudflats, to rocky headlands, to dense forests, to sandy beaches—all within a few miles of each other. The bay's north spit is one of the last strongholds of the **snowy plover,** which has its habitat protected during nesting season. The mudflats beneath the south side of the US 101 bridge are host to a variety of **migrants.** Pony Slough, a finger of Coos Bay surrounded by North Bend, is a good spot to see **shorebirds.** It's a dependable place to watch for **great egrets** and **snowy egrets** during summer and fall.

The South Slough National Estuarine Reserve, a southern arm of Coos Bay, is home to a wide variety of birds as well as **Roosevelt elk** and **black-tailed deer. Raccoon** and **black bear** often leave their tracks in the mud when the tide goes out (see Kayaking/Canoeing, above).

Large numbers of male **California sea lions** rest offshore from Shore Acres State Park (see Parks/Picnics, above) during summer on Simpson Reef. **Harbor seals** are present on the reef throughout the year and give birth from March through May. **Steller sea lions** also visit the reef, as do **northern elephant seals** in January and February.

The Coquille River estuary at Bandon has produced some surprising finds in recent years—the **Mongolian plover** and **sharp-tailed sandpiper** among them. The best shorebird area is along Riverside Rd just west of US 101 at the north edge of town where 289 acres comprise the Bandon Marsh National Wildlife Refuge, (541) 757-7236. **Harbor seals** are seen frequently inside the bar.

Coastal headlands, numerous in Coos County, are good places to watch for the offshore parade of wildlife that inhabits the islands and reefs of the Oregon Islands National Wildlife Refuge system. **Tide pools** can be found at Sunset Bay and Cape Arago State Parks (see Camping, Parks/Picnics, above), Five-Mile Point off Seven Devils Rd, and Coquille Point on the west edge of Bandon. Designated **California gray whale** viewing sites are Shore Acres State Park near Charleston and Face Rock

Wayside at Bandon (see Parks/Picnics, above). For an unusual whale-watching opportunity, take a flight from Aerial Photo and Sightseeing of North Bend, (541) 756-2842.

The Bandon fish hatchery, on Ferry Creek 5 miles east of town, has a year-round show pond for large **rainbow trout.** Adult **coho salmon** return from October through February and **steelhead** from December through March. **Wood ducks** live in the area year-round and can be seen at the intake reservoirs.

Surfing/Windsurfing

Surfers, windsurfers, and surf kayakers occasionally share the same waves off the Oregon Coast. It's not a situation that surfers embrace fondly, but it's a reality due to the explosion of high-adrenaline sports in the late 20th century.

Surfers were the first to discover the best locations: Charleston's **Bastendorff Beach** and Bandon's **Bullards Beach.** Surf kayakers have added **Lighthouse Beach** and **Sunset Bay** near Charleston. Windsurfers, at least the ones who are sufficiently skilled, can sail through the offshore waves with the surfers and can also glide over the water of the bays when the winds are sufficiently strong.

Good windsurfing spots are just inside the entrance to **Coos Bay** along the north spit, **Whisky Run Beach,** north of Bandon, and **Face Rock Wayside** in Bandon. The beach at Face Rock is difficult to reach when carrying sailing equipment, but when the wind is good the effort is rewarded.

Local surf shops are Rocky Point Surf Shop in Coos Bay, (541) 888-9370, and Northwest Surf Shop in North Bend, (541) 756-5792. Adventure Kayak Tours of Ashland, (541) 488-1914, uses Bay Area beaches to teach surf-kayaking classes.

outside in

Attractions

The south bay's port city and formerly the world's foremost wood-products exporter, **Coos Bay** has been undercut by a sagging timber industry and the political struggle to control the Northwest's forests. But it's still the Oregon Coast's largest city and the finest natural harbor between San Francisco and Seattle. It's currently making the painfully slow transition from an economy based on natural resources to one that's more service-based (but still a bit rough around the edges).

The **Coos Art Museum,** 235 Anderson, (541) 267-3901, offers many exhibits of big-city quality. Southwestern Oregon Community College, 1988 Newmark, (541) 888-2525, schedules art shows and musical performances. The **Oregon Coast Music Festival** happens every summer; (541) 267-0938. Score coffee drinks and fresh-baked scones at The Scenery, 190 Central, (541) 267-5600, and pizza, pastas, and calzones at Pizza Crazy, at 274 S Broadway, (541) 269-2029.

Charleston's docks moor the bay's commercial fishing fleet. Fresh fish is inexpensive, the pace is slow, and the location central. **Oregon Institute of Marine Biology,** (541) 888-2581, is the University of Oregon's respected research station. Visit Chuck's Seafood, 5055 Boat Basin Dr, (541) 888-5525, for fish, and Qualman Oyster Farms, 4898 Crown Point Rd, (541) 888-3145, for oysters.

The town of **Bandon** looks—and feels—newly painted, freshly scrubbed, and friendly. Some locals believe Bandon sits on a "ley line," an underground crystalline structure that is reputed to be the focus of powerful cosmic energies. Certainly there's magic here.

Begin in **Old Town,** where there are a number of **galleries,** including the Second Street Gallery, 210 Second, (541) 347-4133, and the Clock Tower Gallery, 198 Second, (541) 347-4721. Also in Old Town, buy fish 'n' chips at **Bandon Fisheries,** 250 First SW, (541) 347-4282, and nosh at the public pier. For another treat, try the New York Times–touted handmade candies at **Cranberry Sweets,** First and Chicago, (541) 347-9475 (they're generous with free samples). At **Brewmaster's,** 375 Second, (541) 347-1195, you can taste a handful of beers from among the 100 recipes in the repertoire. On Bandon's north end, sample the famous cheddar cheeses (especially the squeaky cheese curds) at **Bandon Cheese,** (680 Second, (541) 347-2456.

Bandon's **cranberry bogs** make it one of the nation's largest producers. Call (541) 347-9616 or (541) 347-3230 for a tour May through November. The berries grow in cleared fields of peat that are covered with sand. Berries are harvested from late September through November by flooding the fields and scooping the berries off the top of the water. For a bog tour and visit to a tasting room, check with Bandon's Faber Farms, (541) 347-1166.

South of Bandon 6 miles, the West Coast Game Park Safari is a special "petting" park where you can view lions, tigers, and elk, among others; (541) 347-3106.

Restaurants

Andrea's ☆☆ A piano player at breakfast? It can happen at this Old Town landmark with massive wooden booths. Breakfast is first-rate, lunch includes substantial sandwiches, and for dinner there is a plethora of unusual choices. *160 Baltimore (1 block east of ocean in Old Town), Bandon; (541) 347-3022; $$.*

Bank Brewing Company This inviting bank-turned-microbrewery has a spacious floor, high ceilings, and balcony seating. Sweet Wheat or Gold Coast Golden Ale top the craft-beer list. Enticing pub grub and a congenial pub atmosphere. *201 Central Ave (corner of 2nd), Coos Bay; (541) 267-0963; $.*

Blue Heron Bistro ☆☆☆ This bistro with European flair has airy atmosphere, sidewalk tables, and an innovative menu. People drift in for waffles and strong coffee in the morning, for salads or sandwiches at lunch, and for pasta or Continental cuisine for dinner. *100 W Commercial (US 101 and Commercial), Coos Bay; (541) 267-3933; $$.*

Harp's ☆☆ Don't expect a harpist—the name comes from chef/owner Michael Harpster. Do expect a new, bigger, spectacular seafront location. And do look for some wonderful halibut, a sweet onion soup, mozzarella appetizers, and an excellent wine list. *130 Chicago St (a half-block east of harbor, in Old Town), Bandon; (541) 347-9057; $$.*

Lord Bennett's Though across Beach Loop Drive from Bandon's ocean-front cliffs, the saltwater vistas from here are still stunning. Shellfish selections are darn appetizing, also. *1695 Beach Loop Dr (next to Sunset Motel), Bandon; (541) 347-3663; $$.*

Portside ☆ It's dark and cavernous inside, so you'll notice the lighted glass tanks containing live crabs and lobsters. Naturally, fresh seafood, simply prepared, is the house specialty. For something different, try the "cucumber boat." *8001 Kingfisher Rd (just over Charleston Bridge, in midst of boat basin), Charleston; (541) 888-5544; $$.*

Lodgings

Coos Bay Manor Bed & Breakfast ☆ This Colonial-style home is located on a quiet treed street overlooking the waterfront. The five guest rooms are all distinctively decorated, and upstairs is an open-air balcony patio. Mannerly children are welcome. *955 S 5th St (4 blocks above waterfront), Coos Bay, OR 97420; (541) 269-1224 or (800) 269-1224; $$.*

Lighthouse Bed & Breakfast ☆☆ This contemporary home has windows opening toward the Coquille River, its lighthouse, and the ocean—guests can watch boats, windsurfers, and seals cavorting. There are five guest rooms. Breakfasts are top-notch, the hostess amiable. *650 Jetty Rd (at 1st St), Bandon; PO Box 24, Bandon, OR 97411; (541) 347-9316; $$.*

Sea Star Hostel and Guest House Begun as a hostel, this lodging now includes a four-room guest house, which offers a comparatively lavish alternative to the dormlike accommodations. The former bistro is a brew store. Coffee, tea, and cable TV are included; beer and wine are available. *375 2nd St (take 2nd St off US 101 into Old Town), Bandon, OR 97411; (541) 347-9632; $$.*

Cheaper Sleeps

Blackberry Inn Guests have this Victorian home on a busy street to themselves (the owners stay elsewhere). Breakfast is Continental, but a kitchen is available. Two of the four rooms have private baths—the Rose Room is a bargain ($35 off-season). *843 Central Ave, Coos Bay, OR 97420; (541) 267-6951 or (800) 500-4657; $.*

Sunset Motel A clean room with a limited view is yours for about $50 (an oceanfront unit is more than twice that amount). Opt for economy— you're just across the road from the ocean, anyway, and all rooms have use of the Jacuzzi. *1755 Beach Loop Rd, Bandon, OR 97411; (503) 347-2453 or (800) 842-2407; $.*

More Information

Bandon Chamber of Commerce, Bandon: *(541) 347-9616.*
Bay Area Chamber of Commerce, Coos Bay: *(800) 824-8486.*
Bureau of Land Management, North Bend: *(541) 756-0100.*
Charleston Information Center, Charleston: *(541) 888-2311.*
Lakeside Chamber of Commerce, Lakeside: *(541) 759-3011.*
Myrtle Point Chamber of Commerce, Myrtle Point: *(541) 572-2626.*
North Bend Information Center, North Bend: *(541) 756-4613.*
Powers Chamber of Commerce, Powers: *(541) 439-3861.*
Powers Ranger District, Powers: *(541) 439-3011.*
Siskiyou National Forest, Grants Pass: *(541) 471-6500.*

Southern Coast

From the Coos-Curry county line on the north, east to Agness on the Rogue River and the crest of the Siskiyou Mountains in the Kalmiopsis Wilderness, south to the California border, and west to the Pacific Ocean, including the towns of Port Orford, Gold Beach, and Brookings.

The real reason Oregon runs a state lottery is to give its residents hope that one day they might strike it rich enough to retire to the Southern Coast. What a dream! What a place!

As Big Sur has the reputation of being the most beautiful coastline in California, so does the Southern Coast in Oregon. Now drive the two. See which one you like better. Oregon's Southern Coast demands time to explore, even if only with the eyes. Rushing past is not a good idea. Ask the motorist from California who pulled into an information center at Bandon to inquire about the length of time required to drive to Brookings, the town at the other end of Oregon's most scenic coastline. "You can do it in two hours," the information officer responded. After the man hurried out of the information center, someone who had overheard the conversation muttered under his breath, "I just took four days to drive here from Brookings and thought I was pushing it mighty hard."

The mouth of the mighty Rogue River is at Gold Beach, and the Chetco River joins the Pacific Ocean at Brookings. The Grassy Knob Wilderness is one of only four designated wilderness areas in Oregon within sight and smell of the ocean. (The other three are near Newport.) Cape Blanco near Port Orford is the westernmost point in Oregon, also the state's windiest spot. With frequent gusts measured at more than 100mph when winter storms blow in earnest, it's no surprise the concrete walls at the base of the lighthouse atop the cape are 5 feet thick.

The western side of the Kalmiopsis Wilderness and, in the coastal lowlands, Oregon's only redwood forest are among the other spectacular natural attractions of the Southern Coast. Sunshine and delightful weather are an added bonus. Believe it or not, Brookings occasionally has the warmest temperature during February of the entire U.S. Pacific Coast (except for Hawaii). February temperatures can climb into the 70s and the beach can reach 90° in September when the wind is blowing offshore. The trade-off is that July and August are known for their cool, foggy weather.

While many of the Southern Coast's most beautiful sights are within easy reach of US Highway 101 (US 101) in Samuel H. Boardman State Park, one of the most beautiful places of all is tucked away delightfully out of sight from the highway. Californians driving between Bandon and Brookings in two hours always miss Floras Lake State Park and its spectacular Blacklock Point.

The Southern Coast is a place that makes Oregonians believe they are rich, even if they haven't won the lottery.

Getting There

Visitors from the north often drive US Highway 101 (US 101) south along the coast until they reach their desired destination. Gold Beach, seat of Curry County, is 290 miles southwest of Portland. Brookings is another 30 miles south of Gold Beach and only 5 miles north of the California border. From Interstate 5, take Highway 42 from Roseburg or US 199 from Grants Pass, which dips down into California before returning north on US 101.

Adjoining Areas

NORTH: **Bay Area**

EAST: **The Rogue Valley**

inside out

Camping/Parks

Frantic callers to Reservations Northwest, (800) 452-5687, the campground telephone reservations system that handles the Oregon and Washington state parks, usually have two choices—Cape Blanco and Humbug Mountain, on either side of Port Orford—when, during summer camping season, they try to find a short-notice campsite near the beach in Oregon. Both parks are so far from population centers that they're rarely crowded. Neither, however, is on the reservation systems, so an open spot can't be guaranteed. But both parks are worth a try. Just give them a call and ask the park staff how the weekend is shaping up.

Distance can have its advantages. Besides usually having campground space available, the two parks are surrounded by miles of beautiful, uncrowded coastal scenery.

Cape Blanco State Park, (541) 332-6774, is 9 miles northwest of Port Orford on Cape Blanco Hwy (turn west from US 101). The campground is set far enough back from the tip of the cape, tucked into the coastal forest, that the area's famous winds are bearable. Like Oregon's other coastal state park campgrounds, Cape Blanco is open for camping year-round. The campground has 58 electrical sites, including one that is accessible for campers with disabilities. The park has a hiker/biker camp, plus a reservable horse camp with corrals, a 150-acre open riding area, and a loop horseback trail to the beach.

Cape Blanco's famous lighthouse, the oldest on the Oregon Coast, was built in 1870. The light remains active and can be seen 21 miles out to sea. The 59-foot-high tower sits at the edge of the cape surrounded by grassy meadows. Tours are available April through October, Thursday through Monday (call the park number listed above). Although the grassy areas around the lighthouse are closed to hikers, the 1,880-acre state park has an extensive trail network that leads from the headland down to beaches to the north and south. The park also has a boat ramp on the Sixes River. Special evening tours of the lighthouse, complete with costumed guides and tall tales, are available by reservation from Siskiyou Coast Escapes of Port Orford, (541) 332-2750.

Humbug Mountain State Park, (541) 332-6774, is tucked behind 1,756-foot Humbug Mountain, away from the fury of the coastal storms. Located 6 miles south of Port Orford on US 101, the 1,842-acre park has 30 RV campsites, 78 tent sites, and a hiker/biker camp. One of the park's major attractions is a 3-mile trail that climbs to the summit of Humbug Mountain. The hike is particularly pretty in May when the rhododendrons are blooming, but the coastal forest is too thick to offer extensive views of the ocean.

Harris Beach State Park, (541) 469-2021, is located at the north edge of Brookings west of US 101 in the middle of Oregon's so-called "Banana Belt." The southern part of Curry County is the most temperate region in the state because a thermal trough known as a heat low is often pulled north from California by high-pressure systems in northwest Oregon. The coastline around Brookings has a stronger east-west slant than anywhere else in Oregon, so it's frequently sheltered by headlands from the cool marine air that moves down from the north. The Harris Beach Campground is on the state park reservations system and is frequently fully booked when Brookings has another of its good-weather spells. The park is close to California and the Redwoods Hwy, so visitors are numerous and they tend to stay for awhile. Campsites can be booked 11 months in advance by calling (800) 452-5687. Harris Beach has 86 RV sites, 66 tent sites, 4 yurts, and a hiker/biker camp. The disabled have access to 1 campsite and a yurt. The 173-acre park has a large picnic area and day-use access to the seastack-studded beach. Campers wind up spending much of their time touring the day-use sites of Samuel H. Boardman State Park to the north, fishing out of the Chetco River, hiking in the redwoods, or enjoying America's largest fields of spring lilies, which are cultivated in the coastal lowlands.

Alfred A. Loeb State Park offers inland campsites near Brookings, 10 miles up Chetco River Rd. The 320-acre riverside park sits amid an old-growth grove of myrtlewood trees (which grow only on the southern Oregon Coast and in Palestine) that are surrounded by redwoods. The park's **Riverview Trail** (easy; .75 mile one way) connects to Siskiyou national forest's **Redwood Nature Trail** (easy; 1.25-mile loop), where trees are as old as 800 years. The largest is 286 feet tall with a circumference of 33 feet. Harris Beach State Park manages Loeb Park's 53 electrical camping sites; call (541) 469-2021 for information. One site has access for the disabled. The campground is open all year but is not on the reservations system.

Little Redwood Campground, a Forest Service camp with a dozen sites, is 5 miles up the Chetco River from Loeb State Park. Siskiyou National Forest's Chetco Ranger District, (541) 469-2196, manages national forest recreation opportunities near Brookings. Most of its campgrounds are scattered among its river drainages, and all are small. Much of the camping in the forest is of the dispersed variety outside developed areas.

Winchuck River Campground, nestled along the river farthest south on the Oregon Coast, has 12 national forest campsites 16 miles southeast of Brookings on County Rd 896. **Ludlum House,** 1 mile farther up the Winchuck River, is one of 3 national forest facilities available for overnight use within Siskiyou National Forest. The Ludlum House was built in 1939 from scrap lumber from an old hotel near Brookings. The house holds up to 15 people and is available for rent year-round for $20 per night.

Packers Cabin, located 25 miles northeast of Brookings on Long Ridge, can also be rented throughout the year. The three-room cabin rents for $20 per night and holds up to 10 people. **Snow Camp Fire Lookout** is available to rent May through October; it's snowed in during winter. The lookout is 33 miles northeast of Brookings and commands a view from the Pistol River drainage in the Kalmiopsis Wilderness all the way to the Pacific Ocean. The view adds $10 to the nightly rental rate compared to the other two, but $30 is still a good deal.

Reservations for all three must be made through the Chetco Ranger District, (541) 469-2196. Renters need to supply their own food, bedding, and drinking water. Cooking utensils are provided. All of the sites can be reached by car. A list of items to bring, as well as detailed driving directions, are provided by the ranger district with the rental agreement.

Siskiyou National Forest's Gold Beach Ranger District maintains two campgrounds up the Rogue River east of Gold Beach. **Lobster Creek Campground** has 7 sites at the forest boundary, 8.5 miles east of town, and **Quosatana Campground,** the largest national forest campground in southwest Oregon, has 43 sites 11.5 miles east of Gold Beach. Both camps have access to the Rogue River. The **Shrader Old-Growth Trail** (easy; 1-mile interpretive trail) is 2 miles south of Lobster Creek Campground, and the **Myrtle Tree Trail** is a mile to the north across the Rogue River. The short trail leads to Oregon's largest myrtle tree, 88 feet tall and 42 feet in circumference.

The Bureau of Land Management (BLM)'s Coos Bay District Office manages only a few scattered parcels of land in Curry County. Developed facilities are limited to 25 campsites at **Edson Creek Campground** and 22 campsites at **Sixes River Campground,** both up the Sixes River east of Cape Blanco State Park on County Rd 184. Edson Creek, 4 miles east of US 101, is popular for swimming and fishing. It has a launch for small boats and its group picnic and camp areas can accommodate up to 200 people by reservation with the BLM's Coos Bay office, (541) 756-0100. Sixes River Campground is 7 miles upstream from Edson Creek. Recreational miners and fishermen are the most frequent users. Panning for gold is allowed year-round, and dredging is permitted during summer with a permit.

Curry County's **Boice-Cope Park,** (541) 332-8055, on Floras Lake, 3 miles west of US 101 and the community of Denmark on Floras Lake Rd, is one of the best-kept secrets on the Oregon Coast. The park's facilities don't come close to those of coastal state park campgrounds, but few parks can match the setting of Floras Lake. The county campground on the lake sits at the edge of undeveloped Floras Lake State Park, with its 2-mile chain of 150-foot cliffs that rise steeply above a wave-sculpted beach. The cliffs end at Blacklock Point, with its spectacular view of Cape Blanco. The seldom-visited coastal beaches between the New River and the ocean begin near Floras Lake. Both experiences are available by walking from the campground past the lake to the beach. Turn south for the cliffs or north for the New River.

Picnics

When traveling south of Bandon on US 101 (see Bay Area chapter), Port Orford is the next town of any size. An incorporated city with 1,050 residents, Port Orford looms large only when comparing it to its surroundings. Like so many Oregon coastal cities, Port Orford is strung out along US 101, but the oldest settlement on the Oregon Coast has much more to offer than gas stations, fast food, and motels. Built east of the Heads of Port Orford for protection from storms, the city's harbor lies in a south-facing protected cove. The **Port Orford Heads State Wayside** has a commanding view of the harbor, plus some wind-protected spots that are great places for dining on the fresh crab that can be purchased at one of the local markets. Agate Beach stretches north of the Heads of Port Orford and **Battle Rock City Park** and beach anchors the city to the south. To reach the wayside, turn west from US 101 on Ninth St, then south on Coast Guard Rd. A path leads to a viewpoint that takes in Cape Blanco to the north and Humbug Mountain to the south.

A pullout along US 101 invites lingering at the **Geisel Monument,** 7 miles north of Gold Beach, which commemorates the slaying of John Geisel and his sons during the 1856 Rogue River Indian War. **Otter Point,** 3 miles south of the monument, has a trail to a beachside rockhounding area. Hike the trail only at high tide to avoid going somewhere that you can't get back from during low tide.

Cape Sebastian and **Pistol River** command scenic stretches of US 101 south of Gold Beach, but both have limited picnic facilities. Cape Sebastian is famous for its views and hiking trails (see Hiking/Backpacking, below), while Pistol River offers outstanding beachcombing and windsurfing (see Windsurfing/Surfing, below).

Samuel H. Boardman State Park has numerous day-use waysides strung out over 11 miles of coastline. The 1,471-acre park begins at Burnt Hill Creek, 2.5 miles south of the mouth of the Pistol River, and extends to within 4 miles of Brookings. Picnic areas are located at Arch Rock, Whalehead Cove, and Lone Ranch Beach at Cape Ferrelo, all marked along the highway. Each has outstanding views of the rugged coastline, plus access to beaches and the Oregon Coast Trail. The Oregon Coast Highway crosses **Thomas Creek Bridge** near milepost 348, 16 miles north of the California border. At 345 feet above the creek, the bridge is the highest in Oregon.

Good outdoor lunch spots in Brookings include **Harris Beach State Park, Chetco Point, Azalea State Park,** and the **Chetco River boat basin.** Azalea State Park is just east of US 101. Fragrant Western **azaleas** bloom in May, alongside wild strawberries, fruit trees, and violets; you can picnic amid all this splendor on hand-hewn myrtlewood tables. Myrtlewood grows only on the southern Oregon Coast and in Palestine and can be seen in groves in Loeb Park (see Camping/Parks, above). Brookings is occasionally spelled with a hyphen, as in Brookings-Harbor; Brookings is located on the north side of the Chetco River, while Harbor is on the south side of the river. **McVay Rock** and **Winchuck Waysides** provide beach access and picnic opportunities on the Harbor side of the river.

Hiking/Backpacking

Oregon's Southern Coast and the inland areas of Curry County offer some of the best hiking opportunities in the state. Better yet, many of the best hikes cover fairly short distances and can be combined with other activities during the day. If hiking is the primary objective, several different destinations can be squeezed into a single day. (Also see Camping/Parks, above, for additional hiking suggestions.)

Coast and beaches

The **New River** runs north along the coast, separated from the beach only by a line of sand dunes, for 9 miles north of Floras Lake. Land along the river, actually more like a coastal marsh, is being acquired by the BLM as a wildlife refuge. Although recreation opportunities are limited, it doesn't take much more than a stroll along the beach and the dunes to enjoy the area's wild setting. Aleutian geese frequent the area during their migrations in March and November. To reach the New River, either hike north along the beach from Floras Lake (see Camping/Parks, above) or head for the BLM's facilities at the old Storm Ranch, 5 miles north of Langlois on US 101 and 2 miles west on Croft Rd.

Floras Lake State Park, 3 miles southwest of Langlois, is where the developed part of the **Oregon Coast Trail** begins at the north end of Curry County. The trail along this part of the coast is managed by Cape Blanco State Park, (541) 332-6774. The hiking route enters the county on the north along New River Beach, then switches to a maintained path at Floras Lake (see Camping/Parks, above). The trail follows the beach to the south end of the lake, then climbs into the coastal woods where the impressive line of cliffs begin. The trail continues heading south, following an old Coast Guard telephone line along the inland side of Blacklock Point. Spur trails lead west to views from the point. The Coast Trail drops south off the point down to the beach and continues to Cape Blanco State Park.

Hiking the Southern Coast is a constant challenge and it's prudent to have alternate routes planned in advance. The **Sixes River** poses a hazard midway along the beach between Blacklock Point and Cape Blanco. High flows during the rainy season (usually November through May) make the river's mouth too hazardous to cross. During the summer dry season, a sandbar usually blocks the river from entering the ocean at all. Depending on its flow, the Sixes River can be crossed at low tide. The **Elk River** poses a similar crossing dilemma south of Cape Blanco on the way to Port Orford. Across the river, Agate Beach leads to the north side of the Heads of Port Orford, although the outlet for Garrison Lake can pose a crossing problem along the way.

The easiest route to **Blacklock Point** is from Cape Blanco State Airport, a mile-long strip of blacktop set amid the coastal forest. The airport, which is seldom used, is 2.8 miles west of US 101 and 7 miles north of Port Orford on County Rd 160. Park outside the locked gate at the airport's entrance and follow the trail north through thick coastal brush. At the first signed junction, the route to Blacklock Point turns left and the Coast Trail continues straight. After turning left, the next junction leads to two approaches to the point: the left fork to the grassy headlands that look south to Cape Blanco and the right fork to the overlook of the line of cliffs that head north to Floras Lake. From the cliff view, continue hiking north .25 mile to a stream that plunges off a 150-foot cliff to the beach below. The distance from the airport to the point is 1 mile.

The Coast Trail follows US 101 much of the way to **Humbug Mountain,** where it joins an abandoned stretch of the coast highway for a 3.6-mile ramble through Humbug Mountain State Park (see Camping/Parks, above). The coastline to the south is a mixture of long sandy stretches broken by rugged headlands that surround pocket beaches. US 101 begins to stick like glue to the coastline as it heads south of Humbug Mountain. Although the beach is publicly owned, access is not guaranteed through private property. To avoid trespassing, begin hiking from designated parking areas along US 101 and stay on established paths.

South of Humbug Mountain, the coast has long stretches of sand between **Ophir** and **Nesika Beach;** on either side of the **Rogue River** at Gold Beach; between **Cape Sebastian** and **Pistol River;** and south of the **Chetco River** at Brookings to the California border. All are easy to find when driving US 101, but some of the beaches are interrupted by headlands that require low tide for passage.

While beach walking can be rewarding, the hikes that make the Southern Coast special are the short trails from the highway to views from the rocky headlands and down to pocket beaches. **Cape Sebastian State Park** is a convenient side trip from US 101, 6 miles south of Gold Beach. The access road climbs steeply to a choice of two viewpoints, one to the north and another to the south. Both are spectacular. Cape Lookout is on the northern horizon, 43 miles away, and California's Point St. George can be seen to the south, 50 miles away. The 1,104-acre park has a 2.5-mile trail that drops 720 feet in elevation south to the beach at Meyers Creek.

Samuel H. Boardman State Park runs for 11 miles along US 101 between mileposts 341 and 352. The park has many short trails that lead from highway pullouts to scenic viewpoints. **Indian Sands Trail** at milepost 349.2 leads .5 mile through a wooded area to a sand dune cliff. **Whalehead Beach** is the largest day-use facility in the park at milepost 349. A rock formation in the cove resembles the shape of a whale's head, complete with the blowhole that spouts water when the waves hit it just right. The path to the south leads to some abandoned mining equipment and to a beach where rumrunners landed illegal booze during prohibition.

Cape Ferrelo and **Lone Ranch Beach,** both near milepost 352, mark the southern end of the designated route of the Oregon Coast Trail. The 250-foot-high cape, a good spot to fly a kite, is connected by a 1.5-mile trail north to the House Rock viewpoint. Lone Ranch Beach is a popular spot for tide-pool exploration and beachcombing.

Inland hikes

The Gold Beach Ranger District, (541) 247-3600, maintains a network of trails appealing enough to draw hikers inland from the coast. The **Lower Rogue River Trail** (difficult; 12 miles one way) isn't a match in beauty for the longer trail upriver that follows the wild section of the Rogue (see The Rogue Valley chapter), but it has appeal as a hiking or backpacking route. The lower trail begins near the Old Agness Post Office, 34 miles upriver from Gold Beach on the Lower Rogue River Hwy, and runs west to Forest Rd 3533-340 near Silver Creek. Although the lower Rogue River has a highway along it, the trail is on the north side of the river across from the road and offers a remote experience. The trail crosses a series of creeks, with a scenic waterfall at Auberry Creek, and passes 500-year-old Douglas fir trees. The trail is open to mountain bikes.

The **Pine Grove Trail** (difficult; 5 miles one way) begins 27 miles up the Rogue River from Gold Beach at the Illinois River Bridge. The trail follows a divide between the Rogue River and Fox and Lawson Creeks as it climbs from 600 to 2,700 feet above sea level. It offers views of the Illinois River Valley and passes through an old-growth pine grove along the way before ending on a spur road 3 miles east of Quosatana Campground. Two short nature trails are located close to Lobster Creek Campground near the west boundary of Siskiyou National Forest along the Rogue River.

The Chetco Ranger District, (541) 469-2196, covers the west slope of the Klamath Mountains east of Brookings, where an 18.5-mile self-guided forest-ecology tour leads through an old-growth forest along the Chetco River. One of the interpretive sites along the driving tour is at a trail that leads to an unusual site. The **Bomb Site Trail** (easy; 1 mile one way) begins at the end of Forest Rd 1250 and leads to the first bombing of mainland U.S. territory by enemy aircraft. On September 9, 1942, a Japanese airplane dropped an incendiary bomb in hopes of starting a forest fire. Due to wet conditions, the small fire was easily contained by firefighters. The plane, which was assembled and launched from the deck of a submarine, dropped three more bombs near Port Orford, but they did not ignite. The plane's pilot has returned to the area twice in peace. In 1962 he presented a 400-year-old family sword to the people of Brookings, and in 1992 he planted a redwood seedling as a symbol of peace between Japan and America. The sword is on display in Brookings' Chetco Community Library.

The **Chetco Gorge Trail** (moderate; 1.7 miles one way) crosses the Chetco River during the low water of summer and follows it upstream to Eagle Creek. Popular for swimming and fishing, the trail is 22 miles east of Brookings via County Rd 800.

Wilderness hikes

The 179,655-acre **Kalmiopsis Wilderness** is one of the most rugged and wild parts of Oregon. The wilderness is so large that it takes four ranger districts to manage it. Check with the Chetco Ranger District, (541) 469-2196, or the Gold Beach Ranger District, (541) 247-3600, for information on western approaches (see The Rogue Valley chapter for eastern approaches).

Located in the Klamath Mountains, the Kalmiopsis Wilderness provides the headwaters for the Chetco, Illinois, and North Fork Smith Rivers, all protected under the National Wild and Scenic Rivers Act. The Kalmiopsis is characterized by deep canyons, sharp ridges, and clear streams, and is extremely hot during summer. The wilderness is known for its wide variety of plants. Kalmiopsis is a unique shrub, a relic of the pre–Ice Age. The Kalmiopsis is served by 13 trailheads. Major entrance routes from the west are from Game Lake in the Gold Beach Ranger District and the Upper Chetco and Vulcan Peak trailheads in the Chetco Ranger District.

Game Lake is just outside the northwestern tip of the wilderness, 18 air miles east of Gold Beach. Access is up Hunter Creek Rd No. 3680 (which begins east of US 101 as County Rd 635 at the south end of Gold Beach). The **Pupps Camp Trail** (difficult; 6 miles one way) heads east into the wilderness and ends at Collier Bar on the Illinois River. The **Game Lake Trail** (difficult; 9 miles one way) skirts the north edge of the wilderness and reaches the Illinois River at north Oak Flat, the normal white-water takeout. The Illinois River is usually safe to ford during low water from July through September.

The **Upper Chetco Trail** (difficult; 17.5 miles one way) begins near Packers Cabin on Quail Prairie Mountain on Forest Rd 1917 (see Camping/Parks, above). The trail passes the upper reaches of the Chetco before crossing the east boundary of the wilderness. The **Mislatnah Trail** (difficult; 3.5 miles one way) begins at another trailhead 2 miles northwest of Forest Rd 1376. The trail leads to Mislatnah Peak and connects with the Tincup Trail that leads past the Big Craggies Botanical Area, an area renowned for its variety of vegetation. The combined Kalmiopsis Wilderness/Wild Rogue Wilderness map and the Siskiyou National Forest map, both available at ranger stations and local book and outdoor stores, are vital for anyone hiking or backpacking into the Kalmiopsis.

The **Vulcan Peak Trail** (moderate; 1.1 miles one way) leads to Vulcan Lake, nestled beneath the peak's 4,655-foot summit. The trailhead begins off Forest Rd 1909, which follows the Chetco River drainage from Brookings before ending at the middle of the western edge of the wilderness. One mile beyond the Vulcan Peak Trail the road ends at the trailhead for the **Johnson Butte Trail** (difficult; 6.3 miles one way) and the **Gardner Mine Trail** (easy; 2.6 miles one way). Johnson Butte is a good spot to view the Kalmiopsis flower blooming during spring. The mine trail ends at an old chrome mining area.

Compared to the Kalmiopsis, the 17,200-acre **Grassy Knob Wilderness** is small indeed. Administered by the Powers Ranger District, (541) 439-3011, in the northwest corner of Siskiyou National Forest, the wilderness is covered by thick brush and occasional old-growth Port Orford cedar and Douglas fir trees. The **Grassy Knob Trail** (easy; .8 mile one way) ends atop 2,342-foot Grassy Knob, the former site of a lookout tower. To reach the trailhead, turn east from US 101 on Grassy Knob Rd just south of the turnoff for Cape Blanco State Park. The trailhead is 7.9 miles east of US 101 at the end of Forest Rd 5105.

Cycling

The 80 miles of US 101 along Oregon's Southern Coast are filled with stunning scenery and enticing side trips. The highway is also fairly wide and traffic is light compared to more populated parts of the coast farther north. Brookings, only 4.8 miles from the California border, has one of the better networks of bike lanes of any of the coastal cities.

Paved side trips worth taking include **Floras Lake, Cape Blanco State Park,** and the **Elk River,** all marked along US 101 north of Port Orford (see Camping/Parks, above) and the **Lower Rogue River Highway** east of Gold Beach. County Rd 700, which heads into the hills to Carpenterville, at first appears to be an enticing detour from a busy stretch of US 101. While a cyclist can avoid some traffic this way, all the splendid scenery of Boardman State Park will be missed.

With **mountain bikes** not allowed on the Oregon Coast Trail or inside wilderness areas, single-track opportunities are somewhat limited.

Trails open to bikes include the **Lower Rogue River Trail** east of Gold Beach and the **Chetco Gorge and Bombsite Trails** east of Brookings (see Hiking/Backpacking, above).

Discover Oregon of Brookings, (800) 924-9491, offers guided, interpreted mountain-bike tours on forest roads and easy trails in Siskiyou National Forest along the coast. Trips last from a few hours to several days and include bike rentals and meals.

Fishing

In simple terms, fishermen visiting the Rogue River at Gold Beach concentrate inland while those who choose the Chetco River at Brookings spend their time offshore. That's oversimplifying the situation, but it gives a pretty good indication of how the ports are used.

The **Port of Gold Beach,** (541) 247-6269, operates a full-service, 184 wet-slip marina on the south bank of the Rogue just inside the jetty. Jot's Resort, (541) 247-6676, adds another 25 wet slips and 100 feet of transient dock on the north side of the river at Wedderburn. While the Rogue offers an active offshore charter-boat fishery for salmon, lingcod, and rockfish, most fishers wait for schools of salmon to enter the river. The Rogue can be difficult to cross, so small craft usually congregate on the 34 navigable miles east upstream to Agness.

The **Rogue River** earns its reputation as a great river for fishing again and again during its journey from the Cascades to the Pacific. The lower river, from Agness to the mouth, is no exception. Much of the action occurs in the 9 miles of tidewater, but the river's numerous riffles upstream produce many a fish for the river's drift boaters.

The Rogue's narrow estuary provides outstanding fishing for chinook and steelhead, in season, as well as for crab and perch near the river's mouth. When the salmon are running, Gold Beach fills with anglers. The stretch of river between Gold Beach and Agness probably has more professional **fishing guides** than anywhere in Oregon. Many are registered with the Gold Beach Visitors Center, (541) 525-2334. Although most success is had fishing from a boat, hundreds of motor-home occupants park on the lower river's gravel bars and fish from shore. Spring chinook are in the bay from March through July, with peak catches coming in May. The bay's major fishery is for fall chinook from August through October. Summer steelhead begin arriving in July and winter steelhead in November, but most angling occurs upriver above tidewater.

Besides offering great fishing, the lower Rogue teems with interesting places to stay. The river is lined with quaint resorts and lodges that cater to fishermen and vacationers. Lodges accessible by boat or trail upstream from Agness are Paradise, (800) 525-2161; Half Moon Bar, (541) 247-6968; and Clay Hill, (800) 525-2161 (see Rogue River Lodges in The Rogue Valley chapter). Lodges near Agness and along the lower Rogue are Cougar Lane, (541) 247-7233; Lucas Pioneer, (541) 247-7443; Santa Anita, (541) 247-6884; Shasta Costa, (541) 247-7554; Singing Springs, (541) 247-6162; and Tu Tu'Tun, (541) 247-6664. For fishermen who arrive in Gold Beach without a rod, rental equipment is available from Rogue Outdoor Store, (541) 247-7142.

Down the coast at Brookings, the **Port of Brookings,** (541) 469-2218, has more than 900 wet slips that serve the port's active charter industry and the private boaters who flock to the Chetco when chinook are present during fall. The port also has an RV park with some ocean-view sites. The Chetco's relatively safe bar helps make it one of Oregon's top ports for small boats. Upriver from the harbor, the Chetco's small bay soon gives way to the flowing river. Drift boats use the Chetco River, but it's off-limits to jet-boats. The Chetco River flows only 50 miles from the Kalmiopsis Wilderness to the ocean, while the Rogue River journeys more than 200 miles from its headwaters near Crater Lake National Park.

The **Chetco River** usually has a short-notice chinook fishery each fall. Catch limits and seasons vary, but when the season is open, fish are easy to catch. The reefs just offshore are productive year-round for bottom fish. The river's south jetty has a fishing pier for fishers with disabilities. The port has separate basins for recreational and commercial fleets. The large commercial trawlers head far offshore to harvest crab, shrimp, salmon, albacore, and bottom fish.

Port Orford has the Southern Coast's only other offshore fishery. The **Port of Port Orford,** (541) 332-7121, maintains Oregon's only marina that is directly open to the ocean. Boat moorage is available in 75 dry spaces. A handicapped-accessible pier gives everyone a chance to go home with a fish. Port Orford is the center of the region's sea urchin industry. Divers use boats to travel to productive areas, then sell the roe as a delicacy to Japan.

Digging for **clams** often requires plenty of work on the Southern Coast, which lacks the muddy tidal flats of the bays found farther north. Butter and gaper clams are most frequently taken from rocky shorelines and razor clams from sandy beaches. Best places to dig include **Rocky Point** south of Port Orford, the beaches near **Ophir,** and the beaches north of **Gold Beach.**

The Southern Coast has numerous other streams besides the Rogue and Chetco that contain wild runs of fish. Chinook are most frequently available from October through December, steelhead from October through March, and cutthroat trout from May through October.

Boating

The **Rogue River** is synonymous with **jet-boats.** Thousands of visitors leave Gold Beach each year with big smiles on their faces, more than content with their view of the river from a 1,000-horsepower jet-boat. The river also has a jet-boat tour industry based upstream at Grants Pass, but only the run from Gold Beach can mix the sights and smells of salt water with the excitement of the river's rapids.

Tours upriver from Gold Beach are available from May through October. Turnaround points are usually 32 miles at Agness, 80 miles at Foster Bar, or 52 miles at Paradise Bar Lodge. Pilots are experts at locating the native wildlife, whether it's a harbor seal, a black bear, or a river otter, and are happy to share the lore of the river. Cost for a trip ranges from $30 to $75. The trip to Paradise Bar includes lunch and, with the proper planning, can include an overnight stay. The boats dance through some of the Rogue's challenging whitewater rapids, but tours aren't allowed to enter the river's biggest rapids at Blossom Bar.

Four local companies give tours, although two dominate the market and have their brochures available in hotels and visitors centers from San Francisco to Seattle. Rogue River Main Boat Trips, (800) 458-3511, operates out of a dock on the Wedderburn side of the Rogue, and Jerry's Rogue Jets, (800) 451-3645, operates out of Gold Beach on the south bank of the Rogue. Smaller companies are Court's Whitewater, (541) 247-6022, and Rogue River Safari, (541) 247-7497. Rogue River Reservations, (800) 525-2161, is a booking agent for jet-boat and whitewater tours on the Rogue.

Wildlife

Do **California gray whales** become Oregon gray whales when they cross the state line near Brookings? Probably not, but these migrants from California are positively welcome in Oregon. An estimated 23,000 California gray whales swim past the Southern Coast each year—going north to Alaska's Bering Sea in March and south to the lagoons off Baja California in December. A few of the whales even take up year-round residency off the Oregon Coast.

Curry County's designated whale-watching sites are Cape Blanco Lighthouse, Bandon's Battle Rock City Park, Cape Sebastian, Cape Ferrelo, and Harris Beach (see Camping/Parks, above). All are signed along US 101. Designated sites simply mean that trained volunteers are on hand from 10am to 1pm each day during school vacations at Christmas and spring break. The volunteers help spot the whales and share some of the knowledge they acquire during the training sessions. Designated sights are marked by signs that say "Whale Watching Spoken Here." Whales can be seen from many other coastal headlands, but the designated sights usually have a higher concentration of watchers with binoculars so that the odds are better that passing groups of whales will be seen. The best way to spot whales is by looking through binoculars, anywhere from the surf break to 3 miles offshore. The telltale sign is the spout of mist a whale blows 6 to 12 feet in the air when it surfaces to breathe.

In addition to the large mammals, the Southern Coast is home to the myriad of small creatures that make their homes in the tide pools. The **tide pools** with easiest access can be found in Cape Blanco State Park; at the Heads of Port Orford; at Rocky Point, 3 miles south of Port Orford; at Arizona Ranch Beach, 12 miles south of Port Orford and accessible through a private campground for a fee; at Lone Ranch Beach, 5 miles north of Brookings; at Harris Beach State Park; and on Winchuck Beach, .75 mile north of the parking lot on the north side of the Winchuck River (see Camping/Parks, above).

The mouths of the Rogue and Chetco Rivers are frequented during peak fish runs by **California sea lions** and **harbor seals.** Fishermen don't like to see the marine mammals, but hikers walking along the jetty usually find they make a rewarding view.

Many of the Southern Coast's offshore islands are part of the Oregon Islands National Wildlife Refuge system. Although public entry is prohibited, views of the bird colonies are frequently good from the headlands. Goat Island, at 21 acres the largest offshore island in Oregon, was the first to be protected in the refuge system. Located offshore from Harris Beach State Park (see Camping/Parks, above), the island has nesting colonies of **puffins, auklets, guillemots, murres, gulls, cormorants**, and **storm-petrels.**

Horseback Riding

The steady parade of visitors attracted to the Southern Coast by the Rogue River and the coastal scenery keeps a couple of riding stables busy near Gold Beach and Pistol River. Indian Creek Trail Rides, (541) 247-7704, leads tours of the coastal mountains and its abundant opportunities to see wildlife. The stable is located on the south bank of the Rogue River east of Gold Beach on the Lower Rogue River Highway.

Hawk's Rest Ranch, (541) 247-6423, has rides on the beach, through the dunes, and on the ranch's land at Pistol River. Located up North Bank Rd from the Pistol River Store in Pistol River, the riding stable is on a family-owned and -operated ranch. Sunset rides on the beach are a highlight.

Windsurfing/Surfing

High-end windsurfing began in Oregon in the Columbia River Gorge, but it didn't take long for the best sailors to find other outstanding places to sail. One of the very best is the stretch of coastline south of **Cape Sebastian** to **Pistol River.** A June wave bash competition at **Meyers Creek Beach,** the stretch of sand between Pistol River and the cape, has been drawing up to 100 entrants, some journeying from distant lands where wave sailing is a way of life.

The best sailing site depends on where the wind is blowing or how the surf is breaking, but it's usually somewhere between mileposts 334 and 339 on US 101. Facilities are limited to portable toilets and rugged trails that lead from the highway out onto the beach. Gold Beach is 10 miles to the north and Brookings 20 miles to the south. Good sailing conditions occur throughout the year, but spring and early summer are best. The wind usually picks up sufficient strength for sailing to begin around noon. Beaches to the south are angled to the southeast, effectively blocking the prevailing northwesterly winds.

Floras Lake, 2 miles east of US 101 near Port Orford, is the Southern Coast's teaching spot. Floras Lake Windsurfing, (541) 348-9912, provides the lessons, and Big Air Windsurf and Surf Shop, (541) 348-2213, at Langlois sells the gear. The 250-acre lake can be a very windy spot. The best sailors on the Southern Coast love Floras Lake during spring gales when the ocean is too rough but the wind gusts over 30 knots at the beachside lake.

With many offshore seastacks, the coastal break off Southern Oregon is not always conducive to good surfing conditions. The best surfing spots are **Sporthaven Beach** at the south jetty of the Chetco River, **Pistol River,** and the stretch of coast near Port Orford between **Humbug Mountain** and **Battle Rock.** Boogie-board riders can have a good time on the waves at **Harris Beach State Park.** Surf shops in the Brookings area are Sessions, (541) 412-0810, and the Escape Hatch, (541) 469-2914.

outside in

Attractions

The Southern Oregon coast's oldest town, **Port Orford** is a town far removed from big-city nuances—sheep ranching, fishing, sea-urchin harvesting, and cranberries dominate town life. Yet it's hip in its own way, especially considering the seasonal proliferation of surfers and board sailors. And—bonus of bonuses—Port Orford marks the beginning of Oregon's coastal "Banana Belt," which stretches to the California border and means warmer winter temperatures, an earlier spring, and more sunshine than other coastal areas. One warning: From here south, poison oak grows close to the ocean. Watch out for it at Battle Rock.

Named for the gold that was found here in the 19th century, **Gold Beach** is famous as the town at the ocean end of the Rogue River, a favorite with whitewater enthusiasts (*The River Wild*, with Meryl Streep, was filmed here). It's also a supply town for hikers heading up the Rogue into the remote Kalmiopsis Wilderness. Catch some angling tips, or rent clam shovels and fishing gear at the Rogue Outdoor Store, 560 N Ellensburg, (541) 247-7142.

Situated just 6 miles north of the California line, **Brookings** enjoys the state's mildest winter temperatures and is encircled by breathtaking beauty. Because of the favorable climate, most of the Easter lilies sold in North America are grown here. Brookings also boasts the Oregon Coast's safest harbor—and therefore it's a busy port. Soak up the Chetco harbor ambience, and scarf an order of halibut 'n' chips, at **Pelican Bay Seafoods,** 16403 Lower Harbor Rd, (541) 469-7971. The entire Brookings area has been inundated by retirees: the hills are hummin' with new housing, and the real-estate market is red hot.

Restaurants

Bistro Gardens ☆ This storefront scrunched into a tired-looking shopping strip is crowded with diners. The decor is simple, but the menu is expansive. All the entrees (such as baked chicken with apples and mozzarella) showcase the chef's culinary talents. No alcohol. *1130 Chetco Ave (west side of US 101, at north end of town), Brookings; (541) 469-9750; $$.*

The Captain's Table ☆ This funky-looking structure overlooking the highway and ocean is an old favorite. Nothing's breaded or deep-fried, and the beef is meat you can't often get on the coast. Though the dining area can get smoky, the staff is courteous and speedy. *1295 S Ellensburg Ave (on US 101, south end of town), Gold Beach; (541) 247-6308; $$.*

Hog Wild Cafe ☆ This restaurant's gone hog-wild on the pig theme, but the food is worth a pig-out. Muffins are giganto, and you might even give the Hog Slop (chocolate-caramel) mochas a try. *16158 US 101 S (west side of US 101, 1 mile south of Brookings-Harbor Bridge), Harbor; (541) 469-8869; $.*

Nor'Wester ☆ From the windows you may watch fishermen delivering your meal. Most seafood is correctly cooked and served garnished with a simple topping (forgo the more complicated, saucy preparations). You can also find a decent steak or chicken. *Port of Gold Beach (on waterfront), Gold Beach; (541) 247-2333; $$.*

Cheaper Eats

Rubio's This gaudy-yellow restaurant along US 101 is your best bet for Southern Coast Tex-Mex. There are some top-notch choices, and the salsa is outstanding (available by the bottle, too). For something different, try the Seafood à la Rubio. *1136 Chetco Ave, Brookings; (541) 469-4919; $.*

Lodgings

(For Rogue River Lodges, check listings here and see also both Rafting/ Kayaking and Lodgings in The Rogue Valley chapter.)

Beachfront Inn If you want an oceanfront motel room in Brookings, this is the closest you can get. Every unit is beachfront with a private balcony. Amenities? A heated pool and an outdoor spa. *16008 Boat Basin Rd (off Lower Harbor Rd, south of Port of Brookings), Brookings; PO Box 2729, Harbor, OR 97415; (541) 469-7779 or (800) 468-4081; $$.*

Castaway by the Sea This affordable, bluff-top motel sits on top of ancient Indian artifacts and the former site of the oldest military installation on the coast. All rooms enjoy ocean views, and rates begin in the $40 range (even cheaper off-season). Suites are also reasonably priced. It's an easy stroll to the beach or shops. *545 W 5th (between Ocean and Harbor Drs), Port Orford; PO Box 844, Port Orford, OR 97465; (541) 332-4502; $.*

Chetco River Inn ☆☆ This secluded, alternative-energy retreat sits on 35 forested acres, so isolation is guaranteed (there are no phones). Read by propane lights and watch TV via satellite. The main floor offers views of the river and wildlife. Breakfast is included; a deluxe sack lunch or a five-course dinner is available on request. *21202 High Prairie Rd (follow North Bank Rd 16 miles east, left after South Fork Bridge, take second guest driveway on left), Brookings, OR 97415; (541) 670-1645 or (800) 327-2688 (Pelican Bay Travel); $$.*

Gold Beach Resort Stay here for in-town beachfront accommodations. All the rooms and condos in this complex have private decks and ocean views. There's an indoor pool and spa, and a private trail to the ocean. *1330 S Ellensburg (US 101, near south end of town), Gold Beach, OR 97444; (541) 247-7066 or (800) 541-0947; $$.*

Inn at Nesika Beach ☆☆☆ Occupying a bluff overlooking the ocean, this neo-Victorian is grandly decorated and boasts lovely landscaping, a wraparound porch, and an enclosed oceanfront deck. All rooms enjoy ocean views, feather beds, and private baths with spas. *33026 Nesika Rd (west off US 101, 5 miles north of Gold Beach), Gold Beach, OR 97444; (541) 247-6434; $$$.*

Jot's Resort ☆ Spread along the bank of the Rogue River, this resort's 140 rooms are all tastefully decorated. There's an indoor pool, spa, and weight room; guided fishing trips leave from the dock. Angling gear, bikes, and boats can all be rented. *94360 Wedderburn Loop (at Rogue River Bridge), Gold Beach; PO Box J, Gold Beach, OR 97444; (541) 247-6676 or (800) 367-5687; $$.*

Cheaper Sleeps

Battle Rock Motel This nothin'-fancy motel is on the wrong side of US 101, but your room ($40 or less for cheapest) is a stone's throw from Battle Rock Wayside Park. Whale watching and a stretch of uncrowded beach await. *136 S 6th St (PO Box 288), Port Orford, OR 97465; (541) 332-7331; $.*

Ireland's Rustic Lodges Ireland's is really two motels. The original cottages are rustic and inexpensive, without an ocean view but with log walls, fireplaces, and gardens. The newer units are not so rustic, have a view, and cost a bit more. *1120 Ellensburg Ave (PO Box 774), Gold Beach, OR 97444; (541) 247-7718; $.*

Snow Camp Lookout This fire lookout sits atop 4,223-foot Snow Camp Mountain in Siskiyou National Forest, 21 miles northeast of Brookings. No electricity or water, but there's a wood-burning stove and table and chairs; a pit toilet is outside. You bring the rest. Drive to within sight of the lookout, then hike the final 200 yards to the summit. Reservations are taken in January each year—and it's popular. Call for an application. *Chetco Ranger District, 555 5th St, Brookings, OR 97415; (541) 469-2196; $.*

More Information

Brookings-Harbor Chamber of Commerce, Brookings: *(800) 535-9469.*
Bureau of Land Management, North Bend: *(541) 756-0100.*
Chetco Ranger District, Brookings: *(541) 469-2196.*
Gold Beach Ranger District, Gold Beach: *(541) 247-3600.*
Gold Beach Visitors Center, Gold Beach: *(800) 525-2334.*
Port Orford Chamber of Commerce, Port Orford: *(541) 332-8055.*
Powers Ranger District, Powers: *(541) 439-3011.*
Siskiyou National Forest, Grants Pass: *(541) 471-6500.*

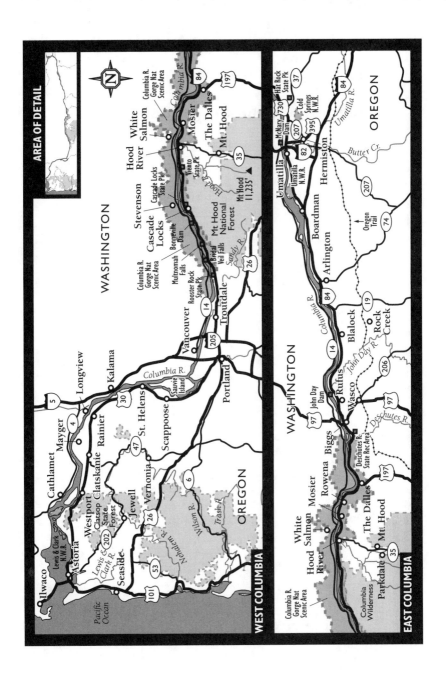

Columbia River

Columbia Basin   295

Hood River and the Gorge   307

Lower Columbia   330

Columbia River

Columbia Basin

From where the Columbia River enters Oregon near Hat Rock State Park on the east, south to the route of the Oregon Trail, west to Hood River, and north to the border with Washington, including the Umatilla National Wildlife Refuge and the towns of The Dalles, Arlington, Boardman, Umatilla, and Hermiston.

Sensing the end of their journey was near, pioneers hurried as fast as their tired oxen would take them through the Columbia Basin country in their bid to reach the Willamette Valley before the onset of winter. Modern travelers often do the same thing as they race along Interstate 84 between Portland and the cities of Eastern Oregon.

The reason for the pioneers' haste was more justified than that of modern vacationers, many of whom take one look at the summer-browned hills east of The Dalles and bump the cruise control up another 5mph.

It doesn't have to be that way because the Columbia Basin has plenty of recreation opportunities, and travelers can pull off the freeway into one of numerous riverside parks and spend a few days. Because of the temperature extremes during a typical summer day, most of the recreation from May through September occurs near water—either the Columbia River or the Deschutes or John Day Rivers, which join the mighty River of the West in Columbia Basin country.

Windsurfing is one of the most colorful activities on the Columbia during summer. Although Hood River in the Gorge is the center of board sailing in the Northwest, many of the busiest beaches are east of town in the Columbia Basin. East Rowena,

The Dalles, Celilo Park, and Arlington have their ardent corps of sailors.

While windsurfing may be the most visible form of recreation in the Basin, it's by no means dominant. Its numbers are small compared to those who fish the Columbia for walleye or sturgeon and those who pitch tents or park an RV in a campground under the shade of a tree. When salmon are in the river, a flotilla of fishing boats can be seen prowling off the mouth of the Deschutes. Cruise ships ply the river from Astoria all the way to Lewiston, Idaho, giving thousands of visitors long, leisurely looks at the massive hills that rise from the river to the wheat fields of the Columbia Plateau 2,000 feet above.

The Columbia is impounded in a series of lakes by three dams in this section of the Columbia Basin—McNary, John Day, and The Dalles. As science has learned in the 1990s, the dams made a fine mess of the anadromous fish runs. But when dam building began back in the 1930s, engineers believed the benefits from power production and recreation far outweighed any possible damage to the environment.

The dams have become so much a part of the Columbia that it's difficult to imagine what the river would be like without them, although possible solutions for improving the declining salmon runs propose removal of the John Day Dam. The Oregon Trail pioneer travelers would have seen the river that way, although they may have been in too much of a hurry to notice. Modern travelers, ironically, have more leisure time than their ancestors but are usually in an even bigger hurry. The Columbia Basin is a good place to force yourself to slow down.

Getting There

Interstate 84 follows the south shore of the Columbia River from Portland in the west to Boardman in the east. Where the freeway dips south toward the Pendleton Grain Belt country and begins its climb into the Blue Mountains, US Highway 730 (US 730) sticks with the south bank of the Columbia to the town of Umatilla, 181 miles from Portland. The Dalles, the main commercial center along this stretch of the Columbia since the 1840s, is 83 miles east of Portland.

Adjoining Areas

SOUTH: **Lower John Day River, Lower Deschutes River**

EAST: **Pendleton Grain Belt**

WEST: **Hood River and the Gorge**

inside out

Camping

A string of camping opportunities awaits travelers in Oregon's Columbia Basin country. From Hat Rock State Park, near where the Columbia begins forming Oregon's border with Washington, to Memaloose Island, east of Hood River, developed campgrounds are rarely far apart.

Hat Rock Campground and store, (541) 567-0917, is one of the busiest camps on the Oregon shore of Lake McNary, the impoundment formed by McNary Dam near the town of Umatilla. The private campground is located 10 miles east of Umatilla on US 730, near a day-use state park of the same name. The camp has 40 tent sites and 30 drive-through sites for any size RV. The Port of Umatilla operates **Umatilla Park,** (541) 922-3939, near the dam. The park has overnight facilities and a marina.

Hermiston is a prosperous farming community 5 miles south of the Columbia River and McNary Dam. With a population of 10,330, Hermiston is next in size to The Dalles' 11,325 among the towns of Oregon's Columbia Basin country. RV camps in the Hermiston area include the **Umatilla County Fairgrounds,** (541) 567-6121.

Lake Umatilla, the pool behind the John Day Dam, has a nice mix of day and overnight facilities on both shores of the river. **Boardman Park,** (541) 481-7217, is operated by the local recreation district and has camping .5 mile north of I-84's exit 164 at Boardman. Even though Boardman is 250 miles upriver from Astoria, the town's elevation is only 400 feet above sea level. The river level itself is 265 feet as it passes the town of 2,145 residents. Boardman Park has 63 RV sites with full hookups.

Phillippi Park Campground is a US Army Corps of Engineers campground 50 miles down the Columbia from Boardman at I-84 exit 114, where the John Day Dam floods the lower part of the John Day River. The park is only accessible by boat, 4 miles up the east bank of the John Day River. **LePage Park Campground** is a drive-in facility on the west bank of the John Day at the same freeway exit. The park has 71 campsites. For information on both parks, contact the Army Corps at (541) 296-1181. Most parks located in the hot spots of the Columbia Basin country have developed swimming facilities, including Boardman, Phillippi, and LePage. Don't count on seeing lifeguards.

Just below John Day Dam, **Giles French Park,** (541) 296-1181, strings out along the Columbia River near Rufus for several miles. Enter the park from Rufus exit 109 from I-84. Camping is spread out along the shoreline in dispersed sites for self-contained RVs and tents. The park has long grassy areas punctuated by some shade trees. Because of the turbulent water that comes out of the John Day Dam, swimming is not advised.

Deschutes River State Recreation Area, (541) 739-2322, sits on the east bank of the Deschutes River where it joins the Columbia. The park is an inviting stop along I-84, but it doesn't have a freeway exit. To reach the park, either exit at Biggs on the east or Celilo on the west and from either direction drive a two-lane road that parallels the freeway 4 miles to the park. The recreation area has 89 primitive campsites, with 30 feet the maximum trailer length. The campground is open all year but does not accept reservations. The park sits at the eastern boundary of the Columbia River Gorge National Scenic Area and is located near just about every form of recreation that makes the Gorge famous, including trails for cycling, hiking, and horseback riding. Heritage Landing on the other shore of the Deschutes is a popular launch site for fishermen and a takeout for rafters. The US Army Corps of Engineers maintains Celilo Park for day use 4 miles to the west on I-84; it's especially good for windsurfing.

Memaloose State Park, (541) 478-3009, is conveniently located along I-84 between The Dalles and Hood River, but the only access is from the westbound lanes at exit 72. To reach the park while driving east, take Rowena exit 76, get back on the freeway, and head west to exit 72. (The Memaloose rest area, however, on the south side of the freeway is accessible to eastbound traffic.) The park has 43 sites with full hookups, with a maximum RV length of 60 feet, plus another 67 tent sites. The park accepts reservations, (800) 452-5687, during its April through October camping season.

Experienced hikers, intimately familiar with ownership of the land, have a route they call "the Memaloose Hills" that follows the ridge tops 10 miles east from the rest area to a lookout over The Dalles. The federal government has been buying land for the Columbia River Gorge National Scenic Area, but hasn't developed a trail system to open it to public use.

The **Wasco County Fairgrounds,** (541) 296-2231, at The Dalles has a campground with 200 sites for RVs and tents. With a group camping area for up to 300, the fairgrounds can be a busy place when the rodeo is in town.

Parks/Picnics

Traffic on I-84 doesn't need to rush nonstop between Portland and Pendleton. Besides the campgrounds, most of which also have shady picnic tables, the shores of the Columbia River are lined with day-use picnic parks.

Hat Rock State Park, 9 miles east of Umatilla off US 730, is a day-use area named for a landmark noted by Lewis and Clark when they passed by in 1805. Irrigon, 9 miles west of Umatilla on US 730, has a recreation district that manages **Irrigon Park** on the river, plus a city park where self-contained RVs are welcome to spend the night. Other day parks on the pool behind the John Day Dam are **Quesnel Park,** 4 miles east of Heppner Junction at exit 151; **Arlington Park,** a pleasant city park and marina at exit 137; and the visitors facilities at the **John Day Dam** at exits 109 and 114. Facilities at the dam include self-guided tours of the power-house and fish viewing.

Arlington is famous for being the boyhood home of former **Tonight Show** bandleader Doc Severinson. A monument in the city's park tells of the high school years of the trumpet player, who still returns home to visit now and then. Arlington is also the site of a large refuse depository, also known as the biggest garbage dump in Oregon. The site is located well south of town and most visitors who spend some time on Arlington's riverfront will not even be aware of it, unless they notice the continual parade of trucks hauling Portland's garbage.

Celilo Park is located near the midway point of Lake Celilo, the impoundment behind The Dalles Dam, at exit 97. The US Army Corps of Engineers park has lots of shade and grassy areas to spread out a blanket. Although not officially a campground, the park is an appealing spot for self-contained freeway travelers to spend the night.

The Dalles Dam attracts visitors to **Suefert Park** at exit 87/88, where they ride a free tour train to the powerhouse and fish viewing station. US 197 crosses the Columbia near the dam on The Dalles Bridge. Don't tell anyone, but the Washington side of the river just across the bridge has two small, pleasant parks that have water access. As with all parks in the Gorge, expect to be serenaded by the rumble of passing locomotives, as railroad tracks parallel the river and highway much of the way.

The Dalles's **Riverfront Park** at exit 85 is just below the dam at the east end of town. The park is usually busy with windsurfers and picnick-ers on summer weekends, although when the Columbia is at full pool, waters of the river will be lapping at the legs of the picnic tables.

Rowena, the first exit off I-84 west of The Dalles (exit 76), has **East Rowena State Park** for windsurfers to the east and **Mayer State Park** for fishermen and picnickers to the west. The old Columbia River Scenic Highway climbs the bluff above the parks for a postcard view of the Columbia River Gorge from Rowena Crest. **Koberg Beach State Recreation Area** is a small day-use park accessible from a westbound exit 1 mile east of Hood River.

Stone's Ski and Sport, (541) 298-5886, at 500 E Second St, is a good place to pick up camping and other outdoor clothing and equipment in The Dalles.

Wildlife

One of the largest concentrations of wintering and migrating waterfowl along the Columbia River can be found from October through January in **Umatilla National Wildlife Refuge,** (541) 922-3232. The headquarters is in the post office building in Umatilla at Sixth and I Sts. The refuge is a temporary home to nearly all the species of **ducks** found in the west, except for sea ducks. The largest number of ducks on the refuge at one time was estimated to be 458,000 on November 13, 1983. An estimated 90,000 **Canada geese** also congregate on the refuge.

Despite the plethora of waterfowl, viewing is limited on the Oregon side because most of the refuge lies across the river. Washington has many good viewing spots. Hunters are allowed to approach closely in season. A boat can also be helpful. The best viewing in Oregon is at McCormack Slough. Located 7 miles east of Boardman along US 730 north on Paterson Ferry Rd, the slough has a small observation area with interpretive signs and refuge brochures. Besides migrating ducks and geese, the slough is host to many local nesting species, among them **Virginia rail, American bittern,** and **marsh wren.** The mixture of marshland and sagebrush provides habitat for **barn owls** and **long-eared owls.** The refuge was created in 1969 to help restore habitat when 76-mile-long Lake Umatilla was created by the construction of the John Day Dam. Other good viewing locations are the farm fields around Umatilla and Irrigon, where waterfowl wander off the refuge to feed.

Another refuge in the area is **Cold Springs National Wildlife Refuge,** (541) 922-3232, located 7 miles east of Hermiston off Hwy 207. The refuge is a tree-lined reservoir in a desert that has been converted to irrigated farmland. It doesn't take much more than that to attract up to 45,000 wintering waterfowl. The size of the pool dwindles during the irrigation season from 1,550 acres to 200 acres, but the exposed lakebed provides abundant vegetation that is used by the waterfowl. **Bald eagles** keep tabs on the weakest waterfowl and can often be seen in winter in the northwestern part of the refuge. The summer season isn't the busiest time of year, but sharp eyes can usually spot nesting **wood ducks, songbirds, mule deer,** and **beaver.**

McNary Dam has a wildlife park below the dam, as well as state-of-the-art fish-viewing facilities at the dam's visitors center on the Oregon shore in Umatilla. The wildlife park is a former gravel pit that has been reconstructed into a system of marshes, sloughs, woodlots, and open fields. The park has picnic facilities and some short trails where sightings are possible of **mourning doves, great blue herons,** and the rare **Bewick's wren.**

The Oregon Department of Fish and Wildlife has two fish hatcheries at Irrigon that welcome visitors. The Irrigon Fish Hatchery, (541) 922-5732, raises **steelhead** and the Umatilla Fish Hatchery, (541) 922-5659, produces **spring** and **fall chinook salmon,** as well as **steelhead.** The Irrigon hatchery also has a show pond for **sturgeon** and both hatcheries have good fishing at their outfalls. The Irrigon hatchery is at the Columbia River on W Eighth St in Irrigon, while the Umatilla hatchery is 3 miles to the west at the end of Paterson Ferry Rd. Both are just north of US 730.

Boating

The Columbia Basin country is a classic example of a wind funnel. Boaters must know local conditions, as well as their own skill and equipment, before challenging the powerful conditions of the Columbia on a mid-summer afternoon. Winds can be brisk throughout the year, and it's not uncommon for waterfowl hunters to swamp their boats and have to swim for their lives.

Marinas are located at Umatilla Park, (541) 922-3939; Irrigon Park, (541) 922-4933; Boardman Park, (541) 481-7217; Arlington, (541) 454-2868; and The Dalles Boat Basin, (541) 298-4146. **Boat ramps** are located at Quesnel Park, Blalock Canyon (exit 112), LePage Park, Giles French Park, and Heritage Landing. **Mayer State Park** west of The Dalles also attracts boaters. (For more information, see Camping and Parks/Picnics, above.)

Windsurfing

Controlled access along I-84 limits beach access in places, but windsurfers always seem to find a way to get to the best water. Volunteers from the Columbia Gorge Windsurfing Association even helped renovate **East Rowena State Park** into a day-use facility because of the good sailing conditions found just offshore.

Heading east upriver from Hood River, **the best windsurfing beaches** are at the town of Mosier at exit 69; East Rowena State Park at exit 76; The Dalles's Riverfront Park at exit 85; Celilo Park at exit 97; the town of Biggs at exit 104; Giles French Park at exit 109; Arlington at exit 137; Quesnel Park at exit 151; and Boardman Park at exit 164. All of the windsurfing sites are less than a mile from the freeway and are marked by brown highway signs pointing the way.

Depending on the time of year, launch points east of The Dalles tend to be less crowded than those closer to Hood River. The use pattern is for good reason because the most reliable winds during summer are usually in the heart of the Gorge, between 55 to 75 miles east of Portland. Sailors, however, will drive a long way east looking for wind when it's not blowing in the Gorge.

So why did Hood River become the windsurfing mecca instead of The Dalles? In a word, geography. Hood River lives in a relatively long east-west stretch of the Columbia River, where the wind is really able to pick up force. On the west side of The Dalles, the river makes a big northwest-southeast bend that takes some of the punch out of the winds. Riverfront Park at The Dalles is one of the better places in the Columbia Gorge for beginners to learn how to windsurf, but they must be alert for some rocky islands that poke above the river's surface when the river level drops in summer.

For current **wind conditions,** call the toll line for Windsight, (900) 860-0600, or check with a local windsurfing shop (see Hood River and the Gorge chapter). To order a copy of the *Gorge Guide,* a comprehensive annual guide to windsurfing in the Columbia River Gorge, call (541) 386-7440.

Fishing

The days when Native Americans used to spear and trap chinook salmon by the hundreds at Celilo Falls are long gone, but the Columbia Basin country still provides some outstanding fishing opportunities. The wild runs of salmon and steelhead have dwindled nearly to extinction in some cases, but the **Columbia River** and its tributaries now offer outstanding fishing for walleye and other warm-water species, including bass, crappie, bluegill, and channel catfish.

Celilo Lake, the impoundment behind The Dalles Dam, is considered to be the best overall fishery in the area, with good fishing year-round for walleye, which tend to be a little sluggish when the water is cold. The lake is also home to a healthy population of sturgeon. The busiest fishery in the Columbia Basin is usually at the mouth of the **Deschutes River** on Celilo Lake, where chinook salmon and summer steelhead congregate to find relief in the cold water of the tributary. The summer run of chinook is usually in the river during August and September, while the summer steelhead run begins in June. Most successful anglers find a boat necessary to fish out in the Columbia, although some anglers meet success from the banks of the Deschutes when the river is open. Camping is at Deschutes River State Recreation Area on the east shore of the Deschutes River, and the boat launch is at Heritage Landing on the west bank (see Camping, above).

The state's largest walleye was taken from **Lake Umatilla** near Arlington. Tipping the scales at 19 pounds, 15 ounces, the catch is expected to be just one step along the way toward even larger fish in one of the most rapidly expanding fisheries in Oregon. The best fishing on Lake Umatilla for the summer runs of salmon and steelhead tends to be at the mouths of the **John Day and Umatilla Rivers** and just below **McNary Dam.**

Anglers who concentrate on warm-water fish have plenty of ponds, sloughs, and bays in which to test their luck. The backwaters were created by construction of the highways and railroads and are connected to the Columbia by culverts and other drainage systems. Unlike on the Columbia itself, a boat isn't always necessary to meet with success on the ponds that line the river. Heading downriver west from Umatilla, best bets include the **McNary Ponds** beneath McNary Dam in Umatilla; **McCormack Slough** on the Umatilla National Wildlife Refuge (see Wildlife, above); **Giles French Park** and the **Rufus gravel ponds,** both near Rufus at exit 109; the **Celilo Park ponds** at exit 97; **Taylor Lakes** at the west end of The Dalles at exit 82; **Mayer State Park** at exit 76; and **Mosier** at exit 69.

The Columbia Basin country is a big place, and hiring a guide service can be a smart move. Outfitters based in The Dalles include Oregon Guide Service, (541) 296-2744; River Bend Outfitters, (541) 296-5949; and Young's Fishing Service, (541) 296-5371.

Hiking/Walking

Lack of public land keeps the Columbia Basin country from offering much hiking, but the few trails the region does have are well worth walking.

One of Oregon's classic hikes, right up there on a lot of hikers' top-10 lists, is the **McCall Point Trail.** Named after Tom McCall, Oregon's beloved governor from the late 1960s and early 1970s, the trail begins at Rowena Overlook on the historic Columbia River Highway and crosses land owned by The Nature Conservancy. Spring wildflowers, plus the awesome views of the Columbia River Gorge, make the hike especially beautiful from March through May. A moderate trail climbs to the south 1.5 miles and gains 1,000 feet to reach McCall Point. Another trail drops 200 feet over .75 mile to the edge of a cliff overlooking the river. Both trailheads are accessible from the circular parking area at Rowena Point, 3.4 miles west of Rowena exit 74 from I-84.

The **Deschutes River State Recreation Area** has an easy 4-mile loop trail along the river that climbs 600 feet to a high point at Ferry Springs. The trail begins at the campground on the east bank of the Deschutes where it joins the Columbia. Several other short loop trails follow the river's shore upstream (see Camping, above).

From the northeast side of Irrigon, a riverside path follows the Columbia River for 6 miles upstream. The path begins as a trail in the riverside picnic area in **Irrigon Park** (see Parks/Picnics, above) and has several other access points off US 730 that are marked with wildlife signs by the Oregon Department of Fish and Wildlife. The path was developed by users over the years (fishermen, hunters, wildlife watchers), so it's not a continuous, easy-to-follow route. It winds through the Irrigon wildlife area, between the Columbia River and US 730, so getting lost is not an option. The eastern end is at the mouth of the Umatilla River at Umatilla.

The Dalles, named for the French word that means "flagstone" and refers to the rock formations along the Columbia River, is the oldest town east of the Cascades in Oregon and was formerly the county seat of the largest county in the country. Wasco County has since been sliced up into smaller chunks, but much of the history of the city and county remains. Established in 1850 as Camp Drum, The Dalles has some fine old buildings that are connected on a walking tour. Among them are the 1859 county courthouse, the 1875 St. Paul's Chapel, and the 1898 St. Peter's Landmark Church. History of the area is preserved in the Fort Dalles Museum, formerly the surgeon's quarters and the last building remaining from the 1856 construction of Fort Dalles. Pick up the "Historic Walking Tours of The Dalles" booklet at the chamber of commerce, (800) 255-3385, at 404 W Second St.

Biking

Summer gets plenty hot in the Columbia Basin country, so any bike ride should make use of the cooler morning and evening hours. A shortage of public land limits mountain-bike riding, and the big hills to the south plague road-bike riding. Neither situation provides justification for leaving bikes at home during a long weekend or vacation in the Columbia Basin.

Some of the popular road-bike rides include a 6-mile jaunt from **Hat Point State Park** west to McNary Dam (see Camping, above); the roads around **Cold Springs National Wildlife Refuge** (see Wildlife, above); and the paved roads and sidewalks at **Giles French Park** that offer 4 miles of riding (see Camping, above).

The Dalles is in the process of building a 10-mile paved **Riverfront Trail** from its Riverfront Park on the east side of town to the Columbia River Gorge Discovery Center west of town. The Discovery Center opened in 1997 at exit 83 off I-84 and has 38,800 square feet of indoor display space, as well as 80,000 square feet of outdoor exhibits. Needless to say, it will be one of the focal points for visitors to the Gorge for many years to come.

Another bike riding opportunity under development is the conversion of the historic **Columbia River Highway** from Hood River to Mosier into a bike and pedestrian path. The trail will offer a 10-mile ride on pavement when the $2 million reconstruction of the Mosier tunnels is complete. The tunnels are 5 miles east of Hood River. Ride Old Columbia River Rd east from the four-way stop where it crosses Hwy 35 just south of exit 64 from I-84 at the east side of Hood River.

Off-road mountain bikers have limited riding opportunities in the Columbia Basin because of the lack of large blocks of public land. The most popular ride is a 20-mile, one-way trip along a closed road up the east bank of the **Deschutes River** (see Camping, above, and Lower Deschutes River chapter). The trail begins at Deschutes River State Recreation Area. Another road closed to vehicles, but open to mountain bikes, is along the west bank of the John Day River at **LePage Park** (see Camping, above).

The Dalles has developed a mountain-bike racecourse at **Sorosis Park** south of town. Most of the course is on private land and is open only for special events. Check with Life Cycles, (541) 296-9588, to see when you might be allowed on it.

outside in

Attractions

The Dalles is the historical stop along this stretch (see Hiking/Walking, above), especially now that the long-awaited $21.6 million Columbia Gorge Discovery Center has opened at Crate's Point. For centuries, this area was the meeting place for Native Americans. In the early 1800s, Hudson's Bay Company trappers (Edward Crate was one of them) lived here. In the 1840s, it was the official end of the Oregon Trail. Later it served as the only military fort in the Northwest and the county seat of Wasco County, then a 130,000-square-mile vastness that spread from the Cascades to the Rockies.

At the **Columbia Gorge Discovery Center,** 5000 Discovery Dr, (541) 296-8660, you can learn about 40 million years of geology and natural history and the last 10,000 years of human occupation of the Columbia Gorge. The best exhibit (among the covered wagons, longhouses, Lewis and Clark camp, cannery, and boardwalks) is a 33-foot working model of the Columbia River that removes Columbia River dams to expose Celilo Falls, an immense basalt chasm of roaring waterfalls east of The Dalles that was completely submerged and silenced when the dam was built in the 1950s.

Uphill from downtown are irrigated cherry orchards; Wasco County is the largest cherry producer in the United States and celebrates its Cherry Festival in mid- to late April; (541) 296-2231.

Restaurants

Baldwin Saloon ☆ Built in 1876, this place is now a restaurant and bar. The food is what impresses us most: oysters on the half shell, smoked salmon mousse, thick sandwiches, filet mignon, and homemade desserts. *205 Court St (at 1st St), The Dalles; (541) 296-5666; $.*

Ole's Supper Club ☆ Ole's isn't glamorous, but the consistent quality of the food and the commitment to good wine make Ole's notable. The restaurant has established its reputation on beef (the house special is a superb prime rib). *2620 W 2nd St (exit 84 off I-84, go west 1 mile), The Dalles; (541) 296-6708; $$.*

Lodgings

Williams House Inn ☆☆ An arboretum surrounds this classic 1899 house, which boasts Oriental rugs and musical instruments. The innkeepers serve a fine breakfast, and happily share an encyclopedic knowledge of the area's history. *608 W 6th St (corner of Trevett), The Dalles, OR 97058; (541) 296-2889; $$.*

More Information

Columbia River Gorge Visitors Association, The Dalles: *(800) 984-6743.*

Greater Hermiston Chamber of Commerce, Hermiston: *(541) 567-6151.*

The Dalles Area Chamber of Commerce, The Dalles: *(800) 255-3385.*

Umatilla National Wildlife Refuge, Umatilla: *(541) 922-3232.*

Hood River
and the Gorge

From Hood River on the east, south through the Hood River Valley to Mount Hood, west to Troutdale at the edge of the Portland metropolitan area, and north to the Washington border, including the north side of the Mount Hood Wilderness Area, the Mark O. Hatfield Wilderness, the western half of the Columbia River Gorge National Scenic Area, and the towns of Hood River and Cascade Locks.

Summer mornings usually dawn quiet and clear in the Columbia River Gorge. As the sun begins to rise above the wheat fields of eastern Washington and move south toward Oregon, only a cool breeze ripples the water of the Columbia offshore at Hood River.

As the heat begins to build by midmorning, the wind begins to steadily increase in velocity. Riverside parks begin to fill with visitors from around the world, who scurry about rigging sails in preparation for another day of windsurfing. The wind usually builds to 15 knots, with occasional gusts of 25 knots. A few days even see gusts upward of 40 knots. It's these days when the winds are called "nuclear," a weary reference to the Hanford Nuclear Reservation that lies upstream in Washington and sends who knows what down the Columbia River.

If windsurfing had not been invented in California in the 1960s, someone surely would have discovered it in the Gorge. Besides having incredibly reliable winds, the Gorge had a network of water parks that were just waiting to find some users. The parks had been built by port districts, which were flush with money that river commerce brings, or as part of the hydroelectric projects funded by the formerly deep pockets of the federal government. Local residents used the parks selectively throughout the year, but anyone who visited the Gorge in the late 1970s before the windsurfing boom remembers how forlorn the parks were when the wind was blowing "nuclear."

Not any more. Windsurfing may have reached its zenith as a sport, but it's still king of the Gorge during summer. It's true that on any given day, there will be far more people hiking trails in the area than windsurfing, but it's the sailors out on the river who can so easily be seen from Interstate 84 and leave a lasting impression on travelers.

Three factors combine to give the Gorge such reliable winds: (1) During summer the west side of Oregon often has a higher barometric pressure than the east side. Wind moves from high to low pressure and is strongest where the gradient changes rapidly, which just happens to be in the heart of the Gorge. (2) Oregon's east side heats up more quickly and to a higher temperature than the west side. As the hot air rises, cool air flows from the Pacific Ocean east up the Columbia River to take the rising air's place. (3) The slot created by the Columbia River as it passes through the Cascade Range constricts the flow of air, resulting in an example of the scientific principle called the Venturi effect. Because a large volume of air is passing through a narrow channel, the air speeds up. The principle is the same as when a wide, placid river comes to a narrow channel and turns into a whitewater inferno.

Couple all this eastward-flowing wind with a westward-running river current, and sailors can zoom back and forth all day on the Columbia and never go anywhere. Despite its reputation, however, wind doesn't always howl through the Gorge each summer day. In fact, the wind may not blow at all, or often is not powerful enough to let the expert sailors pull out the tiny sails they affectionately call postage stamps. These no-wind days have forced the Gorge's boardheads, a young, athletic lot, to seek out other thrills. Now, instead of arriving in Hood River with just their sailboards in tow, they bring kayaks, mountain bikes, paragliders, snow skis and snowboards, rock and mountain climbing gear, even personal watercraft. The Gorge has made the transition from a windsurfing destination into one of the best areas in the country for a complete package of year-round outdoor recreation.

The mild breezes of a summer morning in the Gorge may stay gentle all day long, but boardheads—and others—will find plenty of things to do.

Getting There

Portland is less than an hour's driving time away from the heart of the Gorge, with Hood River lying 64 miles east via Interstate 84. The Historic Columbia River Highway provides a slower alternative east of Troutdale, past Multnomah Falls to where it rejoins the freeway, about 8 miles west of Cascade Locks (just east of Ainsworth State Park). The Hood River Valley can be reached by driving Highway 35 north from Mount Hood or south from Hood River.

Adjoining Areas

    SOUTH: **Mount Hood**

    EAST: **Columbia Basin, Lower Deschutes River**

    WEST: **Greater Portland**

Scenic Drives/Picnics

Since it opened in 1915, the **Historic Columbia River Highway** has been one of the showpieces for tourism in America. Celebrated as the engineering marvel of its age, the scenic highway has been largely replaced by I-84, a ribbon of commerce that connects Portland to the string of cities in central and Eastern Oregon and to the Eastern states. Large parts of the historic highway remain in place, even though large portions wind up being closed most of the winter for frequent major repairs needed because of storm damage. A favorite outing for Portlanders, especially when out-of-town guests visit, is to drive the historic highway east from Troutdale to Multnomah Falls, then return by I-84.

The Historic Columbia River Highway leaves the east edge of the Portland metropolitan area at **Troutdale,** where I-84 crosses the **Sandy River** at exit 18, then heads east to **Corbett** where the constant parade of sites begins. Each is dazzling in its own right. **Portland Women's Forum** and **Crown Point,** both day-use state parks, have awesome hilltop views of the west end of the Gorge. Between the two is the turnoff for Mount Hood National Forest's Rd 20, which leads to the 4,056-foot summit of **Larch Mountain** with terrific views of its own. Crown Point is capped with **Vista House,** which sits 733 feet above the river. Built in 1916 and remodeled in 1997, the art-deco-style structure must surely be one of the most frequently photographed buildings in the northwestern United States. Most of the parks along the scenic highway are managed either by the Rooster Rock office of Oregon State Parks, (503) 695-2261, or the Hood River headquarters of the Columbia River Gorge National Scenic Area, (541) 386-2333.

Just east of Crown Point, the scenic highway dips back to river level and begins passing numerous waterfalls and trailheads: **Latourell Falls** (249 feet high), **Bridal Veil Falls** (100 feet high), **Wahkeena Falls** (242 feet high), **Multnomah Falls** (620 feet high), and **Oneonta Gorge** and **Horsetail Falls** (176 feet high). All are marked along the highway, between 25 to 33.5 miles east of Portland, and can be seen either without leaving the car or after a short walk. The historic highway rejoins the interstate just east of **Ainsworth State Park,** 37 miles east of Portland.

Other short sections of the old highway parallel I-84 and give access to **Elowah Falls** (289 feet high, 2 miles east of exit 35), **Wahclella Falls** (100 feet high, at Bonneville Dam, exit 40), and the **Herman Creek Trail** (midway between exits 47 and 51) (see Hiking, below). Mountain Shadow Ranch, (541) 374-8592, on the south side of the old highway near milepost 50, operates the only horseback trail rides on the Oregon side of the Gorge. Formerly a chicken ranch, Mountain Shadow raises a herd of goats that feeds the migrant workers in the Hood River Valley. The goats are good weather predictors because they scurry for cover at the first sign of a sprinkle.

On I-84 east of Portland, instead of on the Historic Columbia River Highway, **Rooster Rock State Park,** (503) 695-2261, beckons travelers at exit 25. With 1,430 parking spots, Rooster Rock is one of the largest day-use parks in Oregon. The park has acres of shaded grass and, when the river level is low enough, a couple miles of sandy beach. The park also has a marina. The park's namesake is a vertical rock formation just north of I-84 that is popular with technical rock climbers. The park also has a clothing-optional beach at its east end.

Multnomah Falls, accessible from exit 31 on I-84, has been a favored picnic area with travelers over the years. Falling in two cascades (542 feet and 78 feet), it is the fourth-highest waterfall in the country. Recent harsh winters, however, have brought down lots of rock and ice that have made it difficult to keep facilities in full operation. The trail to the top of the falls has been closed more often than it's been open in recent winters, but don't worry about the future of the state's number-one free tourist attraction. The Forest Service is spending $1.2 million to build a new sewage treatment facility that will be close enough to Multnomah Falls Lodge (see Attractions, below) to handle the waterfall's 3 million annual visitors, but far enough away not to become an eyesore.

A pleasant spot for a picnic close to Multnomah Falls is the grassy park at the **Port of Cascade Locks's marina.** Cascade Locks, located in Hood River County just west of the Multnomah County line, is the historic center of the Gorge and the location of the Bridge of the Gods. The toll bridge opened in 1926 and carries the Pacific Crest Trail between Washington and Oregon. The span is 1,131 feet long as it crosses 135 feet above the Bonneville Pool of the Columbia River. To reach the park at the marina, take exit 44 when traveling from the west or exit 47 when driving from the east, follow the road into Cascade Locks, and watch for signs in the center of town for the turnoff to the marina.

Freeway rest stops accessible to eastbound travelers at **Starvation Creek** (near milepost 54) and **Mitchell Point** (near milepost 58) would be pleasant for picnics if it weren't for the noise from the highway and rail-road. The good news is that Portland International Airport is out of ear-shot 40 miles to the west. Both rest areas serve as trailheads for ties into the Gorge's trail network.

Despite the significance of the Historic Columbia River Highway, it wasn't the first tour route developed in Hood River County. That honor goes to the **Mount Hood Wagon Road,** which led to the mountain's northeast side as early as 1884. **Cloud Cap Inn** was constructed in 1889 at the end of the road and is the oldest standing structure on Mount Hood. The historic structure, formerly an overnight inn at the 6,000-foot timber-line on the mountain's northeast side, is used as a base by the Crag Rats, Hood River's volunteer search and rescue organization. Gravel over Forest Service Rd 3512's final 10 miles, from Cooper Spur at the head of the Hood River Valley to Cloud Cap, keeps the area from becoming another Timberline Lodge, where more than a million people visit each year. When the road is free of snow from June through October, the Mount Hood Wagon Road to Cloud Cap Inn continues to be used by several thousand hikers and climbers more than a century after it was built. The unplowed road is open to skiers during winter.

Much of the beauty of the **Hood River Valley** can be seen from a seat on the Mount Hood Scenic Railroad, (800) 386-3556, which runs 22 miles from Hood River to Parkdale as it follows the West Fork of the Hood River. The train operates six days a week during summer (closed Mondays) and on a less frequent schedule the rest of the year. Views from the railroad and nearby Hwy 35 take in the valley's orchards, its river canyons, and the always impressive north face of Mount Hood. (On Hwy 35, head .5 mile south of town and follow the left turnoff up to **Panorama Point.**) The peak blossom time, when the valley's pear and apple trees are covered by white blossoms, is usually late April. Fresh fruit becomes avail-able in September.

Visitors who want to leave the driving to knowledgeable locals can take a tour of the Gorge, Mount Hood, and the Hood River Valley with Pioneer Expeditions of Hood River, (541) 387-4734, or Northwest Day Trips of Portland, (503) 255-5558.

Hiking

Columbia River

The way some hikers (usually from Portland) talk, it's easy to think the **Columbia River Gorge National Scenic Area** is the *only* place worth hiking in Oregon. But the truth of the matter is that the Gorge is probably the only place *they* hike in Oregon.

The Gorge is truly a beautiful setting for hiking, but anyone who hikes the Gorge to the exclusion of all other places is walking up a creek without a hiking stick. For one thing, several of the most beautiful hikes in the Gorge are on the Washington side. With its southern exposure, the Washington side gets more sunshine and has many more open vistas than the Oregon side. And hiking in the Gorge means noise from the freeway and railroads, steep trails, crowds, thick forests that may give desert hikers claustrophobia, severe winter storm damage to the trails, and car clouting at the trailheads.

If the hiking experience is so bad, why do people love hiking in the Gorge so much? For Portlanders, the proximity of the trails in the Gorge is hard to beat. So are its magnificent wildflowers, eye-popping waterfalls, year-round access, and wide-ranging selection of trails. At the end of a day of hiking in the Gorge, the benefits usually far outweigh any negatives and most hikers can't wait to return.

Most trails in the Gorge are managed either by the Oregon Parks and Recreation Department, (503) 695-2261, or the Columbia River Gorge National Scenic Area, (541) 386-2333. Designated by Congress in 1986, the 292,615-acre scenic area on both sides of the river protects urban as well as natural areas from overdevelopment. Most hikers are not aware of who manages which trail, or where trail management changes—they just start walking. The boundaries of the national scenic area extend from Troutdale on the west to the Deschutes River on the east. Volunteers help answer visitor questions about the Gorge at Multnomah Falls, accessible at exit 31 on I-84 (the parking lot is between the traffic lanes, and a paved path leads beneath the freeway to Multnomah Falls Lodge).

The Oregon side of the Gorge has 77 waterfalls, many accessible from the Historic Columbia River Highway (see Scenic Drives/Picnics, above). Most can be seen without leaving the car or are within a 1-mile walk of the numerous trailheads. Dozens of beautiful waterfalls are tucked away in the higher canyons, and dozens more unnamed falls appear out of nowhere when spring rain melts winter snow.

From west to east along the Historic Columbia River Highway, the Gorge's most popular trails (with round-trip or loop distances) between Corbett and Bonneville are **Angels Rest** (moderate; 4.4 miles); **Wahkeena Spring** (moderate; 4 miles); **Multnomah Falls/Wahkeena Falls Loop** (moderate; 5 miles); **Multnomah Falls** (moderate; 2.2 miles of pavement to the upper viewing platform); **Larch Mountain** (difficult; 13.6 miles); **Oneonta Gorge** (moderate; 4 miles); **Horsetail Loop** (easy; 2.7 miles); **Elowah Falls** (easy; 1.4 miles); **Wahclella Falls** (easy; 1.8 miles); and **Eagle Creek** (easy; 6.6 miles to High Bridge). With so many trails to pick from, Gorge hikers usually carry the "Trails of the Columbia Gorge" map that is available from map stores and Forest Service offices.

The trail that climbs Angels Rest for a view of the Gorge from Troutdale to Bonneville begins on the south side of the scenic highway at the first stop sign from exit 25 of I-84. The Wahkeena Falls, Multnomah Falls, Oneonta Gorge, and Horsetail Falls trailheads are can't-miss stops along the scenic highway (see Scenic Drives/Picnics, above). The 4,000-foot climb up Larch Mountain begins at Multnomah Falls and reaches the top of 4,050-foot Larch Mountain at the rim of the Gorge. The trail to Elowah Falls begins in John B. Yeon State Park, located on a frontage road 2 miles east of exit 35 before the road reenters the freeway eastbound. Wahclella Falls is reached from the parking lot on the southwest side of exit 40.

The Eagle Creek Trail, located 1 mile south of exit 41 at the end of the access road, is one of the few long-distance trails in the Gorge that doesn't climb steeply. The trail goes 13 miles up the drainage to reach the Pacific Crest Trail at Wahtum Lake. While the upper part of the trail is for backpackers, day hikers throng the trail's lower 5.5 miles to see Punchbowl Falls, High Bridge, and Tunnel Falls, all high on the list of the most beautiful sights in the Gorge. If Oregon has a trail anything like the Milford Track in New Zealand, it's the Eagle Creek Trail.

In addition to the main trail, most trailheads have secondary trails that lead to less-traveled destinations. Plan to spend a couple of years hiking nowhere else but on the Oregon side of the Gorge if you want to become intimate with all the trails.

The Gorge is a great place to get into shape for bigger climbs. A favorite conditioning hike among mountaineers is the 12-mile round-trip hike up **Mount Defiance** from Starvation Creek State Park (a freeway rest area near milepost 54). The hike gains 4,960 feet, even though the mountain is only 4,815 feet high, the highest point on the Oregon side of the Gorge. Many of the Gorge trails interconnect with one another to offer interesting loops, especially if a car shuttle is available.

Pacific Crest Trail

The Pacific Crest National Scenic Trail (PCT) enters the Hood River Valley at 3,440-foot Lolo Pass, on Forest Rd 8 northwest of Mount Hood, and travels 14 miles to Wahtum Lake and Forest Rd 1310. From the lake, the trail begins a gradual, then steep, 16.5-mile descent to cross the Columbia River over the Bridge of the Gods at Cascade Locks. The trail stays high on a ridge as it passes 1 mile west of Lost Lake (see Camping, below) and works its way to Wahtum Lake where it enters the 39,000-acre **Mark O. Hatfield** (formerly Columbia) **Wilderness**. Although the PCT meets the needs of long-distance hikers, day hikers usually find more scenic trails to walk in the Gorge. The only major trailheads in this 30.5-mile section of the PCT are Lolo Pass, Wahtum Lake, and beneath the south approach for the Bridge of the Gods at Cascade Locks. The trail is managed by the Hood River Ranger District, (541) 352-6002, and the Columbia River Gorge National Scenic Area, (541) 386-2333.

Hood River Valley

Hiking opportunities are limited in the Hood River Valley because most of the land is privately owned and has been used for many years to grow pears and apples. The Hood River Ranger Station, (541) 352-6002, is located 12 miles south of I-84 on Hwy 35 in the tiny town of Mount Hood. The ranger district administers most of the land in the Hood River Valley that is too high up to be suitable for growing fruit. Some of the best hiking on Mount Hood is on its northeast slope near Cloud Cap, where the 47,100-acre **Mount Hood Wilderness Area** is only a few steps away in either direction on the 37.6-mile **Timberline Trail** that circles Mount Hood (see Mount Hood chapter). The trail passes Cloud Cap Inn just below the 6,000-foot elevation as it makes its way around the mountain. To reach the trailhead, first drive 9 miles south on Hwy 35 from the Hood River Ranger Station. Turn east on Forest Rd 3510 and follow signs to Cooper Spur, site of a lodge and restaurant, a small ski area, and several homes. Turn south at Cooper Spur Inn toward Cooper Spur Ski Area, drive 2 miles, and turn west on Forest Rd 3512 just before the entrance to the ski area. The steep, narrow gravel road is okay for passenger autos but is free of snow only from mid-June through October. It ends 19 miles above the ski area at Cloud Cap. Self-issued permits are available at all Mount Hood Wilderness Area trailheads.

One of Oregon's best beginner backpacking trips after snow melts in mid-July is to walk the trail 1 mile to the east to the ridge south of Tilly Jane Creek. Continue along the Timberline Trail through sparse trees to any of a number of possible campsites above or below the trail. Water is available in Tilly Jane Creek. The above-timberline view toward Washington's Mount Adams is spectacular, and the amount of energy expended is minimal. Water can usually be obtained from melting snowbanks.

Hikers who want to venture a little farther from the road can walk 4 miles west to Elk Cove, another spectacular campsite above timberline on Mount Hood's north side. The crossing of a snowfield that often extends from Eliot Glacier can be dangerous, so bring and know how to use an ice ax.

Lower down in the forest from Cloud Cap, popular hikes along the East Fork of the Hood River and Hwy 35 are **Tamanawas Falls** (easy; 1.4 miles one way) and **Cold Springs** (difficult; 8.8 miles to Elk Meadows).

Both begin 1 mile north of Sherwood Campground on the 9.8-mile East Fork Trail, which connects Sherwood and Robinhood Campgrounds as it follows the highway and the river. Mount Hood's spectacular north side, which appears to be of Himalayan proportion when covered with snow and peeking above the Hood River Valley on a midwinter day, can be approached from the end of logging roads via the **Elk Cove Trail** (moderate; 3.9 miles one way) and **Pinnacle Ridge Trail** (moderate; 3.4 miles one way). See the Mount Hood National Forest map for driving directions from Forest Rd 2840 at Laurance Lake.

A small portion of climbers who attempt to reach **Mount Hood's summit** begin from Cloud Cap. Their numbers are limited because the road isn't usually clear of snow until mid-June. Popular routes are **Cooper Spur** and **Sunshine.** Both are steep, technical, and fit only for an experienced party. Descent on either route is uncomfortably steep, so most parties climb down the south side where they have a car waiting at Timberline Lodge. To climb Cooper Spur, walk south from Cloud Cap for 1.4 miles to where the Cooper Spur Climbers' Trail leaves the Timberline Trail. Hike 2.6 miles to a tie-in rock, where most parties rope up for the final 2,000-foot climb up the spur between the Eliot and Newton Clark Glaciers. The Sunshine route requires crossing the entire north face of the mountain on the Eliot Glacier and finishing the climb from the west on the upper part of Cathedral Ridge. Self-issued permits are available from the Hood River Ranger Station on Hwy 35.

Adventure Out, (541) 387-4626, is a Hood River guide service that offers all types of mountain trips.

Camping

Columbia River

The shores of the Columbia River have fewer places to camp than might be expected for such a popular tourist destination. While the Gorge has outstanding recreation opportunities, camping isn't always pleasant because it's next to impossible to get away from the noise of I-84 and the busy transcontinental rail line. Anyone camping in the Gorge has to deal with the incessant summer wind and, during winter, the frigid east wind.

The oldest campground in the national forest system, built in 1916, is **Eagle Creek Campground** (see Hiking, above). The campground has 18 sites, a few with barrier-free facilities, and the maximum trailer size is 22 feet. The campground is near one of the most popular trails in the Gorge, the Eagle Creek Trail. Other Forest Service campgrounds along the Columbia River are **Wyeth** and **Herman Creek Horse Camps,** both on the old scenic highway east of exit 47 and Cascade Locks. Wyeth has

17 sites and Herman Creek has 8. Campers with horses are welcome, as are all campers. All Forest Service campgrounds in the Gorge are managed by the Columbia River Gorge National Scenic Area, (541) 386-2333, located at 902 Wasco St in Hood River.

Oregon State Parks picks up the slack by offering camping at Ainsworth State Park and Viento State Park. Neither is on the reservations system and both are open March through October. **Ainsworth State Park** is located at exit 35 of I-84. Access to nearby trails is the main attraction for Ainsworth, which has 45 campsites with full-utility hookups. **Viento State Park** is 8 miles west of Hood River at exit 56 and has 17 tent sites, 58 electrical sites, and some handicapped-accessible campsites. Viento's main attractions are access to hiking trails and a Columbia River beach that was built in a cooperative project by park staff and Gorge windsurfers. Information about both parks is available through Oregon Parks and Recreation Department at Rooster Rock, (503) 695-2261.

The Port of Cascade Locks Marine Park, (541) 374-8619, on the waterfront in central Cascade Locks at exit 44 (or exit 47 from the east), has 45 camping spaces and a 500-foot beach.

Hood River Valley

The shortage of camping opportunities in the Gorge is made up for by campgrounds in the Hood River Valley, where the wind and noise aren't as bad and campers are still within driving distance of the attractions of the Gorge. Hood River County has only 16,903 residents, but somehow manages to have one of the best county park camping systems in Oregon. Multnomah County, the neighbor to the west with 620,000 residents, should be so lucky.

Campgrounds operated by Hood River County are Tucker, Kingsley, Toll Bridge, and Rouston. **Tucker Campground,** just 5 miles south of town on Tucker Rd (Hwy 281), is a 36-acre county park with 46 campsites. **Kingsley Campground** is located on a reservoir west of town on Kingsley Rd, where plans are underway to increase the size of its 20-site campground. **Toll Bridge Campground,** located 1 mile south of the community of Mount Hood just west of Hwy 35, is the largest of all with 80 sites. Next to Lost Lake, Toll Bridge has the most facilities of any campground on the northern side of Mount Hood. **Rouston Campground** has 20 campsites 7 miles south of the community of Mount Hood on the east side of Hwy 35. The county parks department, (541) 386-6323, can provide information about all its parks and takes reservations for Toll Bridge and Tucker.

Lost Lake Campground, located at an elevation of 3,200 feet 20 miles southwest of Hood River via Hwy 281 and Forest Rd 13, is one of the major camping destinations in the Mount Hood National Forest.

Operated by a concessionaire, the resort has 91 spaces with a maximum trailer length of 24 feet. Call Lost Lake Resort, (541) 386-6366, for reservations in one of the camp loops and at the resort's seven cabins. Other facilities include a wooden boardwalk with two barrier-free fishing piers, paddle boat and canoe rentals, and a store. In addition to the driving route from Hood River, Portland travelers can reach Lost Lake from the south by driving bumpy, dusty forest roads over Lolo Pass.

Two Forest Service camps that are kept busy by their convenient locations on Hwy 35 are **Sherwood Campground** and **Robinhood Campground,** both located along the East Fork of the Hood River. Sherwood, with 14 sites, comes first when driving south from Hood River, 11 miles north of the Hood River Ranger Station, (541) 352-6002. Robinhood is 4 miles farther south and has 24 sites. The 9.8-mile **East Fork Trail** connects the camps, which both have wheelchair-accessible toilets.

Other Forest Service camps near the Hood River Valley are small—fewer than a dozen sites—but located in scenic settings. Hikers like to camp at **Tilly Jane and Cloud Cap Campgrounds,** both located near Cloud Cap Inn (see Hiking, above), because of the access to the Timberline Trail around Mount Hood. The same holds true for **Wahtum Lake,** because of its location on the Pacific Crest Trail (see Hiking, above).

Windsurfing

The Columbia River Gorge is famous for windsurfing throughout, but its biggest winds usually happen at only a few launch sites. Most happen to be on the Washington side at Swell City and the Hatchery (both a few miles west of the Hood River Bridge) and at Doug's Beach (3 miles east of Lyle, Washington). The Washington side doesn't necessarily have better winds than the Oregon side, but it doesn't have the controlled access of an interstate highway and its beaches tend to be more accessible.

Sailors with somewhat lesser skills than those required to ride the big water on the Washington side can usually find fun sailing on the Oregon shore. When the wind is blowing, parking lots are filled by noon with vehicles and beaches are littered with clothing and gear. To call something a beach along the Columbia River is a bit of a misnomer. Rather than sandy beaches, which constantly have to be resupplied as the river's current sweeps the sand away, launches along the Columbia are more likely to be over basalt rocks of varying sizes.

Newcomers to the Gorge, who think they're good enough to sail in the area's big winds, often launch their sailboards at Hood River, then wind up blown across the river to Washington where they wash up on **Bozo Beach.** Thankfully, river windsurfing is relatively forgiving, at least as far as life-and-death situations go. Sailors use a flotation vest and a wet suit. Hypothermia shouldn't be a problem during the prime summer sailing season when air temperatures reach the 90s and water temperatures climb into the 70s. The major threat to life and limb is the river's constant barge traffic, some of which tows log booms with steel cables that are difficult to see against the gray froth of the river.

Hood River, especially the port district, has embraced windsurfing with open arms. Until the sport was invented, the port had a beautiful park that few people used when the wind was blowing strong during summer. Hood River sailing areas are the **Sailpark** at exit 64 off I-84 and the **Event Center** and **the Hook,** both at exit 63. Beginner lessons are taught in the marina next to the Sailpark and in a wind-sheltered beach just upriver from the **Hood River Inn,** also at exit 64. Hood River's major sailboard shops offer rentals and lessons on site at the Sailpark.

Many of the best windsurfing sites are located east of Hood River in the Columbia Basin country, or across the Hood River toll bridge on the Washington shore of the Columbia. The bridge toll for a car is 75 cents, an amount that can add up with multiple daily crossings during a two-week sailing vacation. I-84 makes the Columbia River relatively difficult to access west of Hood River. The best places to sail west of Hood River are **Viento State Park, Cascade Locks,** and **Rooster Rock State Park** (see Camping and Scenic Drives/Picnics, above). Rooster Rock is a little too far west to be in the best summer wind zone, but when the east wind is howling during winter a few sailors can be seen out on the water even when ice covers the shore.

Hood River's main **sailboard shops** are Big Winds, (541) 386-6086, at 505 Cascade; Hood River Windsurfing, (541) 386-5787, at 101 Oak St (both have windsurfing schools); and Windance, (541) 386-2131, at 108 Hwy 35. Rhonda Smith's Windsurfing Center, (541) 386-9463, at the Port Marina Park has a **windsurfing school** and rentals.

Hood River has become the American capital for the **design and manufacture** of sailboarding equipment. Because of the sport's seasonal nature, businesses have expanded their production into snowboarding and outdoor clothing and accessories. More than a few people travel to the Hood River area just to shop. Hood River's concentration of outdoor equipment stores is rivaled in Oregon only by Bend.

Hood River factories with retail shops include Airtime, (541) 386-5788, at 111 Oak St; Body Skins, (541) 386-3637, at 110 Fourth St; Gorge Animal, (541) 386-5524, 509A Cascade; High Gear, (541) 386-7456, at 1100 E Marina Way; Hood River Outfitters, (541) 386-6202, at 1020 Wasco St; Kerrits, (541) 386-1145, at 316 Oak St; Oceanic Sails, (541) 386-1428, at 416 Cascade; Visual Speed, (541) 386-7877, at 489 N Eighth St; and

Windwing Designs, (541) 386-3861, at 315 Oak St. Other Hood River man-ufacturers that don't offer on-site retail but sell gear around the world include Aunt Mable's, Da Kine, North Shore, and Shred Alert.

For an update on wind conditions each morning, listen to K105.5 FM in Hood River, (541) 386-1336, or Q104 FM in The Dalles, (541) 386-3300. Both stations have free wind condition information on telephone recordings. The most current wind conditions are available for a fee by calling Windsight at (900) 860-0600. To purchase a copy of the annual windsurfing guide to the Gorge, call *Gorge Guide* at (541) 386-7440.

Fishing

Due to its proximity to Portland, the **Columbia River** is heavily fished all the way from St. Helens in the Lower Columbia country upstream to Bonneville Dam in the Gorge and beyond to the Deschutes River in the Columbia Basin country. Most fishing upstream from Troutdale is for chi-nook salmon, steelhead, and sturgeon, although seasons and catch limits have been drastically reduced in recent years as the fishery has dwindled. Other fish of choice are walleye and shad, plus the ubiquitous squawfish. The squawfish is not pursued for its taste but rather for the reward that it carries on its head. The fish usually brings a bounty to draw fishermen away from the salmon and steelhead smolt making their runs for the Pacific Ocean. Other fish species taken from the ponds and backwaters located along I-84 include smallmouth and largemouth bass, crappie, and trout.

Chinook are usually in the Columbia River during spring and after August. The steelhead are around from June into winter. The sturgeon live in the river year-round but are easiest to catch when smelt appear in February (in the rare years when smelt appear). Most fishing on the Columbia is by boat, although plenty of anglers park their cars well off the shoulders of I-84 and hike down to the river. The Columbia below **Bonneville Dam** is often the busiest fishing spot in this stretch of the Gorge. The 20-mile pool above Bonneville is lightly fished, partly because it's frequently buffeted by winds during summer and fishing is often better elsewhere. Walleye are frequently taken above the Hood River Bridge along the Washington shore. The side of the river where you launch a boat determines which state license (Oregon or Washington) you must have. Check the state fishing synopsis for a full list of regulations, or call The Dalles district office of the Oregon Department of Fish and Wildlife, (541) 296-4628.

Rivers, creeks, and streams that enter the Columbia in the heart of the Gorge have limited fishing opportunities because of the numerous waterfalls that block passage a few miles from the Columbia. The best bet for trout from April through October and for steelhead all year is **Eagle**

Creek near Bonneville. The **forks of the Hood River** are good for native and hatchery trout and for summer and winter runs of steelhead.

Lakes in the Hood River Valley have cutthroat, brown, brook, and rainbow trout, plus some kokanee at 290-acre **Lost Lake** (see Camping, above). Other large lakes are **Laurance** (104 acres, in the upper Hood River Valley on Forest Rd 2840), **Wahtum** (57 acres, at the edge of the Hatfield Wilderness on Forest Rd 1310), and **Kingsley Reservoir** (48 acres; see Camping, above).

Lost Lake is one of those magical places common throughout Oregon that somehow manages to live up to its reputation. The lake has a picture-postcard view of Mount Hood's northwest side, a photo that has graced more than a few calendars and coffee-table books. Recent upgrades have made the lake into one of the best wheelchair-accessible fishing spots in Oregon. To find the lake, drive south into uptown Hood River and follow signs for 20 miles on Hwy 281 and Forest Rd 13 to Lost Lake.

Every lake worth its salt (or fresh) water needs a resident monster. For Lost Lake, the monster's name is "Walter." At home in the jet-black darkness at the bottom of the 167-foot-deep lake, Walter has been known to rise to the surface to steal bait and torment anglers. The fish is rumored to weigh 50 pounds (or possibly more) and wears a full beard made up from a fortune of lures and broken lines. Everyone who visits the lake tries to land Walter, but nobody wants another fisherman to be so lucky.

For anglers who need to come home with a fish on days the wild ones aren't biting, they may want to try the **trout pond** at Phoenix Pharms, (541) 352-6090, located west of Hwy 35 on Baldwin Creek Rd between Odell and the community of Mount Hood. The Gorge Fly Shop, (541) 386-6977, at 201 Oak St is Hood River's retail **fishing shop** and **guide service.** Luhr Jensen, (541) 386-3811, manufactures much of its fishing tackle in Hood River for sale around the world. The factory has an outlet store at 550 Riverside, Hood River.

Wildlife

Three state fish hatcheries, plus the fish ladder at Bonneville Dam, are the only developed wildlife-viewing locations on the Oregon side of the Gorge. Common sightings along the Columbia include **osprey** and, in the side canyons, the ever-popular **water ouzel,** also known as the **American dipper.**

State fish hatcheries are located at Bonneville Dam (exit 40), (541) 374-8393; Cascade (exit 41 at Eagle Creek), (541) 374-8381; and Oxbow (exit 44 just east of Cascade Locks), (541) 374-8540. Bonneville is popular for its display pools of large **rainbow trout** and 6-foot-long **white sturgeon.** The hatchery raises **fall chinook** and **coho salmon,** which can be seen as they return to spawn August through October. Cascade raises coho. During fall, chinook and coho can be seen spawning below Fish Rock at the bridge crossing Eagle Creek. Oxbow raises coho fingerlings. Adult salmon can be seen spawning near Oxbow at Herman Creek from September through November.

The US Army Corps of Engineers visitors facilities at Bonneville Dam, (503) 326-6021, include stops at the navigation lock, the powerhouse, and the underwater fish-viewing windows at the Bradford Island Visitors Center on the Oregon shore. Best times to view **chinook** are from April through September and for **steelhead** July and August.

Mountain Biking

Hood River mountain bikers usually head up the Hood River Valley to do their riding. The trail along the top of **Surveyor's Ridge** is one of the most famous single-track rides in Oregon and, thankfully, beginners can enjoy it as well as experts. Beginners can make the ride downhill from south to north, then use Forest Rd 17 for an easy return. Experts can ride the trail round-trip or set up a car shuttle to finish the ride with steep descents of either the Dog River or Oak Ridge Trails.

To reach the southern Surveyor's Ridge trailhead, drive south of Hood River on Hwy 35 for 26 miles and turn east on Forest Rd 44. Drive uphill 3.5 miles to gravel Forest Rd 620 and park where the trail crosses the road. The Dog River Trail also begins here. The Surveyor's Ridge Trail travels north across the ridge for 12.6 miles to the junction with the **Oak Ridge Trail.** The elevation is fairly constant, beginning at 4,200 feet and dropping to 3,640. Beginners can ride for 11 miles, then turn east on Forest Rd 680 for the short ride out to Forest Rd 17 and the easy return south. Experts can drop down to Hwy 35 via the Oak Ridge Trail, or ride the full 16.8-mile length of Surveyor's Ridge by continuing north and climbing **Bald Butte.**

The Surveyor's Ridge Trail passes several openings in the forest for impressive views of Mount Hood's towering north face. The orchards of the Hood River Valley lie far below. Be careful at a barbed-wire gate crossing at 9.6 miles that comes at the bottom of a short downhill.

The **Dog River Trail** is a classic in its own right. The 6.3-mile trail, which begins at the same trailhead as Surveyor's Ridge, descends a heavily timbered canyon, steeply at times, but at other times the trail is relatively gentle. Be careful not to carry too much speed into the switchbacks. The trail drops from 3,800 feet on Surveyor's Ridge to 2,150 feet. The lower trailhead is 20 miles south of Hood River on Hwy 35. Turn east on a gravel road for 100 yards before crossing the East Fork of the Hood

River. The trail begins (or ends) where the road turns left and begins to climb.

The **East Fork Trail,** between Robinhood Campground on the south to a bridge just north of Sherwood Campground (see Camping, above), follows the East Fork of the Hood River and Hwy 35. Popular because its elevation change is only 300 feet, the continuation of the trail north of Sherwood Campground is closed to bikes.

The 8-mile **Knebal Springs Trail** makes a loop south of a campground by the same name on the east side of Hwy 35. The route is fairly level as it follows Trails 474 and 455 just east of The Dalles watershed. See the Mount Hood National Forest map for directions or stop at the Hood River Ranger Station, (541) 352-6002, at the community of Mount Hood for information on all Forest Service trails open to biking.

The place in Hood River to head for **bicycling supplies** is Discover Bicycles, (541) 386-4820, at 1020 Wasco St. Pacific Crest Mountain Bike Tours, (800) 849-6589, is based in Bend but leads several multiday tours each summer from Mount Hood to the Gorge. Local tour operators who package multisport adventures include Odyssey, (800) 789-2770, and Hood River Trails, (541) 354-5888.

Many of the trails in the Columbia River Gorge National Scenic Area are open to bikes, but the steepness of most trails and conflicts with other users generally keep bikers off the Gorge's trails along the Columbia River. An exception is **Gorge Trail No. 400,** which parallels the freeway throughout much of the Gorge but nevertheless has plenty of climbing. Steep, rocky, and narrow sections make the ride suitable for experts, except the Bonneville to Cascade Locks stretch that has been tamed by a long strip of blacktop. Access to Gorge Trail No. 400 is from nearly all trailheads along the Historic Columbia River Highway.

Cycling

Road rides in the Gorge are limited only by the amount of hills cyclists want to climb. It's legal to cycle on **I-84** outside the Portland metro area, although the traffic volume is beyond most cyclists' tolerance. A popular tour, however, runs east out of Portland on **Marine Drive** and its bicycle paths, joins the freeway at **Troutdale,** and continues to **Multnomah Falls.** The Historic Columbia River Highway can also be used to reach the falls, but instead of staying at river levels along the freeway cyclists have to make the 700-foot climb over Crown Point.

The **Hood River Valley,** with its network of paved roads and outstanding scenery, can be a beautiful place to ride. The only problem is making the big climb out of Hood River to reach the orchards. A good way to avoid the uphill ride is to take the Mount Hood Scenic Railroad from Hood River to Parkdale (see Scenic Drives/Picnics, above), then coast the backroads into town.

Boating/Cruises

Cascade Locks and **Hood River** both take advantage of their beautiful settings and their large marinas to attract cruise ship lines that ply the **Columbia River,** as well as private motor cruisers and sailboats. The Port of Cascade Locks operates Marina Park, (541) 374-8619, and the Port of Hood River operates Port Marina Sailpark, (541) 386-1645. Cascade Locks has a 120-foot transient dock, while Hood River has 131 open wet slips and a 60-foot transient dock.

The cruise line industry sends large ships on journeys up the Columbia River from Astoria to the head of navigation at Lewiston, Idaho. Occasionally during times of peak runoffs the cruise ships take the Snake River from Pasco, Washington, to Lewiston because of dangerous water levels. Cruising the Columbia isn't about to put the Alaska cruise industry out of business, but enough people plan vacations around Columbia cruise trips to keep the ships busy from spring through fall. Multiday trips are available from Great Rivers Cruises, (800) 720-0012; Adventure Cruises, (800) 613-2789; and the *Queen of the West* stern-wheeler, (800) 434-1232. Day and dinner cruises are available from Stern-wheeler Riverboat Tours, (503) 223-3928, at Cascade Locks, which operates on the Columbia River during summer and on the Portland waterfront the rest of the year. Another day-trip opportunity is with Columbia River Gorge Cruises of Hood River, (541) 296-8437.

The **forks of the Hood River** provide the only **rafting** and **kayaking** opportunities on the Oregon side of the Gorge. The Hood River is a spring-runoff river with lively rapids and should only be run by experts who have scouted the river in advance for logjams. The river has no commercial guide service.

Vacationers don't need to travel far from the Gorge if they must have some **whitewater** thrills. Washington's White Salmon River is just across the Columbia River from Hood River and the lower Deschutes River is only an hour-and-a-half drive away (see Lower Deschutes River chapter). Both rivers run dependably throughout the summer. Local whitewater guides of the White Salmon include Phil's Guide Service, (800) 366-2004, and AAA Rafting, (800) 866-7238, both of Husum, Washington.

Hang Gliding/Paragliding

Not surprisingly, Hood River has a group of hard-core adventurers who fly through the air on days when they don't have enough wind to fly over the water on their windsurfers. **Bald Butte,** the 3,779-foot summit at the north end of Surveyor's Ridge, is a favorite launching site for paragliders and hang gliders. The butte is on the east side of the Hood River Valley, across Hwy 35 from the Hood River Ranger Station at the community of Mount Hood. Most of the other favorite launch sites in the Gorge are on the Washington side.

Any type of self-launched flight in the Gorge has the potential to be dangerous because of the powerful winds that rip through the area. Pilots from outside the area should learn the ropes from the local **flight school,** Gorge Air Paragliding, (509) 493-2070.

For those who want to leave the flying to an experienced pilot, Flightline Services, (541) 386-1133, offers scenic **airplane tours** and **glider rides** daily during the summer from the Hood River Airport on the southwest side of town.

Skiing

Mount Hood's north side offers some less-crowded skiing opportunities than the mountain's south side, where the big ski areas that cater to Portland are located. **Cooper Spur Ski Area,** (541) 352-7803, is a small family ski area served by a rope tow and T-bar on the northeast side of Mount Hood. The vertical drop is only 500 feet, but local skiers from the Gorge keep Cooper Spur hopping on weekends and midweek nights when the lifts are running. The ski area also has a sliding hill. The ski area lost its day lodge to a fire in 1996 but rebuilt it in time for the 1997–98 ski season. Cooper Spur is 30 miles south of Hood River via Hwy 35 and roads that head up the Hood River Valley (see Hiking, above).

Nordic skiers often launch backcountry tours from the Cooper Spur Ski Area, climbing 2,100 feet to Cloud Cap via the **Tilly Jane Trail.** To reach the trailhead, drive the one-way road to Cooper Spur Ski Area, continue 150 yards, and watch for the cross-country trailhead at a wide spot in the road. The Cloud Cap area has four buildings that allow overnight use, but the proper club affiliation comes in handy when booking space. Check with the Hood River Ranger District, (541) 352-6002, for reservations procedures.

The **Little John Snow Play Hill,** located 31 miles south of Hood River on the east side of Hwy 35, was the first snow play hill designed and built by the Forest Service in Oregon. The hill is not patrolled or maintained and sliders must bring their own equipment. With an altitude of 3,300 feet, adequate snow is not always reliable.

Gear for winter sports and other outdoor adventures is available from Hood River Outfitters, (541) 386-6202, at 1020 Wasco St, a surprisingly well-stocked outdoor store for a town with only 4,632 year-round residents.

outside in

Attractions

The old **Historic Columbia River Highway** (US 30), above and paralleling the freeway, is for take-your-time wanderers. This 22-mile detour traverses the waterfall-riddled stretch from Troutdale to Ainsworth Park (see Scenic Drives/Picnics, above, for an overview of this beautiful drive). **Multnomah Falls Lodge,** (503) 695-2376, at the foot of the falls, was designed in a rustic stone-and-timber style in 1925 by Albert E. Doyle of Benson Hotel fame. Now a National Historic Landmark, the lodge houses a popular naturalists and visitors center and has a large restaurant that is a good stop for breakfast, but dinners are unremarkable (better to go just for dessert).

Bonneville Dam, (541) 374-8820, the first federal dam on the Columbia, offers self-guided tours of the dam, the fish ladders (seen through underwater viewing windows), and the navigational locks. You can tour the Bonneville Fish Hatchery (next to the dam) year-round, (541) 374-8393; however, the best times are in September and November, when the chinook are spawning.

Before there were dams here, there were rapids. And before the rapids, there was a natural stone bridge over the river—a sacred and mythical place for Native Americans. The dams smoothed out the waters for riverboats, and a brochure at the now steel **Bridge of the Gods** in Cascade Locks explains the legend of the rapids. There are also the Port of Cascade Locks Visitors Center (with a fine little museum that has more information on the Bridge of the Gods; closed in winter), a sailboard launch, and oodles of picnic spots (see Scenic Drives/Picnics, above).

The town of **Hood River** is ideally located on the climatic cusp between the wetter west side and the drier east side of the Cascades, so it gets sun and enough moisture (about 31 inches annually) to keep the creeks flowing and the orchards bearing. Thirty miles to the south,

11,235-foot Mount Hood dominates the horizon; however, from the town itself, the views are to the north, of Washington's Mount Adams, the Columbia River, and its ubiquitous windsurfers. In town, you're as likely to see orchard workers as boardheads, 2-inch steaks as espresso. New restaurants, inns, and shops are constantly opening (and closing) in flux with the high and low seasons.

As locals strongly attest, there was life in Hood River before board sailors descended. Native American artifacts are on exhibit in the **Hood River County Museum**, (541) 386-6772, Wednesday through Sunday, April through October, or when flags are flying. The town's **Visitors Information Center** is another good source of information about the area and is open every day of the week (except winter, when it's closed on weekends); (541) 386-2000 or (800) 366-3530.

Orchards and **vineyards** are the valley's other economic mainstays. The wonderful small-town Blossom Festival (mid-April) celebrates the flower-to-fruit cycle. From Hwy 35 you can catch the vista of the orchards fanning out from the north slopes of Mount Hood (see Scenic Drives/Picnics, above). You can buy the fruit bounty at The Fruit Tree, 4030 Westcliff Dr, (541) 386-6688, near the Columbia Gorge Hotel, or at River Bend Country Store, 2363 Tucker Rd, (541) 386-8766 or (800) 755-7568; the latter specializes in organically grown produce. Or visit the tasting rooms of Flerchinger Vineyards, 4200 Post Canyon Dr, (541) 386-2882, or Hood River Vineyards, 4693 Westwood Dr, (541) 386-3772, known for its pear and raspberry dessert wines.

Beer aficionados head for the Full Sail Tasting Room and Pub, 506 Columbia St, (541) 386-2247, for handcrafted Full Sail ales and appetizers. The outdoor deck provides a fitting place for tired board sailors to unwind while keeping the river in sight.

Mike's Ice Cream, 405 Oak St, (541) 386-6260, makes a great summer stop for fresh huckleberry shakes. Waucoma Bookstore, 212 Oak St, (541) 386-5353, has a good selection of titles, especially on Oregon and the Northwest. Get a custom, made-to-your-measurements swimsuit at Kerrits, 316 Oak St, (541) 386-1145, a unique locally owned shop and mail-order business that also has active, equestrian, and baby wear.

Restaurants

Big City Chicks ☆ What began as a concession stand is now a real restaurant furnished in art deco style. The menu incorporates wraps and satays from Thailand, curries from India, Mexican moles, and Italian pastas. *1302 13th St (at B St), Hood River; (541) 387-3811; $.*

The Mesquitery ☆ The mesquite grill takes center stage here. There are mounds of baby back ribs, a chicken combo, and fresh fish. The service, the bill, and the apple crisp are all dandy. A good place to bring the kids. *1219 12th St (at B St), Hood River; (541) 386-2002; $.*

Purple Rocks Art Bar and Cafe Despite its name (a self-evident boarder's term), we like this local hangout, which offers delicious, mostly vegetarian fare (sandwiches, quiches, burritos). Dinner is offered in summer only. *606 Oak St (west on Oak from downtown), Hood River; (541) 386-6061; $.*

Stonehedge Inn ☆ The owner of this turn-of-the-century estate serves tender steaks and fresh seafood in myriad dining areas. The stuffed potato is deservedly famous. Sincere service and general high quality keep this on our list. *3405 Cascade Dr (exit 62 off I-84), Hood River; (541) 386-3940; $$.*

Tad's Chicken 'n' Dumplings An Oregon institution, this country restaurant is popular with kids, bargain-hungry families, tourists, and fanciers of chicken. The place is usually packed. *943 SE Crown Point Hwy (exit 18 off I-84), Troutdale; (503) 666-5337; $.*

Cheaper Eats

Big Horse Brew Pub Climb the stairs to this very social spot where people come to dine on bountiful burgers, oodles of noodles, and heaping salads. Match it all with one of their own microbrews, and hope for some live local music. *115 State St, Hood River; (541) 386-4411; $.*

Coffee Spot If you're looking for a hefty sandwich (and maybe an espresso to go) this is your spot. Chow down at one of the few tables or take it down the hill to the park. *12 Oak St, Hood River; (541) 386-1772; $.*

El Sombrero Nothing like a great margarita after a hot day in the sun. And this place certainly knows how to make them—not to mention all the Mexican *especiales* that go along with. *1306 12th St, Hood River; (541) 386-7300; $.*

Hood River Restaurant Hood River's favorite Chinese chow. There are pages and pages of choices, but families should turn to the family page and pick the meal that's best suited for them. Lunch offers especially great deals. *108 2nd St, Hood River; (541) 386-3966; $.*

Lodgings

Columbia Gorge Hotel ☆ This 1921 luxury hotel is a favorite of honeymooners and tourists, and, while it can't compete with the luxury of 1990s hotels, it does have some pluses (and a colorful past). Public rooms are large, elegant; guest rooms are rather small. *4000 Westcliff Dr (exit 62 off*

I-84), Hood River, OR 97031; (541) 386-5566 or (800) 345-1921; $$$.

Hood River Hotel ☆☆ A restoration revived this hostelry's past as a country hotel. Thirty-two rooms (nine with kitchen suites), come with four-poster, sleigh, or brass beds. Pasquale's Ristorante, a small dining room, serves reasonably priced meals strong on Italian specialties and local fish. *102 Oak St (at 1st), Hood River, OR 97031; (541) 386-1900 or (800) 386-1859; $$.*

Hood River Vacation Rental Looks like everything's full, or you want a week-long rental? This service specializes in vacation rentals—from riverfront homes and in-town cottages to condominiums and B&Bs. *823 Cascade Ave, Hood River, OR 97031; (541) 387-3113.*

Lakecliff Estate ☆☆ Historic Lakecliff is sheltered by woods but has an astonishing view of the Columbia River. The manse features stone fireplaces, an inviting living room, and a dining room where guests linger to watch windsurfers below. Fine hospitality in outstanding surroundings. Closed in winter. *3820 Westcliff Dr (exit 62 off I-84, .5-mile west of Hood River), Hood River; PO Box 1220, Hood River, OR 97031; (541) 386-7000; $$.*

McMenamin's Edgefield ☆☆ This former poor farm has been transformed into a brewery, winery, and vineyard. There's a pub, restaurant, and movie theater; the main lodge is where most people stay (there are also men's and women's dorms). All rooms are stocked with beer glasses and a canning jar (you may carry brew back to your room). Guests share baths. *2126 SW Halsey (Wood Village exit off I-84, south to Halsey, turn left, drive .5 mile to Edgefield sign), Troutdale, OR 97060; (503) 669-8610, (800) 669-8610, or (503) 492-3086 (restaurant); $$.*

Vagabond Lodge The front building faces the highway. Ask for a room in the back riverfront building—it has the same view as the Columbia Gorge Hotel, but rooms are twice the size and a fraction of the price. Pets are allowed. *4070 Westcliff Dr (exit 62 off I-84), Hood River, OR 97031; (541) 386-2992; $.*

Cheaper Sleeps

Gorge View Bed and Breakfast Regular rooms toe the cheapster limit, but the "bunk room" is where the surfers like to stay. For about $35 per boardhead, you get a bunk and access to the hot tub. Breakfast is often a carbo-loader. *1009 Columbia St, Hood River, OR 97031; (541) 386-5770; $.*

Prater's Motel A short strip of seven rooms on the main drag, Prater's boasts an unhindered view of the Columbia River and Mount Adams. The rooms are small but versatile, clean, and very reasonable. *1306 Oak St, Hood River, OR 97031; (541) 386-3566; $.*

Scandian Motor Lodge These are large, woodsy rooms with bright colors and tiled baths. A clean upstairs room with a river view is reasonably priced ($46 in summer). Reserve ahead in summer. *307 Wa-Na-Pa St (PO Box 217), Cascade Locks, OR 97014; (541) 374-8417; $.*

More Information

Columbia River Gorge National Scenic Area, Hood River: *(541) 386-2333.*

Friends of the Columbia Gorge, Portland: *(503) 241-3762.*

Hood River County Chamber of Commerce, Hood River: *(800) 366-3530.*

Hood River Ranger District, Mount Hood–Parkdale: *(541) 352-6002.*

Mount Hood National Forest, Sandy: *(503) 668-1700.*

Oregon Parks and Recreation Department, Rooster Rock: *(503) 695-2261.*

Port of Cascade Locks Visitors Center, Cascade Locks: *(541) 374-8619.*

Troutdale Area Chamber of Commerce, Troutdale: *(541) 669-7473.*

Lower Columbia

From the mouth of the Columbia River and along the Washington border on the north, east to Sauvie Island at the edge of the Portland metropolitan area, south into the Coast Range, and west to US Highway 101, including Columbia County, the northern portion of Clatsop County, the Lewis and Clark National Wildlife Refuge, and the towns of Astoria, Clatskanie, Rainier, St. Helens, Scappoose, and Vernonia.

T he winter morning dawns clear and cold on Sauvie Island, a flat expanse of land just downstream from Portland that uses a network of dikes to keep the Columbia River at bay. While the city is buffeted by a brutal east wind, perhaps the most unpleasant weather it experiences all year, Sauvie Island is tucked inside a bend in the Columbia and the fury of the wind doesn't reach it.

That's good, because the thermometer reads 20°, an unusually cold temperature in northwest Oregon, and wintering flocks of geese and ducks gather here in search of food.

The birds' annual migration draws a regular parade of human visitors to the island, part of which is managed by the Oregon Department of Fish and Wildlife to provide food for wildlife. Each winter wildlife watchers enjoy the waterfowl but also eagerly await hungry bald eagles. America's national symbol preys on the injured or weak ducks and geese, with more than 40 eagles setting up shop at the island from late December through March.

The bald eagles usually spend the night in the tall timber that graces Portland's northwest skyline. The birds leave their roost at first light of day and head for Sauvie Island's numerous lakes, sloughs, and canals where they hope to find an easy meal. With so many eagles on hand at any one time, Portland has to be one of the few large American cities so close to such a spectacle. After the eagles fly over the island's western shore, they fan out across the island. During the day, they can be seen singly perched in trees, or flying in pairs overhead, as they look for some fuel to help them get through the cold night that lies ahead.

Sauvie Island offers a multitude of outdoor recreation opportunities only 12 miles from downtown Portland and its urban population of 1.7 million. Besides the outstanding bird-watching, the island is popular for cycling, canoeing, hiking, and fishing. The island also has some of the Portland area's best beaches, including long stretches of sand where clothing is optional.

Sauvie Island is just the beginning of a marvelous chain of paddling and camping opportunities that continue unabated downstream to Astoria, the oldest European settlement in Oregon. This is the route pioneered by the Lewis and Clark Expedition in 1805. With a little imagination, modern explorers can envision the land as first seen by the great overland pathfinders. The network of islands in the Lewis and Clark Wildlife Refuge, just upstream from Astoria, looks, at a glance, as though the explorers passed through only yesterday.

The inland portion of the Lower Columbia is not nearly so wild, because just about every tree that existed when Lewis and Clark passed through has long ago been sent to a sawmill. Despite the lack of old-growth forests, the low mountains of the Coast Range do harbor some outstanding recreation opportunities and wildlife viewing. The Roosevelt elk herd at Jewell Meadow Wildlife Area is one of the largest in Oregon and the Banks-Vernonia Linear State Park offers more than 20 miles of rails-to-trails riding and hiking.

In the dead of winter, an early morning trip to see bald eagles and an afternoon view of Roosevelt elk evoke the outdoor essence of the Lower Columbia and the enduring spirit of Lewis and Clark.

Getting There

US Highway 30 (US 30) heads northwest out of Portland, passes Sauvie Island after 12 miles, and continues 95 miles to the mouth of the Columbia River near Astoria, the Clatsop County seat. St. Helens, the Columbia County seat, is 29 miles from Portland on US 30. US Highway 26 (US 26) from Portland to Seaside is an alternative route to Astoria via the coast. US 30 crosses numerous county roads that approach the Columbia lowlands, including the crossing of Multnomah Channel on Sauvie Island Bridge to reach the Sauvie Island Wildlife Area. Highway 47 cuts through the Lower Columbia area north to south, and Highway 202 east to west between US 30 and US 26.

Adjoining Areas
 SOUTH: **Wine Country, Tillamook**
 EAST: **Greater Portland**
 WEST: **Northern Beaches**

inside out

Wildlife

Sauvie Island's 12,000 acres of state-protected wildlife, land, water, and swamps comprise much of the downriver portion of the island. Access is along Gillihan and Reeder Rds on the Columbia River (east) side and on Sauvie Island and Steelman Rds on the Multnomah Channel (west) side. Much of the upriver portion of the island is private property and is used for farming. Although there are plenty of viewing opportunities through-out the island, respect the rights of the property owners by observing wildlife from the roads. The island has a continual conflict between those who live there to enjoy the rural setting and the thousands of Portlanders who go there each weekend to recreate. The state-owned portions of the island require a $3 per day parking permit, which is available at the con-venience store on the island side of the Sauvie Island Bridge, at other area stores, and at ticket offices at G.I. Joe's stores in Portland. For information about the island's wildlife areas, call the Oregon Department of Fish and Wildlife office, (503) 621-3488, or stop at the information kiosk outside the office at 18330 NW Sauvie Island Rd.

The daily winter morning fly-out of the **bald eagles** is best observed from the end of Steelman Rd. The bald eagles leave the large conifer trees in the hills across US 30 and fan out across the island. Just about any place on the island is good for viewing later in the day when eagles are hunting. Be sure to bring binoculars and a spotting scope to identify birds at a dis-tance. Oak Island on Oak Island Rd and Coon Point on Reeder Rd are well-known wildlife congregation areas along the shores of Sturgeon Lake, the large body of water that floods the lower part of the island.

In addition to the eagles, Sauvie Island attracts five subspecies of **Canada geese.** Other waterfowl that show up in numbers include **snow geese, sandhill cranes, trumpeter swans,** and all kinds of **ducks.** When the waterfowl have migrated north, the action turns to watching **great blue herons, red-tailed hawks,** and various types of **warblers** and **sparrows.** Up to a dozen species of **seagulls** have been spotted on the island, as well as the rare **red-throated loon.** Mammals that live on the island include **black-tailed deer, beaver, nutria,** and **coyote.**

Scappoose Bottoms, northwest across Multnomah Channel from Sauvie Island, is another productive bird-watching area. Reach the bottoms by turning east onto Dike Rd off US 30, about .75 mile north of the Columbia-Multnomah county line.

Further down the Columbia River, the Lewis and Clark National Wildlife Refuge presents an even bigger wildlife spectacle than the one at Sauvie Island. The refuge consists of 20 islands on the Oregon side of the Columbia River, beginning west of Westport and continuing downriver to Astoria. The east side of the refuge is adjacent to the **Julia Butler Hansen National Wildlife Refuge** for the Columbian White-tailed Deer. The refuge lies mostly on the Washington shore, but Oregon has a large section on Tenasillahe Island. Headquarters for both refuges are in Cathlamet, Washington. For information, call (360) 795-3915. The refuges are managed for the benefit of wildlife, and facilities for visitors are limited.

While Sauvie Island's wildlife spectacle is easy to watch from roads, the same can't be said about the Lewis and Clark refuge. The winter wildlife congregation on the numerous islands requires a boat to visit at a time of year when few people choose to boat the Columbia River. Paddlers who live nearby can pick out a good day and drive to the boat launch at Aldrich Point near Knappa, a good jumping-off point for exploration. To reach Aldrich Point, drive 1 mile east of Knappa Junction on US 30, turn north on Aldrich Point Rd, and drive 5 miles to the river's edge. The refuge also attracts a few dozen **bald eagles** during winter, as well as **tundra swans. Ducks** include **mallard, canvasback, bufflehead, redhead, scaup,** and **goldeneye.** Peak waterfowl viewing seasons are October through January.

One of the few locations from which to get a good look at the islands of the refuge is **Twilight Eagle Sanctuary,** 9 miles east of Astoria on US 30 and 1 mile north on Twilight Rd. The sanctuaries' wooden platform also has an outstanding view of the Columbia River's estuary.

Jewell Meadows Wildlife Area is a 1,150-acre preserve on the south side of Hwy 202 in the Coast Range near Jewell. The resident herd of **Roosevelt elk,** largest of the North American elk species, can be seen almost daily from September through March. The best time to look for the big bucks is during hunting season, because they know hunters can't touch them when they stay put in the wildlife area. Besides elk, the surrounding forest harbors **black-tailed deer, coyotes, birds of prey,** and **songbirds.** The staff invites visitors to watch the daily feeding of the elk in season. Call (503) 755-2264 for daily feeding times.

Other productive wildlife-watching areas in the Lower Columbia country include the grounds of the shut-down Trojan Nuclear Power Plant near Rainier, the west Rainier dike lands, the open meadows and park lands around Vernonia, and the marshes near Clatskanie and Deer Island. The Oregon Department of Fish and Wildlife operates the Klaskanine Fish Hatchery 12 miles southeast of Astoria on Hwy 202. The best time to visit the hatchery, which raises coho salmon and steelhead, is from late September to March when adult fish are returning.

Boating/Sailing

It may not be as exciting as a paddle-it-yourself trip, but cruising is the number-one way people see the islands of the Lower Columbia from the water. **Cruising on the Columbia** was almost unheard of a decade or two ago, but the rapid growth of the tourism industry around the world has helped spawn a cruise-ship market on the river. For a trip between Astoria and Portland, check with Great River Cruises, (800) 720-0012, or American West Steamboat Co., (800) 434-1232. The sailing season is May through October. The Astoria Chamber of Commerce, (503) 861-1031, can recommend shorter waterfront cruises and tide-dependent tours that explore the marshlands of the Lower Columbia.

The Columbia River sees lots of pleasure cruising in sailboats and powerboats, in addition to heavy traffic by commercial and private fishing boats. The river is also busy with oceangoing tankers and freighters that travel upriver to Portland, so boaters need to be careful when crossing the main shipping channel. Marinas and moorages that cater to pleasure craft on the Oregon shore of the Lower Columbia are numerous. Portland has five private moorages across from the southwest tip of Sauvie Island. Just downstream is **Hadley's Landing,** an Oregon State Parks facility that is accessible by boat or by foot on the upper west side of Sauvie Island on Multnomah Channel.

Another 15 moorages, mostly private, line the Columbia between Scappoose and Rainier, including city-owned facilities at Scappoose, St. Helens, and Rainier. St. Helens also has a 638-foot county-owned transient dock in front of the **Columbia County Courthouse** in downtown St. Helens 1 mile east of US 30. Other popular facilities that are publicly owned include the city of St. Helens's **Sand Island Marine Park,** (503) 397-5520; transient moorage and a campground offshore of St. Helens; Columbia County's **Gilbert River** boat ramp near the northern tip of Sauvie Island off Reeder Rd; and the county's **J. J. Collins Marine Park,** transient moorage and a campground offshore from Scappoose at river mile 8 of the Multnomah Channel. For information on Columbia County parks and moorages, call (503) 397-2353.

Continuing downriver from Rainier, the Oregon town across the Columbia from Longview, Washington, public ramps along US 30 include

Rainier Marina at Rainier; **Beaver Landing** at Clatskanie; **Westport Ramp,** 1 mile north of Westport at the Puget Island ferry terminal; **Aldrich Point** near Knappa (see Wildlife, above); the **John Day River,** 5 miles east of Astoria; and the **17th Street Transient Float** at Astoria's Columbia River Maritime Museum. Astoria has two large private marinas for pleasure craft, as well as boat launches on the Klaskanine and Young Rivers that merge with the Columbia River in Youngs Bay just west of town.

Motor cruisers and sailboats can pick from plenty of self-contained boat camping spots. **Private moorages** around Scappoose include Happy Rock, (503) 543-7464; Rocky Pointe, (503) 543-7003; Casselman's Wharf, (503) 543-5183; River's Bend, (503) 543-6223; Brown's Landing, (503) 543-6526; Multnomah Channel Yacht Club, (503) 543-5005; and Scappoose Moorage, (503) 543-3939.

St. Helens Marina, (503) 397-4162, comes next downriver, followed by Scipio's Goble Landing south of Rainier, (503) 556-6510. US 30 loses contact with the Columbia River between Rainier and Astoria, partially accounting for the lack of commercial marinas downriver until Astoria. The Port of Astoria, (503) 325-8279, has overnight facilities at the East Mooring Basin at the foot of 36th St and the **West Mooring Basin** beneath the Astoria-Megler Bridge.

The Oregon State Marine Board, (503) 378-8587, publishes several free booklets about Oregon's public and private facilities. Among the best are "Oregon Marina Guide," "Oregon Boating Facilities Guide," and "Boating in Oregon Coastal Waters." With a steady stream of revenue from boater registration fees, the Marine Board seems to be one of the few public agencies that provide outdoor recreation in Oregon that isn't constantly teetering on the brink of financial disaster.

Kayaking/Canoeing

Although Captain Robert Gray was the first American to visit the Columbia River, in 1792, members of the Lewis and Clark Expedition were the first American explorers to float the Lower Columbia country. Many more explorers are expected to head down the same path as Oregon prepares to celebrate the 200th anniversary of the Lewis and Clark Expedition, which arrived at the mouth of the Columbia in November 1805. Incredible paddling opportunities already await sea kayakers and canoeists in the Lower Columbia, but things could get better with development of the **Lewis and Clark Columbia River Water Trail.** The 100-mile water route from Portland to Astoria is being improved in stages in a partnership between the Oregon History Center, the Oregon Marine Board, Columbia and Clatsop Counties, and volunteers from local paddling clubs. Lead planner has been the Oregon History Center, (503) 222-1741, with a project for the bicentennial celebration.

The plan behind the water trail is to develop suitable campsites for paddle craft and shallow-draft motorboats. Many existing locations already meet the needs of paddlers. Other sites will need to be developed, although project leaders are aware that undeveloped sites are currently being used. Paddlers don't need much to set up a place to camp, just a dry spot above the high-water mark. Many of the islands in the lower river are at least partly composed of sandy dredge soils, so they make great camping places. A string of rest rooms, plus formal recognition of availability for public use, are all that's preventing the water trail from becoming one of the most popular canoe and sea kayak paddling routes in the country.

Paddling downriver on the Columbia is usually easy, because the current clips along at a steady 3mph. Occasionally a paddler can find it difficult to make progress, though, because of tidal influences and the afternoon winds that often blow upriver. Add to that the constant parade of oceangoing freighter traffic, and the Columbia becomes a paddling place that demands respect and attention. Day trips are popular from many of the boat launches. Upriver trips are also possible, especially when timed to coincide with the incoming tide. After all, Lewis and Clark paddled both ways on the Columbia.

The journey can begin anywhere in the North Portland harbor, including **Kelley Point Park** where the Willamette River merges with the Columbia River. Permits are not required. The paddling route downstream to Astoria avoids the open water of the Columbia as much as possible, so it takes the Multnomah Channel route around the west side of Sauvie Island instead of following the Columbia River route on the east side.

Because camping is not allowed on Sauvie Island, the first downriver camp spot below Portland is **J. J. Collins Marine Park** on the west side of Coon Island. The 23-acre park is operated by Columbia County and has moorage, camping, and picnic facilities. **Scappoose Bay Marina,** (503) 397-2888, 57420 Old Portland Rd, is a mile up Scappoose Bay, but its large boat landing and campground are used to access the water trail.

Continuing downriver, paddlers encounter one of the best river parks in the Lower Columbia when they reach **Sand Island Marine Park** offshore from St. Helens. The city park was rebuilt in 1996 following the devastating 100-year flood that occurred in the Lower Columbia earlier that year. Facilities include a campground, transient dock, picnicking, and hiking trails.

The water trail continues downriver, hopscotching between developed and undeveloped facilities. **Sandy Island,** offshore from Kalama, Washington, is privately owned and has been used to store rafts of logs for transit to mills in Longview; **Prescott Beach Park,** near the Trojan Nuclear Power Plant, is a picnic facility that Columbia County wants to turn into a campground; the town of **Rainier** has transit moorage and, just offshore, 100-acre **Dibblee Island** was dedicated in 1997 as a Columbia County water park.

A couple more privately owned dredge-spoil islands downstream from Longview are eyed as possible sites for development. Past that area, the water trail begins passing through the island zone near the Columbia-Clatsop county line. First comes **Puget Island,** an agricultural area connected by a bridge to Washington and a ferry to Oregon and protected from flooding by dikes. The upper part of the island is dredge spoils and would make a good riverside camp for paddlers on the water trail.

The water trail crosses into Washington at Puget Island to make use of facilities at Cathlamet and Skamokawa. It crosses back into Oregon at **Tenasillahe Island,** where an upstream part of the island is outside of the Julia Butler Hansen National Wildlife Refuge (see Wildlife, above) and has been used for camping. Overnight use is not allowed anywhere within either the Hansen or the Lewis and Clark refuge.

Other stops along the water trail include existing facilities at **Aldrich Point,** the northernmost part of Oregon's mainland; and boat ramps at **Knappa,** the **John Day River,** and **Astoria.** To solve the problem of the no-camping zone in the wildlife refuges, a small campground is proposed on state land at **Calendar Island** near Knappa.

Clatskanie, located 2 miles inland from the Columbia, is already on board with the concept of a water trail. The city has developed facilities at **Beaver Slough Boat Ramp and Park** to help paddlers gain access to the sloughs that connect the town with the Columbia. A portage is being developed that will connect Beaver Slough with Westport Slough and complete the missing link in a wind-protected route from Clatskanie to Westport. Beaver Slough leads into the Columbia near Puget Island.

Away from the proposed river trail, the channels, lakes, and sloughs of **Sauvie Island** provide some outstanding paddling opportunities, although an outgoing tide during the low water of summer can leave an unpleasant view of acres of mudflats on several of the lakes. A good first paddling experience on the island is to launch at Columbia County's **Gilbert River Boat Ramp,** not on the Gilbert River where the motorboats go but on **Little McNary Lake** nearby. The lake is more than 2 miles long, and a network of dikes makes sure the tide never drains the water completely. The Gilbert River is on the west side of the island, .5 mile down a gravel road from big, sandy **Walton Beach.** Note that where Reeder Rd switches from pavement to gravel at Walton Beach, the sandy shores of the Columbia River switch their dress code to clothing optional.

Windsurfing

When sailors discovered that the wind doesn't blow every summer day in the Columbia River Gorge, they fanned out across Oregon to find other good places to sail. One of the first to be discovered and one of the best windsurfing locations outside the Gorge or the Coast is **Jones Beach,** located 5 miles west of Clatskanie off US 30. It may seem like an unlikely spot, but Jones Beach has many of the same physical attributes as Hood River. It's located on a narrow section of the Columbia River, where the river runs east-west instead of making one of its numerous bends. The river is fairly constricted in the area, with cliffs more than 500 feet high on each shore. The Washington shore across from Jones Beach is called Cape Horn after the famous tip of South America.

Jones Beach is blessed with long sandy beaches, something the wind-surfers wish they could take back with them to Hood River. The wind usually picks up during the afternoon; sailors learn to be patient, because a quiet, no-wind day can turn into a maelstrom at the drop of a dime.

Another place in the Lower Columbia known for good windsurfing and sailing conditions is **Youngs Bay,** located at the west edge of Astoria. The wind isn't as dependable or powerful as at Jones Beach, but Youngs Bay has a lot more things to do nearby on days when the wind decides not to blow.

Camping

With a shortage of public land in the Lower Columbia area, camping opportunities are limited. Sauvie Island does not allow overnight use of its public lands because of their status as a wildlife management area. RVs can stay on Sauvie Island at Reeder Beach RV Park, (503) 621-3098, or Sauvie Island RV Cove Park, (503) 621-9881.

Some of the best camping opportunities in the Lower Columbia are available only with a boat. Publicly owned water-camping opportunities have already been described (see Kayaking/Canoeing, above). Some private moorages offer overnight space for self-contained boat camping (see Boating/Sailing, above).

Campers needing a bit of solid earth have a choice of five county campgrounds in Columbia County. Check with the county parks office, (503) 397-2353, for information on the parks, a brochure that gives driving directions, and reservations at the larger parks. **Big Eddy Park** has 32 sites on the Nehalem River north of Vernonia; **Hudson/Parcher Park** has 36 sites near Rainier; **Scaponia Park** has some primitive sites on the road between Scappoose and Vernonia; **Camp Wilkerson** is popular with large groups, who stay in the camp's Adirondack shelters in the forest northeast of Vernonia; and **Scappoose Airport Park** caters to private pilots and RVs.

Fort Stevens State Park, 20 minutes northwest of Astoria off US 101, (503) 861-1671, is a 3,500-acre outdoor wonderland of paved bike paths, forest trails, a freshwater lake, and uncrowded beaches—including the permanent resting spot of the hull of the *Peter Iredale,* wrecked in 1906. The 604 campsites make Fort Stevens Oregon's largest publicly owned campground (see Northern Beaches chapter).

Parks/Beaches/Picnics

Just about any of the public beaches along the Lower Columbia can be a good spot for a picnic. Even during the fall, it's always worth packing a picnic basket and heading out to observe one of the Northwest's best fall-color spectacles. The Columbia River's vast stands of deciduous trees turn golden from mid-October to mid-November. Wait for one of the rare, blue-sky days to bring out the most brilliant colors. Note, too, that while fog has a tendency to obscure sights along the river in fall, areas a few miles inland are basking in the sun.

Trojan Park, located at the site of the former nuclear reactor, is a popular summer picnic park 6 miles south of Rainier on US 30. The park has a playing field, picnic shelters, and fishing along the nearby shore of the Columbia River. Columbia County's **Prescott Beach Park** is 1 mile north of Trojan Park. The park has covered picnic areas, horseshoe pits, and a volleyball court. Prescott Beach can also be used for windsurfing when it's too windy for a comfortable picnic. **Laurel Beach,** located 1.5 miles south of Rainier on Laurel Wood Rd, is another county park with river access.

Astoria has one of the prettiest picnic sites in Oregon atop 600-foot **Coxcomb Hill** at the base of the **Astoria Column** at the end of Coxcomb Dr. Signs throughout town point the way to the column, the city's can't-miss, signature landmark. Be sure to walk the 164-step spiral staircase to the top of the 125-foot column before you eat. The reward is a breathtaking view of the Columbia River estuary and Oregon's oldest city. Another popular picnic spot in Astoria is the **Sixth Street Viewing Platform** on the downtown waterfront one block north of US 30. The south side of Astoria has picnic grounds near the town swimming pool at **Tapiola Park** and at **Shively Park.** For information on Astoria city parks, call (503) 325-7275.

Bradley State Scenic Viewpoint, 22 miles east of Astoria on US 30, is another picnic spot that has a commanding view of the Lower Columbia country. **Mayger Beach,** (503) 728-3350, has Columbia River access 7 miles northeast of Clatskanie on Mayger Rd. The City of **Clatskanie,** (503) 728-2622, also has a city park at 95 N Nehalem with picnicking and camping.

Hiking/Walking

Sauvie Island's hiking opportunities (see Wildlife, above) are occasionally submerged by high water, both during spring runoff and whenever the area is pelted by winter rain. The best bet is to play it safe and hike on the island during late spring and summer. Access is limited to licensed hunters on parts of the island's wildlife area during the fall goose and duck hunting seasons.

Sauvie Island's **Warrior Rock Lighthouse** is a miniature version of the famous lighthouses of the Oregon Coast. To reach the lighthouse, drive Reeder Rd to its end along the Columbia River. The lighthouse is a 3-mile walk to the north, sometimes on sandy beach but more frequently up and over fallen alder trees and through blackberry thickets. Enough hikers (and cattle) make the trek that the route is never too bad.

The **Oak Island Loop,** a pleasant 2.5-mile tour, follows a peninsula that juts between Sturgeon and Steelman Lakes. The hike begins at the end of Oak Island Rd near the center of Sauvie Island. Hike north on an unmarked path through a grassy area and make a clockwise loop on an obvious system of roads and paths used for wildlife management.

The 2.3-mile **Virginia Lake Trail** starts along Sauvie Island Rd, 1 mile north of the island's wildlife-management headquarters. Walk around either lobe of Virginia Lake, or cross the boardwalk down the middle of the marsh. Hadley's Landing on Multnomah Channel just west of the lake's southern lobe is at the end of a short spur trail.

Other short hiking opportunities along the Lower Columbia can be found at **Fox Creek** near Rainier, **Carcass Creek Falls** near Clatskanie, and the **Bradley Wayside** near Astoria (see Parks/Beaches/Picnics, above). The Clatskanie Chamber of Commerce, (503) 728-3350, can help visitors make arrangements with a local resident for free tours to Fox Creek and Carcass Creek Falls.

Astoria, which dates to the founding of a fur trading post in 1811, is the oldest permanent Northwest settlement west of the Rocky Mountains. Affectionately referred to as the "Little San Francisco of the Northwest," the city celebrates its legacy of Victorian architecture with a designated walking route that passes 74 sites. A tour description is available from the Astoria Chamber of Commerce, (503) 325-6311, 111 West Marine Dr. Hollywood has taken note of Astoria's unique character, and video stores are filled with movies filmed in town, including *Free Willy I* and *II, The Goonies,* and *Kindergarten Cop.*

Besides hiking along the Astoria waterfront, another popular in-town hike is the **Cathedral Trail,** a route through Astoria's urban forest that begins east of the Astoria Column (see Parks/Beaches/Picnics, above).

Columbia County has the distinction of containing the lowest high point of Oregon's 36 counties. Located east of Vernonia, **Long Mountain,** 2,265 feet high, is the tallest hill in Columbia County. It gets few visitors, other than the locals who know the maze of logging roads required to visit it. Clatsop County has the third-lowest high point among Oregon's counties, but 3,283-foot **Saddle Mountain** is an impressive piece of rock no matter how it's measured. (For the hike up Saddle Mountain, see Northern Beaches chapter.)

Fishing

With so much water everywhere, fishing must be pretty good in the **Lower Columbia.** Right? Well, it's not as good as it used to be, especially because of the depleted salmon and steelhead runs, but there will always be some kind of fish to catch in the Columbia and its tributaries. (Fishing downstream of the Astoria-Megler and Young's Bay Bridges is described in Northern Beaches chapter.)

The Columbia River from Portland to St. Helens sees tremendous fishing pressure, partly because the river is so productive, but mostly because so many people live close by the river here. The river and its sloughs around **Sauvie Island** have a good spring chinook salmon run, plus plenty of sturgeon. Shallow bays and channels are productive for largemouth bass and panfish, especially near jetties, pilings, and log booms.

Good fishing spots below Scappoose can be found around **St. Helens,** in the sloughs of **Deer Island,** at **Prescott Beach,** at the mouth of Washington's **Cowlitz River,** at **Rainier Beach,** and offshore along any of the **islands of the lower river.** Boats are usually needed for salmon and sturgeon, but bank anglers often meet success by casting from any of the numerous sandy beaches, jetties, and pilings that they can reach. (See Boating/Sailing and Kayaking/Canoeing, above, for the best places to access the water.)

Most of the Columbia's protected sloughs have good warm-water fishing, including **Blind, Brownsmead, Prescott,** and **Santosh.** Brownsmead produced a state-record yellow perch that weighed 2 pounds, 2 ounces.

Biking

Next to the Willamette Valley, the Lower Columbia country is one of the least hilly parts of Oregon—provided you stay close to the river. Cyclists who don't like hills should bring along their bicycles when visiting **Sauvie Island, Astoria, Vernonia,** and other parts of the peninsula of northwest Oregon.

The longest designated bike path is the 21-mile **Banks-Vernonia Linear State Park,** Oregon's first rails-to-trails conversion. The trail begins in Anderson City Park in Vernonia and is paved for 7 miles to just beyond where it enters Washington County. Anderson City Park, which offers the only camping along the way, is 2 blocks west of Hwy 47 in downtown Vernonia. Another trailhead in Columbia County is at **Beaver Creek,** where parking and a rest room sit next to Hwy 47 and mile 4 of the trail. The **Tophill** trailhead is 2 miles south into Washington County at trail mile 8, where the old railroad wound its way out of the coastal Nehalem River drainage into the Willamette Valley. The trail continues to a dead end just before arriving in Banks, south of US 26 (see Wine Country chapter).

Sauvie Island's network of paved roads draws dozens of bicyclists on sunny weekends, especially during spring when Portlanders are itching to get outside but don't want to travel too far. The parking lot at the island side of the Sauvie Island Bridge is the most popular beginning spot. Cyclists who want to leave the car behind can also place their bicycles, two at a time, on a Tri-Met bus and ride from Portland to Sauvie Island any day but Sunday. Popular trips on the island are anywhere the paved roads go. Gillihan, Reeder, Sauvie Island, and Oak Island Rds are the main thorough-fares on the island.

Portland cyclists who want to rack up the miles often choose Sauvie Island as the setting for their first 100-mile ride, also known as a century. The Portland Wheelmen, (503) 257-7982, a Portland cycling club, annu-ally stages an event the first weekend of October in which cyclists ride designated loops on Sauvie Island, pedal US 30 to Trojan Park near Rainier, then return to the island. The premeasured distance covers 100 miles, all without a major hill.

Astoria's busy waterfront can be one of the more distracting places, in a pleasurable sense, to ride or hike in Oregon. A work in progress, the **Astoria River Trail** stretches 5 miles from **Tongue Point** on the east to **Smith Point** on the west. The trail is 30 feet wide and was a former rail-road line. The route isn't paved and prepared like the state trail at Vernonia, but it's good enough to give users a view of the busy harbor without having to ride along US 30. A good place to enter the trail is the Columbia River Maritime Museum at 1792 Marine Dr, a distinctive building with a large parking lot and river access.

The **Astoria-Megler Bridge,** the 4.1-mile span that opened in 1966 over the Columbia River estuary, is a vital link on the **Pacific Coast** bicy-cle trail (see Northern Beaches chapter).

Astoria is also the western terminus of the cross-country **Bike-centennial Trail,** a route pioneered in 1976 between Virginia and Oregon. For information, call the Adventure Cycling Association in Missoula, Montana, (406) 721-1776. Road cyclists looking for something a little shorter than a border-to-border ride across the country can try the 20-mile loop from Astoria to **Fort Clatsop National Memorial,** the 25-mile loop to **Youngs River Falls,** the 52-mile loop to **Nasell** in Washington, or the 92-mile loop to **Mist** in Columbia County. Check the Astoria-Warrenton area visitor guide for suggested routes. The guide is available from the chamber of commerce, (503) 325-6311.

Astoria has some single-track urban trails for mountain bikers and is only 25 miles west of the **Wauna Trail** system, a swath of state land criss-crossed with riding opportunities near the Wauna Mill at Taylorville. For the latest information on single-track riding, check with Bikes and Beyond, (503) 325-2961, 1089 Marine Dr, Astoria.

outside in

Attractions

Astoria likes to tout its history. The bustling waterfront—once the locale of canneries and river steamers—is now an active port for oceangoing vessels and fishing boats. The **Columbia River Maritime Museum,** 1792 Marine Dr, (503) 325-2323, is the finest of its kind in the Northwest. Restored small crafts are displayed in the Great Hall, and seven thematic galleries depict different aspects of the region's maritime history. The light-ship *Columbia,* the last of its kind on the Pacific Coast, is moored outside (there's a self-guided tour).

Named for a prominent 19th-century businessman and Columbia River bar pilot, the Captain George Flavel House, Eighth and Duane Sts, (503) 325-2563, is the city's best example of ornate Queen Anne architecture. Both it and the restored Heritage Museum, eight blocks away at 1618 Exchange St, (503) 325-2203, feature local history.

Six miles southwest of Astoria, off US 101, Lewis and Clark's 1805–06 winter encampment is re-created at the **Fort Clatsop National Memorial,** (503) 861-2471. Besides audiovisuals and exhibits in the visitors center, there are living history demonstrations (musket firing, candle making) during the summer.

Restaurants

Cannery Cafe ☆ Sitting on pilings over the Columbia River, this airy cafe specializes in baked goods, lunch fare, and a bevy of dinner choices. Sandwich selections vary and salads are creative. Sunday brunch is the best in town. *1 6th St (foot of 6th St), Astoria; (503) 325-8642; $$.*

Columbian Cafe ☆☆ The more publicity this small, vegetarian-oriented cafe gets, the more crowded it becomes. Still, it continues to be Astoria's best bet for good grub. Soups are satisfying, and the seafood and pasta dinners are perhaps the finest on the coast. *1114 Marine Dr (at 11th St, next to the movie theater), Astoria; (503) 325-2233; $.*

Ira's ☆☆ With a storefront setting on a bustling street, Ira's is part luncheonette and part dinner house. Bagel sandwiches and pastas are excellent lunch options, dinner may be grilled tuna, with star-shaped grit cakes as a side dish. Desserts are inviting. *915 Commercial St (between 9th and 10th), Astoria; (503) 338-6192; $$.*

Rio Cafe ☆ Instead of the usual Tex-Mex fare, this cantina offers inspired south-of-the-border cuisine. Salads feature assorted fruits and veggies, tiny shrimp, and a zingy jalapeño dressing. Three snappy salsas are a perfect match for the huge, handcrafted crisp chips. *125 9th St (a block from the Columbia River), Astoria; (503) 325-2409; $.*

Lodgings

Columbia River Inn ☆ This restored Victorian offers four guest rooms (all with private baths) and elegant furnishings. The gracious hostess serves a full breakfast; outside there's a terraced garden with gazebo, benches, and Columbia River vistas. *1681 Franklin Ave (corner of 17th), Astoria, OR 97103; (503) 325-5044 or (800) 953-5044; $$.*

Crest Motel The best alternative to B&B lodging in Astoria, and the best motel view in town. Unwind in the whirlpool. Pets are welcome; so is smoking in one section. *5366 Leif Erickson Dr (2 miles east of downtown), Astoria, OR 97103; (503) 325-3141; $$.*

Rosebriar Hotel ☆☆ This rambling inn has beautifully furnished guest rooms (small but with private baths), and a full breakfast is included in the rates. The common rooms are spacious, the grounds gardenlike, and the front-yard benches afford Columbia River views. *636 14th St (at Franklin), Astoria, OR 97103; (503) 325-7427 or (800) 487-0224; $.*

More Information

Astoria/Warrenton Area Chamber of Commerce, Astoria: *(800) 875-6807.*

Clatskanie Chamber of Commerce, Clatskanie: *(503) 728-2502.*

Lewis and Clark National Wildlife Refuge, Cathlamet, Washington: *(360) 795-3915.*

St. Helens–Scappoose Chamber of Commerce, St. Helens: *(503) 397-0685.*

Sauvie Island Wildlife Area, Portland: *(503) 621-3488.*

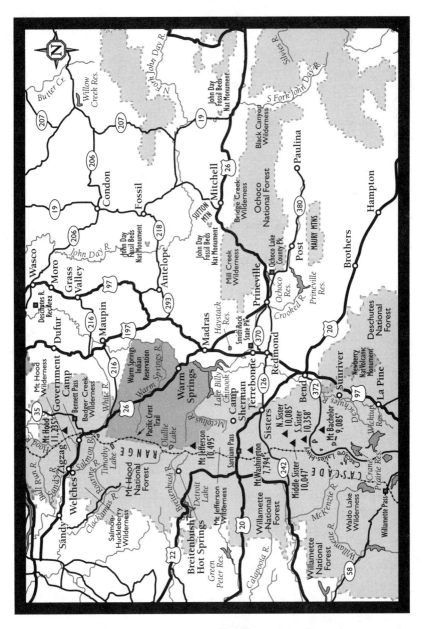

Northern Cascades and Central Oregon

Mount Hood   349

Lower Deschutes River   373

Lower John Day River   391

Mount Jefferson and the Metolius River   400

Crooked River   412

Santiam Pass and Mount Washington   429

Bend and the Upper Deschutes River   441

Three Sisters and Cascade Lakes   464

Northern
Cascades
and **Central**
Oregon

Mount Hood

From the Hood River Valley on the north and east, south to the Clackamas River, and west to the edge of the Portland metropolitan area, including the Mount Hood, Salmon-Huckleberry, and Badger Creek Wildernesses, the towns of Sandy and Government Camp, and the collection of communities known as Hoodland (Brightwood, Wildwood, Wemme, Welches, Zigzag, and Rhododendron).

As the visual backdrop for Oregon's biggest city, and as the state's highest mountain, Mount Hood is under enormous pressure to meet the recreational needs of the 2 million people who live within a couple hours' drive of it.

For the most part, Mount Hood succeeds admirably. Despite the crowds who adore it, the mountain somehow manages to maintain a certain grace and dignity. The glaciers that adorn the 11,235-foot-high volcano capture the spirit of Mount Hood. Their icy, snow-covered surfaces seem to say, "Look at me, play on me, but take care of me for future generations to enjoy."

About the only time Mount Hood is overwhelmed is during winter weekends, when it seems everyone wants to go skiing. Mount Hood, unfortunately, has a monopoly on downhill skiing in northwest Oregon. US Highway 26, the gateway to the mountain from the west, can get packed tighter than a Portland freeway when the Rose Festival fleet sails up the Willamette River each June.

Those gridlock days are rare, perhaps fewer than a dozen per year, but they sure are annoying. During winter, Mount Hood is the only game in town for Portland's downhill skiers and snowboarders, unless they take the extra time to visit Mount Bachelor in Central Oregon. Cross-country skiers and snowmobilers add to the crowds on the highway to Mount Hood, but they have alternate destinations in the forests of southern Washington.

Once they arrive, skiers and snowboarders have a clear choice among the Mount Hood ski areas. Mount Hood Meadows carries the most cachet and is the only place where Portland's trendy skiers want to be seen. Timberline Lodge is friendly to families during winter and is famous worldwide for its summer ski season. Mount Hood Skibowl is a throwback to another era, when fashion didn't matter and skiers let their skis do the talking. Summit and Cooper Spur are small ski areas, suitable for beginners and kids.

Nordic skiers fan out around Mount Hood, picking and choosing from more than a dozen cross-country trailheads, depending on the weather and snow conditions. Snowmobilers head to the Frog Lake and Skyline Sno-Parks.

The Mount Hood recreation scene is less concentrated during summer, although two of the ski areas are just as busy as they are during winter. Timberline Lodge is the only ski area in North America capable of offering skiing any day of the year, while Skibowl runs a summer park with mountain-bike trails, an alpine slide, and bungee-jumping towers.

US Highway 26, the blacktop ribbon that kisses the south side of Mount Hood before dipping south into Central Oregon, feels less crowded during summer than winter because visitation disperses to many different recreation areas. Backpackers head for the Timberline Trail that circles the mountain; hikers seek out the huckleberry fields on Tom Dick and Harry Mountain; campers enjoy the magnificent old-growth forest at Green Canyon Campground along the Salmon River; and fishermen, canoeists, and mountain bikers seek out their favorite spots.

For a mountain that has so many people wanting a piece of it, Mount Hood usually manages to please while holding enough in reserve for future generations to enjoy.

Getting There

Mount Hood is a 55-mile drive southeast of Portland on US Highway 26 (US 26). Highway 35 traverses the east side of the mountain from Hood River. Mount Hood National Forest roads provide access into the surrounding forest. The Mount Hood Information Center, on the south side of US 26 at Welches, can answer questions and sells maps of the area.

Adjoining Areas

NORTH/EAST: **Hood River and the Gorge**

SOUTH: **Mount Jefferson and the Metolius River**

WEST: **Cascade Foothills, Greater Portland**

inside out

Downhill Skiing/Snowboarding

Mount Hood isn't much different from the rest of the Cascades when it comes to winter sports. The snow is wet and heavy and there is lots of it. There is so much snow that skiing goes on and on and on. . . .

Mount Hood's Timberline Lodge is the only ski area in North America that can offer skiing any day of the year. When its upper chairlift was converted to a detachable quad for the 1997 season, Timberline began bridging the gap between what had been a Labor Day closing with its usual season opener in early November. The ski area typically closes for routine maintenance for a few weeks in mid-September, before reopening the last weekend of the month. So if you really need to go skiing in early October, Mount Hood is the place for you.

While Mount Hood's summer ski season is unrivaled on the continent, just how good is skiing during winter?

A ski area manager who moved from Wyoming to Mount Hood Meadows several years ago said his new ski area has as many good skiing days as Rocky Mountain resorts. If skiing at Jackson Hole is good 80 percent of the time during a 120-day season, it has 96 good days. Because 96 good days are spread over a 192-day season at Mount Hood Meadows, skiing would be good 50 percent of the time. Weather is always the wild card when skiing at a mountain so close to the Pacific Ocean, but careful selection by skiers and snowboarders can result in some awesome days of skiing. Those who don't pick carefully end up wearing a lot of plastic to keep the rain at bay.

Timberline Lodge

The magnificent 1930s lodge is Oregon's only full-service on-mountain ski resort. The lodge's 59 rooms are booked to capacity on many weekends throughout the year, but midweek reservations are usually available on short notice. The lodge is a delightful place to spend a long winter's night, either in the excellent dining room, around the grand fireplace, in the large Jacuzzi, or outside skiing under the lights.

Most skiing during winter, all beginner and intermediate, occurs below the lodge's elevation of 6,000 feet. The Victoria Station and Pucci chairlifts haul skiers back up to the lodge, while the Betsy chair serves beginners just east of the lodge. Half of the Blossom chair's 1,000 vertical feet climb above the lodge. The Magic Mile Express rises to 7,000 feet, and the Palmer Express tops out at 8,500 feet. The two upper lifts have been upgraded in recent years to high-speed quads and provide outstanding, wide-open skiing, when weather allows them to operate. The Magic Mile is open regularly throughout the winter, but it takes some time to dig out Palmer from the mountain's massive snow accumulation. Breaks between storms frequently are too short to open Palmer and its runs for strong intermediate skiers.

The **upper lifts** are the setting for the summer ski season, with the Palmer snowfield large enough to offer a mile-long run on days when the thermometer hits 100° in Portland. As the snowfield shrinks by late summer, skiing is limited to the upper .5 mile. The grooming crew packs snow during winter into Mile Canyon so that a narrow finger of snow descends to within walking distance of the lodge into late August, longer in some years. Skiers who don't want to ski the lower runs can ride the Magic Mile down to the lodge.

On sunny days during summer, Timberline attracts ski racers and snowboarders from around the world. Recreational skiing can be outstanding early in the summer, but by July 4 the snow begins to dwindle. The Palmer snowfield is divided up into race training slots to serve summer ski camps, so public skiing is confined to a 200-foot-wide slot just east of the chairlift. Summer skiing is an interesting novelty, but its main appeal is to ski competitors, not recreational skiers out to have a good time.

The knock against Timberline, besides its southern exposure, is that its terrain is too flat low down and too uniform higher up. There's no getting around either situation, but no other ski area in Oregon can offer 3,500 vertical feet of skiing. For **information,** contact Timberline Lodge, (503) 231-7979, or the Ski Report, (503) 222-2211. Timberline is a 6-mile drive up Forest Rd 50. Turn north from US 26 at the east edge of Government Camp.

Skiers and hikers need to be aware that the south slope of Mount Hood drops slightly to the southwest, not directly back to Timberline Lodge. Several snowboarders in recent years have found themselves in trouble and have spent the night outside after straying beyond the ski area boundary.

Mount Hood Meadows

Big and varied, Mount Hood Meadows is one of the country's premier day-ski areas. The resort once had Forest Service permission to build lift-side lodging on Mount Hood's east side but gave up the bid because of litigation.

Meadows (as Portland skiers affectionately call it) has 11 chairlifts, including 3 high-speed quads that serve its 2,777-foot vertical drop. The two day lodges at the base get unbearably cramped when the weather is blustery on busy days, but an on-mountain restaurant is in the planning stages. For **information,** contact Mount Hood Meadows, (503) 337-2222, or the Ski Report, (503) 227-7669. The ski area is 2 miles north of Hwy

35 on Forest Rd 3555, 6.8 miles from Hwy 35's junction with US 26.

The ski terrain has something for everyone—a segregated beginner area, long cruising runs for intermediates, and steep powder skiing in Heather Canyon for experts. The east side has the Yellow chair, which leaves from near the day lodges, as well as the Hood River Express chair, which starts way down the road along Hwy 35. The Shooting Star and Heather Canyon chairs also feed the upper eastside runs. The ski area's lower section has two parallel lifts that run to midmountain from the day lodge, one of them a high-speed quad. Daisy, Red, and Buttercup, all nicely tied together on the lower west side, serve beginners and intermediates.

The **Cascade Express** serves the upper slopes above timberline. Formerly called Texas, the chairlift's top terminal is positioned so that skiers can use the chair to reach nearly every run in the ski area. Terrain to the west is through big, open bowls. Skiers who head east drop into the head of Heather Canyon for some of Oregon's most challenging ski terrain. A sno-cat can take skiers another 1,000 feet above the chairlift's top terminal to 8,300 feet, but Mount Hood's harsh weather most frequently keeps skiers confined to the chairlifts.

Opened to the public in 1968, the ski area's development spurred completion of Hwy 35 and opened the east side of Mount Hood to recreation. Meadows has been paying for it ever since by being forced to fight with preservationists every time it wants to make some kind of change. Of course, management hasn't always done itself a favor by the way it runs things. The ski area's "solar ski season," which used to run in June, was shut down by the district ranger when salt spread over the snow to improve ski conditions was dispersed too far and killed some wildflowers.

The loss of a June ski season was hardly missed by Portland skiers, who get plenty of opportunities to ski during Meadows's typical mid-November to early May season. The ski area is also open for skiing five nights a week and has Oregon's only nighttime high-speed quad.

Unable to develop overnight lodging, Meadows has committed itself to upgrading its facilities, becoming more customer friendly, and taking better care of the environment. A lift ticket at Meadows might cost as much as $10 per day more than Mount Hood's other ski areas, but skiers don't seem to mind paying it because of the outstanding terrain and top-to-bottom coverage by high-speed chairlifts. Mount Hood Meadows works with lodging properties in Hood River to attract multiday visitors, especially from Seattle.

Mount Hood Skibowl

Closest to Portland, Skibowl saves skiers and snowboarders about a half hour's driving time each way when they decide not to drive to Timberline

Lodge or Mount Hood Meadows. Skibowl is situated on the south side of US 26 at the west edge of Government Camp. Because of the Bowl's base elevation of 3,500 feet, skiers usually check it out before they decide whether they want to stop or head for higher terrain.

Skibowl is divided into halves. The western side is served by the Lower Bowl and Upper Bowl chairlifts, which climb 1,500 feet to the top of the ski area. The eastern side is the old Multorpor ski area, which merged with Skibowl in the late 1950s; it is also served by two chairlifts. Both sides have full services, although **Skibowl West** is the major base area and is open longer hours than **Skibowl East.**

Terrain here is great for beginner skiers, as long as the snow is sufficient, and expert skiers have some of the most exciting skiing in Oregon in the Upper Bowl. Intermediates find most of the runs too short to be satisfying, although the Reynolds run is one of the best high-speed cruises in the state. The Outback, an ungroomed area that stretches a mile west of the Upper Bowl along Tom Dick and Harry Ridge, has some of the most challenging ski terrain in the state. The Outback is usually open only on weekends and holidays, when the ski patrol staff is sufficiently large to monitor it.

Skibowl is located on US 26 at Government Camp, 55 miles east of Portland. For information, contact Mount Hood Skibowl and its ski report, (503) 222-2695.

Summit Ski and Snow Play Area

A family and beginner ski area, **Summit** is best known for its inner-tube hill. Skiing is on a 400-vertical-foot double chairlift on the north side of US 26 at the east end of Government Camp. The chairlift operates only on weekends and holidays, but the sliding hill is open daily. For information, call Summit at (503) 272-0256.

The day lodge is open daily and rents inner tubes for use on the sliding hill, which is tucked away at the east edge of the ski runs so different type of users are well separated. Summit also operates another sliding hill 2 miles to the east on US 26 at **Snow Bunny.** It's open on weekends and holidays.

Cross-Country Skiing

Plenty of Nordic skiers give Mount Hood their best shot, but they run into the same problems as their alpine brethren. Let's face it: Mount Hood is a stormy, unpleasant place to be for much of the winter, with a freezing level that mimics the ups and downs of the stock market. During much of the winter, the only place to be that's worse than Mount Hood is working in rainy Portland. As bad as the weather gets on Mount Hood, the rain of Portland keeps sending skiers up to the mountain.

Mount Hood Meadows operates the only full-service Nordic center on Mount Hood. Its Nordic facilities will improve greatly when a 4,000-square-foot lodge is completed in 1998. The Nordic center, (503) 337-2222, grooms 15 kilometers of trails at its Hood River Meadows parking lot, 1 mile past the main turnoff for the ski area on Hwy 35.

Teacup Lake, across Hwy 35 from Mount Hood Meadows, is a week-end Nordic center operated by the Oregon Nordic Club. Facilities include a warming trailer and a 20-kilometer trail system. Trails are groomed for the weekend, but rentals are not available, so pick up rental equipment beforehand at the numerous ski stores in Portland, Sandy, Government Camp, or Mount Hood Meadows. Both of Mount Hood's east-slope Nordic centers are situated near the 4,500-foot level, usually high enough to have good snow—but not always.

Mount Hood has 16 Oregon Department of Transportation sno-parks that cater to cross-country skiers. Strung out like beads of a rosary along US 26 and Hwy 35, the sno-parks have an extensive marked, but ungroomed, interconnecting trail system (see Oregon Outdoor Primer for details on the sno-park system). The busiest sno-parks are **Trillium Lake,** on the south shoulder of US 26 east of Government Camp 2 miles, at 3,700 feet; **White River,** situated at 4,200 feet 4.7 miles north on Hwy 35 from its junction with US 26; and **Bennett Pass,** the highest at 4,647 feet and just across Hwy 35 from the entrance to Mount Hood Meadows.

Other popular sno-parks are **Glacier View** (3,600 feet, where the Enid Lake tour begins across US 26 from the entrance to Skibowl); **Highway Maintenance** (4,000 feet, on the south side of Government Camp); **Snow Bunny** (3,700 feet, across US 26 from Trillium Lake); **Clark Creek** (4,100 feet, 1 mile north of Teacup Lake); and **Frog Lake** (3,950 feet, 4 miles south of the US 26–Hwy 35 junction). Stop at the Mount Hood Information Center at Welches to pick up a handout that describes the mountain's cross-country ski trails and sno-park trailheads.

Hiking/Backpacking

Mount Hood summit climb

Oregon's highest mountain is often referred to as the second most frequently climbed glaciated peak in the world. A specious claim at best—there is no way to verify the number of Mount Hood summit climbers because too many decline to register despite a Forest Service requirement that they do so (because they are entering the Mount Hood Wilderness). A generally accepted estimate is that 10,000 hikers attempt to reach the summit in a given year, with a 60 percent success ratio. (The total pales in comparison to the estimated 80,000 who annually reach the top of Japan's

Mount Fuji.) Climbers should register and obtain a mandatory wilderness permit in the climbing room (open 24 hours) of Timberline's Wy'east day lodge. At present, climbing permits are free and there is no daily quota, although both situations may change in the near future.

The popular **south side** climbing route on Mount Hood, which rises to 11,235 feet and is the high point of both Clackamas and Hood River Counties, is considered a walk-up, although most climbing parties use ropes, ice axes, and crampons. The best time to climb is during periods of good weather from April into early July. Later than that, the mountain is notorious for its rockfall—all that most sane climbers need to see is a base-ball-size rock hurtling past their head at 100mph to decide they really don't want to climb the south chute when the rocks aren't frozen together.

The climb starts at 6,000 feet in the parking lot at **Timberline Lodge** around 2am. The first couple hours are spent hiking up the slopes of the Magic Mile and Palmer chairlifts, from where the route continues north for a mile from 8,500 to 10,500 feet to the base of a snow slope called the **Hogsback.** Most parties rope up here, then wait their turn to work their way up the 45-degree slope to the summit. Heavy use usually leaves a sequence of steps, much like the rungs of a ladder, all the way to the top. The climb usually takes 5 to 7 hours up, plus a 3-hour descent, for the 7-mile round trip.

The mountain's convenient location near a paved road means that more than a few climbers wind up in trouble. Besides the problem with altitude gain that climbers who come from sea level have, the mountain is notorious for brewing up intense storms. A May 1986 whiteout claimed the lives of eight climbers, one of America's worst climbing disasters. The accident spurred the development of a rescue beacon called the "Mountain Locator Unit," which can be rented inexpensively at Portland mountain shops and in Government Camp at the Mount Hood Inn. The device is only used on Mount Hood because of the expensive tracking equipment and training required for searchers. Still, not even the locator unit is foolproof. Three climbers were benighted by a storm in 1997 and survived because they dug a snow cave and spent two nights in sleeping bags. The tracking equipment was unable to locate the locator beacon they activated.

For a safe climb, wait for predictable spells of good weather in spring, start early, climb fast, and turn around at the first hint of a change in the weather. Remember also that the slope of the mountain veers west of Timberline Lodge and that a map, compass, and altimeter are required to navigate a safe route in poor visibility.

Steve Boyer, a Portland physician, holds most of Mount Hood's speed-climbing records. Boyer has run to the summit and back from Timberline Lodge in 2 hours and 6 minutes. His round-trip time from Government

Camp is 3 hours and 13 minutes. He even holds the record from Portland, riding a bicycle from the Ross Island Bridge, climbing the mountain, and returning to town in 10 hours and 16 minutes.

For a guided climb, contact Timberline Mountain Guides, (800) 464-7704, the only guide service with both an office and mountain shop at Government Camp. Recreation on the south side of Mount Hood is managed by the Zigzag Ranger District, (503) 622-3191. The mountain has 14 other climbing routes, but all require more experience than the south-side route.

Pacific Crest Trail

The Pacific Crest National Scenic Trail (PCT) passes through some of its most accessible miles as it crosses the Mount Hood country. The trail's Mount Hood section runs 40 miles between the **Warm Springs Indian Reservation** on the south (see Mount Jefferson and the Metolius River chapter) and **Lolo Pass** on the north (see Hood River and the Gorge chapter). The trail is accessible from major roads at **Clackamas Lake,** on Forest Rd 42, 8 miles south of its junction with US 26; at **Timothy Lake,** 2 miles north of Clackamas Lake; at **Wapanitia Pass** on US 26, 4.5 miles south of the Hwy 35 junction; at **Barlow Pass,** 2.6 miles north on Hwy 35 from its junction with US 26; at **Timberline Lodge,** 6 miles north of Government Camp; and at **Lolo Pass,** 10 miles northeast of Zigzag and US 26 on Forest Rd 18.

Some of the popular day hikes in the Mount Hood area connect with the PCT, at least for short distances. The most heavily used part is north from Timberline Lodge, where it passes through the Mount Hood Wilderness and makes up part of the Timberline Trail, which circles the mountain. The Forest Service publishes three topographic maps that show the trail in detail throughout Oregon. The map called "Oregon Northern Portion" shows the trail in the Mount Hood area. Pick up a copy at the Mount Hood Information Center, (503) 622-7674, at Welches.

Timberline Trail

Every great mountain should be circled by a trail. The trail that goes around Mount Hood is the 40-mile Timberline Trail. Runners have covered the distance in as little as 12 hours, but most backpackers prefer to spend three nights or more among the many spectacular campsites that are nestled in the trees at timberline, where harsh weather sets the upper limit of their growing area. Water is never far away, although it's prudent to carry the Forest Service's Mount Hood Wilderness map to plot the next reliable source of drinking water. The only roads that intersect the trail are at Timberline Lodge and at Cloud Cap on the northeast side (see Hood River and the Gorge chapter).

A popular way to do the circuit is to begin in a clockwise direction from Cloud Cap, get the highest and driest part of the trail out of the way early, stop at Timberline Lodge to resupply, then continue past the wildflower meadows at Paradise Park, the cool spray of Ramona Falls, and the meadows on the mountain's north side—Cairn Basin, Wy'east Basin, and Elk Cove. For anyone contemplating a single backpack of four days in Oregon, forget all the others and walk around Mount Hood. The best time is from early August through September. Stream and snowfield crossings can be dangerous through July, depending on the year. Black flies are a nuisance on the mountain's western slopes but aren't a big problem on the east.

The trail is jointly managed by the Zigzag Ranger District, (503) 622-3191, and the Hood River Ranger District, (541) 352-6002. Pick up a route description from the Mount Hood Information Center at Welches. Permits are self-issued at the trailheads. For the entire circuit, expect to gain and lose 10,000 feet in elevation while crossing canyons that go as low as 3,200 feet (Sandy River on the southwest side) and climbing ridges that top out at 7,320 feet (Lamberson Spur on the northeast).

Mount Hood's west side

Oregon's biggest city is less than 50 miles away on US 26, so the Hoodland area sees plenty of day hiking, especially on weekends and throughout the summer. The most famous day hike is the **Ramona Falls Loop** (easy; 7.5 miles round trip) from Old Maid Flat. The trail ends at a spectacular waterfall that cascades 50 feet down a wide, moss-covered basalt cliff. The waterfall on Ramona Creek is right on the Pacific Crest Trail, which also serves as the Timberline Trail on this part of Mount Hood, so don't expect to find solitude. A trail continues from Ramona Falls up **Yocum Ridge** (difficult; 6 miles round trip from the falls), for a stunning view of Mount Hood's western glaciers. To reach the Old Maid Flat trailhead, turn north from US 26 at Zigzag on Lolo Pass Rd (Forest Rd 18). Drive 5 miles to Forest Rd 1825, turn right, and follow signs past three campgrounds to the trailhead. For the trail up Yocum Ridge, follow the PCT north from the falls for .5 mile and turn right on the Yocum Ridge Trail.

The **Castle Canyon Trail** (difficult; 2 miles round trip) is a steep climb to some castlelike rock formations. The trailhead is on Forest Rd 1819, .25 mile west of Rhododendron. **Hidden Lake Trail** (easy; 4 miles round trip) begins on Kiwanis Club Rd (Forest Rd 2639), which veers off the north side of US 26, 2 miles east of Rhododendron. The .25-mile trail to **Little Zigzag Falls** begins at the end of Kiwanis Club Rd. Pick up a free, six-page information guide called "Day Hikes Around Mount Hood" at the Mount Hood Information Center in Welches.

Most of the visitors to the 44,600-acre **Salmon-Huckleberry Wilderness** enter on the **Salmon River Trail,** 5.2 miles south from US 26 at Zigzag on Salmon River Rd. The trail continues through the wilderness area to the east, where it joins the road system south of Government Camp, but most hikers walk only a mile or two along the river to enjoy its many pools and viewpoints. A popular turnaround point is at 3.2 miles where a spur trail leads to an overlook of the Salmon River gorge. The **Old Salmon River Trail** (easy; 2.5 miles one way) follows the river downstream from the trailhead, passing through the old-growth forest of Green Canyon Campground.

Trails that enter the Salmon-Huckleberry Wilderness from the US 26 corridor on the north climb to the tops of ridges. The high point tops out at 5,000 feet, not quite enough to get above the trees, but a few rocky outcrops allow for views along the way. The **Hunchback Mountain Trail** (difficult; 2.5 miles to ridge top) begins in the parking lot at the Zigzag Ranger District on US 26. The trail climbs steeply for 3,000 feet for views of the Zigzag Valley, then continues along the ridge to the summit of 5,045-foot Devils Peak.

Mount Hood's east side

The 24,000-acre Badger Creek Wilderness lies east of Mount Hood and can be entered from the west on a few steep trails or from the east from some gentler trails (see Lower Deschutes River chapter). The quickest way into the wilderness from the west is via the **Gumjuwac Saddle Trail** (moderate; 2.5 miles to the saddle), which begins 4 miles south of the turnoff to Mount Hood Meadows across from Robinhood Campground on the east side of Hwy 35.

Lookout Mountain, at 6,525 feet the second-highest peak in the Mount Hood National Forest, is a moderate 2-mile hike north from Gumjuwac Saddle.

A popular backpack trip on Mount Hood's eastern flank is the moderate, 8-mile loop to **Elk Meadow,** the largest on Mount Hood. The trail begins at Hood River Meadows (see Cross-Country Skiing, above). Camping is not allowed in Elk Meadow; use established sites in the trees at the edge of the meadow. Hikers share many more trails on Mount Hood's eastern side with mountain bikers (see Biking, below).

Mount Hood's south side

Hikers share trails with fishermen at **Timothy Lake** and with mountain bikers on the **Frazier Trail,** both located south of Mount Hood in the upper reaches of the Clackamas River drainage. For best access drive east past Mount Hood on US 26 and turn south on Skyline Rd (Forest Rd 42), 8 miles south of the junction with Hwy 35. To reach Timothy Lake, one of the major camping locations in the forest, drive south for 7 miles on Skyline Rd, turn west, and drive 2 miles on Forest Rd 57 to the lake. The Frazier trailhead is 8 miles west of Timothy Lake (see Mountain Biking, below).

Clackamas Lake (see Pacific Crest Trail, above) is circled by a 1-mile trail in a historic part of the Mount Hood National Forest. The lake's ranger station was built by the Civilian Conservation Corps in 1933–34. The lake is also the setting for a cabin built by a Portland dentist in 1900, a grove of old-growth timber, an archway over the Pacific Crest Trail, a meadow, and the springs that feed the lake.

Llama trekking

Mount Hood doesn't have a horse packing station like those in the Wallowa Mountains of northeast Oregon, but llamas are available for hire for those who rightly believe there's a better way to enter the wilderness than by carrying everything in a backpack. Moonshine Acres, (503) 667-4301, offers **guided llama trips** on weekends and holidays into the 47,100-acre Mount Hood Wilderness. The llamas can carry 80 to 90 pounds, and hikers are left with only a daypack to carry. One of Moonshine's more popular one-night trips is on Trail No. 778 from Kiwanis Club Rd to **Paradise Park** on the southwest shoulder of Mount Hood. With the llamas doing most of the work, the hikers have plenty of time to explore the outstanding flower gardens after arriving at camp in midafternoon.

Scenic Drives

Next to US 101 along the Oregon Coast, the **Mount Hood/Columbia Gorge Loop** is the most popular scenic drive in Oregon. Portland residents often treat their visitors to a tour of at least part of the loop. The Historic Columbia River Highway section is usually the first choice (see Hood River and the Gorge chapter), but more than a million visitors find their way to **Timberline Lodge** each year on **Mount Hood.**

The tour route can begin or end anywhere in the Portland area, although the formal start/end point is the **Oregon Trail Interpretive Center,** (503) 657-9336, at 1726 Washington St in Oregon City. The tour route has three components—the Historic Columbia River Highway, Hwy 35 along the east side of Mount Hood, and US 26 between Portland and Mount Hood. The 160-mile route requires more than a day for full enjoyment, but a one-day visit is better than no visit at all.

Long before tourists set their sights on Mount Hood, during the pioneer migration that began in the 1840s, the mountain's flanks served as a branch route of the Oregon Trail. After reaching The Dalles, settlers were faced with the choice of running the Columbia River or tackling the **Barlow Road,** the old wagon route around the east and south sides of Mount Hood, to reach the Willamette Valley. Neither route was without difficulty at the end of a cross-continent journey and both live in the lore of Northwest migration. Numerous historic sites along the Barlow Road are marked along Mount Hood's highways and forest roads.

The Barlow Road left The Dalles, traveled south, and turned to follow the White River to enter the Mount Hood country. The 150th anniversary of the Oregon Trail, celebrated in 1994, brought a series of signposts and displays to help modern visitors retrace the route. Interpretive sights in the Mount Hood area include **Barlow Pass,** the crest of the Cascades on the Oregon Trail, on Hwy 35, 2 miles east from its junction with US 26; **Pioneer Woman's Grave,** where an emigrant is buried in a wagon box, .5 mile east on a side road south of Hwy 35 near its junction with US 26; **Laurel Hill,** a short walk south of US 26 at milepost 50.9, where a rock chute is an example of what the wagon trains descended; and **Tollgate,** a replica of the final fee-collection site on the Barlow Road near Tollgate Campground off US 26 1 mile east of Rhododendron.

Remnant ruts of the westward march can be seen near Pioneer Woman's Grave, Trillium Lake Sno-Park, Skibowl ski area, and on the Pioneer Bridle Trail below Enid Lake (see Downhill Skiing/Snowboarding and Cross-Country Skiing, above).

Camping

The Mount Hood corridor is by no means bereaved of campgrounds, but compared to other Oregon mountain playgrounds it doesn't have a lot of them in relation to the size of the population that lives nearby. Portlanders tend to do their camping on the coast or in Central Oregon and visit Mount Hood on day trips. Obviously there are plenty of exceptions to that rule, especially along the western base of the mountain in the Welches corridor and around Timothy Lake well south of Government Camp.

Reservations are accepted for many of the larger campgrounds in the Mount Hood National Forest through the national reservations system at (800) 280-2267.

Heading east from Portland on US 26, visitors run into a string of communities collectively known as **Hoodland.** Each retains a piece of its identity, whether through a famous pizza parlor, roadhouse, or resort, along 7 miles of the highway just before it makes its climb to Government Camp at Mount Hood's southern base.

The Mount Hood RV Village, (503) 253-9445, is a big sprawling commercial campground, but it plays a larger role than that. The **Mount Hood Information Center,** located at the entrance to the RV village, has several meeting rooms that serve the needs of the community. While big RVs are king, the campground has year-round tenting facilities, plus access to national forest trails and fishing on the Salmon River.

Campgrounds on the south side of US 26 in the Hoodland area are **Green Canyon** on the Salmon River Rd (see Hiking/Backpacking, above) and **Tollgate** and **Camp Creek,** both just off US 26 a few miles east of Rhododendron. If you don't like highway noise, Green Canyon is your only choice.

North of US 26 up the Lolo Pass Rd from Zigzag (see Hiking/Backpacking, above), Forest Rd 1825 leads to **McNeil Campground** and **Lost Creek Campground,** plus **Riley Horse Camp.** While a horse camp is designed specifically for horse owners, other campers are allowed to stay there if they want to put up with the noise and smell of the animals. Lost Creek is designed for wheelchair use and has a barrier-free fishing platform and trail system. A sunny weekend spent at these camps makes one wonder why so many Portlanders pass them by and drive an extra hundred miles to camp amid the crowds of Central Oregon. The largest Forest Service campground on Mount Hood's west side is Camp Creek with its 34 spots. RVs longer than 22 feet should use the Mount Hood RV Village.

Up at Government Camp, **Trillium Lake Campground's** 54 spots, 2 miles south of US 26 on Forest Rd 2650, are usually first to fill up. **Alpine Campground** has 16 spots 1 mile below Timberline Lodge and **Still Creek Campground** handles the overflow with 27 spots on the south side of US 26 at Government Camp. All of the above campgrounds are managed by the Zigzag Ranger District, (541) 622-3191.

Campers looking for solitude fan out on forest roads southeast of the mountain in small camps at **Barlow Creek, Barlow Crossing, Grindstone,** and **White River Station.** Each has only 5 spots and all are part of the Barlow Ranger District, (541) 467-2291. The Mount Hood National Forest map shows their locations.

The Oak Grove Fork of the Clackamas River can be reached by driving east from Estacada on Forest Rds 46 and 57, or west from US 26 on Forest Rd 42 (also known as Skyline Rd). The February flood of 1996 wiped out much of the road network above Estacada, but it was repaired and reopened in 1998. It doesn't matter much which way Portlanders go—either up the winding route along the Clackamas (see Cascade Foothills chapter) or down the faster but longer route from US 26 east of Mount Hood. Popular camps on US 26 before the turnoff to Skyline Rd are **Frog Lake** (33 sites, 4 miles south of the Hwy 35 junction) and **Clear Lake** (28 sites), 3 miles south of Frog Lake on Forest Rd 2630.

Timothy Lake adorned a recent cover of *Sunset* magazine as one of the 10 best camping spots in the West, so don't expect to pull in on a Saturday in July and pick up a lakeside spot. Four camps with 170 spots surround Timothy Lake, 2 miles west of Skyline Rd on Forest Rd 57. **Oak Fork,**

Gone Creek, and **Hoodview** are the largest. **Joe Graham Horse Camp** is located nearby, as are camps at **Clackamas Lake, Little Crater Lake, Lake Harriet,** and a handful of smaller camps with 5 or fewer sites. A base camp at Timothy Lake gives campers the opportunity to tie into the Clackamas-Breitenbush scenic byway (see Cascade Foothills and Mount Jefferson and the Metolius River chapters) to the Olallie Lake Scenic Area. Campgrounds south of Mount Hood are managed by the Barlow Ranger District, (541) 467-2291, on the east slope and the Clackamas Ranger District, (541) 630-6861, on the west slope.

The Mount Hood National Forest has actively worked to improve its campgrounds to accommodate people with disabilities. Camps near Mount Hood with the best barrier-free facilities are Lost Creek, Clear Lake, Little Crater Lake, Clackamas Lake, Gone Creek, Hoodview, Timothy Lake, Harriet Lake, and Trillium Lake.

Fishing

With its location so near a major metropolitan area, the Mount Hood region needs to produce plenty of fish, so it relies primarily on hatcheries to provide a bite at the end of a line. The lower **Sandy River** and lower **Clackamas River** are the major exceptions. Both have strong runs of wild steelhead and chinook salmon (see Greater Portland and Cascade Foothills chapters).

The **Salmon River,** which joins the Sandy at Brightwood, is good for wild cutthroat and has a summer run of steelhead from June through December. Spawning salmon also enter the river, but they are protected from fishing. Best fishing access is along the Old Salmon River Trail (see Hiking/Backpacking, above) and from the Wildwood Recreation Area. The **Sandy River** is good for chinook salmon and steelhead, but most fishing occurs below the Mount Hood country from Revenue Bridge, 1 mile north of Sandy, to the Columbia River (see Greater Portland chapter). The stretch just upstream from Marmot Dam produces summer steelhead from May through August. Marmot Rd follows the north side of the Sandy River and provides a quiet alternative to busy US 26, which runs south of the river. The Sandy runs milky from glacial melt during summer and the best trout fishing is in the clear tributaries, especially the Salmon.

Mount Hood's lakes are heavily planted with rainbow trout and also produce some wild rainbow and cutthroat. Some of the best fishing lakes are **Timothy, Clear, Trillium,** and **Harriet.** All have campgrounds around their shores (see Camping, above). Best fishing is during spring and fall, and trolling large spinners and worms usually works best. Bank anglers count on small spinners and lures to attract bites. Timothy, Trillium, and Harriet Lakes all have fishing piers and other barrier-free facilities for the handicapped.

For families that want a guaranteed bite, the Rainbow Trout Farm, (503) 622-5223, waits just east of Sandy near milepost 32 on US 26. A license is not required. Fishermen who want to seek out the salmon and steelhead in the Sandy River might want to try one of the Hoodland guide services, like Reel Adventures, (503) 622-5372, or Hook Up, (503) 666-5370. When you just can't get anything to bite, head for Welches and the Fly Fishing Shop, (503) 622-4607, where more than a few anglers from Portland find the right answer. Check the state fishing synopsis for regulations, or call the Columbia Region office of the Oregon Department of Fish and Wildlife, (503) 657-2000.

Timothy Lake is one of the best places to go **crawdad** fishing in Oregon. Also known as crayfish, the creatures look like miniature lobsters and live in fresh water throughout Western Oregon. The crawdad is one fish that won't rise to a fly. They are caught by the dozens in traps that resemble crab pots with smaller openings and are usually eaten as a fresh, tasty supplement during a summer barbecue. Anyone trying to survive on the creatures would indeed need to catch a lot of them. Cracking open a crawdad's body yields only a tiny bite of meat.

Biking

Cycling

US 26 has **bike lanes** as it climbs 30 miles to Government Camp from Sandy. Lots of Portland cyclists use it for conditioning. With the ever-constant auto traffic, the ride isn't particularly pleasant, but it offers a good workout. Before leaving Sandy, ride north .5 mile past the high school on Bluff Rd to **Jonsrud Viewpoint** for a spectacular view of the Sandy River and Mount Hood. Bluff Rd is at the west end of Sandy, where the lanes of US 26 come together after being separated as one-way streets through the center of town.

Speaking of workouts, the 6-mile, 2,200-foot hill climb from Government Camp to **Timberline Lodge** is one of Oregon's ultimate road-bike challenges. Again, it usually has plenty of auto traffic and isn't the most pleasant place to ride on a sunny summer weekend. A good alternative is to ride paved **West Leg Road,** a little-used forest road between Government Camp and Timberline. The road begins on the north side of US 26, across from the highway maintenance station, and joins Timberline Rd just below the ski area's maintenance shop.

One of the most pleasant rides in the Mount Hood area is along **Marmot Road** on the north side of the Sandy River. While hundreds of cars speed past a mile or two away on US 26, Marmot Rd is delightfully empty. The road can be reached from Zigzag and Brightwood by crossing any of the three highway bridges in the area over the Sandy River. The west end of the road comes out at Sandy, or it can be used as a relatively uncongested route to connect with I-84 at Troutdale. The view of Mount Hood over farm fields is outstanding when riding east along Marmot Rd.

Mountain biking

Just about everything on the west side of Mount Hood is named Sandy— a glacier, a river, a town. Since sand doesn't make for good single-track mountain-bike riding, you'll find most trails on the south and east sides of Mount Hood.

Mount Hood Skibowl's Action Park (see Action Park, below) is the center of mountain-bike activity on Mount Hood. Three of the ski area's four chairlifts are equipped to carry bikes and riders during summer. Popular rides off the ski trails are the 8-mile loop of Summit Meadow and Trillium Lake to the east (see Cross-Country Skiing, above) and the 10-mile descent (with shuttle vehicle waiting) of **Still Creek Road** to Rhodo-dendron on the west. Action Park provides a free bicycle trail map.

In addition to rides out of Skibowl, the south side of Mount Hood sees plenty of bike activity by summer residents and the visitors from around the world who attend summer ski and snowboard camps at Timberline Lodge. Besides mountain biking in their free time, summer campers will have an 8,000-square-foot indoor recreation center to play in when construction is completed in 1998. The building will be located at Skibowl East, formerly known as Multorpor Ski Area, just south of Government Camp via the bridge over US 26 from the center of town.

Favorite Government Camp mountain-bike trails are the **Cross Town Trail,** a 3-mile ride from Glacier View Sno-Park west of Government Camp to the Summit Ski Area on the east side of town; a 9-mile loop on roads and trails at **Snow Bunny Snow Play Area;** and the **Alpine** and **Glade Trails** from Timberline Lodge to Government Camp (see Downhill Skiing/Snowboarding and Cross-Country Skiing, above). The area also has virtually unlimited riding opportunities on lightly used forest roads. Mountain bikes are welcome on ski trails at Skibowl, but they must stay on roads at the mountain's other ski areas. Stop at the Mount Hood Information Center in Welches to pick up a free information sheet on the mountain-bike trails of the Zigzag Ranger District.

On the east side of Mount Hood, south of Forest Rd 44 (which leaves Hwy 35 and heads east to Dufur), bikers head for the **Gunsight Trail,** a 4.5-mile singletrack on the ridge west of Badger Lake; the **Bennett Pass Trail,** a 4-mile ride that parallels Forest Rd 3550; the 3.6-mile loop of **Sahalie and Umbrella Falls** near Hood River Meadows; the 5.8-mile **East Fork Trail** between Robinhood and Sherwood Campgrounds; and the 8-mile **Fifteen**

Mile Creek Trail that heads downhill to the east from Fifteen Mile camp. The Hood River Ranger District, (541) 352-6002, actively manages for mountain-bike recreation and publishes trail guides.

The **McCubbins Gulch** area, located between the White River and the Warm Springs Indian Reservation at the southeast edge of the Mount Hood National Forest, is designated for off-highway vehicles. Mountain bikers can use the trails when the ATVs and motorcycles aren't around. Everyone needs to stay off land owned by the tribes. For information on McCubbins Gulch, check with the Barlow Ranger District at (541) 467-2291.

The **Frazier Trailhead,** an end-of-the-road spot 14 airline miles south of Welches, sits at the edge of a roadless area that overlooks the Roaring River. Although the river is part of the National Wild and Scenic Rivers System, the area has not been declared a wilderness and mountain bikes are welcome, as long as they stay out of the adjacent Salmon-Huckleberry Wilderness. Several tours begin at the Frazier trailhead, which can be reached by driving Forest Rd 57 east from Ripplebrook or west from Timothy Lake to Shellrock Creek Campground. Turn north on Forest Rd 58 near the camp, drive 5.8 miles, turn left on Forest Rd 4610, drive 1.2 miles, turn left on Spur Rd 240, and drive 4 miles to the Frazier turnaround at the edge of the Rock Lake Basin. This is one of the most isolated spots reachable by road in the Mount Hood National Forest.

Rides from Frazier include 4.7 miles to **Shining Lake;** 4 miles to **Serene Lake;** 8.5 miles for a loop of the **Rock Lakes Basin;** and 9.6 miles to **Grouse Point.** All are for skilled riders, and together they offer one of the better three-day vacation opportunities for mountain-bike riding in the forest. Check with the Clackamas River Ranger District, (503) 630-6861, for information.

Action Park

It will never be mistaken for Disney World, but the summer action park at **Mount Hood Skibowl** does a pretty good job of providing the young and eager from Portland something to do for thrills when the snow is melted and it's roasting in the mountains. It all began with the construction in the late 1970s of the only dual alpine slide in the Cascades. Sliders reach the starting point by riding the Lower Bowl chairlift to a midway unloading station, then hop aboard a wheeled plastic sled for a ride down the curvy cement trough in the bottom half of the Lower Bowl.

The man who built the slide envisioned it as a way to stabilize the yo-yo economy of a low-elevation ski area that all too often suffered through long rainy winters. The owner was right, but it ended up putting him out of business because a few years of drought left him in financial arrears. After another ownership change, a young man from Portland bought the Bowl and realized he had something no other ski area in Oregon has—private land near the ski lifts. Virtually all of Oregon's ski facilities are on national forest lands and, as such, have limited opportunity for development.

Skibowl is different because of the private land on the east side of the ski area, now called Skibowl East but long known as Multorpor (short for MULTnomah County, ORegon, PORtland). In an effort to counterbalance its winter season, Skibowl began developing a summer action park. With easy access to Portland via US 26, the park has met with overwhelming success. It boasts more than two dozen attractions, some that would look right at home on a carnival midway and others that work pretty well in a mountain setting.

The carnival-type rides include the tallest **bungee-jumping** tower in Oregon, a rapid-riser bungee, go-carts, miniature golf, batting cages, and the ever-popular (with kids) velvet fly trap. **Horseback rides,** company picnics, outdoor concerts, scenic chairlift rides, and **mountain biking** work well in the mountain setting. The ski area maintains a full-service bike shop with rentals (call ahead for reservations in summer), leads guided tours, and is the only place in Oregon where bikes are loaded on chairlifts. Trails are steep, and inexperienced riders should know that downhills can be just as difficult as riding uphill. The ski area is host each summer to several regional mountain-bike races.

For information on Action Park, call (503) 222-2695.

Canoeing/Kayaking/Boating

Boating is rather limited on Mount Hood, although that doesn't stop Portlanders from bringing along their car-toppers, canoes, and sailboats when they visit **Trillium, Frog, Timothy, Clear, and Harriet Lakes** (see Camping, above). Timothy Lake has four and the other lakes each have one boat ramp.

The upper **Sandy, Salmon, Zigzag, and Bull Run Rivers** provide some whitewater thrills, more so for kayakers than for rafters because of their narrow, rocky channels. All are advanced runs good only during the winter rainy season and spring runoff. The 12-mile run on the Sandy from Marmot Dam to Dodge Park (see Greater Portland chapter) goes through the **Sandy River Gorge** and the upper stretch has four rapids that can become choked with logs. Access to Marmot Dam is on a power company road off Marmot Rd, 5 miles east of Sandy. The lower river is managed by the BLM, (503) 375-5646.

One of the safest ways to see this beautiful section of river through the gorge is to wait for the river level to drop in late summer. By then, most of the water it carries is melt from the glaciers on Mount Hood. The current isn't powerful enough to pin a boater under a log jam, but the water level isn't high enough to float a boat, either. Boaters float the river in **inner tubes** and carry them around rocks. Be sure to wear a wet suit (and life vest) for protection from the cold water and the inevitable bumps that happen along the way. This is strictly a do-it-yourself activity.

Mushroom and Berry Picking

Mount Hood's most famous berry is the huckleberry, which grows on a small bush and ripens from mid-August through early September. The huckleberry is just about the best-tasting wild berry there is.

One of the best spots for huckleberries in the Mount Hood National Forest is the **Mirror Lake Trail** to Tom Dick and Harry Mountain on the south side of US 26, .5 mile west of Government Camp. The higher you hike above Mirror Lake, the better the picking is. This is an overused area because of its proximity to Portland, so check with the Mount Hood Information Center in Welches to find other good picking locations. The best spots vary year to year, even week to week.

Other reliable picking areas, all described in a berry-picking handout available from the information center, are **East Zigzag**, along the Zigzag Mountain and Burnt Lake Trails; **West Leg Road** and the **Alpine Trail; Sherar Burn,** on Forest Rd 2613 near Government Camp; and **Frog Lake Buttes,** along either side of Forest Rd 2610 at the Frog Lake turnoff from US 26.

Mushrooms are nothing to trifle with because, to the inexperienced, poisonous ones can look just like the edible ones. For pickers who know which is which, the Mount Hood National Forest offers good picking in spring and fall.

During spring (usually early April), morels grow in sandy places under cottonwood trees along the **Zigzag, Sandy, Clackamas, and Salmon Rivers.** Morels, along with the poisonous helvella, also grow in conifer forest, especially where burning occurred the previous year. Areas around **Clear Lake Campground** are noted for their big spring coral mushrooms. Best picking is just after a spring rain.

During fall (usually after the first rains), look for matsutake mushrooms in the **Old Maid Flat** area and around **McNeil Campground.** Collecting is not allowed in campgrounds. Timothy Lake also has good hunting. Since you need a permit anyway, check with the local ranger district before picking any mushrooms.

Berry picking for personal consumption is allowed without a permit, but mushroom collectors and those who gather forest greens need a free permit from a ranger station. Stop at the Mount Hood Information Center in Welches for a permit and detailed descriptions of the best collecting areas.

Wildlife

Raptors by the hundreds use a flyway east of Mount Hood for their annual fall migration from Canada and Washington to the warmer climes of California and Mexico. A long, uninterrupted ridge follows the Hood River Valley south for 35 miles to where it finally ends at the White River. The birds use the uplift created by winds hitting the west side of the ridge to speed their journeys to the south.

Hawk Watch International, a Utah-based conservation group, sets up an annual monitoring station atop Bonney Butte to count the number of birds going south. It's not unusual for the volunteers to spot more than 100 eagles, hawks, and vultures winging their way south each day. Visitors are always welcome because another pair of eyes behind binoculars increases the number of sightings. Volunteers from Hawk Watch International are on-site in September and October. Contact the Hawk Watch Salt Lake City office for more information, 555 E South Temple, Salt Lake City, UT 84110; (801) 524-8511.

A recent year's count tallied 2,368 raptors, including 873 **sharp-shinned hawks**, 528 **red-tailed hawks**, 310 **Cooper's hawks**, 236 **turkey vultures**, 81 **golden eagles**, and 40 **bald eagles**. Other common sightings include **merlins, osprey**, and **northern harriers**. Volunteers also spotted 5 **peregrine falcons.**

To reach the 5,600-foot summit of Bonney Butte, exit Hwy 35 at White River East and drive 7 miles south on Forest Rd 48. Turn left on Forest Rd 4890 and drive 3.75 miles, then turn left on Forest Rd 4891 for 4 miles to Bonney Meadows Campground. The road is rough in places but passenger cars can reach the campground. Park at the campground and walk 200 yards beyond the entrance to a spur road that leads .5 mile to the summit. Pick a sunny day, bring a lawn chair and a picnic lunch, and plan to spend the day, which more often than not will be sunny and warm during September with a million-dollar view of Mount Hood. The brilliant red of the vine maple leaves on the road along the way provides one of the best fall color displays in all of Oregon.

Anyone who spends enough time on Mount Hood will spot plenty of wildlife, even though it isn't known for particular concentrations (except the raptors) as are other parts of the state. Little Crater Lake, a tiny, crystal-clear lake fed by an artesian spring, is surrounded by a meadow known for its birding opportunities. Located near Timothy Lake (see Camping, above), Little Crater Lake can be depended on for **yellow warblers** and

red-winged blackbirds in its willow patches. Timothy Lake is another good birding spot and is famous for hosting all four loon species that visit Oregon, including the only inland sighting of a **yellow-billed loon.**

outside in

Attractions

At 11,235 feet, **Mount Hood** may not be the highest in the chain of volcanoes in the Cascades, but it is one of the best developed, with five ski areas and plenty of facilities to equip the mountaineer, hiker, or skier. The lower slopes are ablaze with rhododendrons (peaking in June) and wildflowers (peaking in July), easily reachable from trails that spread out from Timberline Lodge. (See the appropriate Inside Out sections, above.)

US 26 divides into one-way avenues through the town of **Sandy** on the way to Mount Hood. Named for the nearby river, Sandy offers a white-steepled church, antique shops, a weekend country market, ski rentals, and big stands purveying local produce, wines, juices, and filberts. In short, this is a nice stop en route to the mountains.

The Oregon Candy Farm, 5.5 miles east of Sandy on US 26, (503) 668-5066, features Bavarian truffles along with hand-dipped chocolates and caramels. Kids can watch the candy makers in action.

The pretty little town of **Welches** was named after Samuel Welch and his son Billy, who built the Old Welches Inn. For excellent coffee, stop by Mount Hood Coffee Roasters, 64235 E Brightwood Loop, (503) 622-5153, where Serene Elliott-Graber will show you how she roasts coffee beans from around the world.

Oral Hull Park, (503) 668-6195, actually a conference center and lodge on 23 acres, is designed for the blind, with splashing water and plants to smell or touch; it is a moving experience even for the sighted. You may walk through the garden only by permission if you aren't a guest.

Restaurants

Chalet Swiss ☆☆   This is Oregon's version of Switzerland, where you'll find Swiss specialties: Bundnerfleisch (paper-thin slices of beef salt-cured in alpine air), traditional fondues, and raclette (broiled cheese served with pickles and onions). Reservations suggested. *24371 E Welches Rd (US 26 and E Welches Rd), Welches; (503) 622-3600; $$.*

The Elusive Trout Pub   The owners have kept the original slangy menu at this popular pub: the Keeper, Eastern Brookie, and German Brown are all names for better-than-average sandwiches. Nineteen brews are on draft. *39333 Proctor Blvd (corner of Hoffman Ave), Sandy; (503) 668-7884; $.*

Mount Hood Brew Pub The theme is universal—trout fishing and beer—in this knotty-pine brewpub. Try the popular Iceaxe IPA with a gourmet pizza. The burgers are excellent choices too. *87304 E Government Camp Loop (take Government Camp Loop off US 26), Timberline; (503) 272-3724; $.*

Cheaper Eats

Barlow Trail Inn If the place looks like it has been around for over seven decades, it's because it has. Zigzaggers stop here for fried chicken, a T-bone steak, taco salad, or breakfast—served until 11pm. You get the idea. *69580 E US 26, Zigzag; (503) 622-3112; $.*

Michael's Bread and Breakfast When you only do one thing, you usually do it well. And Michael's only does breakfast. Hikers heading to the hills stop here for a carbo load. Big pancakes and bushels of baked goods will keep you going all day. *24525 E Welches Rd, Welches; (503) 622-5333; $.*

Lodgings

Falcon's Crest Inn There are three secluded hideaways on the top floor of this family-friendly inn, but be prepared for rooms done in themes. A big breakfast is cooked up and, with 24 hours notice, a satisfying dinner served ($30, by reservation only; open to the public). *87287 Government Camp Loop (take Government Camp Loop off US 26), Government Camp, OR 97028; (503) 272-3403 or (800) 624-7384; $$$.*

The Resort at the Mountain ☆☆ Its proximity to Mount Hood, its 27-hole golf course, and the tennis courts, heated pool, fitness center, and *much* more make this resort a good choice for the active traveler. Reserve a fireplace room with forest-facing deck. *68010 E Fairway Ave (.5 mile south of US 26 on E Welches Rd, turn on E Fairway), Welches, OR 97067; (503) 622-3101 or (800) 669-7666; $$$.*

Timberline Lodge ☆☆ Built in 1937, this National Historic Monument has massive beams and a huge, octagonal lobby. Options here range from private rooms with a fireplace to budget-oriented bunk rooms. The Cascade Dining Room's strong point is Northwest cuisine; food in the Ram's Head Lounge is not as good. Adventurous types can bring sleeping bags and rent bunks in the Silcox Hut, 7,000 feet up the mountain. *Timberline Ski Area (60 miles due east of Portland off US 26), Timberline, OR 97028; (503) 272-3311 or (800) 547-1406; $$.*

Cheaper Sleeps

Thunderhead Lodge The management rents out privately owned condominiums here, complete with fully furnished kitchens. For larger groups, they can be a great deal: $89 for 4 people, $290 for 10. Call to see what's available. *PO Box 129, Government Camp, OR 97028; (503) 272-3368; $.*

More Information

Barlow Ranger District, Dufur: *(541) 467-2291.*
Bear Springs Ranger Station, Maupin: *(541) 328-6211.*
Bureau of Land Management, Salem: *(503) 375-5646.*
Clackamas County Tourism Development Council, West Linn: *(800) 647-3843.*
Clackamas River Ranger District, Estacada: *(503) 630-6861.*
Hood River County Chamber of Commerce, Hood River: *(800) 366-3530.*
Hood River Ranger District, Mount Hood–Parkdale: *(541) 352-6002.*
Mount Hood Information Center, Welches: *(503) 622-7674.*
Mount Hood National Forest, Sandy: *(503) 668-1700.*
Northwest Weather and Avalanche Center, Portland: *(503) 326-2400.*
Oregon Road Conditions, Ontario: *(541) 889-3999.*
Oregon Ski Report, Portland: *(503) 222-9951.*
Sandy Area Chamber of Commerce, Sandy: *(503) 668-4006.*
Zigzag Ranger District, Zigzag: *(503) 622-3191.*

Lower Deschutes River

From where the Deschutes River joins the Columbia River on the north, east to US Highway 97, south to Culver, and west to US Highway 26, including the east-side trailheads for the Mount Hood National Forest and Badger Creek Wilderness, Lake Billy Chinook, the Warm Springs Indian Reservation, and the towns of Maupin, Warm Springs, Madras, and Culver.

When summer temperatures soar to 100° and Oregonians begin looking for a place to relax and cool off near water, more than a few wind up in the canyon of the Lower Deschutes River. In addition to the estimated 125,000 annual boaters on the Deschutes, an unknown number of sun seekers evacuate Oregon's cloudy western valleys and swarm the Deschutes to camp, bird-watch, hike, ride mountain bikes and horses, and fish from the river's banks.

The Deschutes's lower 100 miles, from Warm Springs to its confluence with the Columbia River, give Portlanders something few big-city residents can enjoy: an easily accessible whitewater river that runs clear and cold even during the baking heat of summer. As if that weren't enough, the Deschutes comes complete with big-time rapids that thrill rafters, enough navigable distance to offer a pair of multiday float trips, and outstanding fishing.

Mother Nature should have been so kind to Seattle.

Unfortunately, on many weekends, the Lower Deschutes River has been too popular. The influx of humanity, most of it looking for a cool river to run by day and a hot party to attend by night, caused river managers to institute a variety of measures to limit use. Future Deschutes River boaters can expect to find increased fees, permits to float the river—even controls on alcohol while boating and on designated places ashore. The Deschutes is one of the few places where federal, state, and county police await the arrival of troublemakers at rafting take-outs, administer breathalyzer tests to inebriated boaters, and haul them away to spend a night in a distant pokey.

Although it will never go away entirely, the party scene on the river has mellowed in recent years. Designated campsites, bans on riverside fires, and the get-tough approach to law enforcement have chased away many of the problems.

Left behind is the spectacular canyon scenery, the great fishing, and the exciting rapids—in short, the things that attracted people to the river in the first place.

The tiny town of Maupin serves as the supply point for the Lower Deschutes River, while Madras is the hopping-off point for boating on Lake Billy Chinook. It's the waters of this reservoir, an impoundment behind Round Butte Dam, that keep the Lower Deschutes River running cool and clear all summer.

Getting There

The small community of Maupin, the center of activity on the Lower Deschutes River, is 95 miles southeast of Portland via US Highway 26 (US 26) over Mount Hood and Highway 216. Madras, the largest town in the Lower Deschutes River country, is 118 miles southeast of Portland via US 26, at its junction with US 97. Maupin is connected to the Columbia River by US 197. The east bank of the Deschutes near Maupin is accessible via the 37-mile Bureau of Land Management (BLM)'s Lower Deschutes River National Back Country Byway, most of it bumpy and dusty.

Adjoining Areas

NORTH: **Columbia Basin**

SOUTH: **Bend and the Upper Deschutes River**

EAST: **Lower John Day River**

WEST: **Mount Jefferson and the Metolius River, Mount Hood**

Rafting/Kayaking

Deschutes River

The Deschutes River runs clear and cold out of **Pelton Dam** near Warm Springs and stays that way until it joins the Columbia River east of The

Dalles. The dam maintains the river's flow between 4,000 and 8,000 cubic feet per second (cfs), ideal water for boating.

Controlling human use, and the inevitable damage it brings to the ecosystem, is an evolving process by the river's managers. Key players are the BLM's Prineville District, (541) 416-6700; the Oregon Parks and Recreation Department's rivers program, (503) 378-6305; and the Confederated Tribes of the Warm Spring Reservation, (541) 553-1161, owners of much of the land on the lower river's west bank. The tribes ask that nontribal members not use their land for camping, picnicking, fishing, or any other reason, except for a few areas such as **Dry Creek,** where a fishing permit purchased from the tribe allows nontribal use.

Since the river's management plan was adopted in 1993, campsites have been designated, fees have increased, and a boating permit system has been adopted. All boaters are required to have a state permit to use the Lower Deschutes River. The $2 collected per boater per day by the state helps maintain visitor facilities and can be purchased through licensed vendors locally and at G.I. Joe's stores statewide. A federal fee for summer weekend use costs an additional $3 per boater per day. Boaters must purchase permits from licensed vendors in advance; they are not available at launch sites, even when river managers are checking for permits. A plan has been adopted to implement user quotas in the future, but for now the river takes all comers.

For the purposes of floating, the lower river begins at the town of Warm Springs at river mile 95, 5 miles below Pelton Dam on US 97. Sherars Falls, an unrunnable torrent at river mile 44, effectively cuts the Lower Deschutes into two separate sections. The **upper section,** which begins at Warm Springs, is used by fishermen and rafters as a multiday trip. The section ends with one of the country's busiest stretches of commercial whitewater, the famous "splash and giggle" section centered on Maupin at river mile 52. The **lower section** below Sherars Falls is another multiday outing for fishermen and rafters, with jet-boats running upriver from Deschutes River State Park (see Columbia Basin chapter) at the Deschutes's confluence with the Columbia River.

Public roads elsewhere along the river are limited to the stretch around Maupin, where Deschutes River Rd follows the east bank of the river for 37 miles, from Macks Canyon at river mile 23 to a locked gate at river mile 60. The locked gate at the south end of the road prevents public entry by vehicles. Landowners have keys to unlock the gate and can drive to North Junction at river mile 73. Public foot traffic is allowed. All but 8 miles of Deschutes River Rd has a bone-jarring gravel surface notorious for the number of flat tires it causes. The paved section runs north from Maupin to Sherars Falls.

The upper launch point on the Lower Deschutes is alongside US 26, just upstream from the highway bridge at **Warm Springs** at a small day-use river access boat ramp (Warm Springs boat ramp) on the river's east bank. Fishermen are more likely than whitewater thrillseekers to launch there because it's about 20 miles to the first major rapids. An alternate launch site is **Mecca,** a small BLM campground 2 miles downstream from Warm Springs where a gravel BLM road ends along the river's east bank. To reach Mecca, follow the gravel road south along the river's east bank from the east side of the US 26 bridge at Warm Springs. **Trout Creek,** another BLM campground, is a popular launch site 8 river miles downstream from Warm Springs. To find Trout Creek, drive 2 miles north of Madras on US 97 and turn left on a county road signed to the Gateway area. Follow the road north 9 miles to Gateway, then continue 3 miles as the road changes to gravel and winds down to meet the river. The launch at Trout Creek puts boaters much closer to Whitehorse Rapids, the first major whitewater on the river below US 26.

Boaters usually pull out on the east bank to scout **Whitehorse Rapids** from the railroad tracks at river mile 75. The Deschutes canyon carries an active freight line and trains pass by regularly, so watch out for rail traffic. Whitehorse is rated Class III, but more than a few rafters have wrapped on the famous rock on the right side of the entry and needed help getting off. The river picks up intensity below Whitehorse and alternates exciting water with long flat stretches.

Boxcar Rapids, another Class III, is 2.5 miles above Maupin, and it's the location where a commercial photography company takes everyone's photo and displays them in town for sale at the end of the day. More than a few people have gone swimming in Boxcar, but a quiet pool where rowers/paddlers, boats, and equipment can easily be reunited follows the rapids' big drop. **Maupin City Park,** just below the US 197 bridge that crosses the river, is a popular lunch spot.

Harpham Flat, 5 miles up from Maupin at river mile 57, is the usual launch point for the river's 12-mile day trip. In addition to a boat launch, Harpham Flat is a BLM campground. The day-trip section ends at **Sandy Beach** at river mile 45, the takeout 1 mile above Sherars Falls. Sandy Beach allows day use only. To reach Harpham Flat, drive the gravel BLM road south along the east bank of the river from Maupin. Sandy Beach is north along the same road, but the road is paved for 8 miles downstream from Maupin.

The day-trip section gives rafters the thrill of warming up with Boxcar and testing themselves on **Oak Springs Rapids** at river mile 47.5, the only Class IV rapids on the Lower Deschutes. Like Boxcar, Oak Springs has dumped more than a few boaters into the river.

Surf City, a kayak play spot .5 mile above Oak Springs, is one of several big splash areas as the river rushes toward the Sandy Beach takeout. Because of the number of rafts floating past on busy summer days, kayakers usually wait until evening to play in Surf City. The sheer volume of boaters, including a lot of inexperienced raft captains, tends to keep Oregon's hard-core rafters away from the Deschutes during summer. The Deschutes's day-use whitewater section from Harpham Flat to Sandy Beach is floated in just about any kind of craft—from inner tubes to rubber duckies and river boards. Fully half the use in the Maupin day-trip section is in **rented rafts** from what must be the country's largest stockpile of rental boats. The biggest rental companies are All-Star Rafting, (800) 909-7238; Deschutes U-Boat, (541) 395-2503; Deschutes River Adventures, (800) 723-8464; and River Trails, (541) 395-2545. All have offices in Maupin. Although the river has no quota on the number of people, river managers have been limiting use by reducing the number of rafts available for rent during busy weeks. Be sure to reserve in advance.

With more than 130 licensed **outfitters,** many of them small fishing guide services, the Lower Deschutes River is an easy place to hook up with a river trip. Many of the day-use boaters book through the big resorts in Central Oregon around Bend. Outfitters who run the Deschutes are listed under rafting in yellow pages telephone directories throughout the Northwest. For additional referrals, contact the BLM, (541) 416-6700, or the Greater Maupin Area Chamber of Commerce, (541) 395-2599.

Although **Sherars Falls,** the 12-foot drop at river mile 44, effectively cuts the Deschutes into two sections, the falls has been run, but only by experts who analyze the situation minutely. The falls must be considered unrunnable for the average boater. Access to the river at Sherars Falls is restricted by the Confederated Tribes, so most whitewater trips below the falls begin at the BLM launch at **Buckhollow** at river mile 42. From Hwy 216 on the east side of the river, turn north on the gravel road to reach riverside recreation areas downstream to Macks Canyon where the road ends at river mile 23. The river is relatively mellow for many miles below Buckhollow, so few day trippers run this section.

With camping accessible by road all the way to Macks Canyon, overnight float trips often continue past Macks Canyon before looking for campsites. This can be a long day, but the current is brisk and the distance is easy to make with an early start. This leaves the second day of a three-day trip to make another 15 miles or so before looking for camp. Practically all the big water on the river's lower 42 miles is packed into the final 6 miles. **Gordon Ridge, Colorado, and Rattlesnake Rapids** all pack Class III punch just before the takeout at **Deschutes River State Park.** While the state park campground is on the east bank at the river's mouth, the takeout at Heritage Landing is on the west bank, just above the confluence with the Columbia.

Warm Springs River

A good way to warm up for the big water of the Lower Deschutes River is to join a kayak trip with Kah-Nee-Ta Kayaks at the Warm Springs Indian Reservation. Tours of the **Warm Springs River** leave several times each day during summer in one- and two-person inflatable kayaks from the Kah-Nee-Ta Resort recreation center, (800) 554-4786. One guide leads the way and another brings up the rear on the 1.5-hour trip. Everyone participates in the paddling and gets used to being wet.

Whitehorse Rafting of Warm Springs, (541) 553-1604, offers an alternate approach to the Deschutes that avoids the slack water between Warm Springs and Trout Creek. Operated by tribal members, trips begin on the peppy Warm Spring River (when water levels allow) and continue all the way to the Deschutes, where Whitehorse Rapids awaits a few miles downriver.

Boating

Round Butte Dam, 10 miles west of Madras, impounds the waters of the Deschutes, Crooked, and Metolius Rivers to form one of Central Oregon's most popular recreation areas—a reservoir 6 square miles in size called **Lake Billy Chinook.** The lake is set in a deep canyon, with its 400-foot walls crowned with rimrock. This is one of the most popular places for waterskiing in Central Oregon, although fishermen's boats are more numerous. Commercial marinas are located on the Crooked River and Metolius arms, while Oregon State Parks operates three additional launch facilities. To reach the lake and its parks, drive west on any of several county roads along the first 20 miles of US 97 south of Madras. The access roads are signed and all eventually lead to the park entrance road, which drops steeply from the rim down to the water, its marinas, and parks. Boat speed limits of 10mph are enforced on Lake Billy Chinook above the road bridges that cross the Crooked and Deschutes Rivers arms of the lake.

Houseboats can be rented from Oregon State Parks by calling Reservations Northwest, (800) 452-5687. A deposit of $400 is required at the time of booking. The boats have sleeping facilities for 10 to 12, with prices ranging from $1,050 to $1,590 for a week. Ski boats, fishing boats, and personal watercraft can be rented from Cove Palisades Marina, (541) 546-3521, located on the Crooked River arm of the lake, or from other rental companies located in surrounding towns.

Formed by Pelton Dam just downstream from Round Butte Dam, **Lake Simtustus** is a smaller, quieter version of Lake Billy Chinook. A marina on the east shore at **Pelton Park,** (541) 475-0517, is operated under concession contract with Portland General Electric, the license holder for Pelton and Round Butte Dams. The 7-mile-long lake has a 10mph boat speed limit, except in the area just above the dam.

Fishing

The **Lower Deschutes River** is world-renowned among anglers for its native redside rainbow trout, its fall run of steelhead, and its spring and fall runs of chinook salmon. Due to the **Columbia River's** dwindling stock of salmon, the season and number of chinook that can be taken are determined annually by the Oregon Department of Fish and Wildlife. Check the state fishing synopsis for current regulations, or call the Oregon Department of Fish and Wildlife at The Dalles, (541) 296-4628, or at Bend, (541) 388-6363. (See Rafting/Kayaking, above, for routes to fishing access at Warm Springs, Mecca, Trout Creek, the 37 miles of Deschutes River Rd between the locked gate and Macks Canyon and to Heritage Landing at the mouth.)

On the Lower Descutes, no angling is allowed from a floating device that supports the angler. Boats are used to reach fishing holes, but the angler must step ashore before casting a line. Trout season is open all year, except for a January 1 to late April closure where the river passes Warm Springs Reservation land. Steelhead fishing is open all year on the river's lower 100 miles. With some exceptions, anglers are restricted to the eastern half of the river where it borders the reservation. Fishing from reservation land, where allowed, requires a tribal license that is available from stores in Warm Springs and from many fishing license outlets in north-central Oregon.

Redside trout are famous for their striking power and fighting ability. The native trout have made a strong comeback since stocking of hatchery fish was halted in the late 1970s and river management focused on improving habitat for the redside. Trout are common in the 8- to 15-inch range, but only trout from 10 to 13 inches may be kept. The daily limit is two trout, but most anglers release all fish unharmed. Best water for trout is between **Warm Springs** and **Harpham Flat,** while salmon and steelhead are best in the lower river from **Sherars Falls** to the **mouth.** Most anglers don chest-high neoprene waders and aggressively work the pools and riffles with an assortment of flies. The river's current is swift and can be dangerous. Steep drops are common along shore.

Matching the correct lure to the current **insect hatch** is the ticket to trout fishing success on the Deschutes. Caddis fly and stonefly hatches can bring big trout to the surface, but they may decide to strike at some unknown insect instead. The fun comes from figuring out what the trout are eating when you happen to be fishing. The salmonfly and golden stonefly hatch in May and June is the best time to fish for trout. Hatches later in the summer include caddis fly, mayfly, and grasshopper. Due to the variety of food the desert environment presents, anglers will need to bring their full bag of tricks to find out what works on a given day.

The most popular fishing water for bank anglers is along a 7-mile trail from **Mecca** downstream to **Trout Creek.** Both areas have small campgrounds and the trailhead is marked. Anglers use boats to reach favorite spots but, again, must pull ashore and step out of their boats before casting a line. Fishing around riverside camps accessible by boat is popular in the mornings and evenings. The stretch of river along **Maupin** is lightly fished during summer due to the crowds of whitewater rafters.

Steelhead, Oregon's oceangoing trout, are frequent in the 5- to 10-pound range. Bigger fish occasionally stop by for a short visit in the cool waters of the lower river as they head past the Deschutes in their journey up the **Columbia River.** The fall run begins entering the Deschutes in mid-July and increases throughout the lower river into September. Fishing can be good into December, including the section around Maupin when the rafters have departed at the end of summer. All wild steelhead (the ones that don't have their adipose fins clipped) must be released unharmed and should not be removed from the water. Bag limit for hatchery steelhead is 2 fish per day, 20 per year. Most steelhead are caught on large and bright spoons and spinners. The Oregon State Police game-regulations unit maintains a corps of cadets who work the Deschutes to enforce regulations during its prime fishing season.

Most fishing on the lower part of the river is accessed either by drift boats from above or by jet-boats from below. Jet-boats launch at **Heritage Landing,** a state park facility on the Deschutes's west bank at its confluence with the Columbia alongside I-84, 15 miles east of The Dalles. Boat operators must pass through some pretty big rapids in this section, so it's not a good place to practice skills. Jet-boats are not allowed during four-day periods on alternating summer weekends in order to give rafters a quiet camping opportunity. Jet-boats frequently prowl the river during fall to provide access for hunters. A limited number of jet-boat permits are available for upriver in the Maupin section outside the heavy summer rafting season. For information, contact the BLM, (541) 416-6700.

Fishing guides are readily available on the Deschutes. With 130 licensed **outfitters** to choose from, the trouble becomes finding the right one for you. The local shop is Deschutes Canyon Fly, (541) 395-2565, on Hwy 197 in Maupin. Fly-fishing shops from Portland to Bend work with outfitters who guide on the Deschutes. If you don't already know how to fly-fish, Trout Magic of Bend, (541) 383-3474, offers lessons taught by Raven Wing, one of the region's most enthusiastic female fly-fishers.

Deschutes reservoirs

Lacking fish ladders, **Lakes Simtustus and Billy Chinook** miss out on the steelhead run in the Lower Deschutes River, but each have plenty of fishing of their own. Kokanee, a landlocked sockeye salmon, thrive in the reservoirs. Rainbow, brown, and bull trout can also be caught, but all occur less frequently. The bull trout in the Metolius River arm of Lake Billy Chinook are legendary (up to 20 pounds), but the species is in decline and it's best to release them unharmed. Tribal permits, available from local tackle stores and tribal offices in Warm Springs, are required on the Metolius River arm of Lake Billy Chinook and on Lake Simtustus. Access is best from marinas on both lakes (see Boating, above).

Camping

Lower Deschutes River

It used to be that campers could pitch a tent just about anywhere on public land along the Lower Deschutes River, but that began to change in 1995 when river managers started designating campsites in the Maupin section. Additional camping restrictions are being enforced from Sherars Falls to Macks Canyon along the BLM's 37-mile Lower Deschutes River National Back Country Byway. For information on riverside camping, contact the Prineville office of the BLM, (541) 416-6700.

In an effort to restrict peak weekend use, during summer the BLM bumps the evening roadside camping fee from $5 to $10 on Fridays and Saturdays. The entire river is under a burning ban from June through October. Fires are allowed only in stoves or grills. Smokers can't even light up, except when they are in a boat on the water or inside a vehicle with the windows rolled up. The police are quick to enforce these regulations.

Campgrounds available by vehicle downstream from Warm Springs include **Mecca** and **Trout Creek,** plus numerous designated campgrounds between the locked gate and **Macks Canyon** along the 37-mile byway (see Rafting/Kayaking, above). Beginning at the locked gate and heading north downstream, campers can choose from Devil's Canyon, Long Bend, Harpham Flat, Wapinitia, Oasis, Blue Hole, Oak Springs, and White River above Sherars Falls. Below the falls, camping is allowed at Twin Springs, Oakbrook, Jones Canyon, Gert Canyon, Beavertail, Rattlesnake Canyon, and Macks Canyon. Facilities are limited to picnic tables, portable toilets, and garbage cans. All can be crowded on summer weekends. As a rule, it becomes less crowded far above or below Maupin.

Deschutes River State Park, where the Deschutes joins the Columbia, is open for camping year-round (see Columbia Basin chapter). **Maupin City Park Campground,** (541) 395-2252, on the east bank of the river in Maupin, handles a major share of tent and RV campers who spend the day playing in the whitewater section on either side of the park. Potable water is available only at Trout Creek, Maupin City Park, Macks Canyon, and Deschutes River State Park campgrounds.

Reservoirs

Cove Palisades State Park, (541) 546-3412, on Lake Billy Chinook is one of the most popular state park campgrounds east of the Cascades. Open year-round, the park has 91 electrical sites at **Crooked River Campground,** plus 94 tent sites and 87 trailer spaces with full hookups at the **Deschutes River Campground** (see Boating, above, for access). The park also rents cabins ($80 per night for up to five people; bring sleeping bags). The Crooked River camp is just below the rim near the park's entrance, while the Deschutes River camp is 5 miles farther into the park on the park's main road. The park has 1 site with full hookup facilities that is fully accessible for handicapped campers. Reservations can be made by calling Reservations Northwest, (800) 452-5687.

The park charges a $3 day-use fee year-round at all its developed sites, including the viewpoints located along the east rim of Lake Billy Chinook. The lake was named after an Indian who guided John Charles Fremont through the area in 1843. The palisades are the tall, columnlike rocks that are part of the basalt rimrock. The campground was built in 1964, along with Round Butte Dam, as part of the federal licensing of the project to the state. The license is up for renewal in 2001.

Deschutes National Forest maintains small campgrounds accessible by vehicles over long, dusty roads at **Perry South Campground** and **Monty Campground** on the Metolius River arm of Lake Billy Chinook (see Mount Jefferson and the Metolius River chapter). Monty in particular has been known as a weekend party spot and the Sisters Ranger District is working to change that. Campsites are closed to protect nesting bald eagles, except for a few spots at Perry South, each year until April 15. Consult the Deschutes National Forest map, available at ranger stations and sporting goods stores, for driving directions to the remote campgrounds.

Pelton Park Campground, (541) 475-0517, has 79 campsites on Lake Simtustus. The park is managed by a concessionaire for Portland General Electric, developer of Pelton and Round Butte Dams.

The Crooked River National Grassland, (541) 475-9272, maintains a small campground (24 sites) along **Haystack Reservoir** on the east side of US 97 south of Madras. The reservoir usually accommodates many additional campers, who park big rigs near the water in dispersed locations away from the campground. Popular activities include fishing, hiking, and birdwatching. To reach the campground, turn east 12 miles south of Madras from US 97 and follow signs to Haystack Reservoir.

Mount Hood National Forest

When the Deschutes canyon gets too hot, savvy campers head for the eastern foothills of the **Mount Hood National Forest** to pitch their tents and settle in their RVs beneath ponderosa pines. Favorite campgrounds in the Barlow Ranger District, (541) 467-2291, for tents and small RVs in Mount Hood's eastern foothills are **Rock Creek Reservoir Campground** (33 sites) and **Bonney Crossing Campground** (8 sites). Rock Creek Reservoir's 100 acres are stocked annually with rainbow trout. The campground is popular enough to be in the national reservations systems, (800) 280-2267. Bonney Crossing is conveniently located at the eastern trailhead for the Badger Creek National Recreation Trail. Rock Creek is 10 miles west of Tygh Valley and US 197 on Forest Rd 48. Bonney Crossing is 5 miles north of Rock Creek via Forest Rds 4810, 4811, and 2710.

Hiking

Deschutes River

The Deschutes River Canyon has a shortage of developed trails, but it has unlimited hiking opportunities. A popular game among rafting parties is the "bet you can't climb that butte and be back before dinner" routine. An unsuspecting neophyte to the river usually swallows the bait, soon remembers with dismay that it's still 90 degrees out, finally realizes that the butte is 2,000 feet high, and returns well after dark. Since this is a canyon where summertime fires are not allowed, there will be no warm glow of a fire guiding the hiker's return. Most reasonable hikes in the river canyon are on footpaths that follow riverbanks between fishing holes.

A few hikers walk 7 miles of the Deschutes River Trail between **Mecca** and **Trout Creek,** but most of the use is by fishermen and cyclists (see Rafting/Kayaking and Fishing, above). A lot of the fishermen on this trail are cyclists who hope they don't snap off the tip of their graphite fly rod as they pedal between the willow trees.

One of the most scenic hikes in the Lower Deschutes River country is along one of its tributaries, the White River in **Tygh Valley State Wayside.** The day-use picnic park is 3 miles west of the Deschutes River bridge at Sherars Falls on Hwy 216. The White River's 100-foot waterfall can be seen on a short walk to a viewing platform from the parking lot, but it warrants further exploration along paths that leave from the platform. Be careful when approaching the river from either above or below the falls—the paths are not maintained and a fall could be fatal. The path below the falls leads to a spectacular viewpoint inside the canyon, especially during May when water thunders over the walls from the snowmelt far away on the east slope of Mount Hood.

Despite its size of 7,000 acres, **Cove Palisades State Park,** comprising Lake Billy Chinook, Deschutes River Campground, and Crooked River Campground (see Boating and Camping, above), has only 8 miles of hiking trails. Until a 5-mile loop trail was built in 1997 to the Peninsula, most of the developed trails connected the two campgrounds to lakeside day-use areas. The new trail was built to mitigate the closure of a spectacular formation called **the Island,** a 3-mile-long plateau that juts into Lake Billy Chinook and is covered with native grasses. Access to the Island is restricted to research groups in order to protect the formation's unique ecosystem, one of the few spots in Central Oregon that hasn't been grazed by cattle. The **Peninsula Trail** (moderate; 5-mile loop) climbs south onto a plateau from Deschutes River Campground. The view from the top is nearly as spectacular as from the Island, but the vegetation includes more nonnative species.

Grasslands

Crooked River National Grassland, (541) 475-9272, administratively part of **Ochoco National Forest,** offers a couple of developed hiking opportunities, but it can be a joy for the off-trail hiker. The grassland's major developed trail is a route along the west slope of Gray Butte. The **Gray Butte Trail** (difficult; 14 miles round trip) begins off Forest Rd 57 at McCain Orchard and ends where the trail joins the high point of Burma Rd at the edge of Smith Rock State Park (see Crooked River chapter). The trail is also open to mountain bikes, but it's a steep climb. To locate the trailhead, drive US 26 southeast of Madras for 11.5 miles and turn west on Laurel Lane. Drive 2.1 miles to Scales Corral and turn south on Forest Rd 57. Drive south for 2.4 miles, ignoring two junctions that lead west, to a Y intersection. Take the east fork of the Y, drive .2 mile, and park at the old orchard. The 5,108-foot summit of Gray Butte is a one-hour, off-trail scramble to the south. The view extends from California's Mount Shasta to Washington's Mount Adams.

The grassland's **Rimrock Springs Wildlife Management Area** (easy; 1.5 miles of trail) is adjacent to US 26 about 10 miles southeast of Madras. Trails lead to two observation decks, one barrier-free with an asphalt surface leading to it, where year-round water attracts resident and migrating birds. Mammals such as mule deer, coyote, and even pronghorn antelope stop in for a morning or evening drink.

A couple of interesting off-trail jaunts on the grassland climb Juniper and Haystack Buttes, which straddle US 97 about 10 miles south of Madras. Both can be accessed by driving Monroe Lane. **Juniper Butte** (moderate; 3 miles round trip) is on the west side of the highway and has an outstanding view of Lake Billy Chinook. Drive .9 mile west of US 97 on Monroe Lane and park. Hop the fence that controls the area for cattle grazing and pick the easiest route to the summit. **Haystack Butte** (moderate; 3 miles round trip) is on the east side of US 97. Drive Monroe Lane for .5 mile east across US 97 to where it meets paved Forest Rd 60. Turn south and watch for the first dirt road that leads east through unfenced land. The dirt road ends after .5 mile and Haystack Butte lies immediately to the east. Part of its summit is private land, so don't cross the fence near the top.

The Nature Conservancy maintains a 378-acre preserve east of the Deschutes River near Shaniko called the **Lawrence Memorial Grassland.** An area of rolling hummocks of native grasses interspersed with outcrops of basalt, the preserve is a rare sample of natural vegetation thanks to the conservative grazing practices of previous owners. Recognized as a national natural landmark, the preserve is used for research and education. The public is invited to walk through, but camping, fires, dogs, and vehicles are not allowed. The preserve is located southeast of Shaniko and south of Ward Creek Canyon. The Portland chapter of The Nature Conservancy, (503) 228-9561, asks that visitors call in advance for directions and permission to visit.

Badger Creek

Most of the runoff that flows east of Mount Hood comes down the White River, but the Badger Creek drainage provides a significant addition to the Deschutes River on the eastern edge of Mount Hood National Forest. Badger Creek is the major feature of the 24,000-acre **Badger Creek Wilderness.** Average annual rainfall dwindles from 75 to 20 inches west to east across the 12-mile wide wilderness, so the east side of the wilderness is a spot where soggy Portlanders go to hike where they have a good chance of being warm and dry.

The 12-mile **Badger Creek National Recreation Trail** begins at Bonney Crossing Campground (see Camping, above) and heads west all the way across the wilderness area. The lower 6 miles are most popular, especially during spring before it gets too hot. A good spot for a backpacking camp is at Pine Creek, 6 miles up the trail near the place where the main trails leaves Badger Creek. The national recreation trail continues to **Badger Lake,** a 35-acre lake surrounded by wilderness boundaries. The lake was left out of the 1984 wilderness designation due to a four-wheel-drive road that is still used to reach a 15-unit campground along its shore. To reach Badger Lake, drive 7 miles west of Rock Creek Campground on Forest Rd 48 (see Camping, above), turn north, and drive 11 miles on a steadily deteriorating Forest Rd 4860. Passenger cars should be able to reach the lake, but expect a rough ride.

More trails fan out into the wilderness from **Flag Point Lookout.** Like Badger Lake, the summer fire watchtower is also surrounded by wilderness and was left outside of the wilderness boundary because there already was a road to the 5,657-foot summit when the wilderness was created. The view from the top takes in a largely unlogged valley, a rare sight indeed in Mount Hood National Forest. The lookout is reached over a maze of logging roads from Tygh Valley, so bring along a Mount Hood National Forest map.

Biking

With summer's typical high temperature near 100°, the canyon of the Lower Deschutes River is not a place where **cyclists** come from miles away to ride. But that doesn't mean no one brings their bikes when they visit the area. Rides along the road from car camps are popular during the cool hours of morning and evening. US 197 and other nearby paved roads in the **Tygh Valley** area can be enjoyable on a road bike, but remember that the road that climbs east out of **Maupin** isn't named "Bakeoven" for nothing.

Two **mountain-bike rides** in particular stand out, especially for neophytes. Both share the name of **Deschutes River Trail** and are differentiated by the segment of river they follow—a 20-mile former railroad grade on the east bank of the river that runs south from the confluence with the Columbia River to just below Macks Canyon, and a 7-mile singletrack that connects Mecca and Trout Creek near Warm Springs (see Rafting/Kayaking, above).

When the railroad was constructed up the Deschutes River Canyon, two companies competed with each other to complete a line on either side of the river. The winning line still operates today, but the losing line has been abandoned and has fallen into disrepair. An occasional game-enforcement vehicle drives the old railbed, but private vehicles are not allowed. This leaves the entire route to cyclists, hikers, and equestrians. Most cyclists begin from the trailhead at the entrance to **Deschutes River State Park,** on the east side of the Deschutes 15 miles east of The Dalles. To reach the park, take exit 97 from I-84 at Celilo and follow the frontage road east 3 miles. Some bikers make it all the way to Macks Canyon, 23 miles away, where they have a shuttle vehicle waiting. The trail is closed by a washout in Harris Canyon at 20 miles, but a few cyclists make it through by shouldering their bikes and walking across the worst sections.

River-running companies have found a way to package cycling with the best rapids of the lower river. Outfitters meet clients at Deschutes River State Park and everyone pedals 7 miles upstream to where rafts are waiting. The river trip includes a descent of Washout Rapids, which was created during a summer thunderstorm in 1995. Cost is less than $100, cheaper if you provide your own bike. Check at Maupin with Ewings'

Whitewater, (800) 538-7238, for its schedule of trips.

The Mecca–to–Trout Creek section of the Deschutes River Trail follows paths created over the years by fishermen hiking to their favorite fishing holes (see Rafting/Kayaking, above). Over the years the trail has become a fairly decent single-track ride. The route passes through private land in a couple of places. To maintain easement privileges, everyone should stay precisely on the trail's grid when they pass through private land.

Rock Collecting

If you've never dug a **Thunderegg,** the Lower Deschutes River country is a mighty fine place to begin. Just what is a Thunderegg? Well, it's Oregon's official state rock. Thundereggs are agate-filled nodules found in various locations throughout the western United States. Perhaps the best place to dig for Thundereggs is a commercial rock-digging ranch. Yes, such things do exist in Jefferson County. Perhaps the most famous of all is Richardson's Recreational Ranch, (541) 475-2680, 10 miles north of Madras on US 97. The ranch has a campground, an impressive rock shop, free use of shovels and buckets, and plenty of proven digging beds. Rock collectors pay by the pound for what they take away. Bulldozers regularly scrape the beds, so the digging isn't too tough.

Thundereggs were formed an estimated 60 million years ago as water containing silica quartz seeped through air pockets left in the lava flows. Over the course of, say, a million years, a pretty pattern of quartz was left behind. Of course, you'll need a diamond-studded rock saw to open them up and see what's inside. The ranch is also know for its **moss agate, jasper, jasp-agate, Oregon sunset,** and **rainbow agate.**

Wildlife

The Lower Deschutes River country offers several wildlife-viewing opportunities, including the state-managed White River Wildlife Area, (541) 544-2126, an interesting mix of ponderosa pines, forests of oaks, and sagebrush flats. **Black-tailed deer** and **Rocky Mountain elk** winter in large numbers in the area. **Wild turkeys** were introduced to Oregon in 1961 here and have maintained the state's largest population. To reach the preserve, head west from the town of Tygh Valley toward Wamic. Bear right on Dodson Rd and drive 2 miles to signs that designate the 41,000-acre management unit. Gravel roads wander through the area, but many are closed during critical habitat seasons. Bring binoculars and watch for signs of wildlife from your vehicle. As with much of the eastern slope of the Cascades, **rattlesnakes** also live here in the lowlands.

Eagle viewing is at its peak in February and March at Lake Billy

Chinook in Cove Palisades State Park. The best viewing locations are the viewpoints just off the paved road that follows the eastern canyon rim. To reach the road, turn north at the entrance to the park just before the park entrance road begins dropping into the canyon. During some years, when mortality is especially high for kokanee salmon, more than 100 wintering **bald eagles** have been counted. Even when food isn't especially plentiful, more than 40 eagles are around, enough to guarantee seeing one on any given day. Seven pairs of bald eagles nest in the area and about a dozen **golden eagles** also call the area home, so America's largest birds of prey can be spotted throughout the year.

A state-run **fish hatchery** at Oak Springs, (541) 395-2546, puts visitors on the quiet west side of the Deschutes River across from its biggest rapids. To reach the hatchery, go 3 miles north on US 197 from its junction with Hwy 216, turn east, and drive 3 miles down to the Deschutes. The hatchery has a picnic area, show pond, and good bird-watching during spring and fall migrations. Trout spawning occurs in the fall.

Cross-Country Skiing/Snowmobiling

Snow comes infrequently to the Lower Deschutes River country and doesn't hang around for long when it does. The exception is the eastern slopes of **Mount Hood National Forest.** It's possible to drive from the east up any of the forest roads into the snow zone and start **cross-country skiing** when the white stuff gets deep enough.

Two reasons skiers elect to visit this part of the forest are the **Five Mile Butte and the Flag Point Lookouts,** both part of the national forest cabin-rental program in the Pacific Northwest. For reservations and directions, call the Barlow Ranger District, (541) 467-2291.

Five Mile Butte Lookout is easier to reach on skis, usually 4 hours from the end of the plowed road during midwinter conditions. Flag Point lookout can take 8 hours to reach on skis, so a **snowmobile** may be a better way to approach it. Both lookouts are 14-by-14-foot cabins built atop towers. They command impressive views and can be rented from November 1 through May 30. The nightly rental fee of $25 goes to maintaining them in good shape for use by the Forest Service during summer fire-watch season. Visitors must bring their own bedding, food, and water.

Mount Hood National Forest's only other overnight rental facility is the **Valley View cabin** at the edge of the Badger Creek Wilderness. It can also be approached from the east via a 4- to 8-hour ski trip and is available through the Barlow Ranger District.

Attractions

For most highway cowboys, **Warm Springs** was just a small bend in the road at the bottom of a pine-studded rimrock canyon on US 26, until the spectacular **Museum at Warm Springs**, (541) 553-3331, opened in 1993. Built by the three Native American tribes (Wasco, Paiute, and Warm Springs) who live on the 600,000-acre reservation, the museum houses a permanent collection (the largest tribally owned collection in the United States) that includes prized heirlooms protected by families for generations, on view to the public for the first time. The Smithsonian Institution has named it the best of its kind in North America. Look here for stunning beadwork that would have been exchanged in a Wasco wedding, baskets, stories of early reservation days, music, and dance. The museum's art gallery has frequently changing shows of Indian art and artists, a small gift shop, and demonstrations during the summer. The architecture has won numerous awards.

Lodgings

Kah-Nee-Ta Resort and Village ☆☆ Owned by the Confederated Tribes of Warm Springs, this resort has a Native American cultural desk, and amenities include a day spa, water slide, 18-hole golf course, stables, and spring-fed swimming pool. (The Confederated Tribes asks that nontribal members use only the reservation lands that are designated for nontribal use, unless accompanied by a tribe member. You may purchase fishing licenses that access five designated areas.) Rooms in the main hotel, tepees, and an RV park are all lodging options. There's a casino and a restaurant/deli/general store. *11 miles north of Warm Springs on Hwy 3 (follow the signs from the Simnasho exit on Hwy 26 or turn onto Hwy 3 from the town of Warm Springs); PO Box K, Warm Springs, OR 97761; (541) 553-1112, (800) 554-4786, or (800) 831-0100; $$.*

More Information

Barlow Ranger District, Dufur: *(541) 467-2291.*
Bear Springs Ranger District, Maupin: *(541) 328-6211.*
Bureau of Indian Affairs, Warm Springs: *(541) 553-2411.*
Bureau of Land Management, Prineville: *(541) 416-6700.*
Confederated Tribes of Warm Springs, Warm Springs: *(541) 553-1161.*
Crooked River National Grasslands, Madras: *(541) 475-9272.*

Dalles Area Chamber of Commerce, The Dalles: *(541) 296-2231.*
Deschutes National Forest, Bend: *(541) 388-2715.*
Greater Maupin Area Chamber of Commerce, Maupin: *(541)*
   395-2599.
Madras–Jefferson County Chamber of Commerce, Madras: *(541)*
   475-2350.
Mount Hood National Forest, Sandy: *(503) 668-1700.*
Ochoco National Forest, Prineville: *(541) 416-6500.*
Sherman County Visitors Association, Moro: *(541) 565-3232.*
Sisters Ranger District, Sisters: *(541) 549-2111.*

Lower John Day River

From the John Day River's confluence with the Columbia River on the north, east to Highway 19, south to the Ochoco Mountains divide, and west to US Highway 97, including the Painted Hills and Clarno Units of the John Day Fossil Beds National Monument and the towns of Moro, Condon, Fossil, and Mitchell.

Once the location of one of the more bizarre episodes in Oregon history, the Lower John Day River country is back to being a quiet backwater.

During the early 1980s, thousands of red-clad visitors from around the world descended on the Big Muddy Fork of the Lower John Day River to participate in a commune led by the late Bhagwan Shree Rajneesh. The guru came from India and preached a brand of spiritualism that included free love and divestment of worldly goods—that is, turn all the goodies over to him. His followers dressed in various shades of red and were easy to spot as they passed through Portland and, especially, the tiny towns of Central Oregon.

Called Rajneespuram, the 64,229-acre commune split apart in 1985 when law enforcement agencies swooped in and arrested just about everyone tied to its leadership. Voter fraud, attempted murder, conspiracy, and dozens of alleged crimes sent the Bhagwan and his band back to where they came from—except for those who landed in federal penitentiaries.

Also quick to disappear were the 120 Rolls Royce automobiles collected by the Bhagwan, the private Lear jets that made regular landings at the commune's air strip, the paramilitary force that kept the curious at bay, and the commune's 3,000 residents. The Bhagwan himself almost got away, but federal marshals forced his jet to land at Charlotte, North Carolina, before it could reach the safety of an offshore island. He was tried and convicted on conspiracy charges, spent some time in prison, and was eventually deported to India. He attempted to resurrect his commune in South America but died before it was anything like his glory days on the Big Muddy.

The commune was, to say the least, totally out of character with the adjoining land, or anything else in Oregon, for that matter. Surrounded by sparsely populated ranch land, the Lower John Day River passes through deep canyons as it carves its way from the Blue Mountains of north-central Oregon to join the Columbia River near the town of Rufus.

Songbirds inhabit the shores of Oregon's longest undammed river, while the elusive chukar partridge makes its home in the canyon breaks. Mule deer commute by season from the farmlands at the canyon's rim to the river bottoms where they spend the winter. Bones of some of Oregon's most ancient residents are buried nearby in two units of John Day Fossil Beds National Monument. The eroded hills of the monument's Painted Hills Unit are among Oregon's most colorful landscapes, especially during May when their reddish hues contrast with the green grasses and wildflowers of spring.

It was red of a different color that brought an end to some of the commune's buildings when a range fire swept the area in 1996. A Montana businessman, who bought the ranch at auction, grazes cattle on the grounds of the former commune, which has been given back its pre-Rajneesh name, the Big Muddy Ranch. He once offered to donate the land to the state as a park, but the idea was rejected partly because of local opposition. The Young Life Ministries, a family and youth church group, has been trying to jump through all the hoops required to assume ownership of the ranch.

No matter what fate awaits the former Rancho Rajneesh, its future may never be as colorful as its past.

Getting There

Much of the Lower John Day River lies at the bottom of a deep, rugged canyon inaccessible by highways. The best access points are on Highway 206, where it crosses the river at J. S. Burres State Park, and Highway 218, which crosses the river at Clarno. Highway 19 parallels the middle part of the river between Service Creek on the west and Kimberly on the east. From Portland, drive Interstate 84 for 103 miles to the exit at Biggs. Head south 50 miles on Highway 206 to Condon, the largest community in the Lower John Day River country, which covers much of Wheeler, Sherman, and Morrow Counties, plus smaller parts of Jefferson and Wasco Counties. Another river crossing is at

Twickenham, a collection of ranches at the bottom of the canyon accessible by paved Twickenham Road, which connects Highways 19 and 207.

Adjoining Areas

NORTH: **Columbia Basin, Pendleton Grain Belt**

SOUTH: **Crooked River**

EAST: **Upper John Day River**

WEST: **Lower Deschutes River**

Rafting/Canoeing

One of the longest undammed rivers remaining in the Lower 48 states, the **John Day River** can be boated throughout much of its length in early season when the river carries sufficient water. The flow usually drops below rafting levels in June when runoff from snowmelt subsides and irrigators begin pumping water onto their alfalfa fields. The Portland phone number for the Oregon River Forecast Center is (503) 261-9246. Recreation on the river is managed by the Prineville office of the Bureau of Land Management (BLM), (541) 416-6700.

This chapter covers 185 miles of the main stem of the John Day River, from Kimberly to its confluence with the Columbia River just above the Columbia's John Day Dam near the community of Rufus. (See Upper John Day River chapter for additional information.) The major hazard to navigation is **Tumwater Falls,** a dangerous drop 9 miles before the river reaches the Columbia. To avoid the falls, most boaters take out at river mile 40 at **Cottonwood Bridge** at J. S. Burres State Park on Hwy 206.

The John Day River offers one of the longest continuous floating opportunities in Oregon—116 miles from **Service Creek to Cottonwood,** although the trip is most frequently done as separate three- or four-day outings by using Clarno as a midpoint takeout/launch. Even longer trips of another 100 miles or more are possible by beginning the trip on the upper reaches of the river's North Fork. Below Service Creek, the river flows with a gentle current and has only one rapid rating a Class III. Boaters on multiday trips usually skip the stretch of river from Kimberly to Service Creek because of the highway along the shore and the irrigated ranch land the river passes through.

Despite this shortage of whitewater, the John Day River has an ardent following of boaters who love the river for precisely what it provides—a gentle, laid-back trip with outstanding camping, fishing, birding, and opportunities for solitude. About the only time the river gets really busy is Memorial Day weekend. Boaters should be prepared to pack out human waste and use fire pans when the fire season allows burning.

Service Creek has two popular launch points—**Muleshoe Campground,** 2 miles east upriver from the Service Creek store on Hwy 19, and an open rocky beach near the bridge over **Service Creek,** .25 mile downriver from the store on Hwy 207. The small BLM campground at Muleshoe is favored by boaters who camp the night before, but boaters who arrive in the morning may find the campground's launch too crowded to prepare their equipment. The Service Creek launch site is large enough to accommodate everyone, but flooding in 1996 washed away most of the sand and left a big field of river cobble. The BLM maintains the site annually, but facilities vary depending on a particular year's runoff and funding for maintenance.

The 47-mile run from Service Creek to Clarno is rife with high desert scenery and irrigated ranch fields, especially around the community of **Twickenham.** Hillsides a thousand feet high line the banks of the river, green and covered with wildflowers during May when most boating occurs. The river has only three Class II rapids in the entire section. Although canoeists and neophyte kayakers may find their hearts pounding as they run the rapids, rafters will barely notice.

Big Muddy Creek empties into the John Day from the left about 7 miles above the **Clarno Bridge** where Hwy 218 crosses the river. Facilities at Clarno are minimal (rest room, parking) and the beach can get crowded during a Sunday afternoon takeout.

The 69 miles of river that begin at **Clarno** and end at **Cottonwood Bridge** are set in an even more spectacular canyon with fewer patches of irrigated land. The BLM has proposed creation of two wilderness areas comprising 33,700 acres in the lower canyons of the John Day. The only legal public access to the proposed wilderness areas is by floating the river. **Clarno Rapids,** 4.4 miles below the launch at Clarno, can vary in intensity from Class II to IV, depending on the river flow. Most rafters take the time to scout the rapids; many canoeists opt to portage them. The takeout at Cottonwood, located on the right just below the highway bridge, is another state park site (J. S. Burres) that is being managed by the BLM.

Commercial shuttles can be arranged either on-site or in advance by calling the Service Creek Trading Post, (541) 442-5433 (it's the only thing at Service Creek on Hwy 19). The BLM can provide additional names of shuttle drivers. **Guided raft trips** are hard to sell on the John Day because of the river's lack of big water, but a few people want to hire an outfitter so they can enjoy the experience while having a guide take care of the logistics. Commercial floats are offered by CJ Lodge of Maupin, (541) 395-2404.

Hiking

Boaters enjoy hiking in the John Day River's **canyons** during the evenings after setting up camp and during layover days on raft trips. Side canyons and the tops of buttes are popular destinations. Elevation in the lower canyon goes from 600 feet at the river to 3,500 feet on the rims, so reaching the wheatfields above the rims is a major objective indeed. One hiker made the mistake of hiking below the rim during summer and passed out due to heat prostration on the way out. The only thing that saved him is that a local search-and-rescue group was practicing nearby and able to reach him with a four-wheel-drive vehicle.

Two of **John Day Fossil Beds National Monument's** three units are located in the Lower John Day country and offer some pleasant hiking. The Clarno Unit is just east of Clarno Bridge where Hwy 218 crosses the river about 20 miles west of Fossil. The Painted Hills Unit, one of the most photographed sites east of Oregon's Cascade Mountains, is 3 miles west of Mitchell and 2 miles off US 26 on Bridge Creek Rd. (Sheep Rock, the monument's third unit and site of the national monument's visitors center, is located near Dayville; see Upper John Day River chapter.) Together the three units comprise 14,000 acres of heavily eroded volcanic deposits that preserve an outstanding fossil record of life in the area from between 45 million and 5 million years ago. The formations were deposited during the Cenozoic Era, also known as the Age of Mammals. Disturbing the ground or collecting specimens is strictly prohibited.

The **Clarno Unit** has two short nature trails located .25 mile west of the Clarno picnic site, plus a connecting trail between the trailhead and picnic area, all on the north side of Hwy 218. The **Trail of Fossils** (easy; .25-mile loop) brings hikers to evidence of ancient forests where plant fossils are preserved in rock along the trail. The trail leads to informational displays that interpret geologic history of the area. The magnificent surroundings of rock spires and high desert scenery make the lesson in geology interesting. A brochure available at the trailhead details 11 stops along the way, including a tree limb that extends 3 feet through a boulder. The **Clarno Arch Trail** (easy; .25-mile round trip) is steep but still easy enough for the entire family. The small arch is a famous erosional formation, but don't expect to be reminded of the arches in Utah's national parks. And while concentrating on views up above, don't forget that this is rattlesnake country down below.

Many visitors to the Clarno Unit are drawn to the area by geology programs offered at the Camp Hancock Field Station through the Oregon Museum of Science and Industry in Portland, (503) 797-4547. Clarno has a few rock spires solid enough to attract technical rock climbers, but few climbers venture this far away from Smith Rock State Park (see Crooked River chapter).

The beauty of the **Painted Hills Unit** is easily seen from automobile pullouts and along the 1-mile road that leads between the colorful buttes. Walking off-trail in the clay soil, which can be a muddy morass when wet, is discouraged because when the ground dries footprints harden and leave ugly scars. Painted Hills is especially scenic during spring when wildflowers are blooming. The best photo opportunities occur in the morning and evening hours. The **Carroll Rim Trail** (easy; 1.5 miles round trip) rewards hikers with a view of the Painted Hills and Sutton Mountain. The **Painted Cove Trail,** a short, 11-stop interpretive trail, has displays that explain how the hills got their color and how the colors change because of weather and time of day. Both trails are easy to find on the dead-end road that leads into the unit.

All units of the national monument allow day use only. Visitors who want to see fossils on display can visit the museum in the Sheep Rock visitors center near Dayville, (541) 987-2333 (see Upper John Day River chapter).

Sutton Mountain, a 4,000-foot-high plateau east of the Painted Hills Unit, is the center of a 40-square-mile tract of land administered by the BLM as a wilderness study area. Hikers who want a stern challenge can try to reach the summit by walking up Black Canyon south of Twickenham. From the bridge over the John Day River on Twickenham Rd, drive 3.1 miles south and park alongside the road at the wide mouth of Black Canyon, which reaches the road from the west. Follow the canyon uphill, passing a side canyon on the right after about 15 minutes and taking the right branch after about a half hour's walking. Continue up the main canyon to where it flattens out on top. Cross the plateau to the west for a view down into the Painted Hills. Sutton Mountain is an exciting off-trail desert hike, but the route is easy to follow and the terrain is never too steep. The only difficulty comes low down where the canyon passes through a short and slick rock section in the basalt. Scramble up and around the bare rock to reach better footing above.

The 5,400-acre **Bridge Creek Wilderness** of Ochoco National Forest, (541) 416-6500, lies in the John Day River drainage, 6 miles south of Mitchell. After the waters of the creek leave the wilderness, they pass through Mitchell, between the Painted Hills and Sutton Mountain, and join the John Day 7 miles below Twickenham near the BLM's Priest Hole Campground. This is *truly* a wilderness, where all human traces are absent, including trails.

An old, unmaintained trail follows Bridge Creek downstream from Pisgah Springs where Forest Rd 2630 passes the southern boundary of the wilderness. The old trail soon disappears, so orienteering skills and the Mount Pisgah topographical map are necessary throughout the wilderness. Elevations in the wilderness range from 5,200 feet along the creek to 6,607 feet at North Point.

Biking

The area's small population keeps the Lower John Day River country from developing a network of mountain-bike trails. Public land is mostly spread out in a checkerboard pattern of square-mile blocks, except where status as wilderness study areas precludes bike riding anyway. The one exception is the north slope of **Ochoco National Forest** in Wheeler County. Pressured mostly from the bike-riding community centered in Bend, the forest has been progressive about developing bike trails.

The best single-track riding opportunity here is **Rock Creek Trail** No. 823 (difficult; 7 miles one way). The trailhead is located on Forest Rd 38 at **Potter Meadow,** 2 miles west of the Black Canyon Wilderness. The ride is remote, challenging, and scenic. The lower 3 miles follow a historic mining ditch as the trail travels north to the forest boundary. Bikers who ride this deep into the middle of nowhere are probably going to want to make a weekend of it and go on another ride. Nearby is an old dirt road that leads to the top of 6,871-foot high **Spanish Peak** (difficult; 5.5 miles to the summit). The 1,500-foot climb is grueling, but the view is spectacular from one of Central Oregon's most isolated spots and the highest point in Wheeler County. Both locations are shown on the Ochoco National Forest map, and information sheets about them are available from the information center at 3160 NE Third St in Prineville, (541) 416-6500.

Road bike riding, again because of the small population, isn't particularly common in the Lower John Day region. The few paved highways usually drop from the canyon rims to the river below, then climb the other side. It's a lot of fun going down, but it's very difficult going up. The one exception is where paved Hwy 19 runs for 25 miles between Kimberly and Service Creek and stays relatively flat along the river, a stretch of the John Day River where boating occurs infrequently.

Camping

The Lower John Day River country is among the least populous areas of Oregon. With a little more than 5,000 residents spread over 3,500 square miles, developed facilities for camping are few and far between. Ochoco National Forest maintains four small campgrounds in Wheeler County—**Ochoco Divide, Wildwood, Barnhouse,** and **Cottonwood. Ochoco Divide Campground** is the only one that's busy, with its 28 sites alongside US 26, 12 miles west of Mitchell. Maximum RV length is 24 feet. The other campgrounds are tiny, with 2 to 6 sites, and are used by hikers and rockhounds. For information, contact Ochoco National Forest, (541) 416-6500.

Shelton State Wayside, (541) 575-2772, situated on the south side of Hwy 19 a dozen miles south of Fossil, is a popular overnight stop for John Day River rafters and travelers. The camp, located along Service Creek, is an easy 10-mile drive from the Service Creek launch site (see Rafting/Canoeing, above). Shelton has 36 primitive camping sites, with a maximum 50 feet for RVs, and a 2-mile hiking trail through the surrounding ponderosa pine forest. Reservations are not accepted, and the camp is open from April 15 to October 29. Many a camper from Western Oregon, unused to the elevation and clear skies of Eastern Oregon, has had a chilling tale to tell about trying to tough it out during an April night in a tent at Shelton on the way to a John Day River raft trip.

Wheeler County, the state's least populous with 1,550 residents, operates small campgrounds at **Bear Hollow Park** (18 sites 7 miles southeast of Fossil on Hwy 19) and at **Donnally** (6 sites 18 miles south of Fossil on Hwy 207). Contact the county parks department at (541) 763-2911.

RV camping in the Lower John Day River country is available at county fairgrounds at Moro (Sherman County), (541) 565-3510, and Condon (Gilliam County), (541) 384-2777.

Much of the camping here occurs on dispersed sites on public land that can be reached by gravel roads. The BLM's Lower and Upper John Day River public land maps, available at the BLM office in Prineville, show roads and land ownership.

Fishing

The **Lower John Day River** is famous far and wide for two types of fishing—steelhead and smallmouth bass. The steelhead are native. The adults usually arrive in late summer and smolts migrate out in spring. The smallmouth bass fishery has become nationally known since the fish were introduced to the river in 1971. Rafts and jet-boats prowl the river looking for the best fishing holes. Best bank access is a 12-mile stretch along the east bank below **Clarno Rapids,** on a bouncy BLM road that threads its way between public land and private ranches, and where highways cross the river at Cottonwood, Clarno, Twickenham, and Service Creek (see Rafting/Canoeing, above). The season is open all year above **Tumwater Falls** to **Kimberly.**

The best bass fishing corresponds with the river's best boating season. Bass are usually in the deep holes during spring, and it takes knowledgeable fishermen to lure them out. They move into riffles and weed beds in June when the water clears. Average size is less than 2 pounds, but 4-pounders are taken occasionally.

An experienced fishing outfitter is the Columbia River Guide Service of Hermiston, (800) 821-2119.

More Information

Big Summit Ranger District, Prineville: *(541) 416-6645.*
Bureau of Land Management, Prineville: *(541) 416-6700.*
National Park Service, Painted Hills Unit, Mitchell: *(541) 462-3961.*
North Central Oregon Tourism Promotion Committee, The Dalles: *(800) 255-3385.*
Ochoco National Forest, Prineville: *(541) 416-6500.*
Paulina Ranger District, Paulina: *(541) 416-6643.*
Sherman County Visitors Association, Moro: *(541) 565-3232.*

Mount Jefferson and the Metolius River

From Olallie Lake on the north, east to where the Metolius River joins the Deschutes River, south to US Highway 20 and west to Highway 22, including the Mount Jefferson Wilderness, the Metolius River Basin, the community of Camp Sherman, and Breitenbush Hot Springs.

So prominent from the east, Mount Jefferson is rarely seen from Oregon's western valleys.

Contrary to local folklore, the reason the 10,495-foot mountain is often hidden from the west is not because of the clouds of mosquitoes that swarm the lakes at the mountain's base. The steep, forested ridges that rise above the forks of the Santiam River block the western view of Mount Jefferson from all but a handful of places where fleeting glimpses can be had.

Now a little more about those mosquitoes.

How bad are Mount Jefferson's skeeters? Well, a climber who ventured north one summer to escape the heat of his Arizona home has never returned to Oregon after his close encounter with the buzzing swarms that inhabit the lakes of Jefferson Park. The Arizonan made it to the park, an idyllic setting at the northern base of the mountain, in the early afternoon of a late July day. He was promptly forced by the mosquitoes into the cramped quarters of a bivouac sack, where he lay through the heat of the afternoon, skipping dinner and delaying bathroom breaks for as long as possible until darkness settled after 9pm.

His miserable night passed quickly because his climbing party awoke at 4am to get the early start required to climb Oregon's second-highest mountain. The standard climbing route from Jefferson Park requires a laborious trudge across the Whitewater Glacier, the largest in Oregon, which blankets the mountain's eastern flank. The temptation is overpowering to call timeout halfway along the glacier, then head straight for the peak up its east-face routes.

As things turned out, the climbing route was even more memorable (and miserable) than the mosquitoes. Mount Jefferson is one of the most crumbly piles of rock in the Cascades and rockfall is a constant problem. Of 500 peaks climbed by the visitor from Arizona, Mount Jefferson, he said, was the most frightening because it was the one mountain where he could have died from a fall without warning. Needless to say, he took the longer, but less dangerous, route down.

Camp was no relief because the mosquitoes were awaiting his return. The buzzing bugs must have been educated in the laws of physics (what goes up must come down). After the exertion of the climb, there was no point in fighting them, so the Arizonan slapped on some repellent, packed up his bivy sack, hit the trail, ran to the highway, and headed home to Arizona.

It was a trip that ended well, but the Arizonan refuses to return to see what he missed. The crisp days of autumn, when the mosquitoes are a blur in memory, not in front of your face, are perhaps the most outstanding time to enjoy Mount Jefferson and its neighbors, the Metolius River and the Olallie Lake Scenic Area.

Getting There

The Mount Jefferson and Metolius River country is easiest to approach on Highway 22 as it heads east from Salem, joins US Highway 20 (US 20), and crosses Santiam Pass. Popular trailheads begin a few miles beyond Detroit, about 100 miles from Portland. Other approaches are via Highway 224 southeast of Estacada and Skyline Road (Mount Hood National Forest Road 42) as it branches off US 26 south of Government Camp. While Mount Jefferson is much more visible from the east than the west, access from the northeast is limited by the Warm Springs Indian Reservation, which requires a fishing permit for travel on reservation land away from main highways. Forest roads that head west from Camp Sherman offer access to the southeast part of the Mount Jefferson Wilderness.

Adjoining Areas

NORTH: **Mount Hood**

SOUTH: **Santiam Pass and Mount Washington**

EAST: **Bend and the Upper Deschutes River**

WEST: **Cascade Foothills**

inside out

Hiking/Backpacking

Pacific Crest Trail

The venerable trail of the Pacific Crest (PCT) travels 38 miles through the **Mount Jefferson Wilderness Area,** 10 miles through the **Olallie Lake Scenic Area,** and then another 22 miles through the **Warm Springs Indian Reservation** before emerging into the Mount Hood National Forest near Clackamas Lake. The rite of passage is guaranteed for non-tribal members through the reservation portion, but hikers must stay within 100 feet on either side of the trail and must camp in existing camp-sites. The camps tend to have fire rings and are near water, so there is no problem abiding with tribal regulations for long-distance hikers.

The PCT traverses the center of the Mount Jefferson wilderness and remains a long way from roads, except at the northern and southern entry points and as it passes Oregon's second-highest mountain on the west. Best access to the trail from the south is at **Santiam Pass,** where the PCT crosses US 20; from the west where trails to **Pamelia Lake** and **Woodpecker Ridge** reach the PCT; and from the north, where the PCT passes **Breitenbush Lake** (see Camping, below). The PCT is not more than a mile or two from roads in the Olallie Lake area and can be included as part of day hiking loops from the area's campgrounds. Due to tribal reg-ulations, the portion of the trail that passes the Warm Springs Reservation should be accessed from Olallie Meadow Campground (see Camping, below) on the south or from Clackamas Lake (see Mount Hood chapter) on the north.

Pamelia Lake trailhead, a convenient access to the PCT from the west side of the Mount Jefferson Wilderness, is located at the end of Forest Rd 2246, 3 miles east of Hwy 22. The turnoff is 12 miles east of Detroit. The **Pamelia Lake Trail** (moderate; 3 miles one way) passes Pamelia Lake before ending at the junction of the PCT. The trailhead is one of two in Oregon that limits day-use access (the other is the Obsidian Trail; see Santiam Pass and Mount Washington chapter). Backpackers are allowed to pass beyond Pamelia Lake without being counted in the day-hiker quota of 30. Everyone needs a self-issuing permit for all wilderness area trails in the Willamette and Deschutes National Forests. To guarantee availability of a Pamelia Lake day-hike permit, make a reservation up to one month in advance with the Detroit Ranger Station, (503) 854-3366.

The **Woodpecker Trail** (moderate; 2 miles one way) is at the end of Forest Rd 040 .5 mile north of the turnoff for Pamelia Lake on Hwy 22. The trail is lightly used and offers access to the Mount Jefferson Wilderness without going through the hassle of the Pamelia Lake quota system.

Mount Jefferson and Three Fingered Jack summit climbs

Mount Jefferson, the highest peak between Mount Shasta in California and Mount Hood, is perhaps the least climbed of the major Cascade volcanoes. Several factors combine to keep Mount Jefferson relatively undisturbed. Since it's not the highest peak in the range or the state, the mountain isn't number one on anyone's list. All but the very strongest climbers require an overnight backpack trip, and access is usually limited to July through September when snow finally melts off the approach trails. Added to that is the difficulty of the climbing routes. Even the tedious route from **Hunts Cove,** the least technical route on the mountain, ends below the 100-foot-high summit pinnacle that turns away more than a few would-be summiteers.

The most frequently used climbing route begins at the **Whitewater Trailhead,** 10 miles east of Detroit and 6 miles up Forest Rd 2243. Climbers usually pack 5 miles and 1,740 feet into **Jefferson Park,** where they make camp in one of the designated campsites according to wilderness regulations. Self-issuing permits are required to enter the wilderness and are available at the trailhead. Backcountry rangers aggressively enforce regulations, which at Jefferson Park also include no open fires. Pamphlets that detail wilderness regulations are available at trailheads.

The climb begins up a rock-choked gully from **Scout Lake,** the large lake on the south end of Jefferson Park. The obvious gully climbs the outlet stream of the **Whitewater Glacier.** From the base of the glacier, traverse the entire eastern flank of the mountain for more than 2 miles to the south ridge. The surface of the glacier is relatively smooth in midsummer and the few crevasses can easily be skirted. Climb north on the loose rock of the south ridge to the base of the pinnacle, which has two horns. The north horn is slightly higher, so traverse across the west face of the pinnacle to a small shoulder from where reasonably solid rock leads to the top. The traverse is exposed below and can have rockfall from above. Climbing parties frequently use ropes for protection, but it can be difficult to locate solid anchors. The return is by the same route for what easily can be a 12- to 14-hour day from camp.

Relatively easy approaches can be made from **Pamelia Lake** and **Hunts Cove** on the mountain's southwest and south sides, but both cross the mountain's seemingly endless southern talus slopes and are exceedingly tedious.

Three Fingered Jack is a 7,841-foot remnant plug of a volcano and the second-highest peak in the Mount Jefferson Wilderness. The least difficult route on the mountain requires crossing a downward-sloping ledge with an 800-foot drop and climbing the 30-foot summit pinnacle. Most parties protect themselves with ropes on both pitches. To reach this south-ridge route, follow the PCT south from Santiam Pass for 5 miles to where a climbing trail heads for the peak's west face. Follow the path up a large talus field to reach the ridge and the base of the sloping ledge. Three Fingered Jack is considered one of Oregon's most dangerous mountains to climb because of the crawl along the sloping ledge. For information on ·either peak, contact the Detroit Ranger Station, (541) 854-3366.

Mount Jefferson Wilderness

The 111,177-acre wilderness is long and skinny (25 miles long and 10 miles across at its widest point), and use is concentrated in Jefferson Park on the north side of the namesake mountain. The wilderness contains 190 miles of trail, 150 lakes, and the high points of Linn and Jefferson Counties (Mount Jefferson) and Marion County (a 9,000-foot shoulder of Mount Jefferson. The most popular entrances are the PCT from the south at Santiam Pass and from the north at Breitenbush Lake (see Pacific Crest Trail, above). The southern entrance is good for long-distance hiking, while the northern entrance makes a nice, 13-mile round-trip backpack to Jefferson Park.

In addition to Pamelia Lake, Woodpecker, and Whitewater (all described above), popular approaches from the west are Marion Lake and Breitenbush River Gorge. The **Marion Lake Trail** (easy; 3 miles to Marion Lake) begins at the end of Forest Rd 2255, which heads southeast of Hwy 22 at Marion Forks. The trail has backpacking opportunities south from the lake 3 miles into Eight Lakes Basin or east for 5 miles to the PCT. The **South Breitenbush Trail** (difficult; 6 miles to Jefferson Park) begins at 3,100 feet elevation on a big bend of Forest Rd 4685, 6 miles south of the entrance to Breitenbush Hot Springs. The Breitenbush Trail also has a lower section along Forest Rd 4685 where it travels for 2.5 miles along Breitenbush Gorge at 2,600 feet elevation.

Eastern approaches from the Camp Sherman side are via Jack Lake, Cabot Lake, and Jefferson Lake. Of the three, the **Jack Lake Trail** (easy; 6.5-mile loop to Canyon Creek Meadows) is farthest south. The trail begins at Jack Lake at the end of Forest Rd 1234 and ends at a spectacular view of the northeast face of Three Fingered Jack. The **Cabot Lake Trail** (difficult; 6 miles to the PCT) begins at the end of Forest Rd 1230 and passes tiny Cabot Lake near the halfway point. The **Jefferson Lake Trail** (difficult; 10 miles one way to the PCT) begins at the end of Forest Rd 1292 and skirts a large lava flow. Another trail begins at the same trailhead and traverses Sugar Pine Ridge before reaching the PCT 10.5 miles from the road.

Other popular hikes are the 2-mile climb from Pamelia Lake to the 5,779-foot summit of **Grizzly Peak** (difficult; 10 miles round trip from Pamelia Lake trailhead); the 6,229-foot summit of **Maxwell Butte** on the Maxwell Butte Trail (difficult; 9.6 miles round trip), which begins at the end of Forest Rd 080 2 miles north of the Santiam Junction on Hwy 22; and the backpacking tour of **Eight Lakes Basin** (moderate, 14 miles round trip), which begins at the Marion Lake trailhead.

Camp Sherman

One of the most surprising hikes in all of Oregon is the stroll down the short paved path to the headwaters of the **Metolius River** near Camp Sherman on Forest Rd 14. The river bubbles up out of the ground from the base of Black Butte and is all at once a full-blown river. The land at the headwaters is privately owned, so stay on the paved path to guarantee future access. Mount Jefferson can be seen over the river to the north. For longer hikes along the Metolius, drive downstream (north) to **Wizard Falls Fish Hatchery.** Hike downstream, cross the river at Lower Bridge, then head back upstream for an easy 6.5-mile loop, or follow the west bank trail upstream for 2.5 miles from the hatchery to the beautiful springs just downstream from Lower Canyon Creek Campground.

Other hikes not to miss near Camp Sherman are the climb to the summit of 6,440-foot **Black Butte** (difficult, 4 miles round trip and a gain of 1,640 feet) and **Canyon Creek Meadows** at Jack Lake (see Mount Jefferson Wilderness, above). Save the Canyon Creek Meadows hike for late July when the wildflowers are at their peak. To reach the Black Butte trailhead, drive north 4 miles on Forest Rd 11 from Indian Ford Campground, then turn west and drive Forest Rd 1110 for 4 miles to the start of the hike. Don't be surprised if you see one of the local paragliders launching from the summit near the restored fire lookout tower.

Olallie Lake Scenic Area

One of the classic views along the PCT is reached by hiking 3.5 miles south of Breitenbush Lake, located on Forest Rd 4220 at the south end of the Olallie Lake Scenic Area, to the summit of **Park Ridge.** From the ridge, the entire north side of Mount Jefferson reveals itself. The route is also a popular 6.5-mile one-way backpack trip into the lakes of Jefferson Park. It's best to approach Breitenbush Lake from Olallie Lake on the north because the portion of Forest Rd 4220 that connects Breitenbush Lake to Forest Rd 46 is 6 miles of bump and grind.

A 3.8-mile trail from Forest Rd 42, 2 miles north of Olallie Lake, leads to the summit of 7,215-foot-high **Olallie Butte,** the highest peak between Mount Hood and Mount Jefferson. Olallie Butte is on land owned by the Confederated Tribes of the Warm Springs Reservation, but hiking is allowed as long as hikers stay on the trail. Camping is not allowed on the summit. Look for the trailhead where a power line crosses Forest Rd 42 at the northwest foot of the butte. There is also a variety of possible loops from Forest Rd 42 to the lakes on the west side of the scenic area. Check with the Clackamas River Ranger District, (503) 630-4256, in Estacada for a free map of the Olallie Lake Scenic Area.

Camping

Metolius River

It's hard to imagine a more perfect spot for camping than along the Metolius River during summer. Long sunny days beneath the magnificent old ponderosa pines on the banks of one of the cleanest and coldest rivers in the state—it doesn't get any better than this. The mosquitoes that plague the high country are hardly noticeable here on the drier east side of the Cascades.

An 86,000-acre conservation area, where various sections are managed for wildlife, scenic views, and natural heritage, protects the Metolius River Basin. The river is well decorated with campgrounds in the 13 miles from its source to where the riverside road turns into a rough dirt track. From south to north, along **Forest Road 14** as it passes Camp Sherman, camps close to the river are Riverside, Camp Sherman, Allingham, Smiling River, Pine Rest, Gorge, Lower Canyon Creek, Allen Springs, Pioneer Ford, Lower Bridge, and Candle Creek Campgrounds.

Indian Ford Campground is located adjacent to US 20, 5 miles northwest of Sisters, and **Jack Creek, Jack Lake,** and **Round Lake Campgrounds** are located on tributary streams on the west edge of the basin. All camps are small, with Smiling River's 38 sites the largest, and all but the smallest few charge an overnight fee.

Monty and **Perry South Campgrounds** are located on the Metolius River arm of Lake Billy Chinook on County Rd 64, a tortuous drive over rough gravel roads from any direction. Both have seasonal closures during spring to protect bald eagle nesting habitat. The eagles are usually finished raising their young by June, allowing the Forest Service to open the camps when they are most needed. Access to the water makes the drive worthwhile. Refer to the Deschutes National Forest map for directions. For information on all campgrounds in the Metolius River Basin, contact the Sisters Ranger District, (541) 549-2111.

RV camping is available at Camp Sherman at Black Butte RV Park, (541) 595-6514, and Cold Springs RV Park, (541) 595-6271.

Highway 22

Most campers heading east on Hwy 22 from Salem wind up pitching a tent along Detroit Lake (see Cascade Foothills chapter) before they enter the Mount Jefferson Wilderness, but if they continue driving east they can pick from 68 campsites at **Whispering Falls, Riverside,** and **Marion Forks Campgrounds.** Each is situated on the North Santiam River and are signed along the highway.

Heading east of Detroit on Forest Rd 46, along the Forest Service's **Clackamas-Breitenbush Scenic Byway,** campers can stop at **Humbug, Cleator Bend,** and **Breitenbush Campgrounds** as they head up to the Olallie Lake Scenic Area. Together they have 60 sites along the Breitenbush River. Breitenbush has the best barrier-free facilities in the area. All campgrounds on the west side of Mount Jefferson are managed by the Detroit Ranger Station, (541) 854-3366.

Olallie Lake Scenic Area

Created by Congress in 1969, the scenic area shrunk to its present size of 10,798 acres in 1972 when Congress settled a longtime land dispute with the Confederated Tribes of the Warms Springs Reservation. The scenic area is located on the crest of the Cascades in the southernmost portion of the Mount Hood National Forest. The area is well endowed with lakes, including many reachable only by trail. The largest are **Olallie and Monon Lakes,** both of which are on the main access road through the area (Forest Rd 42, also called Skyline Rd).

Seven campgrounds have 104 total sites in the scenic area, which is located 70 miles southeast of Estacada, 35 miles northeast of Detroit, and 45 miles south of Government Camp via Forest Rds 46 and 42. The largest is **Peninsula Campground,** with 35 sites on Olallie Lake. Elevation is 4,900 feet, so the camping season usually runs from June into October. The scenic area is managed by the Clackamas River Ranger District, (503) 630-4256.

Olallie Lake Resort, (503) 645-4045, rents cabins, rowboats, and paddle boats, and has a general store. The resort also manages **Paul Dennis Campground** for the Forest Service, the only camp in the area that takes reservations and has running water at campsites. **Breitenbush Lake Campground** sits on a 6-acre lake at the south edge of the scenic area and is within a .5-mile walk on the PCT to the Mount Jefferson Wilderness.

Fishing

The **Metolius River,** nearly all of it federally protected as a Wild and Scenic River, is one of the best trout fly-fishing streams in Oregon. The river has a variety of regulations along its length, but much of it is restricted to fly-fishing with barbless hooks and all fish must be released.

Most fishing is along the bank from the many campgrounds that dot the river between Camp Sherman and Lower Bridge. The best chance for success comes in late spring and early summer when fishermen have the best luck matching the fly hatch. Insect hatches occur throughout the year and vary widely throughout the river. For advice on the best flies to use, check with the Camp Sherman store, (541) 595-6711, or the Fly Fisher's Place in Sisters, (541) 549-3474. John Judy Fly Fishing, (541) 595-2073, is the local **guide service** on the Metolius.

The Metolius River also has a run of spawning kokanee each fall from the waters of **Lake Billy Chinook.** The red-sided fish are easy to spot when they are in the river.

Fishermen are welcome to use designated areas of the **Warm Springs Indian Reservation.** A fishing license must be purchased from GI Joe's stores in Oregon, from other stores that sell fishing licenses in Portland, Salem, Bend, and Redmond, or from tribal offices or vendors in the town of Warm Springs. The fishing license allows nontribal members access to areas that would otherwise be off-limits. Areas that allow fishing for nontribal members are the **high lakes** near Mount Jefferson (Long, Dark, Island, Trout, Boulder, and Harvey Lakes), the **Metolius River arm** of Lake Billy Chinook, **Lake Simtustus,** the **Warm Springs River** near Kah-Nee-Ta, and the **Dry Creek** section of the Deschutes River. Permits cost $15 for the season, or $4 for the day, and come with a complete set of regulations.

Many lakes in the Mount Jefferson Wilderness have good fishing for rainbow, brook, and cutthroat trout. Bank angling is possible at most, but a rubber boat or float tube improves opportunities for success. **Marion Lake** (see Hiking/Backpacking, above) is the largest at 350 acres and has an elevation of 4,109 feet.

Lakes in the Olallie Lake Scenic Area are good producers of rainbow, brook, and cutthroat trout, although the cutthroat tend to be small because their abundance doesn't allow them to put on size. Lakes downstream from Olallie require a tribal fishing permit. **Breitenbush Lake** (see Camping, above), a good producer of brook and rainbow trout, is located on tribal land but does not require a tribal fishing permit. Tribal regulations must be obeyed when on tribal land that allows access for nontribal members.

Rafting/Kayaking

An extremely beautiful river to float, the **Metolius River** receives only light use by boaters because of a particularly brutal shuttle and the fact that owners of the river's north bank consider any nontribal use to be trespassing. The Confederated Tribes of the Warm Springs Reservation controls the river's left bank from Jefferson Creek downstream to where the river joins Lake Billy Chinook behind Round Butte Dam. The Tribal Council voted to close the river to boaters in 1993 after the drowning of a kayaker.

The Deschutes National Forest, which manages the river's right (south) bank, considers the river to be open for boating. The impasse continued through the writing of a river management plan and shows no signs of being resolved. While the Forest Service considers the river to be open, it purposely does little to improve access or encourage use. Boaters who choose to run the river should not touch the river's left bank and should not remove any woody debris for the purpose of improving navigation. They should also be aware that tribal police could cite them for trespassing and confiscate their equipment and the tribal council could impose a $500 fine. The 17-mile trip begins at **Lower Bridge Campground,** 7 miles downstream from Camp Sherman, and ends at **Monty Campground** on Lake Billy Chinook. Because of the numerous springs that feed it, the river runs fast, clear, and very cold throughout the year. The river is rated Class III, but boaters unfamiliar with the river can encounter unexpected trouble because of fallen trees and lively rapids. The cold water makes it necessary to wear protective clothing even during summer's heat.

Boaters who want to avoid the trespass issue can run the upper 13 miles of the river, but this section passes frequent resorts and roads and has little interesting whitewater. It also is lined with private land, and several low bridges may force rafters to portage. For current status and information, contact the Sisters Ranger District, (541) 549-2111.

Biking

Most of the trails here are off-limits to cycling because they are in a wilderness area, so bikers pretty much stick to lightly used dirt roads. The Sisters Ranger District encourages riding in three areas—**Green Ridge,** just east of Camp Sherman; **Castle Rocks,** south of where the Metolius River bends from north to east; and **Black Butte,** a loop ride between Indian Ford and Riverside Campgrounds on the Sisters Tie Trail. All riding is rated more difficult because of distance traveled and elevation gained. Use the Deschutes National Forest map for designing routes, or stop at the Sisters Rangers District, (541) 549-2111, on Hwy 20 at the west edge of town to pick up detailed route information. (See Bend and the Upper Deschutes River chapter for more mountain-bike rides in Central Oregon.)

Cross-Country Skiing

With much of the area tied up in a designated wilderness, the Mount Jefferson and Metolius River country has limited winter recreation opportunities unless a backcountry skier really wants to work for it. The only sno-parks are **Maxwell Butte** and **Big Springs,** located across from each other on Hwy 22 about 2 miles north of Santiam Junction (see Hiking/Backpacking, above). Big Springs has 10 miles of marked trails on the west side of the high-way, and Maxwell Butte has more than 20 miles of trails on the east side. Skiers who want the easier trails use Big Springs, while those with interme-diate and advanced skills stage out of Maxwell Butte. **Snowmobilers** begin trips at Big Springs and head west, but most of their activity is centered at the Ray Benson Sno-Park (see Santiam Pass and Mount Washington chapter).

A unique opportunity in Oregon for skiers is to stay overnight in the **Mountain View Hut,** located 3 miles off the highway from the Maxwell Butte Sno-Park. The hut sleeps 20, has a wood stove for heat, and is used on a first-come basis. Snowmobilers have a similar opportunity at the McCoy Hut, which is located 10 miles west of Detroit. Both huts are maintained by the Detroit Ranger Station, (503) 854-3366, and can be used for free.

While the Camp Sherman area is a beautiful place to ski, snow con-ditions are unreliable due to its elevation of 3,000 feet. When the roads are covered by snow, as they usually are a few times each winter, touring among the orange-barked ponderosa pines is as good as it gets in Oregon.

Wildlife

The **Metolius Fish Overlook** is one of the most popular wildlife-viewing stations in Oregon. Located in the center of Camp Sherman, the pine-shaded viewing platform overlooks the spring-fed Metolius River. Big **rainbow trout** live year-round in the stretch of river near the highway bridge and can be seen in the deep pool beneath the platform. The fish usually face upstream, waiting to pounce on any tasty morsel that floats their way. Feeding of any wildlife is usually frowned on by biologists, but that doesn't stop tourists from walking over to the Camp Sherman store, buying some snack that might appeal to a trout, and tossing it into the river. If the fish are interested, they will streak from the depths of the river and ripple the surface as they gulp down the food.

The Wizard Falls Fish Hatchery, an Oregon Department of Fish and Wildlife operation, is 4 miles downstream from Camp Sherman. The hatchery's parklike setting is one of the most beautiful for any hatchery in Oregon. Display ponds, interpretive signs, and a fish-viewing platform help visitors enjoy the area. **Canada geese** usually nest nearby and the young goslings can be seen in May and June.

Indian Ford Campground, located 5 miles northwest of Sisters, is a popular spot for birding. Look for **white-headed woodpeckers** in the ponderosa pines and **pygmy owls** along Indian Ford Creek.

outside in

Lodgings

House on the Metolius ☆☆ This private fly-fishing resort, set on 200 acres, has exclusive access to a half mile of the Metolius River. Lodgings are seven fully-equipped cabins. Usually open all year, it's hard to get into and reservations are necessary. *Forest Rd 1420 (2.5 miles north of Camp Sherman), Camp Sherman; PO Box 100, Camp Sherman, OR 97730; (541) 595-6620; $$$.*

Metolius River Resort ☆☆ These 11 lodgettes on the west bank of the Metolius are elegant cabins with decks and fireplaces. All have river views, master bedrooms, and furnished kitchens. Don't want to cook? Raves for nearby Kokanee Cafe (open seasonally), (541) 595-6420. *5 Suttle Sherman Rd (5 miles north of US 20), Camp Sherman; HCR Box 1210, Camp Sherman, OR 97730; (541) 595-6281 or (800) 81-TROUT; $$$.*

More Information

Clackamas River Ranger District, Estacada: *(503) 630-4256.*
Confederated Tribes of the Warm Springs Reservation, Warm Springs: *(541) 553-1161.*
Deschutes National Forest, Bend: *(541) 388-2715.*
Detroit Ranger District, Mill City: *(503) 854-3366.*
Metolius Recreation Association, Camp Sherman: *(541) 595-6117.*
Mount Hood National Forest, Sandy: *(503) 668-1700.*
Sisters Ranger District, Sisters: *(541) 549-2111.*
Willamette National Forest, Eugene: *(541) 465-6521.*

Crooked River

From the crest of Ochoco National Forest on the north, east to the headwaters of the Crooked River on the Crook-Grant county line, south to US Highway 20, and west to US Highway 97 at Terrebonne, including Smith Rock State Park and the city of Prineville.

I Lost My Lunch at the Peepshow when Crankenstein Hit Bunny Face with a Double-edged Sword.

Is there anyone who doesn't love the names rock climbers give their routes? Smith Rock State Park, the recreational focal point of the Crooked River country, has hundreds of interesting names bestowed on its numerous crags, chimneys, and faces. Some of the names can even be spoken in polite company.

Smith Rock State Park is in the Ochoco Mountains, the western outlier of Oregon's Blue Mountains range, a vast area of mountains that extend 200 miles in width to Hells Canyon and the Idaho border. Geologic forces graced the Smith Rock area with one of the few massive formations of solid rock in the state. A volcanic rock called "welded tuff" rises 700 feet above the curving Crooked River in the 641-acre state park.

Climbing began at Smith Rock State Park in the 1940s, and in 1960 the first ascent of Monkey Face was made. The park remained popular with local climbers, as well as with escapees from the wet Willamette Valley, into the early 1980s when things began to change rapidly. By then, all the major climbs had been accomplished and everything that remained seemed impossible. That's when Alan Watts arrived on the scene and began exploring new routes with some of his friends from Bend.

Because the tops of most crags are easily accessible by hiking,

Watts rappelled from the top, removed loose rock, and placed bolts on his way down. Then he climbed the routes and a new age was born that would make the park one of the world's most popular rock climbing areas. With bolts already in place, climbers could clip in for protection as they climbed and didn't need to worry as much about life-threatening falls. They could work a route by pushing themselves to the limit, falling, then getting back on and practicing until they got it right. The climbing standards shot up from 5.11d at the end of the 1970s to 5.14a at the beginning of the 1990s. It was like knocking off 30 seconds for the world record in the mile.

As Smith Rock's reputation spread, climbers from around the world made it a point to visit and pushed the climbing standards even further. Several of the country's hottest young climbers moved to Bend to climb at Smith Rock and work at local manufacturing companies that produce the country's best climbing accessories for indoor climbing walls.

In short, Smith Rock has become a world mecca for climbers, but it still caters to Northwesterners who climb far below a world-class level. During spring and fall weekends, when the season for climbing at Smith Rock is perfect, the parking lot overflows with cars. Climbers love the place for its beauty, its challenging climbs, and its convenience. Most climbs are less than a half-hour walk from the parking lot on the park's extensive trail system. A fire swept through the park in 1996 and it will take some time before everything is beautiful again, but the climbing walls were unaffected and the trail system was quickly repaired.

For travelers coming from Western Oregon, Smith Rock is just the beginning of the Crooked River country. The river and its tributaries drain much of 2,991-square-mile Crook County, famous for its uncrowded camping and its colorful scenery. Prineville, the county seat, is the gateway to water recreation on Prineville Reservoir and Crook County's world-famous rockhounding areas.

US Highway 97 acts as a dividing line in Central Oregon. Recreation areas west of the highway along the Upper Deschutes River can be filled to overflowing, while those east of the highway along the Crooked River can be lonely. Smith Rock State Park is the major exception. It must have been one of those beautiful spring days, when Smith Rock's parking lots overflowed with climbers' vehicles, that one of the climbing routes was named "If I Ran the Circus."

Getting There

Prineville, the seat of sprawling Crook County, is 146 miles southeast of Portland via US Highway 26 (US 26). Smith Rock State Park, the recreation hub of the Crooked River country, is 3 miles east of US 97 at Terrebonne and 10 miles north of Redmond. Three highways (Forest Road 27 on the north, US 26 in the middle, and Highway 380) head east out of Prineville for access to Ochoco National Forest and Bureau of Land Management (BLM) lands along the Crooked River.

Adjoining Areas

NORTH: **Lower Deschutes River, Lower John Day River**

SOUTH/WEST: **Bend and the Upper Deschutes River**

EAST: **Upper John Day River, Harney County**

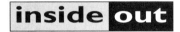

Climbing

Smith Rock State Park's unusual collection of colorful rock formations can be seen far and wide by travelers in Central Oregon as they drive US 97 and other highways between Madras, Prineville, Bend, and Sisters. To find the park, turn east from US 97 at Terrebonne and follow signs for 3 miles on paved county roads.

The view that takes most people's breath away is when they pull into the park's main parking area ($3 day-use fee required), walk 200 feet, and stare across the Crooked River straight at 700-foot-high **Picnic Lunch Wall.** Most visitors swallow hard and think, "They climb *that!*" Well, actually, few climbers bother with doing the big stuff. That's not what climbing at Smith Rock is all about. Most climbs are a single pitch (a 150-foot length of rope), where climbers accomplish unbelievably difficult tasks to achieve their goal of reaching the top of a pitch, not necessarily the top of a cliff.

When you hike down to the river from the parking lot, the footbridge across the river leads directly to Picnic Lunch Wall. From the footbridge (the only bridge over the Crooked River in the park), major climbing areas are located both downstream to the left and upstream to the right.

Besides the main climbing areas, the park has a wealth of bouldering opportunities and short routes through the rimrock that lines the river just upstream from the major rock formations. The park has routes for climbers of all abilities, although in recent years the emphasis has been on establishing super-hard routes. The bible for climbing routes in the park is *Climber's Guide to Smith Rock* by Alan Watts. The book was published in 1992 but remains an effective guide to most of the climbs in the park and is available wherever outdoor books are sold in Oregon or at the climbing shops near the park.

The park's most famous routes are **To Bolt or Not to Be,** the first climb rated 5.14a ever accomplished in America, and **Just Do It,** the park's most difficult climb, rated at 5.14c. To Bolt or Not to Be is in the Dihedrals section and Just Do It is on Monkey Face. Both first ascents were prepped by Watts and completed by Frenchman Jean Baptiste Tribout.

Monkey Face is an exception to the rule that Smith Rock climbers don't care about reaching the top, only about the moves they make along the way. Monkey Face is a 350-foot overhanging spire that, from a southern view, resembles the face of a monkey. Even though most of the difficult climbing comes before climbers reach the monkey's mouth, most continue on and up over the nose, eyes, and forehead so they can tell their friends they stood on the monkey's head. This is one summit at Smith Rock that really matters.

Climbers who run short of supplies or need information can stop at Juniper Junction's Rock Hard store, (541) 548-4786, the climbing shop at the entrance to the park that may be even more famous for its huckleberry ice cream. Redpoint Climbers Supply, (541) 923-6207, one of Central Oregon's best-equipped climbing stores, is located in Terrebonne where the road to Smith Rock heads east from US 97. First Ascent Climbing School and Guide Service, (541) 548-5137, and Vertical Ventures, (541) 389-7937, are **guide services** that operate in the park. Timberline Mountain Guides of Government Camp, (800) 464-7704, runs most of its rock climbing programs out of Smith Rock. The park manager at Smith Rock State Park can be reached by calling (541) 548-7501.

Hiking

Smith Rock State Park

The park's 7-mile trail system is shared by hikers, climbers, bird-watchers, cyclists, and equestrians, so unless the weather is bad (or it's too hot) this is no place to look for solitude. Heavy use has forced park management to build an expensive trail system, with boardwalks and staircases in sensitive areas. The trail system is not just for looks. The park staff expects hikers to use it and stay on it. Erosion quickly follows any off-trail scrambling. Smith Rock is not a place to explore off-trail, except where the rock is solid and the impact of a footprint is minimal.

Most hikers begin by walking down from the parking lot (see Climbing, above) to the river and crossing the footbridge. The trail to the right goes up the Crooked River Gorge and joins Burma Rd. It continues to the high point of Burma Rd, 2 miles from the parking lot, to the southern end of the **Gray Butte Trail** (difficult; 7 miles one way). The north end of the trail is on Forest Rd 57 in the Crooked River National Grassland (see Lower Deschutes River chapter).

The most popular hike at Smith Rock is to the viewpoint for **Monkey**

Face (easy; 2.8 miles one way). Turn left after crossing the bridge over the Crooked River, continue past the highest formation in the park (the Smith Rock Group, 3,230 feet high), round a promontory, turn north, and begin watching for Monkey Face. Just north of the base of Monkey Face, the **Misery Ridge Trail** (difficult; 2 miles one way) climbs over the top of the center of the park and drops down the east side where it meets the bridge across the Crooked River.

Stop at the park's ranger station to pick up a map of the park's trail system.

Ochoco National Forest/Crooked River

Have you ever looked a 350-foot volcanic plug in the eye? That's the feeling you get when you hike the **Steins Pillar Trail** (moderate; 4 miles round trip). Steins Pillar is a formation similar to Monkey Face in Smith Rock State Park, except there are no other big rocks around the pillar. It rises in splendid isolation above Mill Creek, 15 miles northeast of Prineville. The formation can be seen from a road, but to reach it requires crossing private land. To eliminate the problem, the Forest Service built a new trail through the pines that brings hikers to a viewpoint across a gap near the top of the pillar. To find the trailhead, drive US 26 east of Prineville for 9.4 miles and turn north on Mill Creek Rd. Drive 5.2 miles to where the surface becomes gravel. Continue 1.6 miles and turn east on a road marked for Steins Pillar. Drive 2.2 steep miles and park at the trailhead. Technical climbing used to be popular on Steins Pillar, but the private land and the explosion of routes at Smith Rock pretty much put an end to it.

The southeast end of the 17,400-acre **Mill Creek Wilderness** can be reached by continuing 3 miles past the Steins Pillar turnoff on Mill Creek Rd to Wildcat Campground. The wilderness has 20 miles of trail. **Twin Pillars Trail** (difficult; 11 miles one way) begins at the camp, crosses the wilderness, and comes out on the north at Bingham Prairie on Forest Rd 27. **Wildcat Trail** (difficult; 8.5 miles one way) crosses the wilderness between White Rock Campground on Forest Rd 3350-300 on the south and Whistler Spring on Forest Rd 27 on the north. Refer to an Ochoco National Forest map, available from the Forest Service information center at the east end of Prineville on US 26 (3160 NE Third St). The northwest part of the forest is managed by the Prineville Ranger District, (541) 416-6500.

Trails ascend two of the highest mountains in Ochoco National Forest. The **Lookout Mountain Trail** (difficult; 7.5 miles one way) begins at the Ochoco Ranger Station picnic area and ends atop the 6,926-foot mountain. To reach the ranger station, drive US 26 east of Prineville for 16 miles and turn right on County Rd 23. Continue driving east for 7 miles to the ranger station, where the road splits (Forest Rd 22 goes north to

Walton Lake and Forest Rd 42 goes south to Big Summit Prairie).

Round Mountain, 6,753 feet high, lies 5 miles to the north and can be climbed by the **Round Mountain Trail** (moderate; 3.5 miles one way), which begins at Walton Lake Campground 7 miles east of the ranger station. The central part of the forest is managed by the Big Summit Ranger District, (541) 416-6645.

The 13,400-acre **Black Canyon Wilderness** is usually entered from the South Fork of the John Day River (see Upper John Day River chapter), 12.5 miles south on County Rd 42 from Dayville and US 26. The **Black Canyon Trail** (difficult; 12.3 miles one way) travels west through the center of the wilderness. Access into the wilderness from the south is via the **South Prong Trail** (easy; 4.5 miles one way) from Mud Springs Campground. To reach the campground, drive Hwy 380 to Paulina and continue east for 14 miles to Forest Rd 58. Turn right and travel 12 miles to Forest Rd 5840. Travel northwest on 5840 for 6 miles to the campground. The eastern part of the forest is managed by the Paulina Ranger District, (541) 416-6643.

To visit the 20,700-acre **Gerry Mountain Wilderness Study Area,** turn south from Hwy 380 (Post-Paulina Rd), 43.5 miles southeast of Prineville, to reach Camp Creek Rd. Drive 11.6 miles south on Camp Creek Rd and bear left at a Y intersection where the pavement ends. Continue another 1.5 miles and park at the top of a slight rise. **Gerry Mountain,** 5,500 feet high, lies to the west and is thickly covered with juniper. Follow some old vehicle tracks for .5 mile to where they end in dense juniper. Hikers need the US Geological Survey Gerry Mountain map, as well as compass skills, to continue from there. Needless to say, Gerry Mountain provides an outstanding opportunity for solitude.

The **South Fork of the Crooked River,** along with neighboring **Sand Hollow Wilderness Study Area,** has 25,392 acres that the BLM recommends for wilderness designation. To visit the area, drive 9 miles south on Camp Creek Rd from Post-Paulina Rd and turn east on County Rd 6575 near a gravel pit. Drive as far east as you can go, get out and walk east another 2 miles, and you'll be wetting your toes in the South Fork of the Crooked River. To get around safely, it's best to use the USGS Sand Hollow topographic map. The South Fork flows through a remote canyon, lined with interesting rimrock formations and filled with wildflowers in late May and early June. Wilderness hiking on the public lands of Oregon's high desert is one of the few untapped recreation opportunities that remain in the state.

Camping

Crooked River

Prineville Reservoir State Park, (541) 447-4363, is open year-round and is on the state reservations system. Call (800) 452-5687 to book a spot. The campground has 25 tent sites, 23 electrical sites, and 22 trailer spaces with full utility hookups. Maximum RV length is 40 feet. The park also has camping cabins that rent for $45 to $55 per night, as well as several sites for dispersed camping, some of which are accessible only by boat. Another unit of the park has 29 primitive sites at **Jasper Point,** 2.5 miles to the east. Both park units have boat ramps. To reach the reservoir, follow signs 14 miles southeast of Prineville on US 26, Hwy 380, and Juniper Canyon Rd.

The BLM's **Lower Crooked River Recreation Area,** located below Prineville Reservoir 12 miles south of Prineville on Hwy 27, has nine camping areas with 120 sites spread over a 4-mile stretch of river. Fly-fishermen head for these sites and leave the lake campgrounds for the boaters. **Chimney Rock Campground,** located near the center of the elongated camping zone, has a barrier-free fishing platform. It's also the trail-head for a 2-mile hike into the rimrock to the east, popular as an overlook of the area's geology and as a place to photograph the sunset. All the BLM Chimney Rock sites have picnic tables, with toilets nearby. Only Chimney Rock has potable water. Heading upstream from Prineville, campgrounds are Castle Rock, Stillwater, Lone Pine, Lower Palisades, Chimney Rock, Cobble Rock, Post Pile, Poison Butte, and Big Bend. Camping fees are collected and the money goes into maintaining and improving the area. For information, contact the BLM, (541) 416-6700.

The next camping downstream along the Crooked River is at **Smith Rock State Park,** where a bivouac site caters to rock climbers (see Climbing, above). The situation isn't as bad as it sounds. Hot showers are available, but campers must be willing to carry their gear a few hundred yards from the parking lot to campsites spread among the juniper trees. Overflow camping for Smith Rock is along **Skull Hollow Road** (Forest Rd 5710), 5 miles northeast of the park on the way to Lone Pine in the Crooked River National Grassland. Facilities are limited to a portable toilet.

Ochoco Lake County Park, (541) 447-1209, is 7 miles east of Prineville, just off US 26 alongside Ochoco Reservoir. The park has 22 sites, plus a biker camp that caters to long-distance cyclists. Formerly a state park, the facility was turned over to the county in 1996 when the Oregon State Parks system faced a budget crisis.

Ochoco National Forest

The heart of the forest east of Prineville has 12 campgrounds in the Prineville and Big Summit Ranger Districts, of which only four have more than 10 sites. The Ochoco National Forest information center, (541) 416-6700, serves as an information clearinghouse for the various ranger districts, although you could get lucky and talk to someone in a ranger station who has the most up-to-date information.

Antelope Reservoir Campground, with 24 sites, is the showpiece of the Maury Mountains 35 miles southeast of Prineville via Hwy 380 and Forest Rd 17. For visitation numbers, the Maury Mountains are about as low as it gets for the national forests of Central Oregon. The mountains are dusty in summer and are roamed by cattle, but they've got solitude if that's what you want.

Wildcat Campground, a 20-mile drive northeast of town on Forest Rd 33, has 17 sites and sits at the southwest edge of the Mill Creek Wilderness. Hikers enjoy its access to the Twin Pillars and Belknap trailheads.

Ochoco Divide Campground is 30 miles east of Prineville, just off US 26. Set amid the beautiful ponderosa pine forest, the camp is popular with travelers and anyone who wants to get away into the mountains for the night. The camp has barrier-free facilities, as well as a new bike camping area.

With an elevation of 5,100 feet, **Walton Lake Campground** is perhaps the most popular with Prineville locals (see Hiking, above). A 30-mile drive east of town via US 26, County Rd 23, and Forest Rd 22, the 25-acre lake is surrounded by pines and is stocked annually with trout. Anglers use float tubes, canoes, and electric motors to get around. The camp has 25 sites, the lake is circled by a barrier-free trail, and a fishing pier has a reserved handicapped parking place.

Sugar Creek Campground, located 12 miles east of the community of Paulina via County Rds 112 and 113 and Forest Rd 58, is the most developed campground within the Paulina Ranger District, (541) 416-6643. It has 20 sites, including some with barrier-free facilities. A fully accessible trail in the campground follows a stream and has fishing opportunities.

Picnics

Ochoco Creek Park in downtown Prineville, on Elm St 2 blocks north of Main St, has a big grassy lawn, a clear-running creek, and plenty of shade trees—in short, everything that is necessary to qualify as a great picnic spot. The Crook County Chamber of Commerce is located right next to the park, making it an ideal spot to pick up some literature and plan a trip through the Crooked River country.

The park is also the setting of one of the most poignant monuments in Oregon, honoring the people who dedicate their lives to protecting the natural resources that make the western United States one of the best places in the world to enjoy outdoor recreation. Dedicated on June 15, 1996, Prineville's **Wildland Firefighters Monument** honors the 14 young people who were killed by the 1994 Storm King Mountain wildfire near Glenwood Springs, Colorado. Some of the firefighters were born and raised in Crook County and nine belonged to the Prineville Hotshots, one of the nation's elite teams of wildland firefighters. Each of the deceased is honored with a photo and short biography set in stone along the monument's shaded walkway. A large bronze statute, the centerpiece of the monument, honors all wildland firefighters, especially the 28 who died that year.

Biking

Not everyone sets out to ride a bicycle across the United States from the Atlantic to the Pacific Ocean, but a few who do pass through the Crooked River country on US 26. Called the **TransAmerica Trail,** the 4,000-mile route from Virginia to the Oregon Coast clicks off 45 miles through the north end of the Crooked River region on US 26 and Hwy 126. Ride as far as you want.

Other **road-cycling** opportunities include the network of paved roads within the triangle of highways (US 26 and 97 and Hwy 126) that connects Prineville, Madras, and Redmond. Smith Rock State Park is located near the center of the triangle. The roads south of the park are paved and good for road bikes; roads north of the park are gravel and good for mountain bikes. Other reasonably flat paved rides include Forest Rd 27 northeast of Prineville, Post-Paulina Rd southeast of town, and Forest Rd 42 through the center of the Ochoco Mountains east of town. Unfortunately, only the county roads near Smith Rock provide enough variety to avoid the out-and-back riding of the others.

Fueled in general by the population explosion in Bend and Central Oregon, more and more bikers are putting their bikes atop their vehicles and heading east away from the crowds and wilderness areas to find places to ride. They find **Ochoco National Forest** to be mostly open to **mountain-bike** riding.

The forest has more than 5,000 miles of roads over its 847,938 acres. About 3,700 miles of the roads are low-standard roads that are open to motor vehicles but rarely see more than a few each day, except during hunting season. About 600 miles are blocked even from four-wheel-drive traffic, leaving them for anyone who yearns to pedal in solitude. The forest also has some single-track rides, but they all carry the "difficult" label and beginners should stay away. Ochoco National Forest publishes a brochure called "Mountain Biking in Central Oregon" that gives detailed driving and riding directions. Contact the Ochoco National Forest information center, (541) 416-6500.

Punishing hill climbs include **Lookout Mountain Trail** No. 804 and **Round Mountain Trail** No. 805. Both are 7.5 miles of long, grunting uphills that are rewarded with sweeping vistas (see Hiking, above). Other views can be had by riding the **Independent Mine Trial** No. 808, an 8-mile loop that begins just off Forest Rd 42, 7 miles east of the Ochoco Ranger Station.

The **Cougar Creek Trail,** a difficult 8.2-mile one-way ride that begins near Ochoco Divide 30 miles east of Prineville on US 26, was recently reconstructed. Heading north, the first part of the ride is on closed logging roads interspersed with some singletrack. The final 3.5 miles follows a historic pack-and-saddle route used by settlers as they traveled between Prineville and the John Day River. The ride is strenuous in places with some technical riding along ridges and side hills.

To get ready for tougher rides, try out the **McKay Saddle area** on Forest Rd 27, which heads north out of Prineville as Main St, 20 miles northeast of town. Park at the junction with Forest Rd 2720 and begin riding north on the network of forest roads that receive little use by motor vehicles.

The BLM has its Central Oregon headquarters at the east end of Prineville on US 26, but most of its dollars for recreation are spent along the rivers (Deschutes, Crooked, and John Day) to develop camping, boating, and fishing facilities. Although bikers don't have designated trails to ride, they can explore miles of seldom-used roads on BLM land, especially between Prineville and US 20.

Boating/Kayaking

Prineville Reservoir draws boaters for fishing and waterskiing from as far away as the Willamette Valley. Both groups are attracted by the reservoir's numerous bends and twist where, for at least a few minutes a day, a boater may feel like no one else is around. Don't expect to experience the feeling on summer's three-day weekends, however.

The reservoir has six launch ramps, four along the north shore, one near the dam at the west end, and one on the south shore. The busiest launches are at Prineville Reservoir State Park (see Camping, above) and the Prineville Reservoir Resort, (541) 447-7468. The resort has seven motel units (six with kitchens), an 80-slip floating moorage, gasoline, store, restaurant, and boats to rent. The state park offers another 32 wet slips accommodating boats up to 26 feet.

Boating on Ochoco Reservoir is much lower-key than on Prineville

Reservoir, which attracts most of the water-skiers and their high-performance boats. Launching is available at Ochoco Lake County Park (see Camping, above).

The **Crooked River Gorge** packs in 27 wild-and-crazy river miles from just above Smith Rock State Park to where the river ends in a placid pool in Lake Billy Chinook. During times of high water, which may last only a day or two a year, expert boaters risk their life and property to experience one of Oregon most thrilling stretches of whitewater. Check with Bend Whitewater Supply, (541) 389-7191, 413 NW Hill St, for reference to local boaters who are intimate with the river. The only thing in Oregon that compares to the Crooked River for sheer excitement are the steep creeks of the Cascades that kayakers run, but rafters can't enjoy them because their equipment is too large. The Crooked River runs deceptively placid through Smith Rock State Park, where thousands of visitors view it without thinking twice. The steep walls of the canyon complicate important things, such as takeout points and possible rescue assistance. For a ride on water ranging from Class IV to V, call the Ochoco Irrigation District, (541) 447-6449, to find out when releases are scheduled. (Access to the river will be restricted for a year while crews blast abutments for the US 97 bridge; see Climbing, above). The launch is 3 miles east above Smith Rock State Park at Lone Pine Bridge. The river's lower 9 miles, accessible from a four-wheel-drive road on Crooked River Ranch to Lake Billy Chinook, aren't as wild. The lower stretch, however, has a mandatory portage around a dam and ends with a 3-mile flatwater paddle to the takeout at the highway bridge of Lake Billy Chinook's Crooked River arm (see Lower Deschutes River chapter).

Fishing

Most angling interest in the Crooked River country is centered on three types of environments—the wild trout of the north and south forks of the Crooked River, the fly-fishery in the river's main stem below Prineville Reservoir, and the warm-water and trout fisheries in Prineville and Ochoco Reservoirs.

The Crooked River's upper north and south forks are for hard-core fishermen who don't want to see anyone else on the nearby banks and don't mind walking to get there. Both are spring-fed and stay cool despite the desert surroundings. Much of the **South Fork** flows through BLM land, but private ranches limit access (see Hiking, above). The river is best during summer and fall when the water is cool. The **North Fork** is part of the National Wild and Scenic Rivers System and flows through a rugged, roadless canyon. The best approach is from Deep Creek Campground on Forest Rd 42, 20 miles east of the Ochoco Ranger Station (see Hiking, above). Paths created by fishermen follow the river downstream.

The BLM's **Lower Crooked River Recreation Area** below Bowman Dam and Prineville Reservoir is nationally known for its rainbow trout fly-fishing. The right bank has a paved road along it (Hwy 27; follow Main St south out of Prineville) that has access to numerous fishing holes and camping places around Chimney Rock (see Camping, above). Trout grow to 18 inches and frequently weigh 2 to 3 pounds. Best success is early and late in the season. Even if the fish aren't biting, the scenery is spectacular.

The two reservoirs east and south of Prineville rise and fall depending on the spring snowmelt and summer irrigation demands. Both were built to meet the water needs of county irrigators and to control flooding. **Prineville Reservoir's** level fluctuates by as much as 30 feet during the year, and the water surface can shrink from 5 to 3 square miles. The reservoir is good for trout when the water is cold and for largemouth and smallmouth bass during summer. Ochoco Dam gobbled up $30 million in the mid-1990s when the Bureau of Reclamation tried to shore up its earthen wall. The project has been declared a success, but the fishery was lost due to the required drawdown of the reservoir. The reservoir is restocked annually with catchable rainbow trout. **Ochoco Creek** supports its own fishery, above and below Ochoco Reservoir, of wild and hatchery rainbow. Best fishing on both reservoirs is offshore from boats or from shore at the reservoirs' parks (see Camping and Boating/Kayaking, above).

Prineville Sporting Goods, (541) 447-6883, 346 N Deer, is a good place to pick up supplies on the way out of town. Check the state fishing synopsis for regulations, or call the Bend office of the Oregon Department of Fish and Wildlife, (541) 388-6363.

Wildlife

The Crooked River country, with its sagebrush-covered prairies and its ponderosa pine forests, has a mix of vegetation that supports a variety of wildlife. Oregon's state bird, the **western meadowlark,** has become a rarity on the western side of the state due to loss of habitat. When the yellow-breasted denizen of the high desert fills the air with its cheerful song, it's a sure sign that spring is on its way. The bird is easy to spot in the open grasslands by pinpointing its location by its song.

Smith Rock State Park (see Climbing, above) is a good place to begin watching for wildlife in the Crooked River region. The herd of **mule deer** that hangs out near park headquarters is so familiar that the park staff has given each deer a name. Other animals seen frequently in the park include **prairie falcons, common ravens,** and **canyon wrens. Canada geese** and **mallard ducks** nest along the Crooked River.

River otter also live in the Crooked River and can be seen floating along the surface or playing along the banks. Normally at home in clear-running streams, the otters must make an exception to accommodate the Crooked River because the river usually runs a muddy brown through the park.

Big Summit Prairie, an enclave of private land surrounded by Ochoco National Forest, is famous for resident herds of **pronghorn antelope** and **Rocky Mountain elk.** The prairie begins 10 miles east of the Ochoco Ranger Station on Forest Rd 42 (see Hiking, above). With the aid of binoculars, antelope can frequently be seen by looking north toward Johnson Creek while driving Forest Rd 42 at the south edge of the prairie, or on Forest Rd 3010 on the prairie's east side. Elk can be seen along Forest Rd 22 on the north edge of the prairie and Forest Rd 4210 on its west edge. Look for the **beaver** colony where Dudley Creek meets Forest Rd 42 at the southwest edge of the prairie. Up to 60 **wild horses** roam Ochoco National Forest, mostly around Lookout and Round Mountains west of Big Summit Prairie (see Hiking, above). Big Summit Prairie is a former Indian summer encampment. Its 10,000 acres are mostly privately owned and locked to keep out the public, although forest roads skirt its perimeter.

As many as 50 **bald eagles** congregate during December through early April in the upper Crooked River, from Prineville Reservoir east to Post and on up the Crooked River Valley. Best viewing is from 9am to 4pm in February and March, as eagles move to and from their roosts while searching for food during the warmth of the day.

Rock Collecting

It's sort of like the chicken-or-the-egg quandary: did the Crooked River country make rock collecting famous, or did the area's fabulous rock-collecting opportunities make Crook County famous?

The Crook County Chamber of Commerce has been the leading player in development of rock collecting as one of the county's strongest tourist attractions. Here's the opening paragraph from one of the chamber's brochures: "Each year, thousands of rockhounds, pebble puppies, and persons interested in looking for rocks visit Crook County, Oregon. When the earth was created, this area was blessed with the widest variety of rock types found almost anywhere on this continent. Crook County is rightfully known as the rockhound capital of the world."

OK, so you want to look for rocks but you don't own a shovel. What's a person to do? First, stop at the chamber of commerce at 390 N Fairview in Prineville, (541) 447-6304, to load up on free information and then head over to Elkins Gem Stones, (541) 447-5547, at 833 S Main St. If it's a weekend, members of the local Prineville Rockhounds Club will be happy to have you join them for an outing.

A commercial dig is another possible starting place. One of the most famous in Oregon is over by Madras in the Lower Deschutes River country, but Crook County has one of its own called Lucky Strike Geodes, (541) 462-3332. The mine is famous for its **Thundereggs,** the official Oregon state rock, and is located about 40 miles northwest of Prineville. Call for directions to see if the dig is open. Operation is limited to April 20 through October 31 because winter snow closes the road. Commercial digs provide the digging tools and directions to the best digging locations, and charge by the pound for the rock that is taken away. Heavy equipment, including bulldozers, is used to remove soil and vegetation that cover the best digging sites.

Most rockhounds are young families or senior citizens who do it as much for the camaraderie and the camping as they do for the collecting. Serious collectors eventually purchase the cutting saws and polishing tools that are needed to bring out the beauty of a rock, but most openly admit that the rocks decorating their homes were purchased from another collector during the rockhound powwows that are common throughout the western United States.

In order to protect the digging grounds, the Crook County Chamber of Commerce has filed claims over the years on some of the most productive digs on public land within the county's 2,991 square miles. Many digging areas are open to the public, but other sites are closed—even places that look abandoned, because mining claims remain in effect. Mining law passed by Congress in the 1870s protects the rights of small collectors to pursue their hobby on unclaimed public land. While mushroom pickers or even beargrass collectors often need permits these days to use the national forests, rock collectors are free of such restrictions until they begin using power equipment.

The chamber of commerce has 10 mining claims where the public is free to dig. Most sites are located along rugged backcountry roads. Two of the more popular digs are for **limb casts** and **petrified wood.** A limb cast is formed in the cavity of volcanic ash that was once occupied by wood. Heat caused the wood to burn away and later it was filled by deposits of silica.

To find the limb-cast digging area, drive east of Prineville for 2 miles on US 26 and turn south on Post-Paulina Rd (County Rd 380). Drive to milepost 50 along the Crooked River, turn right on a BLM road and drive 5 miles to a digging area to the east. The road can be driven by cars in all weather but is closed during hunting season. Limb casts are usually 18 inches deep, so digging is required, but pay close attention to banks over-looking washes where they may be closer to the surface. Pits and excavations left by other diggers are good places to try your luck.

The Bear Creek Wood digging area is south of Prineville on Hwy 27, the BLM's **Lower Crooked River National Back Country Byway.** Drive 33 miles south on Hwy 27 and turn east on Bear Creek Rd. Travel 5.2 miles and turn left off the road just before a fence. Drive .2 mile to a gate, go a short distance through the gate to a fork, turn right, and go another .5 mile to the dig. Bring picks and shovels. Some pieces are so large that it would take a crane to carry them away. Begin digging where previous excavators look like they met success. The BLM's designated byway covers all 43 miles of Hwy 27, from Prineville on the north to its intersection on the south with US 20 between Millican and Brothers about 36 miles east of Bend. The northern 21 miles are paved, and the remainder of the road is all-weather gravel, although it turns to washboard soon after it is graded.

Cross-Country Skiing/Snowmobiling

With an average of only 80 to 90 frost-free days in Prineville, the Crooked River country has plenty of cold weather to build up sufficient snow for cross-country skiing, snowmobiling, and sledding. The **Ochoco Mountains** don't have the vertical drop needed for a major downhill ski area, so downhill skiers head to the Cascades (see Bend and the Upper Deschutes River chapter). Snow can be spotty in the Ochocos because they are the next range east of the rain shadow cast by the Cascades. But snow can also be deep, like it was nearly everywhere in Oregon during the wet winter of 1996–97. In snowy years the highest roads in the Ochocos can still be blocked by snowdrifts when people head out during Memorial Day weekend in late May for the first big outing of the summer.

Most winter recreation takes places at three sno-parks strung out over a 3-mile section of US 26 about 30 miles east of Prineville at Ochoco Summit. First comes **Marks Creek Sled Hill,** a bring-your-own sledding hill developed by the Forest Service at milepost 28. Next is **Bandit Springs**, a highway rest area that serves as a winter destination for cross-country skiers, followed by 4,720-foot **Ochoco Divide** at milepost 30.5, where an 85-mile network of groomed snowmobile trails begins.

Nordic skiers of all abilities have a 13-mile trail system that begins at Bandit Springs. Trails lead through old-growth ponderosa pines, their bark glowing orange as the sun filters down through their branches. Open meadows grace the area.

Adventuresome skiers head for the ultimate ski tour in the Ochocos—the summit of **Lookout Mountain.** At 6,926 feet, Lookout is the tallest peak in Crook County. Access is limited during winter to times when a timber sale leads to plowing the road, so check with the Forest Service information center in Prineville, (541) 416-6500, before beginning the tour. Drive 16 miles east of Prineville on US 26 and turn south onto County Rd 123. Follow it 7 miles to the Ochoco Ranger Station and drive .5 mile beyond to Forest Rd 42. Drive 6.5 miles and park at Lookout Mountain trailhead. The trail is marked 3.5 miles to the summit, but markings can be difficult to find in open meadows and the climb is 2,200 feet. This is a tour for expert skiers only and is a shorter but steeper route than the 7.5-mile hiking trail (see Hiking, above). The 360-degree view is spectacular, but you may have to share it with snowmobilers who also are permitted to climb Lookout Mountain.

outside in

Attractions

It may come as a surprise to visitors that **Prineville,** founded in 1877 and the oldest town in Central Oregon, is quite an active railroad community. The City of Prineville Railway has been operating since 1918. Of most interest to visitors is the **Crooked River Railroad Company,** (541) 548-8630, which operates excursion runs—featuring dinner or brunch, train robberies, and murder mysteries—year-round on weekends between Redmond and Prineville.

Hundreds of visitors are drawn to Indian Trail Spring, located 2 miles southeast of Big Summit Prairie, for an annual gathering called the **Oregon Star Party,** (503) 357-6163. The event is staged during the August weekend nearest to the new moon. As many as 500 amateur astronomers gather from around the Northwest to gaze at the stars by night—star viewing is good anywhere 50 miles east of Prineville where tree cover is minimal—and hike and enjoy surrounding Ochoco National Forest by day. A few visitors usually travel from overseas just to attend the party. Visitors are invited to gaze at stars through some of the most high-powered amateur telescopes in the Northwest.

Ever since **Crooked County** voted for George Bush in the 1992 presidential election and the rest of the country elected Bill Clinton, rock collecting has been Crook County's main claim to fame. Up until that time, journalists from around the country had descended on the county each fourth fall to see which way the political wind was blowing—as residents of the county had voted for the **winning presidential candidate** every time since the county was founded in 1882. It had been the longest bellwether streak of any county in the nation for the presidential election. To show that they really didn't like the nation's selection in 1992, Crook County residents voted against the winner again in 1996 and instead went with Bob Dole. So much for visits to the county by national journalists.

More Information

Big Summit Ranger District, Prineville: *(541) 416-6645.*
Bureau of Land Management, Prineville: *(541) 416-6700.*
Central Oregon Visitors Association, Bend: *(800) 800-8334.*
Ochoco National Forest, Prineville: *(541) 416-6500.*
Paulina Ranger District, Paulina: *(541) 416-6643.*
Prineville–Crook County Chamber of Commerce, Prineville:
   (541) 447-6304.
Prineville Ranger District, Prineville: *(541) 416-6500.*
Smith Rock State Park, Terrebonne: *(541) 548-7501.*

Santiam Pass and Mount Washington

From US Highway 20 at Santiam Pass on the north, east to Sisters, south to McKenzie Pass and Highway 242, and west to Highway 126, including the Mount Washington Wilderness, the north side of the Three Sisters Wilderness, the town of Sisters, and the resort village at Black Butte Ranch.

Not everyone heads for Bend and Central Oregon when they drive east out of the Willamette Valley across the north-central Cascades looking for outdoor fun. For many, opportunities at 4,817-foot Santiam Pass and the Mount Washington Wilderness satisfy just fine.

A fair number of travelers never venture farther east than Hoodoo, the fun little family ski area at Santiam Pass. Others swear that the resort at Black Butte Ranch, situated in the shadow of the rugged Three Sisters mountains, is even more relaxing than the more famous Sunriver Resort south of Bend. Still others find everything they need in the charmingly sophisticated town of Sisters, without ever setting foot in bustling Bend or Redmond farther east.

The Santiam Pass area, as it turns out, offers just about everything that draws visitors deeper into Central Oregon, but without the longer drives and larger numbers of tourists. During summer, when snow finally retreats to the highest mountains, McKenzie Pass opens for auto traffic and provides a second cross-Cascades route from the Willamette Valley to Sisters. After all, fewer miles in a car can mean more time on the ski slopes or more miles on the hiking trails.

Sandwiched between Santiam Pass to the north and McKenzie Pass to the south is the 46,655-acre Mount Washington Wilderness. Small compared to some of Oregon's other protected mountain areas, Mount Washington nevertheless packs a pretty good punch when it comes to excitement in the backcountry.

The peak itself is a 7,794-foot eroded plug of an ancient volcano. Climbers often warm up on bigger peaks (like Mount Hood, Middle Sisters, or South Sister) before they have the skill and courage to make a summit try on Mount Washington. Visitors who don't aspire to heights can safely enjoy the view of Mount Washington from their campsite along the shore of Big Lake at Santiam Pass.

A barren moonscape of lava rocks lies at the southern edge of the wilderness. Many travelers soak in the view from paved trails at McKenzie Pass on Highway 242, but only the foolish walk off-trail through the sharp-edged lava. Plants may need another thousand years or so to reclaim the rugged ground and soften the surface of the lava.

Getting There

Santiam Pass carries traffic over the central Cascades between Salem and Albany to Sisters and Bend. Portland is 130 miles to the northwest via Interstate 5 to Salem and Highway 22 as it climbs east into the Cascades then joins US Highway 20 (US 20). Highway 242, the McKenzie Pass Highway, provides the quickest route between Eugene and Central Oregon, but the road is closed during winter and its season is limited to June through October. Santiam Pass carries the burdensome numbers of US 20/Highway 126.

Adjoining Areas

NORTH: **Mount Jefferson and the Metolius River**

SOUTH: **Three Sisters and Cascade Lakes**

EAST: **Bend and the Upper Deschutes River**

WEST: **Cascade Foothills**

Hiking

Santiam Pass

Hikers tend to focus their energies on two pursuits—a backpack trip to the Patjens Lakes or a summit climb of 7,794-foot Mount Washington. Both trails begin at **Big Lake** (see Camping, below), a popular camping area 3 miles south of Santiam Pass. (See Mount Jefferson and the Metolius River chapter for hikes from the north side of Santiam Pass.)

Patjens Lakes Trail (easy; 6-mile loop) is a popular family backpack outing but not a place to go for solitude. The trail passes four small lakes, two of them no bigger than ponds. The best view is of Mount Washington's pointy summit to the southeast.

Mount Washington is a prime example of a mountain that, without being extraordinarily tall, is tough to climb. More than 2,500 feet shorter than nearby South Sister, Mount Washington is much more difficult to climb by its standard route. The normal approach is via the Pacific Crest National Scenic Trail as it passes the north side of Big Lake, following it south for 4 miles to where an obvious spur trail branches to the southeast and begins to climb Mount Washington's north ridge. The crux of the climb is the crossing of a break in the cliffs. It doesn't seem too hard on the way up, but the move is awkward on the way down and the drop is frightening. Most climbers prefer the safety of a rope, both up and down. All other routes on Mount Washington are technical, requiring placement of protection and route-finding ability. The mountain is one of the few places in which to climb on solid rock on any of Oregon's Cascade volcanoes.

Continuing down the east side of Santiam Pass on US 20, the blue waters of Suttle Lake can be glimpsed through the trees along the highway. The **Suttle Lake Shore Trail** (easy; 3.2-mile loop) is especially popular with the lake's campers and fishermen. Pick up the trail at any of the lake's three campgrounds (see Camping, below).

Management for recreation in the Santiam Pass area is split down the middle. Land west of the Cascade crest is managed by the McKenzie Ranger District, (541) 465-6522, and land on the east side is managed by the Sisters Ranger District, (541) 549-2111.

Three Creeks Lake area

Deschutes National Forest roads that head south from Sisters have some of the lesser-used trailheads for the Three Sisters Wilderness. Several roads peel off to the west from Forest Rd 16, which begins in Sisters and heads south for 13 miles to Three Creeks Lake where it ends. Popular in winter as a snowmobile staging area, Three Creeks Lake is hemmed in on the south by 500-foot **Tam McArthur Rim.** To reach the top of the rim (moderate; 5 miles round trip), hike east from the campground to reach the tabletop highlands, then south to a 7,730-foot-high perch that looks down on Three Creeks Lake.

One of the most scenic locations in the Three Sisters Wilderness can be reached from the **Pole Creek trailhead** southwest of Sisters. Drive west out of town on Hwy 242 for 1 mile, then turn south and follow Forest Rd 15 for 10 miles to where it ends at the trailhead. The **Chambers Lakes Trail** (difficult; 14.5 miles round trip) begins at the Pole Creek trailhead and is popular with backpackers because of its scenic campsites at Camp Lake. If the mosquitoes aren't biting too badly, it's easy to spend three or four days wandering through the different-colored lakes above tree line or making summit climbs on seldom-used eastern routes on the Three Sisters. The Chambers Lakes get their varying shades of turquoise and green from the type of silt they contain from glacial runoff.

Squaw Creek Falls (moderate; 2 miles round trip) is another scenic trail that heads into the wilderness from a spur road off Forest Rd 16 south of Sisters. Summer snowmelt from the glaciers above make the flow over Squaw Creek Falls a continually changing spectacle. Squaw Creek's cascades are another .5 mile upstream on a scramble path. Just keep Squaw Creek to your right. In the late 1980s, following the eruption of Mount St. Helens in Washington, the US Geological Survey underwent a methodical examination of other Cascade volcanoes. One of the scientists' findings prompted the Forest Service to issue a flash-flood alert for the Squaw Creek drainage in the event of a catastrophic breach of the moraine that holds back the waters of **Carver Lake.** The lake is still in place, although an unforeseen event could cause it to drain in a flash now or a thousand years in the future. The falls section of Squaw Creek is on a different fork of the drainage, but if Carver Lake bursts while you're hiking the trail, your car at the trailhead may turn up missing.

McKenzie Pass

The circuitous **McKenzie Pass Highway,** Hwy 242, gets so much snow that the Oregon Department of Transportation doesn't bother to keep it plowed during winter. When the McKenzie Pass Highway is finally cleared for the summer in June, hikers head for the scattering of lakes just to the west of the pass and the **Pacific Crest National Scenic Trail** (PCT) where it crosses the pass at an elevation of 5,325 feet. The McKenzie Pass Highway is not recommended for vehicles or trailers longer than 35 feet.

As Hwy 242 splits off from Hwy 126 on the west side of McKenzie Pass, the first trailhead comes 6.3 miles east of the junction. The **Proxy Falls trailhead** is marked on the south side of the road, and a .5-mile trail leads to views of the 100-foot upper falls and the 200-foot lower falls on Proxy Creek. The **Obsidian trailhead** comes next, 5 miles farther east on Hwy 242. The major climbing route for Middle Sisters (see Three Sisters and Cascade Lakes chapter), Obsidian is one of two trails in Oregon with day use limited by permit to 30 hikers. Pick up a permit at the McKenzie Ranger Station, (541) 822-3381, in McKenzie Bridge. (The other limited-use trail is Pamelia Lake; see Mount Jefferson and the Metolius River chapter).

The **Scott Lake trailhead** offers a short and long hikes from the north side of Hwy 242, 1 mile east of Obsidian or 6 miles west of the pass. Forest Rd 260 ends at the trailhead, 1 mile west of Hwy 242. **Benson Lake** (easy; 2.8 miles round trip) is a popular destination from the Scott Lake trailhead. With a wilderness permit in hand, keep on going to Scott Mountain (moderate; 8 miles round trip from the road) for an aerial view of the region and Central Oregon's magnificent volcanoes from a former fire lookout at the peak's 6,116-foot summit. On the south side of Hwy 242 near the turnoff to Scott Lake, a hiker symbol along the road points the way to **Four-in-One Cone** (moderate; 8.8 miles round trip). The trail heads east and passes the four cinder cones at 4.4 miles before reaching the PCT in another mile. Hikers planning to enter any of the wilderness areas within the Willamette and Deschutes National Forests must fill out a self-issuing permit at the trailhead.

The **Dee Wright Observatory,** constructed from the lava rock that covers the surrounding area, coaxes travelers to pause for a while atop McKenzie Pass and soak in the impressive view. One of the lava flows covers 65 square miles and is 2,700 years old—barely enough time for the hardiest of plant species to get a foothold. The PCT heads north from McKenzie Pass, reaching Santiam Pass in 20 miles. Most hikers use the PCT to access **Little Belknap Crater** (moderate; 5.2 miles round trip) from McKenzie Pass. The PCT is faint in places as it heads north, but persistence usually pays off when trying to relocate the trail as it passes through the rugged lava. Little Belknap Crater, a .2-mile stroll east of the PCT, is the source of much of the lava in the area. The 6,872-foot high **Belknap Crater,** another major lava source, can be climbed off-trail by continuing on the PCT past Little Belknap. Climb Belknap Crater's north slope after passing through a lava field, which has seen sufficient foot traffic over the years to leave an obvious path through the lava.

Heading south on the PCT from McKenzie Pass, the trail quickly crosses the boundary of the Three Sisters Wilderness. A popular day hike from here leads to **Matthieu Lakes** (easy; 6 miles round trip). Another nearby trail that heads south of the highway begins 3 miles east of the pass near Windy Point. The 7,251-foot summit of **Black Crater** (difficult; 7.6 miles round trip) has outstanding views of the McKenzie Pass lava flows and surrounding volcanoes.

McKenzie River

A circuit of **Clear Lake** (easy; 5 miles round trip) is a popular way to spend a day just outside the northwest corner of the Mount Washington Wilderness along Hwy 126 (just south of US 20). The amazingly clear lake is the headwaters of the McKenzie River, one of Western Oregon's most popular recreational rivers. The lake is not only clear, but it's also very cold. Scuba divers, in full protective gear, venture into the waters of Clear Lake to explore the forest of underwater snags that are mysteriously visible from a few spots on the trail at the lake's north end.

The **McKenzie River National Recreation Trail** (easy when hiked in small sections; 27 miles one way) begins at Clear Lake and follows the river south and west to the McKenzie Ranger District (see Greater Eugene chapter). The trail crosses Hwy 126 south of Clear Lake and in 1 mile reaches a roadside trailhead for scenic **Sahalie Falls** (100 feet) and **Koosah Falls** (70 feet). Both falls are within sight of viewpoints from Hwy 126. The trail continues dropping along the river until it reaches **Tamolitch Falls** (moderate; 9 miles round trip from Sahalie Falls). Tamolitch Falls was 60 feet high until a power generation project diverted its supply of water. At the base of the falls, where the plunge pool used to be, springs rise up from the lava and the McKenzie runs above ground again.

Biking

With its steep hills and vast expanses of lava, the Santiam Pass and Mount Washington country isn't known for its off-road biking opportunities. Throw in a couple of designated wilderness areas and riding isn't allowed at all in much of the area. The **McKenzie River National Recreation Trail** (see Hiking, above) is open to bikes, but the trail's lava rock surface has caused more than a few flat tires in its northern area from Clear Lake to Tamolitch Falls. The riding becomes easier near the trail's western terminus next to Paradise Campground (see Greater Eugene chapter).

One of Oregon's ultimate challenges on a road bike is the 82-mile **McKenzie-Santiam Pass Loop,** a Deschutes and Willamette National Forest Scenic Byway. The route begins at Sisters, follows Hwy 242 over McKenzie Pass, turns north on Hwy 126, then west on US 20 for the climb over Santiam Pass and the descent back to Sisters. Cyclists who can finish this loop in a day are ready to take on the Tour de France.

Camping

Santiam Pass

The largest manager of campgrounds in the Santiam Pass and Mount Washington country is—surprise!—a ski area. **Hoodoo** was one of the region's first ski areas to expand its business into summer by bidding on concession contracts to manage Forest Service campgrounds. Within four years of picking up its first campground in 1993, Hoodoo has grown to manage 55 Forest Service camps and is the sixth-largest campground concessionaire in the country.

Campers may not have hot showers to run to in the morning, but crowds are small, favorite spots are often available, and the cost is low. Call Hoodoo Recreation Services for information, (541) 822-3799.

Campers heading up Santiam Pass from Willamette Valley towns usually cross their fingers and hope they can find a spot at the **Big Lake Campgrounds,** located at the end of Forest Rd 2690, 4 miles south of Santiam Pass. Needless to say, with only 60 sites in two campgrounds (Big Lake and Big Lake West), not everyone gets in. The lucky few enjoy spots near the lake's shore and views across the water to Mount Washington. Maximum trailer length is 28 feet. Big Lake is one of the few camps in the area available on the Forest Service's national reservations system, (800) 280-2267.

Suttle Lake is 7 miles down the east side from Santiam Pass and has 100 sites at **Link Creek, South Shore, Blue Bay,** and nearby **Scout Lake Campgrounds.** All are along Forest Rd 2070, which circles the lake south of Hwy 20. Check with the Sisters Ranger District, (541) 549-2111, for information. Suttle Lake Resort, (541) 595-6662, has campsites, cabins, and a marina. Blue Lake Resort, another private resort nearby, was open to the public for 35 years before it was sold in 1996. The resort is no longer open to the public. Farther east on US 20 toward Sisters, campers turn north and head for Camp Sherman to stay at the many campgrounds along the Metolius River (see Mount Jefferson and the Metolius River chapter). Most campers pulling long rigs over Santiam Pass usually wind up in the Sisters KOA Campground, (541) 549-3021, 2 miles east of town, or the Mountain Shadow RV Park, (541) 549-7275, at the west edge of town. **Graham Corral Horse Camp** is 4 miles northwest of Sisters.

Three Creeks Lake, McKenzie Pass, McKenzie River

Far away from the busy cross-Cascades highways, the Three Creeks Lake area (see Hiking, above) offers a much quieter experience with just a touch of remoteness. Instead of traffic noise, you're more likely to be serenaded to sleep by the call of a great horned owl. **Black Pine Springs, Driftwood,** and **Three Creek Lakes Campgrounds** have only 30 sites among them, so get there early on weekends. All are along Forest Rd 16, which heads south of US 20 at Sisters. For information, contact the Sisters Ranger District, (541) 549-2111.

Five campgrounds line Hwy 242 as it traverses McKenzie Pass— **Limberlost, Alder Spring,** and **Scott Lake Campgrounds** on the west (check with the McKenzie Ranger District), **Lava Camp Lake** at the summit, and **Cold Springs** on the east (check with the Sisters Ranger District). None are larger than 23 sites and trailers are limited to 20 feet in length. Most popular is Cold Springs because of its bird-watching opportunities and because its east-slope location gives it a better chance of being in the sun.

A half-dozen camps line the McKenzie River as Hwy 126 travels between its junctions with US 20 on the north and Hwy 242 on the south. Most popular are **Coldwater Cove Campground** on Clear Lake (see

Hiking, above) and **Trail Bridge Campground,** situated on Trail Bridge Reservoir 8 miles south of Clear Lake on the west side of Hwy 126. Hikers like **Ice Cap Campground** because of its trailhead for Sahalie and Koosah Waterfalls (see Hiking, above). All of the campgrounds are in the McKenzie Ranger District, (541) 822-3381.

Fishing

The **McKenzie River** is one of Oregon's blue-ribbon trout streams. The best fishing is beyond the Santiam Pass and Mount Washington country from Blue River to where it joins the Willamette near Eugene (see Greater Eugene chapter). The river's upper reaches are cold and swift, and fishing is slow. **Clear Lake,** headwaters of the McKenzie, is good for brook trout and planted rainbow (see Hiking, above, for access). The 148-acre lake is uniformly deep (175 feet at the south end), except for some shallows in Coldwater Cove. Best fishing is by trolling.

     Big Lake near Santiam Pass has stocked kokanee, rainbow, and cut-throat, plus some resident brookies in its 225 acres. **Suttle Lake,** largest of the area's lakes at 240 acres, has brown trout, whitefish, and kokanee. (For more on both lakes, see Camping, above.) The fly-fishing specialist in Sisters is the Fly Fisher's Place, (541) 549-3474.

Boating/Kayaking

Other than the snows of winter, lava flows are not particularly good at holding surface water. The main exceptions in the Santiam Pass and Mount Washington country are **Suttle Lake** (waterskiing, fishing, and rental boats), **Big Lake** (waterskiing and fishing), and **Clear Lake** (motors prohibited; rental boats available at Clear Lake Resort). (See Camping and Hiking, above.)

     The upper reach of the **McKenzie River** provides a fun, 9-mile white-water trip from the launch at Olallie Campground, 1 mile south of Trail Bridge Reservoir on the west side of Hwy 126, to the takeout at Paradise Campground (see Greater Eugene chapter). Although the rapids aren't particularly big, the river provides nearly constant action, and this isn't a place to make mistakes. Coming from underground, the river always runs clear and cold. The most difficult rapids is Fishladder. Although the rapids are only rated Class III, newcomers to the river usually make a point of scouting it from a gravel road along the river's west bank. An experienced guide on the McKenzie is Jim's Oregon Whitewater at McKenzie Bridge, (541) 822-6003.

Skiing

Hoodoo Ski Area, located 1 mile south of Santiam Pass, has been a ski center since the 1930s. Small but friendly, Hoodoo has long attracted skiers from the mid–Willamette Valley and has recently been pulling them in from the Central Oregon area—Mount Bachelor's backyard. Hoodoo's lift tickets sell for about $15 less per day than its more famous neighbor. Hoodoo's other major attraction is that it offers weekend night skiing.

With a 1,035-foot vertical drop and four chairlifts, Hoodoo will never be mistaken for Mount Bachelor. You probably won't be seeing many Hoodoo skiers wearing the latest $800 ski suits, either. Hoodoo is a volcanic butte that rises above the fairly flat surrounding pass. The Green chair runs all the way to the 5,703-foot top, giving skiers a full 360-degree option for skiing on the upper mountain. They soon must begin circling back to the base area, although the future installation of the Mambo chairlift will change that.

Like most of Oregon's Cascade passes, Hoodoo is storm country. Wind and snow can dominate for days, only to be followed by a rising freezing level that brings rain. But skiers who visit Hoodoo a lot also know it can offer outstanding powder skiing. The Manzanita chair, a short triple for beginners, can offer powder skiing all day long after the bigger lifts at Mount Bachelor have been skied out. Hoodoo's Crater Face collects prodigious amounts of snow and has some of the best powder skiing along Oregon's Cascades crest, on those rare days when powder snow is the norm.

Hoodoo also has a full-service **Nordic center** with 10 kilometers of groomed tracks, plus a full-service **snowboard center.** Skiers tend to be young at Hoodoo, which prides itself on its family atmosphere and celebrates each New Year's with an alcohol-free evening. The ski area can be reached by calling (541) 822-3799 or (541) 822-3799 (snow report). A good ski shop to visit in Sisters is Eurosports, (541) 549-2471.

Additional cross-country skiing can be found at **Santiam Pass,** which has numerous marked trails over 10 square miles of rolling tabletop plateau. Most skiers begin at the **Ray Benson Sno-Park,** just across the entrance to Hoodoo, 1 mile south of the pass. The sprawling, marked Forest Service trail system heads mostly south and east from the sno-park, which requires a sno-park permit for parking during the November 15 to April 30 winter season (see Oregon Outdoor Primer). The trail system features three shelters—Brandenburg, Island Junction, and Blowout. The extensive system of ski trails is shown on the Santiam Pass Winter Recreation map, available at local ranger stations and sporting goods stores.

Other ski trails in the Santiam Pass and Mount Washington country begin from the **Isaac Nickerson Sno-Park** across from Clear Lake (see Hiking, above). At the closed snow gate west of Sisters on McKenzie Pass Rd, skiers head up unplowed Hwy 242 toward McKenzie Pass. The route to the pass can be windswept and brutally cold, so most skiers wait for clear days in spring. The Three Creeks Lake area (see Hiking, above) offers outstanding views from Tam McArthur Rim, but this is snowmobile country and skiers usually head elsewhere.

Dozens of miles are groomed by volunteers of the local **snowmobiling** clubs for riding in the Santiam Pass and Mount Washington area. Contact the Sisters Ranger District, (541) 549-2111, for club representatives and rental information.

The backcountry specialist in Sisters is Mountain Supply of Oregon, (541) 549-3215.

Horseback Riding

Sisters, located at the edge of Central Oregon's horse ranch country, is host the second weekend of June to the popular Sisters Rodeo. For buckaroos who don't own their own horses, Black Butte Ranch Stables and Pack Station, (541) 595-2061, located 7 miles northwest of Sisters on US 20, offers trail rides and wilderness pack trips into the Cascades. It is the only horse packer licensed to enter Central Oregon's three wilderness areas from the east. Expect to pay $180 per day on a guided trip, or use the service to establish a base camp. A drop camp costs $150 for the packer and $75 per day for each horse.

Rock Springs Guest Ranch, (541) 382-1957, located midway between Sisters and Bend on US 20, maintains a herd of 55 horses for its ranch guests to use. The ranch is famous for its photography seminars during which guests pay to photograph and videotape wranglers as they herd the horses. The photos wind up on calendars and in books around the world.

Wildlife

Some of Oregon's largest herds of wintering **mule deer** can be seen on the less-traveled roads south of US 20 between Sisters and Bend. Frequently seen in groups of 20 or more, the deer graze in open fields and use juniper groves for cover between Plainview and Tumalo. Turn south on any of the paved or gravel roads off US 20 and be on the alert. The deer aren't hard to find.

The beautiful parklike setting of aspen groves and old-growth ponderosa pines west of Sisters is a popular location for viewing migrating **songbirds.** Drive 4 miles west of town on Hwy 242, park at Cold Springs Campground, and walk into the aspen grove. Four types of **woodpeckers** frequent the area.

outside in

Attractions

Named after the three mountain peaks that dominate the horizon (Faith, Hope, and Charity), the little community of **Sisters** is becoming a bit of a mecca for tired urban types looking for a taste of cowboy escapism. On a clear day (and there are about 250 of them a year here), Sisters is exquisitely beautiful. Surrounded by mountains, trout streams, and pine and cedar forests, this little town capitalizes on the influx of winter skiers and summer camping and fishing enthusiasts.

There's mixed sentiment about the pseudo-Western storefronts that are thematically organizing the town's commerce, but then again Sisters does host 56,000 visitors for each of four shows during its annual June rodeo. It also has the world's largest outdoor **quilt show,** with 800 quilts hanging from balconies and storefronts each July. In the early 1970s, Sisters developed the Western theme that by now has grown much more sophisticated. The town, built on about 30 feet of pumice dust spewed over centuries from nearby volcanoes, has added numerous mini-mall shopping clusters with courtyards and sidewalks to eliminate blowing dust. There are several large art galleries; a couple of great bakeries; and even Sisters Coffee Company for freshly roasted coffee beans, (541) 549-0527. Although the population of the town itself is about 1,000, more than 7,500 live in the surrounding area on miniranches.

Restaurants

Hotel Sisters Restaurant and Bronco Billy's Saloon ☆ The social centerpiece of Sisters, this bar and eatery's friendly waitstaff serves up Western-style ranch cooking, with good burgers, fresh seafood, and some Mexican fare. It's a good place for drinks on the deck. *105 Cascade St (at Fir St), Sisters; (541) 549-RIBS; $$.*

Papandrea's Pizza ☆ Papandrea's has built a quality reputation on fresh dough, homemade sauce, real cheese, and fresh vegetables. Because of all this freshness, you wait quite a bit longer for the original thick-crust pies, but there's a you-bake line for takeout. *E Cascade Hwy (east end of town), Sisters; (541) 549-6081; $.*

Lodgings

Black Butte Ranch ☆☆☆ With 1,800 acres, this recreation wonderland remains the darling of Northwest resorts. Rimmed by the Three Sisters, rental condos and private homes draw families year-round to swim, ski, fish, golf, bike, boat, ride horses, and play tennis. Reserve a space by stating the size of your party and whether you want a home or simply a good-size bed and bath. The handsome main lodge serves as dining headquarters. *US 20 (8 miles west of Sisters); PO Box 8000, Black Butte Ranch, OR 97759; (541) 595-6211; $$$.*

Conklin's Guest House ☆☆ One of the best B&Bs in Central Oregon, this remodeled old farmhouse has five large rooms, each with a private bath. One room has been kept a dorm room. Large breakfasts, laundry facilities, and two trout ponds ready for fishing add to the allure. *69013 Camp Polk Rd (across road from Sisters airport), Sisters, OR 97759; (541) 549-0123; $$.*

More Information

Black Butte Ranch, Sisters: *(541) 595-6211.*
Central Oregon Visitors Association, Bend: *(800) 800-8334.*
Deschutes National Forest, Bend: *(541) 388-2715.*
McKenzie Ranger District, McKenzie Bridge: *(541) 822-3381.*
Mountain Supply of Oregon, Sisters: *(541) 549-3251.*
Sisters Area Visitors Information Center, Sisters: *(541) 549-0251.*
Sisters Ranger District, Sisters: *(541) 549-2111.*
Willamette National Forest, Eugene: *(541) 465-6522.*

Bend
and the Upper Deschutes River

From where the Deschutes River enters Lake Billy Chinook on the north, east into the juniper and sagebrush desert to Hampton, south to La Pine, and west to Mount Bachelor, including Newberry Crater National Volcanic Monument and the towns of Redmond, Bend, Sunriver, and La Pine.

When you ask a Willamette Valley resident, during the gloom of a rainy winter, where in Oregon they would most like to live, more than a few would answer "Bend." The secret is out. Oregon's Upper Deschutes River country, from Redmond on the north to Bend in the center and Sunriver on the south, is one of the state's most appealing places to live.

It doesn't take a rocket scientist to figure this one out. Noise from saws and hammers, made by contractors scurrying around while building custom homes, apartment complexes, and shopping malls, can make it hard to carry on a conversation in Bend.

Why do Oregonians love the towns of the Upper Deschutes River? It's simple. The chance of seeing the sun more than doubles on the east side of Oregon's Cascades, compared to the fog-shrouded valleys on the wet western side. It's much easier to get motivated and head outdoors when the sun is shining. Central Oregon had long been famous for its fishing and camping when, in 1958, a group of local visionaries opened Mount Bachelor Ski and Summer Resort. Both the ski area and surrounding towns grew slowly until the mid-1980s, when things began to explode.

Attracted to the area for ski vacations, more than a few people settled in the Bend area and began looking for new ways to enjoy the outdoors. Instead of just skiing downhill, they began skating on Mount Bachelor's cross-country ski tracks, launching off Pine Mountain with a paraglider, screaming down Deschutes National Forest trails on mountain bikes, and running the Deschutes River in fiberglass kayaks. It takes a mighty big garage to store all the toys needed to enjoy the Upper Deschutes River, to say nothing of the versatile automobile roof racks that adorn the tops of resident cars and sport utility vehicles.

The population explosion hasn't been welcomed by some of the old-time residents, but the situation is a fact of life. The boom shows no indication of slowing, and there's no going back to the quieter times of the 1970s.

For those who can't move to the Upper Deschutes River country, the next best thing is to visit it regularly. A steady stream of cars heading east from the Willamette Valley across the Cascade mountain passes each weekend shows that's exactly what's happening.

Getting There

Bend is 160 miles southeast of Portland via US Highway 26 (US 26) and US 97. US 20, another major thoroughfare, passes through Bend on its east-west crossing of Oregon. The resort community of Sunriver is 14 miles south of Bend on US 97, and La Pine is 15 miles south of Sunriver. Redmond is 16 miles north of Bend on US 97. Newberry Crater rises above US 97 east of Sunriver, accessible by Deschutes National Forest Road 21. Century Drive heads southwest out of Bend, reaching the Mount Bachelor ski area in 22 miles and continuing into the Cascade Lakes country. Central Oregon has regional and commuter air service through Redmond Municipal Airport.

Adjoining Areas

NORTH: **Mount Jefferson and the Metolius River, Lower Deschutes River**

SOUTH: **Klamath Basin**

EAST: **Lower John Day River, Lake County**

WEST: **Three Sisters and Cascade Lakes, Santiam Pass and Mount Washington**

inside out

Downhill Skiing/Snowboarding

The first taste most visitors get for outdoor recreation, Upper Deschutes River style, comes at big, friendly **Mount Bachelor Ski and Summer Resort,** Oregon's busiest ski area. Not all expert skiers consider Mount Bachelor to be Oregon's best ski area, but when the full range of services and facilities is weighed, Bend is head and shoulders above anything else in Oregon. So what if Mount Bachelor doesn't have a lot of cliffs to jump off or double black-diamond chutes to scare yourself silly? Most skiers and snowboarders don't want those types of thrills anyway.

Statistics say a lot about Mount Bachelor—3,686 skiable acres, 3,365-foot vertical drop, 11 chairlifts (including seven high-speed quads), 56 kilometers of groomed trails in the Nordic center, 600,000 annual skier visits, and enough snow to operate from early November to July 4.

With an active marketing department and regular exposure in national ski magazines, Mount Bachelor attracts plenty of first-time visitors to Bend. Visitors usually decide to make an encore appearance, whether during the same winter or the following summer, when storm clouds lift and Broken Top and the Three Sisters mountains come into view a few miles north of the ski area.

Most skiers arrive at Mount Bachelor by private automobile. With acres of paved **parking,** it's vital to make a mental note of where you parked your car. The ski area operates $1 bus rides to the mountain from its parking lot on the southwest side of Bend at the intersection of Colorado and Simpson Aves. Free **shuttle buses** connect Mount Bachelor's base lodges every half hour. Central Oregon's big resorts (Sunriver, Inn of the Seventh Mountain, and Eagle's Crest) offer bus service to the ski area for their guests, either at a daily charge or included in the price of a ski package.

Mount Bachelor is 22 miles west of Bend via Century Dr. Numerous signs in town point the easiest way to reach Century Dr, whether from Division St from the north, Franklin Ave from the east, or Colorado Ave from the south. Sunriver is 20 miles away via a separate access road (Forest Rd 45) from the south. Both roads are kept plowed and sanded during winter, making Mount Bachelor one of Oregon's easiest ski areas to reach from its surrounding towns, and one of the few winter resorts in Oregon that does not require the state sno-park permit to park in its lots.

When arriving at the mountain, skiers have a choice of **three base facilities.** First along Century Dr comes Sunrise Lodge, followed by the

Junior Racing Center (formerly the Blue Lodge) and West Village. The Junior Racing Center is a staging area for regular guests of the ski resort who already have their lift tickets. The other two base areas have complete facilities, including day care. West Village is the main part of the resort where skiing began in 1958. The Mount Bachelor Nordic Center is located at the edge of the West Village parking lot (see Cross-Country Skiing, below). Mount Bachelor has no overnight accommodations, other than RV parking, but various lodgings are available nearby.

Not everything is perfect, however, because all that snow must fall sometime. Storms often blow for days at a time off the Pacific Ocean, less than 150 miles to the west, making ski conditions less than ideal. Oregon's freezing level fluctuates widely, meaning a powder-snow day can be followed by a day of rain and fog. Due to its location slightly east of the Cascade crest and its top elevation of 9,065 feet, highest of any Oregon ski area, Mount Bachelor has fewer bad days, however, than most Oregon ski areas. The ski area sells a popular-points **lift ticket** that can be used any day for up to three years, so if conditions turn bad the price of a lift ticket can be spread over a number of days. Cost of a daily lift ticket is in the $40 range ($2 more for the popular-points ticket).

Mount Bachelor's **chairlifts** are spread out one after another east to west on the symmetrical pumice cone that rises 3,000 feet above the surrounding forest. The east side, served by the Sunrise Lodge, has a three-lift complex. Farthest east is the Rainbow chair, a fixed-grip triple that rarely has a lift line. Runs are pretty flat, but most West Coast skiers should feel right at home on a trail called "I-5." The east edge of Rainbow has some good powder skiing in the trees, but skiers need to stay within ski area boundaries. The Carousel chair is a short chairlift for beginners, and Sunrise Express rises to mid-mountain where it feeds the Summit Express.

Skyliner Express at the Junior Racing Center bridges the gap between the other two base areas. The West Village area is served by three long high-speed lifts—Pine Marten Express, Outback Express, and Northwest Express—plus a shorter high-speed lift (Sunshine Accelerator) and two old-style fixed-grip lifts (Yellow and Red). Skiing on the lower mountain is pretty tame, but intermediate skiers who love groomed runs have a ball. The exception is the west side of the lower mountain, where runs begin to steepen at Outback and get long and steep at the Northwest chair. Skiers end up doing a lot of traversing as they cross back and forth on the lower mountain.

Mount Bachelor really begins to shine when the **Summit Express** chairlift is able to operate. The lift is weather dependent, but when it's closed because of weather, you wouldn't want to ride it anyway. Expect to find the Summit open 25 percent of the time during midwinter and

75 percent during spring. The Summit rises 1,725 vertical feet and opens the entire upper mountain to skiing. The exciting photos that make the national ski magazines are usually taken up in Cirque Bowl or from the cornice that crowns the West Ridge run. Built in 1983 as a three-seater, the Summit chairlift was the second high-speed chairlift constructed in North America. When the lift broke down in 1997, the ski area went ahead and replaced it with the latest high-speed quad technology.

The best skiing at Mount Bachelor comes when snow is light enough for skiers to escape the groomed runs and head for the trees. The much-anticipated Northwest Territory, which opened in 1996–97 with 458 acres of new terrain, has some of the best **tree skiing** in the Cascades. When the snow is heavy (it isn't nicknamed "Cascade Concrete" for nothing) and the weather closes the Summit chair, expert skiers quickly get bored at Mount Bachelor. With the ski area's more than 70 named runs and Oregon's biggest fleet of snow grooming machines, however, intermediate skiers can enjoy themselves for days.

Contact the ski area, in Bend, (541) 382-2442, or at the mountain, (541) 382-2607, or call (541) 382-7888 for **snow conditions.** Mount Bachelor Ski and Sports at West Village is Oregon's best on-mountain ski shop. Bend and Sunriver have nearly a dozen ski and snowboard shops that offer quality goods and services in order to stay in business in a highly competitive and knowledgeable market. Some of the oldest in Bend are Bend Ski and Sport, (541) 389-4667, at 1009 NW Galveston Ave; The Powder House, (541) 389-6234, 311 SW Century Dr; and Stowells Ski & Sports, (541) 382-5325, 10th St and Greenwood NE.

Cross-Country Skiing

Mount Bachelor Nordic Center and Century Drive

Home to several U.S. cross-country ski championships, Mount Bachelor sets the standard for Nordic centers in Oregon. Meticulously groomed, the 56-kilometer trail system has everything a Nordic skier could want—flat beginner areas, hills challenging enough to get an expert's heart pumping, even a biathlon target range for competitive shooters. The Nordic center offers complete facilities, from instruction to sales and rentals, and is located at Mount Bachelor's West Village, 22 miles west of Bend on Century Dr. Phone numbers are the same as for the downhill ski area—(541) 382-2442 for the Bend office and (541) 382-7888 for the snow report.

Beginners usually stick near the Nordic center on short loop trails that head north and east toward Century Dr. Intermediates can ski all day on trails named for some of the most famous local skiers—Devecka's Dive (Mike Devecka), Woody's Way (Bob Woodward), and Rich's Range Route

(Rich Gross). Experts pick from Oli's Alley (Dennis Oliphant) or Leslie's Lunge (Leslie Krichko).

The marked but ungroomed Deschutes National Forest trail system is accessible from the West Village parking lot by skiing the "common corridor" north through the Mount Bachelor trail system to the unplowed portion of Century Dr. Skiers who use Mount Bachelor's groomed trail system must have a trail pass. For ski rentals in Bend, check with Mountain Supply of Oregon, (541) 388-0688, at 2600 NE Division St.

The Oregon Department of Transportation's sno-park system has five plowed parking lots between Bend and Mount Bachelor on **Century Drive.** Vehicles using the lots must display an Oregon sno-park permit, or a permit from a neighboring state, to avoid getting a parking ticket. Permits are available at ski shops for about $10 for the season and $2 for the day.

Sno-parks and their milepost numbers west of Bend on Century Dr are **Virginia Meissner** (12), **Wanoga** (15.5), **Swampy Lakes** (16), **Vista Butte** (18), and **Dutchman Flat** (21). The Swampy Lakes area (5,700 feet in elevation) has about 25 miles of marked ski trails, plus two warming shelters, and is connected by ski trail to the Meissner and Vista Butte Sno-Parks. Wanoga is used primarily by snowmobilers. Dutchman Flat is a staging area for skiers and snowmobilers heading deep into the wilderness of the central Cascades.

The Forest Service can provide maps and trail descriptions of its cross-country ski areas. Contact the Bend Ranger District, (541) 388-5664.

More cross-country skiing

Knowing its guests wanted a direct connection to Mount Bachelor, Sunriver Resort helped the Forest Service upgrade Forest Rd 45, which begins at Sunriver and joins Century Dr 3 miles east of Mount Bachelor. The new road allowed Deschutes National Forest to open the **Edison Butte Trail System,** 4 miles south of the junction with Century Dr. Opened in the late 1980s, the Edison Butte system has become one of the most popular Nordic trail systems in the state for intermediate skiers and above. The 20 miles of marked trails wind through an old-growth ponderosa pine forest and a variety of volcanic formations, beginning at 5,100 feet in elevation. The sno-park is 12 miles northwest of Sunriver Lodge's main entrance, 1 mile west of US 97, and 14 miles south of Bend.

The **Skyliners Snow Play Area** on Tumalo Creek, site of the first downhill ski area in Central Oregon, is 10 miles west of downtown Bend on Skyliners Rd. The rope tow has long since disappeared, but people from Bend still drive out to where the winter road plowing ends to enjoy some tubing and cross-country skiing. To visit 97-foot-high **Tumalo Falls,** ski north from the parking area down a gentle hill, cross a bridge over

Tumalo Creek, turn west, and follow a gentle road for 2.5 miles. Cross a second bridge and look for the falls after 100 yards. Sno-park permits are not required at Tumalo Creek. Other beginner-to-intermediate ski opportunities are available from the parking area. Because the valley is tucked behind the big volcanoes to the west, it doesn't always have sufficient snow for skiing despite its elevation of 4,800 feet.

Skiers wanting to escape the crowds on the Mount Bachelor side of US 97 head for **Newberry Crater National Volcanic Monument** (see Camping, below) on the east side of US 97 between Sunriver and La Pine. While Nordic skiers visit in small numbers, snowmobilers frequent the area. The beauty of the monument—the vapor rising from the surface of Paulina Lake, the view from Washington to California from Paulina Peak, and the frozen sides of Paulina Creek Falls—makes putting up with a little snowmobile noise more than bearable. To reach Paulina Lake, drive the monument's access road 10 miles east of US 97 where plowing ends during the winter at **Tenmile Sno-Park.**

Other Winter Activities

Central Oregon is **snowmobile** country. The Oregon State Snowmobile Association and volunteers from the area's two snowmobile clubs groom more than 100 miles of trail every winter. The Moon Country Snowmobile Club takes care of the trails from **Wanoga Sno-Park** on Century Dr, and the La Pine Lodgepole Dodgers handle things up at **Paulina Lake** in Newberry Crater. Each publishes an annual trail guide that is available at snowmobile shops and at the Central Oregon Visitors Association, (541) 382-8334, 63085 N Hwy 97.

With its steady flow of vacationing tourists, the Bend area is one of the easiest spots in Oregon to rent a snowmobile and go for a **guided tour.** Fantastic Recreation Rentals, (541) 389-5640, has on-site rentals at Wanoga Sno-Park, and Paulina Tours, (541) 536-2214, operates out of Tenmile Sno-Park near the entrance to Newberry Crater. Both maintain a fleet of about 30 machines to rent by the hour or the day, guided or nonguided. Snowmobiling isn't cheap (about $160 for an 8-hour ride), but those who do it say the thrills are worth the expense.

For a quieter over-the-snow experience, Mount Bachelor's Sunrise Lodge offers **sled dog mushing** with Jerry Scdoris's Oregon Trail of Dreams kennel. A pair of sleds, with a crew of 48 dogs, keeps going nonstop on weekends. Midweek rides are also available. Scdoris hooks a second sled to each team so his physically fit guests can experience the feel of standing up and mushing a dog team. Others ride in the front sled behind the dogs with a musher in charge. A 1-hour tour costs about $60. Reservations can be made through Mount Bachelor at (800) 829-2442.

Outdoor **ice skating** is available, when the temperature is low enough, at Sunriver Resort and the Inn of the Seventh Mountain (both have skate rentals; see Lodgings, below) and at Shevlin Park, 4 miles west of Bend via Newport Ave (which becomes Shevlin Park Rd).

Volunteers from Deschutes National Forest offer guided winter interpretive tours on weekends and holidays at Mount Bachelor. The **snowshoe tour** leaves at 10am and 1:30pm from the Ski and Sport Building at West Village. Snowshoes are provided, or they can be rented at the Nordic center for use after the tour. The **Nordic ski tour** leaves at 10am from the Nordic lodge, and the **downhill ski tour** (featuring a discussion on geology) meets at the West Village information center at varying times. Skiers need to provide their own equipment and lift tickets. For information on the tours, call the Bend Ranger District, (541) 388-5664.

Cycling

The new 11-mile **Bend Parkway,** a $90 million project, will siphon some of the traffic from overloaded US 97 as it passes through Bend. The parkway's northern portion opened in late 1997, but the southern part won't be ready until 2001. The parkway, which cuts through the middle of Bend between US 97 and downtown, will have bike lanes along its entire length. The city has 21 miles of paved bicycle lanes, 60 miles total in the Urban Growth Boundary, plus another 34 miles of unimproved paths along the river and irrigation canals.

Deschutes County, (541) 388-6581, publishes a **bicycling guide** that is widely available in the half-dozen bike shops scattered around the Upper Deschutes River country. The guide is informative when spread out on a table, but don't expect to use it as a navigation aid while riding the county's roads. The county's drivers tend to be courteous, perhaps because they also may be cyclists.

The shoulders of the Upper Deschutes River country highway system are an easy way to rack up a lot of mileage. Cyclists who live in Bend think nothing of going on a 40-mile round-trip ride to visit a neighboring community. The county's network of paved secondary roads (Cline Falls Hwy, Alfalfa Market Rd, Powell Butte Hwy) provides an excellent way to get away from highway traffic and enjoy sights of the rapidly urbanizing county. The topography is relatively flat, making long-distance cycling easy, except when climbing a cinder cone or riding west into the Cascades.

A popular hill climb right in Bend is **Pilot Butte State Park,** located just off US 20 a few blocks east of US 97. The day-use park has a paved road that circles the butte as it winds to the top. The 300-foot climb is enough to get the heart pumping and is high enough for a 360-degree panorama of Bend and the Upper Deschutes River country. Sunset over the

Three Sisters mountains to the west can be quite incredible. Pilot Butte is closed to vehicular traffic during winter, but bicycles can use the road when it's not blocked by snow.

Another similar hill climb is **Lava Butte** at Lava Lands Visitors Center 10 miles south of Bend on US 97 (see Camping, below). Lava Butte also has a stunning view of the area. During summer, the Forest Service closes the road to motor vehicles, but cyclists should watch for the shuttle bus that cruises up and down the butte.

For visitors staying in central Bend's numerous motels, a popular ride follows the park system upriver **along the Deschutes.** Begin at Pioneer Park, where Portland Ave crosses the river, ride south upstream to join the multi-use path along Century Dr, then curve west as far as you care to ride toward Mount Bachelor. The route climbs gradually all the way, making for an easy downhill cruise back to town to complete the tour.

Sunriver Resort maintains Deschutes County's best network of bicycle paths. Sunriver's 33-mile bike trail system is popular with families and children, so it's not a good place for high-speed cruising. The trails are designed for resort residents and overnight guests, but visitors can enter the trail system where it passes through Sunriver Mall just inside the resort entrance (see Cross-Country Skiing, above).

Mountain Biking

If the sport of mountain-bike riding hadn't been invented in California's Marin County, someone surely would have figured it out in Central Oregon. With the exception of Utah's slickrock country, trail riding around Bend is about as good as it gets.

When snow locks up the mountains west of Bend, cyclists head for the extensive dirt-road system east of town. Much of the land is publicly owned and has good riding during winter when there's enough moisture in the ground to keep the dust down. The trail system is undeveloped, so bikers stick to the dirt roads until they learn where they like to ride. A big part of the wide-open spaces east of Bend is designated as an **off-highway-vehicle trail system.** Dirt bikes and four-wheel all-terrain vehicles congregate in Deschutes National Forest's East Fort Rock trail system (110,000 acres), south of US 20 and east of Newberry Crater along Forest Rd 18, and the Bureau of Land Management (BLM)'s Millican off-trail vehicle area (64,000 acres), 22 miles east of Bend on US 20 on the north side of the highway near the Millican store. Cyclists can use the off-highway trail systems, but most prefer to head elsewhere when motorized use is heavy. Popular mountain-biking areas east of Bend include **Horse Ridge,** 18 miles east of town on the north side of US 20, and **Pine Mountain** (turn south on Forest Rd 2017 at the Millican store). A map called "Mountain Biking Central Oregon," available in local cycling shops, shows all the best riding areas around Bend. For more information, contact the Prineville office of the BLM, (541) 416-6700, or the Bend/Fort Rock Ranger District, (541) 388-5664.

Another popular ride open most of the year is a 5-mile loop trail of Tumalo Creek at **Shevlin Park.** The park is 3 miles west of the entrance to Central Oregon Community College on Shevlin Park Rd at the outskirts of Bend. Most cyclists ride the road from town, make the upstream loop through the park, and ride back to town.

Unfortunately, single-track riding away from dirt roads that can be handled by beginners is a rarity. While expert mountain bikers, complete with scars on their chins and ham hocks for legs, revel in the challenges of steep uphills, beginners are left begging for a few thrills they can handle without fearing that death lurks around every bend in the trail.

There is one major exception. The Meadow–to–Benham Falls section of the **Deschutes River Trail** near the Inn of the Seventh Mountain may be the best single-track ride in Oregon for beginners. A single afternoon riding a rented bike on the trail has probably led to the purchase of hundreds of mountain bikes, only for the new owners to discover there is nothing else around quite so enjoyable.

The 10.5-mile Deschutes River Trail begins at **Meadow picnic area,** 5 miles west of Bend and 1 mile south of Century Dr (watch for the marked turn less than a mile before the turnoff for the Inn). The trail follows the west bank of the Deschutes past three waterfalls—Lava Island, Dillon, and Benham—before ending at the **Benham Falls** trailhead 5 miles from Sunriver. The trail is used heavily, especially on weekends, by hikers, horse riders, and bikers. In places, each user group has its own separate track. Due to the trail's constant branching, it's hard to know if you're on the right branch or not. Follow the trail upstream, yielding to hikers and equestrians, until you cross the wooden footbridge over the Deschutes above Benham Falls. Then turn around and pedal back to your car.

It's a very special place, especially when the aspens across the river turn gold in late September. The first part of the trail from Meadow has a couple of steep, rocky sections that could intimidate a beginner. To avoid them, drive west of the turnoff to the Inn to Forest Rd 41, signed for **Deschutes River Recreation Sites.** Turn south, then head toward the river on any of several marked roads to Lava Island Falls (.8 mile from Century Dr), Aspen and Big Eddy (1.9 miles), Dillon Falls or Slough Camp (3 miles), and Benham Falls (3.7 miles). Get on your bike and ride south along the river. Your face will carry a smile the rest of the day.

The hard bodies who disdain the easy pedaling along the river have plenty of alternatives—**Phil's Trail, Rockless Ridge Loop,** or **South Fork**

Trail, all off Skyliners Rd near Tumalo Falls, and **Swede Ridge Loop** at Swampy Lakes (see Cross-Country Skiing, above). Stop at the Bend Ranger Station, 1230 NE Third St, Suite A-262, to pick up the brochure called "Mountain Biking in Central Oregon" (west of Bend) for route details. Another Forest Service brochure for trails south of Bend points the way to rides in Newberry Crater, again mostly for experts. Local bike shops sell the "Mountain Biking Central Oregon" **map** that has plenty more suggestions.

One of the best ways to learn the local trails is to hire a guide. Because of its constant flow of tourists, the Upper Deschutes River country is one of the few places in Oregon where a mountain-bike **guide service** can hang up a shingle and make a go of it. Pacific Crest Mountain Bike Tours, (541) 383-5058, offers a variety of rides, anywhere from a few hours to four days. A popular sampler is the Three Sisters Country downhill tour for about $50. High Cascade Descent Guide Service, 541-389-0562, leads a downhill tour past a half-dozen waterfalls to Paulina Lake. If you're in the area long enough, you might be able to join a ride organized by the four Bend bike clubs listed on the *Deschutes County Bicycling Guide,* available at stores listed here.

For **bike rentals,** check out Hutch's Bicycle Store, (541) 382-6248, 820 NE Third St, and Mount Bachelor Bike & Fitness Shop, (541) 382-4000, 1244 NW Galveston Ave, both in Bend, or The Village Bike Shop, (541) 593-2453, Building 21 at the Sunriver Village Mall.

Camping

The Upper Deschutes River country is often passed through by campers heading into the Cascade Lakes area west of Mount Bachelor, except for **Newberry Crater National Volcanic Monument** where the scenery and fishing tempt visitors to enjoy long stays. Congress created the 56,000-acre monument in 1990; user fees were initiated in 1997 under a three-year demonstration program. Developed areas in the monument (Newberry Crater and Lava Lands Visitors Center) charge $5 for a five-day pass or $20 for an annual pass. **Lava Lands Visitors Center** is on the west side of US 97, 11 miles south of Bend, and has barrier-free facilities. **Newberry Crater** is 8 miles south of the turnoff for Sunriver and 14 miles east of US 97 on Forest Rd 21. For information, contact monument headquarters at Lava Lands Visitors Center, (541) 593-2421.

Newberry Crater is what remains of an ancient volcano that collapsed like the one that created Crater Lake in Oregon's Southern Cascades. It's been said that if Oregon didn't have Crater Lake, Newberry Crater would have been designated as Oregon's only national park. Newberry Crater is

5 miles in diameter, has two large lakes inside its walls, and is crowned on the south by 7,984-foot Paulina Peak. The crater area has seven Forest Service campgrounds, including a group and horse camp, plus two small walk-in campgrounds on the shore of Paulina Lake. The campgrounds are managed by Northwest Land Management, (541) 433-2309. Reservations are available at the largest campgrounds by calling the Forest Service's national reservations system, (800) 280-2267.

Paulina Lake, with an elevation of 6,331 feet, makes up the west side of the crater. The lake's campgrounds are **Paulina Lake Campground** (71 sites) and **Little Crater Campground** (51 sites).

East Lake, 5 miles farther east into Newberry Crater, is home to **East Lake** (31 sites) **and Hot Springs Campgrounds** (43 sites). Campers in the Upper Deschutes River country are served by a pair of state parks— **Tumalo State Park,** 1 mile south of US 20 at Tumalo on Tumalo Creek Rd, and **La Pine State Recreation Area,** 8 miles south of Sunriver on the west side of US 97. Both parks are managed by the Bend state parks office, (541) 382-3586, and are situated on the Deschutes River. Tumalo has 65 tent campsites and 22 trailer spaces with full utility hookups. La Pine has 145 sites, most with full utilities. Because most campers head for Central Oregon's mountain lakes (see Three Sisters and Cascade Lakes chapter), the parks usually have openings even on summer weekends. Spaces at both can be reserved through the Oregon State Parks reservations system, (800) 452-5687. Tumalo is open all year, while La Pine is open March through October.

The Deschutes River hosts several small campgrounds as it runs between Sunriver and Bend. Although situated in scenic settings, the camps are small and lack full services. To locate them, drive 1 mile west of the Inn of the Seventh Mountain on Century Dr and turn south on Forest Rd 41 at the sign for Deschutes River Recreation Sites. Watch for signs to **Dillon and Slough Campgrounds** 3 miles from Century Dr. Because of the damage camping brings to riparian areas, the Forest Service will be phasing out camping along the river. The area is managed by the Bend Ranger District, (541) 388-5664.

Picnics

Seasoned travelers to the Upper Deschutes River country bring a blanket and a picnic basket filled with food everywhere they travel because it's never difficult to find a beautiful spot to stop for lunch. Riverside parks popular for picnics in Bend are **Drake Park** on Mirror Pond in downtown Bend, **Pioneer Park** on Newport Ave, and **Robert Sawyer State Park** on O. B. Riley Rd, which heads northwest from US 97 at the north end of town and continues to Tumalo State Park. For a picnic with a view, drive to the top of **Pilot Butte State Park** on the east side of Bend just north of US 20.

Cline Falls State Park is a delightful day-use area 5 miles west of Redmond on Hwy 126. The park sits on the Deschutes River, where a hungry beaver has been working to cut down a riverside tree fully 3 feet in diameter. The beaver still has a long way to go.

Tumalo State Park, 5 miles northwest of Bend on O. B. Riley Rd (see Camping, above), has a lovely picnic area across the entry road from the campground. The park charges a $3 day-use fee, so its picnic grounds frequently sit empty while crowds fill nearby **Shevlin Park** (see Winter Sports, above) and Cline Falls State Park.

Fishing

Record-size German brown trout lurk deep in the waters of **Paulina Lake** and **East Lake** of Newberry Crater National Volcanic Monument. Oregon's official record was taken from Paulina Lake in 1993 and weighed 27 pounds, 12 ounces. A 35-pound, 8-ounce German brown was netted while it recovered near the Paulina Lake shore after it broke a fisherman's line. Paulina Lake covers 1,320 acres and has a maximum depth of 250 feet. East Lake covers 1,050 acres and has a maximum depth of 150 feet. Boat launches are at the campgrounds (see Camping, above).

Fishing for the big German browns is best near shore, or by boat in shallow water, after the ice leaves the lakes early in spring, then again in fall when the fish build their reserves for winter. The big ones typically go deep during summer to reach the colder waters. While a German brown weighing more than 20 pounds is a rarity, the lakes regularly produce fish weighing 7 to 10 pounds. The lakes are also home to foot-long rainbow trout and the state's biggest kokanee (landlocked sockeye salmon). The record kokanee was caught in 1989 and weighed 4 pounds, 2 ounces.

Trolling is the most popular fishing method. Rental boats are available at marinas on both lakes at the Paulina Lake (541) 536-2240 and East Lake (541) 536-2230 Resorts. Speed limit is 10mph and fishing season lasts from Oregon's traditional trout opener on the last Saturday of April to October 31.

More than 70 miles of the **Deschutes River** are in the Bend area, from where the river leaves Wickiup Reservoir (see Three Sisters and Cascade Lakes chapter) to where it forms Lake Billy Chinook in the impoundment behind Round Butte Dam (see Lower Deschutes River chapter). Much of the river offers outstanding fly-fishing for trout, although access is not always easy because of private land in the lower reaches. The river is open all year from Lake Billy Chinook upstream to Benham Falls, but only from the last Saturday of April through September 30 from Benham Falls upstream to Wickiup Reservoir. Most angling is done from the bank because the river's current and hidden drops make wading too dangerous. Water level fluctuates during summer's irrigation season when much of the river's flow is diverted through Central Oregon's canal system.

Fishermen who enjoy a challenge in getting to the water head for the section of river below **Lower Bridge** near Terrebonne. From Lower Bridge, the Deschutes runs 15 miles through a rugged, roadless canyon before reaching Lake Billy Chinook. Access is by foot along the river after parking at the end of the road system in the Crooked River Ranch, a real-estate development set on a narrow strip of land (with the Crooked River to the east and the Deschutes River to the west), 5 miles west of US 97 at Terrebonne on Lower Bridge Rd. The river access path starts at a small BLM campground just above Steelhead Falls (see Hiking, below).

Local **fly-fishing shops** include the Fly Box, (541) 388-3330, 1293 NW Third St, and the Patient Angler, (541) 389-6208, 55 NW Wall St, both in Bend. At Sunriver, look for The Hook, (541) 593-2358, in the Village Mall. Check with the shops to learn what lures the trout are biting and what **guide services** are available. Regulations are outlined in the state fishing synopsis. For information, contact the Bend office of the Oregon Department of Fish and Wildlife, (541) 388-6363.

Wildlife

Wildlife-watching opportunities can be found at the High Desert Museum, (541) 382-4754, 4 miles south of Bend on US 97, and the Sunriver Nature Center. The museum displays captive native animals that help visitors learn what to watch for in the wild. **River otters** are among the most popular captives, although daily presentations of native raptors (**eagles, hawks, and owls**) come in a close second. The museum maintains its 150 acres to provide habitat for free-roaming species, especially migrating **songbirds, squirrels,** and **chipmunks.** See Attractions, below.

The village of Sunriver prides itself on maintaining a variety of native wildlife habitats among its expensive homes and golf courses. The Sunriver Nature Center, (541) 593-4394, has 7 acres set amid lodgepole and ponderosa pines where many birds and small mammals live and pass through. The nature center includes a lake, marsh, amphitheater, and observatory, plus the only native botanical garden east of Oregon's Cascade Mountains.

Wildlife can be seen just about everywhere in the Upper Deschutes River country. An amazing sight occurred along the shore of the Deschutes

River just below Benham Falls. This is one of the river's most awesome sections, with powerful undercurrents that keep all but the region's very best kayakers away. Movement along the river's west bank proved to be a **mink.** Without hesitation, the mink leaped into the river, disappeared beneath the wild whitewater, popped its head above the surface midway across, dived in again, and emerged on the other shore. About a foot long, the mink was such a powerful swimmer that the river's current barely pushed it downstream during its crossing.

Rafting/Kayaking/Canoeing

Unlike the Lower Deschutes, the **Upper Deschutes River,** with some notable exceptions, is rarely boated. Whitewater thrills that make the lower river a rafting playground are restricted on the Upper Deschutes to a short 3-mile section called the **Big Eddy** run. The rest of the river is either too flat for rafting or too dangerous for commercial operations.

Rafting trips are easy to book through the activity desk for guests at the region's major resorts (Sunriver, Eagle Crest, Inn of the Seventh Mountain; see Lodgings, below). Sun Country Tours, (541) 382-6277, located at the Sunriver Marina, helps visitors staying elsewhere climb aboard a paddle raft and get wet. Tours depart six times daily during summer from Bend and Sunriver. An outing takes only 3 hours from Sunriver or 2 hours from Bend, including vehicle shuttles, and costs $34. Hemmed in by waterfalls on either side, the short run gives paddlers the opportunity to experience Big Eddy's Class III rapids and decide whether they want to head for Maupin on the Lower Deschutes River for a full day of excitement. For a list of the half-dozen outfitters that operate on the Bend section of the Deschutes, check the yellow pages under rafting or contact the Bend Ranger District, (541) 388-5664.

Central Oregon's flotilla of hard-shell kayakers often spends an entire day surfing the hole at the bottom of Big Eddy. Why go elsewhere when it's as good as this? To see the kayakers in action, drive a mile west of the Inn of the Seventh Mountain, turn south on Forest Rd 41, signed for the **Deschutes River Recreation Sites,** and follow signs to Big Eddy. The parking lot is 200 yards back from the river.

Now a disclaimer about other parts of the Deschutes near the Big Eddy section: Don't even think of boating it, unless you have world-class skills and the water conditions are ideal. A few local kayakers run what is called the "Triple Crown" (Benham, Dillon, and Lava Island Falls), and a team of the best paddle rafters in Oregon has safely negotiated the section. But more often than not, when word filters out about boating on this part of the

Deschutes, it has more to do with courageous rescues by the county sheriff department's search-and-rescue team or, unfortunately, about drownings of boaters foolish enough to try it.

Above Benham Falls, the Deschutes has more than 40 miles of placid, Class I canoe water. The 9-mile float from **Wickiup Reservoir** to **Pringle Falls** is especially beautiful (see Three Sisters and Cascade Lakes chapter). The key to enjoying this part of the Deschutes is knowing in advance precisely where to take out your canoe to avoid log jams and waterfalls. Hazards are marked, but there is no room for error. Check with Bend Whitewater Supply Co., (541) 388-0361, 413 NW Hill St, for up-to-date information. The safest places to paddle on the Deschutes are at **La Pine State Recreation Area** (see Camping, above), at the **Sunriver marina,** and on **Mirror Pond** in downtown Bend's Drake Park.

From Bend to Lake Billy Chinook, the river doesn't always carry enough water for boating during the summer irrigation season. When the flow picks up in the fall, adventuresome kayakers head for **Steelhead Falls** (see Hiking, below), where they make the 18-foot plunge over and over. This is not an adventure for beginners. A few boaters run all the way to Lake Billy Chinook, but once they hit the lake's flat water and have to paddle 3 miles to the road, they don't often repeat the trip.

Hiking

The eastern portion of Deschutes National Forest lies within the **Fort Rock Ranger District.** Most of the land is volcanic with little surface water, except for the lakes in Newberry Crater National Volcanic Monument, so backpacking is rare. Trails are clustered near Lava Lands Visitors Center, within Newberry Crater, and the Swamp Wells complex southeast of Bend. The Fort Rock and Bend Ranger Stations share the same offices at 1230 NE Third St, Suite A-262, and the same telephone number, (541) 388-5664.

Lava Lands has a half-dozen short interpretive trails from the visitors center (see Camping, above) and Lava Butte that teach visitors about the lava flows that formed the area. The most popular are **Lava Butte Trail,** which loops around the top of the crater rim of a cinder cone; **Trail of the Whispering Pines,** which skirts the edge of a lava flow; and the trail through **Lava Cast Forest.** The visitors center is open from April through October, although Forest Service budget problems change the schedule every year.

The ultimate hike at Newberry Crater (see Cross-Country Skiing and Camping, above) is the 20-mile **Crater Rim Loop.** It has many access points from the crater's roads, including Paulina Lake Lodge, but there is no water except for snowbanks.

The **South Paulina Peak Trail** (difficult; 6.5 miles round trip) offers a trail experience, rather than a road, to reach the highest point on the caldera. The north side of the peak has a gravel road to the summit that begins at Paulina Lake Lodge. To reach the trailhead, turn south from Forest Rd 21, 1 mile before entering Newberry Crater, onto Forest Rd 2121. Drive south 4 miles, turn east onto Forest Rd 2225, and drive 2 miles to the trailhead.

The **Peter Skene Ogden National Scenic Trail** (difficult; 8.5 miles one way) leads from Ogden Group Camp at 4,300 feet in elevation on Forest Rd 21, 3 miles east of US 97, all the way to Paulina Lake Resort at 6,250 feet. The trail passes several waterfalls on Paulina Creek, including 80-foot-high **Paulina Creek Falls** just below the lake's outlet. A short trail leads up **Big Obsidian Flow,** one of the largest exposed piles of black volcanic glass in Oregon, from a signed parking area inside the crater on Forest Rd 21, 2 miles east of Paulina Lake Resort.

The **Swamp Wells complex** is in the forested lava flats southeast of Bend along Forest Rd 1610. Much of the use comes from people visiting the area's lava tubes. Many of the trails are too long to hike as one-way routes, but mountain bikers and equestrians can easily cover the distances.

The **Bend Ranger District,** located west of Bend and Sunriver, packs most of its hiking and backpacking opportunities into the high Cascades (see Three Sisters and Cascade Lakes chapter). A major exception is the Meadow–to–Benham Falls section of the **Deschutes River Trail** (moderate; 10.5 miles one way). Hikers usually enjoy small parts of the trail, while bikers get it all (see Mountain Biking, above).

The Upper Deschutes River country has some hiking opportunities where locals rarely encounter visitors from outside the area. **Steelhead Falls,** an 18-foot-high, riverwide waterfall, is less than a mile from a small BLM campground adjacent to the Crooked River Ranch. Locating the trailhead is anything but easy. From Crooked River Ranch headquarters, turn west on Badger Rd. Drive .6 mile and turn right on Bullhead Rd, drive .6 mile and turn left on Ermine Dr, drive 1.3 miles and turn left on Quail Rd. Drive .4 mile and turn right on River Rd, drive 1.1 miles, and park. If all else fails, ask for directions at the ranch's real-estate office. To find the falls, walk north on the river's east bank for less than 1 mile.

The lava country east of Bend along US 20 is popular during the off-season when snow locks up the high country to the west. **Dry River Canyon,** just north of the highway at milepost 17.9, begins near a highway department gravel pit. Drive through the piles of gravel to the east and reach the mouth of the canyon in 1.25 miles. Park and hike as far as you want (moderate; 4 miles one way to the end of the canyon) beneath the canyon's 300-foot walls. The western juniper trees are especially fragrant after the first rains of fall. Other public land in the area tempts hikers to venture cross-country, but the terrain is without distinguishing features and a compass may be needed to return to your starting point.

Other hiking opportunities include the resort trail systems at **Sunriver** and **Eagle Crest** (see Lodgings, below) and the cross-country ski systems that begin at the **sno-parks** on the way to Mount Bachelor (see Cross-Country Skiing, above). Interestingly, skiers used to hike to the summit of **Mount Bachelor** before the Summit chair was built in 1983. It's still possible to hike to the top via any of the downhill ski trails when skiing is closed for summer. The elevation gain is a hefty 3,000 feet. The **Tumalo Butte Trail** (moderate; 3 miles round trip) begins on Century Dr, just north of the entry for Mount Bachelor's West Village lodge. The butte rises to 7,775 feet and gives an outstanding view of the Three Sisters area.

Caving/Climbing

Oregon's **lava tubes,** many of them located on Deschutes National Forest land southeast of Bend, offer some underground fun, especially during summer when the outside temperature pushes toward 100°. The interior of a lava tube maintains a year-round temperature of 50°.

The cave most explorers start with is **Lava River,** a 1.5-mile tube located at a marked turnoff just east of US 97 near the north entrance to Sunriver. The Forest Service's concessionaire offers tours and lantern rentals during summer. Visitors who want to explore the cave on their own should bring reliable light sources. There's really no way to get lost because the cave is a single tube with a 15- to 20-foot-high ceiling and an improved trail along the floor. Stop at the Lava Lands Visitors Center, (541) 593-2421, 2 miles north on US 97, for information and to buy the Deschutes National Forest map, which shows the locations of many other caves in the area.

After acquiring a taste for caving, explorers can decide for themselves whether they want to seek out the numerous other caves in the area. Some of the more popular ones are **Arnold Ice Cave, Boyd Cave, Skeleton Cave,** and **Wind Cave,** all clustered close to each other 12 miles southeast of Bend on Forest Rd 18, and **South Ice Cave,** 24 miles east of La Pine on Forest Rd 22. All are shown on the Deschutes National Forest map. Forest Service roads pass within a short, well-trod walk to the entrance of the caves. Again, be sure to carry and use multiple light sources. One of the scariest adventures in the Upper Deschutes River country can happen when you've been crawling around in a cave and can't find the way back out. Cave topography occasionally hides the light that filters through the entrance, so be prepared to mark your route in any cave that splits into multiple channels.

Central Oregon's growing number of **rock climbers** have found that the entrances of lava tubes provide them some interesting challenges, especially when weather makes it difficult to climb on local crags. Spelunkers alerted land managers about the nontraditional use, and these managers placed a moratorium on use of permanent bolts by rock climbers. Most bolts that were already placed were allowed to stay at Skeleton, Wind, and Arnold Caves. The bolts are used to protect climbers from falls, especially as they climb around the overhang at the mouth of a cave.

Central Oregon's most beautiful cave is **Lavacicle Cave.** One of the few lava tubes in the world that has stalactites, the cave's entrance is protected by a locked gate. The Forest Service used to lead regular tours of the cave, but the program has been discontinued due to lack of funding. The Lava Lands Visitors Center, (541) 593-2421, occasionally gives the key to groups that can be trusted to leave the cave the way they found it and may lead unscheduled tours.

Hang Gliding/Paragliding

Pine Mountain, site of a mountaintop observatory, has long been known as a launch point for hang gliders. The 6,405-foot mountain is located 25 miles southeast of Bend. Turn south from US 20 at Millican to reach Pine Mountain (see Mountain Biking, above).

The latest group to use Pine Mountain for flying is paragliders. Still a tiny sport in Oregon, paragliding continues to grow slowly. Bend's Skyhook Sports, (541) 389-4086, has been teaching paragliding for a decade. An annual September fly-in draws more than 50 pilots from around the Northwest. Oregon's distance record in a paraglider is 68.6 miles on a launch from Pine Mountain. Desert thermals east of Bend can make for some pretty bumpy air currents, so Pine Mountain is not an area for beginners. (Skyhook Sports also offers beginner lessons on the Oregon Coast.)

Mount Bachelor became the first Oregon ski area in 1996 to allow lift-assisted paragliding. Due to the weather, the flying season is usually during the summer. The Summit chair remains open for sightseers through Labor Day. Permission to fly must be obtained from the Desert Air Riders club through Skyhook Sports.

Flight-seeing tours of the Upper Deschutes River country are available from Sun Air at the Sunriver Airport, (541) 593-1860; the Flight Shop in Bend, (541) 382-3801, at Bend Airport, 63132 Powell Butte Rd; and Rainbow Helicopters in Redmond, (541) 548-3255, at 2135 SE Airport Way.

outside **in**

Attractions

Bend was a quiet, undiscovered high-desert paradise until a push in the 1960s to develop recreation and tourism tamed Bachelor Butte (later renamed Mount Bachelor) into an alpine playground. Then came the golf courses, the airstrip, the bike trails, the river-rafting companies, the hikers, the tennis players, the rockhounds, and the skiers. Bend's popularity and its population (more than 50,000) have been on a steady increase ever since, propelling it into serious-destination status. The main thoroughfare, 10 miles of uninspired strip development, bypasses the historic town center, which thrives just to the west between two one-way streets, Wall and Bond. Part of the charm of the town comes from the blinding blue sky and the pine-scented air. The other part of its appeal is its proximity to a multitude of outdoor activities.

The **High Desert Museum,** 59800 US 97, Bend, OR 97702, (541) 382-4754, is an outstanding nonprofit center for natural and cultural history, located 4 miles south of Bend. Inside, visitors can walk through 100 years of history, featuring excellent dioramas from early Native American times through the 1890s. A "desertarium" exhibits desert animals, including live owls, lizards, and Lahontan cutthroat trout. Twenty acres of natural trails and outdoor exhibits offer replicas of covered wagons, a sheepherder's camp, a settlers' cabin, and an old sawmill and support three resident river otters, three porcupines, and about a half-dozen raptors (animal presentations daily). The museum's Rimrock Cafe serves better-than-average deli lunches, 11am to 5pm.

The **Deschutes Historical Center** (corner of NW Idaho and Wall) features regional history and interesting pioneer paraphernalia but keeps limited hours (open Tuesday through Saturday), (541) 389-1813.

Pine Mountain Observatory, 30 miles southeast of Bend on US 20, (541) 382-8331, is the University of Oregon's astronomy research facility and is open to the public in summer (the observatory is closed during winter). One of its three telescopes is the largest in the Northwest.

Restaurants

Alpenglow Cafe   The alpenglow they're referring to is probably the warm feeling in your belly after you eat their mountain of breakfast (served all day). Orange juice is fresh squeezed, bacon is locally smoked, and breads are homemade. *1040 NW Bond St (next to Deschutes Brewery), Bend; (541) 383-7676; $.*

Cafe Rosemary ☆☆ This tiny restaurant serves up wonderful food. Appreciative diners have been known to applaud both the meal and the chef, who serves up simple, magical lunches and dinners. All food can be prepared to go. *222 NW Irving (call for directions), Bend; (541) 317-0276; $$.*

Deschutes Brewery & Public House This is still the best brewpub in town. The beer is dark or light, as you like it: a robust Obsidian Stout or a hoppy Cascade Golden Ale. There's bar food for midday and a full dinner menu—most folks come for the brew. *1044 NW Bond St (near corner of Greenwood), Bend; (541) 382-9242; $.*

Honkers ☆ You're bound to see Canada geese flying over the Deschutes River, so reserve a window seat. Most diners enjoy the charbroiled salmon, and pork chops with apple and raisin chutney. Decor pays homage to a bygone lumber-mill era. *805 SW Industrial Way (east bank of Deschutes, just off Colorado Ave), Bend; (541) 389-4665; $$.*

Pine Tavern Restaurant ☆☆ Fifty years of history—and a reputation for quality—make the Pine Tavern truly established. Eat in the main dining room and marvel at the tree growing through the floor. The prime rib is the restaurant's forte. *967 NW Brooks (foot of Oregon Ave downtown at Mirror Pond), Bend; (541) 382-5581; $$.*

Rosette ☆☆ The dining room looks so light and airy that it's surprising to see such hearty dishes and a mostly meat dinner menu. Wash it all down with a stout beer. Lunches take a lighter, more Asian turn. *150 NW Oregon Ave (between Bond and Wall), Bend; (541) 383-2780; $$.*

Cheaper Eats

Cafe Sante Cyclists and in-line skaters whiz by this cafe on the edge of Drake Park. Main attractions are healthy grub (vegetable stir-frys, barbe-cued rock shrimp) and a kicked-back ambience. Sidewalk tables make lounging easy. *718 NW Franklin Ave, Bend; (541) 383-3530; $.*

Mexicali Rose This celebrated Tex-Mex eatery sits on one of Bend's busiest intersections. Order the steak, chicken, or veggie picados or any of the combo meals and ask for black beans. *301 NE Franklin Ave, Bend; (541) 389-0149; $.*

Lodgings

Entrada Lodge ☆ Weary travelers and avid skiers looking for a firm mattress, a shower, and a clean room will get that and more at this ranch-style motel. Pets are allowed (some restrictions). *19221 Century Dr (3 miles from Bend), Bend, OR 97702; (541) 382-4080 or (800) 528-1234; $$.*

Inn at Eagle's Crest ☆☆ Visitors choose a hotel room or a condo (a better deal) at this full resort, which sports an 18-hole golf course; miles of trails; tennis courts; an equestrian center; and a recreation center with indoor tennis, squash, and racquetball courts, workout room, masseuse, and heated outdoor pool. *821 S Sixth St (5 miles west of Redmond on Hwy 126, turn south on Cline Falls Rd), Redmond; PO Box 867, Redmond, OR 97756; (541) 923-2453 or (800) MUCH-SUN; $$.*

Inn of the Seventh Mountain ☆☆ The closest accommodations to Mount Bachelor, the inn is popular with families due to the vast menu of activities built into the multicondominium facility and the reasonable price tag. It has a large ice rink, a coed sauna, hot tubs, and heated swimming pools. The Inn does a terrific job of social planning and offers great off-season rates. Plenty of good eating, too. *18575 SW Century Dr (7 miles west of downtown), Bend; PO Box 1207, Bend, OR 97702; (541) 382-8711 or (800) 452-6810; $$$.*

Lara House Bed and Breakfast ☆ One of Bend's oldest homes, this is a bright, homey bed and breakfast, remodeled with new private bathrooms in all rooms. A big breakfast is served, and there's a spa tub. There's also a two-bedroom apartment. *640 NW Congress (at Louisiana), Bend, OR 97701; (541) 388-4064; $$.*

Mount Bachelor Village ☆☆ What this development has over neighboring resorts is spacious rooms. Every unit has a furnished kitchen, a wood-burning fireplace, and a private deck. Amenities: two outdoor Jacuzzis, tennis courts, a nature trail, and Scanlon's restaurant. *19717 Mt Bachelor Dr (toward Mt Bachelor on Century Dr), Bend, OR 97702; (541) 389-5900 or (800) 452-9846; $$$.*

The Riverhouse ☆ The Riverhouse is an institution, offering comfortable stays at more reasonable rates than the resorts. Amenities are many: swimming pools, saunas, whirlpools, exercise room, 18-hole golf course, and tennis courts. The lounge rocks, so avoid nearby rooms unless you plan to dance all night. *3075 N Hwy 97 (across from Bend River Mall), Bend, OR 97701; (541) 389-3111 or (800) 547-3928; $$.*

Sunriver Lodge ☆☆☆ Sunriver is an organized community with its own post office, chamber of commerce, realty offices, grocery store, and more than 1,500 residents. The specialty of the unincorporated town (sprawling over 3,300 acres) is big-time escapist vacationing, and this resort has all the facilities to keep you busy all week long, year-round—from golf to whitewater rafting to horseback riding to skiing. For the best bargain, deal through the lodge reservations service, request one of the large and contemporary homes, and split expenses with another family. *Off US 97,*

15 miles south of Bend, Sunriver; PO Box 3609, Sunriver, OR 97707; (541) 593-1000 or (800) 547-3922; $$$.

Cheaper Sleeps

Bend Alpine Hostel This large, boxy structure sits within walking distance of the (free) Mount Bachelor ski shuttle. Dorm-room beds are $14 a pop and private rooms are $14 a person (kids are half price). Bring sleeping bag and towels. Guests have access to the kitchen, laundry, and storage. *19 SW Century Dr, Bend, OR 97702; (541) 389-3813 or (800) 299-3813; $.*

Westward Ho Motel The Westward Ho, where rooms run less than $40, is the best value of the traditional-motel bunch on US 97. Most rooms are far enough off the highway, and there's a small indoor pool and Jacuzzi, and plenty of TV channels. *904 SE 3rd St, Bend, OR 97701; (541) 382-2111 or (800) 999-8143; $.*

More Information

Bend Chamber of Commerce, Bend: *(800) 905-2363.*
Bend Ranger District, Bend: *(541) 388-5664.*
Bureau of Land Management, Prineville: *(541) 416-6700.*
Central Oregon Visitors Association, Bend: *(800) 800-8334.*
Deschutes National Forest, Bend: *(541) 388-2715.*
Fort Rock Ranger District, Bend: *(541) 388-5664.*
Metro Parks and Recreation, Bend: *(541) 389-7275.*
Mount Bachelor (central reservations), Bend: *(800) 829-2442.*
Newberry Crater National Volcanic Monument, Sunriver:
     (541) 593-2421.
Redmond Chamber of Commerce, Redmond: *(800) 574-1325.*
Sunriver Area Chamber of Commerce, Sunriver: *(541) 593-8149.*

Three Sisters
and Cascade
Lakes

From Highway 242 near McKenzie Pass on the north, east along the Cascade Lakes Highway (Forest Road 46), south to Highway 58 near Willamette Pass, and west into the central Cascades, including the eastern and southern approaches to the Three Sisters Wilderness and Cascade Lakes resorts.

The $64,000 question every spring in Central Oregon is "When will the Cascade Lakes Highway open for the season?" Closed each winter by abundant snowfall, the road is usually plowed so that it's ready to open in time for the annual Memorial Day migration of campers and fishermen to the lakes that line the highway. Hikers and backpackers intent on visiting the Three Sisters Wilderness have to wait for summer's next holiday, the Fourth of July, when most backcountry trails finally melt free of snow.

The Cascade Lakes Highway, a 93-mile national scenic byway that loops into the mountains west of Bend and La Pine, is one of the busiest summer mountain-vacation destinations in Oregon. Convenient to US Highway 97, the beginning of the Cascade Lakes loop is four hours' or less driving time from most of Oregon's major cities. By the time road crews begin punching out a route in mid-May, an average winter's snow will have settled on the highway to a depth of 10 feet or more. It takes the big plows a couple weeks to clear the way, but when the weather warms the snow disappears amazingly fast.

The highway changes direction from east-west to north-south when it reaches a big bend at Sparks Lake, 25 miles west of Bend. Most of the land to the north and west is part of the Three Sisters Wilderness, the most heavily used wilderness in the state for hiking and backpacking. Then comes the continuous string of scenic lakes—Devils, Elk, Hosmer, Lava, Little Lava, Cultus, Little Cultus, Crane Prairie, Twin, and Wickiup. It's a miracle that the mosquitoes aren't worse than they are.

Some visitors see the sights in a day, content to marvel at views of the Three Sisters volcanoes and to pause for a picnic at the Deschutes River's headwaters at Little Lava Lake. Others set up camp for a week at a time, with only summer's vigorous crop of mosquitoes discouraging them from staying longer.

Mountain bikers, equestrians, fishermen, windsurfers, and sailors all have their favorite spots to recreate along the Cascade Lakes Highway. The lakes at the southern part of the loop are lower in elevation, so the highway is usually open by the last Saturday of April—Oregon's annual kickoff to the trout-fishing season.

After a busy summer of pristine alpine fun along the Cascade Lakes Highway, crowds thin out quickly in September. By October, everyone has another question on their minds: "When will the coming winter's snow close the Cascade Lakes Highway?"

Getting There

Smack in the center of the Oregon Cascades, the Three Sisters and Cascade Lakes country is approached by most visitors via Deschutes National Forest roads from Bend, Sunriver, or La Pine and US Highway 97 (US 97) from the east. Portland is a 190-mile drive away via Bend to the first lakes at the north end of the loop.

Adjoining Areas

NORTH: **Santiam Pass and Mount Washington**

SOUTH: **Willamette Pass**

EAST: **Bend and the Upper Deschutes River**

WEST: **Greater Eugene**

inside out

Scenic Drives

The **Cascade Lakes Highway** is a designated Forest Service scenic byway. The 93-mile partial loop provides recreation access to **Mount Bachelor,** the **Three Sisters** and other volcanoes, and numerous lakes, lodges, and wilderness trailheads. The byway can be entered from the north at **Bend,** from the center at **Sunriver** or **La Pine,** or from the south on Hwy 58 near **Davis Lake.** The western part of the byway, where it passes the Three Sisters Wilderness on the west and the numerous lakes on the east, is usually open from Memorial Day weekend to late October. Other parts melt out earlier or are kept plowed of snow all year. Officially named Forest Rd 46 of the Deschutes National Forest, the 93-mile Cascade Lakes Highway continues south past the string of lakes to reach Hwy 58, 10 miles southeast of Willamette Pass. The highway also has connections to US 97 that make for shorter loops—Forest Rd 40 to Sunriver, Forest Rd 43 to La Pine, and Forest Rd 61 to Crescent.

When driving west from Bend, the route begins as Hwy 372, better known as Century Dr. The scenery begins to change noticeably at Mount Bachelor, shortly before the name changes to the Cascade Lakes Highway where the road makes its big bend to the south. Where the highway crosses **Dutchman Flat,** adjacent to the Mount Bachelor Ski Area parking lot, the views open up because trees are unable to grow in the small pumice desert. Views of **Broken Top** and the **Three Sisters,** the most impressive alpine scenery in Oregon, mix with idyllic lakeside settings. The highway passes turnoffs for Todd, Green, and Sparks Lakes before making its south turn. While several wilderness trailheads line the highway to the west, the route begins to pass the area's many lakes—Devils, Elk, Lava, Crane Prairie, Wickiup, and Davis, plus several others that are on spur roads a short way off the highway. (See Fishing, below, for more on individual lakes.)

Boating/Canoeing

All kinds of boating are available in the Three Sisters and Cascade Lakes country, but it's important to know which lake is best for what type of boat. **Fishing boats** with motors are allowed on Sparks, Elk, Hosmer (electric only), Lava, Little Lava, Little Cultus, Crane Prairie, and Davis. All but Davis have 10mph speed limits, but the engine must be turned off when fishing on Davis. Because of the speed limits, **water-skiers** are limited to Cultus Lake and designated areas on Wickiup Reservoir.

Sailors and **windsurfers** head for Elk Lake, a fairly dependable location for afternoon winds. Due to lighter winds, sails and boards are usually larger than the windsurfing equipment used in the Columbia River Gorge near Hood River. Shelter Cove is the staging area for windsurfers, while a marina on the lake is the summer home of a small fleet of sailboats. Cultus Lake also gets enough afternoon wind to allow sailing.

Paddlers, either in **canoes** or **sea kayaks,** head for Sparks, Hosmer, Lava, Little Lava, Little Cultus, Crane Prairie, North Twin, South Twin, and Wickiup Lakes. Sparks, Little Lava, and Little Cultus are favorites among the paddling camping crowd.

Todd Lake is a short walk from the nearest road, so about the only boating it sees is a fisherman in a float tube. At 23 acres in size, Devils Lake is too small to attract much boat use.

The **Deschutes River,** which has its headwaters in Little Lava Lake and flows through Crane Prairie and Wickiup Reservoirs, has a popular 9-mile Class I **canoe** route from Wickiup Dam to Pringle Falls. To reach the takeout, drive Forest Rd 43 7 miles west of US 97 from the La Pine area. Follow Forest Rd 4370 southwest to the launch at the dam. Pringle Falls requires a portage, as does the Tetherow log jam 4 miles below the falls. Paddlers who don't mind making portages can continue to Benham Falls, where the placid river turns into a raging torrent of whitewater (see Bend and the Upper Deschutes River chapter.)

(For additional information on the lakes, see Fishing and Camping, below.)

Fishing

The first lake past Mount Bachelor is **Todd Lake,** located 2 miles west of the ski area, 1 mile north of the Cascade Lakes Highway on Forest Rd 370, and a .25-mile hike to the north from a signed trailhead. The lake is good for brook trout, especially the first few weeks after the snow melts. A trail circles the lake and a small campground is on the west shore.

Sparks Lake, 3 miles west of Mount Bachelor, is slowly dying. There is no need to worry because this natural death is part of life for all lakes. The shallow lake is slowly being transformed into a meadow. The lake covers 400 acres, but its maximum depth is only 12 feet. The lake is open only to fly-fishing for brook trout, which grow big and plump in the nutrient-rich lake.

Devils Lake is located in the crook of the bend that the Cascade Lakes Highway makes when it passes South Sister, 27 miles west of Bend. The 23-acre lake is shallow and nutrient poor, but catchable rainbow trout are stocked regularly during season and kids find the fishing to their liking.

While **Elk Lake,** 31 miles from Bend, is a sailor's playground, most fishermen pass up its unproductive waters and head next door to **Hosmer Lake,** 1 mile to the east. One of the few Western lakes stocked with Atlantic salmon, Hosmer is also a good producer for big brook trout. Fly-fishing is on barbless hooks for catch-and-release only on the salmon, which are usually found cruising the canal between the lake's two lobes.

Next up along the Cascade Lakes Highway are **Lava Lake** and **Little Lava Lake,** 36 miles from Bend. Both are spring fed, but only Little Lava has an outlet. The water that flows south from Little Lava is the beginning of the Deschutes River, one of the most beloved rivers in a state famous for its rivers. Lava Lake is a better choice for fishing than Little Lava, with lots of big rainbow and brook trout being hauled from its water. The upper waters of the Deschutes are popular with fly-fishermen for rainbow and native brook trout, but the fishery that makes the river world famous is found below Pelton Dam in its last 100 miles before it joins the Columbia River (see Lower Deschutes River chapter).

All the lakes south of Sparks are on the east side of the highway, until **Cultus Lake** and **Little Cultus Lake.** Both are 2 miles west of the highway, across from Crane Prairie Reservoir, and 43 miles from Bend. Cultus Lake, deepest along the highway at 200 feet, has a healthy population of lake trout, also known as mackinaw. The lake is also productive for hatchery rainbow. Little Cultus, one of the quietest lakes along the highway, is good for native rainbow and stocked brook trout.

Crane Prairie Reservoir sprawls over 3,420 acres at full pool, second-largest in size along the highway. The shallow lake, only 20 feet deep, is extremely productive for rainbow trout, brook trout, and largemouth bass. The bass were illegally introduced but haven't placed the trout fishery in danger. Bluegills and crappie have also been illegally stocked, and biologists are keeping a wary eye on the result. The reservoir was created in 1920 when its rising waters flooded the surrounding forests. Many snags are still standing.

Fishermen get a lesson in geology when they visit **South Twin Lake** and **North Twin Lake,** which sit next to each other between Crane Prairie and Wickiup Reservoirs. Both Twin Lakes are classic examples of volcanic maars (craters). They are symmetrical in shape, have no inlets or outlets, and are about 60 feet deep. Both lakes have good fishing for stocked rainbow, which makes them among the most popular for families along the Cascade Lakes Highway. Former President Herbert Hoover used to stay in a cabin at South Twin in the 1940s after he left the White House.

At 10,000 acres, **Wickiup Reservoir** is the giant along the Cascade Lakes Highway. The reservoir gets its name from the wickiup poles that were left standing by the Indians who fished and hunted the areas seasonally. The teepee poles were still present when the reservoir was flooded in 1949. Wickiup has good fishing for kokanee, brown trout, and native rainbow, as well as whitefish in the channel on its west side. Much of the lake is only 20 feet deep, except for a 60-foot-deep channel carved by the Deschutes River where it used to run under the reservoir. The Deschutes below Wickiup produced small rainbow trout and an occasional large brown trout.

The big lakes at the south end of the Cascade Lakes Highway are most easily approached by driving US 97 for 3 miles south of Sunriver. Turn west on Forest Rd 42 and drive 18 miles to where it passes between Crane Prairie and Wickiup Reservoirs. All of the lakes (except Davis) are managed by the Bend Ranger District, (541) 388-5664.

Largest of the natural bodies of water along the Cascade Lakes Highway is **Davis Lake,** 4 miles southwest of Wickiup Reservoir on Forest Rd 46 and inside the Crescent Ranger District, (541) 433-2234. Davis Lake, at times, can also be one of the smallest lakes along the highway. Covering 3,000 acres when full, the lake's porous volcanic bottom allows so much water to escape that it can go nearly dry in drought years. The lake was created about 3,000 years ago when a volcanic eruption deposited a 100-foot-high wall of lava a mile wide across Odell Creek. Water seeps beneath the dam into Wickiup Reservoir, but two recent wet winters have allowed the fishery to rebound. The lake is managed as a fly-fishery for native trout and the same Atlantic salmon that have found a home in Hosmer Lake.

The Cascade Lakes Highway is well endowed with lakes, but their number pales in comparison to the 300 or more lakes that dot a map of the **Three Sisters Wilderness** like spots on a Dalmatian. Many of the wilderness lakes have been planted frequently with rainbow, cutthroat, and eastern brook trout over the years. The brookies have become unwanted recently, due to their nonnative status, and fishery managers place no limit to the number or size taken from streams. A float tube is a big help when fishing the backcountry lakes. Most of the east side of the wilderness is managed by the Bend Ranger District, (541) 388-5664.

Other than the Deschutes itself, **Fall River** is one of the few streams that flow through the porous lava characteristic of the land east of the Cascade Lakes Highway. The river emerges from springs 2 miles north of the Deschutes at Pringle Falls and flows only 10 miles before merging with the Deschutes. Fall River runs cold and fast and is a popular fly-fishing stream for rainbow, brook, and brown trout.

The **Little Deschutes River,** which meanders nearly 100 miles to cover 30 miles between Crescent and Sunriver, is the major tributary of the upper Deschutes. Most of the river runs through private land, so be sure of your access before going after the river's famous brown trout.

For the fishermen who want to learn where the big fish hide without wasting a lot of time, **guide services** are readily available through the fly-fishing shops in Bend and Sunriver and at the lakeside resorts (see Camping, below). The largest guide service on the Cascade Lakes is Garrison's Fishing, (541) 593-8394, based in Sunriver. For more information, check the synopsis of fishing regulations, available where fishing licenses are sold, or call the Central/Southeast Region office of the Oregon Department of Fish and Wildlife in Bend, (541) 388-6363.

Hiking/Backpacking

Three Sisters and Broken Top summit climbs

The Three Sisters have all been climbed in the same marathon day, but mere mortals tend to do one climb at a time, thank you. All of the mountains have multiple routes—some are easy (if gaining 5,000 feet can ever be easy), some are moderate, and some are downright dangerous. North Sister, along with Mount Jefferson, has a well-deserved reputation as one of the most difficult peaks to climb among Oregon's glaciated volcanoes. Entry into all Deschutes National Forest wilderness areas requires a self-issuing permit, available at the trailhead. For information, contact the Bend Ranger District, (541) 388-5664.

South Sister, at 10,358 feet, is the third-tallest mountain in Oregon and its summit is the highest point in Deschutes and Lane Counties. The mountain is frequently climbed from a backpacking camp in the Green Lakes Basin, but it also makes an outstanding day hike from Devils Lake. The **South Sister Climbers' Trail** (difficult; 5.5 miles one way) begins at Devils Lake on the north side of the Cascade Lakes Highway, 27 miles west of Bend. It follows a shaded draw called Hell Creek up to the Wickiup Plain, a large expanse of pumice where the trees grow sparsely. The mountain comes into view and the climbers' trail heads relentlessly north toward it. The trail passes left of the Lewis Glacier at 8,900 feet and continues up a long rocky slope to the big rounded summit. The high point is across the snow-covered crater on the northeast side. Most hikers make the trip in 12 hours or less, but an early start is always the best way to guarantee a return before darkness. By early August the route is usually snow free to the summit rim.

The **Middle Sister,** 10,047 feet, is 3 miles north of South Sister across the beautiful Chambers Lakes Basin. The standard north-ridge climb is approached via the **Obsidian Trail** from Frog Camp on the McKenzie Pass Highway (Hwy 242) (see Santiam Pass and Mount Washington chapter). Trail use is limited to 30 hikers per day, so make a reservation up to one month in advance with the McKenzie Ranger District, (541) 822-3381. The climb is either a long day or a short backpack, often in conjunction with a climb of the North Sister. Follow the Obsidian Trail 4.1 miles to its junction with the Pacific Crest National Scenic Trail (PCT). Cross the PCT and continue on the climbers' trail up to the saddle between the Middle and North Sisters, an easy route to follow in good weather but a nightmare during whiteout conditions. Climb the ridge to the summit. The only difficulty is a short steep slope where crampons might come in handy, although enough steps are usually punched in that they aren't necessary. Be sure to carry an ice ax. Good campsites can be found just across the PCT.

To climb 10,085-foot **North Sister,** return to the saddle and follow the climbers' trail up the south ridge. The going is easy until the first of North Sister's three summit pinnacles bars the way. The highest point, of course, is the farthest-north pinnacle. The crux of the climb is a 100-foot crossing of a steep, icy slope between the pinnacles. Prudent climbers are prepared with crampons and an ice ax, plus a rope to use for belaying and fixing in place while the climbers cross one at a time. More than a few climbers have plunged to their deaths on the Collier Glacier below.

Broken Top, a multiheaded remnant of a massive volcano, is one of the most beautiful peaks in the Cascades and a very rewarding climb. The peak is only 9,175 feet high, eighth highest in the Oregon Cascades, but the view down the north side onto the Bend Glacier is a sight to behold. Climbers usually hike 4.5 miles north from Forest Rd 46, 4 miles west of Mount Bachelor, where they establish camp in the Green Lakes Basin. The climb is east up the peak's massive northwest ridge. Follow the ridge to the summit pinnacle. Climb a short pitch to a broad south-sloping ledge, take the ledge around a corner, and then scramble to the summit over loose, rotten rock. The climb is short, but it's low class 5 and some climbers appreciate the security of a rope. For information, contact the Bend Ranger District at (541) 388-5664.

Pacific Crest Trail

The PCT enters the Three Sisters Wilderness from the south at **Taylor Lake,** at the end of Spur Rd 600, 5 miles west of Little Cultus Lake, and winds its way more than 50 miles through a maze of lakes to **Dee Wright Observatory** at McKenzie Pass and Hwy 242 where it leaves the wilderness (see Santiam Pass and Mount Washington chapter). Most of the route is on the west side of the Cascade crest in Willamette National Forest. The closest it comes to a road the entire way is when it passes within 1 mile of Elk Lake near the north end of the Cascade Lakes Highway.

The trail is never far from a lake in the southern portion of the wilderness, which also means hikers are never far from a buzzing swarm of mosquitoes during the warm days of summer. The trail crosses some dry lava flows as it passes the Three Sisters, but lingering patches of snow ensure continued breeding of the buzzing pests. An interesting side trip is a 2-mile, off-trail scramble to 7,524-foot **Husband,** a lonely volcanic peak west of the trail and the Middle and South Sisters.

Three Sisters Wilderness

The 29-mile-long Three Sisters Wilderness covers 283,402 acres (second-largest wilderness in Oregon; the Eagle Cap Wilderness in Wallowa County is larger with 360,000 acres) and offers hikers and horseback riders 240 miles of trails. Many of the most popular entry routes begin on the west side (see Greater Eugene chapter) and, especially, the north side (see Santiam Pass and Mount Washington chapter).

The busiest trailheads along the Cascade Lakes Highway are Green Lakes on the north and Horse Lake and Blow Lake, the latter two across the highway near Elk Lake. The three **Green Lakes** lie near the southeast base of South Sister, a very appealing (and overcrowded) location. The lakes are a 4.5-mile walk from Forest Rd 46, 4 miles west of Mount Bachelor, and draw lots of weekend backpackers. Permits are self-issuing at the trailhead. Camping is in designated sites with no open fires allowed.

The 5-mile hike to **Horse Lake** begins from a trailhead on the west side of Forest Rd 46 near the northwest corner of Elk Lake (see Fishing, above, for driving access). The trail crosses the crest of the Cascades into Lane County and continues into the **French Pete area.** Added to the Three Sisters Wilderness in 1977, the French Pete area stretches nearly 20 miles west of the crest as a big bulging lobe of the wilderness. It offers one of the most remote backpacking opportunities in the Oregon Cascades because of its distance from roads. To plan a trip, consult the Three Sisters Wilderness map, widely available in sporting goods stores or from ranger stations in Central Oregon.

The **Blow Lake Trail** (difficult; 8.5 miles one way to Mink Lake) begins 1 mile south of Elk Lake on the west side of the highway. Most hikers stop along the way at any of several lakes and never make it to Mink Lake, one of the largest in the wilderness.

Moraine Lake Trail (easy; 4.5 miles round trip) can be reached by following the South Sister climbing trailhead that begins at Devils Lake Campground. The lake is a short walk east of the trail once you reach the Wickiup Plain (see South Sister climbing route, above). **Sisters Mirror Lake Trail** (moderate; 8 miles round trip) is also reached from Devils Lake but via a trailhead different from the South Sister Climbers' Trail. From Devils Lake Campground, look for a short spur road on the northwest side of the Cascade Lakes Highway and drive .4 mile to the Wickiup Plains trailhead. **Broken Top Crater Trail** (moderate; 6.5 miles round trip) is accessible via Spur Rds 370 and 380, 4 miles northwest of Todd Lake (see Fishing, above). The roads are rough and narrow, but passenger cars can negotiate them. Access to the **Eileen and Husband Lakes Trail** (difficult; 19.5 miles round trip) is from the Obsidian trailhead off Hwy 242 on the west side of McKenzie Pass. Hike 5.5 miles southeast to the PCT, follow it south for 2 miles, and turn west on a side trail that heads to the lakes beneath a 7,524-foot peak called the Husband.

Biking

Campers who remember to bring their **road bikes** find paradise riding between the lakes of the **Cascade Lakes Highway.** The road isn't striped for cycling, but traffic is usually pretty light (except for the big arrival and departure times around the weekend). Once you've finished the climb from 3,623 feet in Bend to 5,900 feet at Dutchman Flat near Mount Bachelor, the riding is downhill nearly all the way to Wickiup Reservoir at 4,300 feet. Forest Rds 40, 42, and 43 offer paved connections from the central and southern lakes to US 97 near Sunriver and La Pine.

For an area with a lot of land off-limits to entry by **mountain bikes** because of its wilderness status, the Three Sisters and Cascade Lakes region has a lot of off-road riding. About the only places mountain bikes aren't allowed besides the wilderness are the downhill ski runs at Mount Bachelor and in lakeside meadows. Mount Bachelor Ski and Summer Resort, (541) 382-2442, rents bikes during its summer season and most riders promptly head west to sample trails around Sparks Lake. (For more on Mount Bachelor, see Bend and the Upper Deschutes River chapter.)

The **Sparks Lake/Lava Lakes Trail** is a 10-mile single-track ride between Soda Creek and Lava Lake Campgrounds (see Camping, below), with a 13.5-mile return trip on pavement on Forest Rd 46. The entire trail is downhill, but some rough rock and the long distance give the ride a more difficult rating. Another popular ride from Lava Lake is a 10-mile trail that heads east through the forest to Edison Butte Sno-Park on Forest Rd 46. The route travels uphill to the east and has some technically challenging sections, followed by long climbs and fast descents.

Crane Prairie Reservoir (see Fishing, above) has a 23-mile loop around it, with all but 1.5 miles on double-track dirt. The **Twin Lakes/Wickiup** circuit is 30 miles, again with the majority of it on doubletrack. The loop around **Cultus Lake** is 12 miles, with 5.5 miles of singletrack to give beginning riders a good taste of the sport. Drive to any of the access points along the lakes to begin the rides. The **Lemish Lake Loop** begins at Little Cultus Lake and heads southwest. Of the 14 miles, 8 are single-track riding.

Some of the best trails are tucked away in the high country between Davis and Waldo Lakes. The **Charlton Lake Loop** is a 22-mile ride split between singletrack and doubletrack. The ride begins just east of the Cascade Lakes Highway at the junction with Forest Rd 4290 south of Crane Prairie Reservoir.

Other popular rides are to **Maiden Lake** and **Maiden Peak,** both beginning at the end of Forest Rd 4664-100, 2 miles west of Davis Lake; the **Metolius-Windigo Horse Trail** at the southwest shore of Davis Lake; and the **Moore Creek Trail** to Bobby Lake, which begins at the end of Forest Rd 4652-400, 3 miles northwest of Diamond Lake. The Moore Creek Trail is a 7.5-mile one-way singletrack that gains only 600 feet. It's another one of the best beginners' rides in the Three Sisters and Cascade Lakes country.

For detailed route descriptions of mountain-bike rides, pick up **information** sheets from the Bend Ranger Station at 1230 NE Third, Bend, or the Crescent Ranger District at Crescent on US 97.

Camping

Once you get past Mount Bachelor at 22 miles west of Bend, it's never very far to a campground along the Cascade Lakes Highway. Except for Davis Lake, all campgrounds are managed by the Bend Ranger District, (541) 388-5664, and most are operated by concessionaires. The national forest camps along the Cascade Lakes Highway do not accept reservations. The best way to guarantee a campsite for an RV is to book a spot with one of the commercial lodges (see below). Campgrounds at Davis Lake are part of the Crescent Ranger District, (541) 433-2234.

Following is a description of campgrounds along the Cascade Lakes Highway from north to south; all are marked along the way.

Campers in need of a quick spot to bed down as they drive west of Mount Bachelor can find small camps at **Todd Lake, Soda Creek** at Sparks Lake, and **Devils Lake Campgrounds,** all between 22 and 27 miles from Bend. With only 27 sites between them, the camps are only tantalizing appetizers of what lies ahead. Soda Creek's sites are reachable by vehicles, but the others are for walk-in tent campers.

Elk Lake, 31 miles from Bend, features **Elk Lake Campground, Point Campground,** and **Little Fawn Campground,** with 53 sites total. Little Fawn also has a group camp that can be reserved from High Lakes Contractors, (541) 382-9443. Sunset View and Beach are picnic sites with access to the lake. Hosmer Lake, 1 mile east of Elk Lake, has 35 campsites at **Mallard Marsh Campground** and **South Campground.** The best horse camp in the area is **Quinn Meadow** near Elk Lake. Call High Lakes Contractors for a reservation.

Lava Lake and **Little Lava Lake,** 36 miles from Bend, each have a campground named after it. Together they have 53 sites, of which all but 10 are at Lava Lake. Camps along Forest Rd 46 and the Deschutes River as it leaves Little Lava Lake are **Mile Campground** and a group camp at

Deschutes Bridge. Together they have 22 sites that usually are less busy than the lakeside camps.

Crane Prairie Reservoir is the busiest fishing lake along the highway and thus has the most campgrounds. Camps clockwise from the north end of the reservoir are **Cow Meadow, Crane Prairie, Quinn River,** and **Rock Creek.** Crane Prairie is the largest, with 146 of the reservoir's 239 total sites, and it is the largest campground in Deschutes National Forest.

Across the Cascade Lakes Highway from Crane Prairie, 43 miles from Bend, campers hang out at **Cultus Lake Campground's** 70 sites, as well as at a dozen sites at the lake's west end that require a boat or a good pair of hiking shoes for access. **Little Cultus Lake** has 10 spots in its campground. The horseback crowd is attracted to **Cultus Corral Horse Camp.**

Wickiup Reservoir is a big sprawling lake, and its campgrounds end up being a long way from each other by road. **Sheep Bridge Campground,** located on the Deschutes River arm of the reservoir, is the quietest, but it only has 18 sites. **Gull Point Campground,** located where the Deschutes enters the main part of the reservoir, is largest, with 81 sites. Other camps, with 53 sites among them, are **Wickiup Butte, Reservoir,** and **North Davis Creek.**

The **North and South Twin Lakes** have three campgrounds with 53 sites. **Davis Lake** has 70 sites in its three campgrounds.

Campers who want to get away from the often crowded lakes head downstream of Wickiup Reservoir for riverside camping at **Bull Bend, Wyeth,** and **Pringle Falls Campgrounds** on the west side of the Deschutes along Forest Rds 4360 and 4370, and at **Fall River** on Forest Rd 42 (see Fishing, above). **La Pine State Recreation Area** just downriver on the Deschutes is the closest state park campground (see Bend and the Upper Deschutes River chapter).

Lakeside lodges

Oregon is famous for its casual, comfortable fishing lodges that are found in many parts of the state and that offer camping facilities, as well. In addition to the two recommended under Lodgings, below, visitors find the motherlode when they drive south along the Cascade Lakes Highway.

Lava Lake Lodge, (541) 382-9443, is 5 miles south of Elk Lake. It specializes in full hookups for RV camping, as well as some tent sites. The lodge rents boats and fishing equipment and its store sells gas and groceries.

Crane Prairie Resort, (541) 383-3839, is on the northeast side of Crane Prairie Reservoir, a 6-mile drive off the Cascade Lakes Highway. The lodge has an RV park, camping, boat rentals, general store, gas, and fishing tackle.

Twin Lake Resort, (541) 539-6526, is 44 miles southwest of Bend via Wickiup Junction on US 97. Lowest of the Cascade Lakes resorts at 4,300 feet, Twin Lake has a lodge, general store, restaurant, cabins, gas, boat rentals, and RV park with full hookups. The resort is conveniently located to Wickiup Reservoir, one of the busiest fishing destinations along the highway.

Cross-Country Skiing/Snowmobiling

The only designated state sno-park in the Three Sisters area is **Dutchman Flat,** located next to Mount Bachelor where plowing of the road ends during winter. Backcountry skiers and snowmobilers use the parking area for staging long trips to the frozen lakes. Elk Lake Resort is the only Cascade Lakes lodge that remains open during winter. Skiers who find the 9-mile access route a bit too much can arrange for the lodge to carry either themselves or their baggage aboard a sno-cat to the snowed-in lodge. (See Lodgings, below, for more information.)

Spring is the most popular time for backcountry skiing into the Three Sisters Wilderness. Daylight lasts longer, snow conditions have stabilized, avalanche danger decreases—even the sun has been known to poke through the cloud cover once in a while. Popular tours from the Dutchman Flat Sno-Park go to **Green Lakes, Sparks Lakes,** and **Tam McArthur Rim** via Todd Lake (see Hiking/Backpacking and Camping, above), but all require a commitment of a full day or an overnight trip. All the Three Sisters have been climbed and descended on skis.

One of the most unusual skiing opportunities in the Lower 48 states is a big patch of snow between **Broken Top** and **Ball Butte.** Nordic skiers have trained in August by driving to the wilderness boundary (see Broken Top Crater in Hiking/Backpacking, above), then carrying their skis a mile or two (depending on the size of the remaining snowfield) and setting up a cross-country training course. Mount Hood has year-round downhill skiing, but its terrain is too steep for cross-country skiing. The Ball Butte snowfield is the closest thing that Oregon has to Nordic skiing throughout the summer.

Snowmobilers also frequent Elk Lake Resort during winter when they go for all-day rides on the groomed trail over the snow-covered highway. The nearest snowmobile rental service is at Wanoga Sno-Park, 5 miles east of Mount Bachelor on Forest Rd 46. Fantastic Recreation Rentals, (541) 389-5640, often has all its machines booked on weekends so it's wise to make a reservation. One of the snowmobilers' favorite play areas is Moon Mountain, a popular hill climb north of Mount Bachelor.

outside in

Lodgings

Elk Lake Resort This remote fishing lodge—access is via sno-cat or cross-country skis in winter—33 miles southwest of Bend consists of a dozen self-contained cabins, most with sleeping quarters for two to eight people. It's nothing grand, but the scenery is wonderful. Phone direct, a year in advance, to make reservations both for cabins and the dining room. Other facilities include a store, boat rentals and gas, and paddleboats, which are popular with the kids who camp with their parents nearby. *Century Dr (also known as Cascade Lakes Hwy; look for signs to Elk Lake), Bend; PO Box 789, Bend, OR 97709; (541) 317-2994; $$.*

Cheaper Sleeps

Cultus Lake Resort This resort is situated alongside a lake popular with anglers, boaters, board sailors, and swimmers (it's the only lake in the area that has shallow sandy beaches). Only open from mid-May through mid-October, the resort offers cabins at $52 and up. A restaurant and small grocery store are in the main lodge, and watercraft rentals are available. *Hwy 46 (PO Box 262), Bend, OR 97709; (541) 389-3230 (winter), (541) 389-5125, wait for beep, then 037244 (summer), or (800) 616-3230 (information); $.*

More Information

Bend Ranger District, Bend: *(541) 388-5664.*
Central Oregon Visitors Association, Bend: *(800) 800-8334.*
Crescent Ranger District, Crescent: *(541) 433-2234.*
Deschutes National Forest, Bend: *(541) 388-2715.*
Lane County Visitors Association, Eugene: *(800) 547-5445.*
McKenzie Ranger District, McKenzie Bridge: *(541) 822-3381.*
Oakridge Ranger District, Westfir: *(541) 782-2291.*
Willamette National Forest, Eugene: *(541) 465-6521.*

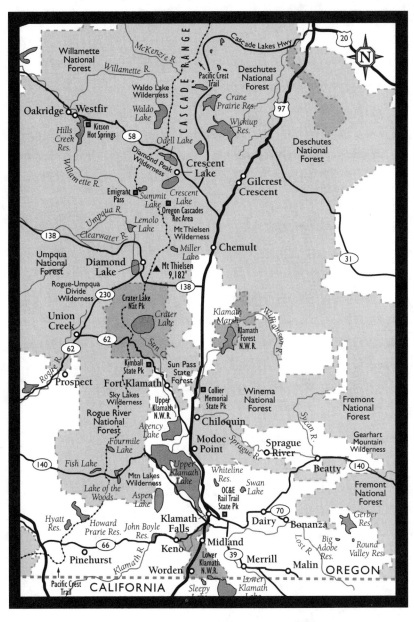

Southern
Cascades
and the Klamath
Basin

Willamette Pass 481

Diamond Lake 494

Crater Lake National Park 503

Mountain Lakes 512

Klamath Basin 525

Southern
Cascades
and the Klamath
Basin

Willamette Pass

From the Waldo Lake Wilderness on the north, east to Cascades Lakes Highway and US Highway 97, south to the Willamette-Umpqua divide and west into Willamette National Forest near Oakridge, including Diamond Peak and Waldo Lake Wildernesses, and the communities of Westfir, Oakridge, Crescent Lake, Crescent, and Gilchrist.

Willamette Pass, famous for its big lakes and fast skiers, somehow maintains an aura of peacefulness when neighboring vacation areas are bursting at the seams with activity. Crowds congregate in the Three Sisters and Cascade Lakes country to the north and the Diamond Lake country to the south, while Willamette Pass can feel empty. Instead of focusing attention on one large lake or a cluster of smaller ones, the Willamette Pass country spreads its visitors out around the shores of three of Oregon's big lakes. Each lake is within a half hour's drive of the others, but all have their own access roads from Highway 58 and serve as self-contained vacation destinations.

Waldo Lake, the biggest of the lakes here, at 6,298 acres (nearly 10 square miles), is amazingly clear and deep. With a maximum depth of 420 feet, the only lake deeper than Waldo in Oregon is Crater Lake. Waldo has a thrilling 22-mile mountain-bike trail around its shore, with the edge of the trail bordering the Waldo Lake Wilderness. It's as close as most mountain bikers get to legally riding in a designated wilderness. The trail is just one of the reasons nearby Oakridge lays claims to being the fat-tire bike capital of Oregon.

Waldo is the only lake protected by Oregon's Scenic Waterway Act, which also protects 19 rivers as a supplement to the National

Wild and Scenic Rivers Program. The North Fork of the Middle Fork of the Willamette River, the outlet for Waldo Lake, is protected both by the state and the federal government in recognition of its status as the most scenic of the many headwater streams of the Willamette River system.

Crescent Lake and Odell Lake, each covering about 6 square miles, combine to keep visitor pressure off Waldo, however, by offering myriad recreation activities of their own. Each of the lakes is among the half-dozen largest natural bodies of fresh water in Oregon.

To contrast all that flat expanse of water, the Willamette Pass country has some steep mountain slopes. The Diamond Peak Wilderness encompasses a big chunk of the Cascades just beyond the shores of Crescent and Odell Lakes. Diamond Peak, the namesake of the wilderness, rises to 8,744 feet and is the highest mountain for 50 miles, from Mount Bachelor on the north to Mount Thielsen on the south.

Willamette Pass Ski Area has a super-steep ski run on the southwest side of 6,666-foot Eagle Peak where it once staged a World Cup speed skiing race. The competition established the state record for fast skiing—112mph. That's faster than most skiers would want to go, unless they are fishermen and the fish are biting in the Willamette Pass lakes.

Getting There

Willamette Pass is an easy 180-mile drive south from Portland via Eugene on Interstate 5, then southeast into the Cascades on Highway 58. Many long-haul truckers who run from Puget Sound and Portland to California take Willamette Pass Highway to avoid the numerous hill climbs on I-5 in southern Oregon. Access from the east is via US Highway 97 (US 97). National forest roads lead into the scenic country along Willamette Pass Highway, including the Robert Aufderheide Memorial Drive (Forest Road 19).

Adjoining Areas

NORTH: **Three Sisters and Cascade Lakes**
SOUTH: **Diamond Lake**
EAST: **Bend and the Upper Deschutes River**
WEST: **Greater Eugene**

Hiking/Backpacking

One cardinal rule applies to hiking throughout this area: the ratio of mosquito repellent should be directly proportional to the number of miles walked from mid-June to early September.

As a long-distance route, the **Pacific Crest National Scenic Trail** (PCT) serves the Willamette Pass country admirably, less so for day hikes. A favored one-day outing on the PCT follows the trail north from Summit Lake into the Diamond Peak Wilderness and a summit climb of **Diamond Peak.** At 8,744 feet, Diamond Peak sticks up high enough to rise above tree line but doesn't have glaciers. Permanent snowfields make it prudent to bring along an ice axe for the climb. To reach Summit Lake, drive Forest Rd 60 from Hwy 58 along the north shore of Crescent Lake. Turn west on Forest Rd 6010 and drive 5 miles to the Emigrant Pass trailhead on the PCT. Hike north on the PCT for 4 miles to where the trail crosses the southeast shoulder of the peak at 6,880 feet. Scramble northwest up the ridge 2 miles to the summit. The ascent makes for a long day and should be attempted only when the weather is good. For information, contact the Crescent Ranger District, (541) 433-2234.

Another day hike along the PCT begins at the Willamette Summit trailhead on Hwy 58, .25 mile east of the ski area. From the north side of the highway, hike the PCT east and then north to **Rosary Lakes** (easy; 7 miles round trip to the third lake). The lower, southern lake is the largest of the three Rosary Lakes.

The Willamette National Forest portion of the **Eugene-to-the-PCT Trail** starts near Lowell on Lookout Point Reservoir east of Eugene (see Greater Eugene chapter), runs south of Waldo Lake, and meets the PCT near Bobby Lake, 5 miles north of the Rosary Lakes. The route can be picked up on the eastern outskirts of Oakridge on Dunning Rd. The trail follows forested ridges into the high country, offering some day-hike opportunities from a few forest roads that approach the trail from the south. For information, check with the Oakridge Ranger District, (541) 782-2283.

The **Waldo Lake Wilderness** covers 37,162 acres, but not Waldo Lake itself. The most convenient entry points into the wilderness are from the ends of paved roads on the north and south shores of the east side of the lake. Another half-dozen gravel forest roads provide access to the wilderness from the west. To reach the east shore of the lake and its north and south recreation areas, turn north from Hwy 58 onto Waldo Lake Rd (Forest Rd 5897), 3 miles west of Willamette Pass. Shadow Bay at the south end of the lake is 8 miles from Hwy 58 and North Waldo is 13 miles.

Popular destinations from the North Waldo trailhead are the **Eddeeleo Lakes** (moderate; 9 miles round trip) and the **Rigdon Lakes** (moderate; 8-mile loop). The South Waldo picnic shelter is a 2-mile walk from the end of the road at the Shadow Bay boat ramp, so most hikes turn out to be out-

and-back strolls along the lake's shore. The Waldo Lake Trail (difficult; 22 miles around) circles the lake (see Biking, below).

The Klovdahl Headgate and Tunnel, in retrospect one of the most irresponsible attempts at development in Oregon history, can be viewed on a 3-mile hike from **South Waldo** picnic area along the lakeshore trail. The project, begun in 1914 and abandoned in 1933, was designed to divert the waters of one of the most pure large lakes in the world to irrigate Willamette Valley farms and provide hydroelectric power.

Popular destinations from the west side of Waldo Lake Wilderness are **Lillian Falls** (easy; 2.5 miles round trip) and **Waldo Mountain Lookout** (difficult; 8-mile loop and 2,000-foot climb). The Lillian Falls trailhead begins at the end of Forest Rd 2421, a 25-mile backcountry adventure from Oakridge. The trailhead for Waldo Mountain is at the end of Forest Rd 2424. Consult a Willamette National Forest map, available from the Oakridge Ranger Station, (541) 782-2283.

The 14 miles of the PCT that pass through the 36,637-acre **Diamond Peak Wilderness** receive the bulk of the use, but the wilderness is not the only worthy destination. Other popular destinations are off-trail rambles to the summits of **Mount Yoran,** 7,100 feet, and **Lakeview Mountain,** 7,065 feet. Yoran requires some third-class scrambling to reach its summit. Hike south for 7 miles from the Willamette Summit trailhead on Hwy 35 and scramble up the peak from the east. To reach Lakeview Mountain, hike 3.8 miles south from Odell Lake Resort to Fawn Lake, then 1.4 miles northwest to Stag Lake for views of the mountain's steep cliffs.

Water destinations inside the wilderness include **Fawn, Yoran, and Midnight Lakes,** each within a 3-hour hike of a road. Consult the Diamond Peak Wilderness map, available at local ranger stations. **Diamond View Lake** near the center of the wilderness is midway along the 14.3-mile **Whitefish Creek Trail,** which begins at Trapper Creek Campground on Odell Lake and ends at Whitefish Horse Camp on Crescent Lake (see Camping, below). The southern half of the trail gets heavy horse use.

The **Timpanogas Lake** area, located at the headwaters of the Willamette River's Middle Fork, has hikes to **Indigo Lake** (easy; 1.9 miles one way), including an off-trail scramble to 7,301-foot **Sawtooth Mountain;** and an old-growth forest walk to **Big Swamp Grove** (easy; 2 miles one way). To reach Timpanogas Lake, take Forest Rd 21 (also known as Diamond Dr) southeast from Oakridge for 40 miles, following the Middle Fork all the way. Indigo Lake and Sawtooth Mountain are both south of the lake on Trail No. 3649, while Big Swamp Grove is 3 miles south of Forest Rd 21 on Rd 2253.

Much of Diamond Dr is paralleled by the 25-mile **Middle Fork**

Willamette River Trail, which can be accessed from several locations along Diamond Dr. The trail begins at Sand Prairie Campground, near the upper end of Hills Creek Reservoir at 1,200 feet in elevation. It passes additional camping opportunities at Campers Flat, Sacandaga, and Indigo Springs, before ending at Lake Timpanogas, at 5,400 feet the headwaters for the Willamette's Middle Fork.

Other summit hikes near Willamette Pass are 7,144-foot **Fuji Mountain** (moderate; 3 miles round trip) near the south end of Waldo Lake and 7,818-foot **Maiden Peak** (difficult; 5.8 miles round trip), 3 miles north of Odell Lake. The Fuji Mountain trailhead is at the end of Forest Rd 5883 in Willamette National Forest, while Maiden Peak is approached from Davis Lake on the east via Forest Rd 4660-100 in Deschutes National Forest. **Twin Peaks** (moderate; 6.6 miles round trip), a shorter climb than the trail to Maiden Peak, has a view equally good with its elevation of 7,362 feet. The trailhead is along Waldo Lake's east-side road, .5 mile south of the turnoff for Shadow Bay.

No visit to the Willamette Pass country is complete without hiking to **Diamond Creek Falls** (easy; 3.4-mile loop). The trail begins on the south side of Hwy 58 at the viewpoint for 286-foot **Salt Creek Falls,** third highest in Oregon. The turnoff for Salt Creek Falls is marked on the south side of Hwy 58 just east of an 800-foot highway tunnel and 6 miles west of Willamette Pass. A 150-foot-long trail leads from the highway to a viewpoint of the falls. For Diamond Creek Falls, follow the loop trail southwest to viewpoints for the segmented falls that drop more than 200 feet out of sight from the highway. A passing train on the nearby railroad tracks will provide a reminder that Willamette Pass is the main north-south rail corridor in Oregon.

Biking

Oakridge's claim to being the **"Fat Tire Capital"** of Oregon is based on the community's embrace of mountain biking, its annual July bike festival (call (541) 782-4228 for info), and its numerous riding opportunities, many on the area's extensive network of logging roads.

The Willamette Pass country's most famous ride is the 22-mile **Waldo Lake Trail.** Rated most difficult by Willamette National Forest because of its mileage, the trail never strays far from the lake's shore and its elevation change isn't as brutal as a lot of trails that are rated as less difficult. Count on about 800 feet of ups and downs along the way, but nothing is consistently long. The main danger is to beginners who are lured into riding the circuit and decide they want to bail out midway along the ride. Wrong! Once you start, you've got to keep going. The best way to make the circuit is to begin at North Waldo (see Hiking/Backpacking, above) and ride in a counterclockwise direction. This leaves the easiest part of the ride for the end—a downhill, through-the-woods section along the lake's east shore from Shadow Bay to Islet Point.

The other outstanding riding opportunity in the Willamette Pass country is in the **Oregon Cascades Recreation Area,** a roadless area south of Crescent Lake. Also known as **Windy Lakes,** the area is relatively flat and offers some easy riding on the Windy Lakes, Metolius-Windigo, Oldenberg Lake, Snell Lake, and Summit Lake trails. Cyclists have access to more than 30 miles of trail, but remember to stay out of the Diamond Peak Wilderness and off the Pacific Crest Trail. Access is from the south side of Crescent Lake. Check with the Crescent Ranger District, (541) 433-2234, for detailed route descriptions.

Bikers who don't want to stray far from Oakridge often head for **Larison Rock** and **Larison Creek** at the southwest edge of town. Larison Rock requires a climb of 2,400 feet on Trail No. 3607, so a better choice may be the 400-foot climb along Larison Creek. The latter ride covers 6.5 miles along a tributary that enters the northwest side of Hills Creek Reservoir, accessible on Forest Rd 21.

Camping

The western gateway to the Willamette Pass country, the twin communities of Oakridge and Westfir are 41 miles southwest of Eugene on Hwy 58. Population is 5,000 and elevation is 1,200 feet. The timber communities have been serving travelers and tourists since the 1870s when the Oregon Central Military Wagon Road used the Middle Fork of the Willamette River to travel between central Oregon and the Willamette Valley. The towns have seven trailer parks, most of which accept overnight travelers.

National forest campgrounds close to town are **Blue Pool Campground,** a 29-site camp along Hwy 58 only 8 miles east of Oakridge, and **Salmon Creek Falls Campground,** with 17 sites 5 miles east of town on Forest Rd 24. The falls are not spectacular at 10 feet high, but the camp's cool forested setting is welcome on a hot summer day.

Forest Service campgrounds in the Willamette Pass country are not on the reservation system. To guarantee a spot for an RV, arrange to stay at one of the commercial campgrounds operated by resorts at Crescent and Odell Lakes. For information on campgrounds west of Willamette Pass, call the Oakridge Ranger District, (541) 782-2283.

In spite of poor fishing because of a lack of nutrients, Waldo Lake has the largest campgrounds in the Willamette Pass country. Located 4 air miles north of Hwy 58 west of the Cascade crest, Waldo Lake has highway access to its eastern side, but its other shores are in a designated wilderness. **Shadow Bay Campground** (92 sites) is on the south side of the lake. **Islet Point Campground** (59 sites) and **North Waldo Campground** (62 sites) are on the lake's northeast shore. All are accessible off Forest Rd 5897. Campers with horses head for **Harralson,** 1 mile east of North Waldo. Maximum trailer length at the campgrounds is 30 feet. Waldo Lake's campgrounds are in the Oakridge Ranger District, (541) 782-2283.

    Gold Lake, 1 mile north of Hwy 58 on the way to Waldo Lake, has one of the best handicapped-accessible campgrounds in the Willamette Pass country. The camp has 24 sites.

Odell and Crescent Lakes

The two large lakes on the east side of Willamette Pass both have a wide selection of camping opportunities. Recreation facilities east of the pass are managed by the Crescent Ranger District, (541) 433-2234, while Northwest Land Management, (541) 433-2309, operates most campgrounds on Crescent and Odell Lakes as a concessionaire with the Forest Service.

    At Odell Lake, **Princess Creek** (46 sites) and **Sunset Cove Campgrounds** (21 sites) are tucked between Hwy 58 and the lake's north shore along Hwy 58. **Trapper Creek Campground** (32 sites) at the west end of the lake and **Odell Creek Campground** (22 sites) at the east end offer quieter spots away from the highway.

    Crescent Lake, situated 2.5 miles south of busy Hwy 58, is popular with campers who want a little buffer from the highway corridor's busy truck traffic. The largest campgrounds are **Crescent Lake Campground** (47 sites) on the north end and **Spring Campground** (68 sites) on the south end. **Contorta Point Campground** has 15 primitive sites on the south end, and **Whitefish Campground** attracts most of the horse camping with its 19 box stalls. To reach Crescent Lake, turn south from Hwy 58 onto Forest Rd 60, 7 miles east of Willamette Pass.

    Crescent Creek Campground has 10 campsites on the outlet stream for Crescent Lake, midway between Hwy 58 and US 97 on County Rd 61. **Summit Lake,** 5 miles west of Crescent Lake on Forest Rd 6010, has a small campground used by hikers preparing to enter the Diamond Peak Wilderness.

    Klamath County runs a small campground .25 mile west of Crescent on County Rd 61 called **Cy Bingham Park,** (541) 883-4697, ext. 696. The park was donated by the Gilchrist Timber Company and has 10 campsites. The Gilchrist Garden Club has planted the 2.5-acre park with flowers and shrubs.

Middle Fork and Hills Creek Reservoir

Following the Middle Fork of the Willamette River on Diamond Dr upstream from Oakridge to Timpanogas Lake is a quiet alternative to visiting the Willamette Pass country without competing with the long-haul truck traffic on Hwy 58. The route begins 3 miles east of Oakridge, where Forest Rd 21 follows the river southeast along the west shore of Hills Creek Reservoir to the headwaters of the Willamette River system at Timpanogas Lake.

Drivers can either retrace the route to Oakridge or connect to forest roads that reach Crescent Lake to the north or Lemolo Lake to the south (see Diamond Lake chapter). The 40-mile route is well supplied with more than a half-dozen campgrounds, plus any number of beautiful spots for dispersed camping. The largest camps are **Packard Creek Campground** (33 sites on Hills Creek Reservoir), **Sand Prairie Campground** (21 sites near the head of the reservoir), and **Sacandaga Campground** (17 sites halfway between Oakridge and Timpanogas Lake). Check in Oakridge with the Rigdon Ranger District, (541) 782-2283, for the Diamond Dr tour brochure and other sights along the Oregon Central Military Wagon Road, the historic route along the Willamette's Middle Fork that was built to herd cattle across the mountains.

Fishing

Odell Lake covers 3,558 acres and is 287 feet deep. The lake stretches out for 6 miles along Hwy 58, a tantalizing sight for travelers heading east from Oregon's cloudy interior valleys because Odell Lake is often where they get their first glimpse of sunshine on the Cascade's drier east side. The lake is famous for its trophy-size mackinaw trout, has some of Oregon's best kokanee fishing, and has plenty of rainbow trout. The success rate is usually quite high. And just how large is a trophy-size mackinaw, also known as a lake trout? Odell Lake produced the state record of 40 pounds, 8 ounces, in 1984. Boat launches are at Princess Creek, Sunset Cove, and Trapper Creek Campgrounds (see Camping, above) and Shelter Cove resort.

Crescent Lake, located 2 miles south of Hwy 58 on Forest Rd 60, covers 4,000 acres and has a maximum depth of 280 feet. The lake has a large population of mackinaw, brown and rainbow trout, plus whitefish and kokanee. Motorboat rentals and moorage slips are available at Crescent Lake Lodge on the lake's north shore. Crescent Lake, Spring, and Contorta Point Campgrounds all have boat launches (see Camping, above). **Crescent Creek,** which drains Crescent Lake to the Little Deschutes River, is a fair trout stream over its 40-mile length. Access to its upper end is along County Rd 61.

Waldo Lake itself is too pure to provide good fishing habitat, but the lake's outlet is a good fly-fishing stream for trout. Burdened by the clumsy name of **North Fork of the Middle Fork of the Willamette River,** the lake's outlet runs 40 miles to join the Middle Fork of the Willamette River and is referred to locally as the North Fork. Access is along Forest Rd 19, the Robert F. Aufderheide National Scenic Byway (see Greater Eugene chapter). Best fishing in the North Fork is after July when the frigid water warms slightly. The river drops 2,400 feet in 3 miles below Waldo Lake in the Waldo Lake Wilderness and has 34 separate waterfalls.

Salt Creek, another tributary of the Middle Fork, flows 28 miles from Gold Lake to Oakridge. The creek is alongside Hwy 58 much of the way and sees a fair amount of fishing, but its steep character provides little habitat for wild trout. It's pretty hard for fish to live in a 286-foot waterfall (see Hiking/Backpacking, above). **Gold Lake** is a good trout lake for fly-anglers. Motorboats are not allowed, but some type of floating device comes in handy because of the brushy shore. Gold Lake is one of the few places in Oregon frequented by solitary sandpipers.

Hills Creek Reservoir, the pool where the Middle Fork of the Willamette is collected to provide electricity, is fished frequently because national forest roads follow each side of the 8-mile-long reservoir. Forest Rd 21 follows the west shore and Forest Rd 2118 lines the east shore. The lake is stocked with rainbow, which bite during winter when the water temperature drops. Native cutthroat trout, as well as crappie, occasionally wind up on an angler's hook. The Willamette's **Middle Fork,** the longest of its major tributaries, runs west of the Cascade crest south of Willamette Pass (see Hiking/Backpacking and Camping, above). The river above Hills Creek Reservoir is stocked with rainbow, but fishing opportunities are limited during summer because of low water flows. Spring and fall rainy seasons are the best times to try.

Fishermen who want to camp at Waldo Lake usually hike to back-country lakes to do their fishing. **Betty Lake** is near Shadow Bay on the south shore and **Upper and Lower Eddeeleo Lakes** are convenient to North Waldo. Betty Lake is a .5-mile trail hike, and fishermen with float tubes usually catch some rainbow. The Eddeeleo Lakes, two of the larger bodies of water in the Waldo Lake Wilderness, provide a 4-mile hike and are good producers of brook trout for fishermen with float tubes.

Check the state fishing synopsis for current regulations. Fishing on the west side of the crest is managed by the Oregon Department of Fish and Wildlife's Corvallis office, (541) 757-4186, and on the east side by the Bend office, (541) 388-6363.

Downhill Skiing/Snowboarding

Skiing at the **Willamette Pass Ski Area** dates to the 1930s, but it wasn't until the 1980s that a new owner came on board, pumped some money into facilities, and turned it into a respectable ski area. It ranks among the best midrange ski areas in the state, along with Mount Hood Skibowl and Ski Ashland. Willamette Pass has a 1,525-foot vertical drop with a top elevation of 6,666 feet.

Although Willamette Pass is by no means a one-dimensional ski area, the thing that sets it apart from other Oregon ski areas is its steep terrain. Locals like to tease Mount Bachelor skiers by telling them to visit the Pass once they get bored with the runs at Oregon's biggest ski area.

The R.T.S. run at Willamette Pass averages 45 degrees of steepness over a 1,400-foot length. It was the scene of the state speed skiing record. Much faster speeds have been reached elsewhere, mainly in Europe, but only because those courses are longer, not steeper, than R.T.S. To celebrate its challenging terrain, the ski area operates a Black Diamond Club through its ski school. Anyone who can ski R.T.S., Success, and Northern Exposure without stopping or falling wins a T-shirt. By the way, R.T.S. is the initials of a former owner of the ski area, but skiers think it stands for "real tough stuff" (or another word that begins with "s").

Willamette Pass has five chairlifts, including the Sleepy Hollow lift for beginners that is well isolated from the steep upper slopes. Intermediates have their own chairlift in the trees, called Twilight, to the west of the main bowl, or mix they can with everyone on the Midway lift in the wide-open runs of the lower part of Eagle Peak. The Summit lift takes skiers to the steep runs atop Eagle Peak, but Rosary run winds back to the bottom along the eastern edge of the ski area and allows skiers of moderate ability to use the chairlift. The backside of the mountain, an outstanding combination of glades, bowls, and cut runs for advanced intermediates, is served by the Peak 2 chairlift.

Despite its 5,141-foot base elevation, the highest of the Cascade pass ski areas in Oregon, Willamette Pass can be short on snow due to its southern exposure. Oregon's largest snow-making system can cover the lower slopes, although the state's moderate temperatures don't always allow it to operate, and the backside faces north and can usually be skied early in the season. Open seven days a week, with night skiing on weekends, Willamette Pass was the first ski area in Oregon to offer women-only ski workshops. It also has day care for children in its Cascade Summit Lodge. Contact the ski area in its Eugene office, (541) 484-5030, or listen to its snow conditions report at (541) 345-7669.

Cross-Country Skiing/Snowmobiling

The **Willamette Pass Nordic Center** is a full-service cross-country ski area with 20 kilometers of groomed skiing just west of the ski area's downhill runs on the north side of Hwy 58. The ski area's fee trail system has a connecting trail to Willamette National Forest's Gold Lake Road Sno-Park (see below). The large parking lot at Willamette Pass, one of a half-dozen designated sno-parks in the corridor, can fill to overflowing on popular weekends. Nordic skiers head for the west end of the parking lot where the Nordic center, (541) 484-5030, sells trail passes and rents equipment.

Sno-parks located west to east along Hwy 58 in the Willamette Pass corridor are Salt Creek Falls, 6 miles west of the pass; Waldo Lake Road, 4 miles west of the pass; Gold Lake Road, 1 mile west of the pass; the downhill and Nordic ski areas at Willamette Pass; and Royce Mountain and Crescent Lake Sno-Parks east of the pass.

The majority of the Nordic ski activity begins from **Gold Lake Road Sno-Park,** from where trails lead from the sno-park's nordic ski patrol base to three day-use shelters. The Westview Loop Trail system from Gold Lake Road Sno-Park leads to a shelter and views over the west end of Odell Lake. Shelter Cove Resort at the east end of Odell Lake grooms 5 miles of Nordic ski trails.

Salt Creek Falls Sno-Park is the lowest in the area, at 4,080 feet, and doesn't always have reliable snow. **Waldo Lake Road Sno-Park** is the hopping-off place for winter tours to the lake, but with a 10-mile one-way trail the tour is too much for all but the most experienced skiers. A map called "Willamette Pass Cross-Country Ski Trails" is available at local ranger stations and sporting goods stores.

Warner Mountain Lookout is an isolated retreat for skiers and snowmobilers on the west slope of the Cascades 33 miles south of Oakridge off Forest Rd 21. The fire lookout stands atop Warner Ridge at 5,800 feet. Depending on snow conditions, it can require as much as a 12-mile over-the-snow trip to reach it. The 14-by-14-foot cabin sits atop a 41-foot tower and is available for rent from December 1 through May 10. For reservations and directions, contact the Rigdon Ranger District, (541) 782-2283.

Royce Sno-Park, 7 miles east of Willamette Pass at Crescent Lake Junction on Hwy 58, and the **Crescent Lake Sno-Park,** 2.5 miles south of the highway at the junction, are frequented by snowmobilers who come to ride trails that connect with Elk Lake to the north along the Cascade Lakes Highway and with Diamond Lake to the south. Crescent Lake Lodge, (541) 433-2505, caters to snowmobilers and has some machines to rent.

Canoeing/Kayaking/Boating

Canoeists love **Larison Cove,** an area designated for the paddle sport 6 miles south of Oakridge on Forest Rd 21 (see Biking, above). Larison Cove is a sheltered backwater of the large **Hills Creek Reservoir,** a lake on the Middle Fork of the Willamette River. The canoe area has a ramp for nonmotorized boats and a swimming area on the south side of the cove. Four paddle-accessible picnic areas, tucked away in the forest along the shore of the lake, offer a feeling of solitude. Canoeists who like to mix paddling with hiking can head for the **Larison Creek** trailhead on the north side of the cove and walk 6 miles upstream to where the trail meets a road. Hills Creek Reservoir has an elevation of 1,200 feet, so it can be paddled year-round.

Waldo Lake, elevation 5,414 feet, is one of the most pure large lakes in the world. Because the lake is too sterile to support a significant population of fish, paddlers pretty much have the lake to themselves without having to compete with fishermen. The lake's motorized speed limit is 10mph, too slow for water-skiers and personal watercraft. Waldo Lake is one of the most popular inland **sea kayak** destinations in the state, with most launches occurring from the three campgrounds and boat ramps on the lake's east shore (see Camping, above). Overnight camp spots abound on the lake's 21 miles of shoreline. Under certain lighting conditions, canoeists have reported seeing their shadow on the floor of the lake 100 feet below.

A few expert kayakers and rafters boat the **North Fork of the Middle Fork of the Willamette River,** the outlet for Waldo Lake, during the spring rainy season. The only other river kayaking in the Willamette Pass area is on what kayakers call "steep creeks," extremely technical runs that come into shape only during the right combination of rain and snowmelt.

Odell Lake and **Crescent Lake** resorts both have marinas and see plenty of boating. Fishermen ply the shores during the morning and early afternoon. When the winds pick up later in the day, sailors and wind-surfers can be seen skimming across the lakes' surface. Both lakes are big and exposed and the afternoon winds whistling through the Cascades at Willamette Pass should not be underestimated. Water-skiers usually opt for more hospitable (and warmer) lakes down the west side of Willamette Pass, including Hills Creek Reservoir near Oakridge and other reservoirs closer to Eugene.

outside in

Lodgings

Odell Lake Lodge and Resort This resort on Odell Lake is ideal for the fisher, hiker, and skier in all of us. Sports equipment is for rent, and the restaurant is open year-round. Request a lakeside room or cabin. Pets okay in cabins only; some minimum-stay requirements. *From Oakridge, head east on Hwy 58 for 30 miles, take E Odell Lake exit; PO Box 72, Crescent Lake, OR 97425; (541) 433-2540; $$.*

Westfir Lodge ☆☆ This pleasant inn anchors the tiny community of Westfir, with its English country ambience. Guests are served a full English breakfast (complete with bangers and scones). The longest covered bridge in Oregon is just across the road. Closed for a month in spring. *47365 1st St (3 miles east of Hwy 58 near Oakridge), Westfir, OR 97492; (541) 782-3103; $$.*

More Information

Central Oregon Visitors Association, Bend: *(800) 800-8334.*
Crescent Ranger District, Crescent: *(541) 433-2234.*
Deschutes National Forest, Bend: *(541) 388-2715.*
Lane County Visitors Association, Eugene: *(800) 547-5445.*
Oakridge Ranger District, Westfir: *(541) 782-2283.*
Oakridge-Westfir Chamber of Commerce, Oakridge: *(541) 782-4146.*
Oregon's Outback Visitors Association, Klamath Falls: *(800) 598-6877.*
Rigdon Ranger District, Oakridge: *(541) 782-2283.*
Willamette National Forest, Eugene: *(541) 465-6521.*

Diamond Lake

From the Willamette-Umpqua Divide on the north at Windigo Pass, east to US Highway 97, south to Crater Lake National Park, and west into Umpqua National Forest, including the Mount Thielsen Wilderness, the north end of the Rogue-Umpqua Divide Wilderness, the Oregon Cascades Recreation Area, Diamond Lake Resort, and the community of Chemult.

As diamonds go, this area is a little rough around the edges and not polished to perfection. But among Oregon's mountain resorts, it's the jewel in the crown because it offers just about the biggest variety of outdoor recreation—winter and summer—available at any single location.

When you want to take an exhilarating snowmobile ride to the edge of world-famous Crater Lake, or to the 8,368-foot summit of Mount Bailey, head for Diamond Lake and rent a machine.

When you want to enjoy Oregon's best powder skiing, head for Mount Bailey at Diamond Lake.

When you want to cross-country ski to the local pizza parlor for lunch, go for an inner-tube ride on the sliding hill, or take a spin on ice skates over the frozen surface of a lake, head for Diamond Lake's Nordic center.

When you want to rent a rowboat, take it for a spin on a 3,214-acre lake, and catch a creel full of trout, head for Diamond Lake and its marina.

With more than 90 cabins and motel rooms, Diamond Lake Resort is the largest mountain resort in Oregon. While Mount Hood's Timberline Lodge is as majestic as a monument in Washington, D.C., Diamond Lake in Oregon's Southern Cascades is as comfortable as a pair of old slippers. A warm fire crackles in the lodge's gathering room on all but the warmest summer days, friendly staff members regale guests with tales of past adventurers, and a guest's dog wanders through the parking lot looking for a scratch behind the ears.

Oregon's Southern Cascades, however, have more outdoor gems than Diamond Lake Resort and Lemolo Lake Lodge 9 miles to the north. This is where the mighty Rogue and Umpqua Rivers rise, before they head west through contorted canyons and bludgeon their ways to the Pacific Ocean. The Mount Thielsen Wilderness's 51,000 acres are protected from motorized entry, while just to the north lie 157,000 acres of the Oregon Cascades Recreation Area that Congress created in 1984 to enhance recreation opportunities—both motorized and nonmotorized.

About 30 miles of the Pacific Crest National Scenic Trail pass through the Diamond Lake area, usually within sight of 9,182-foot Mount Thielsen. Called the "Lightning Rod of the Cascades," the mountain comes to a preposterously pointy peak. During winter, when snow accentuates the mountain's outline, Thielsen looks sharp enough to cut open the underbelly of any airliner that passes too close. In fact, the mountain is so sharp that it must have been cut by a diamond, just like the lake that lies at its feet.

Getting There

Diamond Lake Resort, a self-contained village, is reached from the west on Highway 138 from Roseburg, or from the east, also on Highway 138, from near the community of Chemult and US Highway 97 (US 97). Portland is about 250 miles away on either approach. Forest Service roads fan out across the area, including routes to the north that connect Lemolo Lake Lodge with Windigo Pass and the Middle Fork of the Willamette River. For information, contact the resort at (800) 733-7592

Adjoining Areas

NORTH: **Willamette Pass**

SOUTH: **Crater Lake National Park**

EAST: **Klamath Basin**

WEST: **The Umpqua Valley**

inside out

Hiking/Backpacking

The **Pacific Crest National Scenic Trail** (PCT) covers 30.3 miles from the north side of Crater Lake National Park to Windigo Pass where it leaves the Diamond Lake country. The trail stays within the boundary of the Mount Thielsen Wilderness for 26 of the miles. The wilderness is long and narrow (rarely more than 5 miles wide), so the PCT can easily be reached from roads to the east and west. The PCT's southern trailhead in the Diamond Lake country is on Hwy 138 at North Crater, 1 mile east of the north entrance to Crater Lake National Park. The northern trailhead at Windigo Pass is 12 miles east of Lemolo Lake Lodge on Forest Rd 60.

The only significant eastside trailhead for the Mount Thielsen Wilderness is the **Miller Lake Trail,** 14 miles west of Chemult on Forest Rd 9772. Trails follow both shores of Miller Lake until they merge and enter the wilderness .5 mile west of the lake. The trail joins the PCT 3 miles from Digit Point Campground on the lake's south shore, crosses the divide from Klamath to Douglas Counties, and begins its 79-mile journey as the **North Umpqua Trail,** which ends in Glide (see The Umpqua Valley chapter).

Diamond Lake, located west of the Mount Thielsen Wilderness, has many hiking opportunities. Some visitors never venture beyond the lakeshore trail (see Biking, below), but they miss out on a lot. The **Howlock Mountain Trail** (difficult; 7 miles one way to the PCT) begins near the horse corrals at the entrance to the resort. The trail forks near its midpoint, with the Howlock Mountain Trail going northeast and the **Thielsen Creek Trail** heading southeast. Both join the PCT after climbing 1,830 feet from the trailhead.

Continuing in a clockwise direction around Diamond Lake, next you encounter the Mount Thielsen trailhead, 2.5 miles south of the resort entrance on the east side of Hwy 138. The **Mount Thielsen Trail** (most difficult; 4.4 miles one way) climbs from 5,190 feet to the upper reaches of the 9,182-foot peak where a difficult, third-class scramble is required to stand on the top pinnacle. Most climbers enjoy the security of a rope and a belay. The southeast ridge of the 80-foot pinnacle is easiest to climb. Along the way, just after climbing out of the trees, head north around a cleaver of rock to avoid a particularly unstable pumice slope that is better for using on descent.

The **Horse and Teal Lakes Trail** (easy; 1.6 miles one way) leaves from the South Shore Picnic Area and circles Horse and Teal Lakes, two shallow ponds covered with water lilies. Wildlife frequents this area of Diamond Lake.

Mount Bailey, 8,363 feet high, can be climbed via the **Mount Bailey Trail** (difficult; 5 miles one way) on the west side of Diamond Lake. Drive Forest Rd 4795 through the South Shore Picnic Area for 1.5 miles to Forest Rd 300. Turn left and watch for the trailhead on the right in 1.3 miles. The trail gains 3,113 feet and only the last mile rises above timberline. **Silent**

Creek Trail (easy; 1.4 miles one way) can be reached by continuing .3 mile on Forest Rd 4795 beyond the turnoff for the Mount Bailey Trail.

For an easier mountain to climb, head for the **Rodley Butte Trail** (easy; 3.2 miles one way) at the northwest corner of Diamond Lake near the head of Lake Creek. The trail gains only 400 feet as it swings around the north side of the butte.

Three miles north of Diamond Lake Resort on Hwy 138, Forest Rd 4793 heads east toward the Thielsen Wilderness and climbs to 6,417-foot Cinnamon Butte Lookout. **Tipsoo Trail** (moderate; 3.1 miles one way) can be reached by driving 1 mile on Forest Rd 4793, then continuing 3 miles up Forest Rd 100 (instead of driving to Cinnamon Butte). The trail climbs 1,503 feet in a series of switchbacks and has a spectacular view when it reaches the summit. The PCT is a .3-mile scramble down the southeast side of 8,034-foot Tipsoo Peak.

The turnoff for Lemolo Lake is 5 miles north of Diamond Lake Resort on Hwy 138. Forest Rd 2610 leads 4 miles to the lake, with its resort, campgrounds, and hiking trails. The 6.3-mile Lemolo segment of the North Umpqua Trail can be accessed from camps along the lake's north shore. **Lemolo Falls,** an 80-foot-high cascade, is a 2-mile walk down the North Umpqua from Lemolo Lake Resort and Bunker Hill Camp. Another popular hike near Lemolo Lake is a tough, .5-mile scramble up 5,687-foot **Watson Butte,** site of an abandoned fire lookout. The trailhead is at the end of Forest Rd 4780-170, about 3 miles southwest of Lemolo Lake.

Forest Rd 2612 heads east of Lemolo Lake, joins Forest Rd 60, and continues to 5,817-foot Windigo Pass, a little-used high-clearance-vehicle access route to the southern portion of Deschutes National Forest. Hikes on the Umpqua side of the divide include **Calamut Lake Trail** (easy; 1.5 miles one way), via Spur Rd 700; and **Tenas Peak Trail** (difficult; 3.3 miles one way), **Tolo Creek Trail** (difficult; 5 miles one way), and **Windigo Pass Trail** (moderate; 7 miles one way), all accessible from the Kelsay Valley trailhead at the end of Forest Rd 6000-958. Tolo Creek Trail connects the PCT with the North Umpqua Trail, the Windigo Pass Trail is an alternative to driving the road, and the Tenas Peak Trail ascends to near the summit of a 6,558-foot peak.

The **Rogue-Umpqua Divide Wilderness** covers 33,000 acres of forested mountains and high ridges that separate the drainages of the two rivers. Elevations range from a low of 3,200 feet to a high of 6,783 feet at Fish Mountain, one of the highest peaks on the western side of Oregon's Cascades. The **Fish Mountain Trail** can be reached by driving to the end of Forest Rd 3700-870, which snakes its way 3 miles deep into the surrounding wilderness from the northeast of Forest Rd 37. The road was left outside the boundary when the wilderness was created in 1984, but the wilderness is a few feet away on either side. Roads like this are called "cherry stems" because they penetrate a wilderness, where motors are not allowed, but are not actually inside the designated wilderness boundary. Hike the trail .3 mile from the end of the road, then scramble .5 mile off-trail up an open ridge to the summit.

The **Rogue-Umpqua Trail** (difficult; 33 miles one way) traverses the wilderness from northeast to southwest. The trail begins 8 miles north of the wilderness boundary at Garwood Butte, 6 miles west of Diamond Lake. To reach the **Garwood Butte Trail** (difficult; 1.7 miles one way), drive southwest of Diamond Lake on Hwy 230 for 2 miles to Forest Rd 3703. Turn west and drive 6 miles to the trailhead near Three Lakes Camp. The trail climbs 1,024 feet to the summit of the peak and a rundown old fire lookout. The northern terminus of the Rogue-Umpqua Trail is located near the Garwood Butte Trail, or can be picked up within the wilderness at the end of the road near Fish Mountain.

Other nearby trails outside the wilderness boundary, with one-way distances given here, are **Fish Creek Trail** (difficult; 2.6 miles), **Black Rock Trail** (difficult; 1.4 miles), and **Skookum Lake Trail** (difficult; .6 mile). Skookum Lake has brook trout and a resident elk herd, Black Rock Meadows is covered with wildflowers in season, and Fish Creek Trail follows a lush creek bottom that is particularly colorful in fall when vine maple leaves are turning color. For route descriptions of the trails, contact the Diamond Lake Ranger Station, (541) 498-2531, located in the residential area of Toketee in the North Umpqua Valley 20 miles west of Diamond Lake.

Camping

With 446 Umpqua National Forest campsites along its shores, Diamond Lake can be heaven for campers who don't mind crowds. **Broken Arrow Campground** has 148 sites on the south shore, **Diamond Lake Campground** has 238 sites on the east shore, and **Thielsen View Campground** on the west shore adds another 60 sites.

Broken Arrow can take RVs of any length, while Diamond Lake limits the length to 40 feet and Thielsen View to 30 feet. Broken Arrow and Diamond Lake Campgrounds are on the national reservations system, (800) 879-4496. Broken Arrow has 28 modified campsites to accommodate disabled campers, Diamond Lake camp has 8, and Thielsen View has 4. The **South Shore Picnic Area** also has barrier-free facilities.

Lemolo Lake isn't quite so crowded, but it still offers plenty of camping opportunities. **Bunker Hill Campground** (8 sites), **East Lemolo Campground** (dispersed camping), **Inlet Campground** (14 sites), and **Poole Creek Campground** (59 sites) line the lake. Poole Creek Campground is on the national reservations system and has barrier-free rest rooms and drinking fountains.

Campers who want to be in the forest away from the lakes can choose from **Whitehorse Falls Campground** (5 sites) and **Clearwater Falls Campground** (12 sites), both along Hwy 138 a few miles west of Lemolo Lake, or dispersed camping at **Kelsay Valley Campground** on Windigo Pass Rd.

Campgrounds in the Diamond Lake region are managed by the Diamond Lake Ranger District, (541) 498-2531.

Digit Point Campground on the shores of Miller Lake is one of the choice camping spots within the Winema National Forest. Located 14 miles west of Chemult on Forest Rd 9772, the campground has 64 sites and can accommodate rigs up to 30 feet. **Corral Springs Campground,** 2 miles northwest of Chemult on Forest Rd 9774, has 5 spots and offers travelers a convenient camp near US 97. For information, contact the Chemult Ranger District, (541) 365-7001.

Fishing

Over the years, **Diamond Lake** has been one of the most popular mountain fishing lakes in Oregon. Covering 3,000 acres at 5,182 feet in elevation, the lake has a maximum depth of 50 feet. Liberally planted with rainbow trout, the fishing tempts visitors to linger for days on end at the lake's resort, campgrounds, and summer homes. The best fishing usually comes early in the season just after the ice leaves the lake and trout then congregate in the inlets to spawn. Opening weekend is the last Saturday in April, but the ice isn't always gone by then. The boating speed limit is 10mph through fishing season, which ends October 31. A pier on the north side of the lake near the resort is capped with a concrete path and is accessible for fishing.

The lake sees all types of angling, most of it successful depending on how the fish are biting. Fly-anglers find good success in late spring when the lake produces a midge hatch. While most trout are in the 1-pound range, a few manage to avoid the heavy angling pressure. They compete with an introduced fish, a tui chub, for the lake's bountiful food supply. A few trout grow to over 5 pounds, but not nearly as many as there used to be. Fishery managers have proposed treating the lake with chemicals to kill all the fish. They say it's the only way to eliminate the tui chub and allow the lake to rebuild its famous fishery.

Lemolo Lake is a 25-foot-deep reservoir that covers 345 acres. The reservoir is managed for wild brown trout, which can grow to over 10 pounds. The lake shrinks to about a third of its normal size as the water is drawn down in preparation to receive winter's rain.

Miller Lake has one of the best brown trout fisheries in the state, with fish growing to 15 pounds or more. The lake covers 565 acres at 5,616 feet in elevation. Maximum depth is 148 feet. Miller Lake also supports rainbow trout and kokanee, but it's the browns that interest most anglers. A slow troll over deep water works best, although brown trout can be caught in the shallows early and late in the day when water and air temperatures are coolest.

For information on regulations, check the state fishing synopsis, available where licenses are sold. Fishing is managed on the west by the Oregon Department of Fish and Wildlife's Roseburg office, (541) 440-3353, and on the east by the Bend office, (541) 388-6363.

Skiing/Snowmobiling

Mount Bailey Snowcat Skiing uses an over-the-snow-vehicle with covered seating to transport up to a dozen guests up Mount Bailey for untracked runs through powder snow. Cost for a day of skiing, including lunch in a midmountain warming hut, is $175. **Snowboarders** are welcome and need to be of intermediate ability or above.

The machine takes about an hour to transport skiers to the 8,363-foot summit of Mount Bailey, weather conditions permitting, via a snowmobile trail on the mountain's west side. A day of skiing usually includes a half-dozen runs, each a 3,000-vertical-foot drop. The only groomed trail is the swath laid down by the sno-cat, so every run is through powder, or whatever condition the snow happens to be in. Mount Bailey is, after all, located in the Oregon Cascades.

Skiing can be through incredibly beautiful glades of mountain hemlock, or down the scary steeps of the mountain's north face. A downhill ski area has been proposed for Mount Bailey, but the Forest Service has not found a group with sufficient capital to develop the project. The mountain has the kind of terrain that could make skiers switch their allegiance from Mount Bachelor. For information, contact the Mount Bailey Ski Corporation, (800) 446-4555.

Diamond Lake Resort, (800) 733-7593, has some winter fun for everyone. In addition to the state's best powder skiing at Mount Bailey, Diamond Lake has an extensive **snowmobile trail system.** The resort's **Nordic center** offers a full line of ski rentals, grooms 8 miles of trail, and rents skates for use on a prepared surface of the lake when conditions are right. Youngsters aren't forgotten, either, with a rope tow that serves a snowboard and **sliding hill.** The parking lot can also come alive with the sound of barking huskies as their musher prepares to take them on a run.

Diamond Lake's snowmobile trails connect with long-distance riding opportunities far to the north and south. The resort's Hilltop Shop maintains a fleet of 40 snowmobiles to rent and leads **guided rides** to Crater Lake. Another popular ride is to the summit of Mount Bailey, using the track established by the sno-cat. The variety of guided tours can be as short as an hour around the lake or last 8 hours for the ride to Crescent Lake near Willamette Pass.

The resort's ski and snowmobile trails don't require a state sno-park pass because the resort crew plows its own parking lots. Most popular among the area's 100 miles of marked ski trails is the 3-mile groomed track from the lodge along the lake's east shore to the pizza parlor. Be sure to bring a headlamp for the trip home after dark.

Other easy ski trails near Diamond Lake are the 3-mile **Vista Trail,** which heads north from Diamond Lake Lodge; the 4-mile **Silent Creek Trail** and the 4.8-mile **Lake West Trail,** both from the West Diamond Lake Sno-Park at the lake's southwest corner; and the 11.5-mile **circuit of the lake** from the Nordic center. More difficult ski outings follow summer hiking routes to Mount Bailey, Mount Thielsen, and the Pacific Crest Trail (see Hiking/Backpacking, above).

The state maintains four sno-parks near Diamond Lake—**West Diamond Lake,** 3 miles west of Hwy 138 on Hwy 230; **Diamond Lake,** at the south end of the lake at the intersection of Hwys 230 and 138; **North Crater Lake,** on Hwy 138 at the entrance to Crater Lake National Park; and **Mount Thielsen,** on Hwy 138 1 mile north of the intersection with Hwy 230. Contact the Diamond Lake Ranger District, (541) 498-2531, about fees and other information.

The north rim viewpoint of Crater Lake is 9 miles south of North Crater Lake Sno-Park. This can be a bumpy trail because of heavy use by snowmobiles. It takes a strong skier to cover 18 miles to the lake and back in a day. Save this trip for the long daylight hours of spring.

Lemolo Lake Lodge remains open in winter for skiing and snowmobiling (see Camping, above). The lodge works with Umpqua National Forest to groom 10 miles of trail west of the lake, a well-marked system popular with beginners and families.

The town of **Chemult,** 20 miles east of Diamond Lake, offers the best opportunity for winter sports along the entire 300-mile length of US 97 in Oregon. Chemult sits at 4,700 feet in elevation, high enough to have sufficient snow for skiing and snowmobiling. **Walt Haring Sno-Park** is only .5 mile north of town and .25 mile west of US 97. The sno-park has 8 miles of marked ski trails, as well as virtually unlimited trails for snowmobile riding with connections to the Diamond Lake and Crescent Lake trail systems. Favorite ski trails from the sno-park are **Runner Loop** (easy; 2.1-mile loop) and **Twinkle Loop** (easy; 2.2-mile loop). **Jim's Trail** (difficult; 1.9 miles one way) takes off from the northwest tip of Twinkle Loop and climbs to a viewpoint of the Cascade peaks. Most of the skiing is through lodgepole pines, with enough ponderosa pines sprinkled in to keep things interesting. For information on recreation east of the Cascade crest, contact the Chemult Ranger District, (541) 365-7001.

Biking

The **Diamond Lake Bicycle Path** (easy; 11-mile loop) is a paved trail that winds around the lake. The trail is designed for cyclists of all abilities, with a maximum grade of 8 percent. The South Shore Picnic Area has 5 non-motorized campsites for bikers and hikers.

An alternative to riding pavement on the east side of the lake is **Crater Trail** (moderate; 8.4 miles one way). The trail follows an abandoned road and is mainly used in winter by snowmobiles. The trail runs from the Howlock Mountain trailhead on the north to the North Crater trailhead on the south (see Hiking/Backpacking, above), with elevations ranging from 5,290 feet to 6,000 feet. Ride the highway or the bike path back to the trailhead, or make a 21-mile circuit by riding **North Crater Trail,** which parallels Crater Trail much of the way. (The North Crater trailhead provides summer access to the PCT and other trails. It is located on Hwy 138 1 mile east of the North Crater Lake trailhead, which provides winter access to Crater Lake National Park.)

More Information

Chemult Ranger District, Chemult: *(541) 365-7001.*
Diamond Lake Information Center (summer only): *(541) 793-3310.*
Diamond Lake Ranger District, Idleyld Park: *(541) 498-2531.*
Oregon's Outback Visitors Association, Klamath Falls: *(800) 598-6877.*
Roseburg Visitors Information Center, Roseburg: *(800) 444-9584.*
Umpqua National Forest, Roseburg: *(541) 672-6601.*
Winema National Forest, Klamath Falls: *(541) 883-6714.*

Crater Lake National Park

From Highway 138 on the north, east to US Highway 97, south to Fort Klamath, and west to Prospect, including Crater Lake National Park, its southern highway access routes via Highway 62, and the communities of Prospect and Fort Klamath.

Crater Lake, Oregon's only national park, leaves a lasting visual impression on anyone fortunate enough to look down on its surreal beauty. Most people experience the sight along Rim Drive, usually in company with throngs of other tourists. There's nothing wrong with this because everyone knows it will be crowded. But there's a better way to first experience the beauty of Crater Lake. Here's the way.

Enter the park from the north. Soon after driving across the stark Pumice Desert, turn east on Rim Drive. Resist any temptation to head straight to the rim for the highway pullouts and their gorgeous views of the lake. Instead, drive east 1 mile on Rim Drive and park alongside the road. The elevation is 7,400 feet. Walk in a southeasterly direction, across open slopes studded with whitebark pine, to the 8,049-foot summit of Llao Rock. A prominent park landmark, the south cliff of Llao Rock rises 1,873 feet above the surface of the lake. That's only 59 feet less than the lake is deep.

The first sight of the lake from the summit of Llao Rock is guaranteed to be breathtaking, if for no other reason than most people will be huffing and puffing from making the climb at such an elevation. Take your time. Sit down and dangle your feet over the edge of the rock. The face of the rock is so vertical that it almost looks as though a jumper would make a clean splash in the water about .4 mile below. (This is no place for children to roam unsupervised.)

The off-trail hike is less than a mile long, but the little bit of effort required to get there adds much to the appreciation of the lake's beauty. Crater Lake, with a depth of 1,932 feet, is the world's seventh-deepest lake and the deepest in the United States. The lake's diameter ranges from a maximum 6 miles to a minimum 4.5 miles, and its surface covers 20.5 square miles. The area was preserved as a park in 1902 and is the country's sixth-oldest national park.

Geologic forces created the caldera 7,700 years ago when 12,000-foot Mount Mazama went through a series of eruptions and lava flows and eventually collapsed upon itself. With more than 600 inches of snow falling annually, the caldera began filling with water and required only 350 years to reach a stable level. The level of the lake has varied only 16 feet since Europeans first saw it in 1853.

Underground fires continued to burn in the caldera until about 1,000 years ago. One product of their work was Wizard Island, a lava cone that rises about 2,700 feet above its base, but only 760 feet above the lake's surface. The lake's only other island is the Phantom Ship, a small rocky point best viewed from Kerr Notch on Rim Drive along the lake's southeast side.

In 1995, Crater Lake Lodge reopened after the National Park Service spent $15 million to bring it up to modern standards. The lodge, first opened in 1915, closed in 1988 and sat empty for a few years while Congress decided whether to fund the remodeling or tear down the lodge and build a new one away from the rim.

Most visitors get their first view of the incredibly blue lake from near the lodge at Rim Village, situated at 7,076 feet above sea level. That's not a bad way to see the lake for the first time. It's just not the best way.

Getting There

Year-round access to Crater Lake National Park is from the south—either via Highway 62 from Medford, or from US Highway 97 (US 97) and Highway 62 from Klamath Falls. Both cities are about 65 miles from park headquarters and Rim Village, both on the park's south side. The northern entrance road from Diamond Lake is usually accessible from June, when snow melts out for the summer, through October. The quickest summer access from Portland is to drive south on Interstate 5 to Roseburg, travel east on Highway 138 to Diamond Lake, then head south into the park through the north entrance gate. The distance from Portland by this route is 280 miles.

Adjoining Areas
    NORTH: **Diamond Lake**
    SOUTH: **Mountain Lakes**
    EAST: **Klamath Basin**
    WEST: **The Rogue Valley**

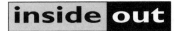

Hiking/Backpacking

Crater Lake National Park and Rim Drive

Since a road was punched around Crater Lake's rim in 1911, walking the circuit of the rim is one trip hikers don't normally bother with. They leave that to skiers and cyclists. **Rim Drive,** which is normally plowed free of snow only from mid-June to mid-October, does pass, however, hiking trails that climb to many of the high points along the rim, as well as the only trail that descends to the water; hiking within the caldera anywhere except the Cleetwood Cove Trail is dangerous and illegal.

After hikers take in the scenery at Rim Village, they often choose the nearby **Garfield Peak Trail** (moderate; 1.7 miles one way). The trail climbs about a thousand feet to the peak's 8,054-foot summit. Other trails near Rim Village and the Steele Center at park headquarters are **Castle Crest Wildflower Garden** (easy; 1-mile loop) and **Dutton Creek Trail** (easy; 2.4 miles downhill to the Pacific Crest Trail).

Driving clockwise from Rim Village, the next major trail is **Watchman Lookout** (easy; .7 mile one way). The trail climbs 450 feet to another dynamite view of the lake.

Cleetwood Cove Trail (difficult; 1.1 miles one way) begins 4.5 miles east of the north-rim access road junction. The trail drops 674 feet to reach the lake. The grade is 11 percent, something hikers soon notice when walking up the trail from the boat landing. The Cleetwood dock at the end of the trail is the launch point for the **lake's tour boat.** Private craft are not allowed on the lake. The number of daily tours fluctuates from three to eight, depending on the season. Tickets are purchased at the dock and reservations are not taken. The first tour usually leaves at 10am. Cost for an adult is $10. Boats stop at **Wizard Island,** where it's possible to remain ashore and take a later boat back. You may need to wait until the last boat of the day to leave the island if all the other boats are full and none of the passengers want to trade places. The island has two hiking trails, including a 1.1-mile trail to its summit.

Continuing in a clockwise direction from the Cleetwood Cove Trail, another popular hike is to the summit of Mount Scott. The **Mount Scott Trail** (moderate; 2.5 miles one way) begins at 7,670 feet and ends atop the highest peak in the park, at 8,926 feet. On a sparklingly clear day, Mount Shasta can be seen 105 miles to the south and Mount Jefferson 120 miles to the north. Less than 1 mile beyond the Mount Scott trailhead a side road climbs to a turnaround and a viewpoint atop 8,070-foot **Cloudcap,** the highest point along the rim.

After Rim Drive passes through **Kerr Notch,** with its view of the **Phantom Ship,** it passes a junction with another road that travels 6 miles southeast into Pinnacle Valley and ends at the **Pinnacles Overlook.** The volcanic layers of pumice and ash are eroded into a weird assortment of 80-foot-high cylindrical shapes.

Sun Notch comes next along Rim Drive. Other than a boat tour, it offers the best view of the Phantom Ship. Hike .25 mile north of the road to the low point in the notch, then go a short way either north or south to see the lake's small island.

Crater Peak Trail (difficult; 2.5 miles one way) begins 2 miles beyond Sun Notch. The trail climbs steeply to the south to gain the summit of the 7,265-foot-high cinder cone, a climb of 775 feet.

The **Pacific Crest National Scenic Trail** (PCT) covers 32.4 miles as it passes through the 183,224-acre national park. Because the PCT stays well below the rim, through-hikers usually use the Dutton Trail to climb to the rim from the PCT and get a view of the lake. The summit of **Union Peak** is a worthy objective along the PCT. The 7,698-foot peak dominates its surroundings southwest of the lake. From where the PCT crosses Hwy 62 near the park's southside Annie Springs entrance station, hike south on the PCT for 2.9 miles. Turn west at an old road, walk 1.6 miles to the base of the peak, and then climb 1 mile of switchbacks to the summit.

Crater Lake National Park requires free backcountry use **permits** for all overnight stays. Pick them up at Rim Village or park headquarters. Pets are allowed only on the PCT, not on spur trails. For information on the park's trails, contact Crater Lake National Park, (541) 594-2211.

Rogue River National Forest

The most popular trail in the Prospect Ranger District is the 42-mile-long **Upper Rogue River Trail.** The trail's southern end is near the town of Prospect and the northern end is at **Crater Rim Viewpoint** on Hwy 230, at the northwest edge of Crater Lake National Park. The trail shares the canyon with busy highways and is not usually hiked as a through route. Most frequently, use is short hikes from the various campgrounds and picnic areas that are common in the area. For information, contact the Prospect Ranger District, (541) 560-3400.

The trail leads to an unusual feature in the gorge of the **North Fork of the Rogue River** near Union Creek Resort, 12 miles north of Prospect on Hwy 62. At **Natural Bridge,** on the west side of Hwy 62, 2 miles south of the resort, the river flows over lava into a collapsed lava tube and then into an intact tube. Downstream the tubes collapse again and the river returns to a surface channel. The best time to see Natural Bridge is in late summer when the river's flow is low enough to be contained in the collapsed tube. Riverside rocks are slippery, and hiking too close to the water is dangerous. One hiker slipped into the tube in 1983 and his body was never found. The Upper Rogue River Trail is especially scenic for 8 miles downstream from Natural Bridge as it passes through **Takelma Gorge. Mammoth Pines** is a picnic area 3 miles south of Natural Bridge that features a short nature walk with 20 interpretive stops that highlight vegetation in the canyon of the Upper Rogue.

Trails west of Hwy 62 in the Prospect Ranger District include **Anderson Camp Trail** (difficult; .8 mile one way), **Golden Stairs Trail** (moderate; 4.3 miles one way), and **Muir Creek Trail** (easy; 3.9 miles one way). The first two can be reached by driving Hwy 62 for 6 miles north of Prospect to Forest Rd 68 and continuing on to the trailheads. Anderson Camp Trail climbs 880 feet and has outstanding views of the Rogue-Umpqua Divide area. Golden Stairs Trail climbs 1,600 feet to enter the Rogue-Umpqua Wilderness. The Muir Creek Trail is on Hwy 230, 10.4 miles north from its junction with Hwy 62. The trailhead is just south of a highway bridge over Muir Creek. The area is famous for its wildlife-viewing opportunities, its wildflowers, and its berry picking.

Camping

The National Park Service maintains only 2 campgrounds within the boundaries of **Crater Lake National Park,** but campers have many more campgrounds to choose from in the national forests that surround the park. The park charges a $10-per-vehicle entrance fee, good for seven consecutive days; for information, call (541) 594-2211.

The park's **Mazama Campground** is 7 miles south of Rim Village near the 40-unit Mazama Village Motor Inn. The camp has 198 sites, including some that are accessible for disabled campers. The park concessionaire does not take reservations but sites are usually available. The camping season is mid-June to mid-October. The camp has shower and laundry facilities, but no utility hookups. **Lost Creek Campground,** located in the southeast part of the park between Rim Drive and Pinnacles Overlook, has 16 drive-up sites for tents. These sites fill up early.

Rogue River National Forest offers 225 campsites spread among seven campgrounds along Hwys 62 and 230 between Prospect and the national park boundary. Largest are **Union Creek Campground** (78 sites) and

Farewell Bend Campground (61 sites), both on Hwy 62 near Union Creek Resort. **Mill Creek, River Bridge, and Natural Bridge Campgrounds** are on the east side of the Rogue River between Prospect and Union Creek Resort. **Abbott Creek Campground** is on the west side of the river on Forest Rd 68. **Hamaker Campground** is 13 miles north of Union Creek Resort. For information, contact the Prospect Ranger District, (541) 560-3400.

The national park's southeast entrance route from Fort Klamath passes near camps at **Kimball State Park Campground,** (541) 783-2471, with 10 sites 2 miles north of Fort Klamath on Hwy 62 and 1 mile east on Dixon Rd, and Winema National Forest's **Spring Creek Campground,** (541) 783-4001, with 26 sites 6 miles north of Chiloquin and 2 miles west of US 97 on Forest Rd 9732.

The eastern boundary of Crater Lake National Park has about a 4-mile-wide buffer of national forest land that is seldom used for recreation, other than for hunting. A small campground is at **Scott Creek,** 5 miles west of US 97 off Forest Rd 66. None of the forest roads enter the park from the east side. The closest they come is on the park's southeast boundary, where a mile-long hiking trail connects the end of Forest Rd 2304 with the park's Pinnacles Overlook.

Biking

Rim Drive, which circles Crater Lake for 33 miles, is one of Oregon's ultimate road-bike rides, but its difficulty should not be underestimated. The road has no shoulders and many long, steep grades that can be exhausting, especially because of the elevation. The highest point along the road is 7,700 feet near Mount Scott. Cyclists must compete with heavy tourist traffic, including large RVs. About half of the drive is open to one-way traffic only, in a clockwise direction from Cleetwood Cove to park headquarters. Rockfall is a common occurrence. The only water along the way is at Rim Village. For those who want to enter the park by bicycle, the north entrance road from Diamond Lake is much less steep than the southern routes from Medford or Klamath Falls.

Mountain bikes are prohibited on all national park trails. They are welcome, however, on the **Grayback Motor Nature Road,** a one-way route from Lost Creek Campground (see Camping, above) to Rim Drive. The road's 8-mile oiled dirt surface sees light use by motor vehicles.

Mountain bikers also have several riding options outside the park boundary in Rogue River National Forest near Prospect. To find the **Minnehaha Trail,** drive north on Hwy 62 from Union Creek Resort to the junction with Hwy 230 and turn north toward Diamond Lake. Drive 12 miles and turn right on Forest Rd 6530. Go 1 mile to the junction with Forest Rd 800, turn left, and park at a signed trailhead after .1 mile. The

Minnehaha Trail (easy; 3.1 miles one way) takes off to the east. Where the trail ends at Soda Springs, cross the creek and ride west back to the trailhead by using Forest Rds 830 and 800. Elevation gain is 575 feet.

The **Cold Springs Trail** (moderate; 2.6 miles one way) runs near the southwest corner of the national park. From Prospect, travel 1.2 miles east on county roads and turn left on Forest Rd 6205. Drive east 4.5 miles to the junction with Forest Rd 100, turn left, and drive 7.7 miles to the trailhead. The trail drops 260 feet to reach the springs.

Bitterlick is a roadless valley 10 miles northwest of Prospect. The upper trailhead is at 4,200 feet and the lower one at 2,000, so that should help you decide which way you want to ride. A vehicle shuttle is most frequently part of the deal. **Bitterlick Trail** (difficult; 5.5 miles one way) requires seven stream crossings, so the ride is recommended only when the creek is low. The upper trailhead can be reached by driving the Elk Creek Rd, 5 miles northeast of Shady Cove via Hwy 62, for 14 miles to Forest Rd 66. Turn left and drive 4 miles to the end of the pavement. Continue another 4 miles north on Forest Rd 6640 to the trailhead. The lower trailhead can be found 13 miles up Elk Creek Rd by turning left on Forest Rd 6620. Drive 1.5 miles to the junction with Forest Rd 050, 1 mile north on a four-wheel-drive road. The Prospect Ranger District, (541) 560-3623, publishes information sheets called "Recreation Opportunity Guides" for its bike trails.

Fishing

The good news is that **Crater Lake National Park** doesn't require a fishing license. The bad news is that the park has few fishing opportunities. Access to the lake is limited to **Cleetwood Cove,** where the only trail drops down to the lake from the rim, and at **Wizard Island** via the tour boat (see Hiking/Backpacking, above). The lake and the park's streams were stocked frequently until the 1930s, but fish now are allowed to develop on their own. Crater Lake has kokanee and rainbow and brown trout, while dolly varden live in park streams. The lake has no aboveground outlet, so the streams carry little water during summer.

Park visitors who simply must wet a fly usually fish outside the park boundaries. The **North Fork of the Rogue River** and its tributaries near Prospect have wild rainbow, cutthroat, brown, and brook trout. Legal rainbow trout are stocked beginning in May near the picnic areas and campgrounds. **Union Creek,** a 15-mile-long tributary, is famous for its large brown trout (7 to 8 pounds). Best fishing is from May until July, when flow diminishes.

Check the state synopsis for regulations, or call the Oregon Department of Fish and Wildlife's Roseburg office, (541) 440-3353, for west-side information, or the Bend office, (541) 388-6363, for the east side.

Cross-Country Skiing

One of the most glorious mountain sights in Oregon is **Crater Lake** on a blue-sky day during spring with 200 inches of snow covering the ground. All that snow has to get there sometime, so be sure to wait for the right day if you want the best views. Most winter recreation begins in the park at Rim Village, the only plowed access road. The park staff attempts to keep the road open, but occasionally the road is closed when snowfall overwhelms the plowing crew. Snowmobiling in the park is limited to the north entrance road (see Diamond Lake chapter).

The park has no groomed ski trails, but several of the more popular routes are marked with blue diamonds. By far the most popular trail in the park is the **Wizard Island Overlook Trail** (easy; 5 miles one way). Head north along the rim from Rim Village. Great views are frequent and you don't need to ski all 5 miles. **Watchman Overlook Trail** (moderate; 10 miles one way) continues 5 miles farther along the rim. A good one-way downhill trail, if you have someone willing to pick you up by car at the lower end, is the **Dutton Creek Trail** (difficult; 4.6 miles one way). This trail heads south out of Rim Village, joins the PCT, then continues to Hwy 62.

When storms are blowing on the exposed cliffs of the rim, most skiers stay down in the protected areas of the forest. The most popular trail below the rim is **Sun Notch** (easy; 4.5 miles to the rim), which starts at the park museum. Feel free to turn around any time. The climb to the rim covers 625 feet.

The ultimate ski tour in the national park—perhaps in all of Oregon— is the 33-mile circuit of **Crater Lake Rim.** While the trail can be skied in a day by an extremely fit skier when the snow surface is consolidated, most skiers plan for at least three days. It could take several more if bad weather hits. Registration with the park staff is mandatory. The route follows the unplowed Rim Drive but is not marked. Avalanche rescue gear is advised. Most circuits are done clockwise from Rim Village.

Skiers must bring their own gear to the park, or rent it from shops outside the park. Rim Village has a restaurant that's open year-round, and rangers lead free **snowshoes tours** at 1pm most winter weekends. Snowshoes are provided (but are not available for rent separately). Crater Lake does not require vehicles to display the Oregon State sno-park permit.

When ski conditions are good lower down, skiers don't need to drive all the way up into the park. Union Creek Resort, (541) 560-5565, stays open all year and in winter caters to skiers and snowmobilers. The resort is 3,500 feet in elevation, high enough to get plenty of snow but low enough to mix in a lot of rain. **Farewell Bend Sno-Park** is 1 mile north of the resort on Hwy 62 and is favored by skiers and sliders. It has an excellent hill for **snow tubers,** a shelter with three covered picnic tables and a 6-mile

Nordic trail that leads to views of the Rogue River. Snowmobilers head for **Thousand Springs Sno-Park,** 8 miles north of Union Creek.

outside in

Cheaper Eats

Beckie's Cafe Beckie's is a fixture, and it enjoys gorgeous Rogue River National Forest scenery. Recreationists stop here for basic eats: pie, a hot beef sandwich, or a filling pork chop dinner. *56484 Hwy 62, Prospect; (541) 560-3563; $.*

Lodgings

Crater Lake Lodge ☆☆ This historic wood-and-stone building, perched at 7,076 feet on the rim of the caldera, has had a $15 million makeover, and all the rooms have great views. The menu in the dining room is contemporary (advance reservations required for dining, too). Closed winters. *Crater Lake National Park (via Hwy 138 or Hwy 62), Crater Lake; PO Box 128, Crater Lake, OR 97604; (541) 594-2511 or (541) 830-8700; $$$.*

Cheaper Sleeps

Prospect Historical Hotel The century-old hotel is now a bed and breakfast, motel, and restaurant complex. The B&B rooms are attractive but expensive. Cheaper are the basic (smallish) motel rooms out back. The restaurant serves reasonably priced dinners. *391 Mill Creek Dr, Prospect, OR 97536; (541) 560-3664 or (800) 944-6490; $.*

More Information

Chemult Ranger District, Chemult: *(541) 365-7001.*
Chiloquin Ranger District, Chiloquin: *(541) 783-4001.*
Crater Lake Lodge: *(541) 594-2511 (summer), (541) 830-8700 (winter).*
Crater Lake National Park: *(541) 594-2211, ext. 402.*
Klamath County Department of Tourism, Klamath Falls: *(800) 445-6728.*
Oregon's Outback Visitors Association, Klamath Falls: *(800) 598-6877.*
Prospect Ranger District, Prospect: *(541) 560-3400.*
Rogue River National Forest, Medford: *(541) 858-2200.*
Winema National Forest, Klamath Falls: *(541) 885-3400.*

Mountain Lakes

From Crater Lake National Park on the north, east to Upper Klamath Lake, south to the California border, and west to the edge of the Rogue River National Forest, including the Sky Lakes and Mountain Lakes Wildernesses, Howard Prairie Lake, the community of Butte Falls, and mountain resorts at Lake of the Woods and Fish Lake.

When the temperature soars above 100° in Medford, as it can on practically any day from mid-June to mid-September, the thoughts of the 200,000 people who make their home in the Rogue Valley turn toward the cool mountain breezes that await them a few miles away in the Mountain Lakes country of the Southern Oregon Cascades.

When the weekend begins, they load their pickups and recreational vehicles with camping, hiking, and fishing gear and head east. The air is fresh and pure, a marked contrast to what they breathe below, and the trout are waiting to rise to a temptingly placed fly. Raining or snowing for much of the year, the mountains can go for weeks at a time without hint of a threatening cloud during summer. Several well-situated resorts on Lake of the Woods, Fish Lake, Howard Prairie Lake, and Hyatt Reservoir help bring fishing and paddling opportunities to people who don't own boats. Trail worshippers—the hikers and cross-country skiers—would need to spend years in the area to experience all the trails.

The Mountain Lakes country isn't without a downside, however. The area can be thick with two particularly annoying nuisances—lodgepole pine trees clustered together like the hairs on a dog's back, and hordes of buzzing mosquitoes. Mosquitoes can be dealt with by applying repellent, wearing a head net, or swatting furiously, but the lodgepoles are another matter. Forest Service officials typically frown on people caught carrying chainsaws into the wilderness to clear away a few pines so they can see more than a couple feet beyond their noses.

Thankfully, the lodgepoles give way when you climb high enough or reach the shore of a lake. And those views make up for the claustrophobia the trees bring to the miles of trails behind you. Lodgepoles never lose their needles either, so their foliage is always there to put a cloak over the view. At least mosquitoes perform a valuable public service by dying off at the first hint of frost in September.

Autumn just might be the best time of all in the Mountain Lakes country. Aspen trees that live on the east side begin changing their leaves to a golden yellow, while the vine maples on the west side try to steal the show by changing color to brilliant red. Cool, crisp days make it much easier to haul a heavy backpack deep into the wilderness than during the hot and dusty days of summer.

Trails are less crowded during fall, because heat is gone from the valley below, living conditions are more bearable, and people don't need to head for the high country to escape the heat, although more than a few folks dream up whatever excuse they can to spend another weekend in the Mountain Lakes country.

Getting There

Three Oregon highways—62, 140, and 66—cross the Southern Cascades between the Rogue Valley on the west and Klamath County on the east. Highway 62 heads northeast to Crater Lake National Park, Highway 140 passes between the Sky Lakes and Mountain Lakes Wildernesses on its run from Medford to Klamath Falls, and Highway 66 heads east out of Ashland toward Howard Prairie Lake and Hyatt Reservoir. Portland is 310 miles away, via Medford, from Lake of the Woods Resort, the hub of recreation in the Mountain Lakes country and the southernmost Oregon Cascades.

Adjoining Areas

NORTH: **Crater Lake National Park**

EAST: **Klamath Basin**

WEST: **The Rogue Valley**

inside out

Hiking/Backpacking

The **Pacific Crest National Scenic Trail** (PCT) enters the Mountain Lakes country after it crosses Interstate 5 south of Ashland, climbs past 6,091-foot **Soda Mountain,** and turns north toward Hyatt Reservoir. From the Soda Mountain area, the next 85 miles of the trail are located in the Mountain Lakes country until the trail enters Crater Lake National Park. Hikers attempting to cover the trail's entire 2,500-mile distance from Mexico to Canada try to enter the Mountain Lakes country by early July.

Day-hiking opportunities along the trail can be found at **Green Springs Summit** on Hwy 66, about 15 miles east of Ashland; at **Hyatt and Howard Prairie Reservoirs,** where the trail passes close to each; along **Dead Indian Road** (County Rd 722), 30 miles from Ashland; and at **Cascade Summit,** 2 miles east of Fish Lake on Hwy 140. Once the PCT heads into the Sky Lakes Wilderness for its 35-mile run to Crater Lake, only small bits of it are close enough to a road to offer day-hiking opportunities.

Day hikers' most frequent encounter with the PCT in the Mountain Lakes country comes when they hike the **Mount McLoughlin Trail** (difficult; 5 miles one way) in the Sky Lakes Wilderness. With an elevation of 9,495 feet, Mount McLoughlin is the highest peak in all of southern Oregon. It can be seen for many miles from any direction, especially when deep snow blankets its summit. Mount McLoughlin is one of Oregon's easiest major Cascade peaks to climb, requiring only the ability to stay on a somewhat confusing trail and gain 4,000 feet in elevation. The trailhead is on Forest Rd 3650, 2.5 miles north of Hwy 140. The turnoff is 2 miles east of Fish Lake. Within a mile from the trailhead, the trail to the summit joins the Pacific Crest Trail. It soon leaves the PCT, less than 2 miles from the trailhead, and strikes out to the west across a boulder-strewn forest. Watch for blazes on the trees to know that you're on the trail. At timberline, the trail follows piles of rock cairns along a ridge that continues west to the summit. An old Forest Service telephone line that used to serve the summit fire lookout marks the way.

On the way down, avoid descending the easy scree slope that leads to the south. The south side only gets climbers in trouble, because it heads nowhere near where they parked their cars. If you lose the trail, keep heading east during the descent so that you eventually cross the PCT or hit one of the roads. The best way to avoid problems coming down is to be alert on the ascent and take mental notes of the terrain and landmarks.

The **Sky Lakes Wilderness** covers 113,590 acres south of Crater Lake National Park in a rectangular shape roughly 27 miles long and 6 miles wide. Congress created the Sky Lakes Wilderness in 1984 as part of the Oregon National Forest Wilderness Protection Act. It has three major clusters of lakes: **Blue Canyon Basin,** at the southern end of the wilderness just north of Fourmile Lake; **Sky Lakes Basin,** in the south-central part of the wilderness; and **Seven Lakes Basin,** a few miles north of Sky Lakes Basin. The upper 9 miles of the wilderness are largely without lakes, although the **Middle Fork of the Rogue River** cuts a deep canyon as it begins its march to the Pacific Ocean.

Western approaches to the wilderness are managed by Rogue River National Forest, Butte Falls Ranger District, (541) 865-2700; eastern and southern approaches by Winema National Forest, Klamath Ranger District, (541) 885-3400; and northern approaches by Crater Lake National Park, (541) 594-2211.

Blue Canyon Basin can be reached from a trailhead at the end of Forest Rd 3770 at the west edge of the wilderness. Turn north from County Rd 821, 9 miles east of Butte Falls, onto Forest Rd 37 and drive 10 miles to the junction with 3770. Turn southeast and drive 5 miles to the trailhead. When approaching Blue Canyon Basin from the west, the **Blue Canyon Trail** (moderate; 11-mile loop to Island Lake at the east edge of the basin) can be either a day hike or the beginning of a long backpack deeper into the wilderness.

The **Long Lake Trail** (moderate; 6 miles one way to Island Lake) is the main access route from Fourmile Lake at the south end of the wilderness. To reach the Fourmile Lake trailhead, turn north from Hwy 140 at Lake of the Woods onto Forest Rd 3661. The trailhead is on the lake's south side 5 miles from the highway. For a 15-mile backpack loop, hike along the north side of Fourmile Lake to Island Lake. Pick up the Pacific Crest Trail just east of Island Lake and follow it south to the Twin Ponds Trail, which travels south of Fourmile Lake to the trailhead.

Sky Lakes Basin can be reached from three Winema National Forest trailheads—**Cold Springs** (moderate; 6 miles one way to Margurette Lake), **Cherry Creek** (moderate; 5.5 miles to the lake), and **Nanny Creek** (moderate; 6 miles to the lake). **Margurette Lake** is located at the very heart of the wilderness where several loop trips are possible among the area's many lakes. The Sky Lakes Trail heads south to join the Pacific Crest Trail in 6 miles. Midway along the way is **Lake Notasha,** which was judged by a water survey team in the early 1980s to have the most pure lake water found on earth. Cold Springs trailhead is 8 miles north on Forest Rd 3651 from Hwy 140, 4 miles east of Lake of the Woods Resort. Cherry Creek and Nanny Creek are located at the ends of spur roads off Forest Rd 34, which travels along the lower eastern flank of Winema National Forest in the upper Klamath Basin. The trailheads are labeled on the national forest map, available at ranger stations and sporting goods stores.

Seven Lakes Basin can be reached from the east via **Sevenmile Marsh Trail** (moderate; 7.8 miles one way to Alta Lake) on Forest Rd 3334 or from the west via **Seven Lakes Trail** (easy; 4.1 miles one way) on Forest Rd 3780 or via the **Alta Lake Trail** (moderate; 5.3 miles one way) on Forest Rd 3785. Selecting a trailhead frequently comes down more to the road you need to drive rather than the trail you will hike. Trailheads from the east are readily accessible from roads along the west side of the upper Klamath Basin (Forest Rd 34/County Rd 531). Approaches from the west require long drives on rough mountain roads to reach the trailheads and require reference to a Rogue River National Forest map. When visiting Seven Lakes Basin, be sure to scramble up 7,582-foot **Devils Peak,** the obvious peak that juts above timberline at the south edge of the basin. The approach is made via the PCT.

Before heading east of Prospect and Butte Falls to the Forest Service trails that lead up toward the Sky Lakes Wilderness, hikers should explore a scenic spot along the Rogue River near Prospect. The **North Fork of the Rogue River** plunges through a wildly scenic canyon, easily viewed from Mill Creek Rd, which parallels the river just south of Hwy 62. To reach Mill Creek Rd, turn south from Hwy 62 at Cascade Gorge, 5 miles southwest of Prospect.

Even more impressive than the wildly churning Rogue are the side-creek waterfalls across the Rogue canyon. **Mill Creek Falls** plunges 173 feet from atop the canyon rim to join the Rogue River below. About 200 yards downstream, **Barr Creek Falls** drops 200 feet from the same plateau. A large sign on Boise Cascade Corporation land marks the trailhead on Mill Creek Rd. Mill Creek Falls is .3 mile from the trailhead.

The easiest approaches to the Sky Lakes Wilderness are described above, but three other trails are worth exploring—the **Red Blanket Trail** (moderate; 3.9 miles into the far north section of the wilderness), the **Middle Fork Trail** (difficult; 9.75 miles to Alta Lake), and the **South Fork Trail** (moderate; 5.1 miles to Blue Canyon Basin). All pass through a vegetation zone not found elsewhere in Mountain Lakes country: Douglas fir and western hemlock dominate the forest, rather than the Englemann spruce and western white pine found farther up. The trails can be accessed by the network of forest roads southeast of Prospect; stop at the Prospect Ranger Station for directions.

Wilderness areas come in a variety of shapes and sizes in Oregon, but only the **Mountain Lakes Wilderness** comes in a 6-mile square. It was created in 1964 under the original wilderness act that set aside wilderness areas around the country. The goal of most hikers is to reach the 9-mile **Mountain Lakes Loop Trail** in the center of the wilderness, which gives access to the wilderness lakes. Where the loop trail crosses an alpine ridge 1 mile south of Lake Harriette, the summit of 8,208-foot Aspen Butte—the highest point of the wilderness—is an easy 1-mile off-trail scramble from the loop trail south up the ridge.

The most popular entry route into the wilderness is the **Varney Creek Trail** (moderate; 4.3 miles to the Mountain Lakes Loop Trail). Next in popularity is the **Mountain Lakes Trail** (moderate; 5.4 miles one way), followed by the **Clover Creek Trail** (moderate; 4.5 miles one way). Varney Creek enters from the north on Forest Rd 3664, Mountain Lakes from the west on Forest Rd 3660, and Clover Creek from the south on Forest Rd 3852. Most lakes in the wilderness are within a three-hour hike from one of the trailheads. The wilderness is administered by Winema National Forest, which gets its name from an Indian word that means "woman of a brave heart." The forest publishes a Mountain Lakes Wilderness map.

Camping

Rogue River headwaters

Rogue River National Forest roads lead to several small campgrounds and hiking trails in the block of land bounded by Prospect and Butte Falls on the west, the Sky Lakes Wilderness on the east, and Hwy 140 on the south. For information, contact the Butte Falls Ranger Station, (541) 865-2700.

Campgrounds along Forest Rd 3065, which heads north from County Rd 821, 9 miles east of Butte Falls, include **Whiskey Springs.** Located .5 mile north on Forest Rd 3065 from the junction, Whiskey Springs is the largest campground in the area with 17 tent sites, plus 19 sites that can accommodate trailers to 30 feet. The campground has a barrier-free nature trail that makes a 1-mile loop around a beaver-created wetland. A boardwalk leads to a viewpoint over the wetlands, where great blue herons, wood ducks, and sandhill cranes are occasionally seen. **Fourbit Ford and Snowshoe Campgrounds** have 12 sites combined and are within 5 miles of Whiskey Springs on Forest Rd 3065.

Forest Rd 34, which heads east from County Rd 992, 7 miles northeast of Butte Falls, has camping at **Imnaha, South Fork, Big Ben, and Parker Meadows Campgrounds.** The largest has only 4 sites. Imnaha Campground, 22 miles east of Butte Falls, has the **Imnaha Guard Station,** available for overnight use from the Forest Service from May 16 through November 9. The cabin can squeeze in six people and rents for

$50 per night from the Butte Falls Ranger Station, (541) 865-2700. Be prepared to fill out paperwork that is only slightly less involved than taking out a second mortgage on your home. The government requires a special use permit, not just a nightly rental agreement. Be sure to tidy up the place when you leave.

Willow Creek Reservoir, 9 miles southeast of Butte Falls via County Rds 821 and 965, is the site of 927-acre Jackson County park, a resort with cabins and boat rentals, and several picnic areas. The campground can accommodate 77 trailers (21 with full hookups). Call (541) 865-3229 for reservations.

Lake of the Woods corridor

Fish Lake, with its resort and campgrounds, comes first while traveling Hwy 140 east from Medford. In addition to cabins and camping at private Fish Lake Resort, (541) 949-8500, Rogue River National Forest has camping at **Willow Prairie Campground,** north of County Rd 821, and at **Fish Lake, Doe Point, and North Fork Campground,** all along the south side of the highway near Fish Lake. Fish Lake (16 sites) and Doe Point (25 sites) both have spots right on the lake. **Beaver Dam** and **Daley Creek** are small forest camps about 6 miles south of Fish Lake on Forest Rd 27, which heads south to Howard Prairie Lake. Recreation around Fish Lake is managed by the Ashland Ranger District, (541) 482-3333.

Lake of the Woods is 6 miles east of Fish Lake, across Cascade Summit on Hwy 140. On its northeast side, the lake has two Winema National Forest campgrounds, as well as cabins and camping at Lake of the Woods Resort, (541) 949-8300. The Forest Service's **Sunset Campground** has 67 sites for tent and trailers, while **Aspen Point Campground** has 5 of its 61 sites reserved for tents. **Rainbow Bay** is a popular picnic area on Lake of the Woods, which also has a visitors center with a small historical museum. For information on campgrounds east of Cascade Summit on Hwy 140, contact the Klamath Ranger District, (541) 885-3400.

Fourmile Lake, the big lake at the southern edge of the Sky Lakes Wilderness (see Hiking/Backpacking, above), has a campground with 16 tent sites and 5 sites for trailers. The lake is 6 miles north of Lake of the Woods on Forest Rd 3661.

The Rogue River and Winema National Forests do not participate in the national campground reservations systems, so the only guaranteed camping spots are at private resorts. Better plan to get out of town early on Fridays to find a camp spot. Make your move when the thermometer hits 90; don't wait until it tops 100.

BLM reservoirs

When Rogue Valley residents want to get serious about camping, they head up to Howard Prairie Lake and Hyatt Reservoir in the foothills east of

Ashland. One is called a lake and the other is called a reservoir, but both are Bureau of Reclamation projects and are big and busy, with complete facilities for an extended camping, boating, and fishing outing. Visitors can even go for a walk if they want because the PCT passes the south shore of both.

Howard Prairie Lake can be reached by taking exit 14 off I-5 in Ashland. Drive 1 mile east, then turn left on Dead Indian Rd (County Rd 722) for 17 miles to the reservoir turnoff. The lake is surrounded by pine and fir forest. An afternoon wind usually picks up during the summer, strong enough that sailors can use the lake to stage regattas. The lake has 19 miles of shoreline, but only boats can reach the east side.

Howard Prairie Lake Resort, (541) 826-3122, is one of the most developed county park facilities in Oregon. The Jackson County park covers 155 acres and has 220 campsites (78 with water and electricity), plus 19 "prairie schooner" covered-wagon rentals. Other facilities include a store, restaurant, showers, marina, gasoline sales, fish-cleaning station, boat ramps, and docks. The lake even has a floating rest room called "The Island."

The county also operates 59-acre **Willow Point Park,** also on the west shore of the lake, 3 miles south of the resort by road or 2 miles by speedboat. The park has 40 camping sites, but no hookups. Farther south, near the reservoir's dam, **Klum Landing Park** has 30 sites set on 156 acres. Just north of the reservoir, the county's **Lily Glen Horse Camp** has 26 campsites on 40 acres, plus corrals and a barn. For information on Jackson County parks, call (541) 826-8101.

Hyatt Reservoir is 3 miles southwest of Howard Prairie Lake, but is 600 feet higher in elevation. **Main Campground,** part of a BLM recreation complex, includes 29 drive-through sites (no water hookups or electricity), 18 drive-in tent sites, 7 walk-in tent sites, a group shelter that can be reserved, and an equestrian facility for use by reservation only. **Wildcat Campground,** another part of the recreation complex, has 12 additional drive-in sites (no hookups available). For information, contact the BLM's Medford office, (541) 770-2200.

Campers Cove, (541) 482-1201, is a private resort on the west shore of Hyatt Reservoir. The resort has full-hookup camping, showers, a bait and tackle store, and a full-service restaurant and bar. Hyatt Lake Resort, (541) 482-3331, has full resort facilities, including camping, cabins, and a store.

Wildlife

It may not seem possible during summer, when auto traffic floods the roads and speedboats tar up the water of the lakes, but the Howard Prairie Lake/Hyatt Reservoir area is one of the best locations in Oregon to spot the

great gray owl. Southern Oregon and Northern California are the southern extent of the owl's range. The best way to spot an owl is to drive the side roads off Dead Indian Rd (County Rd 722, which connects Ashland with Lake of the Woods), especially the ones that border open meadowlands along the east shores of Hyatt Reservoir and Howard Prairie Lake. Areas where the owls are frequently seen are the junction of Dead Indian and Howard Prairie Lake Rds, the turnoff to Howard Prairie's marina, and along the east side of Hyatt Reservoir Rd. Owls are usually seen in the most isolated meadows just before dusk and just after dawn.

Fishing

There's no better spot to begin a fishing report on the Mountain Lakes country than at **Fish Lake,** the first big lake travelers encounter when heading up Hwy 140 from Medford, at milepost 30. Fish Lake covers 350 acres and has a depth of 25 feet. Fishing for stocked rainbow and brook trout is good. Fish Lake Resort, (541) 949-8500, offers moorage space, rental boats, and six cabins on the east shore of the lake.

Lake of the Woods is 6 miles east of Fish Lake along Hwy 140 on the way to Klamath Falls. Recreational anglers have visited the 1,113-acre lake for a hundred years. Lake of the Woods Resort, (541) 949-8300, was established in the late 1800s and was rebuilt in 1960. The resort rents eight cabins, boats, and moorage space. With a depth of 52 feet, the lake supports a population of rainbow and brook trout, as well as kokanee, largemouth bass, and brown bullhead. There is no limit on the bullhead, which make up half the lake's fish population. Water-skiers also use the lake.

Backcountry lakes abound in the Sky Lakes Wilderness, which has more than 200 pools of water ranging in size from ponds to lakes of 30 to 40 acres. **Fourmile Lake,** the largest in the area, is not part of the wilderness but is surrounded by designated wilderness. The lake covers 740 acres at 5,744 feet in elevation. Maximum depth is 170 feet. Fishing is good for kokanee and rainbow and brook trout. Boats are launched at the beach in the campground (see Camping, above). Many Sky Lakes Wilderness lakes have resident populations of rainbow and brook trout and are stocked on alternating years. Best fishing is with flies from the bank early or late in the day.

Howard Prairie Lake and **Hyatt Reservoir** (see Camping, above) are recovering from the drought cycle of the early 1990s and are again becoming productive for stocked rainbow trout. Howard Prairie Lake covers 2,000 acres at 4,500 feet in elevation. Hyatt covers 900 acres and is at 5,100 feet elevation. Bank access is good at Hyatt because it has a road around it, but a boat for trolling is a big help at Howard Prairie. Bank anglers congregate around the dam at the southeast end of Howard Prairie, down to Klum Landing.

Willow Creek Reservoir southeast of Butte Falls (see Camping, above) covers 340 acres and is productive for rainbow trout, largemouth bass, and black crappie. Fishing is best just before and after the heat of summer.

Two of the **Rogue River's forks** rise in Rogue River National Forest west of the Sky Lakes Wilderness. The Middle Fork joins the main North Fork near Prospect, and the South Fork joins a few miles below in Lost Creek Reservoir (see The Rogue Valley chapter). Fishing in the headwaters of the middle and north forks is fair for native rainbow, cutthroat, and brook trout, with an occasional large fish taken out of slack pools.

Mountain Biking

The two national forests of the Mountain Lakes area have worked jointly to develop a 9.3-mile one-way mountain-bike trail called the **High Lakes Trail.** The trail connects Lake of the Woods to Fish Lake via a route that's far enough south of Hwy 140 to be out of earshot of highway traffic noise. Not a singletrack for the hard-core rider, the trail is wide and fairly flat. Although still relatively undiscovered, the trail is expected to receive high use in the future.

The High Lakes Trail has four access points: Fish Lake on the west (mile 0 in Fish Lake Campground), Brown Mountain (mile 6 on Forest Rd 3640), Aspen Point (mile 7.5 in Aspen Point Campground), and Great Meadows (mile 9.3 at the turnoff to Lake of the Woods Resort from Hwy 140 to County Rd 533). The trail is level between Great Meadows west to Aspen Point and is accessible to wheelchairs. The trail's surface is compacted gravel throughout.

For one-way rides on the High Lakes Trail with a car shuttle, bikers can start at Lake of the Woods Resort at 4,949 feet in elevation, reach a high point of 5,220 feet midway along the route, and descend to Fish Lake at 4,634 feet. The last 3 miles is a fast, fun descent. Bikers can add another 3 miles west of Fish Lake by continuing to North Fork Campground on Forest Rd 37.

The east side of the trail begins at Great Meadows, which is alive with wildflowers in late spring and early summer. Beyond Lake of the Woods, the trail passes through an old-growth forest of mixed conifers and the austere lava flows of 7,311-foot Brown Mountain to the south. Cyclists should take some time to enjoy the views of Mount McLoughlin to the north and to watch for bald eagles and osprey around the lakes. The trail is also open to hikers.

After an easy day on the High Lakes Trail, bikers may want to try a more difficult 7.8-mile single-track ride or a 15-mile loop using forest roads south of Brown Mountain. The trail begins at 4,850 feet on Forest Rd 3705 southwest of Lake of the Woods at the **Browns Mountain trail-head.** The ride climbs to 5,730 feet before reaching Forest Rd 700. Riders can either return to the trailhead by following gravel roads that are shown on the Rogue River National Forest map, available at ranger stations and sporting goods stores, or they can make a one-way ride by continuing on the trail down to Lake of the Woods. Riding opportunities in the area are somewhat limited because bikes aren't allowed on the PCT or in the nearby wilderness areas.

The Butte Falls Ranger District has a 15-mile round-trip bike ride between **Nichols Creek Picnic Area** and the 6,208-foot summit of **Rustler Peak.** The ride requires a climb of 2,200 feet. If you're still interested, head for the picnic ground via Forest Rds 34 and 37, about 12 miles northeast of Butte Falls. Ride 2 miles south on paved road 37, then 3 miles on lightly traveled dirt Forest Rd 800 to **Parker Meadows Campground.** Just outside the campground, turn west and ride for a little more than 2 miles on Forest Rd 830 to the lookout atop the peak. On the way down, take gravel Forest Rd 640 to Forest Rd 37, then ride past the campground and back to the picnic area. Starting at the campground can shorten the ride.

For **guided mountain-bike rides,** check with Ashland's Adventure Center, (541) 488-2819. The company uses several local outfitters to package all sorts of outdoor recreation, southern Oregon–style, for travelers who don't have quite enough space to haul around their raft, hot air balloon, mountain bike, and horse and buggy when they head out on vacation.

Cross-Country Skiing/Snowmobiling

The Rogue River and Winema National Forests jointly publish "Jackson-Klamath Winter Trails," a map and guide, available at local ranger stations, to the vast network of ski and snowmobile trails in the area. The Oregon Department of Transportation maintains 11 sno-parks in the Southern Cascades for winter recreation.

Heading east up Hwy 140, Nordic skiers from the Medford area come to the **Fish Lake ski trails** first (30 miles east of Hwys 62–140 junction at Eagle Point) and may decide to spend the day if the snow is good. Elevation is 4,634 feet. The 9.5-mile **Lollipop loop trail system,** mostly easy to moderate terrain, begins at Fish Lake Sno-Park, heads around the east end of the lake, then loops through terrain to the south. Detailed **maps** are available at the sno-park and at Fish Lake Resort on weekends; the resort also **rents skis,** (541) 949-8500.

Summit Sno-Park is another 2 miles east on Hwy 140. Trails link it to Fish Lake on the north and south sides of the highway. The most popular tour from Summit is into the 12.1-mile **High Lakes ski trail system** northeast of the sno-park. Summit ski shelter is situated along the High Lakes trail system's **McLoughlin Trail.** Skiing is mostly easy to moderate, with cutoffs that can shorten or length loops through the High Lakes system.

Fourmile Sno-Park, on Hwy 140 just north of Lake of the Woods, has 2 trail systems that head north, plus link trails to Summit and Lake of the Woods. From the sno-park, the **Upper Canal Trail** goes north for 6.5 miles and ends at Fourmile Lake. **Billie Creek loop** is a 6.6-mile ski trail system that makes it halfway to Fourmile Lake.

Lake of the Woods Resort has a couple of trails perfect for beginners and families. **Family Ski loop** is 2 miles long and **Lake of the Woods–Sunset** connects the resort with the Sunset boat launch 2.7 miles away. **Rental skis** are available at the resort, (541) 949-8300.

Easiest winter access to the Mountain Lakes Wilderness is via the **Mountain Lakes Trail** that begins near Lake of the Woods (see Hiking/ Backpacking, above). The trail is not marked for skiing but is easy to follow. This is usually an overnight trip for experienced backcountry skiers.

Table Mountain is the BLM's winter recreation area in the Mountain Lakes country, 23 miles east of Ashland at 5,000 feet in elevation. To reach this winter play area, take exit 14 from I-5 at Ashland and drive Hwy 66 for 17 miles to Green Springs Inn. Turn north and drive 4 miles to Hyatt Reservoir, and then continue 2 miles along the lake's shore to the parking area. State sno-park permits are not required. The play area is designed for **snow tubing,** with snowmobile and cross-country **ski trails** that begin nearby. The tubing area has a rest room and a place to build a fire, but you'll need to bring wood.

Most skiers who use the BLM land leave Table Mountain to sliders and snowmobilers and instead head for **Buck Prairie Sno-Park,** 13 miles east of Ashland at the summit of Dead Indian Rd (County Rd 722, which connects Ashland with Lake of the Woods). The sno-park has 17 miles of interconnected trails for beginner and intermediate skiers.

Southern Oregon is **snowmobile** country, with groomed trails that link Fish Lake and Lake of the Woods resorts with Diamond Lake Resort north of Crater Lake National Park. For the most part, ski and snowmobile trails are segregated and users avoid conflict. Lake of the Woods Resort, (541) 949-8300, rents snowmobiles, skis, and ice skates.

More Information

Ashland Chamber of Commerce, Ashland: *(541) 482-3486.*
Ashland Ranger District, Ashland: *(541) 482-3333.*
Bureau of Land Management, Medford: *(541) 770-2200.*
Butte Falls Ranger District, Butte Falls: *(541) 865-2700.*
Crater Lake National Park, Crater Lake: *(541) 594-2211.*
Klamath Ranger District, Klamath Falls: *(541) 885-3400.*
Medford Visitors and Convention Bureau, Medford: *(800) 469-6307.*
Oregon's Outback Visitors Association, Klamath Falls: *(800) 598-6877.*
Prospect Ranger District, Prospect: *(541) 560-3400.*
Rogue River National Forest, Medford: *(541) 858-2200.*
Southern Oregon Visitors Association, Medford: *(800) 448-4856.*
Winema National Forest, Klamath Falls: *(541) 883-6714.*

Klamath Basin

From the Deschutes-Klamath county line near La Pine on the north, east to the Klamath-Lake county line, south to the California border, and west to the shore of Upper Klamath Lake and US Highway 97, including Klamath Marsh, Upper Klamath and Bear Valley National Wildlife Refuges, and the towns of Chiloquin, Beatty, Klamath Falls, and Merrill.

More than a million ducks and geese can't be wrong: the Klamath Basin country of south-central Oregon is a great place to hang out for a while.

Oregon's largest concentration of migrating waterfowl usually is in place for a couple months each winter, making use of the national wildlife refuge system on both sides of the Oregon-California state line. Following these migrants from the north is the largest concentration of wintering bald eagles in the Lower 48 states: more than 300 congregate in the area to dine on the inevitable injuries that such huge waterfowl flocks include. Wildlife-viewing opportunities are spectacular in Klamath County on winter days, especially when the fog that is so common during winter doesn't blanket the ground and drop visibility to a few feet.

Even when the birds are nesting up north in Canada and Alaska during summer, the Klamath Basin country has an abundance of recreation opportunities. And the area's full potential is now on the verge of being recognized with the development of the Running Y Ranch on the shores of Upper Klamath Lake.

The 3,600-acre vacation resort, complete with condos, homesites, and plenty of on-site recreation, is a long way from becoming another Sunriver, but the potential is there. Winema National

Forest is studying the resort's proposal for a day-use ski area on nearby Pelican Butte. A decision is expected in 1999. If approved, the ski area would be built over two summers and would become Oregon's first new downhill ski area since 1968.

Growth from Oregon's southern neighbor, aka California (a dirty word in much of Oregon), had hopscotched over the Klamath Basin country in its rush to reach Bend and Sunriver, but that situation has begun to change. The good folks of the Klamath Basin country know that uncontrolled growth can spoil a place as fast as an eagle pounces on a dead duck. They know their land is blessed with great natural beauty and they aim to keep it that way. Their winter visitors from the north will never forgive them if they don't.

Getting There

Klamath Falls is the hub of Klamath County and its 6,135 square miles. The easiest driving route from Portland is to take Interstate 5 to Eugene, cross the Cascades on Highway 58 over Willamette Pass, and continue south on US Highway 97 (US 97). It's 279 miles from Portland to Klamath Falls. Kingsley Field in Klamath Falls is served by regional and commuter air service. Klamath County is crossed north-south by US 97 and east-west by Highway 140. Redding, California, is 111 miles south via US 97 and Interstate 5.

Adjoining Areas

NORTH: **Bend and the Upper Deschutes River**

EAST: **Lake County**

WEST: **Mountain Lakes, Crater Lake National Park, Diamond Lake, Willamette Pass**

Wildlife

The 3,600-acre **Gerber Reservoir** is a good place to begin watching for wildlife while you refine your technique before heading to the larger expanse of the national refuge system in the Klamath Basin. Built by the Bureau of Reclamation and managed by the Bureau of Land Management (BLM), the reservoir rises and falls depending on the water year and irrigation needs. When full, the reservoir is home to dozens of water birds, songbirds, and the birds of prey that feed on them. The BLM has a watchable **wildlife auto tour** through the area that is open from April 15 through November 15. Roads are closed during winter to protect them from damage. Gerber Reservoir is 35 miles east of Klamath Falls. Drive Hwy 70 to Bonanza and follow county roads to the reservoir. Visit the Klamath Falls BLM office, (541) 883-6916, at 2795 Anderson Ave, Bldg. 25, for information and to pick up a copy of the brochure.

The Oregon Department of Fish and Wildlife operates the **Klamath Fish Hatchery,** (541) 383-2278, located 8 miles west of US 97 on Hwy 62. The hatchery is best to visit from mid-October through May when its stock of rainbow and cutthroat trout is growing. The hatchery also raises desert trout for release in the warm, alkali waters of southeast Oregon.

Visitors to the area can leave the driving to a professional and learn where to go in the future by booking a **guided tour** with Oregon Natural History Tours, (541) 356-2353, or Outback Adventure Tours, (541) 882-2348, both in Klamath Falls. Dude ranches that specialize in wildlife viewing from the back of a horse are the Circle 5 Ranch, (541) 545-6736, and the Gem Limousin, (541) 545-6111, both outside Bonanza.

Klamath Basin National Wildlife Refuge Complex

The Klamath Basin, including parts of California, has six national wildlife refuges—Klamath Marsh, Upper Klamath, and Bear Valley in Oregon; Lower Klamath, on the state boundary, but mostly in California; and the Tule Lake and Clear Lake units in California. The complex is managed out of Tulelake, California. For information, call (916) 667-2231.

Klamath Marsh, northern Klamath County's national wildlife refuge, lies 6 miles east of US 97, about 17 miles south of Diamond Lake Junction or 45 miles north of Klamath Falls where Silver Lake Rd (County Rd 676) leaves the highway and heads east through the marsh. The 37,600-acre reserve, which is managed from a Chiloquin office, (541) 783-3380, protects nearly all of the Klamath Marsh and part of the surrounding ponderosa and lodgepole pine forest. The refuge is undeveloped for visitors and viewing is done from cars on roads around the perimeter of the refuge, as shown on the Winema National Forest map. Much of the refuge is covered with tule and cattail marshes.

The spring and fall migration seasons are best for viewing **ducks** and **geese.** Summer residents include **pelicans, osprey,** and **sandhill cranes.** Wocus Bay, the southeast arm of the marsh, is a popular viewing spot for **shorebirds.** The surrounding forest harbors **Rocky Mountain elk, mule deer,** and **great gray owls.** The Williamson River, one of Oregon's blue-ribbon trout streams, passes through the marsh.

The **Upper Klamath National Wildlife Refuge** includes 14,000 acres of freshwater marshes and open water at the northeast edge of Upper Klamath Lake. The refuge is managed out of the California office and access to the refuge is by boat only. The lake itself covers 64,000 acres and is connected by the 1-mile-long Agency Straits to 8,200-acre Agency Lake. The state of Oregon also maintains four game management areas in the Upper Klamath Basin.

Oregon's largest expanse of fresh water provides vital forage for thousands of migrating **waterfowl,** plus critical nesting habitat for **white pelicans, herons,** and **egrets.** Oregon's largest concentration of nesting **bald eagles** (more than 20 pairs) lives in snags in the old-growth forest that lines the lake's western shore.

Due to the lake's huge size, spotting the abundance of waterfowl is not always easy. US 97 abuts part of the lake's east shore and has some wildlife-viewing turnouts, but this is open water and birds can be miles offshore. Hwy 140 passes the lake's west shore as it travels from Klamath Falls to Medford. Wildlife viewing is best where the highway passes marshes and the meadows at the edge of Winema National Forest.

The 4,200-acre **Bear Valley National Wildlife Refuge,** situated on the east edge of a forest overlooking California's 53,600-acre Lower Klamath National Wildlife Refuge, is where many of the area's wintering bald eagles roost for the night. The highest number of **bald eagles** counted in the Klamath Basin was 780, once the birds began their comeback after DDT was banned. A typical year sees the count in the 300 to 400 range, with the peak number occurring in February. The refuge is managed out of the California office and is 12 miles southwest of Klamath Falls, 1 mile west of Worden and US 97.

Watching the eagles fly out each winter morning is one of the great wildlife-watching spectacles in Oregon. Viewers arrive just north of the state line before dawn, when the temperature can be well below freezing, and park west off US 97 near the community of Worden. As light begins to brighten the eastern sky, the eagles leave their roosts in the big trees at the edge of the forest and fan out throughout the basin to feed on injured ducks and geese. Watching several dozen bald eagles fly overhead a few hundred feet above the ground is a sight that won't soon be forgotten. It doesn't always work that way, though. The Klamath Basin can be covered for days with a tule fog—named after the tule bullrushes that grow in the marshes—that blankets the land like a down comforter. The fog may lift in the afternoon, but watching eagles return to their roosts for the night never provides as many sightings as the morning fly-out when so many leave at the same time.

After watching the Bear Valley fly-out, wildlife watchers can drive just across the California state line on US 97 and turn east on California 161. The paved road travels 20 miles along the northern edge of the **Lower Klamath National Wildlife Refuge,** following the state line much of the way, before joining Hwy 39 near the border town of Merrill. Bald eagles and the waterfowl they feed on are frequently seen along the road. Most of the Lower Klamath's 53,598 acres are in California.

Boating/Canoeing

Believe it or not, the 100 square miles covered by **Upper Klamath Lake,** the largest lake in Oregon when dry years keep Malheur Lake within its banks, has an average depth of only 7 feet. The shallow nature of the lake makes it extremely rich and productive for fish, but it's not a place a lot of water-skiers are interested in visiting. Most boating is of two types— self-propelled craft, such as canoes, for wildlife viewing, or powerful boats that can search out the best fishing spots and cover the lake's vast area. Most boating occurs near shore because it doesn't take much wind to churn the surface of the lake into whitecaps.

Canoeists concentrate on the northwest side of the lake near the marshes of Upper Klamath Basin National Wildlife Refuge (see Wildlife, above). Popular launch points include Rocky Point Resort, (541) 356-2287, and Harriman Springs Resort, (541) 356-2331. Both resorts are within 2 miles of Hwy 140 on County Rd 531 at the lake's northwest corner.

The 9.5-mile **Upper Klamath Canoe Trail** begins at the Rocky Point boat launch at **Pelican Bay** on Upper Klamath Lake. Another launch point is 3 miles to the north at **Malone Springs** on County Rd 531 (also called Westside Rd). The trail winds through four named segments—Recreation Creek, Crystal Creek, Wocus Cut, and Malone Springs. A common plant in the area is the wocus, a large-leafed yellow water lily. Canoeists can paddle the distance in a half day by paddling at 2mph, but the bird-watching opportunities for the 250 species seen in the area usually make the outing an all-day affair. Both resorts have canoes and other boats for rent, plus overnight moorage. Only the **Wocus Cut Trail** is off-limits to powerboats, but the speed limit is 10mph around marinas and in arms of the lake.

Upper Klamath Lake has 11 boats launches, most of them along Hwy 140, plus 3 more on the west side of **Agency Lake** near Chiloquin. Klamath Falls is an active boating community, with a yacht club and rowing club. **Sailboats** ply the lower waters of Upper Klamath Lake near town. **Powerboats** stage trips from Pelican Marina, (541) 882-5834, and Lakeside Yachts, (541) 884-5731, both large marinas on the southwest shore of the lake at the edge of town on Lakeshore Dr. The Ewauna Lake Rowing Club stages an annual regatta on Lake Ewauna, an impoundment of the Klamath River just south of town. The 1-mile-long Link River connects Upper Klamath Lake and Lake Ewauna.

The Klamath Lake Touring Company, (541) 882-8150, can show visitors who don't own a boat the beauty of Upper Klamath Lake.

Rafting/Kayaking

The mighty **Klamath River** begins its 250-mile run through both the Cascade and Coast Ranges at Lake Ewauna. It soon becomes a California river after leaving the lake, but not before giving rafters two of the most exciting stretches of whitewater in Oregon. A 7-mile stretch of river between **Keno Dam** and **Boyle Reservoir** is popular with expert local paddlers. The river is in a deep canyon and scouting is difficult. The water is usually a frothy brown, because of runoff from upstream farming, so kayakers try to keep their mouths closed in the event of a roll.

The Klamath River below the Boyle powerhouse is the most exciting commercial river-running day trip in Oregon. The Lower Deschutes River is like a kid's bicycle with training wheels compared to the Klamath's titanium-framed mountain bike. The run on the Upper Klamath is 15 miles long, with 11 miles of it in Oregon before the river crosses the California state line. All of the big rapids are in Oregon. This part of the river was added to the National Wild and Scenic Rivers Program in 1996, giving Oregon 40 federally protected rivers.

The Klamath River is one of Oregon's most predictable whitewater rivers during summer. The river's flow is regulated to pass through two powerhouses operated by Pacific Power and Light (PP&L). Peak electricity generation is needed in the middle of the day during summer to meet residential air-conditioning demands in the power system network. That means the Klamath River flows with a mere trickle of water until about 10am, when the powerhouses are turned on. By late afternoon, the water is held back again. The situation is ideal for rafters, guaranteeing the exact amount of water they need at precisely the moment they need it. The dependable flow runs throughout the summer.

Before packing up a raft and heading for the river, however, a word of caution is in order. The river has 20 rapids rated Class III or better, including a pair of Class Vs, plus another 25 Class II rapids. In addition to the challenging whitewater, the river requires a hellish shuttle of 150 miles at the end of the day to return to Klamath Falls. You'll be a lot closer to Mount Shasta in California midway through the shuttle than to your vehicle back in Klamath Falls. The difficult water and the long shuttle means most river use is by commercial outfitters who have the logistics down pat. Fully 90 percent of the river's use is by guided trips. The Oregon part of the Klamath River sees about 4,500 user days annually with commercial guides and 500 by private boaters. The Lower Deschutes River, by comparison, has more than 125,000 annual user days.

The Klamath has about two dozen **outfitters** licensed by the BLM. The vast majority are based in California, where action dries up during summer along the Northern California coast and the Sierra Nevada, and shifts to the reliable water source of the Klamath. The only local Klamath Falls outfitter is Cascade River Runners, (541) 883-6340. Ashland and Medford also supply a lot of Klamath River boaters because the end-of-the-day shuttle is actually closer to Medford than Klamath Falls. Commercial outfitters from the Medford side of the Cascades are Rogue Klamath River Adventures, (541) 779-3708, Noah's World of Water, (541) 488-2811, the Adventure Center, (541) 535-2116, and Arrowhead River Adventures, (541) 830-3388.

Expect to pay more on the Klamath River than for any other day trip on an Oregon river. The long shuttle, the requirement of a wet suit in the event of a swim, and the proximity to the more expensive California market conspire to put the price for a day trip near $100. But it's usually worth it.

The whitewater trip below the Boyle powerhouse begins relatively easily, allowing plenty of time for paddlers aboard commercial rafts to get to know each other and bond as a team. The guide at the back of the boat will be watching to determine which paddlers he wants up front when the big water begins just below the normal lunch stop at Frain Ranch. **Caldera,** one of only four Class V rapids commercially run in Oregon, is just downstream and can be scouted during lunch. It may be hard to keep a sandwich down after getting a look at Caldera. **Hell's Corner** waits a couple miles below, a Class V rapids that ushers in the river's most intense stretch of whitewater.

From Caldera to **State Line Falls,** the river packs in 6 intense miles of water with an average gradient of 76 feet per mile. Caldera is 200 yards long, but the boat captain has all the moves planned in advance and most paddle teams come through with smiles on their faces and eager for more excitement. They don't have to wait long because 350-yard-long Hell's Corner isn't far away. After running the big Class V rapids, the Class IV rapids seen tame. The trip usually ends at **Copco Lake** in California, a beautiful end-of-the-road setting that tempts rafters to return for some much quieter fishing and camping.

To keep track of PP&L's planned water releases in the Klamath River canyon, call the company's recreation line, (800) 547-1501. The river is managed by the Klamath Falls office of the BLM, (541) 883-6916.

Hiking

The Klamath Basin country east of US 97 has access from the west to two roadless areas—the 25,000-acre **Yamsay Mountain** semiprimitive, nonmotorized recreation area and the 22,800-acre **Gearhart Mountain Wilderness.** Both areas are most frequently visited from the east (see Lake County chapter).

At 8,196 feet high, Yamsay Mountain is the tallest point in Klamath County east of the Cascades and rises in splendid isolation above many square miles that are rarely higher than 6,000 feet. The western approach to **Yamsay Mountain** (difficult; 3.5 miles one way) follows an abandoned road at the end of Forest Rd 4973 near Jackson Creek Campground. To reach the campground, drive Forest Rd 49 east of Klamath Marsh (see Wildlife, above). The old road has some fallen trees across it to keep out vehicles and climbs steeply to reach the summit, the site of an old fire lookout. For information, contact the Chiloquin Ranger District, (541) 783-4001.

Gearhart Mountain is 8,364 feet high and lies just east of the Klamath County border in Lake County. The Boulder Spring entrance into the Gearhart Mountain Wilderness begins at the end of Forest Rd 18 in Fremont National Forest, 10 miles northeast of the community of Bly. The **Boulder Spring Trail** (easy; 2.6 miles one way) provides a quick entrance into the wilderness and ends where it joins the main Gearhart Trail 2 miles north of the high point of the range. The trail is a fine day hike, as well as a possible beginning point for a backpack trip. For information, contact the Bly Ranger District, (541) 353-2427.

(For hiking west of Upper Klamath Lake on the east side of the Cascades, see the Mountain Lakes chapter, and for trails suitable for walking, see the OC&E Woods Line State Trail in Biking, below.)

Biking

Rail banking is a system of land-management transfer that allows a railroad to be converted to another use, but the original owner maintains the right to redevelop it as a rail line in the future. Rail banking usually results in removal of the ties for sale as scrap steel, with some of the money going to improve the surface of the right-of-way to accommodate bicycling, hiking, and horseback riding. Facilities, such as trailheads and rest rooms, must be developed to avoid conflict with adjacent private landowners.

The **OC&E Woods Line State Trail,** Oregon's longest rail-trail conversion, begins in Klamath Falls and extends 110.4 miles into Fremont National Forest to Thompson Reservoir in Lake County. The line began operating in 1917 as the Oregon, California and Eastern and was the last timber-hauling railroad in the state. The 65.4-mile segment that begins in Klamath Falls was rail banked by the Weyerhaeuser Company under agreement with the Oregon Department of Parks and Recreation in 1992.

The 45-mile extension that begins at Bly was part of the Woods line, another timber-hauling railroad. It was rail banked by Fremont National Forest. The first 3.5 miles of the trail are heavily used since it was dedicated and paved in 1997 between the Avalon Ave and Crosby St trailhead (1 block south of Hwy 39 on Washburn Way in central Klamath Falls) to Hwy 39 at Henley High School, 2 miles south of town. Additional improvements are continuing in an effort to open more of the trail to recreational use. Undeveloped access to the trail is along roads that cross the abandoned rail line (consult a Winema National Forest map).

Mountain bikers looking for a spot to ride on BLM land near Klamath Falls are directed to **Topsy Road** on the east side of the Klamath River canyon (turn south from Hwy 66 on the east side of the river 5 miles west of Keno). The old stagecoach road begins near Spencer Bridge at the Boyle powerhouse and follows the river downstream all the way to California. The road is rutted, rough, and suitable only for high-clearance vehicles, so motorized traffic is light. Bikers can drop down to the river on any of several side roads, including one that goes to **Frain Ranch** where rafters begin the Class V whitewater run.

For a screamer downhill, drive to the top of 6,596-foot **Hamaker Mountain** south of Keno on BLM Rd 40-7E-1 and ride down to the river at Spencer Bridge on a jeep road and trail, crossing 6,349-foot Chase Mountain along the way. This is a 7-mile ride that requires a car shuttle, because not many people would want to ride it back uphill.

Klamath Falls has a system of bike paths and lanes that cross the city north and south along the Alameda Bypass and east and west from Oregon Institute of Technology at 3201 Campus Dr to Moore Park on Lakeshore Dr at the southwest end of Upper Klamath Lake. The **A Canal Trail** connects the OIT campus with the start of the OC&E Woods Line State Trail. The county publishes a bicycle trail map available from the tourism office at 1451 Main St.

Camping

The Klamath Basin is the type of place vacationers are apt to stay a while, so don't be surprised if you run into more campsites designed for recreational vehicles than for tents. Tent campgrounds are popular in the mountains to the west, but it's the RV parks that are spread throughout the Klamath Basin. Also, many of the area's tent campgrounds are very small—only two sites—but that's just about perfect, as long as you're friends with your neighbors.

Many commercial RV and tent camps are located near Chiloquin, where the Sprague and Williamson Rivers join. Chiloquin and Fort Klamath serve as a southern gateway to Crater Lake National Park and are stopping places for vehicles that don't want to pull their trailers up into the park.

The Klamath Basin is the home of **Collier State Park,** (541) 783-2471, located on the Williamson River 35 miles north of Klamath Falls on US 97. The park has 18 tent campsites, 50 trailer spaces with full hookups, and barrier-free campsites for disabled campers. A short trail system winds through the park's camping and day-use areas, including an outdoor museum with one of the country's finest collections of logging equipment. The campground is closed during winter, but the day-use areas are open all year. Camping reservations are not accepted.

Most of Winema National Forest's campgrounds lie to the west (see Mountain Lakes chapter), but four serve vacationers in the Upper Klamath Basin. **Odessa Campground** has 6 sites on the west shore of Upper Klamath Lake, 22 miles northwest of Klamath Falls on Hwy 140. **Williamson River Campground** has 10 sites on its namesake, 1 mile north of Collier State Park on US 97. **Head of the River Campground** has 6 sites, 27 miles northeast of Chiloquin on County Rd 600. The campgrounds are managed by the Chiloquin Ranger District, (541) 783-4001.

Jackson Creek Campground has 12 sites to serve visitors exploring Yamsay Mountain (see Hiking, above), part of the Chemult Ranger District, (541) 365-7001.

Klamath County offers camping at **Eagle Ridge,** a small campground on the west shore of Upper Klamath Lake at 17300 Eagle Ridge Rd, and **Hagelstein Park,** 10 miles north of Klamath Falls on US 97. Contact the county at (541) 883-4697, ext. 696.

The BLM's most popular campgrounds in the Klamath Basin are at **Gerber Reservoir,** where 50 sites are clustered along the north and south shores of the lake (see Wildlife, above), and along the upper Klamath River, where **Topsy Campground** offers a dozen sites for small RVs (see Biking, above). The BLM, (541) 883-6916, has several other small camp-sites in its block of land south of Gerber Reservoir. Gerber and Topsy both have barrier-free facilities for camping and fishing.

PP&L, (800) 547-1501, maintains **Keno Campground** on the Klamath River just above Boyle powerhouse where Hwy 66 crosses the river 5 miles west of Keno. The park has 26 campsites and 21 picnic tables in a beautiful setting but for some reason is one of the lesser-used parks in the power company's seven-state camping network. The power company's other recreation facilities include **Pioneer Park,** a picnic site near Keno Campground, plus a 1-mile nature trail along the west bank of **Link River** in Klamath Falls (the connection between Upper Klamath Lake and Lake Ewauna).

Fishing

Upper Klamath Lake

Trophy-size rainbow trout lurk in the shallow waters of massive Upper Klamath Lake, a 26-mile-long body of water with more than 100 miles of shoreline. County and Forest Service campgrounds and day-use areas are scattered around the lake. Private resorts offer boat rentals, camping, and, most importantly, tips for the best way to locate the lunkers. For regulations in the Klamath Basin, check the state fishing synopsis or call the Klamath Falls office of the Oregon Department of Fish and Wildlife, (541) 883-5732.

Trout grow fast in the lake's nutrient-rich waters, with average fish running 18 to 23 inches and weighing 3 to 5 pounds. Trout are occasionally taken in the 10- to 15-pound range, and rainbow reach a length of 20 inches in only three years. And the lake's trout fishery is entirely natural after past stocking attempts failed due to bacteria in the lake. Seven streams feed the lake, with the **Williamson and Wood Rivers** on the north. Fishing is best where the rivers enter the lake and fish congregate to escape the warm lake water of summer. **Pelican Bay** near Rocky Point Resort (see Boating/Canoeing, above) is usually another good producer.

Bank angling is possible near the lake's outlet on Lakeshore Dr in Klamath Falls during cool parts of the year. Troll fishing begins in April in the northern part of Upper Klamath Lake. Fly-fishing lasts through summer when the trout move from the lake's warm waters to cool tributaries, or cluster around underground springs. Lake fishing is open all year, with a one-trout-per-day limit.

Crystal Creek Anglers, (541) 356-2385, runs **fly-fishing schools** and **guided trips** from Rocky Point to the Klamath Basin country's trophy waters. Other local fishing guide services are Hughes of Klamath Falls, (541) 883-3307, and Miranda's of Rocky Point, (541) 356-2141.

Klamath, Williamson, and Sprague Rivers

Trout fishing can be outstanding on the 38 miles of the **Klamath River** from Lake Ewauna to the California state line. Fishing is closed from June 16 to September 30 between Keno Dam and Boyle powerhouse because of the river's warm water. Regulations call for catch-and-release for trout from below the powerhouse to the state line during the same period.

The river below the powerhouse sits in a deep, rugged canyon and can be approached in a few places by high-clearance vehicle along Topsy Rd, or on foot or by bicycle (see Biking, above). Fishing is good in the early morning and evening, when the water isn't being pumped through the turbines. That's one of the reasons rafters rarely see fishermen: when rafters are on the river, fishing isn't at its best. It's not uncommon for anglers to catch and release 20 trout in a day, but they have to work for it because of the canyon's difficult access. Fishing below Keno Dam is restricted to artificial lures.

John C. Boyle Reservoir, the impoundment of the river that is crossed by Hwy 66, is a popular warm-water fishery, with 16-inch largemouth bass common. Kids can usually hook onto a crappie or bluegill.

The **Williamson River,** one of Oregon's blue-ribbon trout streams, has its best access from Williamson River Campground and Collier State Park (see Camping, above). Canoes and drift boats float the river between the two, but angling from a floating device is not allowed in this section. The river is open to angling from late May to late October, with the opening a month earlier above **Kirk Bridge** on Forest Rd 43. Fly-fishing for brown and rainbow trout is the major fishery, with best prospects for the biggest fish during the summer when they escape the warm waters of Upper Klamath Lake. All trout are native and respond best during the caddis fly and mayfly hatches of June and July. The river also hosts the Lost River sucker, also known as mullet, a protected species that must be released.

The Yamsi Ranch, (541) 783-2403, near the headwaters before the river disappears into Sycan Marsh, offers fun for the family while dad fishes for 25-inch rainbow. The Lonesome Duck, (800) 367-2540, is another riverside resort that packages lodging with guided fishing trips.

Half of the problem in fishing the Williamson is figuring out how to access public lands while respecting private property. The other half of the problem is deciding which of the day's big trout to keep. Williamson River Anglers in Chiloquin, (541) 783-2677, sells **supplies** and offers **fishing tips**.

A public-private partnership is funding, to the tune of $5.5 million, an effort to restore 3,600 acres of wetlands to help improve wildlife habitat and fish spawning grounds on the **Williamson River Delta** at the north end of Upper Klamath Lake. The Nature Conservancy purchased the land in 1996, with help from the US Natural Resources Conservation Service, PacifiCorp, and New Earth Company.

The 100-mile-long **Sprague River** has its headwaters on the west slope of Gearhart Mountain, but the best fishing is in its lower reaches that share the exciting wild rainbow trout fishery of the Williamson River. Private land makes access difficult, even though the Sprague River Rd (County Rd 858) follows the river all the way from Chiloquin, near the river's mouth, to the town of Sprague River. Largemouth bass are common from Sprague River upstream to Beatty, but access is difficult. **Sprague River Picnic Area** 5 miles east of Bly on Hwy 140 provides access to trout fishing in the river's upper section.

BLM reservoirs

Similar to the history of Western settlement, **Gerber Reservoir** goes through its boom and bust cycles. In the early 1980s, when the West was dry, the reservoir nearly dried up. When the US Fish and Wildlife Service held water back to preserve habitat for the endangered Lost River sucker, some ranchers who depended on irrigation water from the reservoir went out of business. Their resulting lawsuit went all the way to the U.S. Supreme Court, which ruled in 1997 that economic interests are a legitimate basis to sue in cases involving the Endangered Species Act. By the time the court issued its decision, the weather cycle had changed back to wet and Gerber was brimful of water.

Before the drought, Gerber Reservoir produced a state-record white crappie of 4 pounds, 12 ounces. The record was subsequently lost, as was much of the fishery. The wet years of 1996–97 helped bring the fishery back, but such things take time. Rainbow trout are planted annually, and bass, perch, and brown bullhead are frequently caught. **Ice fishing** is popular in winter. For information, contact the BLM, (541) 883-6916.

Willow Valley Reservoir, 11 miles south of Gerber and just north of the state line, is another good producer of bass. Fishing in several other irrigation reservoirs nearby will pick up as stocking resumes.

Skiing

Most winter sports activity around Klamath Falls takes place in the Cascade Mountains to the west (see Mountain Lakes and Crater Lake National Park chapters). Skiing is limited east of US 97 because of lack of suitable terrain, abundance of private land, and inconsistent snowfall. One exception is the **Jackson Creek Ski Trail system,** developed by the Alla Mage Skiers Club of Klamath Falls. To reach the trailhead, drive US 97 north of Klamath Falls for 45 miles, turn east on Silver Creek Rd and drive 21.5 miles, turn southeast on Forest Rd 49, and drive 4.5 miles to Jackson Creek Campground. The parking area is not within the Oregon sno-park system but is usually kept plowed during winter because of ranch traffic. This is rugged, remote country, a long way from developed facilities. But it also is one of the state's best opportunities for uncrowded skiing. The parking lot is situated at 4,675 feet in elevation. The ultimate challenge is to ski to the top of Yamsay Mountain, a 3,430-foot climb of over 8.5 miles one way. Easier trails follow roads near the parking area. The Chemult Ranger District, (541) 365-7001, can provide a description of all the trails.

Nordic skiers won't be overlooked if Winema National Forest allows development of ski facilities on **Pelican Butte,** an 8,036-foot-high peak that stands in isolation above Upper Klamath Lake east of the midsection of the Sky Lakes Wilderness. The Forest Service expects to decide in 1999 whether to allow development of a downhill and cross-country ski area. Construction would take two years after approval before the ski area could open.

The evolving master plan for Pelican Butte calls for downhill ski development on 612 acres that would be served by a gondola, four chairlifts, and a summit surface tow. The vertical rise would be 3,800 feet and the peak capacity of skiers would be 5,560. Nordic facilities would be based at the midmountain day lodge, with a 15-kilometer system of groomed trails.

Although **snowmobiles** climb to the top of Pelican Butte, skiing on the butte is limited to those hardy enough to cover long distances. If developed, Pelican Butte would be the first new downhill ski area in Oregon since Mount Hood Meadows opened in 1967. The Pelican Butte Corporation, a subsidiary of Jeld-Wen, Inc. of Klamath Falls, proposes the development. Other property held by the company includes Silver Mountain ski area near Kellogg, Idaho; Eagle Crest Resort near Redmond; and the Running Y Resort near Klamath Falls. For information, contact the Pelican Butte Project Office, (541) 883-8858.

outside in

Attractions

Klamath Falls, a city of 17,000 people and the largest for 70 miles around, is so isolated that it once led a movement to secede from Oregon and become the state of Jefferson. Now its residents happily welcome tourists, bird-watchers, and sportsmen from both Oregon and California (just 25 miles south). It's a pretty drive through the high desert from Bend, or over the mountain passes from Medford or Ashland. Seemingly dormant for years, the geothermally heated town has bubbled to life in the past few years with a flurry of construction, including chain hotels and the $250 million Running Y Ranch Resort, with its planned 250-room hotel, Arnold Palmer golf course, and condo development on 9,000 acres 10 miles out of town; call (888)797-2624 for current information. The Klamath Indian Tribe also shook things up shortly after the last earthquake when it announced plans to build its **Kla-Mo-Ya Casino** on US 97 at Chiloquin; the casino is now open just a few miles north of Klamath Falls International Airport.

The **Favell Museum of Western Art** is a true Western museum, with arrowheads, Indian artifacts, and the works of more than 200 Western artists, 125 W Main St, (541) 882-9996. The **Klamath County Museum** exhibits the volcanic geology of the region, Indian artifacts from all over Oregon, and relics from the Modoc wars, 1451 Main St, (541) 883-4208. The **Baldwin Hotel Museum,** in a spooky 1906 hotel, retains many fixtures of the era; it is open June through September at 31 Main St, (541) 883-4207.

Take Hwy 139 south a few miles to the **Lava Beds National Monument** visitors center in Tulelake, California, (916) 667-2282, and walk through the moonscape where Captain Jack and 60 Modoc Indian men defended themselves and their families during a four-month siege in 1872 by the US Cavalry.

Restaurants

Chez Nous ☆ The name may be French, but Chez Nous really serves more of a Continental menu. A favorite with locals, it's pretty standard but nicely done. *3927 S 6th St (follow 6th St south, a few blocks past Altamont), Klamath Falls; (541) 883-8719; $$.*

Fiorella's ☆ Residents of Klamath Falls appreciate the Northern Italian fare at Fiorella's. The pasta is homemade and delicious. Reservations welcome. *6139 Simmers Ave (S 6th St to Simmers), Klamath Falls; (541) 882-1878; $$.*

Lodgings

Aspen Ridge Resort ☆ This resort in high-meadow country has both log cabins and a main lodge. The resort is adjacent to a cattle ranch, which influences the restaurant's menu. *Fishhole Creek Rd (18 miles SE of Bly), Bly; PO Box 2, Bly, OR 97622; (541) 884-8685; $$.*

Thompson's Bed and Breakfast by the Lake ☆ This first B&B in town is still the best. Four bedrooms each have a private bath. Sunsets over the Cascade Range and Upper Klamath Lake are spectacular. *1420 Wild Plum Court (call for directions), Klamath Falls, OR 97601; (541) 882-7938; $$.*

More Information

Bly Ranger District, Bly: *(541) 353-2427.*
Bureau of Land Management, Klamath Falls: *(541) 883-6916.*
Chemult Ranger District, Chemult: *(541) 365-7001.*
Chiloquin Ranger District, Chiloquin: *(541) 783-4001.*
Crescent Ranger District, Crescent: *(541) 433-2234.*
Deschutes National Forest, Bend: *(541) 388-2715.*
Fremont National Forest, Lakeview: *(541) 947-2151.*
Klamath County Department of Tourism, Klamath Falls: *(800) 445-6728.*
Klamath Ranger District, Klamath Falls: *(541) 885-3400.*
Oregon's Outback Visitors Association, Klamath Falls: *(800) 598-6877.*
Upper Klamath National Wildlife Refuge, Tulelake, California:
    (916) 667-2231.
Winema National Forest, Klamath Falls: *(541) 883-6714.*

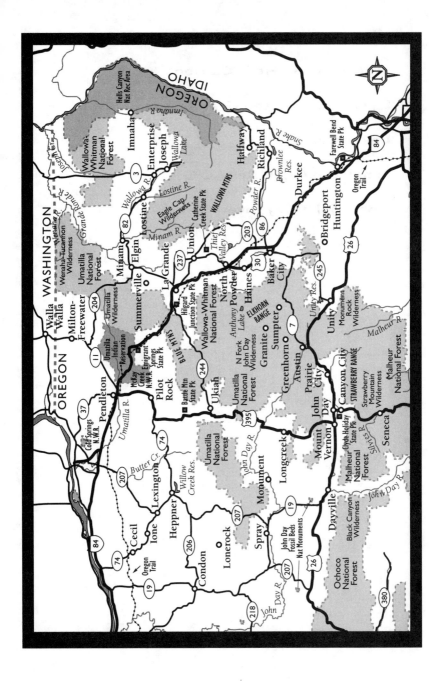

Northeast Mountains

Wallowas and Hells Canyon   543

La Grande and the Grande Ronde River   560

Baker County   574

Pendleton Grain Belt   590

Upper John Day River   602

Northeast Mountains

Wallowas and Hells Canyon

From the Washington state line on the north, east to the boundary with Idaho in Hells Canyon, south to the Wallowa-Baker county line, and west to the Wallowa-Union county line, including the Eagle Cap Wilderness, the Hells Canyon National Recreation Area, and the towns of Wallowa, Lostine, Enterprise, and Joseph.

If Bend is where Oregon mountain lovers dream of living, then Enterprise and the Wallowa Mountains are where they dream of vacationing. While a booming economy makes it possible to relocate in central Oregon, the northeast is a much tougher nut to crack. The county's reliance on timber, ranching, and tourism limits the year-round population to 7,150, and only tourism shows any sign of growing. But for now, lack of a destination resort, or a big-time ski area, has kept the Wallowas relatively unspoiled, which is just fine for the thousands of visitors who spend parts of their summers here. They love it exactly the way it is.

The scenery is outstanding, especially the snowcapped peaks of the Eagle Cap Wilderness and the deep canyons of the Snake and Imnaha Rivers. Recreation opportunities are nearly unlimited: stream and lake fishing, wildlife watching, hiking, backcountry skiing, horse packing, and whitewater rafting are as good as they get in Oregon. Peak baggers can finish the high points of Oregon's Cascades in a few weeks, but they can climb for several seasons in the Wallowas. So what if the only golf course in the county's 3,153 square miles has only nine holes?

Wallowa Lake, the recreation hub of the county, sits at the end of the road south of Joseph. The 1,508-acre lake ranks right up there with the most beautiful in Oregon. Its forested west shore presents a stark contrast to its grass-covered east shore. Both of the lake's sides are moraines left by a series of glaciers that flowed out of the high peaks to the south. Some of the tourist attractions at the lake are on the tacky side, but the go-carts and bumper boats don't overwhelm the beautiful natural setting.

Trails climb steeply south out of Wallowa Lake to reach the alpine lakes that lie beneath the high peaks of the Eagle Cap Wilderness. Most of the peaks have relatively easy scrambling routes to their summits. The Wallowas contain 23 of Oregon's 35 named peaks that rise above 9,000 feet.

Wallowa Lake can feel crowded on summer weekends. Trails can get busy with horses and hikers; campgrounds and lodges can fill up early. But just a few miles east of Joseph, crowds quickly thin out as you head into remote and spectacular Hells Canyon. The Wallowas and Hells Canyon country is one of those special vacation places worth dreaming about.

Getting There

Relatively isolated from the rest of Oregon, Wallowa County is reached by many vacationers by driving south into Oregon from Lewiston, Idaho, via Washington Highway 129, which becomes Highway 3 at the Oregon border. Travelers from Portland drive Interstate 84 to La Grande, then take Highway 82 to Enterprise. Distance from Portland to the county seat of Enterprise is 317 miles. Highway 350 leads northeast from Joseph to Imnaha, the northern gateway to Hells Canyon National Recreation Area. A network of Wallowa-Whitman National Forest and Wallowa County roads lead to Eagle Cap Wilderness trailheads and tourist sites along the rim of Hells Canyon. The Wallowa Mountain Loop Road heads south from Joseph as Forest Road 39, crosses the recreation areas at Salt Creek Summit, and continues to circle the Wallowas before joining Interstate 84 at Baker City.

Adjoining Areas

SOUTH: **Baker County**

WEST: **La Grande and the Grande Ronde River**

Scenic Drives

As Oregon counties go, Wallowa County isn't extraordinarily large. The county's 3,150 square miles rank it only ninth in size among Oregon's 36 counties. But if someone were to take a giant rolling pin and smooth out all the mountains and canyons, the county would rank right up there with

Harney as the state's largest. An area with so many attractions takes some getting used to, and a vehicle tour is a good way to find out what's worth coming back to explore in depth.

The only designated scenic byway in the Wallowas and Hells Canyon region is the Forest Service's **Hells Canyon National Scenic Byway.** Stop at the Wallowa Mountains Visitors Center, (541) 426-4978, at 88401 Hwy 82 in Enterprise to load up with printed information about sites along the byway. The 314-mile loop makes a circuit of the Wallowas but really only scratches the surface of the area. The byway passes between the Wallowas and Hells Canyon National Recreation Area on the Wallowa Mountain Loop Rd, which was devastated during the New Year's Day flood of 1997. The road has undergone massive reconstruction ever since and is open for one-lane travel led by pilot car until the project is completed late in 1998.

Hells Canyon is frequently referred to as the deepest gorge in North America and occasionally as the deepest in the world. Reality is that Hells Canyon is the deepest river-carved gorge in the United States. The depth of the canyon at Hat Point on the Oregon side is 5,632 feet. When measured from the Seven Devils in Idaho, the canyon is 8,043 feet deep. Alaska's Great Gorge in Denali National Park and Washington's Lake Chelan both are deeper, although one remains covered by ice and the other by waters of a lake. Glaciers carved both. The world's deepest river gorge is Tibet's Yarlung Tsango Gorge, more than 3 miles deep.

For those who want to leave the driving to a **guide,** Wallowa County companies that offer scenic tours include Eagle Cap Fishing Guides, (541) 426-3493, Rim Roads Scenic Tours, (541) 426-4913, and Moffit Brothers Transportation, (541) 569-2284.

The byway's 314-mile semi-loop begins either at La Grande or Baker City on I-84. It circles the Wallowas to the east before returning to the freeway, primarily on Hwy 82 on the north, Forest Rd 39 on the east, and Hwy 86 on the south. The byway has many detours along the way that warrant exploration.

Lostine Canyon Road leaves the byway at the small town of Lostine on Hwy 82, 10 miles northwest of Enterprise, and follows the Lostine River south upstream to several wilderness trailheads. A designated National Wild and Scenic River, the Lostine rises in the Lakes Basin in the center of the Eagle Cap Wilderness and flows through a deep, rugged canyon to join the Wallowa River at Lostine. The Wallowa-Whitman National Forest's auto tour describes 21 sights along the 18-mile route, which ends at Two Pan Campground where trails lead into the high country.

The **Joseph Canyon Overlook** is 29.5 miles north of Enterprise on Hwy 3. The 2,000-foot-deep canyon would be one of the county's major scenic destinations if it weren't sandwiched between Hells Canyon on the east and Grande Ronde Canyon on the west. Joseph Creek is another of the eight National Wild and Scenic Rivers in Wallowa County.

The farthest north of Hells Canyon's viewpoints is **Buckhorn Overlook,** an off-the-beaten-track location 43 miles northeast of Enterprise on Forest Rd 46. Just inside the national recreation area boundary, the viewpoint is a good destination for anyone visiting the northeast part of Wallowa-Whitman National Forest where few tourists bother to go. The forest is a delightful mix of meadows and ponderosa pines, but lacks the captivating beauty of areas farther south.

Hat Point Road, which begins at the town of Imnaha, has views of Hells Canyon at **Saddle Creek** (mile 18.8 from Imnaha) and at the end of the road at Hat Point (mile 23.5). Forest Rd 4240 has been improved over the years to a good gravel surface, but can be difficult driving in an RV because of its steepness. The road was one of the few on the east side of the Wallowas that escaped largely unscathed during the 1997 flood. Due to Hat Point's elevation of 6,982 feet, Hat Point Rd is usually open only from early July to late October. Spur Rd 315 branches east for the last mile to Hat Point, while Forest Rd 4240 continues another 4 miles where it ends at Warnock Corral.

The view from Saddle Creek along the way takes in a big chunk of Hells Canyon, but you'll need to keep going to Hat Point to see all the way to the bottom and the Snake River. Hat Point's paved overlook offers a view down to **Rush Creek Rapids** on the Snake River. The fire lookout tower offers the same view a little higher up.

The easiest viewpoint to reach along the Oregon rim of Hells Canyon is **Hells Canyon Overlook,** 43 miles southeast of Joseph or 30 miles northeast of Halfway. The overlook is 3 miles east of Forest Rd 39 on Rd 3965. The road is paved to the overlook, then turns to gravel and continues along the rim for more views of Hells Canyon, the Snake River, and the Seven Devils Mountains across the way in Idaho.

Hiking/Backpacking

Eagle Cap Wilderness

First-time visitors to the Wallowa Valley should stop at the **Wallowa Mountain Visitors Center,** (541) 426-4978, an impressive log structure located on a small hill just north of Hwy 82 on the west edge of Enterprise. The visitors center's main structural support comes from a 383-year-old ponderosa pine. In addition to slide shows and changing exhibits, the visitors center disseminates a wealth of information about the Eagle Cap and Hells Canyon backcountry and has a large scale-model display that clearly shows just how rugged the country is. Hikers who still want to tackle the steep trails after seeing such a graphic display usually head for one of three main trailheads, all on the north side of the Wallowas: **Wallowa Lake,** at the end of Hwy 82, 7 miles south of Joseph; **Hurricane Creek,** at the end of Forest Rd 8205, 9 miles south of Enterprise; and **Lostine River,** at the end of Forest Rd 8210, 18 miles south of Lostine.

Most trails in the Wallowas are continuous routes. Once a hike begins, hikers can walk for days if they want, choosing virtually any other trail to exit the wilderness if a shuttle has been arranged. All the multiday hikes into the backcountry should be considered difficult and require proper equipment and conditioning. Hikers are asked to register at the trailhead, but none of the trails have use limits.

The **Wallowa Lake trailhead** begins at the end of the road at Wallowa Lake, south of the motels, the tram, and the horse-packing station. The trail branches after 200 yards to follow the east and west forks of the Wallowa River. A frequent destination on the **East Fork Trail** is **Aneroid Lake** (difficult; 6 miles to the lake, 2,850-foot gain). The trail keeps going across 8,500-foot-high Tenderfoot Pass, 2 miles south of the lake, and enters the Imnaha River drainage.

The **West Fork Trail** (difficult; 11.6 miles to the basin, 3,500-foot gain) heads into Lakes Basin, the most popular spot in the wilderness. Backpackers often spend several days hiking among the lakes, but don't go there during peak season if you want to escape the crowds. A popular branch from the West Fork Trail is the trail to Ice Lake (difficult; 5.5 miles to the lake from the parking lot, 3,250-foot gain). Ice Lake, one of the most beautiful lakes in the Wallowas, sits beneath the three highest mountains in the range (the sixth-, seventh-, and eighth-highest in Oregon): 9,838-foot Sacajawea, 9,826-foot Matterhorn, and 9,776-foot Hurwal Divide. Each is a nontechnical scramble from a campsite along the lake, and some hikers bag them all on the same day. Sacajawea is listed on maps as the high point of Wallowa County, but some Forest Service information lists Matterhorn as taller. Better climb them both if you want to say you reached the high point of the Wallowas. The latest, best source for technical information on the Wallowas is the Wallowa Mountains map by Imus Geographics of Eugene, available at the visitors center.

Easy mountain climbs that can be finished in a day are a rarity in the Wallowas, but the Wallowa Lake trailhead offers a couple of interesting opportunities. Chief Joseph Mountain, at 9,616 feet the seventh tallest in the range, can be climbed via the **Chief Joseph Trail,** a signed spur that branches from the West Fork Trail .3 mile from the parking lot. Leave the trail after 4.5 miles at an open grassy slope, walk up the slope, then scramble up an avalanche chute to the top of the summit ridge. Turn west and follow the ridge to the summit. Elevation gain is 5,000 feet over 6 miles, a long, tough day for most peak baggers.

The **Wallowa Lake Tramway,** (541) 432-5331, is the ticket to an interesting three-peak ridge run that ends atop Aneroid Mountain, at 9,702 feet the fourth tallest in the range. After parking at the Wallowa Lake trailhead, walk down the road .5 mile to the tram station and purchase a ticket for the first car of the day at 9am. Ride the tram 3,700 feet to near the summit of 8,241-foot **Mount Howard.** After exploring Howard's summit trails and enjoying the view of the valley, begin walking south from the tram up the ridge toward 9,280-foot East Peak, climb over 9,495-foot Hidden Peak (unnamed on maps), and continue to the summit of Aneroid Peak, 5 miles from the tram. Descend down Aneroid Peak's northwest scree slope, pick up the East Fork Trail near Aneroid Lake, and walk back to the trailhead. Only fit climbers should attempt this 11-mile ridge run from tram to peak to trailhead.

The Hurricane Creek trailhead is one valley to the west of Wallowa Lake. The **Hurricane Creek Trail** (difficult; 12.1 miles, 2,700-foot gain) ends at Mirror Lake in the Lakes Basin area. One-day trips include summit climbs of 9,673-foot **Twin Peaks** on the west side of the valley and Sacajawea on the south side. Both climbs are long and tiring but not technically difficult (except for the summit block of Twin Peaks). Matterhorn Mountain shows off its awesome 1,800-foot western face to hikers at the 6-mile mark on the Hurricane Trail.

Lostine River Rd leads to several trails, the most popular being **Two Pan** at the end of the road (see Scenic Drives, above). Trails earlier along the road climb quickly to lakes in the high country on either side of the valley. Two trails leave from the Two Pan trailhead—the **East Fork Lostine River Trail** (difficult; 7.3 miles, 2,000-foot gain) climbs to Mirror Lake at the edge of Lakes Basin, and the **West Fork Lostine River Trail** (difficult; 5.5 miles, 1,800-foot gain) climbs to Minam Lake and the headwaters of the Minam River.

Eagle Cap, the namesake of the wilderness but only the eighth-tallest peak at 9,572 feet, can be climbed from the southwest side of Lakes Basin. Plan for a three- to five-day trip from any of the trailheads. The easiest route is via the East Fork Lostine River Trail to Mirror Lake. From a camp in Lakes Basin, continue south over 8,400-foot high **Horton Pass** and make an easy scramble up Eagle Cap's south slope (moderate; 3 miles one way, 2,000-foot gain). The mountain is the high point of Union County.

Hells Canyon and Joseph Creek Canyon

With more than 900 miles of trail (many of the miles are in Idaho) in the designated recreation and wilderness areas that surround Hells Canyon, hikers could walk for years. Some of the trails are in rough shape, however, due to lack of maintenance funds to repair substantial damage caused by forest fires throughout the extended drought of the 1990s.

The **Nee-Me-Poo National Recreation Trail,** located in the lower Imnaha River Canyon on the road to Dug Bar, is a 3.7-mile trail that follows the path of the Nez Perce Indians as they embarked on their historic flight to freedom in 1877. Young Chief Joseph led his band 1,800 miles on a journey to Canada, only to surrender to US Army troops a few miles from the border in the Bearpaw Mountains of Montana. The Wallowas and Hells Canyon country is replete with poignant tales of the brave chief and his band of followers. To reach the trailhead, drive County Rd 735 north from Imnaha. The road switches designation to Forest Rd 4260 in 7 miles at French Creek and becomes increasingly steep and narrow. Passenger cars can use the road during dry weather. Continue 10 miles to the trailhead. Dug Bar on the Snake River is another 5 miles farther along the road.

Other popular trails and their trailheads, especially for horse packing, on the Oregon side of Hells Canyon are the **Freezeout Saddle Trail** (difficult; 10.7 miles to the Snake River), which begins at the end of Forest Rd 4230, 3 miles east of County Rd 727 and 12 miles south of Imnaha; the **Bench Trail,** a 63-mile route from Freezeout Saddle to Dug Bar on the Snake River; Warnock Corrals, 4 miles north of Hat Point, where the **Summit Ridge Trail** travels 35 miles north to Dug Bar; and P.O. Saddle at the end of the Hells Canyon Overlook Rd (see Scenic Drives, above), where the 8-mile **Salisbury Trail** climbs a saddle and drops to the river at Hells Canyon Dam (see Baker County chapter). The **Snake River National Recreation Trail** travels along the river for 35 miles on the Idaho side from the park at Pittsburgh Landing to Hells Canyon Dam (the shoreline on the Oregon side is too rugged to accommodate a long-distance trail). The Wallowa Mountains Visitors Center, (541) 426-4978, in Enterprise also provides recreation information for Hells Canyon.

The section of Joseph Creek that is designated as a National Wild and Scenic River is reached by trails that follow Davis and Swamp Creeks. Both trails are long enough to require a backpack trip for hikers who want to spend time at the bottom of Joseph Canyon. The trailhead for both is 9 miles south of the **Joseph Canyon viewpoint** on Hwy 3, or 20 miles north of Enterprise, on the east side of the highway across from the turnoff for Forest Rd 3035. The trail begins by following an abandoned road east for 1 mile, then turns north to follow Davis Creek down to Joseph Creek. One-way distance is 12 miles, with a 2,000-foot loss in elevation, to Joseph Creek. The trail in Swamp Creek Canyon, the next drainage to the east of Davis Creek, joins the **Davis Creek Trail** midway along the descent to Joseph Canyon. To reach the **Swamp Creek Trail,** continue hiking east for 2 miles over Starvation Ridge instead of turning north and hiking down Davis Creek. The route down Swamp Creek adds 2 miles to the distance, but it also provides an alternate route for a backpack trip. Only about 6 miles of Joseph Creek, not counting its numerous twists and turns, is in public ownership. Private ranch land restricts access directly down or up Joseph Creek. Check with landowners for permission to cross, either by driving to ranch houses or by calling the visitors center in Enterprise for owners' names.

Horseback Riding

The **Eagle Cap** and **Hells Canyon Wilderness Areas** draw horse owners from around the Pacific Northwest for long trail rides and camping trips during summer vacations and fall hunting seasons. Trailheads with stock facilities are located at Indian Crossing, on the east side of the Wallowas off Forest Rd 39, and at Warnock Corrals near Hat Point on the rim of Hells Canyon. Other popular horseback staging areas are the Wallowa Lake and Lostine River trailheads (see Hiking/Backpacking, above). The Wallowa Mountain Visitors Center, (541) 426-4978, can provide information for self-sufficient riders and referrals to licensed outfitters.

A word of warning from the professional wranglers who ride horses every day in the Wallowas: horses that look good and ride well in the Cascades or on the Oregon Coast can have a difficult time in the Wallowas because of the altitude and the steepness of the trails. Horses need to be paced, just like people.

Most visitors who enter the Eagle Cap Wilderness by horseback do so with High Country Outfitters, (800) 432-4145, which operates the **Eagle Cap Pack Station** at Wallowa Lake. Visitors may arrive at the state park campground not knowing there's a horse anywhere around, but once they discover how steep the trails are, many are all too eager to let a horse do the work. The pack station offers all kinds of trips—from a few hours to as many days as you want—and the loading station can handle riders with disabilities. First-time buckaroos are also more than welcome to ride the surefooted horses. High Country Outfitters also has a deluxe camp 10 miles into the wilderness south of Wallowa Lake. A staff person remains in camp to cook for clients. The horses are kept available for daily rides.

The ultimate outing to the backcountry is to hire horses and mules for the ride high into the mountains, then have the wranglers come back at a prearranged time for the ride out. This style of horse packing is called a

drop camp and is offered by most outfitters. It's popular with older hikers, who still love to day hike on mountain ridges and camp at the wilderness lakes but don't much appreciate carrying a heavy backpack the half-dozen miles and 3,000 feet to get there. Drop camps are easy to spot in the wilderness. The campers in drop camps are the ones eating steak, drinking bottled beer, sitting on comfortable chairs, and sleeping in wall tents. Not even the Wallowas' famous mosquitoes can spoil this type of camping.

The lower slopes of **Hells Canyon** are ridden during spring, but the rim country, just as in the Wallowas, isn't ready for riding until July because of snow. **Outfitters** in Hells Canyon are game to try any type of outing by combining horse travel with vehicle shuttles, jet-boat rides, or raft trips. Other local horse packers permitted by the Forest Service to work in the Wallowas and Hells Canyon country are Hells Canyon Packers of Union, (541) 853-2341; Cornucopia Pack Station of Richland, (541) 742-5400; Diamond W Outfitters of Imnaha, (541) 577-3157; Millar Pack Station of Wallowa, (541) 886-4035; Moss Springs Pack Station of Cove, (541) 568-4823; Steen's Wilderness Adventures of Joseph, (541) 432-5315; Backcountry Outfitters of Joseph, (800) 966-8080; and Outback Ranch Outfitters of Joseph, (541) 426-4037.

Each outfit tends to have a specialty, whether it's the type of trip it offers or the trailhead where it enters the wilderness. Diamond W Outfitters has day rides on its Imnaha River ranch lands; Steen's packages three-day raft trips with two-day horse trips; and Outback Ranch Outfitters has a working cattle ranch where guests can stay overnight and help with the ranch work. Pricing an overnight trip is somewhat complicated because outfitters vary their price by distance, number of people, number of horses or mules required to carry gear, etc. When everything is tallied, horse packing in Oregon tends to be far less expensive than similar trips in the Rocky Mountains states. For instance, Eagle Cap Outfitters charges about $225 per person for a drop camp of three people or fewer.

Llama packing at the north end of the Wallowas is handled by Hurricane Creek Llama Treks, (800) 528-9609. The business operates out of Enterprise and offers a variety of predesigned trips in the Wallowas and Hells Canyon. Llamas can carry the same heavy loads carried by horses and mules, but people aren't allowed to ride llamas.

Camping

Campers leave the Willamette Valley towns by the thousands to spend summer weekends at the Oregon Coast, probably because **Wallowa Lake State Park Campground** is too far away to reach on a Friday night from Portland. As good as the coastal campgrounds are, it's hard to beat the experience of camping at Wallowa Lake. The campground is located .5 mile east of Hwy 82 at the south end of the lake, 76 miles from the nearest freeway. It has a gorgeous 1,508-acre mountain lake at its front door and 9,616-foot Chief Joseph Mountain at its back door. Get the picture?

The largest state park campground in Eastern Oregon has 90 tent campsites and another 121 trailer spaces with full utility hookups. Two campsites are fully accessible for disabled campers. The campground is open mid-May through October and accepts reservations at (800) 452-5687.

Wallowa Lake has all the amenities of the finer Oregon state parks campgrounds—hot showers, picnic areas, large play fields—and is close to outstanding fishing, boating, and hiking. Wallowa Lake village has enough pizza parlors and amusement parlors to keep the kids happy. The park has to be one of the state's safer places to let children roam on their own, provided they are warned to stay away from the fast-moving Wallowa River as it rushes out of the mountains to join Wallowa Lake. The resort area has a half-dozen motels and lodges, all of which can guarantee a quiet, comfortable night's sleep.

Wallowa-Whitman National Forest campgrounds on the north side of the Eagle Cap Wilderness are **Hurricane Creek Campground,** 6 miles south of Enterprise (see Hiking/Backpacking, above); **Two Pan Campground,** at the end of Lostine River Rd (see Scenic Drives, above); and **Boundary Campground,** at the end of Forest Rd 8250, 7 miles south of Wallowa. Each has 8 campsites. Dispersed camping opportunities on public land away from developed campsites are limited south of Enterprise. The best places to look are along Lostine River Rd, which has many sites, and within the national forest boundary southeast of Joseph just south of the Wallowa Mountain Loop Rd.

The Wallowa Mountain Loop Rd southeast of Joseph has campgrounds at **Lick Creek** (12 sites), **Blackhorse** (16 sites), and **Ollokot** (12 sites), while **Coverdale** (11 sites), **Hidden** (13 sites), and **Indian Crossing** (14 sites) are located on Forest Rd 3960, which leaves the loop highway to travel west up the Imnaha River Valley. All are within Hells Canyon National Recreation Area. Imnaha River Rd below its crossing of the Wallowa Mountain Loop Rd passes through private ranch lands along the river bottom and has limited camping opportunities. RVs have the best choices at the camps located along the paved loop road.

Camping along the rim of Hells Canyon is developed at two viewpoints—**Buckhorn** (8 sites) and **Saddle Creek** (7 sites) (see Scenic Drives, above). **Hat Point** is officially a day-use area, but its large gravel parking lot and its rest room facilities tempt a few campers to remain overnight in order to watch the sunrise the following morning. Dispersed camping is widely available along the Hells Canyon road system, but campers should take note of the numerous areas of scorched timber. Fire danger is high during most summers, and there is a very real possibility of being forced to evacuate during an emergency closure.

The Joseph Creek/Chesnimnus Creek part of Wallowa-Whitman National Forest north of Enterprise has campgrounds at **Dougherty Springs** (12 sites), **Coyote** (29 sites), and **Vigne** (7 sites). Although located in a beautiful pine forest surrounded by clear streams, these camps are rarely busy except during hunting seasons because the tourists flock to the more popular spots to the south. By the time you look for these campgrounds, you'll probably have already purchased a Wallowa-Whitman National Forest map. Berry picking and hiking are the main summer attractions, as well as driving west of Coyote onto **Table Mountain** via Forest Rd 4650 for views down into Joseph Canyon from the east.

For information on all national forest campgrounds in the Wallowa Mountains and Hells Canyon National Recreation Area, contact the Wallowa Mountains Visitors Center, (541) 426-4978, in Enterprise.

Fishing

The **Eagle Cap Wilderness** has more than 50 named lakes, most of which support healthy populations of rainbow and brook trout. Angling is best in late summer when trout are eager to take flies. Most lakes are a long way from trailheads, anywhere from 5 to 10 miles, so anglers must plan to carry gear for an overnight trip or hire a horse-packing guide service.

Wallowa Lake is easily accessible by boat, or by road on its north, east, and south sides. Launch facilities are available at the northern end of the lake near Joseph, where water-skiers tend to congregate, and the southern end near the state park, where motorboats, rowboats, and paddle boats, as well as canoes, can be rented from Wallowa Lake Marina, (541) 432-9115. Wallowa Lake has a large population of **kokanee,** which bite in late spring and early summer, and hatchery **rainbow trout.**

Like the lakes of the Eagle Cap Wilderness, the **Snake River** is difficult to approach for Oregon anglers. The only road from the Oregon side that reaches the river below Hells Canyon Dam travels northeast out of Imnaha to Dug Bar (see Hiking/Backpacking, above). The road is maintained for high-clearance vehicles only and can be impassable due to mud during any part of the wet season. Most angling in the Snake occurs from boats, either rafts that launch at Hells Canyon Dam (see Baker County chapter) or jet-boats that prowl the river from Forest Service facilities at Idaho's Pittsburgh Landing, (208) 628-3916. The Snake can have outstanding angling for **smallmouth bass, rainbow trout,** and, during winter, hatchery **steelhead.** The river also holds some big **channel catfish** and **sturgeon,** although the sturgeon must be released without removing them from the water.

The **Imnaha River,** a 75-mile-long tributary of the Snake River (see Hiking/Backpacking and Camping, above), is good for wild rainbow in late summer and steelhead during winter. The **Lostine River** (see Scenic Drives, above) is good for wild trout, but wood debris and overhanging trees make it difficult to fish. The **Wallowa River** below Wallowa Lake along Hwy 82 is a good fly-fishing river for rainbow in late summer and fall and for steelhead from February through April.

A local fishing outfitter is Eagle Cap Fishing Guides, (541) 426-3493, of Enterprise, which also runs the Wallowas Outdoors Store. Check with the Hells Canyon National Recreation Area headquarters, (509) 758-0616, in Clarkston, Washington, for a full list of guides on the Snake River.

The Oregon fishing synopsis, available at tackle stores, details regulations. When fishing on the Snake River, you must be licensed by the state from where you access the river. For additional information, contact the Oregon Department of Fish and Wildlife office at Enterprise, (541) 426-3279.

Rafting/Jet-Boats

From Hat Point, high atop the rim of Hells Canyon, the **Snake River** looks like a tiny ribbon of water glistening in the sun. Reality is so very different.

When viewed from a raft or jet-boat, the Snake River is very big water indeed, far bigger than any other whitewater river in Oregon. Whether the Snake pumps through Hells Canyon at 80,000 cubic feet per second (cfs) during spring or 5,000cfs in late summer, the river is big and powerful. The river's surface is frequently a couple hundred yards or more wide. **Granite Creek and Wild Sheep Rapids** fluctuate between Class IV and V, depending on the water flow. Both pack awesome power, more like rapids on the Colorado River in the Grand Canyon than those on other Oregon rivers such as the Rogue or Deschutes.

Despite the Snake's feistiness, the river has a long tradition of boating. When paddlewheel steamships ruled the Columbia River in the late 1800s, one was able to cruise all the way up the Snake through Hells Canyon. Residents of the canyon still receive weekly deliveries of mail and supply by jet-boats.

The Snake River has four primary launch sites for jet-boats: the **Lewiston-Clarkston** area, where the river passes between Idaho and Washington; **Heller Bar,** a Bureau of Land Management (BLM) launch in Washington (26 miles south of Clarkston); **Pittsburgh Landing,** 20 miles east of White Bird, Idaho (72 miles upriver from Clarkston); and **Hells Canyon Dam** on the Oregon side of the river (104 miles upriver from Clarkston). The Oregon border is 33 miles upriver from Clarkston.

Most jet-boat tour rides originate at Lewiston/Clarkston, from where it takes a 10-hour day to make the round trip to the river's protected wild section. Check with the Lewiston Chamber of Commerce for a list of outfitters.

Boating from Oregon begins at the Hells Canyon Dam launch site, a spectacular end-of-the-road location set deep in the heart of Hells Canyon (see Baker County chapter). To reach the dam, drive Hwy 86 east from I-84 at Baker City for 70 miles. Cross into Idaho and drive Forest Rd 454 north for 22 miles along Hells Canyon Reservoir. The road ends just after it crosses over the top of the dam and reenters Oregon. Facilities include a visitors center and cement boat ramp. **Jet-boat tours** from there are operated by Hells Canyon Adventures, (541) 785-3352. The company also operates the only day-rafting trips in the canyon by sending rafts down in the morning, then collecting them in the afternoon and running back upriver with a jet-boat.

Raft trips usually plan to run the 32 miles to Pittsburgh Landing in three days. The lower float to Heller Bar is anticlimactic, with few big rapids and frequent afternoon headwinds. Oregon rafting companies licensed to operate on the Snake are Canyon Outfitters, (541) 742-4110, of Halfway; Peer's Snake River Rafting, (541) 742-2050, of Halfway; Oregon Trail Adventures, (541) 534-5393, of La Grande; HCA Raft, (541) 523-6580, of Baker City; and Steen's Wilderness Adventures, (541) 432-3315, of Joseph.

Private rafters and jet-boaters should apply for permits from the Hells Canyon office on the river at Clarkston, Washington, (509) 758-1957. Applications for private raft trips are taken each winter between December 1 and January 31 for trips through the wild section the following summer, from late May through mid-September. A strict quota means not everyone can go on their chosen date. Jet-boats are also being restricted, although limits on their use are currently under appeal to the Forest Service.

Mountain Biking

Mountain bikers looking for an introductory ride should head 18 miles southeast of Joseph to Salt Creek Summit for a 10-mile single-track and dirt-road loop called the **Tenderfoot Wagon Trail**. From the trailhead parking on Forest Rd 3920, just off the Wallowa Mountain Loop Rd, ride south 5 miles on the old wagon road, cross Big Creek, turn east and ride back north either on the paved loop road or on a lightly used forest road farther east. The Salt Creek Summit area has other riding opportunities on the trails that are marked for skiing during winter.

The **Imnaha River Trail** begins on the lower Imnaha River Rd where the road leaves the river and veers east 4.5 miles to meet the Snake River at Dug Bar (see Hiking/Backpacking, above). The Imnaha River Trail continues down the Imnaha to meet the Snake River at Eureka Bar. If you really want to know how Hells Canyon got its name, ride this trail during the heat of a summer day. But if you want to live to ride another day, save the ride for spring, fall, or very early morning. The single-track trail drops 300 feet from Imnaha River Rd to reach the Snake River, plus some ups and downs along the way. The typical 100° heat of a midsummer day may not seem so bad after you've finished dodging the trail's rattlesnakes, poison ivy, and tire-piercing thorns.

When it's too hot to ride the lower Imnaha, cyclists drive up toward **Hat Point** and look for trails to ride in the cool lodgepole pine forest atop the rim of Hells Canyon. **Warnock Corral,** at the end of Forest Rd 4240, 4 miles north of Hat Point (see Scenic Drives, above), has good views and some fun single-track riding. One trail here travels **Windy Ridge** to the northeast and circles back to the corral on the **Summit Ridge Trail** at the very rim of Hells Canyon. The ride covers a 17-mile loop and drops 800 feet, with another 800 feet of up and down along the way. A locked gate occasionally blocks the road to Warnock Corral during fire season, so you might need to begin riding on Forest Rd 4240 just north of Hat Point.

For cyclists who don't want to ride through hell alone, Hells Canyon Bicycle Tours and Crosstown Traffic Bicycle Shop, (541) 432-2453, of Joseph is a **guide service** with the motto "We bring 'em back alive." Outings last anywhere from one to four days. The company warns that any of its guests who have trouble riding through poison ivy, spiders, rattlesnakes, or extreme heat should have the courtesy of warning their tour guide beforehand. Otherwise, have a nice day.

Wildlife

At times it seems like Wallowa County is one big wildlife refuge, teeming with herds of **Rocky Mountain elk, mule deer, white-tailed deer,** and **bighorn sheep.** Although not located on one of the major flyways, the county sees plenty of **migratory birds,** and other feathered residents call the place home during summer. The varied habitat around Wallowa Lake (see Fishing, above) has produced sightings of 195 species, including seven types of **owls, white pelicans,** and **double-breasted cormorants.** Birds are usually of secondary interest to the campers at the state park (see Camping, above), who marvel at the close approach of members of the local deer herd. Although the bucks grace many a photograph, they occasionally prove their wildness by accidentally injuring someone they find annoying.

The Wallowa Fish Hatchery, (541) 426-4467, a state facility 1 mile west of Enterprise on Fish Hatchery Lane, is a good place to see nesting **geese** during spring. A .25-mile-long trail leads from the hatchery to the pond where waterfowl nest. The hatchery raises **rainbow trout** and **steel-**

head. Spring Branch Wildlife Area, (541) 426-3279, is farther down the Wallowa River 2 miles east of the town of Wallowa on the north side of Hwy 82. Watch for **mule deer** browsing in the meadows at dawn and dusk; **mink, muskrat,** and **river otter** inhabit the marshy areas.

Oregon's largest herds of **Rocky Mountain bighorn sheep** inhabit the breaks of Joseph Canyon and the ridges of the high Wallowas. The ruggedness of Joseph Canyon, plus the large blocks of private land, limit the number of people who try to spot the canyon's sheep. The Wallowas' bighorns, as well as its herd of **mountain goats,** can be seen by anyone adventuresome enough to scramble off-trail to the high ridges of the Hurricane and Hurwal Divides. An unusual place to spot a bighorn is aboard a jet-boat on the Snake River, the method preferred by wildlife managers for transplanting sheep into Hells Canyon. The canyon has supported a population of 500 bighorn when the herd is healthy, but wildlife officials hope it will grow to more than 2,500.

The Imnaha River Canyon is also good bighorn sheep habitat. More accessible by roads than the Snake River, the lower Imnaha (see Hiking/ Backpacking, above) is a good place to watch for **California quail, chukar, golden eagles,** and **turkey vultures.** While looking for things in the sky, don't forget to look underfoot for **Pacific rattlesnakes. Black bear, bobcats,** and **mountain lions** are common throughout the Imnaha, Snake, and other canyons of the Wallowas and Hells Canyon country.

One of the best drives for seeing the variety of wildlife that lives in the area is to follow **Crow Creek Road** downstream from Joseph and Enterprise. The road leaves Hwy 82 midway between the two towns, travels north 1 mile, heads east for 3 miles, then heads north for 20 miles to where Crow and Chesnimnus Creeks join to form Joseph Creek. The road down Joseph Creek continues downstream for high-clearance vehicles before it ends at a private ranch.

Crow Creek mixes a marshy creek bottom with wheat fields and is a good place to look for **ringed-neck pheasant, magpie,** and **California quail.** The Chesnimnus area is one of the largest producers of **Rocky Mountain elk** in Oregon. Where Crow Creek changes direction from east to north just beyond Enterprise, the road up OK Gulch continues to the east and winds up at the Buckhorn Viewpoint of Hells Canyon.

Skiing/Snowmobiling

Ferguson Ridge, a 10-mile drive southeast of Joseph on Tucker Down Rd, serves as the county's ski hill. The ski area is privately owned and is operated by the Eagle Cap Ski Club. For information, contact the Wallowas Outdoor Store in Enterprise, (541) 426-3493. The ski area has one T-bar with 640 vertical feet of skiing. Some years Ferguson Ridge offers out-standing powder snow skiing; during other years it barely has enough snow to meet its weekend and holiday operating schedule. One thing it does have is views, from the vast expanse of canyon lands at the edge of Hells Canyon to Idaho's Seven Devils Mountains.

Salt Creek Summit, the only Oregon state sno-park in Wallowa County, is 28 miles southeast of Joseph on the Wallowa Mountain Loop Rd. The sno-park is host to most winter snow play in the county with its 150-mile groomed snowmobile trail system and 18 miles of marked cross-country ski trails. The Wallowa Mountain Loop Snowmobile Guide Service, (541) 426-4261, is the place to go for guided snowmobile tours and rentals in Wallowa County. Most riding is on the east side of the Wallowas and to the Hells Canyon viewpoints.

Wilderness Trails of Moscow, Idaho, (800) 545-5537, has been guiding backcountry **ski tours** into the **McCully Basin** for more than 20 years. Tours start from the McCully trailhead next to the Ferguson Ridge ski area and ascend 2,000 feet over 6 miles to a yurt camp in the Eagle Cap Wilderness.

Wind Ridge Ski Tours of Joseph, (800) 646-9050, has guided and do-it-yourself ski tours to a system of permanent shelters near Salt Creek Summit. Touring and telemarking opportunities are unlimited. The company also leads special tours monthly into private cabins at **Aneroid Lake.**

The **Lostine Guard Station,** 12 miles up the Lostine River from Lostine and 6 miles beyond the end of the plowed road (see Scenic Drives, above), can be rented December 15 through March 31 from the Eagle Cap Ranger District, (541) 426-4978. The cost is $25 per night.

outside in

Attractions

Joseph is the fabled land of the Wallowas, ancestral home of **Chief Joseph,** from which he fled with a band of Nez Perce to his last stand near the Canadian border. Although Chief Joseph's remains are interred far from his beloved "land of the winding water," he saw to it that his father, Old Chief Joseph, would be buried here, on the north shore of Wallowa Lake. The town itself is becoming something of an art colony. David Manuel, official sculptor for the state's Oregon Trail Celebration, opened the Manuel Museum and Studio on Main St, (541) 432-7235. Valley Bronze of Oregon has built a **bronze foundry** and a showroom in Joseph. Tours are offered on weekdays; phone (541) 432-7551 for information.

Restaurants

Vali's Alpine Deli and Restaurant ☆ Don't let its "deli" status mislead; dinner here usually requires reservations (the menu is prix fixe and varies nightly). Hungarian-German food is interspersed with authentic renditions from other cuisines. Open seasonally—call for details. *59811 Wallowa Lake Hwy/Hwy 82 (5 miles south of Joseph, near Wallowa Lake State Park), Joseph; (503) 432-5691; $.*

Lodgings

Wallowa Lake Lodge ☆ Rooms in this historic lodge are small—reserve one with a lake view, or a cabin on the lake. The fireplace in the lobby is magnificent, and the deck is splendid. Cabins are available year-round; the lodge and restaurant close in winter. *60060 Wallowa Lake Hwy (near Wallowa Lake State Park), Joseph, OR 97846; (541) 432-9821; $$.*

More Information

Bureau of Land Management, Baker City: *(541) 523-1256.*
Eastern Oregon Visitors Association, Baker City: *(800) 332-1843.*
Hells Canyon National Recreation Area, Clarkston, Washington, *(509) 758-0616.*
Lewiston Chamber of Commerce, Lewiston, Idaho: *(208) 743-3531.*
Pine Ranger District, Halfway: *(541) 742-7511.*
Wallowa County Chamber of Commerce, Enterprise: *(541) 426-4622.*
Wallowa Valley Visitors Center, Hells Canyon National Recreation Area, Eagle Cap Ranger District, and Wallowa Valley Ranger District, all in Enterprise: *(541) 426-4978.*
Wallowa-Whitman National Forest, Baker City: *(541) 523-6391.*

La Grande and the Grande Ronde River

From the Washington state boundary on the north, east to the Union-Wallowa county line, south to the Union-Baker county line, and west to the Union-Umatilla county line, including the Grande Ronde River, the Wenaha-Tucannon Wilderness, the west slope of the Eagle Cap Wilderness, and the towns of La Grande, North Powder, Union, and Elgin.

The Grande Ronde River begins as a tiny mountain stream in the Anthony Lakes area of the Blue Mountain's Elkhorn Range, about 30 miles southwest of La Grande. The river slowly gathers itself as it winds north out of the mountains, then abruptly switches directions to run east along Interstate 84 just west of La Grande. Drivers clipping along at 65mph have just enough time to say, "Hey, Mabel, there's a pretty river," and the Grande Ronde disappears from sight. The river continues to twist and turn as it winds past the outskirts of La Grande, passing near Island City, Imbler, and Elgin as it continues its journey north through Union County. Portions of the upper river are scenic and interesting, but they are nothing like what lies downriver where the river runs through its impressive canyon.

Meanwhile, high in the Wallowa Mountains, the Minam and Wallowa Rivers drain the northern portion of the Eagle Cap Wilderness. The two rivers join forces at Minam Junction, then tumble downstream another 10 miles where they join the Grande Ronde at Rondowa.

The combined flow of the three rivers creates one of Oregon's most relaxing wilderness river float trips. Beginning at Minam, and ending 90 miles downstream at the Snake River in Washington, the Grande Ronde passes through magnificent canyon habitat. The sides of the canyon are forested with ponderosa pines along the river's upper reaches, then are covered with grass and scrub oak in its lower canyon as it nears the Snake. The sky overhead can alternate with blue sky and white clouds, followed in a few hours by dark gray clouds and bolts of lightning during the thunderstorms of late spring and summer.

One of the longest continuous floating opportunities in the Pacific Northwest, the Grande Ronde River manages to stay relatively uncrowded. The fact that the river has only a few Class III rapids over its entire 90 miles dissuades hard-core boaters from pinpointing it as a destination for whitewater thrills. Their loss is the gain of families, fishermen, hikers, and campers. River runners not in a hurry to get anywhere, whose eyes are not cast on the end of the trip, love the Grande Ronde for its ambience and its gentle, forgiving nature.

From Rondowa to the Oregon-Washington border, 26.4 miles of the river are protected as wild and another 17.4 miles are designated as recreational, under the National Wild and Scenic Rivers Act. As long as big rapids aren't too important, boating doesn't get much better than the Grande Ronde.

Getting There

La Grande, the Union County seat, is 259 miles east of Portland via Interstate 84. Lewiston, Idaho, is 45 miles north of where the Grande Ronde River leaves Oregon and enters Washington beyond the community of Troy. State highways connect La Grande to Starkey to the west, Elgin to the north, and Union and Medical Springs to the south.

Adjoining Areas

SOUTH: **Baker County, Upper John Day River**

EAST: **Wallowas and Hells Canyon**

WEST: **Pendleton Grain Belt**

inside out

Rafting/Kayaking

The lower **Grande Ronde River** float trip usually begins at the Bureau of Land Management (BLM) launch at Minam, site of a motel and store where the Minam and Wallowa Rivers converge head on beneath a bridge along Hwy 82. After the Minam and Wallowa merge, they flow together as the Wallowa for 9 miles to join the Grande Ronde at Rondowa. The 90-mile float ends where the Grande Ronde meets the Snake River at Heller Bar in Washington. The BLM is the lead management agency on the river, even though its land holdings in the La Grande and the Grande Ronde River country are relatively minor. A BLM staff member is usually at the launch site and a crew lives nearby seasonally. Self-issuing permits are required, but the river has no quotas or use limitations, other than for commercial outfitters. All floaters must carry a fire pan and a portable toilet. To reach the river office during boating season, call (541) 437-5580. The entire 90-mile float can be done in three days during spring, when the current is clipping along, but it's better to plan for five days and enjoy it.

The merged **Minam and Wallowa Rivers** continue downstream from the Minam launch and carry the name of the Wallowa until they reach the Grande Ronde. This stretch has some of the liveliest water on the river, including the **Minam Roller.** A famous kayak play hole, the roller has the reputation of being one of the more challenging rapids on the Wallowa when flows exceed 5,000 cubic feet per second (cfs). It's not so much a rapids as a boat-eater. Avoid it altogether by running around it to the right. When the river rangers run their annual rescue clinic, they delight in sending county sheriff deputies and state police officers swimming through the roller while friends are stationed below with throw bags to retrieve them.

House Rock and **Blind Falls** are Class II rapids just before the Wallowa's confluence with the Grande Ronde. The volume of water in the Grande Ronde more than doubles after the confluence because of the reliable flows carried out of the Eagle Cap high country by the Wallowa and Minam Rivers. Sheep Creek at river mile 79 and Martin Misery at river mile 70 are the only Class III rapids before the midpoint of the 90-mile float at Troy. Competent canoeists usually have little problem with the river, especially if they wait for the river flow to drop in summer.

The river channel shrinks drastically where the flow is constricted by the **Narrows,** 6 miles above the Snake River and the biggest rapids on this float. Basalt ledges cramp the river's flow into a narrow channel, but a pool at the bottom makes it easy to collect swimmers and gear from any boats unfortunate enough to flip. The Narrows is usually Class III, but can become Class IV during the big water of spring. The takeout is .5 mile down the Snake on river left at **Heller Bar,** a large Forest Service/BLM site that caters to jet-boats, as well as rafters, on the Grande Ronde, Snake, and Salmon Rivers. To reach Heller Bar, drive Hwy 129 south of Clarkston, Washington, for 7 miles to Anatone, then follow the west bank of the Snake River south for 25 miles.

Fine camp spots line the Grande Ronde, although campers need to stay off private land and avoid rattlesnakes and poison ivy.

Much of the riverbank near Troy is privately owned, so rafters should not plan to begin or end theirs trip there. BLM boat launches nearby are **Wildcat,** 7 miles upriver near Powwatka Bridge, and **Mud Creek,** 6 miles upriver, via County Rd 500. To reach Troy, drive 44 miles north of Enterprise on Hwy 3, turn west toward Flora, and continue driving 21 miles to the bottom of the canyon. Another convenient launch/takeout is **Boggan's Oasis** where Hwy 129 crosses the Grande Ronde in Washington just north of the Oregon border. Weekend rafters can begin at Boggan's and float 27 miles to the Snake, with all the distance in Washington. Raft rentals and shuttles are available at the Minam launch from the Minam Store, (541) 437-1111, or upriver from T. R. T. Raft and Rentals, (800) 700-7238, at Elgin.

Wildlife

The Oregon Department of Fish and Wildlife maintains the 12,300-acre Wenaha Wildlife Area, (541) 828-7721, in the transitional benchlands between the summit ridges of the Blue Mountains and the canyon bottoms of the Grande Ronde and its tributaries. Winter offers the best opportunity to see herds of mammals when they migrate to get out of the snow in the highlands and congregate on the benches to browse. **Mule deer, Rocky Mountain elk,** and **bighorn sheep** can be seen on the Eden Bench southwest of Troy. Forest Rd 62 climbs the bench from Troy and a county road follows its base along the Grande Ronde River. **Bald eagles** can be seen near the river and **wild turkeys** frequent the openings along roads.

During winter, herds of **Rocky Mountain elk** are so common in the foothills of the Elkhorn Range south of La Grande that a commercial operation has been modeled along the lines of the elk-viewing trips of Wyoming's Teton Range. The Oregon Trail Trolley, (541) 856-3356, offers tours in horsedrawn hay wagons to within a few yards of the massive creatures in the state-managed Elkhorn Wildlife Area, (541) 898-2826. Tours run on weekends and holidays from December through February. Between 150 and 200 elk are fed daily by state game managers. Elk pass through the area and can be seen year-round. Interpretive signs explain the life cycles of elk and the reason behind the supplemental feeding. It's not uncommon to get within 10 feet of the impressive creatures during winter feeding. The Oregon Department of Fish and Wildlife provides feed for deer and elk during winter to keep the animals away from farmers' fields. The 7,772-acre site is divided into two units, both well marked by highway signs on River Rd, 8 miles west of North Powder at exit 285 of I-84.

Ladd Marsh Wildlife Area, (541) 963-2138, located 5 miles south of La Grande, is a 3,208-acre state wildlife area that can be reached from exit 268 of I-84. The entrance is 2 miles south on Foothill Rd. **White-tailed deer, mule deer,** and **Rocky Mountain elk** use the marsh seasonally, but the marsh's major attraction is migrating and nesting waterfowl. The marsh is the largest hard-stem bulrush marsh remaining in northeast Oregon. Because the area is designed to protect waterfowl, public access is restricted to viewpoints and a 1-mile nature trail. Exceptions are for licensed hunters during waterfowl season and educational groups by permit. Facilities include observation points along Foothill Rd and a photo blind near Hot Lake Mineral Springs. Common bird sightings include **bald eagle, sandhill crane, American avocet, northern shoveler, bobolink, western screech owl,** and numerous **hawks, waterfowl,** and **songbirds.** Bring a pair of binoculars and spend several hours watching activity in the marsh. Watch for **coyotes** and **beaver,** too.

The Grande Ronde Valley is a birder's paradise as the river flows out of the Elkhorn and Blue Mountains, through the heavily farmed valley between La Grande and Elgin, and through its deep canyon as it journeys to join the Snake River. Unusual sightings include **gray catbird, veery, and red-eyed vireo,** all eastern U.S. species that are rare in Oregon. **Marsh wrens, yellow-headed blackbirds,** and **Virginia rails** are common in the valley.

Perhaps the most famous winged resident of the Grande Ronde country is the **great gray owl.** The largest owl in North America, great grays congregate in Wallowa-Whitman National Forest's Spring Creek Great Gray Owl Management Area 12 miles west of La Grande. From the Spring Creek exit off I-84, follow Forest Rd 21 south for 3 miles. Common nesting sites are from .25 mile to 1 mile on either side of the road. The best way to spot an owl is to visit between mid-May and early June when the young are leaving the nest. Young birds are very vocal during morning and evening, and the hunting adults are kept busy feeding them. Listen and watch for activity to locate the nests. Check with the La Grande Ranger District, (541) 963-7186, for specific driving directions for nests that are known to be occupied.

The congregation of great gray owls was first noticed in the early 1980s when the area was logged and large, parklike stands of ponderosa pines were left undisturbed. The owls moved into vacant northern goshawk nests and have since taken up residence on 2-foot-square artificial platforms built 30 to 50 feet high in trees by wildlife biologists. The population includes up to eight nesting pairs in a 4-square-mile area.

The Starkey Elk Project is a large, fenced enclosure in the northwest part of Union County where **deer** and **elk** are studied in their natural surroundings. The Starkey project can be seen on the north side of Hwy 244, midway between I-84 and Ukiah.

Hiking/Backpacking

A short hike located 16 miles north of La Grande follows the Oregon Trail at the **Oregon Trail Interpretive Park** at Blue Mountain Crossing, the jewel of the visitors facilities managed by the La Grande Ranger District, (541) 963-7186. Take exit 248 from I-84 and follow signs west to Kamela. After .5 mile, turn right on Forest Rd 600 and drive 2.5 miles to the trailhead. Two side loops branch from the main trail, covering a distance of a little more than a mile. The .5-mile interpretive trail is barrier free and explains the major feature of the site—ruts of the Oregon Trail left by pioneers in the 1840s. A picnic area is located .5 mile west of the interpretive trail, which is open only from Memorial Day to Labor Day when staff can be on hand to protect the sensitive nature of the site.

The tiny community of Troy, with its population of about 50, is the main Oregon gateway to 177,412-acre **Wenaha-Tucannon Wilderness** (see Rafting/Kayaking and Wildlife, above). Oregon has 66,417 acres of the wilderness and the remainder are in Washington. The highest peak in the wilderness is Oregon Butte at 6,401 feet, but it's a good 7 miles north of the border into Washington.

The **Wenaha River Trail** begins at the edge of Troy and continues west upstream 31 miles to Timothy Springs Campground, a remote spot on Forest Rd 6415 in the Umatilla National Forest on the southwest edge of the wilderness. The trail climbs from 1,600 to 4,600 feet. Day hikers usually walk a few miles, drop down off the trail to soak their feet in one of Oregon's most beautiful streams, and head back to Troy. To find the trailhead, drive the road northwest out of Troy that is signed for Pomeroy, Washington. Park after .3 mile where the road makes a sharp right turn. The signed trailhead has a few parking spots.

Three trails that drop down to the Wenaha from its southern rim can be accessed on Forest Rd 62 as it heads west from Troy. From east to west one way to the Wenaha, the trails are **Hoodoo Trail** (moderate; 3.2 miles), **Cross Canyon Trail** (moderate; 3.3 miles), and **Elk Flats Trail** (moderate; 5 miles). The Elk Flats trailhead in particular makes an ideal backpack trip, with prearranged car shuttle, because it drops down to the river's forks where the Wenaha can easily be crossed for a 20-mile walk downstream to Troy.

The Minam River, protected in the National Wild and Scenic Rivers Program, drains the northwest portion of the **Eagle Cap Wilderness.** The 45-mile Minam River Trail follows the river south from near Hwy 82, 4

miles west of Minam (see Rafting/Kayaking, above) to its headwaters at
Minam Lake, at the west edge of Lakes Basin (see Wallowas and Hells
Canyon chapter). The trail begins 9 miles south of Minam Summit on Hwy
82 on a road that is best driven in a four-wheel-drive over the last 4 miles.

Moss Springs Trail is the most popular westside approach to the
Wallowas in Union County. The trailhead and campground (see Camping,
below) are 10 miles up steep Forest Rd 6220 from Cove. This is horse
country and the trailhead has eight 16-by-6-foot holding stalls. The main
trail heads east, but it soon branches and the north fork leads to Minam
Lodge, (541) 432-4145, and the Minam River. The lodge is open for
overnight guests during the summer, usually people who land at the
lodge's airstrip or pack in on horseback. The south branch of the Moss
Springs Trail follows the Little Minam River. A 20.5-mile loop can be made
using the two trails and connecting them with the trail on Jim White
Ridge.

For extended trips into the Eagle Cap backcountry, consult the
Wallowa Mountains map by Imus Geographics. The map is available
through ranger stations and sporting goods stores.

Other western approaches to the Wallowas begin from the end of the
roads at **Catherine Creek** and at **Buck Creek,** both about 30 miles southeast of La Grande. Drive Hwy 203 southeast of Union for 10 miles to
Catherine Creek State Park. Two miles past the park, Forest Rd 7785 splits
off to the east and follows the north fork of Catherine Creek to the trailhead. Buck Creek trailhead is at the end of Forest Rd 7787, the junction of
which is 5 miles up from Hwy 203. A 12-mile loop that is accessible from
either trailhead can be a challenging day hike, or backpackers can continue
into the wilderness and walk for days and never retrace their steps. Main
places of interest are **Diamond and Tombstone Lakes,** 8 miles from Buck
Creek trailhead. Fishing is good for brook trout in many Eagle Cap lakes in
August and September. The highest peak in the area is 8,679-foot **Granite
Butte.** Bring the Imus map of the Wallowas for an extended trip.

Camping

Like any better-than-average outdoor recreation mecca, La Grande is
surrounded by campgrounds. Most of the camps are clustered on the west
flank of the Wallowa Mountains, around irrigation reservoirs in the southern part of the La Grande and the Grande Ronde River country, and in the
west along Hwy 244 near Starkey.

Moss Springs Campground, 10 miles east of Cove on a steep gravel
road, is situated at 5,400 feet and has 11 sites for tents. Most campers use
it to stage trips into the Wallowas, either on foot or by horse. **Catherine
Creek State Park Campground,** (541) 523-2499, is in a beautiful creek-

side setting 8 miles southeast of Union on Hwy 203. The camping area has 18 primitive sites. Ice caves can be found on federal land just east of the park where natives used to catch steelhead and pick huckleberries. The Forest Service's **North Fork Catherine Creek Campground** is 6 miles due east of the state park at 4,400 feet. The small campground has a half-dozen spots for tents and small trailers, but the trailhead is another 2 miles up the road. Forest Service campgrounds around La Grande are managed by the La Grande Ranger District, (541) 963-7186.

The Union County Parks Department, (541) 963-1001, maintains small campgrounds at **Thief Valley, Wolf Creek,** and **Pilcher Reservoirs** in the southern part of the county near North Powder. The parks also have boat ramps, picnicking, fishing, and wildlife watching. Access is convenient to I-84. The largest is Thief Valley, with a dozen camping sites, 12 miles south of Union and 18 miles east of North Powder. Wolf Creek is 6 miles west of North Powder, and Pilcher Creek is 9 miles west of North Powder. **Morgan Lake,** a 60-acre reservoir, 5 miles southwest of La Grande, has some camp spots, is wheelchair accessible, and has good fishing for kids. For information, check with the La Grande–Union County Chamber of Commerce, (800) 848-9969, at 1912 Fourth St, Suite 200, La Grande.

Campers heading out of La Grande toward Starkey usually leave I-84 at Hilgard Junction, 8 miles northwest of town at exit 252. They are immediately confronted with a decision: should they stay and camp at **Hilgard Junction State Recreation Area,** or head farther south on Hwy 244 and try their luck at three La Grande Ranger District camps farther away?

Hilgard Junction Campground, (541) 523-2499, offers camping in 18 primitive sites, none very far from I-84. The Grande Ronde River flows through the park and helps muffle the freeway noise. The park was another important stop for pioneers on the Oregon Trail. A park shelter outlines some of the pioneer adventures and explains how the wagon trains came down the hill facing the park. An overflow camping area is 5 miles south on Hwy 244 at **Red Bridge,** a day-use state park.

While in the area, campers should explore the **Oregon Trail Interpretive Park** at Blue Mountain crossing, 4 miles northwest of Hilgard Junction at exit 248 off I-84 (see Hiking/Backpacking, above). Other Oregon Trail interpretive points in the area are at **Charles Reynolds Rest Area,** on I-84 at milepost 268, and in La Grande at **Birnie Park.** The emigrants were pleasantly pleased with the Grande Ronde Valley because of its running water and fertile grazing lands, after they had passed through hundreds of miles of baking-hot sagebrush lands on the Snake River Plain.

Forest Service campgrounds south of Hilgard Junction are **Spool Cart Campground** (16 sites) and **River Campground** (6 sites), both along Forest Rd 51. Where Hwy 244 veers west toward Ukiah 9 miles from the freeway, Forest Rd 51 continues south and follows the Grande Ronde River. The road continues south for 30 miles, passing several other roads that lead west to the North Fork John Day River drainage (see Upper John Day River chapter) or east into the Elkhorn Range (see Baker County chapter). The Union County side of the Elkhorn Scenic Highway (Forest Rd 73 west of North Powder) has one campground near Anthony Lakes Ski Area at **Grande Ronde Lake.** The lake contributes to the headwaters of its namesake river and has 8 campsites for tents, 1 mile north of Elkhorn Dr and 1 mile west of Anthony Lakes. Situated at 6,800 feet, Grande Ronde Lake is heavily fished for stocked rainbow trout. Campgrounds are managed by the La Grande Ranger District, (541) 963-7186.

Minam State Recreation Area, (541) 523-2499, is located 15 miles northeast of Elgin and offers pleasant camping among giant pine trees along a beautiful rushing river. The park is a 2-mile drive north on a gravel road along the west bank of the Wallowa River from the Hwy 82 bridge at Minam (see Rafting/Kayaking, above). The park has 12 primitive campsites. Fishing for trout and steelhead can be productive and the park has two boat launches. Be aware, however, that the Wallowa River is a brisk mountain stream as it passes the park, and any boat that is launched may need to be picked up a long way downstream.

In addition to its campgrounds, Wallowa-Whitman National Forest in the La Grande area has one cabin rental. **Fry Meadow Guard Station** is 50 miles north of La Grande in the Walla Walla Ranger District, (509) 522-6290. Located near the southern edge of the Wenaha-Tucannon Wilderness, the guard station is a good base from which to explore the roads that approach the wilderness, including the view from **Big Hole** high on the rim above the Wenaha River. The guard station is available to rent year-round by reservation, but skis or a snowmobile are normally required to reach it from mid-November to mid-May. It costs $25 per night for up to four people, and campers need to supply their own food, water, and bedding.

Fishing

For an area without a lot of lakes, the La Grande and the Grande Ronde River country nevertheless has some mighty fine fishing. The Grande Ronde, Minam, and Wenaha Rivers, each protected under the National Wild and Scenic Rivers Program, guarantee good fishing opportunities.

The **Grande Ronde River** flows about 180 miles from its beginning in the Elkhorn Range to its meeting with the Snake River. The river's lower 35 miles are in Washington. Fishing in the river above La Grande is good for wild and stocked rainbow trout in the upper section that runs through national forest land. Access is on Forest Rd 51 (see Camping, above). The river below Starkey has been degraded by logging activity and heats up during summer, forcing the fish to migrate upstream.

The **Lower Grande Ronde** below Miman (see Rafting/Kayaking, above) offers rainbow trout, whitefish, and an occasional dolly varden. The fish that makes the lower river famous is the steelhead, mostly reared in hatcheries because dams, agriculture, and forestry practices have played havoc with the native population. Steelhead bound for the Grande Ronde enter the Columbia during summer. By the time they swim through eight dams over 500 miles, it can be anywhere from late fall to early spring when they make it upriver to the Grande Ronde. Most fishing is accessed by drift boats. Fly-fishing is difficult because of the river's current. Wild trout and steelhead must be released without removing them from the water.

Much of the commercial river running on the Grande Ronde is built around fishing. The river's gentle nature makes it easy for floaters to conduct their own trips safely, but some fishermen turn to guides to learn the location of the choice fishing holes on the river. **Local guides** include Little Creek Outfitters, (541) 963-7878, and Oregon Trail Adventures, (800) 527-8787, both of La Grande. Little Creek Outfitters has a riverside lodge where its clients can stay. When visiting La Grande, look for fishing **gear and tips** at the Four Seasons Fly Shoppe, (541) 963-8420.

The **Minam River** has plenty of native rainbow, plus some brook trout and a few bull trout. A remnant from the last ice age, bull trout must be released. Fishing is from the roads that follow the river's lower 9 miles, or from the trail that continues up 45 miles to the river's headwaters in Minam Lake (see Hiking/Backpacking, above).

The 35-mile-long **Wenaha River** flows mostly through a designated wilderness before joining the Grande Ronde near Troy. Nearly all access is by trail (see Hiking/Backpacking, above). The river runs deep and swift with many pools that hold steelhead, rainbow trout, and whitefish. The river is managed as a wild trout stream, with the best trout fishing lasting from midsummer through fall. Rainbow average 10 to 15 inches. Wild rainbow can be kept, but wild steelhead must be released.

Thief Valley Reservoir is a desert impoundment that can dry up completely in drought years. The lake is planted periodically with trout fingerlings that grow to 20 inches within a few years. The **Powder River** naturally restocks the reservoir with crappie, bass, and bullhead. The reservoir is 10 miles east of North Powder. **Wolf Creek Reservoir,** 5 miles west of North Powder, and **Pilcher Creek Reservoir,** 2 miles farther west, are small impoundments that offer fishing for rainbow and crappie. Trout are stocked annually. Both reservoirs can go dry in drought years (see Camping, above).

Check the state synopsis for regulations, or call the Oregon Department of Fish and Wildlife's Baker City office, (541) 523-5832.

Biking

If the Grande Ronde Valley was in Wyoming, it would be called a "hole." That's "hole," as in Jackson Hole. "Hole" is the word fur trappers used to describe a depression between mountain ranges. With the Blue Mountains flanking the valley on the west and north and the Wallowa Mountains (locals call them the Eagle Mountains) doing the same on the east, the Grande Ronde Valley is a large expanse of relatively flat land situated at 2,800 feet above sea level. The conditions couldn't be much better for road cycling.

Lightly used county roads north, east, and south of La Grande offer a variety of loop riding opportunities. A good way to begin to explore the possibilities is a tour along **Foothill Road** to the Ladd Marsh Wildlife Area (see Wildlife, above). Begin at **Birnie Park** on Fourth St in La Grande. Turn right onto C Ave, which becomes Gekeler. At .8 mile, turn right onto Foothill Rd and ride 6 miles past viewpoints to the wildlife area's nature trail. Return to town the same way.

A 42.5-mile **Valley Loop** heads east on Hwy 82 from Island City, a small community 2 miles east of La Grande. At 4.5 miles, turn right on Market Lane and follow it as it changes to Lower Cove Rd and turns south to reach Cove. Take Hwy 237 west out of Cove, then follow the highway as it turns south to reach Union. Hwy 203 leads back to La Grande. Bring a bathing suit because this tour passes Cove swimming pool, (541) 586-4890, where warm mineral water flows through a gravel opening in the pool bottom into an immaculate 60-by-60-foot pool.

After catching a glimpse of scenic Union, cyclists may want to return to make a 72.5-mile tour south through **Medical Springs,** west to Haines, and back north through North Powder to Union. The entire route is on state highways that carry little traffic because nearby I-84 handles the bulk of the load.

Another popular tour near La Grande is a 31.4-mile loop that begins in town at **Riverside Park** (on Spruce St just north of I-84), heads north to Summerville, and passes through Imbler before returning to town.

As home to Eastern Oregon State University, La Grande has more than its share of mountain-bike riders among the students. A good introductory ride is in the **Spring Creek** area, where the great gray owls nest (see Wildlife, above). Riding is easy to moderate on dirt-road doubletracks from 3,100 to 3,500 feet in elevation. Loops of 5 and 7 miles are possible on the south side of Forest Rd 27, about 3 miles south of exit 248 on I-84.

Telephone Ridge just north of **Mount Emily** offers a nice downhill ride of 1,200 feet over 6 miles, but the elevation must be regained on the return. Mount Emily, at 6,063 feet in elevation, is La Grande's signature mountain, just as Mount Hood is for Portland. Located 8 miles due north of town, the peak has a four-wheel-drive road to its summit. Before beginning the tour, stop at the La Grande Ranger District, (541) 963-7186, at 3502 Hwy 30 in La Grande, to pick up a packet of cycle tours, the best information on biking available from any Oregon ranger district. The information is provided jointly with the local chamber of commerce. The bike tour begins at Indian Rock Shelter, 2 miles north of the summit, on Forest Rd 3120. The tour switches to Rd 450, then takes Trail 1860 to the end of Long Ridge, from where the view takes in Five Points Creek drainage to the west and Fiddlers Hell Creek to the east.

Across the Grande Ronde Valley east of Mount Emily, the towns of Cove and Union are located near a pair of bike tours. The **Cove** tour begins just east of town at the entrance to Moss Springs Campground (see Camping, above). Follow Forest Rd 6220 north as it switchbacks up 7,155-foot **Mount Fanny.** At the 6-mile mark, turn left on Rd 500, ride 1 mile west, then turn right on Trail 1917. Ride the trail to the 10-mile mark from the trailhead and turn right on Trail 1936. This trail leads east and rejoins Rd 6220. Turn right and head south to complete the 21-mile loop. This ride requires two separate climbs of more than 1,000 feet. Expect to see lots of huckleberries, and maybe bears feeding on them, in August. Bring along the brochure available from the La Grande Ranger District.

The **Bald Mountain** ride begins 14 miles east of Union at the junction of Forest Rds 2036 and 2038. The 19-mile loop tour heads north and uses a combination of gravel and dirt roads, as described in the Forest Service brochure, to connect with 3 miles of single-track riding. Elevation gain is 1,600 feet.

Horseback Riding

Oregon has three wildernesses that see a lot of overnight horse-packing trips, and the Grande Ronde River country has access to two of them—the Oregon half of the **Wenaha-Tucannon Wilderness** and the western entrances for the **Eagle Cap Wilderness.** The third is Hells Canyon (see Wallowas and Hells Canyon chapter).

Much of the packing into the Wenaha-Tucannon Wilderness happens during hunting season. Outback Ranch Outfitters, (541) 426-4037, of Joseph leads horse pack trips into the Wenaha-Tucannon Wilderness.

Vacationers who want to go for a summer horse-packing trip usually pick the Eagle Cap Wilderness because the high lakes offer respite from the heat in the valleys below. Outfitters who operate on the west side of the Eagle Cap, mostly out of the **Moss Springs** trailhead near Elgin (see Hiking/Backpacking, above), are Eagle Cap Pack Station at Joseph, (800) 681-6222, and Moss Springs Packing, (541) 568-4823. Moss Springs is based in Cove and is the local westside outfitter.

Eagle Cap Pack Station is based at Wallowa Lake, but it uses an east-side trailhead to take guests to Minam Lodge, one of the few lodges open to public use in Oregon that is entirely surrounded by a designated wilderness. Minam Lodge, (541) 432-4145, is accessible by horseback, airplane, or foot. Located on the Minam River, the lodge is often found by vacationers to be the ultimate mountain retreat in Oregon. Rustic cabins have showers, bathrooms, and wood heat. Dining is in the central lodge, which is located at 3,600 feet near the banks of the Minam River.

Llama trekking out of La Grande is offered by Sandy Ryman, (541) 963-8268.

Cross-Country Skiing

The Grande Ronde River country is blanketed with snow during much of the winter but until 1977 had only one designated Oregon sno-park. **Oregon Trail Sno-Park,** 1 mile south of I-84 at exit 248, is at the summit of the Blue Mountains between La Grande and Pendleton, near Kamela. The sno-park's snowmobile trail system connects to Tollgate on the north and Lehman Hot Springs on the south (see Pendleton Grain Belt chapter). Nordic skiing is on unmarked trails. Backcountry ski tours can begin as far up a snow-covered national forest road as a skier wants to drive.

The **Meacham Divide Sno-Park,** the second in the area, opened in 1997 at the same freeway exit, 2 miles east on Forest Rd 31. The new sno-park is the setting for the Meacham Divide Ski Area, a 15-kilometer groomed network of cross-country ski trails at the 4,200-foot level. Trails are mostly beginner and intermediate and lead to views of the Blue Mountain canyons. The ski area is groomed by the La Grande Nordic club and recreation is managed by the La Grande Ranger District, (541) 963-7186. Facilities are limited to plowed parking, groomed trails, and portable toilets. Trail use is free, although donations are welcome.

Skiers can find help with information and equipment in La Grande at Anson Ski Shop, (541) 963-3660, 112 Depot St, and One Track Mind, (541) 963-6643, at 1306 Adams Ave.

Restaurants

Mamacita's House specials at lunch are usually the best things coming out of the kitchen. Dishes are not overly spiced and not as fat-laden as Mexican food often is. Wine margaritas and a wall adorned with bright splotches of Mexicana complete the experience. *110 Depot St (near Adams), La Grande; (541) 963-6223; $.*

Ten Depot Street ☆ This is the locals' pick for an evening out. Lunches feature superior salads and sandwiches; dinners can be a burger or beef tenderloin heaped with mushrooms. The daily blue plate special is under $5. *10 Depot St (2 blocks west of Adams), La Grande; (541) 963-8766; $$.*

Lodgings

Stang Manor Inn ☆☆ This house on the hill behind town has a sweeping staircase leading up to four bedrooms. The owners have given personal attention to an already nurturing environment. Cookies with tea await you at check-in. Breakfasts are served on china and crystal. *1612 Walnut St (corner of Spring), La Grande, OR 97850; (503) 963-2400; $$.*

More Information

Bureau of Land Management, Baker City: *(541) 523-1256.*
Eagle Cap Ranger District, Enterprise: *(541) 426-4978.*
Eastern Oregon Visitors Association, Baker City: *(800) 332-1843.*
La Grande Ranger District, La Grande: *(541) 963-7186.*
La Grande–Union County Chamber of Commerce,
    La Grande: *(800) 848-9969.*
Pomeroy Ranger District, Pomeroy, Washington: *(509) 843-1891.*
Umatilla National Forest, Pendleton: *(541) 278-3716.*
Walla Walla Ranger District, Walla Walla, Washington:
    (509) 522-6290.
Wallowa-Whitman National Forest, Baker City: *(541) 523-6391.*

Baker County

From the Baker-Union county line on the north, east to the Idaho border, south to the Baker-Malheur county line, and west into the gold-mining areas along the Baker-Grant county line, including Anthony Lakes, the Elkhorn Range, the southern entrances to the Eagle Cap Wilderness and Hells Canyon National Recreation Area, and the towns of Haines, Sumpter, Unity, Baker City, Richland, Halfway, and Huntington.

The hike started out as an innocent overnight backpack trip into some of the most beautiful terrain in Oregon's northeast mountains. Before the hike was over, the outing had become an ordeal that was mercifully finished within the day because it made no sense at all to stretch the misery into the night.

The objective of the trip was to hike the 22.6-mile Elkhorn Crest Trail, a skyline hiking route along the top of the highest range in Oregon's Blue Mountains. The Elkhorn Range is the impressive ridge that can be seen west of Interstate 84 when driving through the North Powder River Valley in Baker County. The Elkhorns aren't as vast as the Wallowa Mountains east of the freeway, but they pack much of the same scenery in a smaller, easier-to-reach package. The Elkhorns have high mountain lakes, headwaters of wild rivers, wilderness, and Oregon's best chance for powder snow at a developed ski area.

To make the hike into a one-way trip required a vehicle shuttle. The southern trailhead for the Elkhorn Crest Trail is located in the hills above Baker City at Marble Pass. The northern trailhead is near Anthony Lakes Ski Area above North Powder. In between is a high-country trail that never dips below 7,100 feet, a fairly lofty elevation in Oregon.

A telephone call to the Baker City Ranger District found a young county resident willing to run the shuttle. "You want to pay me $80 to pick you up at Anthony Lakes, drive you 30 miles, and drop you off at Marble Pass?" he asked incredulously as he pocketed four $20 bills.

The money turned out to be well spent because, as the day turned out, it became quite comforting to know that our camper-van was waiting at the end of the trail. As the shuttle driver's four-wheel-drive pickup disappeared from sight, pellets of snow began falling from the clouds that swirled among the peaks of the crest. With no other vehicles anywhere in sight, there was nothing to do but begin walking north. It was midsummer, for gosh sakes, so surely the snow wouldn't last all day.

By midday the temperature had warmed up enough for the snow to change to rain. The rain wasn't very heavy, but it was wet enough to work its way through the Gore-Tex as the layers of clothing chafed against each other over the miles.

Locating water to drink can be difficult on a ridge top, so the only spot with a flowing spring required a decision—would it be best to pitch a tent or to keep hiking? Since it was only 3pm, and summer's light would last another six hours, the decision was made to keep hiking. A lake along the way offered the next available water, but by then it was only 3 miles to the end of the trail. There wasn't much point in unpacking a tent when a dry van was within reach.

As darkness began to fall, the one-day backpack trip mercifully came to an end at the van parked at Anthony Lakes. As it turned out, there had been no need to carry the tent, a sleeping bag, a stove, and food for an overnight trip. The 50-pound backpack could have been replaced with a 10-pound daypack, but then the misery wouldn't have been so much fun.

Getting There

Baker City is 304 miles east of Portland on Interstate 84. A network of state and county highways connects Baker City with other towns in Baker County, while Wallowa-Whitman National Forest and Bureau of Land Management (BLM) roads probe the forested mountains and desert hills. Sumpter is just off Highway 7 west of Baker; Haines is north on US Highway 30 (US 30), Richland and Halfway are east on Highway 86, and Huntington is southeast via Interstate 84. Unity is on US 26 southwest of Baker as the cross-state highway slips through a corner of Baker County.

Adjoining Areas

NORTH: **La Grande and the Grande Ronde River**

SOUTH: **Malheur County**

EAST: **Wallowas and Hells Canyon**

WEST: **Upper John Day River**

inside out

Scenic Drives

Similar to the way Oregon Trail pioneers experienced the Baker country, many a modern-day visitor enjoys sights of northeast Oregon from within a moving vehicle. Speeds are a little higher these days, but the country is big and mobility is necessary to see everything. The Baker area is home to three designated scenic byways, as well as other routes designated by the state for their historical interest. Drop by the Baker County Visitors and Convention Bureau, (541) 523-3356, 490 Campbell St, to pick up information for all the tours.

Managed by the BLM, the **Snake River/Mormon Basin National Back Country Byway** makes a 130-mile circle east of Baker City, passing through Richland on Hwy 86 and Huntington before heading back to town through Bridgeport on a county road that follows the Burnt River. Highlight of the tour is a 38-mile road, mostly gravel, that parallels the **Snake River Canyon** between Richland and Huntington. The road is passable most of the year, but snow and mud during winter and spring make it best to drive during dry weather. Old mining and pioneer towns, most of which stand empty and forlorn these days, encountered along the way are Amelia, Clarksville, and Eldorado. All are in Mormon Basin in the extreme north part of Malheur County south of Bridgeport. Stop at the Baker City BLM office, (541) 523-1256, at 1550 Dewey Ave, Room 215, to pick up a copy of a route guide.

Elkhorn Drive, a Forest Service scenic byway, makes a 106-mile loop west of Baker City. When traveling clockwise from town, the tour passes Phillips Lake, Sumpter, Granite, Anthony Lakes, and Haines as it follows Hwy 7, County Rd 24, Forest Rd 73, and US 30. Snow closes the loop west of Anthony Lakes from November through May. The Baker City office of Wallowa-Whitman National Forest, (541) 523-4476, is at 3165 Tenth St.

The southern leg of the **Hells Canyon tour,** also a Forest Service byway, travels through Baker County between Halfway and Baker City on Hwy 86. The rest of the 314-mile loop passes through La Grande and Enterprise (see La Grande and the Grande Ronde River and Wallowas and Hells Canyon chapters). A side trip at the southeast part of the byway follows Hwy 86 and the Snake River downstream east from Halfway, crossing to the Idaho side at **Oxbow.** This route gives access to the remote northeast corner of Baker County along the Snake River Canyon. Old mining towns along the Baker country part of the route are Sparta, Cornucopia, Copperfield, and Homestead. From Oxbow, a road leads north 24 miles on the Idaho side before crossing Hells Canyon Dam back into Oregon where it ends at a visitors center and boat launch.

The **Sumpter Valley Railway** is a Malheur National Forest tour that begins in Baker City and covers 65 miles, mostly on Hwy 7, before ending in Prairie City (see Upper John Day River chapter). The tour traces the history of the railroad that was used for mining and log hauling. The Sumpter Valley Railway, (541) 894-2268, offers the chance to relive a bit of history with summer weekend rides on a restored narrow-gauge railway between Sumpter and Phillips Lake. Several old mining towns of Baker and Grant Counties are in the mountains that surround Sumpter. **Auburn** is 10 miles southwest of Baker via Hwy 7 and County Rd 722. The abandoned townsite was founded in 1862 and was once the county seat. The **Bourne** townsite is 6 miles north of Sumpter, and a few buildings remain from what once was a thriving hard-rock mining town. The buildings are privately owned and are used as summer residences. An interpretive sign just off Hwy 7 at the north entrance to **Whitney** describes the ghost town's mining, logging, and cattle ranching history. **Greenhorn,** 11 miles northeast of Austin Junction, is Oregon's smallest and highest incorporated town. The town's elevation is 6,270 feet and the population is listed at 3, far below the 500 townsfolk and 2,000 miners who lived around town in the mining heyday of the 1890s.

The state of Oregon's 230-mile **Unity Lake tour** takes in parts of the other tours south and west of Baker City, but pushes the loop down to Ontario (see Malheur County chapter) on I-84 and up to Austin (see Upper John Day River chapter) on US 26. Old settlements along the way include Pleasant Valley, Durkee, Weatherby, and Lime. **Rye Valley,** 30 miles south of Baker City and 11 miles west of I-84, is site of an old cemetery that got more than a few of its customers from a famous hanging tree.

Hiking/Backpacking

The Oregon Trail

The Baker country offers outstanding hiking in the Elkhorn Range, northwest of Baker City, and the Eagle Cap Wilderness, east of town. But for most visitors, the only hiking they'll do comes at the Oregon Trail visitors center at Flagstaff Hill. A worthy destination in its own right, the National Historic **Oregon Trail Interpretive Center** at Flagstaff Hill 6 miles east of Baker City on Hwy 86 interprets the events of the westward migration with displays, murals, and live programs put on by local actors.

The visitors center has a 4.2-mile loop trail system around the grounds. The building itself and parts of the trail are barrier free for wheelchair access. The trail system leads to Panorama Point, for a view of the valley that the settlers worked so hard to cross, and to wagon ruts that are carved into the landscape by the passing of thousands of emigrants. More than 7 miles of Oregon Trail ruts have been identified in the area. The BLM's center is open daily, except Christmas, and can be reached at (541) 523-1843.

The visitors center's paved **Flagstaff Hill Trail** (easy; .5-mile loop) leads to viewpoints of the Blue Mountains, the first sign of green the settlers had seen for many miles; to an overlook of Virtue Flat, an arid tableland where 7 miles of trail still exist; and to a view of the Flagstaff Mine, a gold mine discovered in 1895 that still produces modest results today. The **Living History Trails** include a loop around a hard-rock mine north of the visitors center (easy; 1 mile one way) and a tour of an emigrant encampment just south of the top of Flagstaff Hill.

Panorama Point is at the end of a 1.25-mile trail northwest from the visitors center. Other trails lead down off the hill, where the visitors center is situated, to view the Eagle Valley Railroad grade, a BLM obelisk that marks ruts of the original trail, and to the Auburn–Burnt River wagon road ruts. A stop along the way explains how Ezra Meeker, a pioneer who passed through the area in 1853, returned in 1906 to retrace the trail from west to east.

Elkhorn Range

The highest range in the Blue Mountains, the Elkhorn Mountains dominate the view west of I-84 from the Powder River Valley. For information, stop at the Baker Ranger District, (541) 523-4476, at 3165 Tenth St in Baker City.

The 22.6-mile **Elkhorn Crest National Recreation Trail** traverses the range from Anthony Lakes on the north to Marble Pass on the south. **Anthony Lakes** is 32 miles northwest of Baker (see Scenic Drives, above) on Forest Rd 73. The trailhead is located just east of the Anthony Lake campground. **Marble Pass** is 15 miles west of Baker City via Pocahontas Rd and Forest Rd 6510. The last 8 miles to Marble Pass are suitable only for high-clearance vehicles.

The Elkhorn Crest Trail stays remarkably close to the ridge top, leaving it along the west side more frequently than on the east. **Rock Creek Butte,** the highest peak in the range at 9,106 feet, is an easy scramble from the trail 4.5 miles north of Marble Pass. Mountain goats frequent the area around Rock Creek Butte. The Wallowas are the only other mountains that the nimble goats inhabit in Oregon. The crest trail climbs 1,000 feet in the first 2 miles out of Anthony Lakes, then maintains a fairly constant elevation all the way to Marble Pass.

Shorter trails around the Anthony Lakes area (all mileages are one way) are **Van Patten Lake** (difficult; .5 mile with a 1,015-foot climb) on Forest Rd 130, 2 miles east of Anthony Lake; **Anthony Lake Shoreline** (easy; 1 mile) and **Black Lake** (easy; 1 mile), both at Anthony Lake Campground; **Hoffer Lake** (easy; 1 mile), from the Anthony Lake Shoreline Trail; **Lakes Lookout** (moderate; .7 mile with a 722-foot climb) and **Crawfish Basin** (easy; 2 miles), both on Forest Rd 210 just west of the Elkhorn Summit, and **Crawfish Lake**, (easy; 2 miles) on Forest Rd 320 west of the Elkhorn Summit. With so many trails, hikers usually run out of time before destinations.

The Baldy Creek Unit of the **North Fork John Day Wilderness** lies just west of the Elkhorn Crest. Forest Rd 73 travels past its north side and Spur Rd 380, 7 miles west of the summit, penetrates the wilderness to the Forest Service guard station and trailhead in **Peavy Canyon.** Popular hikes are **Cunningham Cove** (difficult; 3.3 miles) and **Peavy** (moderate; 3.7 miles), both beginning from Peavy trailhead, and **Baldy Creek** (difficult; 7.4 miles), which crosses the wilderness unit north to south.

Trails leading into the Elkhorns from Sumpter on the south are **Twin Lakes** (difficult; 4 miles) on Forest Rd 6550-030 and **Pole Creek Ridge** (difficult; 2 miles) on Forest Rd 5536-150. Both require a high-clearance vehicle to negotiate roads that lead to the trailhead. The shortest route to the summit of **Rock Creek Butte** is via Twin Lakes. Continue hiking above Twin Lakes to reach the **Elkhorn Crest Trail,** turn north, and immediately plot a scramble route up the large mountain to the right. The climb to the highest point in the Elkhorns covers 3,500 feet over 6 miles one way.

Trails that lead into the Elkhorns from the east are **Dutch Flat** (difficult; 9.5 miles), **Red Mountain Lake** (difficult; 1.3 miles, elevation gain of 2,977 feet), **Summit Lake** (moderate; 3.3 miles), **Killamacue Lake** (difficult; 3.2 miles), **North Powder** (difficult; 2.6 miles), and **Rock Creek Lake** (difficult; 3.5 miles). These trails lie between the North Fork John Day Wilderness on the west and Haines on the east, and are lightly used. Consult a Wallowa-Whitman National Forest map for access.

Monument Rock Wilderness

Monument Rock lies 12 miles southwest of Unity and sees relatively light use, except along the cherry-stem road that climbs to the lookout atop 7,815-foot **Table Rock.** Roads that penetrate wilderness areas are administratively left outside the boundaries to comply with wilderness standards, thus earning the nickname of "cherry-stem" roads. The main trails in the 19,620-acre wilderness are **Little Malheur River** (moderate; 7.5 miles from Spur Rd 457 to Elk Flat), accessible from Forest Rd 16 on the south, and **Bull Run** (difficult; 5.5 miles), from Forest Rd 1695 on the north. The Bull Run Trail climbs through the northeast corner of the wilderness, passing just beneath the high point—7,873-foot-high Bull Run Rock, one of the many glacial horns found in the area. The Forest Service sells a topo map of the wilderness (it's on the reverse side of the Strawberry Mountain

Wilderness map). Stop at the Unity Ranger Station, (541) 446-3351, in Unity, to buy a copy.

Eagle Cap Wilderness

The Wallowas' southern side has seven major trailheads, none of them heavily used compared to the north-side trailheads near Joseph (see Wallowas and Hells Canyon chapter). From west to east, **trailheads** at the southern end of the Wallowas are West Eagle (Forest Rd 77-500), Main Eagle (Forest Rd 7755), East Eagle (Forest Rd 7745), all up the Eagle Creek drainage northwest of Richland; Summit Point (Forest Rd 7715) north of Richland; Cornucopia (County Rd 413) north of Halfway; Deadman at Fish Lake and Twin Lakes (both Forest Rd 66) north of Halfway. For information, check with the Pine Ranger District, (541) 742-7511, at Halfway and consult the Wallowa-Whitman National Forest map for driving directions. The West Eagle and Main Eagle areas are managed by the La Grande Ranger District, (541) 963-7186.

Each trailhead has one or more trails that lead into Oregon's largest wilderness. The trails connect with the interior loop trail system and eventually lead out the other side. As an example of the possibilities, it's a 30-mile hike from East Eagle, through Lakes Basin, and out the north side at Wallowa Lake in the Wallowas and Hells Canyon country.

How does a hiker choose from such largesse? The only decent thing to do is to return again and again to experience all the possibilities. **West Eagle Trail** leads to Echo and Traverse Lakes in 6 miles; **Main Eagle Trail** climbs to Eagle Lake in 6.9 miles; **East Eagle Trail** is 14 miles from Lakes Basin, the most direct route among the southern trailheads; **Summit Point Trail** is 6.5 miles from Crater Lake, from where 9,555-foot **Red Mountain,** highest peak in Baker County, can be climbed via a tough 2-mile scramble to the northeast; **Cornucopia Trail** is 8.8 miles to the Wild and Scenic South Fork of the Imnaha River, but the distance may best be left to the horse traffic that frequents the trailhead; **Deadman Trail** is 3 miles from the wilderness boundary, from where a 4-mile trail leads down Deadman Canyon to Imnaha Falls; and **Twin Lakes Trail** is 3.1 miles from the Imnaha's south fork.

Hikers looking for a way out of carrying their heavy gear can hire a horse from Cornucopia Wilderness Pack Station, (541) 742-5400, or a llama from Wallowa Llamas, (541) 742-4930, in Halfway. The **horse-packing station** is based at the Cornucopia trailhead. The West Eagle trailhead has recently been improved for horses, with the addition of 5 stock campsites and holding pens or high lines. (For additional packing options, see Wallowas and Hells Canyon chapter.)

Camping

Perhaps the best way to describe camping opportunities in Baker County's 3,089 square miles, as well as adjacent lands that fit nicely into the county's package of recreation opportunities, is to begin at Anthony Lakes and proceed clockwise. Anthony Lakes would be at 11pm on the clock.

Anthony Lake Campground (see Scenic Drives and Hiking/Backpacking, above) has 37 sites, including 16 for trailers, and is busy during its short summer-fall season. **Mud Lake Campground** nearby handles the overflow with 8 campsites. The Anthony Lakes Ski Area also has some RV hookups. **Peavy Cabin,** located 10 miles down the west side of the Elkhorn Crest, is available to rent year-round from the Baker Ranger District. Plan to get there by snowmobile in winter. For information on the Anthony Lakes area, contact the Baker Ranger District, (541) 523-4476.

Skipping east across I-84 and the Powder River Valley, the southeast flank of the Wallowas looms on the horizon. Forest Rd 77 and its extension (7755) in the main Eagle Valley north of Richland (see Hiking/Backpacking, above) has small campgrounds at **Tamarack, Two Color** (the largest, with 14 sites), and **Boulder Park. Two Color Guard Station** can be rented from the La Grande Ranger District, (541) 963-7186.

Eagle Forks Campground, 9 miles northwest of Richland on Forest Rd 7735, has 12 campsites and is a designated gold-panning site. Campgrounds from here east are managed by the Pine Ranger District in Halfway, (541) 742-7511. National forest roads lead to a half-dozen small campgrounds on the south flank of the Wallowas. Largest are **McBride Campground,** with 19 sites on Forest Rd 77 north of Richland, and **Fish Lake Campground,** with 15 sites on Forest Rd 66 north of Halfway.

The Hells Canyon National Recreation Area (see Wallowas and Hells Canyon chapter) has two campgrounds in the Baker Country. **Duck Lake** (off Forest Rd 66) **and Lake Fork** (on Forest Rd 39) **Campgrounds** have a dozen spots between them and are conveniently located for a day trip on Forest Rd 3965 to the viewpoints at Hells Canyon Overlook. The road to the viewpoints leaves Forest Rd 39, the Wallowa Mountains Loop Rd, 1 mile inside the Baker County line, from where it travels north to the overlooks (see Wallowas and Hells Canyon chapter).

Campgrounds abound along the Snake River and its Powder River arm up toward Richland on Brownlee Reservoir. Richland has RV camps at Eagle Valley, (541) 893-6161, and the county's Hewitt Park, (541) 893-6147. Down on the Snake River, Idaho Power, (541) 785-3323, maintains **Woodhead Park** on Brownlee Reservoir, **McCormack Park** on Oxbow Reservoir, and **Copperfield and Hells Canyon Parks** on Hells Canyon Reservoir. Copperfield is in Oregon, but the others are in Idaho. Call (800)

422-3143 to reserve sites in Idaho Power parks, which have 309 campsites and can accommodate the handicapped.

Farewell Bend, located at the southeastern tip of Baker County, was where Oregon Trail pioneers got their last look at the Snake River before heading across the dried hills that make up the southern part of today's Baker County. **Farewell Bend State Park Campground,** (541) 869-2365, 1 mile east of I-84 at exit 353, is open year-round and takes reservations at (800) 869-2365. Popular with freeway travelers, the park is well situated on the Snake River and worth more than just a one-night stand. The park has 93 electrical hookup sites, one of which is handicapped accessible, and 45 tent camping sites. It also rents covered camper wagons and tepees for overnight use. Park recreation facilities include a boat dock, horseshoe pits, fish-cleaning station, trails to the river, and a sand volleyball court. The Birch Creek ruts of the Oregon Trail are 1.5 miles west of the Farewell Bend freeway interchange. Other Oregon Trail displays can be seen at freeway rest areas at mileposts 336 and 295.

Farewell Bend's **camper wagons** may be designed to look like the wagons that passed through the area 150 years ago, but they are probably outfitted a lot more comfortably. The wagons have two full-size beds with mattresses, a bedside table, indoor lights, a coffeepot, smoke detector, fire extinguisher, and a view of the Snake River. Guests who rent the wagons should bring their own bedding, plus a flashlight and cooking utensils. The wagons come with an outdoor picnic table, running water, and a fire ring.

Unity Reservoir is the location of a popular state park on the Burnt River, about 45 miles southwest of Baker City on Hwy 245. Unity is another one of those places that doesn't know whether it's a lake or a reservoir. The state calls its park **Unity Lake State Recreation Site,** (541) 523-2499, and it has 21 electrical hookup sites, plus a hiker/biker camp and barrier-free facilities.

Wetmore Campground (16 sites), **Oregon Campground** (11 sites), and **Yellow Pine Campground** (21 sites) are national forest camps clustered in a 2-mile stretch of US 26, about 10 miles north of Unity. Mountain Rock Wilderness south of Unity has camping at **South Fork Campground** (14 sites) on County Rd 600, 7 miles southwest of Unity. **Antlers Guard Station,** located 17 miles northwest of Unity (2 miles south of Hwy 7 at Whitney on County Rd 529), can be rented from the Unity Ranger District, (541) 446-3351. The two-room cabin sleeps four and is available year-round.

Phillips Lake, 15 miles southeast of Baker City on Hwy 7, is surrounded by campsites. **Union Creek Campground,** (541) 894-2260, on its north shore sees most of the use. Operated by a concessionaire, the national forest campground has 58 sites, 24 with full RV hookups, plus an area for tents. Fishing facilities include a boat launch, bait shop, and cleaning station. Other smaller campgrounds around Phillips Lake are **Southwest Shore and Miller's Lane Campgrounds,** both accessible by turning south from Hwy 7 onto County Rd 667 at the east end of the lake. The south shore also has some hiker/biker/boater campsites on an unroaded part of the lake (see Biking, below). Phillips Lake is part of the Baker Ranger District, (541) 523-4476.

Deer Creek Campground is a small primitive camp 4 miles north of Phillips Lake via County Rd 656 and Forest Rds 9550 and 6530. **McCully Forks** camp is 3 miles northwest of Sumpter on Forest Rd 24. Both camps are located near designated Forest Service gold-panning sites. For a look at the mining history around Sumpter, stop at **Sumpter Dredge State Park** in town. The park is open for day use.

Fishing

Some of the best warm-water fishing in Oregon is in **Brownlee Reservoir,** where the fertilizer settles from agricultural runoff upstream. The fertile mix guarantees that the reservoir's abundant supply of smallmouth bass, crappie, bluegill, and channel catfish rarely miss a meal. The most successful anglers use high-powered boats to reach the best fishing spots on the 60-mile reservoir, the largest inland fishery in Oregon at more than 14,000 acres. Boat launches are at Hewitt Park on the Powder River arm in Richland; at Swede's Landing and Spring, on the BLM's Snake River Rd; and at Farewell Bend State Park near Huntington. Swede's Landing is accessible by driving south from Richland, and Spring is easiest to reach by driving north from Huntington.

Oxbow and Hells Canyon Reservoirs provide the same kind of fish as Brownlee but not nearly in the same quantity. Oxbow is 10 miles long and Hells Canyon covers 26 miles. Road access for both is excellent. Oxbow Reservoir is accessible by driving south along the west shore of the reservoir where Hwy 86 meets the Snake River. For Hells Canyon Reservoir, cross the dam and head north along the Idaho shore. A few old sturgeon lurk in the deep holes, trapped in place by construction of the dams. Anyone hooking onto one of the old warriors must release it unharmed.

The south slope of the Wallowas has two major drainages—the federally protected Wild and Scenic **Eagle Creek,** plus **Pine Creek.** Eagle Creek has good access, either by road or trail, throughout its run in national forest land (see Hiking/Backpacking and Camping, above). The creek passes through Richland before joining the Powder River in Brownlee Reservoir. Fishing in the stream's upper reaches is good for wild and stocked rainbow trout. Pine Creek and its forks are good for wild and planted rainbow in their upper reaches. Pine Creek flows through Halfway before joining the Snake at Copperfield, where Hwy 86 meets the river.

Fish Lake attracts most lake fishermen in the southern Wallowas (see Camping, above). Fishing is good for planted rainbow and native brook trout. **Duck Lake** is 10 miles northeast of Fish Lake, just across the border into Wallowa County. Duck Lake sees a lot less fishing activity because it's a mile hike from the road. At 5,366 feet, Duck Lake is the lowest of the natural lakes in the Wallowas.

The **Powder River** begins in the mountains above Sumpter, is impounded to form Phillips Lake, flows out of Mason Dam through Baker City, and eventually ends its 140-mile journey to the Snake River near Richland where it forms an arm of Brownlee Reservoir. The **North Powder River,** its upper reaches protected in the National Wild and Scenic Rivers Program, joins the Powder River near the town of North Powder. Best fishing in the drainage is for stocked rainbow below Phillips Lake (see Camping, above), for catfish and bass in the lower river, and for native trout in the North Powder, accessible via high-clearance Forest Rd 7310 between Anthony Lakes and the town of North Powder. Phillips Lake, 2,400 acres when full, is a good fishery for stocked trout and is popular for ice fishing because of its convenient location 15 miles southwest of Baker City (see Camping, above).

The Powder River, below Phillips Lake east along Hwy 7, is also the site of a river-accessibility fishing project that provides access for the physically challenged along 2 miles of the river below Mason Dam. The project began in 1990 with placement of three boulder weirs to create pools that improve rainbow trout habitat. The project includes fishing platforms, 3 miles of paved or hardened-gravel surface trails, five bridges, sitting benches, rest rooms, information displays, and picnic and camping areas. State and federal governments have been working in partnership with local ranches, irrigation districts, and even the Powder River Correctional Facility to complete the project.

Four forks of the **Burnt River** merge at **Unity Reservoir,** 4 miles north of Unity, then flow 80 miles to join the Snake River near Huntington. The river and its tributaries have some good trout fishing west of the reservoir, while the lower river near Huntington is known for its smallmouth bass. Best fishing is early in the summer when the water is still cool. The outlet on Hwy 245 below 2,000-acre Unity Reservoir (see Camping, above) is where the largest trout lurk.

Anthony Lake, located at 7,100 feet in the Elkhorn Range, usually keeps its ice until late May. Heavily fished, the lake nevertheless provides good action for planted rainbow and native brook trout. The campground (see Camping, above) has a boat launch, but motors are not allowed. Other nearby lakes—**Van Patten, Black,** and **Crawfish**—require short hikes to reach (see Hiking/Backpacking, above).

Fishing guides in the area include Powder River Tackle, (541) 523-7143, in Baker City and Hells Canyon Anglers and Outfitters, (800) 851-8718, in Halfway. Check the state synopsis for regulations, or call the Oregon Department of Fish and Wildlife's Baker City office, (541) 523-5832.

Biking

Road-bike rides are easy to put together on the system of paved county roads and Hwy 30 from Baker City northeast to Haines and beyond. Terrain is relatively flat as the roads pass through Baker County ranch lands.

The **Oregon Trail Interpretive Center** at Flagstaff Hill (see Hiking/Backpacking, above) is an easy 6-mile ride west of Baker City, although it's a bit of a climb up to the visitors center. Bikes with fat tires can head south from the visitors center to tour **Virtue Flat** and its sage grouse lek, where male grouse battle in March for the right to mate with the females. Virtue Flat is also the site of a 6-square-mile BLM off-road vehicle play area where rest rooms are available.

The national **Bicentennial Bicycle Trail** crosses the Baker country from Brownlee Reservoir on the east to Austin Junction on the west. The route follows Hwys 86 and 7 through Baker County on its cross-country route from Virginia to Astoria.

For the extremely fit rider, one of Oregon's classic 100-mile (century) challenges is available northwest of town over the **Elkhorn Drive** back country byway (see Scenic Drives, above). The 106-mile loop is best done clockwise from Baker City, because the climb up to Anthony Lakes is a little easier from the west than from the east. Once at the crest of the Elkhorns, it's a relatively easy cruise back into town. Elevation at Baker City is 3,441 feet and the high point is 7,400 feet. Due to weather conditions, this is a ride that should be attempted only from midsummer to early fall, times when a cyclist should be in peak condition anyway.

The fat-tire crowd often heads for **Phillips Lake** southwest of Baker via Hwy 7, where bikers can choose from easy scenic tours, grueling long-distance rides, and steep hill climbs. Check with the Baker Ranger District, (541) 523-4476, at 3165 10th St in Baker City for detailed route descriptions.

Roads and trails circle Phillips Lake, but the 6-mile **South Shore Trail** is of most interest to cyclists. Elevation varies little from the lake's 4,080-foot level. The ride begins at Mason Dam, 16 miles south of Baker City on Hwy 7. Turn left on Black Mountain Rd (Forest Rd 1145) and park after .6 mile at the southeast side of the dam. Ride the trail out and back, or pick up the road at the west end of the lake and follow the north shore back to the dam. The north shore also has a singletrack accessible from Rd

300, a spur that heads south from Hwy 7. The **North Shore Trail** adds another 3 miles of singletrack to the 16-mile loop of the lake.

Indian Rock Trail provides an introduction to hill climbing. The trail begins at Union Creek Campground on Phillips Lake (see Camping, above) and heads northeast across Hwy 7, where it climbs 600 feet in 1.6 miles. **Twin Lakes Loop** is the area's ultimate hill climb, gaining 3,800 feet over 17 miles. The ride begins at Deer Creek Campground, 5 miles north of Phillips Lake. It climbs to Marble Pass, follows the Elkhorn Crest Trail north for 4.5 miles, and descends by the Twin Lake Trail.

The ultimate vehicle-shuttle tour in the Baker country is **Huckleberry Mountain–Dooley Mountain Road,** also know as **Skyline Road.** The 25-mile one-way ride begins at 4,440 feet in elevation and climbs to 6,640 feet as it crosses Dooley Mountain, the divide between the Powder and Burnt Rivers. The ride begins on Hwy 7 at Forest Rd 11, about 33 miles southwest of Baker City. The ride ends at Hwy 245, about 18 miles south of Baker City. The route follows an old four-wheel-drive track as it stays atop a ridge between Phillips Lake to the north and Unity Reservoir to the south. Much of the area burned in a 1986 forest fire.

Fish Lake Campground (see Camping, above) north of Halfway is the setting of two short loop rides. The Horse Lake tour to the southwest is a 13-mile loop of moderate difficulty as it follows the **Horse Lake, Buck's Crossing, and Fish Creek Trails.** The ride begins at 6,662 feet, climbs only 300 more feet, but drops down to 5,600 feet near Horse Lake, which is usually dry in summer. The other tour makes a 7-mile loop northwest out of the campground on **Deadman and Sugarloaf Trails.** High point of the tour is 7,487 feet at Russell Mountain Lookout.

Baker City's bike resource is Dick's Bikes and Repairs, (541) 523-7632, at 2815 E St.

Wildlife

Parts of Baker County are still rugged and wild more than 150 years after the first pioneers passed through on the Oregon Trail. Although there is plenty of wildlife, there aren't as many "guaranteed-see" locations as around La Grande. One exception, and probably the best place to see **sage grouse** within a short drive on I-84, is Virtue Flat. The sage grouse lek is located across Hwy 86 from the Oregon Trail Interpretive Center at Flagstaff Hill. Drive 7 miles east of I-84 at exit 302 and turn south on Ruckles Creek Rd .5 mile beyond the visitors center. Drive the gravel road for 2.5 miles to the first side road on the right. The lek is .5 mile down the side road in a fenced area near an old homestead and is privately owned; viewing should be done from cars. The male sage grouse display occurs in

March and April when they fight for dominance and the right to mate with the females.

Downhill Skiing

One thing skiers don't argue much about in Oregon is where to find the state's best snow conditions at a lift-served ski area. **Anthony Lakes** wins hands down. Located on the drier eastern side of the state, with a base altitude of 7,100 feet, Anthony Lakes can have powder conditions as good as anything found in Utah. In fact, one eagle-eyed Oregon skier noticed that the cover photo on a brochure for Utah's number-one destination ski resort was actually taken on Poster Ridge, an out-of-bounds area at Anthony Lakes.

Anthony Lakes once was one of the many locations investigated as the possible site for the ski resort that the Union Pacific Railroad wound up building at Sun Valley, Idaho. Its location means that the Oregon Cascades have already wrung much of the moisture out of Pacific storms, leaving the snow to fall as dry powder when the clouds are uplifted by the Elkhorn Range.

The only thing that keeps Anthony Lakes from earning a national reputation for the quality of its snow is its lack of lift facilities. It's pretty hard to brag too much when all you have to offer is an old **two-seat chairlift** that rises only 900 vertical feet. Ski-area ownership has long dreamed of building a 1,500-vertical-foot chairlift on the backside, which would probably offer the best ski terrain and conditions in Oregon. Although the new chairlift is approved conceptually, its construction hinges on development of a small base motel at the ski area that could serve as a year-round resort. Currently, **sno-cat skiing** is available on weekends (by appointment) on terrain that a new chairlift would serve.

Although it's limited, the terrain Anthony Lakes offers isn't bad. The 900 feet have some serious challenges on Rock Garden, Tumble Off, and Whale's Tale. Beginners love Broadway and Road Run, which flank either side of the ski area. A friendly word of warning is due here: With an operating schedule of Thursday through Sunday, the ski area can be blanketed deep with powder when it opens its four-day week. Be sure the outer runs have been groomed, or you may be thrashing through waist-deep snow when the runs flatten out and you begin heading back for the lift.

Anthony Lakes caters mostly to local skiers, but Portland skiers often try to work it into their itineraries (especially on Thursdays in hopes of finding fresh powder snow) when they drive by on the way to ski vacations in Sun Valley or Utah. A few Portland families even find it to be an ideal place to bring their children on weekends. They can turn the kids loose here and not give them a second thought. Although a hundred miles farther from Portland than Mount Bachelor, a weekend drive to Anthony Lakes is actually still viable because of the interstate highway access and the lack of skier traffic.

In addition to its chairlift, Anthony Lakes has a **poma lift** where it teaches beginner skiers. Food in the **day lodge,** prepared on the spot rather than being brought in bulk from town, is the best at any Oregon ski area. Anthony Lakes also grooms 13 kilometers in its **Nordic center,** with loop tours circling the lakes in the basin.

Anthony Lakes is 32 miles from Baker City and 45 miles from La Grande. North Powder, the hopping-off spot along I-84, is 22 miles east of the ski area via the Elkhorn Drive Scenic Byway (see Scenic Drives, above). The telephone number for the ski area is (541) 562-1038 and its snow report is (541) 963-4599. Flagstaff Sports, (541) 523-3477, at 1719 Main St, and Blue Mountain Sports, (541) 523-5702, at 2101 Main St, serve skiers in Baker City.

outside in

Attractions

Baker City's restful city park, old-time main street, and mature shade trees may give it a Midwestern flavor, but the backdrop is decidedly Northwest. The Baker County Historical Society maintains the **Oregon Trail Regional Museum** here, across from City Park at the corner of Campbell and Grove Sts. A stroll through **historic downtown** Baker City shows the town as a living museum. Several of the town's main buildings are more than 100 years old and, from the outside, look as though they will survive another century or two. The largest nugget of gold ever mined in Oregon is on display in the U.S. Bank branch at Baker City. Pick up a tour guide at the chamber of commerce, 490 Campbell St. If you'd rather ride than walk through town, tours are conducted by the Oregon Trail Trolley Co., (541) 856-3356. Tours meet on Campbell St across from City Park and are in a horsedrawn wheeled trolley, which makes stops at Baker City's historic district Friday through Sunday during summer.

Restaurants

Haines Steak House ☆ There's no mistaking that you're in cattle country, pilgrim. Cowbells add to the ranchlike bedlam, and we like the log booths. Stay with the beef. *910 Front St (on old Hwy 30, a short detour from I-84, exit 285 eastbound or exit 306 westbound), Haines; (541) 856-3639; $$.*

The Phone Company Restaurant Locals call it the finest restaurant in town, and we agree. The menu is small but has a few nice surprises (warm brie with Northwest apples) alongside Eastern Oregon favorites (filet mignon). *1926 1st St (at Washington), Baker City; (541) 523-7997; $$.*

Lodgings

Birchleaf Bed and Breakfast Horse pastures, peach trees, and solitude surround this pretty home tucked against the southern slopes of the Wallowas. Rooms are as simple. Stash the kids in the converted bunkhouse out back. Call ahead for winter schedule. *Rte 1, Box 91 (4´ miles north of Halfway), Halfway, OR 97834; (541) 742-2990; $.*

Geiser Grand Hotel [unrated] The restored three-story 1889 Geiser Grand Hotel is now the town's centerpiece. Restorers spent several years and $6 million to revive the historic building. Antiques and period wallpapers evoke the 19th-century grace in 30 rooms. *1996 Main St (downtown), Baker City, OR 97814; (541) 523-1889; $$.*

Cheaper Sleeps

Depot Inn Its peeled-log exterior helps this inn blend with the ambience of Sumpter, but its boxy design gives it away: it's a motel, pure and simple. Rooms are clean and nicely furnished. *179 S Mill St (PO Box 36), Sumpter, OR 97877; (541) 894-2522 or (800) 390-2522; $.*

Pine Valley Lodge A boardwalk joins the main lodge and the adjacent house; furnishings are arty and luxurious. It's cheaper if you rent a suite with a group. Budget travelers: try the Bunk House with its communal sleeping room and kitchenette ($25 per person). *163 N Main St, Halfway, OR 97834; (541) 742-2027; $.*

More Information

Baker County Visitors and Convention Bureau, Baker City: *(541) 523-3356.*
Baker Ranger District, Baker City: *(541) 523-4476.*
Bureau of Land Management, Baker City: *(541) 523-1256.*
Eastern Oregon Visitors Association, Baker City: *(800) 332-1843.*
Hells Canyon National Recreation Area, Enterprise: *(541) 426-4978.*
Huntington Chamber of Commerce, Huntington: *(541) 869-2019.*
Malheur National Forest, John Day: *(541) 575-1731.*
Pine Ranger District, Halfway: *(541) 742-7511.*
Prairie City Ranger District, Prairie City: *(541) 820-3311.*
Unity Ranger District, Unity: *(541) 446-3351.*
Wallowa-Whitman National Forest, Baker City: *(541) 523-6391.*

Pendleton Grain Belt

From the Washington state boundary on the north, east to the Umatilla-Union county line, south to the Grant County line, and west to Highway 19, including the North Fork Umatilla Wilderness, the Tower Mountain Unit of the North Fork John Day Wilderness, the Umatilla Indian Reservation, and the towns of Pendleton, Milton-Freewater, and Heppner.

The wheat fields that surround the Pendleton area give way to some welcome surprises as tilled land rises into the Blue Mountains of northeast Oregon. Not exceptionally lofty or inspiring as Western mountain ranges go, the Blue Mountains nevertheless give rise to some clear-running rivers and to this day harbor some untrammeled wilderness areas. The Blues' habitat for big game, especially mule deer and Rocky Mountain elk, is famous throughout the state.

The surprising contrast of the mountains with the wheat fields splayed out below is especially pronounced in the waning days of summer, when cowboys and rodeo fans congregate in Pendleton for the city's world-famous Pendleton Round-Up. Rodeo events are comfortably predictable because organizers have the routine down pat from three-quarters of a century of practice. The September weather is equally predictable.

The sun rises each morning in a clear sky over the Blue Mountains, with a haze from the dusty fields below coloring the soft summits with a smoky shade of blue. The stubble of the wheat fields, already harvested by early August, glistens like gold under the noonday sun. A midday cloud over Pendleton in early September is a rarity, with the threat of an afternoon thunderstorm subsiding with the heat of August. Evening brings breezes that cool the heat of an 85-degree September day.

The weather in September is about as good as it gets anytime, anywhere in the Oregon outdoors. Visitors in Pendleton to enjoy the Round-Up can take a day off to head up into the mountains, where they can hike, mountain bike, or fish in the Umatilla or Walla Walla Rivers. Backpackers can find wild canyons far away from crowds in the north forks of both the Umatilla and John Day Rivers.

The Blue Mountains that surround this Pendleton Grain Belt aren't very tall—6,800 feet max—but their ridges seem to go on forever. If there is anywhere in Oregon that resembles the Great Smoky Mountains of North Carolina and Tennessee, the Blue Mountains in the Pendleton Grain Belt are the place.

The mountains hold another surprise in winter when Oregon's weather pattern is turned on its head. Normally, clouds hang out west of the Cascades and sun rules the east, but the situation can be reversed during winter. When the east wind known as the Coho howls through the Columbia River Gorge, it scours out the clouds around Portland. But the Columbia Basin can be coated with a thick layer of ground fog stacked up against the west slopes of the Blues, all the way from Hood River to Pendleton.

The fog can be miserably cold and clammy for days on end, but the mountains can provide relief. The summit of the Blues, easily reached by automobile and by ski chairlift at Spout Springs, usually basks in the sun above the clouds that lie heavy on the wheat fields below. It's just another of the many welcome surprises in the Pendleton Grain Belt.

Getting There

Pendleton is 209 miles east of Portland on Interstate 84, the region's major east-west route. US Highway 395 (US 395) is the major north-south corridor in the area. A network of state highways connect Pendleton, the seat of Umatilla County, to the Pendleton Grain Belt's other major communities. Heppner, the seat of Morrow County, is on Highways 207 and 74, southwest of Pendleton. Milton-Freewater, the farming town just across the Oregon border from Walla Walla, Washington, is on Highway 11 northeast of Pendleton. Pendleton Municipal Airport is served by a regional airline, the only scheduled airline service in Eastern Oregon.

Adjoining Areas

NORTH: **Columbia Basin**
SOUTH: **Upper John Day River**
EAST: **La Grande and the Grande Ronde River**
WEST: **Lower John Day River**

inside out

Hiking/Backpacking

Rather than running around trying to locate ranger stations, it is probably easiest to make one stop at Umatilla National Forest headquarters in Pendleton, (541) 278-3716, at 2517 SW Hailey Ave. "Umatilla" is an Indian word meaning "water rippling over sands."

The **Walla Walla River** forks are usually the busiest trailheads because they are close to the area's population centers and most trails are open to hikers, equestrians, mountain bikers, and motorcyclists. The **South Fork Walla Walla River Trail** (difficult; 18.1 miles one way) is a popular multi-use path that begins at the Elbow Creek trailhead, 10 miles southeast of Milton-Freewater at the end of County Rd 500. Hikers who want to avoid the crowded trailhead but still want to see the Walla Walla's south fork drive up into the high country and hike down to the river on the **Burnt Cabin Trail** (moderate; 3.2 miles to the south fork). The trail begins near Tollgate, an area of varied recreation opportunity 18.5 miles east of Weston on Hwy 204. The trailhead is 3 miles north of Tollgate on Forest Rd 6401-050. Spout Springs Ski Area (see Skiing/Snowmobiling, below), 3.5 miles southeast of Tollgate, is another beginning point for access to the mountains northeast of Pendleton. **Lookingglass Trail** (easy; 2.1 miles one way) begins at Spout Springs and climbs north of Hwy 204 for views of the canyons below.

The **North Fork Umatilla Wilderness** begins just south of Spout Springs. Relatively small with 20,144 acres, the wilderness has a 27-mile trail system. Elevations range from 2,000 to 6,000 feet, so the lower trails are open early and late in the season. Umatilla Forks Campground, 33 miles east of Pendleton on County Rd 900 and Forest Rd 32, is within a mile of wilderness trailheads for Lick Creek to the north, North Fork and Ninemile Ridge to the east, and Buck Creek to the south. All are demanding hikes for anyone continuing into the high country, and hikers should carry the North Fork Umatilla Wilderness map, available at ranger stations. Ridge trails in the area start steep and level off, while creek trails are gentle before climbing steeply to the ridge above. Rewards are camping spots along cool mountain streams that harbor native trout and spawning steelhead or views of the vast system of canyons from the ridge tops.

The **South Fork Umatilla Trail** (moderate; 2.2 miles one way) begins 3 miles past Umatilla Fork Campground on Forest Rd 32 and is best in late season when stream crossings are easier.

The **Tower Mountain Unit** of the North Fork John Day Wilderness is the least used of the four units of the wilderness. Separated from the main unit by Forest Rd 52, it is surrounded by an off-highway vehicle-riding area on its other three sides. The **Upper Winom Creek Trail** and **Lookout Springs Trail** penetrate the wilderness from south to north. Both are long enough (6 to 8 miles) to get away from the noise and the heavier use of trails along the south side of the road in the Upper John Day River country. The Winom Trail begins on the north side of Forest Rd 52, .5 mile west of Winom Creek Campground and 22 miles east of Ukiah. The Lookout Springs hike begins at the end of Forest Rd 5226, a spur from the north side of Forest Rd 52 2 miles east of the campground.

Most hiking in the **Heppner Ranger District** is north of Forest Rd 21 near Madison Butte. Nearby trails are **Skookum** (moderate; 1.75 miles one way), **Alder Creek** (moderate; 3 miles one way), and **Madison Butte** (moderate; 3 miles one way). The trails connect with one another and range in elevation from 4,150 feet to 5,100 feet. The trailheads can be reached by driving south of Heppner on Hwy 207 for 26 miles to Anson Wright County Park. From the park, head east on County Rd 670, which becomes Forest Rd 22. For the Madison Butte Trail, turn left on Forest Rd 2119, follow it for 2.9 miles, and turn left on Forest Rd 21. Continue past the cattle guard and begin hiking up a dirt road on the left just before the Tupper Work Center. The other trails begin 2 miles farther east on Forest Rd 21, on Spur Rds 146 and 140.

Biking

Mountain bikers looking to explore the Pendleton Grain Belt country usually head for **Spout Springs** near Tollgate Summit, 22 miles east of Weston. The ski area's Nordic trail system was converted into a 12-mile system of bike trails before it was put up for sale (see Skiing/Snowmobiling, below). Trails remain useable, although they won't be maintained as they were when the ski area was operating. The **Lookout Grade Trail** climbs 450 feet from the parking lot on the north side of Hwy 204 to the fire lookout and has several loop riding opportunities. The **Stagecoach Trail** loops west of the downhill ski runs, which remain off-limits to biking.

Bikers who can arrange a car shuttle can make use of the 18.1-mile-long **South Fork Walla Walla River Trail**, which begins near Deduct Springs in Washington across the Oregon state line, about 25 miles up Walla River Rd from Walla Walla on County Rd 582 and Forest Rd 65. The trail begins at 5,000 feet and drops to 2,143 feet at Elbow Creek trailhead (see Hiking/Backpacking, above). The lower trailhead was recently reconstructed under a state and federal partnership and has loading ramps for horses and off-road vehicles, barrier-free facilities, and rest rooms. Note that the Elbow Creek trailhead is busy with motorcycles on summer weekends and horses during elk-hunting season. **Rough Fork Trail,** a 3.2-mile trail that connects to the South Fork Trail, begins 15 miles northeast of Tollgate at Moffet Campground on Forest Rd 6403 and provides an alternate starting point without having to leave Oregon.

The Heppner Ranger District has some riding opportunities on its network of timber-sale roads. While exploring the area, cyclists shouldn't miss the **Copple Butte Trail,** a 6.25-mile singletrack that begins at 5,100 feet and climbs to 5,280 feet near the summit of Madison Butte. The gentle climb makes it a good ride for beginners, but the trail still isn't easy. To find it, take Willow Creek Rd south of Heppner for 23 miles to Forest Rd 21. Turn right, drive 3 miles to Ditch Creek Guard Station, and turn right again on Rd 050. Continue driving to the road closure sign at a corral, then hop aboard your bike and ride 1.25 miles across Martin Prairie to Texas Rd 5350. Cross the road and follow an old timber-sale road to a wooden gate where the trail begins. The trail follows a ridge top most of the way and has views of Mounts Hood and Jefferson as it passes Copple, Texas, and Madison Buttes. Like Hansel and Gretel, you might want to leave bread crumbs to mark your way back to your car.

Road-riding opportunities are limited only by the number and size of the hills you feel like climbing. The paved network of county roads north of Pendleton, around **Helix** and **Holdman,** isn't too hilly. Morning rides are a delight as the wheat changes from green in spring to gold during the late July harvest. Check with the Pedaler's Palace, (541) 276-3337, at 318 S Main in Pendleton for other places to ride.

Camping

Travelers on I-84 between Pendleton and La Grande have a convenient place to camp at **Emigrant Springs State Heritage Area Campground,** (541) 983-2277, located at Meacham near the summit of the Blue Mountains 26 miles southeast of Pendleton. The park, along the Oregon Trail where emigrants camped for several days to graze their livestock and refill their water barrels from a spring, is at exit 234 of I-84. The campground is open mid-April through October. It does not accept reservations for campsites but does accept them for two covered camper wagons and the Totem Cabin. The campground has 33 tent sites and 18 sites for trailers with full hookups. The covered camper wagons are designed to look like the Conestoga wagons of pioneer days. Totem Cabin is available year-round and can be reserved by calling (800) 452-5687. The first wave of migrants, about a thousand strong, passed by Emigrant Springs in 1843. A monument was erected to mark the 80th anniversary in 1923, and President Warren Harding was on hand for the dedication.

The **Oregon Trail** continues to be an attraction through the Pendleton Grain Belt as it leaves Emigrant Springs, descends the west side of the Blue Mountains, and heads toward the Columbia River. The **Echo Trail Sites,** located 1.3 miles south of I-84 at exit 188, has eight Oregon Trail sites or markers along a 7-mile corridor. Campers wishing to explore the area can spend the night at **Fort Henrietta Park,** (541) 376-8411, along the Umatilla River at the edge of the town of Echo. The park has tent and RV camping within a block's walk of groceries and a restaurant. The main feature of the Echo area is a 1-mile-long set of trail ruts 5.5 miles west of town. The ruts are located on 320 acres of public land administered by the Bureau of Land Management (BLM). A .5-mile trail leads to an overlook. County museums with Oregon Trail memorabilia can be found in the Pendleton Grain Belt country at Pendleton and Heppner.

The Forest Service's **Blue Mountains Scenic Byway** begins 40 miles west of Echo at Heppner Junction, exit 147 on I-84. The byway heads southeast 130 miles, passing between Heppner and Ukiah as Forest Rd 53. East of Ukiah, it becomes Forest Rd 52, passes the Tower Mountain Unit of the North Fork John Day Wilderness (see Hiking/Backpacking, above), and joins Elkhorn Drive Scenic Byway (see Baker County chapter). In addition to unlimited dispersed camping opportunities, the Umatilla National Forest has three campgrounds within a few miles of the Blue Mountains Byway—**Penland Lake Campground,** 26 miles east of Heppner and 4 miles south of the byway on Forest Rds 21 and 2103, and, southeast of Ukiah on Forest Rd 52, **Winom Creek Campground** (22 miles) and **North Fork John Day Campground** (36 miles). Other campgrounds east of Ukiah are **Bear Wallow Creek Campground** (10 miles) and **Frazier Campground** (16 miles), both off Hwy 244. Bear Wallow Creek has a mile-long barrier-free interpretive trail. Frazier is the largest campground, with 32 sites, while the others have less than a dozen. Penland Lake is within the Heppner Ranger District, (541) 676-9187, and the others are managed by the North Fork John Day Ranger District, (541) 427-3231, in Ukiah.

Morrow County Public Works Department, (541) 989-9500, operates **Cutsforth Park Campground,** a popular camp 20 miles southeast of Heppner on County Rd 678 where the Blue Mountains Byway reaches the west edge of Umatilla National Forest. The full-service campground has 42 sites, some with hookups, and showers.

The community of Dale on Hwy 395 is surrounded by camping opportunities. The North Fork John Day Ranger District has 42 sites at **Gold Dredge Campground,** 7 miles east of Dale on Forest Rd 5506; 4 sites at **Lane Creek Campground,** 9 miles east on Hwy 244; 5 sites at **Oriental Creek Campground,** 12 miles east on Forest Rd 5506; and 7 sites at **Tollbridge Campground,** .5 mile east of Hwy 395 just north of Dale on Forest Rd 56.

The **Ukiah-Dale State Scenic Corridor,** (541) 523-2499, has a campground with 27 primitive sites 3 miles south of Ukiah on US 395.

Campers bound for the Heppner Ranger District, (541) 676-9187, south of Heppner usually wind up at **Bull Prairie Lake Campground,** 34 miles south of Heppner on Hwy 207 and 2 miles east on Forest Rd 2039. The campground has 26 campsites and 40 picnic sites. The lake is popular for boating and fishing and is circled by a .5-mile trail. Morrow County's **Anson Wright Memorial Park,** (541) 989-9500, is 26 miles south of Heppner on Hwy 207. The full-service campground includes 44 sites, some with hookups, and showers.

The North Fork Umatilla Wilderness is close to a half-dozen campgrounds in the Tollgate area, 40 miles northeast of Pendleton in the Walla Walla Ranger District, (509) 522-6290. **Jubilee Lake Campground,** 12 miles northeast of Tollgate on Forest Rd 64, is the largest, with 51 sites. **Target Meadow Campground,** 2 miles north of Tollgate on Forest Rd 6401, has 20 sites. **Moffet, Umatilla Forks, Woodward, and Woodland Campgrounds** are all smaller than 20 sites, but their positioning means campers are never far from a place to pitch a tent. Moffet is 14 miles northeast of Tollgate on Forest Rd 64 and 6403; Umatilla Forks is 33 miles east of Pendleton on Forest Rd 32; Woodward is 18 miles east of Weston on Hwy 204; and Woodland is 23 miles east of Weston on Hwy 204.

Other overnight opportunities in the area are **Summit Guard Station** and **Goodman Ridge Lookout,** Forest Service facilities in the mountains east of the state park at Emigrant Springs. Both are available to rent year-round, although their distance from plowed roads limits winter access to snowmobiles. Both are available through the Walla Walla Ranger District, (509) 522-6290.

A popular resort in Umatilla County is **Lehman Hot Springs,** (541) 427-3015. Located at milepost 17 on Hwy 244 east of Ukiah, the resort has a 9,000-square-foot natural hot mineral pool, plus a dozen cabins, RV camping, and tent camping and a large meeting hall that can be used by groups as a sleeping dorm. Lehman Hot Springs also rents mountain bikes in summer and has ski and snowmobile trails during winter.

Fishing

Pendleton anglers don't need to travel far for good fishing, with the **Umatilla River** running right through town. The river is productive for steelhead, salmon, and trout. Steelhead can be fished only below the Hwy 11 bridge in town and wild fish must be released. Fishing is usually best from October through March for the steelhead. Native chinook runs became extinct in the 1920s, but chinook were reintroduced in the 1980s and occasionally return in numbers. Fishing above Pendleton is best for wild rainbow trout, but a tribal permit (available at local tackle shops and reservation headquarters) is required to fish on the Umatilla Indian Reservation. The Umatilla River has roads along much of its length as it runs west to join the Columbia River at the town of Umatilla. Downstream roads follow the Echo Trail Sites (see Camping, above), while the road network reaches 33 miles upriver of Pendleton to the Umatilla Forks Campground (see Hiking/Backpacking, above). Boaters should become acquainted with the river to avoid running over several dangerous irrigation diversion dams. For current information, check with Pendleton's Blue Mountain Sports, (541) 276-2269, 221 Main St.

Anglers heading into the high country at Tollgate usually travel 12 miles to **Jubilee Lake** in Union County (see Camping, above). A 97-acre reservoir with a boat ramp, campground, and 2.6-mile trail around it, the lake is popular with families because of its convenient access. The lake is stocked annually with rainbow trout and is restricted to boats with electric motors. Canoes and kayaks are also used to access the lake's deepest holes.

An interesting place to visit near Jubilee Lake is the **Big Sink,** a geological formation that looks like a large piece of earth that sank into the ground. Accessible by foot from Forest Rd 63, the sink is 3 miles south of the lake. To add to the mystery of the location, compasses do not always work correctly in the area, causing fits for hikers and hunters. **Jarboe Creek** is 5 miles east of the sink (via Forest Rds 63, 62, and 6236) and has some deep pools that harbor rainbow trout and dolly varden.

Roads that head up out of the wheat fields that surround Heppner lead to some good fishing spots in a quiet part of the state. The 110-acre **Willow Creek Reservoir** sits right on the south edge of town at 1,900 feet in elevation. Fishing is good for largemouth bass, black crappie, and pumpkinseed. Fishermen are encouraged to release bass so that the populations of the other fish are kept in check and the reservoir maintains its balance. Willow Creek flows into the reservoir from Umatilla National Forest, where anglers fish for rainbow trout near Cutsforth Park (see Camping, above).

Penland Lake (see Camping, above) is a 67-acre lake that was built by private landowners but is open to the public for fishing. The lake, situated at 4,950 feet, is stocked with bluegill and rainbow trout, and the fish bite with relish in the mornings and evenings. Access can be difficult over the 2 miles of Forest Rd 2103, so wait until the road's surface dries out for the summer before trying. **Ditch Creek Guard Station** is 2 miles west of Penland Lake on Forest Rd 21 and has some good fishing for brook and rainbow trout in a nearby pond. Penland Lake drains to the south through **Mallory Creek,** where anglers locate some hungry trout near Mallory

Spring at 4,700 feet. The spring is 3 miles southeast of the guard station via Forest Rds 2104 and 2105.

Bull Prairie Lake (see Camping, above) is a 27-acre reservoir set at 4,000 feet. The lake is stocked with bluegill, brook trout, and rainbow trout.

Travelers along US 395 between Ukiah and Dale can try their luck in **Camas Creek,** a 38-mile-long tributary of the North Fork John Day River. A few steelhead and chinook make their way up the creek, but most action is planted rainbow trout. The creek is heavily fished because of its easy access from the highway. Timber rattlesnakes are common in the area.

Check the state synopsis for regulations, or call the Oregon Department of Fish and Wildife's Pendleton office, (541) 276-2344.

Wildlife

The Wildhorse Creek area, a short drive northeast of Pendleton, has some rare **northern bobwhite,** an introduced game bird species that was planted a century ago near Walla Walla, Washington. From Pendleton's northeast side, follow Hwy 11 toward Milton-Freewater and turn north on Wildhorse Rd .5 mile after the bridge over the Umatilla River. Follow Wildhorse Rd for 6.5 miles, turn right, and return to Hwy 11 for a 20-mile loop from Pendleton. Summer evenings are the best time to make the drive.

The McKay Creek National Wildlife Refuge, (541) 922-3232, 8 miles south of Pendleton on the east side of US 395, is home to **migrating waterfowl, shorebirds, small mammals,** and the **raptors** that feed on them. A popular spot for canoeing, the 1,837-acre refuge has a water surface that varies in size from 1,300 to 250 acres, depending on the irrigation season. The refuge's northern section is open to the public from March 1 through September 30. The southern half remains open until the last day of the state waterfowl hunting season.

The Bridge Creek State Wildlife Area, (541) 276-2344, is managed as a winter range for **Rocky Mountain elk.** More than 1,000 elk congregate during winter to avoid snow at higher elevations. The area is 47 miles south of Pendleton on US 395. Turn east on County Rd 244 and drive 1 mile to Ukiah. At the town store, turn south on Forest Rd 52 and drive 4.2 miles to the entrance. The **Ron Bridges Memorial Trail,** a .13 mile path to a viewpoint, is 1 mile beyond the entrance. The wildlife area is open to the public by permit (available from the headquarters) from December 1 to May 1, but the trail is open all year.

Skiing/Snowmobiling

With the future of **Spout Springs Ski Area** in doubt, downhill skiers from Pendleton must travel to Anthony Lakes (see Baker County chapter) or to

Bluewood, south of Dayton, Washington. Spout Springs was put up for sale in 1997, but there were no takers and the ski area sat idle the following winter. Spout Springs has only a 550-foot vertical rise from its base at 5,000 feet, and a succession of owners have found recent winters to be fickle. Facilities include one chairlift and one T-bar that reach the summit, plus another chairlift and rope tow that cater to beginners lower down. Check with the Walla Walla Ranger District, (541) 522-6290, to see whether Spout Springs is operating.

The ski area used to groom a 21-kilometer cross-country trail system that climbs to the summit on the **Lookout Grade Trail.** The trails are still there, but they are no longer groomed and not maintained during the summer.

The Tollgate Summit area is lined with 10 Oregon state sno-parks, all along Hwy 204. They begin on the west at **Tollgate Sno-Park,** 18.5 miles east of Weston, and continue to **Milepost 27 Sno-Park** on the east, 8.5 miles from Tollgate. Sno-parks between the two and their distances east of Tollgate are **Langdon Lake** and **Milepost 20** (both 1 mile); **Morning Creek** (2 miles); **Spout Springs** and **Milepost 22** (both 3.5 miles); **Woodland** (5.5 miles); **Horseshoe Prairie** (7.5 miles); and **Andies Prairie** (8 miles).

Snowmobile use is heavy at most of the sno-parks. The Horseshoe Prairie Sno-Park, 7.5 miles east of Tollgate, has 7 miles of marked trails for skiers. The Andies Prairie Sno-Park, 8 miles east of Tollgate, has areas designated for sledding and winter camping. For information, check with Umatilla National Forest headquarters in Pendleton, (541) 278-3716.

South of Pendleton, **Four Corners Sno-Park** is 20 miles east of Ukiah on Hwy 244 near Lehman Hot Springs Resort (see Camping, above).

Ski resources in Pendleton are Blue Mountain Sports, (541) 276-2269, 221 Main St, and the Pedaler's Palace Cycle and Ski Shop, (541) 276-3337, 318 S Main.

outside in

Attractions

In these parts, the name of the town of **Pendleton** is synonymous with the Wild West. Each September the **Pendleton Round-Up** rolls around—a big event ever since 1910 that features a dandy rodeo. Call (800) 457-6336 for tickets and information.

Hamley's and Company has been selling Western clothing, boots, hats, tack items, and custom-made saddles since 1883. It's a kind of shrine, the L.L. Bean of the West; 30 SE Court St, (541) 276-2321. **Pendleton Woolen Mills** gives tours Monday through Friday and sells woolen yardage and imperfect versions of its famous blankets at reduced prices; 1307 SE Court Pl, (541) 276-6911, penwoolmil@aol.com, www.pendleton-usa.com.

Pendleton Underground Tours provides a 90-minute walk through Pendleton's history—most of it underground—to view the remains of businesses that date back to the turn of the century: bordellos, opium dens, and Chinese jails. Reservations are necessary and should be made at least 24 hours in advance; 37 SW Emigrant Ave, (541) 276-0730. Price is $10 per adult.

After a long struggle for funding, the Umatilla tribe opens in late 1998 the $13 million **Tamustalik** (pronounced ta-MUST-ah-luck) **Cultural Institute** on 640 acres behind the Wildhorse Gaming Resort. For the first time ever, the institute will tell the story of the Oregon Trail—one of the greatest mass migrations in human history, which had an indelible impact on the Indians of the West—from the Indian point of view. Located 5 miles from town via exit 216 from I-84, the Wildhorse Gaming Resort (which has a golf course and an overpriced bare-bones hotel) can be reached at (800) 654-9453.

Restaurants

The Echo Hotel Restaurant and Lounge ☆ This place has a cedar-shake interior, a bar, dining area, and three blackjack tables. Primarily a whiskey-and-ribs spot, the Echo is getting more and more attention for its seafood and Northwest wines. *110 Main St (20 miles west of Pendleton on I-84), Echo; (541) 376-8354; $.*

The Oasis Eavesdrop on the cowboys swapping stories in this 1920s Western roadhouse. Steaks are gigantic, and a breakfast biscuits-and-gravy platter goes for just over $2. *Old Milton-Freewater Hwy and State Line Rd, Milton-Freewater; (541) 938-4776; $.*

Raphael's Restaurant and Lounge ☆☆ Visit the authentic Native American art gallery while waiting for your table. The emphasis here is more on flavor than on presentation, and some of that flavor is incredible. Wild game is featured during hunting months. *233 SE 4th (Court and Dorion), Pendleton; (541) 276-8500; $$.*

Lodgings

Indian Hills Motor Inn This is the most lavish motel in Pendleton, with pool, lounge, and outsized, gaudy Western bas-reliefs in the reception areas. The view over low mountains and fields can be inspiring. *304 SE Nye Ave (exit 210 off I-84), Pendleton; PO Box 1556, Pendleton, OR 97801; (541) 276-6111; $$.*

Parker House ☆☆ This magnificent home with its ballroom and English garden seems out of place in Eastern Oregon, but somehow the clash is welcome. Five rooms sport fresh flowers and thick robes in one of the classier stays this side of the Cascades. *311 N Main St (north on Hwy 11, follow City Center signs to downtown, head north on Main, cross Umatilla River to N Main), Pendleton, OR 97801; (541) 276-8581 or (800) 700-8581; $$.*

The Working Girl's Hotel This nonprofit hotel gets its name from its former incarnation as a bordello. Five rooms are furnished with antiques and share a bath—but that's a small price to pay for such a fun night's stay. Young children are discouraged. *17 SW Emigrant Ave (between Main and SW 1st), Pendleton, OR 97801; (541) 276-0730 or (800) 226-6398; $.*

More Information

Bureau of Land Management, Baker City: *(541) 523-1256.*
Eastern Oregon Visitors Association, Baker City: *(800) 332-1843.*
Heppner Chamber of Commerce, Heppner: *(541) 676-5536.*
Heppner Ranger District, Heppner: *(541) 676-9187.*
La Grande Ranger District, La Grande: *(541) 963-7186.*
North Fork John Day Ranger District, Ukiah: *(541) 427-3231.*
Pendleton Chamber of Commerce, Pendleton: *(800) 547-8911.*
Umatilla National Forest, Pendleton: *(541) 278-3716.*
Walla Walla Ranger District, Walla Walla, Washington:
    (509) 522-6290.
Wallowa-Whitman National Forest, Baker City: *(541) 523-6391.*

Upper John Day River

From Grant County's northern boundary, east to the Elkhorn Mountains near the Baker County line, south into the Malheur National Forest, and west to the South Fork of the John Day River, including the Strawberry Mountain and the North Fork John Day Wildernesses, the Sheep Rock Unit of the John Day Fossil Beds National Monument, and the towns of John Day, Canyon City, Prairie City, Mount Vernon, and Dayville.

The wide-open spaces of the Upper John Day River country make a city slicker want to get on a horse and ride. But before any erstwhile cowboys get carried away, remember that horses are a lot more savvy about how things are done here on the open range than are the beings of supposedly superior intelligence in the saddle.

Here's a tale of an urban cowboy from Portland, who thought he was doing a darn good job herding cattle at one of those ranches that charge big bucks to tourists for the privilege of performing ranch work. The first day of work had gone without a hitch, except for a forced occupation of a ramshackle settler's cabin when visibility dropped to 15 feet during a mid-May snow squall.

Fast-forward to day two and a fenced pasture in the Silvies Valley, 35 miles south of John Day. Ranch hands were moving cattle between pastures and some city dudes were helping out. Puffy clouds dappled the blue sky with white, like colors on a pinto pony.

The real cowboys, the ones who get paid to do ranch work, were cutting and sorting cattle when a momma cow decided she didn't want any part of the action. She followed her calf's lead and bolted for freedom, a step behind the quick-footed calf. The challenge was irresistible to the urban cowboy, who tickled his horse's ribs and flew off in hot pursuit of the fleeing pair.

The cow, knowing she couldn't outrun a horse, suddenly turned around to rejoin the herd. When the calf noticed her defection, the little one's heart dropped out of its escape attempt and it, too, abruptly turned around.

So did the horse.

Caught unaware, the urban cowboy rocked back in the saddle, the heels of his boots coming forward into the horse's ribs. That caused the horse to buck, which sent the urban cowboy farther backward. In fact, he flipped over the back of the horse, just missing the horse's flying feet. Fortunately, the landing was on fairly soft soil, not on the rocks, sagebrush, or barbed-wire fence that cover the area.

Sheepish and chastened, the urban cowboy climbed back aboard and rode back to the ranch, not once admitting to the pain. The ranch hands and other paying guests all had a laugh, and the damage didn't seem to be too serious—except for stabs of pain from bruised ribs after every deep breath and sneeze during the next two months.

The urban cowboy from Portland can't wait to return to the beautiful Western landscape of Grant County's Upper John Day River country. But the next time I visit, I'll go there to hike, camp, and raft and will leave the cattle herding to the real cowboys.

Getting There

John Day, the largest town in Grant County, with a population of 1,900, is 264 miles southeast of Portland via US Highway 26 (US 26), the major east-west corridor in this area. John Day is 127 miles south of Interstate 84 at Pendleton via US 395, the region's major north-south corridor. National forest, state, and county roads cover much of Grant County, tying John Day to other communities—Long Creek, Dayville, Monument, Mount Vernon, Prairie City, and Seneca.

Adjoining Areas

NORTH: **Pendleton Grain Belt, La Grande and the Grande Ronde River**

SOUTH: **Harney County**

EAST: **Baker County, Malheur County**

WEST: **Crooked River, Lower John Day River**

Hiking/Backpacking

North Fork John Day Wilderness

Four units comprise the 121,800 acres of the North Fork John Day Wilderness—the main North Fork Unit, the southern Greenhorn Unit, the northern Tower Mountain Unit (see Pendleton Grain Belt chapter), and the eastern Baldy Creek Unit (see Baker County chapter). Units in the Upper John Day River country are part of the North Fork John Day Ranger District in Ukiah, (541) 427-3231. The John Day River was named for John Day, a member of the Pacific Fur Company who visited the Northwest in 1812.

The **North Fork Unit** features a 25-mile trail along the river through the heart of the wilderness. Most day use begins in the east at North Fork Campground off Granite Creek Rd (Forest Rd 52), or in the west at the end of Forest Rd 5506. Backpack trips across the wilderness require a car shuttle. Several trails from the high country down into the North Fork canyon make good weekend backpack trips. The best trails, with one-way distances to the canyon floor, are **Crane Creek Trail** (difficult; 5.1 miles, 1,100-foot drop) from Forest Rd 73 to the east and **Lake Creek Trail** (difficult; 4.9 miles, 2,200-foot drop) from the south via Forest Rds 10 and 1010-350. Maps for Umatilla National Forest and the North Fork John Day River Wilderness can be purchased at ranger stations.

The **Greenhorn Unit** lies northwest of the community of Greenhorn, an old mining boom town that still has a few summer residents. The best access into the wilderness is from Olive Lake Campground, 12 miles west of Granite, another old mining town, on Forest Rd 10. Granite is 15 miles northwest of Sumpter on Forest Rd 73, the Elkhorn Drive Scenic Byway (see Baker County chapter). The trail begins at 6,700 feet in elevation. It heads 5 miles south from the campground to Dupratt Springs, from where the 7,720-foot summit of Ben Harrison Peak is a .5-mile scramble to the east.

Long Creek Ranger District

The highlight of Malheur National Forest's Long Creek Ranger District, (541) 575-3000, is the **Vinegar Hill–Indian Rocks Scenic Area,** which is shared with Umatilla National Forest. Vinegar Hill is an area of scenic rock outcrops and has an outstanding view from the **Indian Rock lookout.** Much of the area was burned during a 1995 wildfire. The Long Creek and Bear Valley Ranger Stations are both in John Day, where Malheur National Forest headquarters, (541) 575-1731, provides a centralized information service at 139 NE Dayton St.

The Vinegar Hill trail system, with one-way distances, includes **Squaw Rock** (difficult; 11 miles), **Blackeye** (moderate, 2.6 miles), **Sunrise Butte** (moderate; 3 miles), and **Tempest Mine** (moderate; 3.5 miles). The scenic area is 20 miles north of Prairie City, and its trailheads can be reached from north of County Rd 20, which runs northwest from Austin Junction. The trailheads are labeled on the Malheur National Forest map, which is necessary for negotiating the high-clearance-vehicle roads that access the trails. Squaw Rock on the northwest is close to Indian Rock, while Tempest Mine on the east is near Vinegar Hill.

Magone Lake, 10 air miles north of John Day, has 2 miles of trail and is near the **Arch Rock National Scenic Trail** (easy; .4 mile one way), an area of geologic interest, and **Nipple Butte** (intermediate; 3.1 miles one way), known for its views from the 6,156-foot summit. To reach the area, drive US 26 east from John Day for 9 miles and turn north on County Rd 18. The turnoff for Magone Lake is 11 miles up Rd 18 and Nipple Butte is 2 miles beyond.

On the east end of the Long Creek district, the **Davis Creek Trail** (difficult; 9.1 miles one way) covers much of the country north of 7,592-foot **Dixie Butte,** which has a road to the summit. Dixie Butte is 5 miles north of US 26 at Dixie Summit on Forest Rd 2610 (high-clearance vehicles). The turn is 8 miles northeast of Prairie City. The Davis Creek Trail is 6 miles farther east on US 26 near Austin Junction, 2 miles west of the highway on Forest Rd 2614.

Across US 26 from Dixie Butte in the Prairie City Ranger District, (541) 820-3311, is the **Sumpter Valley Railway Interpretive Trail,** a .2-mile paved path with six stations that describe the history of the railroad in the John Day River Valley. Called the Stump Dodger, the railroad climbed out of the John Day Valley in switchbacks over the Dixie Summit as it made its way east to Baker City. The railroad is no longer active.

Strawberry Mountains

The only busy trailhead in the **Strawberry Mountain Wilderness** begins at Strawberry Campground (see Camping, below) at the end of County Rd 60, 10 miles south of Prairie City. The Strawberry Mountains are split east and west by the Prairie City and Bear Valley Ranger Districts. For information and to purchase the Strawberry Mountain Wilderness map, stop at Malheur National Forest headquarters at 139 NE Dayton, in John Day.

The most popular day hike is **Strawberry Basin Trail** (moderate; 5.1 miles one way to the ridge top beneath Strawberry Mountain's summit). Strawberry Lake is 1.2 miles from the trailhead and 40-foot Strawberry Falls is another 1.1 miles. The summit of Strawberry Mountain is a 6-mile, one-way hike from the campground, with a gain of 3,300 feet. This climb from the north is more strenuous than the route from the south (see Onion Creek Trail, below), but it's still the busiest route to the summit because of the easy access from Prairie City. The **Rabbit Ears** rock formation, on the ridge above Little Strawberry Lake east of Strawberry Mountain, provides some technical scrambling opportunities.

Lookout Mountain, 8,033 feet high, is the main hiking destination east of the Strawberry Mountain Wilderness. The mountain looms east of County Rd 62, 15 miles southeast of Prairie City and US 26. Hikers have a choice of four trails that converge on the mountain like spokes of a wheel. All gain about 2,000 feet and are considered difficult (mileages here are one way). **Sunshine Flat Trail** (3.7 miles) approaches from the northwest and **Starvation Trail** (2.1 miles) from the south, both from spur roads off County Rd 62, while **Horseshoe Trail** (6 miles) approaches from the northeast and **Sheep Creek Trail** (5.7 miles) from the east, both from Forest Rd 13. The trailheads are shown on the Malheur National Forest map.

Continuing south, forest roads lead to a pair of trails along forks of the Malheur River outside the wilderness. The **North Fork Malheur Trail** (intermediate; 12.2 miles one way) and the **Malheur River National Scenic Trail** (moderate; 8 miles one way) lead through remote canyons that harbor abundant wildlife. Don't be surprised if you spot elk or antelope. To reach the North Fork trailhead, drive County Rd 62 for 22 miles southeast of Prairie City to the junction with Forest Rd 16 in Summit Prairie. Turn east and drive 15 miles to Forest Rd 1675. Turn south and drive 3 miles to the end of the road. The trail ends where it leaves the national forest boundary, so it has no southern trailhead. For the Malheur River Trail, drive 3 miles west of Summit Prairie, turn south, and drive 7 miles on Forest Rd 1651 to the trailhead.

The 68,700 acres of the Strawberry Mountain Wilderness are most frequently approached from the north, so trails that enter from other directions are liable to be lonely. **Skyline Trail** (difficult; 19.3 miles one way) runs from the wilderness's southeast boundary up into the Lakes Basin at **Slide Lake** before leaving the wilderness at the south side's High Lakes Rim trailhead. If you want to keep going, connecting trails continue to the northeast side of the wilderness for a 42-mile one-way walk. Be sure to have a vehicle waiting and bring along the wilderness map.

Forest Rd 1640 climbs from Forest Rd 16 in the Logan Valley to reach two trailheads at the south-center of the wilderness—**High Lakes Rim** and **Roads End.** The easiest route to the summit of 9,038-foot **Strawberry Mountain,** the highest point in Grant County, is to follow the **Pine and Onion Creek Trails** north for 4.1 miles from the High Lakes Rim trailhead. Elevation gain is a relatively easy 1,100 feet to reach the mountain's summit.

The most accessible day hike from the town of John Day is the **Canyon Mountain Trail** (difficult; 15 miles to the crest). Most hikers walk only the first few miles for the impressive views of the John Day Valley. To find the trailhead, drive south on US 395 to Canyon City, turn east on Main St, and drive 4.5 miles southeast on County Rd 52 and 77.

Aldrich Mountains

The Aldrich Mountains cover nearly 100 square miles, most of it relatively undisturbed, west of the Strawberry Mountains and east of the South Fork of the John Day River. Elevations range from 2,649 feet at the river to 7,363 feet on **Fields Peak.** The area is divided in half by Forest Rd 21, which heads south from US 26 midway between Dayville and Mount Vernon. After Forest Rd 21 crosses the summit of the Aldrich Range, it descends to the south into the beautiful **Murderers Creek Valley.** An area of lush, well-watered meadows, the valley provides some of the best big-game habitat in the state. Murderers Creek acquired its name in the 1860s when Indians killed eight prospectors who were exploring for gold. The area is in the Bear Valley Ranger District, but it's best to call Malheur National Forest headquarters, (541) 575-1731, in John Day for information.

The west half of the Aldrich Mountains is dominated by 6,991-foot **Aldrich Mountain,** which has a road to the summit. A main area of interest is the **Cedar Grove Botanical Area,** a small grove of Alaska cedars that is located more than 100 miles from other similar stands. The **Cedar Grove National Scenic Trail** (easy; 1 mile one way) leads to the 60-acre grove. Drive Forest Rd 21 for 9 miles south of US 26 and turn west on Forest Rd 2150. Cedar Grove is 6 miles away and the summit is 14.

One of the best high-mountain rambles in the Upper John Day country is on the east side of the Aldrich Mountains, between the **McClellan Mountain Trail** to the west and the **Riley Mountain Trail** to the east. A 10.5-mile trail connects the two trailheads, with an opportunity for plenty of high-ridge walking off-trail above timberline between five connected peaks, each above 7,000 feet.

To reach the McClellan trailhead, which was constructed in 1995, drive 8.6 miles south of US 26 on Fields Creek Rd (Forest Rd 21) and turn east on Rd 2160-115. At a junction in .4 mile, turn right onto Rd 2160, take the first available left, and continue to the trailhead at the end of the road. The road is engineered for passenger cars. Hike up an abandoned road east of the trailhead to a saddle where the trail splits. The left fork continues to Fields Peak; the right fork reaches a grassy saddle in 2.5 miles, just below the center of five peaks along the ridge. Hike to the top and go as far as you want in either direction. It's a 3-mile one-way hike to Fields Peak on the left fork, with a gain of 2,000 feet. The Forest Service says hunting season is the busiest time of year at Fields Peak when one party visits every three weeks. The Aldrich Mountains provide some of Oregon's best high-ridge walking with little chance of seeing other hikers. The Riley Creek trailhead to Riley Mountain is at the end of Forest Rd 2190, a northern spur of Forest Rd 21 as it travels through Murderers Creek Valley.

John Day Fossil Beds National Monument

If you only have one day to spend hiking in the Upper John Day River country, it may as well be spent in the **Sheep Rock Unit** of the John Day Fossil Beds National Monument, (541) 987-2333. The park is located 7 miles west of Dayville near the junction of US 26 and Hwy 19. Stop at the park museum to learn something about the geology before driving north 3 miles to the Blue Basin area.

The **Blue Basin Overlook Trail** (moderate; 4-mile loop) ends at a vista high above the Blue Basin, an area of soft clay that is carved into many unusual formations. The trail gains 700 feet. The **Island in Time Trail** (easy; .6 mile one way) leads into the scenic amphitheater that the other trail circles. Displays along the trail show replicas of fossils as they occur naturally in the rocks. The monument is in an area of active research, so don't assume that anyone digging is necessarily a vandal. Only collectors with a permit can dig for fossils or collect rocks or other artifacts.

The John Day formation spans 20 million years and was laid down 100 million years ago at **Goose Rock,** a series of cliffs along the east side of Hwy 19 just south of the Blue Basin area. The **Foree area** north of Blue Basin has two short trails that offer views of the formations, as well as a picnic area. Foot access to the John Day River is provided at several points along the highway, but be careful not to cross private land. Fishing is allowed in the national monument with an Oregon license under state regulations.

Camping

It only takes a few words to describe the campgrounds in the Upper John Day River country—small and lots of them. And that's precisely the way people who take the time to seek out the recreation opportunities here like them.

Beginning in the north, the North Fork Ranger District, (541) 427-3231, has several campgrounds around Dale (see Pendleton Grain Belt chapter), plus others that are farther afield. **Olive Lake Campground,** 24 miles southeast of Dale (see Hiking/Backpacking, above), has only 3 tent spots, even though it's the largest lake in the Upper John Day River country. The campground is scheduled to be expanded. **North Fork Campground,** a popular starting point from the east for hikes into the John Day River's north fork canyon (see Hiking/Backpacking, above), has 5 tent spots.

The Long Creek Ranger District, (541) 575-3000, which comprises the Malheur National Forest north of the John Day River Valley, has 52 sites among its three campgrounds. **Dixie Campground** is 8 miles east of Prairie City on US 26, **Magone Lake Campground** is 10 air miles north of John Day, and **Middle Fork Campground** is 7 miles northwest of US 26 at Austin Junction on County Rd 20 (see Hiking/Backpacking, above). Magone has wheelchair-accessible facilities.

The main entry from Prairie City on the north into the Strawberry Mountain Wilderness (see Hiking/Backpacking, above) has three campgrounds with 18 sites. First comes **McNaughton Campground,** the smallest, followed by **Slide Creek and Strawberry Campgrounds,** the largest, with 11. County Rd 62, which leads southeast of Prairie City, passes a half-dozen small campgrounds. Most popular are **Trout Farm,** 12 miles from town; **Big Creek,** 26 miles from town; and **North Fork,** at the North Fork Malheur River trailhead (see Hiking/Backpacking, above). Contact the Prairie City Ranger District at (541) 820-3311.

Starr Campground has 14 sites along US 395, about 16 miles south of John Day. The **Aldrich Mountains** (see Hiking/Backpacking, above) are ideal for dispersed camping away from developed facilities, especially in the beautiful valley of Murderers Creek. Springtime on Murderers Creek brings some of the greenest underbrush you'll ever find in Oregon. Check with the Bear Valley Ranger District, (541) 575-3400.

Clyde Holliday State Park, (541) 575-2773, is the only state park campground in the Upper John Day River country. Located 8 miles west of John Day on the river's main stem, the park has 30 electrical sites, plus a hiker/biker camp and showers. The campground is open March through November but does not take reservations. Clyde Holliday also has a shaded picnic area that is open year-round. The picnic area has an outdoor amphitheater, which is the setting of interpretive programs throughout the summer. The park does not have a designated swimming area, but more than a few people use the river to cool off during the heat of a summer day.

Depot Park, (541) 820-3605, a city campground in Prairie City, is the setting for another of the interesting museums in the county. The DeWitt Museum is open Thursday through Saturday, May 15 through October 15 and displays artifacts from the county's railroad history. The campground has 21 sites, including RV facilities, showers, and a picnic area.

Fishing

Surprise—most of the fishing in the Upper John Day River country takes place in the **John Day River,** its forks, and its tributaries. Roads follow much of the John Day River and its forks, making the access easy for

where the land is publicly owned. Much of the river's riparian areas, however, are on private ranch land. Permission from owners must be obtained
before attempting to fish. Parts of the John Day's north and south forks are
protected by the National Wild and Scenic Rivers Act. The Middle Fork of
the John Day is included in the Oregon State Scenic Waterways Program.

Perhaps the most popular fishery in the Upper John Day River country is the wild run of steelhead in the **North Fork** and **main stem.** Fishing
is best in the North Fork below the US 395 bridge near Dale from
November to March, although ice can make access difficult. From Dale,
Bureau of Land Management (BLM) roads follow the north bank of the
river for 15 miles. Fishing for steelhead and chinook salmon is not allowed
above the bridge. The North Fork supports the largest natural run of spring
chinook in the John Day system. The Nature Conservancy owns 1,222
acres on the **Middle Fork** and is working with state and federal wildlife
officials to improve habitat for wild runs of summer steelhead and spring
chinook. County Rd 20 follows the Middle Fork closely from Austin and
US 26 on the east to US 395 (13 miles south of Dale) on the west.

Desolation Creek, a tributary of the North Fork, has pools that provide excellent habitat for rainbow trout. Bull trout and spawning chinook
and steelhead also use the creek, but they cannot be kept. Desolation
Creek extends 21.5 miles in Umatilla National Forest, mostly along Forest
Rd 10 from Dale to Olive Lake.

Clyde Holliday State Park is a popular fishing spot on the John Day
River in November and December when the campground is closed.
Fishermen simply hike in past the locked gate. The Middle Fork is best for
stocked rainbow trout and the main stem has smallmouth bass around
Kimberly, as well as wild rainbow in its headwaters.

County Rd 42 along the **South Fork** of the John Day River (see
Hiking/Backpacking, above) is a designated BLM back country byway,
stretching 50 miles south of Dayville to beyond Izee. All but 12 miles is a
well-maintained county road surface. The BLM annually maintains the 12
miles, but it can be rough and impassable during winter and spring thaw.
Fishing in the south fork is best for stocked rainbow. Worms seem to have
the most success. Much of the land is private ranches, but public access is
available in lands set aside as the Murderers Creek Wildhorse Management
Area beginning 10 miles south of US 26. Check the BLM's Upper John Day
public lands map for land ownership, available from the BLM's Prineville
office, (541) 416-6700. The area is home to about 100 horses spread over
150,000 acres and is jointly managed by the BLM and Malheur National
Forest. A primitive BLM campground is located 23 miles south of Dayville.
The camp is large enough to accommodate motor homes, but no facilities
are provided.

The **Malheur River,** which flows east and joins the Snake River, and the **North Fork Malheur** (see Hiking/Backpacking, above) also have protection under the National Wild and Scenic Rivers Act in their upper reaches. The upper Malheur River flows out of Logan Valley and is managed for native redband trout. The river's north fork is east of the main stem and also is managed for native trout. Hiking trails provide access.

Check the state synopsis for regulations, or call the Oregon Department of Fish and Wildlife's John Day office, (541) 575-1167.

Wildlife

Believe it or not, the official bird of Grant County is a sandpiper. More commonly found on coastal beaches, the sandpiper that frequents this area is the **upland sandpiper.** The population in Bear and Logan Valleys, both located in the Great Basin south of the Strawberry Mountain Wilderness, is the largest known population west of the Rocky Mountains. Birds arrive in early May, complete their nesting, and leave by early August.

The **Logan Valley,** a mixture of private ranch land and Malheur National Forest land, is a high-country meadow with an elevation of 5,000 feet. The upland sandpipers are frequently found in the large open meadows on the north side of Logan Valley Rd, just west of Big Creek Campground (see Camping, above). They are easiest to see early in the day and early in the season. The Logan Valley is 17.5 miles east of Seneca and US 395 on Forest Rd 16. To make a circuit of the Strawberry Mountains, drive east through Logan Valley on Forest Rd 16, which becomes County Rd 62 and swings north to meet US 26 at Prairie City.

The valley is also home to **pronghorn antelope,** nesting **sandhill cranes,** and **long-billed curlews.** Prehistoric northern Great Basin Indians used the Logan Valley as long as 10,000 years ago. An interpretive sign on Forest Rd 16 as it crosses the valley describes their hunting, fishing, and gathering activities during their encampments near the headwaters of the Malheur River.

Murderers Creek Wildlife Area, (541) 987-2843, a state-managed area with its headquarters .25 mile east of Dayville on US 26, is a good place to look for **deer** and **elk** when heavy snow keeps them from the high country. The wildlife area includes land along Murderers Creek (see Hiking/Backpacking, above) and in the Aldrich Mountains, where a herd of **California bighorn sheep** makes its home in the crags—mainly on the northwest flank in Smoky Gulch and Oliver Creek Canyon. The Strawberry Mountains are famous for their trophy-size **Rocky Mountain elk.**

Rafting/Kayaking

The Upper John Day River country offers three popular river-running opportunities—two separate segments on the John Day River's North Fork and one on its Middle Fork. Floaters also occasionally run the main stem and the South Fork, but neither packs much whitewater punch. The Prineville office of the BLM, (541) 416-6700, manages the North Fork below US 395 to the west, while the North Fork John Day Ranger District, (541) 427-3231, handles the river above the US 395 bridge at Dale to the east. Due to the short season, no commercial outfitters run the river.

The 40 miles of the **North Fork John Day,** from North Fork Campground (see Camping, above) to Tollbridge Campground (.5 mile east of the US 395 bridge on Forest Rd 55) at Dale, passes through 30 miles of roadless terrain in the North Fork John Day Wilderness. The river is busy with Class III rapids and has one Class V at Granite Creek. Frequent logjams and fallen trees make this a run for experienced whitewater boaters only.

The **lower 45 miles** of the North Fork John Day, from Dale to Monument, is a popular three-day run (especially on Memorial Day weekend) for rafters looking for their best chance to find solitude. Launches are available near where US 395 crosses the river, although many rafters extend the trip by driving Forest Rd 55 for 7 miles upriver from Dale to several unimproved launch sites. The first half of the float follows a roaded canyon, but once past US 395 the road traffic is light. The river leaves the BLM's north-bank gravel road at Mallory Creek, 15 miles west of US 395, and winds through a scenic canyon where vegetation begins the slow process of changing from the forested Blue Mountains on the east to the dry desert hills on the west. The river again picks up a road 5 miles above Monument, located 15 miles east of Kimberly on Kimberly–Long Creek Rd. The North Fork flows another 15 miles to the west to join the main stem at Kimberly. It's a popular stretch for fishing by drift boat, but a road is nearby and it doesn't have much whitewater. Lots of Class II and some Class III water characterizes the North Fork from Dale to Monument. The rapids aren't the most thrilling in the state, but the scenery and camping are outstanding. The BLM maintains a couple of small campgrounds for river users called **Big Bend** and **Lone Pine**, both accessible on the highway between Monument and Kimberly.

The **Middle Fork John Day** has a road along its entire length, except for its last 9 miles before it joins the North Fork below Mallory Creek. Launch sites are available near Galena in Malheur National Forest (on County Rd 20, midway between Hwys 26 on the east and 395 on the west) for a 40-mile run on Class II and III water to join the North Fork. The takeout is another 12 miles down river at Monument. The river runs through mostly private land, so public land managers don't give it much attention.

Biking

Uncrowded roads and trails of the Upper John Day River country offer numerous riding opportunities. Most of Malheur National Forest, (541) 575-1731, is open to mountain bikes, except the designated wilderness areas. Forest headquarters in John Day sells a biking guidebook to its roads and trails. The spiral-bound guide details 22 rides and sells for about $5.

A nice introductory ride to the area is a 14.3-mile loop on paved and gravel roads southeast of **Prairie City**. Ride east out of town on US 26 for 1.9 miles, turn right on County Rd 61, and follow it past some working cattle ranches until it joins County Rd 62. Turn right and head back into town.

A more difficult ride with all types of trail surfaces is a 23.4-mile loop of the **Middle Fork John Day River** from Austin Junction. Head north from the restaurant on Hwy 7 and ride 1.2 miles to County Rd 20. Turn left and ride 9.8 miles to Forest Rd 2050, where the tour begins to head back home. After .3 mile, turn onto Spur Rd 791, which leads to a single-track trail in 2.8 miles. Continue riding south to where the trail joins Forest Rd 2614 along Davis Creek. Follow 2614 to its junction with US 26 and turn left to reach Austin Junction in .3 mile.

The **North Fork Malheur River Trail** (see Hiking/Backpacking, above) is a good choice for experts in search of a long single-track ride. The trail follows the river for 11.1 miles from the end of the road, 1 mile south of North Fork Malheur Campground. The trail ends at the forest boundary, so the only way back to the beginning is to backtrack. Elevation varies from 4,700 feet to 4,200 feet, but some barbed-wire fences and talus slope crossings gives it a most-difficult rating.

Cross-Country Skiing

The Upper John Day River country has only two official Oregon state sno-parks, but adventuresome skiers can head out just about anywhere that snow covers roads not used for driving during winter. To take advantage of the plowed parking lots, most cross-country skiers head for Starr Ridge Sno-Park, 16 miles south of John Day on US 395, or Dixie Summit Sno-Park, 8 miles northeast of Prairie City on US 26.

Starr Ridge Sno-Park and its warming hut have an elevation of 5,152 feet. Most skiing occurs west of US 395 on gently rolling, unmarked trails. The terrain is good for novice skiers, who shouldn't wander too far from the sno-park. **Dixie Summit Sno-Park** is the site of a club-operated rope tow where many Grant County children get their first taste of skiing.

Cross-country skiing is mostly on unmarked trails over unplowed roads. The ultimate challenge is to ski a 4.7-mile marked trail to the top of 7,592-foot Dixie Butte, a climb of 2,340 feet.

Another area that attracts skiers, even though it doesn't have an official state sno-park, is the **Flagtail Peak/Snowshoe Creek** cross-country ski area, 13 miles west of US 395 on the Izee Hwy (County Rd 63). Snowshoe Creek Loop is a 6-mile marked loop on the south side of the highway. Across the highway, a 5-mile trail over an unplowed road leads 1,400 feet up to the 6,584-foot summit of Flagtail Mountain. The climb is rated intermediate, and the Bear Valley Ranger District invites you to bring a sleeping bag because the fire lookout atop Flagtail Mountain is one of three Malheur National Forest facilities available to rent from November 1 to May 30.

Bear Valley Work Center has two cabins to rent along the Izee Hwy. **Murderers Creek Work Center** with one cabin available is more isolated and requires an 11.5-mile over-the-snow approach during winter, making it a better destination for snowmobilers. The three facilities are accessible by roads before and after the snow season. For rental information and directions, contact the Bear Valley Ranger District, (541) 575-3400.

Attractions

You are in the midst of dry cattle country in an area loaded with history: **John Day** is just off the old Oregon Trail, and the whole region was full of gold (during the height of the Gold Rush in 1862, $26 million in gold was mined in the neighboring town of Canyon City).

Kam Wah Chung Museum, off Canton St in John Day on the north side of US 26 (next to the city park), was the stone-walled home of two Chinese herbal doctors at the turn of the century. A tour makes for an interesting glimpse of the Chinese settlement in the West: opium-stained walls, Chinese shrines, and herbal medicines are on display, as well as a small general store. Tours are offered daily, except Friday, May through October.

Cheaper Eats

Ferdinand's The menu is reassuringly familiar: microbrews on draft, build-your-own pizzas, pasta dishes, teriyaki chicken, and barbecued beef ribs. Everything's made in-house. *128 Main St, Prairie City; (541) 820-4455; $.*

Lodgings

Fish House Inn This century-old house was transformed into an inn with three guest rooms, decorated with eclectic pieces such as ice tongs and old fishing rods; a cottage in back has two more rooms. There's a gift store, and breakfast is bountiful. *110 Franklin Ave (on Hwy 26 west of John Day), Dayville; PO Box 143, Dayville, OR 97825; (541) 987-2124 or (888) 286-3474; $.*

The Ponderosa Guest Ranch ☆☆☆ At this bona fide working ranch (4,000 head of cattle on 120,000 acres of rangeland), you may choose to herd calves, fly-fish solo, or soak in the hot tub. Sleep in log cabins and eat hearty ranch fare in the main lodge's dining room. A blend of professionalism and casual friendliness make this place outstanding. Some minimum-stay requirements. *On Hwy 395 halfway between Burns and John Day; PO Box 190, Seneca, OR 97873; (541) 542-2403 or (800) 331-1012; $$.*

More Information

Baker Ranger District, Baker City: *(541) 523-4476.*
Bear Valley Ranger District, John Day: *(541) 575-3400.*
Bureau of Land Management, Prineville: *(541) 416-6700.*
Grant County Chamber of Commerce, John Day: *(800) 769-5664.*
John Day Fossil Beds National Monument, Dayville: *(541) 987-2333.*
Long Creek Ranger District, John Day: *(541) 575-3000.*
Malheur National Forest, John Day: *(541) 575-1731.*
North Fork John Day Ranger District, Ukiah: *(541) 427-3231.*
Ochoco National Forest, Prineville: *(541) 416-6500.*
Paulina Ranger District, Prineville: *(541) 416-6500.*
Prairie City Ranger District, Prairie City: *(541) 820-3311.*
Umatilla National Forest, Pendleton: *(541) 278-3716.*
Wallowa-Whitman National Forest, Baker City: *(541) 523-6391.*

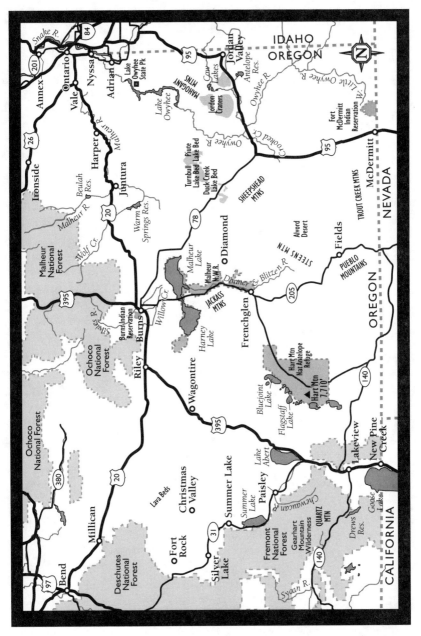

Southeast High Desert

Lake County   619

Harney County   634

Malheur County   647

Southeast **High** Desert

Lake County

From the Lake-Deschutes county line on the north, east to the Lake-Harney county line, south to the California border, and west to the Lake-Klamath county line, including the Gearhart Mountain Wilderness, the Hart Mountain National Antelope Refuge, the town of Lakeview, and Christmas Valley.

L ake County's infinitely varied topography is filled with surprises around every bend and begs to be explored. From the quiet camps high on Winter Ridge in Fremont National Forest, to dry lake beds on the floor of the high desert around Summer Lake, this is a land of delightful contrasts.

John Charles Fremont was the first American explorer to take note of the landscape when in 1843 he explored the forest that would be named for him. Accompanied by the legendary mountain guide Kit Carson, Fremont and his men spent one gray wintry day struggling up the backside of Winter Ridge, only to reach the view from Fremont Point of Summer Lake, an expanse of water shimmering in the sun 3,000 feet below. Their experience led them to bestow names to the lake and its southern ridge that are still appropriate to this day.

Hart Mountain, 80 miles east of Winter Ridge, is also a place held dear for its desert scenery and the wildlife it protects. Managers of the Hart Mountain National Antelope Refuge are currently trying to rebuild its herd of antelope from a high mortality rate among its fawns, but the resident bighorn sheep herd is healthy. The wild sheep are so productive that part of the herd is rounded up annually by helicopter and transplanted to other suitable habitat in Oregon and elsewhere in the West.

Native bighorn sheep were exterminated by 1916 in Oregon's desert mountain ranges, while mountain sheep that lived in wetter regions became extinct by the mid-1930s. The state's present population of California bighorns descends from a successful transplant of 20 sheep from British Columbia to Hart Mountain in 1954. Oregon's Rocky Mountain bighorn sheep were reestablished in 1971 with transplant of a herd from Alberta to the Snake River Canyon. The state's total sheep population has grown to nearly 3,000 animals that live in the central and eastern mountains and canyons.

Spotting a bighorn in the wild is one of the most exciting wildlife-viewing opportunities in the state. Hart Mountain's herd of sheep remains the state's largest, with an estimated 500 head. Hikers who climb to the rim of Hart Mountain are frequently rewarded with views of the bighorns. The big rams often battle for dominance in the flats near the refuge's head-quarters during November's rut, and occasionally visitors don't even need to leave the comfort of their vehicles to see the majestic animals.

Unlike its high-desert neighbors to the east, Lake County is far enough west to pick up plenty of moisture from winter storms off the Pacific. Its large expanse of forests, interspersed with clear-running streams and mountain lakes, provides the ultimate contrast to its desert flats. Frankly, it's hard to beat camping on the desert floor at night, waking to a warm morning sun, driving up into the mountains for a day of hiking or fishing, then returning to camp when the desert cools off in the evening.

Fremont was the first European to notice the contrasts that abound in this area. His one regret was that he looked down on Summer Lake from Winter Ridge, instead of the other way around. Modern-day explorers will just have to decide for themselves what angle suits them best.

Getting There

Lakeview, the county seat and only town of any size in Lake County, is 335 miles southeast of Portland. Drive US Highway 97 (US 97) south of Bend for 25 miles, then turn southeast 2 miles past La Pine on Highway 31. Lakeview is 142 miles from US 97 through the open expanses of Lake County. US 395 runs north-south through Lake County during its journey between Spokane and San Diego. Highway 140 crosses the southern part of the county from east to west. Lakeview calls itself the "tallest town in Oregon" because of its 4,800-foot elevation. The town's population is 2,580. Christmas Valley, the northern hub of Lake County, is 5 miles northeast of Highway 31 on county roads.

Adjoining Areas

NORTH: **Bend and the Upper Deschutes River**

EAST: **Harney County**

WEST: **Klamath Basin**

inside out

Scenic Drives

A lesson in geology awaits explorers who drive the **Christmas Valley National Back Country Byway,** one of two Bureau of Land Management (BLM) tour routes in Lake County. Unlike most geology lessons, this one isn't boring because the forces that created the earth are displayed in so many interesting ways. To pick up the companion brochure, stop at the Christmas Valley Chamber of Commerce or ask to receive one by mail from the BLM's Lakeview office, (541) 947-2177.

The byway begins on Hwy 31, 65 miles southeast of Bend and 29 miles southeast of the junction with US 97 near La Pine. The byway negotiates a series of BLM roads with numbers like 5-10, 5-14E, 6151, 4-14, in addition to the county's numbering system. Don't worry so much about following the numbers; just watch for directional signs at the major junctions that point the way to the attractions.

The first attraction along the way is **Fort Rock State Park,** a picnic area at the base of a circular-shaped rock formation that rises 500 feet above the flat desert floor. The rock has some fun scrambling routes, but some of its cliffs are also steep, so be careful. The view from the top covers hundreds of square miles, with only a few signs of human development anywhere in sight. Fort Rock is home to nesting raptors, including prairie falcons and golden eagles. The remains of 75 sagebrush woven sandals, carbon dated at 9,000 years old, were discovered in 1938 in a cave near Fort Rock. Some artifacts were 3,000 years older than the volcanic ash that buried them when Mount Mazama exploded and formed Crater Lake.

The community of **Christmas Valley** lies near the center of northern Lake County and the route of the designated byway. Although no one seems to know for sure, the town may have gotten its name because Fremont passed through the area during Christmas. Mapmakers made note of the fact and the name has stuck ever since. Christmas Valley was envisioned as a retirement community during the 1960s, but it never quite became the Palm Springs of the north. That may have had something to do with its long, cold winters and the deep water table that have combined to prevent major development. The area's big ranches (along with the roads, one of the few signs of development from a perch atop Fort Rock) pump water from deep inside the ground to irrigate their alfalfa fields. Many of the area's famous geological sites lie to the north and northeast of Christmas Valley.

Crack in the Ground was formed when subterranean lava flows allowed an overlying block of older lava to collapse. Created about 1,000 years ago, the crack is more than 2 miles long and 70 feet deep in places. A footpath follows much of the crack's bottom. Local residents frequently spend the heat of a summer day in cool shade at the bottom of the crack. The BLM recommends that visitors here drive high-clearance vehicles.

The **Christmas Valley sand dunes** cover 15,000 acres and rise to 60 feet in height. Unvegetated parts of the dunes are open to off-highway vehicles and are the setting for an annual gathering every Memorial Day weekend. The **Lost Forest** at the northeast edge of the dunes contains a remnant stand of ponderosa pines that grow 40 miles from the nearest similar forest. The Christmas Valley area formerly was much wetter than it is now, but pines in the Lost Forest continue to thrive on 10 inches of rain annually when they normally require 14 (soil traps the moisture and keeps the pines alive).

Green Mountain, located on Rd 6109 north of Crack in the Ground, offers a stunning view to the north over the **Squaw Ridge lava flow** that reaches to the horizon. An interesting way to leave the byway and return to Bend is to drive north past Green Mountain, turn left on BLM Rd 5-21B, drive 6 miles, then turn north on BLM Rd 6159 toward **Derrick Cave.** The cave is a typical central Oregon lava tube, but the forest that surrounds it makes the area worth a visit.

Two miles north of the cave, after crossing the boundary into Deschutes National Forest, turn left on Forest Rd 800, a bumpy track that leads past one of the largest western **juniper trees** in Oregon. The tree is alongside the road and measures 64 feet tall, 5.5 feet in diameter, and 17 feet in circumference. Larger junipers live in the Lost Forest where they are more difficult to locate. After passing the big juniper, the road meanders through a wonderful stand of old-growth ponderosa pines before reaching Forest Rds 23/22, which head 30 miles west past South Ice Cave (see Bend and the Upper Deschutes River chapter) back to La Pine on US 97.

Lake County's other designated back country byway is the **Lakeview to Steens** route, which climbs past the Warner wetlands to the uplands of **Hart Mountain National Antelope Refuge** (see Wildlife, below) and some of the best wildlife-watching opportunities in south-central Oregon. Start the 140-mile tour 6 miles north of Lakeview. Turn east on Hwy 140 from US 395 and follow the marked byway toward Frenchglen (see Harney County chapter). Drive Hwy 140 for 22 miles and turn north at the Plush/Hart Mountain junction. Go north 20 miles to **Plush,** then turn east for 25 miles to reach the Hart Mountain field station. The gravel road continues east to Frenchglen.

Wildlife

The 275,000-acre **Hart Mountain National Antelope Refuge** was created in 1936 to provide seasonal forage for one of the West's largest herds of **pronghorn antelope.** Hart Mountain provides summer habitat for the antelope. Their winter range is in the Catlow Valley to the east, toward Steens Mountain, and the Charles Sheldon National Wildlife Refuge, across the border in Nevada. Hart Mountain also provides habitat for **bighorn sheep, mule deer, coyotes, black-tailed jackrabbits, sage grouse, golden eagles,** and **red-tailed hawks.** The refuge headquarters, (541) 947-3315, is in Room 301 of the post office in Lakeview, but most visitors stop at the field station 65 miles northeast of Lakeview on the Lakeview to Steens byway (see Scenic Drives, above).

One of the outstanding wildlife observation sites along the byway is the Warner wetlands, a series of lakes, marshes, and potholes that cover 50,000 acres at the western base of Hart Mountain. Most of the wetlands are outside the boundaries of the US Fish and Wildlife Service's refuge, which is located higher up on Hart Mountain. The Warner wetlands, managed by the BLM, are an important resting place for **migrating waterfowl.** The byway passes through the wetlands, and dirt roads leave the byway north and south to give additional access to the lakes at the western base of Hart Mountain. The lakes are also the summer home for dozens of bird species, including **long-billed curlew, western grebe,** and **white-faced ibis.** Facilities include barrier-free rest rooms, two wheelchair-accessible viewing blinds, a .5-mile interpretive trail, and a marked canoe trail between Turpin and Campbell Lakes, 40 miles northeast of Lakeview at the foot of Hart Mountain.

Roads between the wetlands and the base of the mountain are good places to spot Hart Mountain's **California bighorn sheep.** The best way to locate bighorn sheep is to leave the road that climbs up the mountain to the refuge headquarters and drive either north or south along the western base of the mountain. Stop frequently along the way and use 10-power binoculars, plus lots of patience, to spot bands of sheep. Watch either for movement by the sheep or for the sheep's white rump patches that give them away in their otherwise camouflaged environment. Sheep tend to congregate high up the west side of Hart Mountain because they instinctively expect danger to appear from below, not from above. The sheep range widely during the course of the year. The Hart Mountain escarpment rises 3,600 feet, so even the most powerful binoculars won't locate sheep that perch just below the mountain's rim. Poker Jim Ridge, the northern extension of Hart Mountain, is especially productive for large bighorn rams. The cliffs above the stone corral, an unmistakable feature along the dirt road near the base of Poker Jim Ridge, is a good place to stop and watch for sheep. (While driving roads at the base of Hart Mountain, be sure the roads are dry enough to support a vehicle. The rise and fall of the Warner wetlands' lakes create soft spots that can trap vehicles that wander off the road.)

November's rut, which occurs after the limited hunting season of September and October, offers an outstanding opportunity to view the rams battling for dominance. The sheep are usually unafraid of humans during the rut and can be observed from close distances. Look for bands near the refuge headquarters and along the east side of Poker Jim Ridge. November can be extremely cold atop Hart Mountain and snow can temporarily close the road to the refuge headquarters at any time. Visitors must decide whether to brave the elements and camp out or commute from a motel in Lakeview 65 miles away. Most visitors to Hart Mountain arrive from July through September, times when the sheep are most wary; best viewing times are from daybreak to 10am, then again in the evening from 5pm to dusk.

Pronghorn antelope can usually be seen wandering the sagebrush lands on the east side of Hart Mountain. The fastest mammal in North America ranges widely, so the buck you saw in the morning could be the same one you saw in the evening 20 miles away. The fleet creatures can be seen throughout southeast Oregon's high desert, sometimes singly but other times in herds of 50 or more. A suspected cause for mortality among antelope fawns is predation by coyotes. Antelope sightings usually are more a case of being alert to your surroundings rather than actively stalking them like bighorns.

Abert Lake, the third-largest body of salt water in North America, is 18 miles long and 10 miles wide at the base of **Abert Rim**—a massive fault scarp and one of the highest exposed geologic faults in North America, towering 2,000 feet above the lake. The lake is 30 miles north of Lakeview on US 395. It's home to **salt-tolerant birds,** while the rim has the same **large mammals** as Hart Mountain.

Summer Lake Wildlife Area, (541) 943-3152, an 18,000-acre area managed by the Oregon Department of Fish and Wildlife for **migrating and resident waterfowl,** is famous for its large flocks of **snow geese.** The geese are only one of **250 bird species** that have been counted in the area. The wildlife area has an 8.7-mile gravel road that leads visitors to the best viewing sites. Watch for **bald eagles** feeding on **muskrat** carcasses that are trapped and piled where the eagles can enjoy a tasty feast. Best viewing of the snow geese is during March's northward migration, because the wildlife area limits access to hunters during the fall migration. The wildlife area is on the north side of Hwy 31, 70 miles southeast of the junction with US 97.

Large herds of wintering **mule deer** can be seen around Lakeview and at Oatman Flat, 8 miles north of Silver Lake on the southwest side of Hwy

31. Winter and spring are not necessarily safe times to drive at night in Lake County because of foraging herds of deer.

Camping

Campgrounds in the northern part of Fremont National Forest near the community of Silver Lake, 47 miles southeast of US 97 on Hwy 31, are clustered south of the highway near Thompson Reservoir. Check with the Silver Lake Ranger District, (541) 576-2107, before heading south of Silver Lake on either County Rd 4-11 or 4-12 to the reservoir. County Rd 4-11 becomes Forest Rd 27 when it crosses the forest boundary on its way to the west shore of the lake. Road 4-12 becomes Forest Rd 28 on its way to the east shore of the lake.

Silver Creek Marsh Campground has 8 tent sites 11 miles south of Silver Lake on Forest Rd 27. The campground at **Thompson Reservoir Campground** is 4 miles farther south on the northwest corner of the reservoir.

Most lakes and reservoirs of the central and south Fremont National Forest have campgrounds. **Deadhorse and Campbell Lakes,** just west of Forest Rd 28, have two-dozen sites between them that cater to fishermen and hikers planning trips into the Gearhart Mountain Wilderness. To reach Forest Rd 28, drive east of Lakeview for 4 miles on Hwy 140 and turn north on County Rd 2-16. Drive north 5 miles, then turn west where the road soon enters the forest and changes its number. The lakes are managed by the Paisley Ranger District, (541) 943-3114.

Goose Lake State Recreation Area, (541) 947-3111, is the only overnight state park campground in Lake County. Located 14 miles south of Lakeview just off US 395, the park is on the east shore of Goose Lake and has some of the best sunsets this side of the Oregon Coast. The park has 48 sites with electrical hookups. The California border is only a few yards away to the south. Goose Lake also has some outstanding dispersed camping on its western shore, but all the public land is south of the California state line.

The only car camping allowed at Hart Mountain National Antelope Refuge is at **Hot Springs Campground,** 6 miles south of refuge headquarters (see Scenic Drives, above). The campground has a cement pool and a shelter where water from the hot springs keeps campers happy.

Deschutes National Forest extends down from the north to cover a large portion of northwest Lake County. An often overlooked part of the forest, this part of the Deschutes has some interesting sights, including South Ice Cave, Big Hole, and Hole in the Ground. All are easy to explore from Hwy 31 and Forest Rds 22 and 18 east of La Pine. The only campground in the area is at **Cabin Lake,** which has 14 sites on Forest Rd 18, 7 miles south of South

Ice Cave (see Bend and the Upper Deschutes River chapter). Don't bother to bring a fishing pole because Cabin Lake is dry. The turnoff for Big Hole is marked on the south side of Hwy 31, 19 miles southeast of Hwy 97. The turnoff for Hole in the Ground is marked 1 mile beyond, on the north side of Hwy 31. Both are geologic oddities worth exploring. For information, check with the Fort Rock Ranger District in Bend, (541) 388-5664.

Hiking/Backpacking

Gearhart Mountain is located within the Fremont National Forest and was protected as a wilderness in 1964 and expanded to its present size of 22,809 acres in 1984. The eroded rim of an ancient volcano, it rises to 8,345 feet. The view from its summit takes in a forest mixed with lodgepole and ponderosa pines, plus picturesque rock outcrops, lakes, streams, and meadows. In the distance, the Three Sisters are to the north, Steens Mountain is to the east, and California's Lassen Peak is to the south. The wilderness has only 15 miles of trails. Two of its three trailheads are in Lake County on the north and east, and the other is on the west (see Klamath Basin chapter).

The most popular day hike to the summit is via the **Gearhart Mountain Trail** (difficult; 6 miles one way) from **Lookout Rock trailhead** on the south. To reach the trailhead, leave Hwy 140 near Quartz Mountain Pass and travel north on Forest Rd 3660 for 12 miles to the side road to Corral Creek Campground. Turn left, pass the campground and continue to the end of the road. The northern entrance to the wilderness is at the **North Fork Sprague River trailhead,** 3 miles west of Deadhorse Lake (see Camping, above) at the end of Forest Rd 3372-015. An easy 3-mile trail leads to Blue Lake, the only large lake in the Gearhart Mountain Wilderness. The trail continues west of the lake, eventually turning south to climb a ridge to the summit of Gearhart Mountain (difficult; 7 miles from the trailhead).

The tallest peak in Lake County is 8,456-foot Crane Mountain, the high point of Oregon's Warner Mountains southeast of Lakeview. The 31-mile **Crane Mountain National Recreation Trail** can be reached by a four-wheel-drive road that climbs to within .5 mile of the summit, or by a 2-mile hike from the Crane Mountain trailhead. The trail continues 8 miles south of Crane Peak, where it ends at the California border. Along the way it crosses a lightly used area for motorized recreation. To reach the trailhead, drive Hwy 140 east of US 395 for 7 miles and turn south on Forest Rd 3915. Drive south for 9 miles to where the road bends east. Turn south on Forest Rd 4011 and drive 3 miles to the trailhead.

As funding becomes available, Fremont National Forest is constructing the 172-mile **Fremont National Recreation Trail** from Vee Lake near Drake Peak across the forest to Yamsay Mountain. About 95 miles of the trail are complete. Also called the **Southern Oregon Intertie Trail,** the trail will eventually reach from the Pacific Crest Trail (see Mountain Lakes chapter) to the Desert Trail (see Harney County chapter). For information, contact forest headquarters in Lakeview at (541) 947-3334.

Yamsay Mountain's 8,196-foot summit is in Klamath County, but the Fremont National Recreation Trail climbs 16 miles to its summit from Silver Marsh Campground near Silver Lake (see Camping, above). The hike can be shortened to 9 miles one way by starting at the Antler trailhead, where Forest Rd 3038-038 crosses the trail (trailheads are labeled on the Fremont National Forest map).

Diablo Mountain rises to 6,145 feet northeast of Summer Lake Wildlife Management Area. The mountain has an 1,800-foot eastern cliff, but the hiking route approaches from the west. The off-trail hike travels through open desert country and takes six hours for a round-trip hike to the summit from the desert flats. From the Summer Lake store, drive County Rd 4-17, which heads east between the Summer Lake church and rest area, for 6.4 miles to a dirt road on the right. Drive the dirt road 1 mile and park at the edge of a fence line near a sand dune. Hike along the fence for .25 mile, and then continue directly toward a breach in the mountain's western face. The summit is 1 mile east of the prominent western fault block.

Hart Mountain is the massive fault block that rises above the Warner Valley (see Wildlife, above). The high point of the range is **Warner Peak** at 8,065 feet. Hart Mountain's summit is 2 miles south along the rim and reaches 7,710 feet. The best route to Warner Peak begins 1 mile south of Hot Springs Campground on a gravel road. Hike west through open sagebrush for 4 miles and gain 2,000 feet to reach the summit. The refuge brochure is available at the field station. It shows roads but is not a reliable guide for hiking cross-country.

The west flank of Hart Mountain is drained by several steep canyons that are accessible from the roads along the base of the mountain. A favorite west-side hike is **Degarmo Canyon,** which has a 30-foot waterfall about a mile up from the Warner Valley road. Degarmo Canyon is named both on the refuge map and alongside the road. Backpacking is allowed on Hart Mountain, but be sure to pick up a permit at the refuge headquarters.

Visitors who would rather experience the awesome size of Lake County's back country from the seat of a **horse** can hire a ride with Cliff Monchamp Outfitters, (541) 947-5454, of Lakeview.

Fishing

Fresh water is in short supply in parts of Lake County, but the lakes and streams capable of supporting fish often grow them big. Most fishing emphasis is on **Drews Reservoir,** 20 miles west of Lakeview on Hwy 140, and **Thompson Reservoir,** 13 miles south of Silver Lake (see Camping, above). Drews produces an occasional large rainbow, but white crappie, brown bullhead, and yellow perch more frequently rise to the bait. The boat launch is at the south end. Thompson Reservoir has a good population of rainbow and Lahontan cutthroat trout in the 3- to 5-pound range. Both campgrounds have boat launches.

Other fishing getaways are the **Fishhole Lakes Recreation Area,** an area of several lakes 4 miles south of Hwy 140 at Quartz Mountain Pass on Forest Rd 3715; **Deadhorse and Campbell Lakes** near the east side of the Gearhart Mountain Wilderness (see Camping, above); **Dog Lake,** 4 miles southwest of Drews Reservoir on Forest Rd 4017; and **Cottonwood Reservoir,** 7 miles west of Lakeview on Hwy 140 and 5 miles north on Forest Rd 3870. Most are planted with rainbow and brook trout. Dog Lake is best known for its warm-water fishing for largemouth bass and crappie. The Campbell and Deadhorse Lakes basin is at 7,200 feet and is open only from July through October.

The **Chewaucan River,** which flows 50 miles from its tributaries in the Gearhart Mountain Wilderness to Chewaucan Marsh just west of Abert Lake, is a good trout stream by Lake County standards. Best fishing is for planted rainbows in its upper reaches, along Forest Rd 33 south of Paisley. Abert Lake, a delightful desert lake for photographic purposes alongside US 395, is too alkaline to support game fish.

Goose Lake, the 97,391-acre giant that straddles the Oregon-California border on US 395, went completely dry in 1992 and has been closed, along with its tributaries, to allow the surviving native redband trout to repopulate naturally. Goose Lake is another photographer's delight, offering gorgeous desert sunsets almost nightly from May to October.

The **Sycan River** begins on the south flank of Winter Ridge and flows through Sycan Marsh before joining the Sprague River near Beatty. The Sycan is one of Lake County's two federally protected Wild and Scenic Rivers. The Sycan is not heavily fished due to its remote location and rugged access, but fishermen who put in the effort can sample the river's native rainbow and brook trout. Drive Forest Rd 28 for 9 miles south of Thompson Reservoir and turn west on Forest Rd 3239, which crosses the river in 3 miles. The Nature Conservancy owns 19,000 acres of the **Sycan Marsh** and is working with federal agencies and private businesses on a multimillion-dollar wetlands rehabilitation project. The **North Fork of the Sprague River,** also federally protected under the Wild and Scenic Rivers Act, drains the north side of Gearhart Mountain and is a good fly-fishing stream for wild rainbow, brook, and brown trout. Access is best on Forest Rd 3411, just north of the Gearhart Mountain Wilderness.

Fishermen who don't mind driving for the chance to catch big trout head to **Spaulding Reservoir** 85 miles east of Lakeview. The reservoir is one of the best places in Oregon's southeast high desert to latch onto a hatchery rainbow, which grow quickly or don't grow at all in this remote location. The reservoir is 19 miles north into Guano Valley from Hwy 140, about 20 miles east of Adel. Trout up to 20 inches are common.

Check the state synopsis for regulations, or call the Oregon Department of Fish and Wildife's Lakeview office, (541) 947-2950.

Biking

With a population of 7,400 residents spread over 8,359 square miles, Lake County doesn't have much demand for bicycle lanes and other facilities. Paved **road riding** is relatively safe on the county's lightly traveled roads. **Highway 31** between Silver Lake, Summer Lake, and Paisley can be fun to ride, especially near the Summer Lake Wildlife Area (see Wildlife, above). The flat **farmland** west of Lakeview is interlaced by paved county roads that can offer an hour or two of recreation from town. **Drew Creek Picnic Area** (16 miles southwest of Lakeview via Hwy 140, County Rd 1-12, and Forest Rd 4812) is connected by a 2-mile paved bicycle trail to Drews Reservoir. **Black Cap,** the butte on the east edge of Lakeview, offers a stern hill climb with a 1,500-foot elevation gain. Head east out of town up Bullard Canyon and Center St, turn and ride north 2 miles on Black Cap Rd.

Mountain bikes are allowed on many **Fremont National Forest** trails, but so are motorcycles. The mountain-bike trail system will continue to develop as riders from Bend and the Upper Deschutes River country look farther away to find uncrowded places to ride. The only trails closed to bikes are in the Gearhart Mountain Wilderness. To pick up the forest's recreation opportunity guides, stop at the headquarters at 424 North G St in Lakeview.

Hart Mountain National Antelope Refuge (see Wildlife, above) offers mountain-bike riding opportunities on the same roads vehicles use, but a bike may be a better way to watch for wildlife. Off-trail road riding is not allowed on the refuge.

The Fremont National Forest administers about 60 miles of the **OC&E Woods Line State Trail,** which begins in Klamath Falls and runs more than 100 miles to Thompson Reservoir (see Klamath Basin chapter). The abandoned railroad has the rail ties removed and its surface is rock ballast. Large motor vehicles are not allowed, but **four-wheel ATVs** and motorcycles are permitted on the Fremont National Forest part of the trail. Public use of the trail ends where the old railroad crosses private property in **Sycan Marsh.** The area is known locally as "Syco Marsh" because of some of the people who live nearby. Be sure your ATV can top 40mph in order to outrun the resident Rottweiler. The Forest Service has built a small trailhead at Camp Six, 3 miles west of Bly on Hwy 140 and 12 miles north on Forest Rd 30, for access to the rail-trail. It will take many more years and a lot more dollars to convert the trail into a pleasant cycling experience. Check with the Bly Ranger District, (541) 353-3427.

Skiing/Snowmobiling

Although recreation opportunities here are on a much smaller scale than at Oregon's main winter-sports destinations, Lake County offers just about every type of snow play. This sets Lake County apart from its neighbors in southeast Oregon's high desert.

Warner Canyon ski area has a 730-foot vertical drop served by a T-bar. Usually open Wednesday afternoons, weekends, and holidays, the tiny county-owned ski area has better powder snow skiing (when it has snow) than its bigger neighbors in the Cascades can dream of having. The ski runs face north and climb to 6,000 feet. Operated by the local Highlanders Ski Club, the ski area has overhead low enough that it can withstand drought seasons when its operation is limited to a few days all winter. The ski area is 4 miles north of Lakeview on US 395 and 5 miles east on Hwy 140. For information, call the ski area, (541) 947-5001, or the Lake County Chamber of Commerce, (541) 947-6040.

Nordic skiers have a 4-mile groomed course at **Warner Canyon Sno-Park** (adjacent to the ski area), and snowmobilers have 90 miles of trail beginning 2 miles east of the ski area at the snowmobile racetrack.

Quartz Mountain Sno-Park on Hwy 140 about 25 miles west of Lakeview usually has more reliable snow conditions than Warner Canyon due to its westerly location. Snowmobilers can pick from 75 miles of trails that reach far north and south of the highway. Cross-country skiers have more than 10 miles of marked loops on either side of Hwy 140.

Pole Butte Sno-Park, 22 miles south of Silver Lake near Winter Ridge, is one of the most isolated places in Oregon accessible by road during winter. The road is plowed to provide emergency winter access to a nearby power line, but skiers and snowmobilers who want to explore far away from crowds reach the area by driving Forest Rd 28 for 20 miles south of Hwy 31, past Thompson Reservoir to Forest Rd 2916. Turn east and drive 2 miles to the sno-park. The major attraction is **Fremont Point cabin,** a Fremont National Forest rental facility that perches at the edge of Winter Ridge looking down at Summer Lake. The cabin is 9 miles from the sno-park, so most use is by snowmobilers during winter. The cabin is available for rent year-round from the Paisley Ranger District, (541) 943-3114.

Other Forest Service rental facilities are **Bald Butte Lookout** above Paisley, available year-round from the Paisley Ranger District; **Hager**

Mountain Lookout near Silver Lake, available in winter from the Paisley Ranger District; and **Aspen Cabin** northeast of Lakeview, available during summer from the Lakeview Ranger District, (541) 947-3334. Renting cabins and fire lookouts requires users to sign a contract with the Forest Service, at which time a fee is collected (usually $25 per night) and the key is issued.

Hang Gliding

There's no disputing that Lakeview has embraced the sport of hang gliding with open arms since the mid-1980s. Flying in the county began with the occasional pilot from Medford or Portland and has expanded so that vehicles from throughout the western United States and Canada can be seen at the county's wealth of launch sites. Numerous buttes, abundant public land, and reliable summer breezes make it one of the best places for non-motorized human flight in North America from June through September.

Fremont National Forest and the BLM have joined forces with the Lake County Chamber of Commerce to survey and mark launch and landing sites around the county. The county's effort was officially recognized in 1993 when it was chosen to stage the national championships. It was selected as host again in 1997. The county lays claim to being the "Hang Gliding Capital of the West." The longest flight in the area has been 157.5 miles from Sugar Hill to near Burns in Harney County. An information sheet for each of the launch sites describes its location and under what conditions flying is safe. Check with the chamber of commerce, (541) 947-6040, at 126 North E St, Lakeview.

Hang-gliding pilots usually arrive in Lake County fully skilled and in possession of all the equipment they will need. Paragliding pilots also launch from some of the same locations. Instruction in Oregon is available from the Hang Gliding and Paragliding School of Oregon, (541) 223-7448, a mobile **school** that teaches where conditions are the best. Beginner lessons are usually taught on the Oregon Coast.

Rock Collecting

Lake County has the state's only public collection site for the **sunstone,** the official Oregon state gem. Sunstones are feldspar crystals that form in basaltic lava flows. They range in size from thin flakes to as large as a thumb. The official digging area, a 4-square-mile tract set aside in 1972, is 22 miles north of Plush (see Scenic Drives, above) off BLM Rd 6115. Orange plastic posts mark the public collection area. The collecting area has a barrier-free vault toilet, and the hard desert soil will support wheelchairs. Some of the best collecting is on the surface, with a screwdriver coming in handy to separate stones from the soil.

The mountains around Lakeview are productive for **Thundereggs, agate, jasper,** and **petrified wood.** Bullard and Deadman Canyons, both on the eastern outskirts of Lakeview, produce **blue and purple agate.** So does Crane Creek, 5 miles south of town. Digging sites near Dog Lake and Drews Reservoir west of Lakeview produce agate and petrified wood. Hart Mountain is good for a variety of rocks, including **fire opal** on the peaks of the west rim; collectors are limited to 7 pounds per person per day within the refuge.

The easiest place in Lake County—perhaps all of Oregon—to locate collectable rocks is at Glass Buttes in the northeast corner of the county just off US 20. The buttes are made of **black and silver obsidian,** a volcanic glass. **Red and gold obsidian** are also common. Check with High Desert Craft Rock Shop, (541) 947-3237, in Lakeview for the current digging hot spots.

Attractions

At an elevation of nearly 4,300 feet, **Lakeview** calls itself "Oregon's Tallest Town." It's better known for its geyser, **Old Perpetual**—which doesn't exactly rival Yellowstone's Old Faithful but is Oregon's only geyser. It's located in a pond at Hunter's Hot Springs, (541) 947-2127, a 47-acre property dotted by hot-springs pools, on the west side of US 395 about 2 miles north of town. The geyser goes off once every 30 seconds or so, shooting 75 feet into the air for 3 to 5 seconds. It's been erupting regularly for some 60 years, apparently unleashed by someone trying to drill a well.

Lodgings

Summer Lake Bed & Breakfast Inn ☆☆   From the outdoor hot tub of this luxurious B&B, you can see 40 miles in all directions. Stay in the main house or a cabin-style condo. A big breakfast is served, as is dinner with advance notice (there isn't a grocery store or restaurant for miles). *D-7 Ranch, 31501 Hwy 31 (between mileposts 81 and 82), Summer Lake, OR 97640; (541) 943-3983 or (800) 261-2778; $$.*

More Information

Bly Ranger District, Bly: *(541) 353-3427.*
Bureau of Land Management, Lakeview: *(541) 947-2177.*
Deschutes National Forest, Bend: *(541) 388-2715.*

Fort Rock Ranger District, Bend: *(541) 388-5664.*

Fremont National Forest, Lakeview: *(541) 947-2151.*

Hart Mountain National Antelope Refuge, Lakeview: *(541) 947-3315.*

Lake County Chamber of Commerce, Lakeview: *(541) 947-6040.*

Lakeview Ranger District, Lakeview: *(541) 947-3334.*

Oregon's Outback Visitors Association, Klamath Falls: *(800) 598-6877.*

Paisley Ranger District, Paisley: *(541) 943-3114.*

Silver Lake Ranger District, Silver Lake: *(541) 576-2107.*

Harney County

From the Harney-Grant county line on the north, east to the Harney-Malheur county line, south to the Nevada border, and west to the Harney-Lake county line, including the Malheur National Wildlife Refuge, Steens Mountain Recreation Area, and the towns of Burns, Hines, Diamond, Frenchglen, and Fields.

The concept of the Desert Trail was born in Harney County in the early 1970s. Before then, southeast Oregon's high desert was a place for ranchers, hunters, prospectors, and horseback riders. It took a new way of thinking for the desert to be accepted as a place to hike simply for the pleasure of hiking.

The high desert has a way of magnifying beauty. The sunrises and sunsets are more intense, more colorful, and they seem to last longer. The nightly star show, which often features the Milky Way galaxy and the major constellations, is deep and black and brilliant with white lights. The beauty of a field of desert wildflowers is more deeply appreciated in a place where logic defies that delicate flowers should grow. A cool-running stream, shaded by a grove of quaking aspen, has more force in a dry environment than the most powerful of mountain rivers. Wildlife, especially birds and large mammals, are much easier to spot in the wide-open, treeless spaces.

The idea of a Desert Trail that would traverse the dry lands of southeast Oregon came from a high school biology teacher from Burns. Russ Pengelly, who passed away in 1996, dared to think that people would come from the large cities of Oregon to hike in the desert, if they were only shown the way. The result of the visionary thinking of Pengelly, as well as others who shared his vision, was the creation of the Desert Trail. The trail's first section opened in 1980, passing through the Pueblo Mountains of Harney County just north of the Nevada border.

The Desert Trail is not a constructed path like hikers have come to expect in Oregon's Cascades. The openness of the desert terrain made a smoothed-out trail unnecessary, to say nothing of the cost involved in preparing and maintaining a traditional hiking surface. Instead of a designated path, the Desert Trail is designed to be a corridor through public land. The trail's route is marked by rock cairns, built 4 to 6 feet high, that can be spotted on the horizon. When standing alongside a cairn, the next closest cairns forward and backward should be visible. The concept of the Desert Trail makes it less important where a hiker walks than *how* a hiker walks. The Desert Trail's concept spreads use out over the fragile soil while guiding hikers through a defined route that crosses public land.

Originally based in Burns, the Desert Trail Association was formed to guide development of the trail and serve as a liaison among the federal agencies, whose land the trail crosses, and the private landowners, who have graciously granted easements in places where they are needed. The trail has grown over the years to include eight segments—six in Harney County and two in Nevada. The Desert Trail's six Harney County sections already cover 150 miles of land that varies from the dried lake bed of the Alvord Desert to the spectacular heights of Steens Mountain. Ultimately, the trail will stretch from Southern California to Idaho.

Those who have hiked Oregon's beaches and mountains immediately notice a similarity when they first hike here. The desert gives them the same—perhaps even better—open views as they get when walking along a sandy ocean beach or in the mountains above timberline. The Desert Trail gives hikers the chance to compare and decide for themselves if the desert is the kind of place they enjoy.

Getting There

Burns, the seat of Harney County, is 290 miles southeast of Portland. From Bend in central Oregon, Burns is 130 miles east on US Highway 20 (US 20) across the juniper and sagebrush lands of southeast Oregon's high desert. US 20 crosses Harney County east to west and US 395 cuts across the northwest part of the county. Highway 205, paved since the early 1990s, traverses the center of the county from Burns to the Nevada border at Denio, passing Malheur National Wildlife Refuge, Frenchglen, and Steens Mountain Recreation Area along the way. Besides Burns, Hines is the only other town of significant size in the sprawling county, and it's right next door on Burns's west side.

Adjoining Areas
    NORTH: **Upper John Day River**
    EAST: **Malheur County**
    WEST: **Lake County, Bend and the Upper Deschutes River, Crooked River**

inside out

Scenic Drives

Harney County is big, as in 10,228 square miles BIG. The largest county in Oregon by 304 square miles, Harney is the ninth-largest county in the United States outside of Alaska. The sheer size of the county takes some getting used to and, thankfully, the main steward of the land has recognized a system of auto tours that show off the sights of the county. The Bureau of Land Management (BLM) tours can be driven as worthy objectives of their own or used to access the major attractions of the county. The BLM's Burns office, (541) 573-4400, is located at the west edge of Hines on US 20.

Harney County shares the 90-mile **Lakeview to Steens Byway** with Lake County. Only the most ardent defender of Harney County could claim that it has the best scenery on this route (see Lake County chapter). Most of the 40 miles of sagebrush flats that the passenger-car route crosses, between Hart Mountain and Frenchglen, are here. The perspective begins to change as the byway joins Hwy 205, 7 miles south of Frenchglen, which is 65 miles south of Burns. **Frenchglen,** an odd name for a town in Oregon's remote ranching country, is one of the most magical places in the state. Officially little more than a gas station/restaurant/hotel, Frenchglen is so much bigger than the sum of its pieces. The town was named after Peter French, a local ranch foreman who was gunned down more than a century ago by one of his vaqueros. Spread out to the east is Malheur National Wildlife Refuge and magnificent Steens Mountain. Of the hundreds of mountain ranges in the Great Basin, there is only one like Steens Mountain because of its stupendous glacier-carved gorges and its abundance of year-round water.

The BLM's **Steens Mountain Byway,** better known locally as the Steens Mountain Loop Rd, begins at Frenchglen, climbs to just beneath the 9,773-foot summit of Steens on the north loop road, travels 3 miles south along the rim, then circles back west to rejoin Hwy 205, 10 miles south of Frenchglen. The byway's road number is 8244, but signs direct travelers to the Steens Mountain Loop Rd. The southern loop can be rugged and bumpy and usually requires a high-clearance vehicle. The byway is only 66 miles long, but it climbs nearly 5,000 feet, passing through spectacular scenery nearly every mile of the way. Steens Mountain is the highest peak in Harney County and the ninth highest in Oregon. The road to its summit is the highest road in the state.

Main attractions along this route are the glacier-carved gorges— **Kiger, Big Indian, Little Indian, Wildhorse,** and **Little Blitzen,** all of which descend from the rim where the road passes along the summit. Each is a big, U-shaped valley, carved 2,000 feet or more into the mountain's gently sloping 20-mile-long western side. A 30-mile-long fault block mountain, Steens drops precipitously on its eastern side. Within 3 miles it falls 5,000 feet to the dry alkaline lake bed of the **Alvord Desert** below. Contrasting views from the summit rim are nothing short of breathtaking.

The **Diamond Loop Byway** passes the northern flank of Steens Mountain as it covers 69 miles between Hwy 205, 18 miles north of Frenchglen, and Hwy 78 at New Princeton. Major sights along the way include Malheur National Wildlife Refuge, on the east side of Hwy 205; **Diamond Craters Outstanding Natural Area,** 10 miles east of Hwy 205; and the **Peter French Round Barn,** 17 miles east of the highway. One of the last strongholds of open-range ranching, the Round Barn was constructed by Harney County's cowboys in the 1870s and 1880s for their ranch foreman to use for training horses during winter. Built mostly of tough old western juniper trees and local stone, the barn was finished with lodgepole pines hauled in from 100 miles away. The covered barn is 100 feet in diameter and has an interior 60-foot-round stone corral.

The **Malheur National Wildlife Refuge auto tour** covers 42 miles and begins at refuge headquarters, 27 miles south of Burns on Hwy 205 and 5 miles east on the refuge road. A booklet explains the human and natural history of 28 stops encountered along the tour, which heads south from the headquarters on gravel roads a few miles east of Hwy 205 to Frenchglen. Contact the headquarters at (541) 493-2612.

Wildlife

Malheur National Wildlife Refuge is justifiably famous for its flocks of **migrating waterfowl** during spring and fall, but visitors can also expect to see **mule deer** and **pronghorn antelope,** a **bobcat** prowling the ditches along the tour route (see Scenic Drives, above), or any number of **songbirds** that make the place home during summer.

The refuge headquarters, with some barrier-free facilities, is 32 miles south of Burns near the south shore of Malheur Lake. Elevation of the refuge is 4,100 feet above sea level. The refuge is aligned like a giant T, with Harney and Malheur Lakes comprising the horizontal northern part of the T. A narrow 30-mile strip of land south of the headquarters makes up the vertical section. The auto tour heads south from the headquarters, passing a series of dikes that can be used to divert the waters of the Donner und Blitzen River to flood fields as desired.

Birds can be spotted with every turn of the head, and the 185,000-acre refuge encourages spending as much time as possible. Most visitors drive the patrol roads, using their vehicles as blinds and relying on binoculars to bring the wildlife up close. **Sandhill cranes, trumpeter swans,** and **turkey vultures** are some of the large birds seen frequently. Smaller birds include the **killdeer, burrowing owl, whippoorwill,** and **red-winged blackbird.** A total of 232 bird species are seen fairly regularly, with another 59 considered accidental sightings as the birds wander through away from their normal habitat. The **Malheur Field Station,** (541) 493-2629, adjacent to the headquarters, provides a home base for exploring the refuge with meals, dorm rooms, and limited trailer hookups.

An unforgettable sight in Malheur National Wildlife Refuge or along Steens Mountain Loop Rd is the herd of wild **Kiger mustangs.** The Kiger horses are said to be one of the most pure breeds of wild Spanish horses existing today. The BLM maintains two herd-management areas where horses are allowed to flourish naturally. When their number grows too large, they are rounded up and sent to an adoption facility near Burns. The northern herd lives southeast of Diamond and ranges in size from 50 to 80 horses. The southern herd varies in size from 150 to 300 animals. The best viewing spots for the southern herd are from the south branch of Steens Mountain Loop Rd, just before and after Blitzen Crossing (16 miles east of Hwy 205).

One animal on Steens Mountain that is rarely seen from a vehicle is the **California bighorn sheep.** Oregon's second-largest colony of bighorn sheep spends most of its time on the rugged east side of the mountain, away from roads and prying eyes of tourists. Sheep spotting on Steens is usually best in August before the limited hunting season begins in September and the sheep become warier.

Steens is also home to herds of **pronghorn antelope.** It's not unusual to see a band of 40 or more animals just below the summit on the bench land between Big Indian and Little Blitzen Gorges. The east side of the Steens provides great soaring opportunities for a variety of **raptors.**

The Oregon desert harbors the expected assortment of wildlife, including **rattlesnakes.** While snakes are rare and many hiking groups never see them, the memory of a sighting can last a lifetime. One group of

10 hikers was taking a noon rest break. As the hikers sat or stood in a circle, a pair of 5-foot-long western diamondback rattlesnakes, plump as a man's forearm, slithered through the group and continued traveling down to a stream.

Hiking/Backpacking

The Desert Trail

The ultimate goal of the Desert Trail, officially designated a national recreation trail, is to mimic the Pacific Crest Trail and the Appalachian Trail as a long-distance, through-hiking route, although the harsh conditions will make it impossible to hike the entire trail on a single journey. Much of the trail is too hot and too far from water to consider hiking during summer. Alternate summer hiking choices, however, are available through desert mountains, where heavy snow makes the terrain inaccessible during the rest of the year. Signs mark the trail at some of the places where it crosses roads. Outings that require long-distance hiking often involve prearranged vehicle shuttles. Maps of all Desert Trail segments are available from the Desert Trail Association by mail (see More Information, at the end of the chapter), from the BLM, and at many Oregon outdoor stores. Contact the Burns BLM office at (541) 573-4400.

The desert can be full of surprises. Unlike other mountain ranges in the Great Basin, especially Nevada and Utah, Oregon's desert mountains are well watered. Many streams and springs run throughout the year on Steens and in the Pueblo and Trout Creek Mountains. It's hard to beat the beauty of a desert waterfall deep in a canyon where water is so precious. Water may be absent when walking desert flats at the base of mountains, so some sections of the Desert Trail require water to be cached in advance to help hikers make it through long, dry sections.

The Desert Trail begins south of Fields near the Nevada border with the 22-mile **Pueblo Mountains section,** the first part of the trail to be mapped in 1981. A typical fault block range of the Great Basin, the Pueblo Mountains rise to an elevation of 8,634 feet at Pueblo Peak. The trail corridor passes the range's high point to the west, but many hiking groups add an extra day to bag the peak with a 2.5-mile, one-way scramble from 10-Cent Meadow. A through hike in the Pueblo Mountains section usually allows four days. This section has 48 rock cairns, some up to 6 feet tall, that are strategically built atop ridges so they can be seen from a distance to keep hikers on track. The cairns were built before the maps were published, so using the proper map and watching for the cairns is the best way to navigate the trail.

The 25-mile **Alvord Desert section,** the second section in Oregon from the Nevada border, begins at Fields and runs north to Frog Springs, an oasis on the west edge of the Alvord Desert on the east side of Steens Mountain. The corridor has only one water supply along the way at Dixon Spring, but several high-clearance roads cross the corridor and make it possible to cache water in advance. This section is usually hiked in spring or fall when snow locks up the high country. One group that counted on finding water along the way was lucky enough to do so. But to make the water drinkable, they strained it through a bandanna twice, pumped it through a water filter and dropped in some iodine pills. Despite the precaution, they still think it was the water that made them sick after their hike was finished.

The **Steens Mountain section** of the Desert Trail runs north from Frog Springs, climbs through Wildhorse Canyon, and reaches the south loop road on Steens in the cirque between Big Indian and Little Blitzen Gorges. The hike changes 5,000 feet in elevation over 15 miles, so most groups opt to do it down from Steens Mountain rather than up. Any hike up or down Steens Mountain ranks among the most spectacular hikes in Oregon. Locating water is usually not a problem on Steens Mountain because it has three dozen streams that run all year.

The trail's **John Scharff section,** named for a long-time manager of Malheur National Wildlife Refuge, begins atop Steens Mountain and descends 25 to 30 miles over 4,800 feet in elevation to Page Springs Campground near Frenchglen. The corridor concept of the trail allows hikers the option of descending either Big Indian Gorge or Little Blitzen Gorge. Both are deep, scenic canyons filled with wildlife. Dragonflies are welcome residents of Big Indian Gorge. The big insects hang out during the evening around hikers' camps and clean the air of all sorts of nasty little flying things. The lower part of the John Scharff section follows the Donner und Blitzen River on a sagebrush-covered bench west of the federally designated Wild and Scenic River. The canyon bottom, home to a healthy population of mountain lions, is too rugged to hike in for long.

The **Malheur National Wildlife Refuge section** of the trail, the fifth section in Oregon from the Nevada border, runs 30 miles between Page Springs and Diamond Craters. The best hiking season is spring and fall. Summer is when the insect pests appear and the cattails and marsh grasses are too tall for good wildlife viewing. This section can also be hiked in winter when the weather isn't too severe.

The **Riddle Mountain section** of the trail begins at Diamond Crater and travels 30 miles east to reach Hwy 78 at milepost 59 southeast of Burns. The section is easiest to hike east to west because it drops nearly 2,000 feet in elevation. Riddle Mountain is the long, 5,600-foot-high plateau midway along the section. The trail passes along the mountain's northern base for 5 miles.

Work continues on mapping the Desert Trail from Hwy 78 into Malheur County.

Southern Harney County

Much of **Steens Mountain** is publicly owned, so hiking is possible just about anywhere. The area west of **Fish Lake,** north of **Jackman Park** (both along the north loop road; see Scenic Drives, above), and anywhere along the mountain's rim offers good wildlife-viewing opportunities. Descents into the major gorges are popular, but remember to save enough time and energy to climb back out before dark. **Wildhorse Canyon,** just south of the summit microwave tower, makes a good day hike, even though cattle graze around the shore of Wildhorse Lake a thousand feet below the summit road. **Kiger Gorge,** where the north loop road reaches the top, is known for the notch, the only place the glaciers were able to carve through the Steens Mountain rim. The bottom of Kiger Gorge is appealing because its beauty is so evident from above, but much of the bottom of the canyon is privately owned. Probably the best hikes at Steens Mountain start with a drive on the summit road to its end either north or south, then a hike along the rim away from the road. The terrain is rugged, but the view of the Alvord Desert to the east is breathtaking.

The east side of Steens is dissected by a dozen magnificent canyons, most in public ownership but blocked to public access by private ranch lands at the bottom of the canyons. Exceptions are the route used by the Desert Trail, which requires a backpack to get into the interesting high country, and **Pike Creek Canyon,** a steep-walled canyon that begins 2 miles north of Alvord Hot Springs. The hot springs is privately owned, so users should ask for permission at the Alvord Ranch. The hot springs is inside a corrugated metal building alongside Fields-Follyfarm Rd, 23 miles north of Fields.

Access to the **Pueblo Mountains,** other than from the Desert Trail route, is easiest up **Arizona Creek,** 8.5 miles south of Fields where a high-clearance-vehicle road leaves Hwy 205 about midway along the mountain and climbs up Pueblo Peak's eastern face to an old mine. The peak's summit is a 2-mile, 3,000-foot scramble to the west from as high up the road as you can drive. Pueblo Peak doesn't rank among the most difficult peaks to climb in the Great Basin, but it's difficult to find a more scenic climb.

The **Alvord Desert** is an alkaline flat, the remains of an ancient lake bed. With an average of 6 inches of rain per year—the driest spot in Oregon—the Alvord is usually bone dry, but not always. Vehicle access to the lake bed is from **Frog Springs,** 2 miles south of Alvord Hot Springs. The lake is used by land sailors and for towing gliders aloft. The lake bed is an interesting place to camp, but remember that it's virtually impossible to find a way off after dark. The best hiking is on the eastern shore of the circular 7-mile lake bed. Drive across to the low line of sandy hills that harbor native plants, but watch out for wet spots on the playa that can trap vehicles.

A good backpacking base camp in the Trout Creek Mountains is **Little Table Seep,** a spring on Center Ridge between Big and Little Trout Creeks, 4 miles from Little Trout Creek Rd. Drive Whitehorse Ranch Rd, which heads east from Hwy 205, 12 miles north of the Nevada border, for 14 miles. Turn south on Little Trout Creek Rd and drive 2 miles to where a spur road drops to the creek. Park, walk down to the creek, cross it, and continue following an old road as it heads west and then south to climb Center Ridge. Little Table Seep is 4 miles from the parking area, on the east side of the ridge. If you can't locate the seep, drop down east into Little Trout Creek Canyon to camp by running water.

Roads into the Trout Creek Mountains are best to travel with a four-wheel-drive or at least a high-clearance pickup. Bring a second spare tire and fill up with gas at Fields. For information, check with the BLM in Burns, (541) 573-4400.

Hikers worn out by the big country might want to give their feet a rest and go for a **horseback ride.** Steens Mountain Packers, (541) 495-2315, has trail rides out of Frenchglen and overnight trips into the backcountry. The outfitter can also arrange sightseeing trips by helicopter.

Northern Harney County

Developed hiking trails in the Ochoco and Malheur National Forest sections of Harney County are rare. The **Myrtle Creek Trail** is described under Biking, below. The area's only other long trail is **Craft Cabin** (moderate; 9 miles one way). The trail follows Pine Creek in the southeast tip of Malheur National Forest. The trailhead can be reached by driving north on Forest Rd 28 and its spurs from the community of Harney, 12 miles northeast of Burns on US 20.

Camping

Camping is never far away in Harney County, especially if you don't mind camping off the road in a quiet spot with no developed facilities. Much of Harney County is publicly owned and camping is legal just about anywhere, except in Malheur National Wildlife Refuge. Summer mosquitoes can be so bad that camping near the refuge's wetlands would be uncomfortable anyway. As with camping at any location away from a developed campground, use proper procedures for disposing of human waste, be careful with fire, and leave the site cleaner than when you arrived.

A 10,000-square-mile forest of ponderosa pines, the largest in the country, covers the northern part of the county. Most of the expanse of pines is in neighboring Grant County, but enough extends into Harney to offer some cool mountain camping when the desert bakes during summer. The Snow Mountain Ranger District, (541) 573-4300, of the Ochoco National Forest covers northwest Harney County and has three campgrounds: Delintment Lake, Emigrant, and Falls. **Delintment Lake Campground** is the largest with two dozen sites. Access is via County Rd 127, which heads northwest from US 20 at Hines. Drive 16 miles to the forest boundary, where the road splits. Forest Rd 41 travels 25 miles northwest to Delintment Lake, while the county road continues north to another split. Take the left fork, Forest Rd 43, northwest to **Emigrant and Falls Campgrounds.**

The Burns Ranger District, (541) 573-7292, of Malheur National Forest is north of Burns and offers camping at Idlewild and Yellowjacket. **Idlewild Campground** (24 sites) stays busy because of its location just off US 395, about 18 miles north of Burns. **Yellowjacket Campground** (20 sites) is on a reservoir with good rainbow trout fishing (follow County Rd 127 to its second split, turn right on Forest Rd 47, drive 8 miles north, turn east on Forest Rd 37 for 3 miles to the campground).

The BLM, (541) 573-4400, offers camping at **Chickahominy Reservoir,** 35 miles west of Burns on US 20, and at **Mann Lake** on the east side of Steens, 30 miles south of Hwy 78. Both have good fishing, the main attraction for virtually treeless desert campgrounds. Mann Lake has barrier-free camping and a boat launch.

Four BLM camps are well spaced along Steens Mountain Loop Rd: **Page Springs Campground** at the western base of Steens, 3 miles east of Frenchglen on the northern loop road (see Scenic Drives, above); **Fish Lake and Jackman Park Campgrounds,** both 18 miles up the north loop road; and **South Steens Campground** near Blitzen Crossing on the south loop (see Wildlife, above). South Steens is set up for equestrians, but also has 21 family camp spots and drinking water. No BLM camps in the Burns District take reservations, and facilities are limited to outhouses, picnic tables, and fire rings. Fish Lake can have hordes of blackflies during summer. On one trip to the campground, the ravenous flies cleaned a bug-splattered windshield so thoroughly that it looked like the windshield had been through a car wash.

Fishing

Harney County lies at the northwest edge of the Great Basin, an area not known for pristine rivers and great fishing. But the county is big enough to be an exception to the rule. Check the state fishing synopsis, available in tackle shops for regulations, or call the Oregon Department of Fish and Wildlife's district office at Hines, (541) 573-6582.

The **Donner und Blitzen River** (German for thunder and lightning) drains the west side of Steens Mountain and flows through Malheur National Wildlife Refuge before emptying into Malheur Lake. The only natural way for water to escape Malheur Lake is by evaporation. The Donner und Blitzen, a federally protected Wild and Scenic River, is a good trout stream for much of its 40 miles. Native redband are the primary catch. Because it is managed as a trophy fishery, anglers are encouraged to release all fish. Flies and lures are allowed but no bait. Best access is at Page Springs Campground (see Camping, above).

As a result of the early 1990s drought, many of the streams on the east side of the Steens and in the Trout Creek Mountains are still closed to fishing in an effort to rebuild the population of the native Lahontan cutthroat trout.

Krumbo Reservoir, 15 miles north of Frenchglen on Hwy 205, and Fish Lake (see Camping, above) receive much of the angling attention on Steens Mountain's west side. **Krumbo Reservoir** can be good for rainbow trout and largemouth bass before weeds get too thick during summer. (Baca Reservoir nearby is closed to angling.) **Fish Lake** is stocked annually around the Fourth of July with 5,000 rainbow trout. The lake also has naturally reproducing brook trout. **Wildhorse Lake,** just south of the Steens summit near 9,000 feet in elevation (see Hiking/Backpacking, above), has a small population of Lahontan cutthroat and is one of the few places left where fishermen can pursue the desert-adapted fish.

Mann Lake east of Steens is managed as a trophy-fishing lake. Fishing is with flies and lures only; no bait. The native population of Mann Lake cutthroat is supplemented with an annual stocking of 20,000 rainbow trout. Fish in the 20-inch range are not uncommon. The lake has a popular campground and boat launch (see Camping, above).

Most fishing west of Burns is available at **Chickahominy Reservoir** along US 20. The reservoir has an ardent following, who put up with its stark desert conditions and absence of trees to prowl the lake's 530 acres looking for the famous big rainbow that live there.

When it gets too hot down on the desert, anglers head north to the cooler ponderosa pine forests to fish for stocked rainbow trout at **Delintment Lake** and **Yellowjacket Lake** (see Camping, above).

Biking

Big, wide-open Harney County has lots of paved and gravel road-riding opportunities, but singletrack is a rarity in a county without a lot of developed trails. An exception is the 7-mile **Myrtle Creek Trail,** a good opportunity for less-experienced riders to try their hand at trail riding. The trail follow the creek downhill from 5,400 feet in elevation to 4,600 feet at the boundary of Malheur National Forest, where riders must backtrack. To reach the trailhead, drive 1 mile north on US 395 from Idlewild campground (see Camping, above), turn left, and drive 12 miles northwest on Forest Rd 31.

Steens Mountain has few suitable riding areas, other than the loop road itself (see Scenic Drives, above). Cyclists who don't want to pedal the grueling miles to the summit can drive to the top and ride the road between the viewpoints. Riding atop Steens Mountain doesn't provide the excitement of a singletrack, but with an elevation above 9,000 feet this ride is the highest in Oregon and provides a thrill all its own.

Diamond Craters, with some of its roads too rough for most passenger cars, gives an uncrowded road-riding opportunity for mountain bikes. Park along Lava Beds Rd on the Diamond Crater Byway (see Scenic Drives, above) and ride west past Lava Pit Crater and Malheur Maar. The road is mostly flat, with some easy ups and downs. Riding during the middle of a summer day is probably out of the question for most cyclists because of the intense heat.

Rock Collecting

Many of the hills just north of Burns and Hines are made of glass. In this case, it's the jet-black glass called **obsidian.** A favorite among rock collectors, obsidian can be cut into sharp edges to make knives and arrowheads. The best digs are just northeast of Hines. Drive Forest Rd 47 north out of Hines for 4 miles and turn east on a BLM road. Obvious public digging sites soon appear on either side of the road.

The area south of Harney Lake along the BLM road that passes the south shore is known for **agate, jasper,** and **petrified wood.** Pine Creek northeast of Buchanan is known for its **wonderstone,** an unusual variety of rhyolite. Stinkingwater Pass on US 395, 6 miles northeast of Buchanan in eastern Harney County, is a regular producer of petrified wood.

Thundereggs and **Oregon sunstone** can be collected in the area, as well; check with the Highland Rock and Gem Shop, (541) 573-5119, on US 20 in Burns for current information.

outside in

Restaurants

Pine Room Cafe ☆ This cafe has kept the same faithful clientele for 30 years. Careful preparations and interesting recipes are the reason (the German potato-dumpling soup is a favorite). They make their own bread and cut their own steaks in the kitchen. *543 W Monroe St (at Egan), Burns; (541) 573-6631; $$.*

Cheaper Eats

Frenchglen Mercantile   The deli case offers picnic fare, while the dining room offers dinner only, with a very short menu featuring reasonably priced fare (grilled filet mignon, fresh poached salmon). Full bar and a few rooms too. Closed mid-November through mid-March. *Downtown Frenchglen, OR; (541) 493-2738; $.*

Lodgings

Diamond Hotel   This hotel quintuples as general store (with gas), deli, post office, and local watering hole. Five bedrooms share baths and a sitting area. There's always meat, potatoes, vegetables, salad, and bread; desserts are huge. Open mid-March through mid-November. *12 miles east of Hwy 205, Diamond; PO Box 10, Diamond, OR 97722; (541) 493-1898; $.*

Frenchglen Hotel ☆   This historic white frame building has small, plain bedrooms with shared baths. Nothing's very square or level here, and that's part of the charm. Good, simple meals are served; ranch-style dinner is one seating only and reservations are a must. Closed mid-November through February. *60 miles south of Burns, Frenchglen; General Delivery, Frenchglen, OR 97736; (541) 493-2825; $.*

More Information

Bureau of Land Management, Hines: *(541) 573-4400.*
Bureau of Land Management, Vale: *(541) 473-3144.*
Burns Ranger District, Hines: *(541) 573-7292.*
The Desert Trail Association: *PO Box 34, Madras, OR 97741.*
Harney County Chamber of Commerce, Burns: *(541) 573-2636.*
Malheur National Forest, John Day: *(541) 575-1731.*
Malheur National Wildlife Refuge, Princeton: *(541) 493-2612.*
Ochoco National Forest, Prineville: *(541) 416-6500.*
Oregon Outback Visitors Association, Klamath Falls:
  (800) 598-6877.
Snow Mountain Ranger District, Hines: *(541) 573-4300.*

Malheur
County

From the Malheur-Baker county line and US Highway 26 on the north, east to the Idaho border, south to the Nevada, border and west to the Malheur-Harney county line, including the Owyhee River, the eastern half of the Trout Creek Mountains, and the towns of Ontario, Vale, Nyssa, and Jordan Valley.

The scenery around the Owyhee River of Malheur County looks like someone picked up a small part of southern Utah and dropped it in Oregon. Utah has Zion, Bryce, Arches, Canyonlands, and the Escalante. Oregon has the Owyhee. Utah has millions of tourists passing through its parks each year. The Owyhee has only a few thousand. You can decide where you'd rather go to get away from it all.

The Owyhee River rises in the remote desert mountains of southeast Idaho and north-central Nevada. The river's main branches come together at Three Forks, just inside the Oregon border, from where it flows north through a colorful and spectacular canyon to join the Snake River.

It forms Oregon's largest reservoir when its flow is constricted behind Owyhee Dam. The reservoir is 13,900 acres in size, small compared to some on the Snake and Columbia Rivers, but large enough to be the biggest entirely within Oregon's boundaries. The surface of Owyhee Lake provides some of Oregon's best inland boating opportunities. Anyone fortunate enough to have use of a boat also has access to the magnificent side canyons. Many of the Owyhee's canyons are next to impossible to explore from above because of their rugged topography and the long approaches they require from the end of the nearest four-wheel-drive track.

The Owyhee isn't the only attraction of vast Malheur County, which is the second largest in Oregon, with 9,926 square miles. The Trout Creek Mountains, located in the remote southwest part of the sprawling region, come vibrantly alive with wildflowers during late spring and early summer like few other places in Oregon's high desert. Seen only by a few hard-core desert lovers, the canyons and draws of the Trout Creek Mountains offer one of the last true wilderness experiences in Oregon.

The Trout Creek Mountains won't bring to mind Utah's canyon lands, but anyone hiking the Malheur country in summer won't be wishing they were in Utah's desert instead.

Getting There

Ontario, largest town in Malheur County, is 374 miles from Portland and 61 miles from Boise, Idaho, via Interstate 84. The Owyhee River joins the Snake River near Nyssa, a dozen miles south of Ontario. Owyhee Lake is 45 miles southwest of Ontario via state and county roads. The Owyhee River canyon is usually approached from US Highway 95 (US 95) where it crosses the river at Rome, 120 miles southwest of Ontario. The Trout Creek Mountains are 200 miles southwest of Ontario and can be reached via the county's Whitehorse Ranch Road, which passes north of the mountains as it travels from US 95 on the east to Highway 205 on the west. Ontario is linked to the west at Burns by US 20 and to John Day by US 26.

Adjoining Areas

NORTH: **Baker County**

WEST: **Harney County, Upper John Day River**

Rafting/Kayaking

The **Owyhee River's** 103-mile run from Three Forks to the backwaters of Lake Owyhee cuts through a canyon that becomes more and more spectacular the deeper it gets. For convenience of planning, rafters and kayakers divide the Owyhee River below Three Forks into middle and lower sections. The Three Forks launch is 41 miles south of US 95 on a signed Bureau of Land Management (BLM) road 16 miles west of Jordan Valley. Rome, the dividing point of the middle and lower sections, is on US 95, 27 miles west of Jordan Valley. The BLM office and launch is on the east bank of the river, just south of the highway bridge. Leslie Gulch, the takeout for the lower section, is on Owyhee Reservoir, on BLM roads 22 miles northeast from US 95 just after it crosses into Oregon from Idaho.

The Owyhee's **middle section** is often the planned objective for many a raft trip, only to have the destination shift to the lower section due to water level or the condition of access roads. A reading at the Rome gauge of above 4,000 cubic feet per second (cfs) makes the middle section the domain of expert boaters. Anything less than 1,500cfs may be too low for a raft. The 37-mile run of the river's middle section passes through a deep, unroaded canyon, making rescue assistance nearly impossible. In addition to Widowmaker, a Class V rapids that drops 10 feet, other major rapids are Ledge, Half-Mile, and Raft Flip. Each offers a serious challenge. The reward of running the river comes from spending several days in a deep, remote canyon that few people ever experience.

The 66-mile **lower Owyhee** has plenty of exciting rapids. Class IV Whistling Bird is usually the most difficult, but Montgomery and Rock Dam also need to be taken seriously and scouted. The lower river passes many colorful rock formations, including Lambert Rocks just downstream from Rome and Jackson Hole, as well as some old homesteads. A few hot springs along the way are just large enough to warm the toes of rafters on a raw spring day. The best way to find them is to boat with someone who knows.

The Owyhee is a spring snowmelt river, usually at its best for floating from mid-March through Memorial Day weekend, although kayaks can run the river in the lower flows of summer. To check river flow **conditions,** call the Rome launch site of the BLM at (541) 586-2612. When the river rangers are too busy to answer, the river flow is also obtainable by calling the river forecast center in Portland at (503) 261-9246. The launch site isn't staffed after the river's level drops too low for boating.

All river-running parties must have a fire pan and carry and use a portable toilet. Boaters are required to **register,** but there is no restriction on the amount of use by noncommercial parties. The Owyhee is a long way from the nearest boating supply store, so river runners should arrive with all their food and equipment in hand. Rome has a restaurant for a pretrip meal, plus a gas station, but little else. The vast majority of **commercial float trips** run the lower Owyhee from Rome, either to the BLM's Birch Creek takeout above Lake Owyhee or all the way to the Leslie Gulch takeout. Commercial tow operators can be hired to meet parties where the river reaches slack water for the 10-mile tow across the upper part of Lake Owyhee to the boat landing. The BLM's Vale office, (541) 473-3144, can provide a list of commercial outfitters, vehicle shuttle services, and towboat operators. The office also sends out an informative boating guide to the Owyhee.

Camping

The Malheur country is one part of Oregon where no one needs to be shoehorned in with dozens of other campers unless they want to be. Fully 94 percent of the county is classified as grazing land and two-thirds of it is managed by the BLM.

Most campers heading for Malheur County plan to spend a few days at **Lake Owyhee** to relax in the sun, soak up the scenery, and catch a few fish. The lake is located off Hwy 201, 33 miles south of Nyssa. Lake Owyhee Resort, (541) 339-2444, is the center of activity, with motel rooms and cabins to rent, a restaurant, campground, marina, store, and boat rentals. The resort is up the east side of the reservoir 3 miles south of the dam. The 417-foot-high dam has a concrete "glory hole" near its face that can be raised or lowered by hydraulics to control the water level of the reservoir. Water spills down the hole like a giant funnel, no place anybody in a boat wants to be near.

Lake Owyhee State Park, (541) 523-2499, is 1 mile closer to the dam than the resort. The park has 30 tent sites and 10 electrical sites with a 55-foot maximum length for RVs. Open mid-April through October, the park has a barrier-free campsite and shower. Reservations are not accepted. Boat camping along the 52 miles of Lake Owyhee, with its 310 miles of shoreline, is virtually unlimited. Four boat ramps are available at the resort and state park.

The only other state park campground in Malheur County is at **Succor Creek State Natural Area,** (541) 523-2499, where 19 primitive campsites are available. Succor Creek passes through a colorful canyon known for its rock formations and birdlife. The park is on the BLM's Leslie Gulch–Succor Creek National Back Country Byway, a 52-mile gravel and dirt road that runs north-south a few miles inside the Oregon border, with a western spur that drops down to Lake Owyhee through Leslie Gulch. To reach the campground, turn south from Hwy 201 about 3 miles west of the Idaho border and drive 15 miles.

Chukar Park, the only BLM fee site in the area, is 6 miles north of US 20 at Juntura on Beulah Reservoir Rd. It has 18 campsites and the cost per night is $4. The RV length limit is 28 feet.

The BLM has primitive recreation sites spread around the county, most with small campgrounds and picnic areas. **Leslie Gulch** (see Rafting/Kayaking, above) has camping on Lake Owyhee. The 11-percent grade down to Leslie Gulch restricts access for larger RVs and trailers. **Snively Hot Springs,** 12 miles north of the dam on Owyhee Lake Rd, has camping near where hot springs flow from a concrete pipe on the east side of the road. Bathers soak in riverside rock and sand pools.

In the vast area south of Lake Owyhee, the BLM maintains camps at **Rome** and **Three Forks** along the upper Owyhee River (see Rafting/Kayaking, above); at **Antelope Reservoir,** 12 miles west of Jordan Valley on US 95; and at **Cow Lakes,** 8 miles west of Jordan Valley and 8 miles north on Cow Lakes Rd; and at **Willow Hot Springs,** 4 miles southwest of Whitehorse Ranch at the northern edge of the Trout Creek Mountains. Camping is also available near the historic **Birch Creek Ranch,** an alternate rafting takeout owned by the BLM on the Owyhee River above Leslie Gulch. Access during boating season usually requires a four-wheel-drive vehicle, so check with the river rangers before heading to Birch Creek Ranch to camp, an out-of-the-way destination northwest of Jordan Craters. For information on BLM camping, call the Vale office at (541) 473-3144, or visit at 100 Oregon St. BLM maps that cover Malheur County are available at the Vale office for Malheur and Jordan Resource Areas.

Hiking/Backpacking

Although hiking opportunities are abundant in Malheur County, few are developed or designated for that purpose. Hunters and fishermen following trails established by Indians or animals have formed most hiking trails over the years. Residents of southeast Oregon's high desert have been joined in recent years by hikers from urban areas of Oregon and Idaho who want to experience the outdoors in a remote, quiet setting. The wide-open spaces of Malheur County are ideal for that purpose.

   Leslie Gulch, a 5-mile-long canyon with a road at the bottom (see Rafting/Kayaking, above) is a good place for newcomers to begin exploring Malheur County because of its convenient road access and its outstanding scenery. The area was designated in 1983 by the BLM as an area of critical environmental concern to protect its bighorn sheep habitat and rare plant species. Much of the 11,653-acre site has been recommended as suitable for wilderness designation. Hiking usually is easiest up the drainages—**Slocum Creek** to the south of the campground (see Camping, above) near the lake or **Juniper Creek** on the north 3 miles east of the lake. Hikers need not wander far to enjoy the beauty of the country. A worthy goal is to climb to the ridge tops for views of Lake Owyhee snaking its way to the north. Formed by a volcanic rhyolite 15 million years old, the Leslie Gulch area is covered with steep slopes and wind-eroded towers and cliffs in an assortment of browns and yellows.

   The Honeycomb formation just north of the gulch gets its name from the pitted towers that look as though they were home to giant bees. While the formations can be sampled from the Leslie Gulch road, they are at their best several miles north. The center of the Honeycombs is easiest to explore from below on the reservoir by boat, but strong hikers willing to drive some rough roads can enter the formation from above. The best access is through **Painted Canyon,** which can be reached by driving south on Succor Creek Rd for 6 miles from Hwy 201. From Succor Creek Rd, turn west on a dirt road, drive 6 miles, take the right fork for 2 miles and then a left fork for another 2 miles to a watering tank. A four-wheel-drive road leads west from the tank 2 miles to Painted Canyon. Either drive or hike 2 miles to enter the canyon, then continue downcanyon as far as you want or climb slopes on either side for overall views.

The ultimate hike on the west side of the lower Owyhee River is the overlook of **Jackson Hole,** the 1,200-foot-deep canyon where boating parties frequently camp. The 4-mile hike to Jackson Hole is in the Lower Owyhee Canyon Wilderness Study Area. The hike follows an abandoned road for a mile, then a cattle trail east to the overlook. To begin the hike, which requires map and compass skills, drive 25 miles east from Hwy 78 to Crowley. This is the northern extension of Fields-Follyfarm Rd, which travels south along the east face of Steens Mountain. Drive a rough dirt road 8 miles east from Crowley and begin walking where the road becomes too rough to drive.

The middle and upper Owyhee River are primarily accessible by boat, except where vehicles can approach at Rome, Three Forks, and Anderson Crossing. The attraction at Rome is **Chalk Basin,** one of the famous landmarks of the lower river. From the Rome bridge on Hwy 95, drive north on a dirt road 3 miles along the west bank of the river. Park, then hike 2 miles farther north to see Chalk Basin. The road requires high-clearance vehicles and is accessible only when it's dry.

The **Trout Creek Mountains** are an uplifted, eroded plateau that covers a quarter-million acres in six BLM wilderness study areas. Unspectacular when seen from a distance, the mountains need to be explored on foot to enjoy their hidden beauty. Ridges and gullies are covered with mountain mahogany trees, quaking aspen, sagebrush, native grasses, and wildflowers. Snowbanks feed several creeks that flow year-round, and Lahontan cutthroat trout rise to take a fly. Mule deer range widely throughout the mountains. The Trout Creek Mountains are divided roughly in half by the Malheur-Harney county line, with Oregon Canyon, Twelve Mile Creek, Fifteen Mile Creek, Disaster Peak, and Willow Creek Wilderness Study Areas on the Malheur side.

Numerous BLM roads penetrate the high country, but they tend to stay on the ridges and leave the drainages for exploring on foot. A high-clearance vehicle is necessary, a four-wheel drive is helpful, and a second spare tire is prudent for vehicles that venture into the mountains without benefit of a convoy. The BLM's Vale District Jordan Resource Area map shows the roads. Contact the office at (541) 473-3144 for information but feel lucky if you can reach the few staffers that range this far afield.

Mud Spring, a cattle-watering trough 10 miles southeast of the Whitehorse Ranch, is a good place to establish base camp and hike to nearby drainages. To reach the ranch, drive US 95 21 miles south of Burns Junction and turn southwest on gravel Whitehorse Ranch Rd. The ranch comes at 20 miles, where the turn for Mud Spring is on the south side of BLM Rd 6301. From Mud Spring, **Oregon Canyon** to the east, **Antelope Canyon** to the north, and **Whitehorse Canyon** to the southwest are all worthy hiking objectives. USGS topographical maps are necessary for navigation (see Oregon Outdoor Primer chapter). Hiking is on game and cattle trails, unless there happens to be an old four-wheel-drive road nearby. Shorter hikes are also rewarding from vehicle base camps.

Fishing

The Snake, Owyhee, and Malheur Rivers, plus a sprinkling of irrigation reservoirs, give Malheur County more fishing opportunities than might normally be expected for a high-desert environment that averages 9.64 inches of precipitation annually.

The **Snake River** reaches the Oregon border near Adrian, about 30 miles south of Ontario near Hwy 201. It flows north, forming Malheur County's border with Idaho, until it reaches Farewell Bend and begins its run through Hells Canyon. Bends in the river actually leave a small part of Oregon on the east side of the Snake. Fishing is best for channel catfish, smallmouth bass, and crappie. Nyssa and Ontario have boat launches.

The **Owyhee River** provides large rainbow and brown trout in the first 10 miles below Owyhee Dam where the river is accessible from public land along the Lake Owyhee access road (see Camping, above). Other reaches of the river, both above and below the reservoir, have channel catfish and smallmouth bass. **Lake Owyhee** is home to plenty of large bass and black crappie, but naturally occurring mercury makes their flesh dangerous for humans to eat in quantity.

The **Malheur River,** followed closely by US 20 during its run through Malheur County, is most productive for planted rainbow below **Beulah Reservoir** (see Camping, above). **Malheur Reservoir** is an impoundment of Willow Creek in the north part of the county, not the Malheur River. The reservoir is on county roads 15 miles northwest from US 26 at Brogan and is productive for rainbow trout and Mann Lake cutthroat.

Check the state synopsis for regulations, or call the Oregon Department of Fish and Wildlife's Ontario office, (541) 889-6975.

Wildlife

The Lower Owyhee Canyon is designated a watchable-wildlife area by the BLM. Binocular signs, an internationally recognized symbol, mark suggested viewing locations along the road to Lake Owyhee (see Camping, above). Birds are most commonly seen, but a lucky few catch glimpses of **river otter, bobcat,** and **porcupine.** The riparian zone along the river is more productive than the sagebrush uplands above the river. Birds to watch for are **killdeer, common nighthawk,** and **California quail.** A surprise visitor so far from the ocean is the **double-crested cormorant.** A barrier-free picnic area is located along the route.

Soldier Creek, south of US 95 and 17 miles east of Rome, is another of the BLM's designated watchable-wildlife sites.

Succor Creek (see Camping, above) is known for its colony of **white-throated swifts. Golden eagles** and other **raptors** nest in the canyon's cliffs. Leslie Gulch (see Rafting/Kayaking, above) is home to **bighorn sheep, chukar,** and **wild horses.** Trophy-size **mule deer** are common in the northern part of the county near Ironside on US 26 as well as in the Trout Creek Mountains (see Hiking/Backpacking, above), while **pronghorn antelope** roam widely on the county's southern plains.

Rock Collecting

The BLM's Leslie Gulch–Succor Creek National Back Country Byway (see Camping, above) leads to some of the best **Thunдеregg** rock-collecting areas in Oregon. The prime digging location is 19 miles south of Adrian where the road and creek converge. Other rocks worth collecting in the area are **jasper** and **petrified wood.** Nyssa's nickname is the "Thunderegg Capital of Oregon."

outside In

Attractions

Beginning in 1843, emigrants got their first look at what became the state of Oregon where the **Oregon Trail** crossed the Snake River 5 miles south of Nyssa. An interpretive shelter where Hwy 201 crosses the trail describes the dangerous crossing and nearby Fort Boise of the Hudson Bay Company, where the pioneers could purchase needed supplies for exorbitant prices.

Keeney Pass, 5 miles south of Vale on Lytle Boulevard, has a short footpath that leads to wagon ruts carved into the earth by the emigrants' passage. Of an estimated 315,000 emigrants who crossed the Plains between

1843 and 1860, about 65,000 settled in Oregon. Congress designated the 2,000-mile Oregon Trail as a national historic trail in 1978. Other interpretive displays in Malheur County can be found in Vale and at the Ontario rest area for westbound traffic on I-84. The **Four Rivers Cultural Center,** (541) 889-8191, a 10,000-square-foot museum that opened in 1997 at 676 SW Fifth Ave in Ontario, interprets the legacy of settlement along the Oregon-Idaho border after the first wave of pioneers passed through on their way to the Willamette Valley.

Restaurants

Casa Jaramillo This Mexican cantina gives cool respite from the hot Oregon desert. Since 1967, this family has been turning out authentic Mexican fare. Try the enchiladas rancheras. *157 SE 2nd St (2 blocks south of Idaho Ave), Ontario; (541) 889-9258; $.*

More Information

Bureau of Land Management, Burns: *(541) 573-4400.*
Bureau of Land Management, Vale: *(541) 473-3144.*
Eastern Oregon Visitors Association, Baker City: *(800) 332-1843.*
Nyssa Chamber of Commerce, Nyssa: *(541) 372-3091.*
Ontario Chamber of Commerce, Ontario: *(541) 889-8012.*
Vale Chamber of Commerce, Vale: *(541) 473-3800.*

Index

A

Abert Lake, 624
Agate Beach State Recreation Site, 230
Agate Beach State Wayside, 225
Ainsworth State Park, 316
Albany
  fishing, 89
  restaurants, 95
Aldrich Mountains
  camping, 609
  hiking, 607–8
Alfred A. Loeb State Park, 277
Alsea, 238
Alsea Bay
  crabbing, 231
  fishing, 231
Alvord Desert, 637, 639–40, 641–42
Ankeny National Wildlife Refuge, 89–90
Anthony Lake(s)
  camping, 581
  fishing, 584
  hiking, 578–79
  skiing, 587–88
Arch Cape, 182
Arlington, 299
Ashland, 167, 172, 523
  biking, 162
  lodgings, 170–73
  parks, 155
  restaurants, 169–70
  skiing, 165–66
Astoria
  biking, 342–43
  boating, 334
  hiking, 340–41
  lodgings, 344
  parks/beaches/picnics, 339
  restaurants, 344
  windsurfing, 338
Aufderheide Drive, 104, 108–9

B

Backpacking. See Hiking
Badger Creek Wilderness, hiking, 385–86
Baker Beach, 243, 247
Baker City
  lodgings, 589
  restaurants, 589
Baker County, 574–89
  biking, 585–86
  camping, 581–83
  fishing, 583–85
  ghost towns, 577
  hiking, 577–80
  scenic drives, 576–77
  skiing, 587–88
  wildlife, 586–87
Bald Peak State Park, 46
Bandon, 263, 271
  boating, 260
  lodgings, 272–73
  restaurants, 271–72
Bandon State Park, 261
Banks-Vernonia Linear State Park, 42–43, 342
Barlow Road, 360–61
Barrier-free
  camping, 59, 60, 62, 85, 110, 134, 153, 154, 178, 194, 215, 248, 249, 264, 276, 277, 315, 316, 320, 362, 363, 382, 419, 487, 498, 534, 552, 567, 609, 643
  facilities, vi
  fishing, 69, 130, 204, 215, 317, 320, 362, 363, 418, 419, 534, 584
  horseback riding, 91–92, 247
  picnics, 64, 155–56, 230
  trails, 12, 42, 67, 224, 517, 577, 595
Barton Park, camping, 58–59
Barview Jetty County Park, camping, 194–95
Baskett Slough National Wildlife Refuge, 47
Bastendorff Beach Park, 265, 270
Bay Area, 257–73
  beaches, 260–63
  biking, 263–64
  boating, 260
  camping, 264–66
  clam digging, 268–69
  fishing, 268–69
  hiking, 260–63
  horseback riding, 267
  kayaking/canoeing, 259
  lodgings, 272–73
  parks, 266–68
  picnics, 266–68
  restaurants, 271–72
  surfing/windsurfing, 270
  wildlife, 269–70
Bay City, restaurants, 208–9
Beachcombing, 198, 224–26
Beaches
  Bay Area, 260–63
  coastal, vi–vii
  hiking, 280–82
  Lincoln City, 212–13
  Lower Columbia River, 339
  Northern, 177–91
  Oregon Coast, 180–81, 197–99, 200, 212–13, 242–45, 260–63
  Oregon Dunes, 242–45
  Tillamook, 193–95, 197–99, 200
Beachside State Park, 229
Bear Valley National Wildlife Refuge, 528
Beaverton, restaurants, 34
Beggars-tick Wildlife Refuge, 19
Belknap Springs Resort, 116
Bellevue, restaurants, 51
Bend, 441–63
  biking, 448–51
  lodgings, 461–63
  picnics, 452–53
  restaurants, 460–61
  skiing 443–45
  snowmobiling, 447
Berry picking, Mount Hood, 368–69
Beverly Beach State Park, 224, 228, 229–30
Bicycling. See Biking
Big Lake, 431, 435, 436
Big Summit Prairie, 424
Biking, xi–xii
  Ashland, 162
  Astoria, 342–43
  Baker County, 585–86
  Banks-Vernonia Linear State Park, 42–43, 342
  Bay Area, 263–64
  Bend, 448–51
  Camp Sherman, 409
  Cascade Foothills, 68
  Cascade Lakes, 473–74
  Cascade Lakes Highway, 473
  Central Oregon, 397, 420–21, 448–51, 473–74
  central Willamette Valley, 85–87
  Bicentennial Bicycle (Bikecentennial) Trail, 343, 585
  Columbia Basin, 304–5
  Columbia Gorge, 321–22
  Columbia River Gorge National Scenic Area, 322
  Columbia River Highway, 304
  Corvallis, 85–87
  Crater Lake National Park, 508–9
  Crooked River, 420–21
  Deschutes River, 305
  Diamond Craters, 645
  Diamond Lake, 502
  Eugene, 99–103
  Fremont National Forest, 629–30
  Grande Ronde Valley, 570–71
  Harney County, 644–45
  Hells Canyon, 555–56
  Hood River Valley, 321–23
  Klamath Basin, 532–33
  Klamath Falls, 533
  La Grande, 570–71
  Lake County, 629–30
  Lower Columbia River, 341–43
  Lower Deschutes River, 386–87
  Lower John Day River, 397
  Malheur National Forest, 613
  McKenzie Pass, 434
  McKenzie River, 103
  Medford, 162
  Mount Hood, 364–66, 367
  Mountain Lakes, 521–22
  Newport, 228
  Northeast Mountains, 555–56, 570–71, 585–86, 593–94, 613
  Northern Beaches, 183–84
  Oakridge, 485, 486
  OC&E Woods Line State Trail, 532–33
  Ochoco National Forest, 420–21
  Oregon Coast, 183–84, 202–3,

228, 245–46, 263–64, 284–85
Oregon Dunes, 245–46
Pendleton Grain Belt, 593–94
Portland, 4, 5, 14–18, 37
Rogue Valley, 161–62
Roseburg, 139
Santiam Pass, 434
Sauvie Island, 341–42
Seaside, 184
Siskiyou National Forest, 263–64
Sisters, 409
Southeast High Desert, 629–30, 644–45
Southern Cascades, 485–86, 502, 508–9, 521–22
Southern Coast, 284– 85
Steens Mountain, 645
Sunriver, 449
The Dalles, 304–5
Three Sisters, 473–74
Tillamook, 202–3
trails, xii
TransAmerica Trail, 420
Umpqua Valley, 138–40
Upper Deschutes River, 448–51
Upper John Day River, 613
Vernonia, 341–42
Wallowa Mountains, 555–56
Willamette Pass, 485–86
Wine Country, 42–43
Bird-watching. *See* Wildlife
Black Butte, 405, 409
Black Canyon Wilderness, 417
Blue Mountains, 590–91
  camping, 595
  hiking, 574–75
  skiing, 572
Blue River, lodgings, 120
Bly, lodgings, 539
Boardman, camping, 297
Boardman (Samuel H.) State Park, 279, 281–82
Boating, xii–xiii
  Bandon, 260
  Bay Area, 260
  Cascade Lakes, 466–67
  Central Oregon, 422–23, 436–37, 466–67
  central Willamette Valley, 87–88
  Charleston, 260
  Clackamas River, 21, 23, 58
  Columbia Basin, 301
  Columbia Gorge, 323
  Columbia River, 21, 22, 23, 301, 323, 334–35
  Coos Bay, 260
  Crescent Lake, 492
  Eugene, 112–13
  Klamath Basin, 529
  Lincoln City, 217–18
  Lower Columbia River, 334–35
  McKenzie River, 436
  Mount Hood, 367–68
  Ochoco Lake County Park, 421–22
  Odell Lake, 492
  Oregon Coast, 217–18, 253, 260
  Oregon Dunes, 253

Portland, 22–24
Prineville Reservoir, 421–22
Rogue River, 151, 287
Rogue Valley, 151, 152
Southern Cascades, 492
Three Sisters, 466–67
Tualatin River, 49
Upper Klamath Lake, 529
Willamette Pass, 492
Willamette River, 21, 23–24, 49
Yamhill River, 49
  See also Kayaking
Boice-Cope Park, 278
Bonneville Dam, 319, 320–21, 325
Bonney Butte, 369
Boulder Creek Wilderness, hiking, 137–38
Breitenbush Hot Springs, 61
  lodgings, 76
Bridge Creek State Wildlife Area, 598
Bridge Creek Wilderness, 396–97
Bridge of the Gods, 310, 325
Bristow (Elijah) State Park, 108
Brookings
  fishing, 286
  lodgings, 291–92
  picnics, 279–80
  restaurants, 290–91
Brownlee Reservoir, fishing, 583
Bull of the Woods Wilderness, hiking, 65–66
Bull Prairie Lake, camping, 596, 598
Bullards Beach, 270
Bullards Beach State Park, 261, 264
Burns, restaurants, 645–66

C
Camas Creek, 598
Camassia Natural Area, 13
Camp Sherman
  biking, 409
  hiking, 405
  lodgings, 411
Camping
  Aldrich Mountains, 609
  Anthony Lake(s), 581
  Baker County, 581–83
  Bay Area, 264–66
  Benton County, 85
  Blue Mountains, 595
  Boardman, 297
  camper wagons, 582, 594
  Cascade Foothills, 57–63
  Cascade Lakes, 474–75
  Central Oregon, 397–98, 406–7, 418–19, 434–36, 451–52, 474–75
  central Willamette Valley, 84–85
  Clackamas River, 58–59, 362
  Columbia Basin, 297–98
  Columbia County, 338–39
  Columbia Gorge, 315–17
  Columbia River, 315–16, 338–39
  Cottage Grove, 105
  Crater Lake National Park, 507–8
  Crescent Lake, 487

Crooked River, 418–19
Dale, 595
Deschutes National Forest, 382, 625–26
Deschutes reservoirs, 382
Detroit, 60, 61, 407
Diamond Lake, 498–99
dispersed, vi
Estacada, 58–59
Eugene, 103–6
fire lookouts, 141, 277–78, 596, 614
Fremont National Forest, 625
Grande Ronde Valley, 566–68
Harney County, 642–43
Hells Canyon National Recreation Area, 552–53, 581
Henry Hagg Lake, 45
Hermiston, 297
Highway 22, 407
Hood River Valley, 316–17
Howard Prairie Lake, 518–19
Hyatt Reservoir, 519
Jackson County, 152
John Day River, 297–98, 394
Josephine County, 152
Klamath Basin, 533–34
La Grande, 566–68
Lake Billy Chinook, 382, 406
Lake County, 625–26
Lake McNary, 297
Lake of the Woods, 518
Lake Owyhee, 650
Lemolo Lake, 498–99
Lincoln County, 215–16
Long Creek Ranger District, 609
Lookout Point Reservoir, 105
Lower Columbia River, 338–39
Lower Deschutes River, 381–82
Lower John Day River, 397–98
Malheur County, 650–51
McKenzie River, 435–36
Mehama, 60–61
Metolius River, 406
Middle Santiam River, 61–62
Mount Hebo, 195
Mount Hood, 361–63
Mount Hood National Forest, 383
Mountain Lakes, 517–19
national forest, vii
Newberry Crater National Volcanic Monument, 451–52
Newport, 228–29
North Fork Umatilla Wilderness, 596
North Santiam River, 60–61, 407
North Umpqua River, 134–35
Northeast Mountains, 551–53, 566–68, 581–83, 594–96, 608–9
Northern Beaches, 178–80
Ochoco National Forest, 397–98, 418–19
Odell Lake, 487
Oregon Coast, 178–80, 215, 228–29, 248–51, 264–66, 275–78

Oregon Dunes, 248–51
Paulina Lake, 452
Pendleton Grain Belt, 594–96
Phillips Lake, 582–83
Portland, 5, 17–18
Prairie City, 609
Rickreall, 45
Rogue River National Forest,
    151–54, 506–7, 507–8,
    517–18
Rogue Valley, 151–54
Sand Lake, 195
Santiam Pass, 434–35
Silver Lake, 625
Siskiyou National Forest, 153,
    266, 277–78
Siuslaw National Forest, 195,
    248
Snake River, 581
South Santiam River, 62–63
Southeast High Desert, 625–26,
    642–43, 650–51
Southern Cascades, 486–88,
    498–99, 517–19
Southern Coast, 275–78
state park, vi, viii
Strawberry Mountain
    Wilderness, 609
Sweet Home, 62–63
Three Creeks Lake, 435
Three Sisters, 474–75
Tillamook, 193–197
Timothy Lake, 362–63
Umatilla National Forest, 595
Umpqua National Forest, 105
Umpqua Valley, 133–35
Upper Deschutes River, 451–52
Upper John Day River, 608–9
Wallowa Mountains, 551–52,
    566–67, 581
Wallowa-Whitman National
    Forest, 552, 553, 568
Willamette Pass, 486–88
Willamette River, Middle Fork,
    488
Wine Country, 44–45
Winema National Forest, 534
yurts, 178, 194, 228, 248, 264,
    277
See also specific towns, forests,
    and parks
Canby, 96
Cannon Beach, 188–89
    lodgings, 190–91
    restaurants, 189–90
Canoeing. *See* Kayaking; Boating
Canyonville, 140–41
Cape Arago State Park, 267
Cape Blanco State Park, 276
Cape Kiwanda, 198, 199, 200,
    206–7
Cape Lookout State Park
    camping, 194
    whale watching, 192–93, 194,
        200
Cape Meares, 198, 199
Cape Perpetua Scenic Area, 225,
    227, 230, 233, 235
Cape Sebastian State Park, 281
Carl G. Washburne Memorial State
    Park, 226, 229
Cascade Foothills, 56–76

biking, 68
camping, 57–63
fishing, 68–70
hiking, 64–67
lodgings, 76
picnics, 63–64
rafting/kayaking/canoeing,
    72–74
skiing, 71–72
waterskiing, 74–75
wildlife, 70–71
Cascade Head, 201
Cascade Lakes, 464–77
    biking, 473–74
    boating/canoeing, 466–67
    camping, 474–75
    scenic drive, 464–66
    fishing, 467–69
    lodges, 475–76
    waterskiing/windsurfing, 466
Cascade Locks, 310, 316, 318,
    323, 325
    lodgings, 329
Cascadia State Park, 62
Catherine Creek State Park,
    566–57
Cave Junction, lodgings, 171
Caves/caving
    Central Oregon, 458–59
    Lake County, 622
    Lavacicle Cave, 459
    Oregon Caves National
        Monument, 160–61
    Sea Lion Caves, 226, 232–33
    Southeast High Desert, 622
    Upper Deschutes River, 458–59
Celilo Lake, 299, 302
Century Drive, 445–46, 466
Champoeg State Park, 81–82, 84,
    88
Charleston
    boating, 260
    fishing, 268
    kayaking/canoeing, 259
    restaurants, 272
Charlton Lake, 473
Chemult, 501
Chetco River, fishing, 286
Chewaucan River, 628
Chief Joseph Mountain, 547–48
Chimney Rock Campground, 418
Christmas Valley, 621
    sand dunes, 622
Christmas Valley National Back
    Country Byway, 621–22
Clackamas Lake, 360
Clackamas River
    boating, 21, 23, 58
    camping, 58–59, 362
    fishing, 21, 23, 68–69, 363
    hiking, 66
    picnics, 63–64
    rafting/kayaking/canoeing, 25,
        72–73
    waterskiing, 74
Clam digging, 186, 204, 268–69,
    286
Clatskanie
    boating, 337
    parks/beaches/picnics, 339
Clay Creek Park Campground,
    106

Clear Lake, 433, 435, 436
Climbing
    Cascade Foothills, 67
    Central Oregon, 414–15,
        458–59, 470–71
    Menagerie, 67
    Mount Hood, 315, 355–57
    Mount Jefferson, 401, 403
    Portland, 5, 26–27
    Smith Rock State Park, 414–15
    Three Fingered Jack, 403–4
    Upper Deschutes River, 458–59
Cline Falls State Park, 453
Cloverdale, lodgings, 209
Clyde Holliday State Park
    camping, 609
    fishing, 609–10
Coast Range, scenic drives, 262
Cold Springs National Wildlife
    Refuge, 300, 304
Collier State Park, 534, 536
Columbia Basin, 295–306
    biking, 304–5
    boating, 301
    camping, 297–98
    fishing, 302–3
    hiking, 303–4
    parks, 298–99
    picnics, 298–99
    wildlife, 300–1
    windsurfing, 301–2
Columbia Gorge, 307–29
    biking, 321–23
    boating, 323
    camping, 315–17
    fishing, 319–20
    hiking, 311–15
    horseback riding, 310
    scenic drives/picnics, 309–11
    waterfalls, 309–10, 312–13
    wildlife, 320–21
    windsurfing, 307–8, 317–19
Columbia River, 293–345
    biking, 341–43
    wildlife, 330–31, 332–34
    boating/sailing, 21, 22, 24, 301,
        323, 334–35
    camping, 315-16, 338–39
    cruises, 24, 323, 334–35
    fishing, 21, 185, 302, 319–20,
        341
    hiking, 339–40
    islands, 336–37
    kayaking/canoeing, 335–37
    Lewis and Clark Columbia
        River Water Trail, 184-85
    parks/beaches/picnics, 339
    windsurfing, 338
    See also Columbia Basin;
        Columbia Gorge; Lower
        Columbia River
Cooper Spur Ski Area, 324
Coos Bay, 258
    beaches, 260–61
    boating, 260
    clam digging/crabbing, 268
    kayaking/canoeing, 258–59
    lodgings, 272–73
    restaurants, 272
    surfing/windsurfing, 270
Coquille River, 259
    fishing/clam digging/crabbing,

268–69
Corvallis
biking, 85–87
lodgings, 95
restaurants, 94–95
Cottage Grove
camping, 105
fishing, 114
Council Crest Park, 10
Cove Palisades State Park, 382, 383–84
Crabbing, 231, 268, 268–69, 205
Crane Mountain, hiking, 626
Crane Prairie Reservoir, 468, 473, 475
Crater Lake National Park, 503–11, 523
biking, 508–9
boat tour, 505
camping, 507–8
fishing, 509
hiking, 505–7
lodgings, 511
Rim Drive, 505–6, 508
skiing, 510–11
Wizard Island, 505
Crayfish, 364
Crescent Lake, 482
boating, 492
camping, 487
fishing, 488
Creswell, 121
Crooked River, 412–28
biking, 420–21
camping, 418–19
fishing, 422–23
hiking, 415–17
rafting/kayaking, 422
skiing, 426–27
snowmobiling, 426–27
stargazing, 427
wildlife, 423–24
See also Lower Crooked River Recreation Area
Crooked River National Grassland hiking, 384–85
Cultus Lake, 468, 473, 475
lodgings, 477
Cummins Creek Wilderness, 227
Cycling. *See* Biking

D

Dabney State Park, 12
Dale, camping, 595
Dallas, 55
parks, 42
Dams. *See* individual entries
Darlingtonia State Wayside, 251
Davis Lake, 469, 474
Dayton, lodgings, 54
Dayville, lodgings, 614
Delta Campground, camping, 103–4
Denman Wildlife Area, 164
Depoe Bay, 217
lodgings, 221
restaurants, 220
Deschutes National Forest
biking, 449–51
camping, 382, 625–26
hiking, 456–58
scenic drives, 622

Deschutes reservoirs
camping, 382
fishing, 381
Deschutes River
biking, 305, 386–87, 448–49
boating, 378–79
camping, 381–82, 451–52
fishing, 302, 379–81, 453–54
hiking, 383–86, 457
jet-boats, 380
picnics, 452–53
rafting/kayaking/canoeing, 374–77, 386, 455–56
wildlife, 387–88, 454–55
See also Lower Deschutes River; Upper Deschutes River
Deschutes River State Park, 377, 381, 386
Deschutes River State Recreation Area, 298, 303
Desert Trail, 634–35, 639–41, 646
Detroit
camping, 60, 61, 407
lodgings, 76
See also Detroit Lake
Detroit Lake
Detroit Lake State Recreation Area, 60
fishing, 69
waterskiing, 74–75
See also Detroit
Devil's Elbow State Park, 226
Devils Lake, 467, 474
Devil's Lake State Park, 215, 217
Devils Punch Bowl State Park, 216, 224
Diablo Mountain, hiking, 627
Diamond, lodgings, 646
Diamond Craters Outstanding Natural Area, 637
Diamond Lake, 494–502
biking, 502
camping, 498–99
fishing, 499
hiking, 495–98
skiing/snowmobiling, 500–1
Diamond Peak, 483
Drift Creek Wilderness, 226–27
Drives. *See* Scenic drives
Dundee, restaurants, 52–53
Dune buggies, 236, 241–42
Oregon Coast, 195
renting, 242
See also Off-road vehicles
Dunes. *See* Christmas Valley; Oregon Dunes; Sand dunes

E

Eagle Cap Wilderness Area
fishing, 553
horseback riding, 550–51, 572–73
hiking, 546–48, 580
llama/horse trekking, 580
Eagle Creek, 319–20
Eagle Fern Park, 63
East Lake, 452, 453
East Rowena State Park, 299, 301
Ecola State Park, 181, 187, 188
Elijah Bristow State Park, 108
Elk Lake, 466, 467, 474, 476

lodgings, 477
Elk Rock Island, 13
Elkhorn Drive, 576, 585
Elkhorn Range, hiking, 574–75, 578–79
Elkhorn Wildlife Area, 563
Elmira, lodgings, 120
Enterprise, 559
Estacada
camping, 58–59
picnics, 63
waterskiing, 74
Eugene, 97–122
biking, 99–103
boating, 112–13
camping, 103–6
fishing, 112, 113–14
hiking, 109–10
lodgings, 120–21
parks/picnics, 106–8
rafting/kayaking/canoeing, 111–12
restaurants, 118–20
scenic drives, 108–9
swimming, 112–13
waterskiing, 112
wildlife, 115–16
windsurfing, 112

F

Falls City, parks, 42
Farewell Bend State Park, 582
Fern Ridge Reservoir, 105, 106, 112, 114, 115
Feyrer Park, camping, 85
Finley (William L.) National Wildlife Refuge, 89–90
Fire lookouts, 134, 141, 277–78, 491, 596, 614, 630–31
Fish ladders, Umpqua Valley, 130–31, 138
Fish Lake
camping, 518
fishing, 520
skiing, 522
Fishermen's Bend Recreation Site, 60
Fishing, xii–xiii
Albany, 89
Alsea Bay, 231
Anthony Lake(s), 584
Baker County, 583–85
Bay Area, 268–69
Big Lake, 436
Bonneville Dam, 319
Brookings, 286
Brownlee Reservoir, 583
Cascade Foothills, 68–70
Cascade Lakes, 467–69
Celilo Lake, 302
Central Oregon, 398–99, 407–8, 422–23, 436, 453–54, 467–70
central Willamette Valley, 88–89
Charleston, 268
Chetco River, 286
Clackamas River, 21, 68–69, 363
Clear Lake, 436
Clyde Holliday State Park, 609–10

Columbia Basin, 302–3
Columbia Gorge, 319–20
Columbia River, 21, 185, 302, 319–20, 341
Coquille River, 268–69
Cottage Grove, 114
Crater Lake National Park, 509
Crescent Lake, 488
Deschutes reservoirs, 381
Deschutes River, 302, 379, 453–54
Detroit Lake, 69
Diamond Lake, 499
Eagle Cap Wilderness Area, 553
East Lake, 453
Eugene, 112, 113–14
Fish Lake, 520
Fourmile Lake, 520
Garibaldi, 203
Gerber Reservoir, 536–37
Gold Beach, 285
Grande Ronde River, 568–69
Harney County, 643–44
Hells Canyon Reservoir, 583
Hood River, 320
Howard Prairie Lake, 520
Hyatt Reservoir, 520–21
Imnaha River, 554
John Day River, 398–99, 609–10
Klamath Basin, 535–37
Klamath River, 535–36
Lake Billy Chinook, 378, 381, 408
Lake County, 627–29
Lake of the Woods, 520
Lemolo Lake, 499
license, xiii
Lincoln City, 217
Long Tom River, 114
Lost Lake, 320
Lower Columbia River, 341
Lower Deschutes River, 379–81
Lower John Day River, 398
Malheur County, 653
Malheur River, 611, 653
McKenzie River, 113–14, 436
Metolius River, 407–8
Middle Santiam River, 69
Miller Lake, 500
Mount Hood, 363–64
Mount Jefferson Wilderness, 408
Mountain Lakes, 520–21
Newport, 230–31
North Santiam River, 69
North Umpqua River, 127–28
Northeast Mountains, 553–54, 568–69, 583–85, 596–98, 609–11
Northern Beaches, 185–86
Ochoco Reservoir, 423
Odell Lake, 488
Olallie Lake Scenic Area, 408
Oregon Coast, 185–86, 203–4, 217, 230–31, 251–52, 268–69, 285–86
Oregon Dunes, 251–52
Owyhee Lake, 653
Owyhee River, 653
Oxbow Reservoir, 583

Pacific City, 204
Paulina Lake, 453
Pendleton, 595–96
Pendleton Grain Belt, 596–98
Port Orford, 286
Portland, 20–21
Powder River, 584
Prineville Reservoir, 423
regulations, xiii
Rogue River, 162–64, 285–86, 509, 521
Salmon River, 363
Sandy River, 21, 363
Siuslaw River, 114, 251–52
Snake River, 553–54, 653
South Santiam River, 69
South Umpqua River, 128
Southeast High Desert, 627–29, 643–44, 653
Southern Cascades, 488–89, 499–500, 520–21
Southern Coast, 285–86
Sprague River, 536
Steamboat Creek, 128
Three Sisters, 469–70
Tillamook, 203–4
Tualatin River, 48
Umatilla River, 596–97
Umpqua River, 251
Umpqua Valley, 127–29, 138
Upper John Day River, 609–10
Upper Klamath Lake, 535
Waldport, 231
Wallowa Lake, 553
Wallowa Mountains, 583–84
Warm Springs Indian Reservation, 408
Willamette River, 21, 88–89, 114, 489
Williamson River, 536
Willow Valley Reservoir, 537
Wilsonville, 89
Wine Country, 47–48
Woodburn, 89
Yamhill River, 48
Yaquina Bay, 230–31
See also Clam digging; Crabbing; Crayfish
Floras Lake, 289
Floras Lake State Park, 280
Florence, 253
lodgings, 255–56
restaurants, 255
Fogarty Creek State Park, 216
Forest Grove, 51
Forest Park, 7–9, 17
Fort Clatsop National Memorial, 184, 343
Fort Henrietta Park, 595
Fort Rock State Park, 621
Fort Stevens State Park, 178–79, 180, 183, 339, 191
Fourmile Lake, 518, 520
Fremont National Forest, 539
biking, 629–30
camping, 625
hiking, 626–27
Frenchglen, 636
horseback riding, 642
lodgings, 646
restaurants, 646

G
Garibaldi
fishing, 203
Gearhart, 180, 182
restaurants, 190
Gearhart Mountain, hiking, 626
Gearhart Mountain Wilderness, hiking, 532
Gerber Reservoir, 526–27
camping, 534
fishing, 536–37
Gerry Mountain Wilderness Study Area, 417
Geysers, 632
Ghost towns, Baker County, 577
Giles French Park, 297, 304
Gleneden Beach, 213, 218, 219–20
lodgings, 221
restaurants, 220
Gold Beach
fishing, 285
lodgings, 291–92
restaurants, 290
Gold Lake, 489
Golden and Silver Falls State Park, 262, 267
Goose Lake, 628
Goose Lake State Recreation Area, 625
Government Camp
biking, 365
camping, 362
lodgings, 371–72
Grande Ronde River, 560–73
fishing, 568–69
rafting/kayaking, 561, 562–63
Grande Ronde Valley
biking, 570–71
bird-watching, 563–65
camping, 566–68
fishing, 568–69
horseback riding, 571–72
llama trekking, 572
skiing, 572
wildlife, 563–65
Grants Pass
lodgings, 171
parks, 155
restaurants, 169, 170
Grassy Knob Wilderness, 284
Greenway Park, 15
Gresham, 14, 37

H
Haines, restaurants, 588
Halfway, lodgings, 589
Hammond, 185
Hang gliding
Central Oregon, 459
Columbia Gorge, 324
Hood River Valley, 324
Lake County, 631
Lakeview, 631
Oregon Coast, 206–7
Southeast High Desert, 631
Tillamook, 206–7
Upper Deschutes River, 459
Harbor, restaurants, 290
Harney County, 634–46
biking, 644–45
camping, 642–43
fishing, 643–44

hiking, 634–35, 639–42
horseback riding, 642
scenic drives, 636–37
wildlife, 637–39
Harris Beach State Park, 270–71, 289
Hart Mountain, hiking, 627
Hart Mountain National Antelope Refuge, 619–20, 622, 623–24, 629, 633
Hat Point State Park, 304
Hat Rock State Park, 298–99
Haystack Reservoir, 382
Hells Canyon, 543–59
biking, 555–56
camping, 552–53, 581
fishing, 583
hiking, 549
horseback riding, 551
jet boats, 554–55
rafting, 554–55
scenic drives, 544–55, 576–77
Henry Hagg Lake, 42, 45, 47–48, 49
Heppner, 593, 594, 601
Hermiston, camping, 297
Highway 22, camping, 407
Hiking, viii–xi
Aldrich Mountains, 607–8
Anthony Lake(s), 578–79
Astoria, 340–41
Badger Creek Wilderness, 385–86
Baker County, 577–80
Bay Area, 260–63
beaches, 280–82
Blue Mountains, 575–75
Boulder Creek Wilderness, 137–38
Bridge Creek Wilderness, 396–97
Bull of the Woods Wilderness, 65–66
Camp Sherman, 405
Cascade Foothills, 64–67
Central Oregon, 395–97, 402–6, 415–17, 430–34, 456–58, 470–73
central Willamette Valley, 79–84
Clackamas River, 66
Columbia Basin, 303–4
Columbia Gorge, 311–15
Cove Palisades State Park, 383–84
Crane Mountain, 626
Crater Lake National Park, 505–7
Crooked River, 415–17
Crooked River National Grassland, 384–85
Deschutes National Forest, 456–58
Deschutes River, 383–84
Diablo Mountain, 627
Diamond Lake, 495–98
Eagle Cap Wilderness, 546–48, 580
Elkhorn Range, 575, 578–79
Eugene, 109–10
Fremont National Forest, 626–27

gear, ix–x
Gearhart Mountain, 626
Gearhart Mountain Wilderness, 532
Harney County, 634–35, 639–42
Hart Mountain, 627
Hells Canyon, 549
Hood River Valley, 313–14
Illinois River, 159
Jacksonville, 156–57
John Day Fossil Beds National Monument, 395, 608
Joseph Creek Canyon, 549–50
Kalmiopsis Wilderness, 283–84
Klamath Basin, 531–32
Lake County, 626–27
Lava Lands, 456
Lawrence Memorial Grassland, 385
Lemolo Lake, 497
Lincoln City, 213–15
Long Creek Ranger District, 604–5
Lower Columbia River, 339–40
Lower Deschutes River, 383–86
Lower John Day River, 395–97
Malheur County, 651–53
Malheur National Forest, 604–8
Malheur National Wildlife Refuge, 640
McKenzie Pass, 432–33
McKenzie River, 109, 433–34
Metolius River, 405
Middle Santiam Wilderness, 67
Monument Rock Wilderness, 579–80
Mount Bailey, 496
Mount Hood, 355–61
Mount Hood Wilderness Area, 314
Mount Jefferson Wilderness Area, 402–5
Mount Thielsen, 496
Mount Washington, 431
Mountain Lakes Wilderness, 514–17
Newport, 223–27
North Fork John Day Wilderness, 579, 592–93, 604
North Fork Umatilla Wilderness, 592
Northeast Mountains, 546–50, 565–66, 577–80, 592–93, 604–8
Northern Beaches, 181–83
Ochoco National Forest, 416–17
Olallie Lake Scenic Area, 405–6
Opal Creek Wilderness, 64–65
Oregon Coast, 181–83, 200–2, 213–15, 223–27, 242–46, 260–63, 280–84
Oregon Dunes, 242–45
Oregon Trail, 577–78
Pacific Crest Trail, 313–14, 357, 402–3, 432–33, 471, 483–84, 495–96, 506, 514
Pendleton Grain Belt, 592–93
Portland, 7–14

Rogue River, 157–58, 282, 516
Rogue Valley, 156–61
Rogue-Umpqua Divide Wilderness, 497–98
Santiam Pass, 430–32
Sauvie Island, 340
Sky Lakes Wilderness, 514–16
Smith Rock State Park, 415–16
Southeast High Desert, 626–27, 634–35, 639–42, 651–53
Southern Cascades, 482–85, 495–98, 514–17
Southern Coast, 280–84
Southern Oregon, 505–7
Steens Mountain, 640, 641
Strawberry Mountains, 605–7
Sutton Mountain, 396
Table Rock Wilderness Area, 66–67
Three Creeks Lake area, 431–32
Three Sisters Wilderness, 431–32, 472–73
Tillamook, 200–2
Timberline Trail, 357–58
Trout Creek Mountains, 652
Umatilla National Forest, 592
Umpqua National Forest, 110
Umpqua Valley, 136
Upper Deschutes River, 457
Upper John Day River, 604–8
Waldo Lake Wilderness, 483
Walla Walla River, 592
Wallowa Mountains, 546–48, 565–66, 580
Wenaha-Tucannon Wilderness, 565–66
Willamette National Forest, 483
Willamette Pass, 482–83
Willamette River, Middle Fork, 485
Wine Country, 41–42
Yamsay Mountain, 531–32, 627
Hilgard Junction State Recreation Area, 567
Hills Creek Reservoir, 489, 492
Hillsboro, parks, 41
Historic Columbia River Highway, 309–11, 325
Holliday (Clyde) State Park
camping, 609
fishing, 609–10
Honeyman (Jessie M.) Memorial State Park, 248
Hood River, 307–29
boating, 323
fishing, 320
lodgings, 327–29
rafting/kayaking, 323
restaurants, 326–27
windsurfing, 320, 318
See also Hood River Valley
Hood River Valley, 311
biking, 321–23
camping, 316–17
hiking, 313–14
waterfalls, 314–15
winter sports, 324–25
See also Hood River
Hoodoo, camping, 434–35
Hoodoo Ski Area, 437

Horseback riding
  Banks-Vernonia Linear State
    Park, 42–43
  Bay Area, 267
  central Willamette Valley, 80,
    91–92
  Columbia Gorge, 310
  Eagle Cap Wilderness, 550–51,
    572–73, 580
  Frenchglen, 642
  Grande Ronde Valley, 571–72
  Harney County, 642
  Hells Canyon Wilderness Area,
    551
  Horse camping, 104, 194, 197,
    247–48, 264, 265, 276,
    315–16, 362, 435, 487, 519,
    643
  Mount Hood, 360, 367
  Northeast Mountains, 550–51,
    572
  Oregon Coast, 247–48, 267,
    288
  Oregon Dunes, 247–48
  Rogue Valley, 152, 157
  Sisters, 438
  Southeast High Desert, 642
  Southern Coast, 288
  Wallowa Mountains, 551, 580
  Wenaha-Tucannon Wilderness,
    572
Hosmer Lake, 467–68
Howard Prairie Lake
  bird-watching, 519–20
  camping, 518–19
  fishing, 520
Hoyt Arboretum, 8–9
Humbug Mountain State Park, 276
Huntington, 589
Hyatt Reservoir
  bird-watching, 519–20
  camping, 519
  fishing, 520–21

I
Ice Lake, 547
Illinois River, 143
  guided trips, 148
  hiking, 159
  rafting/kayaking, 147–49
Illinois Valley, 172
Imnaha, 544
Imnaha River Canyon
  bird-watching, 557
  fishing, 554
  wildlife, 557
In-line skating. See
  Skating/skateboarding
Irrigon Park, 299, 303–4

J
Jackson Bottom Wetlands
  Preserve, 46–47
Jacksonville, 168
  hiking, 156–57
  lodgings, 172
  restaurants, 169
Jet-boats, 151, 287
  Deschutes River, 380
  Hells Canyon, 554–55
  Northeast Mountains, 554–55
  Snake River, 554–55

Jewell Meadows Wildlife Area, 333
John Day, 614
John Day Dam
  camping, 297
  parks/picnics, 299
John Day Fossil Beds National
  Monument, 392, 395
  hiking, 608
John Day River, 302
  biking, 397, 613
  camping, 297–98, 394, 397–98,
    608–9
  fishing, 398–99, 609–10
  hiking, 395–97, 604–8
  rafting/kayaking/canoeing,
    393–94, 612–13
  skiing, 613–14
  snowmobiling, 614
  wildlife, 611
  See also Lower John Day River;
    Upper John Day River
John Day Wilderness. See North
  Fork John Day Wilderness
Jones Beach, 338
Joseph, 558
  restaurants, 559
Joseph Canyon, 545–46
  wildlife, 557
Joseph Creek Canyon, hiking,
  549–50
Jubilee Lake, 596, 597
Julia Butler Hansen National
  Wildlife Refuge, 333
Junction City, 121
  parks/picnics, 108

K
Kalmiopsis Wilderness, 159–60,
  283
Kayaking, xii
  Bay Area, 259
  Bridge Creek State Wildlife
    Area, 598
  Cascade Foothills, 72–74
  Cascade Lakes, 466–67
  central Willamette Valley,
    87–88
  Clackamas River, 25, 72–73
  Columbia River, 335–37
  Coos Bay, 258–59
  Crooked River Gorge, 422
  Deschutes River, 374–77, 386,
    455–56
  Eugene, 111–12
  Grande Ronde River, 561–63
  Hells Canyon, 554–55
  Hood River, 323
  Illinois River, 147–49
  John Day River, 393–94
  Klamath Basin, 529, 530–31
  Klamath River, 530–31
  Lincoln City, 217–18
  Malheur County, 648
  McKenzie River, 111, 436
  Metolius River, 408–9
  Molalla River, 73
  Mount Hood, 367–68
  Newport, 231–32
  North Umpqua River, 131–33
  Northeast Mountains, 554–55,
    561–63, 612–13
  Northern Beaches, 184–85

Oregon Coast, 184–85, 205–6,
    217–18, 231–32, 253,
    258–59
Oregon Dunes, 253
Owyhee River, 648
Portland, 5, 24–26
Rogue River, 144–47
Rogue Valley, 144–50
Salmon River, 367
Sandy River, 24–25, 367
Santiam River forks, 73–74
Snake River, 554–55
Southeast High Desert, 648–49
Southern Cascades, 492
Steamboat Creek, 132
Three Sisters, 466–67
Tillamook, 205–6
Tualatin River, 25, 49
Umpqua River, 133
Umpqua Valley, 131–33
Upper Deschutes River, 455–56
Upper John Day River, 612–13
Wallowa River, 562
Warm Springs River, 378
Willamette Pass, 492
Willamette River, 87–88,
    111–12, 492
Yamhill River, 49
See also Boating
Kelley Point Park, 13–14
Kimball State Park, 508
Kite flying
  festivals, 211–12, 213
  Lincoln City, 211–12
  Oregon Coast, 212–13
  Portland, 27–28
Klamath Basin, 525–39
  biking, 532–33
  boating/canoeing, 529
  camping, 533–34
  fishing, 535–37
  hiking, 531–32
  rafting/kayaking, 530–31
  skiing, 537–38
  snowmobiling, 538
  wildlife, 526–29
Klamath Basin National Wildlife
  Refuge Complex, 527–29
Klamath Falls
  biking, 533
  lodgings, 539
  restaurants, 539
Klamath Lake. See Upper Klamath
  Lake
Klamath Marsh National Wildlife
  Refuge, 527
Klamath River
  fishing, 535–36
  rafting/kayaking, 530–31
Koberg Beach State Park, 299

L
La Grande, 560–73
  biking, 570–71
  camping, 566–68
  lodgings, 573
  restaurants, 572–73
La Pine State Recreation Area, 452,
  456
Ladd Marsh Wildlife Area, 564,
  570
Lake Billy Chinook

boating, 378
camping, 382, 406
fishing, 408
wildlife, 387–88
Lake County, 619–33
biking, 629–30
camping, 625–26
fishing, 627–29
geysers, 632
hiking, 626–27
scenic drives, 621–22
skiing/snowmobiling, 630–31
wildlife, 623–25
Lake McNary, camping, 297
Lake of the Woods
camping, 518
fishing, 520
skiing, 523
Lake Oswego, 14, 22, 37
Lake Owyhee State Park, 650
Lake Simtustus
boating, 378–79, 381
camping, 382
fishing, 408
Lake Umatilla, 302
Lakeside, 273
Lakeview, scenic drives, 622, 636
Larch Mountain, 309, 313
Laurel Mountain, 41
Lava Beds National Monument,
539
Lava Butte, 449
Lava Lakes, 468, 473, 474–75
Lava Lands
hiking, 456
Visitor Center, 449, 451
Lava River, 458
Lava tubes, Central Oregon, 458
Lawrence Memorial Grassland,
hiking, 385
Lemolo Lake
camping, 498–99
fishing, 499
hiking, 497
skiing/snowmobiling, 501
LePage Park, 297, 305
Lewis and Clark Columbia River
Water Trail, 184–85, 335–37
Lewis and Clark National Wildlife
Refuge, 331, 333, 345
Lewis and Clark State Park, 12
Lewiston (ID), 559
Lighthouses
Cape Arago, 261
Cape Blanco, 276
Cape Meares, 198
Coquille River, 264–65
Heceta Head, 226
Umpqua River, 249, 253
Warrior Rock, 340
Yaquina Head, 224, 225
Lincoln City, 211–21
beaches, 212–13
boating/kayaking/rafting,
217–18
camping, 215–17
fishing, 217
hiking, 213–15
kite flying, 212–13
lodgings, 221
parks, 216
restaurants, 220

surfing, 216, 217–18
wildlife, 218–19
windsurfing, 218
Little John Snow Play Hill, 324–25
Llama trekking. See Horseback
riding
Lodgings. See specific cities for
listing
Loeb (Alfred A.) State Park, 277
Logan Valley, 611
Long Creek Ranger District
camping, 609
hiking, 604–5
Long Mountain, 341
Long Tom River, fishing, 114
Lookout Mountain, skiing, 426–27
Lookout Point Reservoir, camping,
105
Loon Lake Recreational Site, 250,
252
Lost Lake, 316
fishing, 320
Lostine River, 545, 547, 548, 554
Lower Columbia River, 330–45.
See also Columbia River
Lower Crooked River Recreation
Area, 418, 423
Lower Deschutes River, 373–90.
See also Deschutes River;
Upper Deschutes River
Lower John Day River, 391–99. See
also John Day River; Upper
John Day River
Lower Klamath National Wildlife
Refuge, 528–29. See also Upper
Klamath National Wildlife
Refuge

M
Macleay Park, 9
Madras, 374, 390
Malheur County, 647–55
camping, 650–51
fishing, 653
hiking, 651–53
rafting/kayaking, 648
wildlife, 654
Malheur National Forest
biking, 613
hiking, 604–8, 589, 646
scenic drives, 577
Malheur National Wildlife Refuge
hiking, 640, 646
scenic drives, 637
wildlife, 637–38
Malheur River, fishing, 611, 653
Manzanita, 207
lodgings, 210
restaurants, 208
Mapleton, 238
Mark O. Hatfield Wilderness, 313
Marquam Nature Park, 9–10
Marshall Park, 10–11
Marys Peak, 91
Marys Peak Scenic Botanical Area,
83
Maupin, 374, 375, 376, 381–82
Mayer State Park, 299, 303
McCall Point Trail, 303
McDonald State Forest, 86–87
McKay Creek National Wildlife
Refuge, 598

McKenzie Bridge
lodgings, 120
restaurants, 119
McKenzie Pass, 430
biking, 434
camping, 435
hiking, 432–33
McKenzie River
biking, 103
boating, 436
camping, 435–36
fishing, 113–14, 436
hiking, 109, 433–34
parks/picnics, 106–7
rafting/kayaking/canoeing, 111,
436
waterfalls, 434
McMinnville, 51
lodgings, 53–55
restaurants, 51–53
McNary Dam, 297, 300, 302–3
Medford
biking, 162
lodgings, 172
restaurants, 169–70
Mehama
camping, 60–61
picnics, 64
Memaloose State Park, 298
Menagerie, climbing, 67
Merlin, lodgings, 171
Metolius River, 400–11
camping, 406
fishing, 407–8
hiking, 405
lodgings, 411
rafting/kayaking, 408–9
wildlife, 410
Metzler Park, camping, 59
Middle Fork Willamette River. See
Willamette River
Middle Santiam River. See Santiam
River
Middle Santiam Wilderness,
hiking, 67
Mill Creek Recreation Site, 44
Mill Creek Wilderness, 416
Miller Lake, 499, 500
Milo McIver State Park, 58–59
Milton-Freewater
restaurants, 600
Minam River, 560–61, 562,
565–66, 569
lodges, 572
Minam State Recreation Area, 568
Molalla River,
rafting/kayaking/canoeing, 73
Molalla River State Park, 82, 89
Monmouth, lodgings, 96
Monument Rock Wilderness,
hiking, 579–80
Moolack Beach, 224, 234
Mount Bachelor
hiking, 458
lodgings, 462
skiing, 443–46, 448
sled dog mushing, 447
snowshoeing, 448
Mount Bailey
hiking, 496
skiing/snowmobiling, 500
Mount Bolivar, 262

Mount Defiance, 313
Mount Hebo, camping, 195
Mount Hood, ix, xiii–xiv, 311,
    314, 349–72
    biking, 364–66, 367
    bungee jumping, 367
    camping, 361–63
    canoeing/kayaking/boating,
        367–68
    climbing, 315, 355–57
    fishing, 363–64
    hiking, 355–56
    horseback riding, 367
    llama trekking, 360
    scenic drives, 360–61
    skiing, 324–25, 351–55
    snowboarding, 351–55
    summit climb, 315, 355–57
    Timberline Trail, 357–58
    waterfalls, 358
    wildlife, 369–70
    See also Timberline Ski Area
Mount Hood Meadows
    skiing/snowboarding, 352–53,
        355
Mount Hood National Forest, 76,
    329, 372, 411
    camping, 383
    skiing, 388
    snowmobiling, 388
Mount Hood Scenic Railroad, 311
Mount Hood Skibowl
    Action Park, 366–67
    skiing/snowboarding, 353–54
    biking, 365, 367
Mount Hood Wilderness Area,
    hiking, 314
Mount Howard, 548
Mount Jefferson, 400–11
    climbing, 401
    skiing, 409–10
    snowmobiling, 410
    summit climb, 403
Mount Jefferson Wilderness Area,
    402–5
    fishing, 408
Mount McLoughlin, 514–15
Mount Tabor, 11
Mount Thielsen, 501
    hiking, 496
Mount Washington, 429–40
    hiking, 431
Mount Washington Wilderness,
    430
Mountain biking. See Biking
Mountain Lakes, 512–24
    biking, 521–22
    camping, 517–19
    fishing, 520–21
    hiking, 514–17
    skiing, 522–23
    snowmobiling, 522–23
    waterfalls, 516
    wildlife, 519–20
Mountain Lakes Wilderness,
    hiking, 517
Multnomah Falls, 310, 325
Murderers Creek Wildlife Area,
    611
Myrtle Creek, 139, 141, 273

N
National forests
    campgrounds, vii, viii
    parking fees, ix
    See also individual entries
National Park Service,
    information, 399
National Weather Service,
    information, xii
Nature of the Northwest
    Information Center, 13
Neahkanie Mountain, 200
Nehalem, 210
Nehalem Bay State Park, 194, 198
Neskowin, 198, 208
    lodgings, 209–10
New River, 280
Newberg
    lodgings, 54
    restaurants, 52–53
Newberry Crater National
    Volcanic Monument, 447
    camping, 451–52
    hiking, 456
Newport, 222–38, 255
    beachcombing, 224–26
    biking, 228
    camping, 228–29
    fishing, 230–31
    hiking, 223–27
    kayaking/canoeing, 231–32
    lodgings, 237–38
    picnics, 229–30
    restaurants, 235–36
    surfing, 234
    wildlife, 232–33
North Bend, 273
North Clackamas County, 37
North Fork John Day Wilderness,
    hiking, 579, 592–93, 604
North Fork Umatilla Wilderness
    camping, 596
    hiking, 592
North Santiam River. See Santiam
    River
North Umpqua River. See Umpqua
    River
Northern Beaches, 177–91
    biking, 183–84
    camping, 178–80
    canoeing/kayaking, 184–85
    clam digging, 186
    fishing, 185–86
    hiking, 181–83
    lodgings, 190–91
    parks, 180–81
    restaurants, 189–90
    surfing/windsurfing, 187–88
    whale watching, 187
    wildlife, 186–87
Nyssa, 654, 655

O
Oakland, restaurants, 140
Oakridge, 121, 493
    biking, 485, 486
Oaks Bottom, 19–20
OC&E Woods Line State Trail,
    532–33
Oceanside, 198, 207
    lodgings, 209
    restaurants, 209

Ochoco Creek Park, 419–20
Ochoco Lake County Park
    boating, 421–22
    camping, 418
Ochoco Mountains, skiing,
    426–27
Ochoco National Forest, 384–85,
    397–98
    biking, 420–21
    camping, 418–19
    hiking, 416–17
    wildlife, 424–26
Ochoco Reservoir, fishing, 423
Odell Lake, 482
    boating, 492
    camping, 487
    fishing, 488
    lodgings, 493
Off-road vehicles, 196, 203,
    449–50. See also Dune buggies
Olallie Lake Scenic Area
    camping, 407
    fishing, 408
    hiking, 405–6
Ontario, restaurants, 655
Opal Creek Wilderness, hiking,
    64–65
Oregon Cascades Recreation Area,
    486
Oregon Caves National
    Monument, 160–61
    lodgings, 153
Oregon City, 38
Oregon Coast Aquarium, 222, 232
Oregon Coast Bike Route, 183–84,
    228, 246–47, 263
Oregon Coast Trail, 181–82,
    243–44, 261, 280–82
Oregon Department of Fish and
    Wildlife, information, xiii
Oregon Department of
    Transportation, information,
    xvi
Oregon Dunes, 239–256
    beaches, 242–45
    biking, 245–46
    boating/kayaking, 253
    camping, 248–51
    dune buggies, 241–42
    fishing, 251–52
    hiking, 242–45
    horseback riding, 247–48
    lodgings, 255–56
    picnics, 250–51
    restaurants, 255
    waterskiing, 248, 250
    wildlife, 253–54
    windsurfing/surfing, 254
Oregon Dunes National Recreation
    Area, 239–40, 241–45, 255
    fishing, 252
Oregon Shakespeare Festival, 167
Oregon State Parks and
    Recreation, information, xi
Oregon Trail, 360–61, 567, 582,
    600, 654–55
    Applegate Trail branch, 156
    camping, 594–95
    hiking, 577–78
Oswald West State Park, 179–80,
    188
Otter Rock, lodgings, 221

Owyhee Lake, 647
  fishing, 653
Owyhee River, 647
  fishing, 653
  rafting/kayaking, 648
Oxbow Regional Park, 12, 17
Oxbow Reservoir, fishing, 583

P

Pacific City
  beaches, 198
  fishing, 204
  lodgings, 209
  restaurants, 208–9
  whale watching, 204
Pacific Crest National Scenic Trail,
  viii, xii, 109, 158–59, 313–14,
  357, 402–3, 432–33, 471,
  483–84, 495–96, 506, 514
Paragliding
  Mount Bachelor, 459
  Tillamook, 206–7
  Upper Deschutes River, 459
Parasailing
  Columbia Gorge, 324
  Hood River Valley, 324
Parks
  Ashland, 155
  Bay Area, 266–68
  blind, designed for, 370
  central Willamette Valley,
    79–84
  Columbia Basin, 298–99
  Eugene, 106–8
  Grants Pass, 155
  Junction City, 108
  Lincoln City, 216
  Lower Columbia River, 339
  McKenzie River, 106–7
  Northern Beaches, 180–81
  Oregon Coast, 197–99, 216,
    266–68
  Rogue River, 155–56
  Rogue Valley, 151–52, 155–56
  Roseburg, 136
  Tillamook, 197–99
  Umpqua Valley, 135–36
  Willamette River, 107–8
  Wine Country, 45–46
  See also Camping; specific state
    parks
Patjens Lake, hiking, 431
Paulina Lake
  camping, 452
  fishing, 453
Pelican Butte, 537–38
Pelton Park, 378–79, 382
Pendleton, 590–91
  fishing, 595–96
  lodgings, 600–1
  restaurants, 600
  wildlife, 598
Pendleton Grain Belt, 590–601
  biking, 593–94
  camping, 594–96
  fishing, 596–98
  hiking, 592–93
  skiing/snowmobiling, 598–99
Pendleton Round-Up, 590, 599
Penland Lake, 595, 597
Phillips Lake
  biking, 585–86

camping, 582–83
Phoenix, lodgings, 172
Pilot Butte State Park, 453
  biking, 448–49
Pine Mountain, 459, 460
Port Orford, 278–79, 289–90
  fishing, 286
  lodgings, 291–92
  picnics, 279
Portland, 3–38
  biking, 5, 14–18, 37, 38
  boating, 22–24
  buses, 5–6, 10, 11, 14
  camping, 5, 17–18
  cruises, 23
  fishing, 20–21
  gardens, 13–14
  hiking/walking, 6–14
  lodgings, 35–37
  parks, 7–14, 37, 38
  rafting/kayaking/canoeing, 4,
    24–25
  restaurants, 30–35
  rowing, 25–26
  skating/skateboarding, 26–27
  swimming, 27
  weather, 6
  wildlife, 18–20
Powder River, fishing, 584
Powell Butte Nature Park, 11–12,
  17
Powers, 265, 273
Prairie City, 613
  camping, 609
  restaurants, 614
Prineville, 427, 428
  picnics, 419–20
Prineville Reservoir State Park,
  418
  boating, 421–22
  fishing, 423
Promontory Park, 59
Prospect
  lodgings, 511
  restaurants, 511

Q, R

Rafting. See Kayaking; Boating
Ramona Falls, 358
Red Buttes Wilderness, 160
Redmond, lodgings, 462
Reedsport, 253
Restaurants. See specific cities for
  listings
Richardson Park, 105
Richland, 575
Rickreall, camping, 45
Rimrock Springs Wildlife
  Management Area, 384–85
River flow information, xii
Road reports, xvi
Robert Sawyer State Park, 452
Robert Straub State Park, 198
Rock climbing. See Climbing
Rock Creek Wilderness, 227
Rockaway Beach, 210
Rogue River, 142–43
  boating, 144–45, 151, 287
  camping, 151–52, 154, 517–18
  fishing, 146, 162–64, 285–86,
    509, 521
  headwaters, 517–18

Hellgate and Upper sections,
    146–47
  hiking, 157–58, 282, 516
  jet-boats, 151, 287
  lodges, 149–50
  North Fork, 516
  parks, 155–56
  rafting/kayaking, 144–47
  wild section, 144–46
  wildlife, 158
Rogue River National Forest
  biking, 508–9
  camping, 153, 506–8, 517–18
  skiing/snowmobiling, 522–23
Rogue River National Recreational
  Trail, 157–58
Rogue Valley, 142–73
  biking, 161–62
  boating, 151, 152
  camping, 151–54
  fishing, 162–64
  hiking, 156
  horseback riding, 152, 157
  lodgings, 149–50, 170–73
  parks, 151–52, 155–56
  rafting/kayaking, 144–50
  restaurants, 168–70
  scenic drives, 154–55
  skiing, 165–66
  state parks, 151–52, 155
  waterskiing, 152
  wildlife, 164–65
Rogue-Umpqa Divide Wilderness,
  138
  hiking, 497–98
Rooster Rock State Park, 310, 318
Roseburg
  biking, 139
  lodgings, 140
  parks, 136
  restaurants, 140
Rowena, parks/picnics, 299
Rowing
  Portland, 25–26
  Willamette River, 25–26

S

Saddle Mountain, 182–83, 341
Saddle Mountain State Park,
  camping, 179
Sailing. See Boating
Saint Helens, boating, 334, 335
Salem, 77–96
  bird-watching, 90–91
  gardens/parks, 84
  lodgings, 95
  restaurants, 94–95
Salmon River
  fishing, 363
  kayaking, 367
Salmon-Huckleberry Wilderness,
  359
Salt Creek, 489
Samuel H. Boardman State Park,
  279, 281–82
Sand dunes
  Christmas Valley, 622
  Oregon Dunes, 239–56
Sand Hollow Wilderness Study
  Area, 417
Sand Lake, 203
  camping, 195

Sandy, restaurants, 370
Sandy River, 11–13
  fishing, 21, 363
  rafting/kayaking/canoeing,
    24–25, 367
Sandy River Delta, 12–13
Sandy River Gorge, 20, 37
Santiam Pass, 429–40
  biking, 434
  boating/kayaking, 436
  camping, 434–35
  hiking, 430–31
  skiing, 437–38
  snowmobiling, 438
Santiam River
  camping, 60–62, 407
  fishing, 69
  picnics, 64
  rafting/kayaking/canoeing,
    73–74
Sauvie Island, 330–31, 337
  biking, 341–42
  fishing, 341
  hiking, 340
Sawyer (Robert) State Park, 452
Scappoose, boating, 334
Scenic drives
  Baker County, 576–77
  Blue Mountains Scenic Byway,
    595
  Cascade Lakes Highway,
    465–66
  Coast Range, 262
  Columbia Gorge, 309–11,
    360–61
  Deschutes National Forest, 622
  Diamond Loop Byway, 637
  Eugene, 108–9
  Harney County, 636–37
  Hells Canyon, 544–45, 576–77
  Historic Columbia River
    Highway, 309–11, 325
  Lake County, 621–22
  Lakeview to Steens Byway, 622,
    636
  Malheur National Forest, 577
  Mount Hood, 360–61
  Mount Hood Wagon Road, 311
  Northeast Mountains, 544–46,
    576–77
  Rogue Valley, 154–55
  Snake River Canyon, 576
  Southeast High Desert, 621–22,
    636–37
  Steens Mountain Byway,
    636–37
  Umpqua Valley, 129–30
  Wallowa Mountains, 544–46
Scoggins Valley Park, 45
Seal Rock, 235
  restaurants, 236
Seaside, 180, 182
  biking, 184
  lodgings, 190–91
  restaurants, 189–90
  surfing, 188
Seneca, lodgings, 614
Seven Lakes Basin, 515, 516
Shady Cove
  lodgings, 172
  restaurants, 168–69, 170
Shelton State Wayside, 398

Sheridan, lodgings, 54
Shore Acres State Park, 266–67,
  269
Siletz River, 217, 218
Siltcoos Lake, 246, 252
Silver Falls State Park, 79–81, 84,
  91
Silver Lake, camping, 625
Silverton, gardens/parks, 84
Siskiyou National Forest
  biking, 263–64
  camping, 153, 266, 277–78
Sisters, 438
  biking, 409
  horseback riding, 438
  lodgings, 439–40
  restaurants, 439
  wildlife, 410, 438
Siuslaw National Forest, 203, 215,
  245–46
  camping, 195, 229, 248
  picnics, 230
Siuslaw River, 254
  fishing, 114, 251–52
  kayaking, 253
Skating/skateboarding, 26–27.
Ski Ashland, 165–66
Skiing, xiii–xv
  Anthony Lake(s), 587–88
  Baker County, 587–88
  Bend, 443–45
  Blue Mountains, 572
  Cascade Foothills, 71–72
  Central Oregon, 409–10,
    426–27, 437–38, 443–47,
    476
  central Willamette Valley, 91
  Crater Lake National Park,
    510–11
  Crooked River, 426–27
  Diamond Lake, 500–1
  Grande Ronde Valley, 572
  Hoodoo Ski Area, 437
  huts, 410
  Klamath Basin, 537–38
  Lake County, 630–31
  Lemolo Lake, 501
  Lookout Mountain, 426–27
  Mount Bachelor, 443–46, 448
  Mount Bailey, 500
  Mount Hood, 324–25, 354–55
  Mount Hood Meadows,
    351–55
  Mount Hood National Forest,
    388
  Mount Jefferson, 409–10
  Mountain Lakes, 522–23
  Northeast Mountains, 557–58,
    572, 587–88, 598–99,
    613–14
  Ochoco Mountains, 426–27
  Pendleton Grain Belt, 598–99
  Rogue Valley, 165–66
  Santiam Pass, 437–38
  Southeast High Desert, 630–31
  Southern Cascades, 490–91,
    500–2, 522–23
  Three Sisters, 476
  Upper John Day River, 613–14
  Wallowa Mountains, 557–58
  Warner Canyon, 630
  Willamette Pass, 490–91

  See also Snowboarding
Sky Lakes Wilderness, hiking,
  514–16
Skydiving, Cascade Foothills, 75
Skyliners Snow Play Area, 446
Sled dog mushing, Mount
  Bachelor, 447
Smith and Bybee Lakes, 18
Smith River, 245
Smith Rock State Park, 412–13,
  428
  camping, 418
  climbing, 414–15
  hiking, 415–16
  wildlife, 423–24
Snake River
  camping, 581
  fishing, 553–54, 653
  jet boats, 554–55
  rafting, 554–55
Snake River Canyon, scenic drives,
  576
Sno-park permits, xv–xvi
Snow, information, xiv
Snowboarding
  Central Oregon, 443–45
  Mount Hood, 351–55
  Santiam Pass, 437
  Southern Cascades, 490, 500
  Willamette Pass, 490
  See also Skiing
Snowmobiling
  Bend, 447
  Central Oregon, 426–27, 447,
    476
  Crooked River, 426–27
  Diamond Lake, 500–1
  Klamath Basin, 538
  Lake County, 630
  Lemolo Lake, 501
  Mount Hood National Forest,
    388
  Mount Jefferson, 410
  Mountain Lakes, 522–23
  Northeast Mountain, 557–58,
    598–99
  Pendleton Grain Belt, 598–99
  Santiam Pass, 438
  Southeast High Desert, 630
  Southern Cascades, 491,
    500–2, 522–23
  Three Sisters, 476
  Upper John Day River, 614
  Wallowa Mountains, 558
  Willamette Pass, 491
Snowshoeing. See Skiing
South Beach State Park, 225,
  228–29
South Santiam River. See Santiam
  River
South Slough National Estuarine
  Research Reserve, 258–59, 262,
  269
South Umpqua River. See Umpqua
  River
Southern Coast, 274–92
  biking, 284–85
  camping, 275–78
  clam digging, 286
  fishing, 285–86
  hiking, 280–84
  horseback riding, 288

lodgings, 291–92
picnics, 278–80
restaurants, 290–91
wildlife, 287–88
windsurfing/surfing, 288–89
Spanish Peak, 397
Sparks Lake, 467, 473
Spaulding Reservoir, 629
Spout Springs Ski Area, 598–99
Sprague River, 628
  fishing, 536
Springfield, restaurants, 119
Springwater Corridor, 16
Squaw Creek Falls, 432
State parks
  camping reservations, 275
  campgrounds, vi, viii
  See also individual entries
Stayton, 96
Steamboat, lodgings, 140
Steamboat Creek
  fishing, 128
  kayaking, 132
Steens, scenic drives, 622, 636
Steens Mountain, 636
  biking, 645
  hiking, 640, 641
  wildlife, 638–39
Stewart State Park, camping, 152
Straub (Robert) State Park, 198
Strawberry Mountain Wilderness,
  605, 606
  camping, 609
Strawberry Mountains, hiking,
  605–7
Succor Creek State Natural Area,
  650
Summer Lake, lodgings, 632
Summer Lake Wildlife Area, 624
Summit Ski and Play Area, 354
Sumpter
  lodgings, 589
  railroad, 577
Sumpter Dredge State Park, 583
Sumpter Valley Railway, 577, 605
Sunnyside Park, camping, 62
Sunriver
  biking, 449
  hiking, 458
  ice skating, 448
  lodgings, 462–63
  wildlife, 454–55
Sunset Bay State Park, 261, 264
Surfing, xvi
  Bay Area, 270
  Coos Bay, 270
  Lincoln City, 216, 217–18
  Newport, 234
  Northern Beaches, 187–88
  Oregon Dunes, 254
  Seaside, 188
  Southern Coast, 288–89
Sutherlin, 141
Suttle Lake, 431, 435, 436
Sutton Mountain, 396
Sweet Home
  camping, 62–63
  waterskiing, 75
Swimming
  Eugene, 112–13
  Portland, 27
Sycan River, 628

T

Table Mountain, 523
Table Rock Wilderness Area,
  hiking, 66–67
Tenmile Lakes, 260, 268
The Dalles
  biking, 304–5
  lodgings, 306
  parks/picnics, 299
  restaurants, 305–6
  walking, 304
The Dalles Dam, parks/picnics,
  299
Thief Valley Reservoir, 567, 569
Three Creeks Lake
  camping, 435
  hiking, 431–32
Three Fingered Jack, climbing,
  403–4
Three Sisters, 464–77
  biking, 473–74
  boating/canoeing, 466–67
  camping, 474–75
  fishing, 469–70
  skiing/snowmobiling, 476
  summit climb, 470
Three Sisters Wilderness, 110
  hiking, 431–32, 472–73
Tide pools, 187, 199, 218–19, 224,
  233, 269, 288
Tillamook, 192–210
  beaches, 200
  biking, 202–3
  camping, 193–197
  clam digging, 204
  coastal mountains, 195–97
  crabbing, 204
  dune buggies, 196
  fishing, 203–4
  hiking, 200–2
  kayaking, 205–6
  lodgings, 209–10
  off-road vehicles, 195, 196, 203
  parks/beaches, 197–99
  restaurants, 208–9
  whale watching, 192–93, 194,
    199–200
  wildlife, 99–200
Tillamook Head, 182
Tillamook State Forest
  biking, 202–3
  camping, 196–97
Timberline
  lodgings, 371
  restaurants, 370
Timberline Ski Area, xiii–xiv
  biking, 364
  lodgings, 371
  skiing/snowboarding, 351–52
  See also Mount Hood
Timberline Trail, 357–58
Timothy Lake, 362–63, 364, 367,
  370
Todd Lake, 467, 474
Toledo, picnics, 230
Tolovana Park, restaurants, 189
Trailhead parking fee system, ix
Trails, viii–ix
  Bicentennial Bicycle
    (Bikecentennial) Trail, 343,
    585
  Desert Trail, 634–35, 639–41

Lewis and Clark Columbia
  River Water Trail, 184–85,
  335–37
McCall Point Trail, 303
OC&E Woods Line State Trail,
  532–33
Oregon Coast Trail, 181–82,
  243–44
Oregon Trail, 567, 577–78,
  582, 594–95, 600, 654–55
Pacific Crest Trail. See Pacific
  Crest National Scenic Trail
  rating system, ix
Rogue River Trail, 157–58
Timberline Trail, 357–58
TransAmerica Trail, 420
  See also Hiking
TransAmerica Trail, 420
Trout Creek Mountains, 648
  hiking, 652
Troutdale
  lodgings, 328
  restaurants, 327
Tryon Creek State Park, 10–11
Tualatin River
  boating, 49
  fishing, 48
  rafting/kayaking/canoeing, 25,
    49
Tualatin River National Wildlife
  Refuge, 47
Tubing (snow)
  Cooper Spur Ski Area, 324
  Mountain Lakes, 523
  Southern Cascades, 510–11
  Summit Ski and Play Area, 354
Tugman (W. M.) State Park, 249
Tumalo State Park, 452, 453
Twin Lakes, North and South, 468,
  473, 475, 476

U

Ukiah-Dale State Scenic Corridor,
  camping, 596
Umatilla National Forest, 601
  camping, 595
  hiking, 592
  information, 573, 615
Umatilla National Wildlife Refuge,
  300, 303, 306
Umatilla River, 302
  fishing, 596–97
Umpqua Lighthouse State Park,
  249, 253
Umpqua National Forest
  camping, 105
  hiking/backpacking, 110
Umpqua River
  camping, 134–35
  fishing, 127–28, 251
  kayaking, 253
  rafting/kayaking/canoeing,
    131–133
  windsurfing/surfing, 254
Umpqua Valley, 125–41
  biking, 138–40
  camping, 133–35
  fishing, 127–29, 138
  hiking, 136
  lodgings, 141
  parks, 135–36
  rafting/kayaking/canoeing,

131–33
restaurants, 140
scenic drives, 129–30
waterfalls, 137–38
wildlife, 130–31
United States Army Corps of
Engineers, information, 121
United States Forest Service,
information, 38
Unity, 575
Unity Lake State Recreation Site,
582
Unity Reservoir, 584
Upper Deschutes River, 441–63.
See also Deschutes River;
Lower Deschutes River
Upper John Day River, 602–15. *See
also* John Day River; Lower
John Day River
Upper Klamath Lake
boating/canoeing, 529
cruises, 530
fishing, 535
Upper Klamath National Wildlife
Refuge, 527–28, 539
See also Lower Klamath
National Wildlife Refuge

V
Vale, 655
Valley of the Giants, 214
Valley of the Rogue State Park,
151–52
Vernonia, biking, 341–42
Vida, lodgings, 120, 121
Viento State Park, 316, 318
Vinegar Hill-Indian Rocks Scenic
Area, 604–5

W
Wagons, camper, 582, 594
Waldo Lake, 481–82
biking, 485–86
boating, 492
camping, 486–87
fishing, 488–89
Waldo Lake Wilderness, hiking,
483
Waldport, 225
fishing, 231
lodgings, 236–37
Walking
central Willamette Valley,
79–84
Portland, 7–14
The Dalles, 304
See also Hiking
Walla Walla River, hiking, 592
Wallowa Lake, 543–44
fishing, 553
lodgings, 559
tramway, 548
Wallowa Lake State Park,
camping, 551–52
Wallowa Mountains, 543–59
biking, 555–56
camping, 551–52, 566–67, 581
fishing, 583–84
hiking, 546–48, 565–66, 580
llama/horse trekking, 580
scenic drives, 544–46
skiing/snowmobiling, 557–58

visitors center, 546–47
wildlife, 556–57
Wallowa River, 554
rafting/kayaking, 562
Wallowa-Whitman National
Forest, 601
camping, 552, 553, 568
Warm Springs, 376
lodgings, 389
Warm Springs Indian Reservation
fishing, 408
Warm Springs River,
rafting/kayaking, 378
Warner Canyon,
skiing/snowmobiling, 630
Warrenton, 183, 185, 191
Washburne (Carl G.) Memorial
State Park, 226, 229
Washington Park, 8–9
Waterskiing
Cascade Foothills, 74–75
Cascade Lakes, 466
central Willamette Valley,
87–88
Clackamas River, 74
Detroit Lake, 74–75
Estacada, 74
Eugene, 112–13
Lake Billy Chinook, 378
Oregon Dunes, 248, 250
Prineville Reservoir, 421
Rogue Valley, 152
Santiam Pass, 436
Sweet Home, 75
Willamette River, 49, 87–88
Weather, information, 372
Welches
lodgings, 371
restaurants, 370–71
Wenaha River, 569
Wenaha-Tucannon Wilderness
hiking, 565–66
horseback riding, 572
Wenaha Wildlife Area, 563
West Linn, 13, 37
Westfir, 493
lodgings, 493
Whale watching. *See* Wildlife
Wheelchair access. *See* Barrier free
Whisky Run Beach, 261, 267–68,
270
Whitcomb Creek Park, camping,
62
Wickiup Reservoir, 468–69, 475
Wildlife, xiii
Baker County, 586–87
Bay Area, 269–70
Cascade Foothills, 70–71
central Willamette Valley,
89–91
Columbia Basin, 300–1
Columbia Gorge, 320–21
Crooked River, 423–24
Eugene, 115–16
Grande Ronde Valley, 563–65
Harney County, 637–39
Imnaha River Canyon, 557
Joseph Canyon, 557
Klamath Basin, 526–29
Lake County, 623–25
Lincoln City, 218–19
Lower Columbia River,

330–31, 332–34
Lower Deschutes River, 387–88
Malheur County, 654
Metolius River, 410
Mount Hood, 369–70
Mountain Lakes, 519–20
Newport, 232–33
Northeast Mountains, 556–57,
563–65, 586–87, 598, 611
Northern Beaches, 186–87
Oregon Coast, 186–87,
199–200, 218–19, 232–33,
253–54, 269–70, 287–88
Oregon Dunes, 253–54
Pacific City, 204
Pendleton, 598
Portland, 18–20
Rimrock Springs Wildlife
Management Area, 384–85
Rogue River, 158
Rogue Valley, 164–65
Salem, 90–91
Sauvie Island, 330–31
Sisters, 410, 438
Southeast High Desert, 637–39,
654
Southern Coast, 287–88
Steens Mountain, 638–39
Sunriver, 454–55
Tillamook, 192–93, 194,
199–200
Umpqua Valley, 130–31
Upper Deschutes River, 454–55
Upper John Day River, 611
Wallowa Mountain, 555–57
Wine Country, 46–47
Willamette Falls Locks, 23, 25
Willamette Mission State Park, 82,
84–85, 89, 91
Willamette National Forest
hiking, 483
Willamette Pass, 481–93
biking, 485–86
camping, 486–88
canoeing/kayaking/boating,
492
fishing, 488–89
hiking, 482–85
skiing, 490–491
snowboarding, 490
snowmobiling, 491
Willamette Pass Ski Area, 482, 490
Willamette River
boating/canoeing, 20, 23, 49,
87–88, 111–12
camping, 488
cruises, 23–24
fishing, 21, 88–89, 114, 489
hiking, 485
parks/picnics, 107–8
rafting/kayaking, 111–12, 492
rowing, 26
sailing, 24
waterskiing, 49, 87–88
Willamette Valley, central, 77–96
biking, 85–87
camping, 84–85
canoeing/boating, 87–88
fishing, 88–89
gardens, 83–84
hiking/walking, 79–84
horseback riding, 80, 91–92

information, 96
kayaking, 87–88
llama trekking, 92
lodgings, 95–96
parks, 79–84
restaurants, 94–95
waterskiing, 87–88
wildlife, 89–91
William L. Finley National
Wildlife Refuge, 89–90
Williamson River, fishing, 536
Willow Creek Reservoir, 518, 521,
597
Willow Valley Reservoir, fishing,
537
Wilsonville, fishing, 89
Winchester Bay, 251, 255
Windsurfing, xvi
Astoria, 338
Bay Area, 270
Cascade Lakes, 466–67
Columbia Basin, 301–2
Columbia Gorge, 307–8,
317–19
Columbia River, 338
Coos Bay, 270
Eugene, 112–13
Hood River, 302, 318
Jones Beach, 338
Northern Beaches, 187–88
Oregon Coast, 187–88, 254,
270, 288–89
Oregon Dunes, 254
sailboard manufacturers,
318–19
Southern Coast, 288–89
Three Sisters, 466–67
Wine Country, 39–55
biking, 42–43
camping, 44–45
fishing, 47–48
gliding, 50
hiking, 41–42
information, 55
lodgings, 53–55
parks, 45–46
restaurants, 51–53
wildlife, 46–47
Winema National Forest
camping, 534
information, 502, 511, 523,
539
skiing/snowmobiling, 522–23
Wineries
central Willamette Valley, 94
Hood River, 326, 328
information, 51, 55
Rogue Valley, 168
Roseburg, 140
Umpqua Valley, 140
Wine Country, 50–51
Winston
wildlife park, 131
Winter sports, xiii–xvi. *See also*
Skiing; Sled dog mushing;
Snowboarding; Snowmobiling;
Snowshoeing; Tubing
W. M. Tugman State Park, 249
Wolf Creek, lodgings, 172
Woodburn
fishing, 89
gardens/parks, 84

X, Y
Yachats
lodgings, 236–37
restaurants, 236
Yamhill, lodgings, 53
Yamhill River
boating/canoeing, 49
fishing, 48
Yamsay Mountain, hiking, 531–32,
627
Yaquina Bay, 230
fishing, 230–31
Yaquina Bay State Park, 225
Yaquina Head, 224, 234, 238
Yellowbottom Campground,
camping, 62
Yurts, vi, 178, 194, 228, 248, 264,
277

Z
Zigzag, restaurants, 371